POEMS ON AFFAIRS OF STATE

AUGUSTAN SATIRICAL VERSE, 1660–1714

Volume 1: 1660–1678

Guil. Faithorne sculp:

The Second Charles, Heire of y.ᵉ Royall Martyr,
who, for Religion and his Subiects Charter,
spent the best Blood, y.ᵉ uniust Sword ere dyde,
since the rude Souldier pierc'd our Sauiours side:
who such a Father had'st; art such a Son;
redeeme thy people and assume thy Owne.   J. C.

Charles II. From an engraving by William Faithorne.

Poems on Affairs of State

AUGUSTAN SATIRICAL VERSE, 1660–1714

VOLUME 1: 1660–1678

edited by

GEORGE deF. LORD

New Haven & London

YALE UNIVERSITY PRESS

1963

When the sword glitters o'er the judge's head,
And fear has coward churchmen silenced,
Then is the poet's time, 'tis then he draws,
And single fights forsaken Virtue's cause.

—MARVELL

PREFACE

It is a commonplace of literary history that the Restoration of Charles II marks a new epoch in English literature and that the rise of satire in this epoch is a sign of far-reaching changes in poetic sensibility and style. It is not nearly so well known, however, that in the fifty-four years between the Restoration and the death of Queen Anne, satire on public affairs was the dominant poetic genre, and collections of topical verse satire such as *Poems on Affairs of State* were among the most popular poetical miscellanies ever published in England.

In preparing the present edition, the editors have collected some 3,000 verse satires on contemporary events, issues, and personalities from such printed compilations, and as many more from manuscripts. With the exception of the very few pieces by well-known figures like Marvell, Dryden, Rochester, Oldham, and Swift, this mass of material has been unavailable to modern readers. Even if these books and manuscripts were readily available, the highly topical nature of the satires would make them almost inaccessible.

The new collection of *Poems on Affairs of State* stemmed from the idea of exploring and sifting this little-known literary substratum in order to discover how such topical verse satire might illuminate the political, cultural, and literary evolution of England in a critical period. At first, the material was somewhat erroneously regarded as the dunghill from which sprang the flowers of Dryden's satire and Pope's. After the more interesting pieces had been dated and their contemporary allusions understood, however, the dunghill proved to be a gold mine of information about public affairs and literary issues. Not only did it reveal a great deal about the origin and development of satiric techniques, but individual poems were found to illuminate each other and to cast a strong new light on every aspect of the period. No significant event or person in politics, religious affairs, or in court or literary circles escaped notice, and many little-known or forgotten episodes and figures were rediscovered and took on new life. In the meantime the evidence of diaries, letters, and government records revealed how extensively various public figures were involved in these poems, not only as characters, but often as writers and readers.

Perhaps one of the more important functions of the state poems lay in their influence upon a wider reading public. In a day when the only newspapers were official government productions and public affairs were held to be almost exclusively the concern of the king in council, the clandestine information and comment thus provided helped to satisfy a deep hunger and helped also to rally and define opinion on such vital issues as religious toleration, the standing army, or the French alliance.

Probably the most important political function of this material, finally, was as propaganda designed to subvert certain government policies by stirring up effective opposition in Parliament. A notable instance is the anti-French, anti-Catholic fifth column in which Andrew Marvell and John Ayloffe took a leading part during the Anglo-Dutch War of 1672–74.

From a literary standpoint, the growing preoccupation with public affairs is most significantly reflected in changing poetic sensibilities and styles after the Restoration. Public affairs required public standards of value, public viewpoints, and public modes. As the poet became a spokesman, poetry became more oratorical, but this tendency was balanced by the satirist's traditionally keen interest in particulars and personalities. The poetic spirit was thus coarsened and also vitalized by its deep involvement in satire and partisanship.

The poems in this volume represent a small portion of the output between 1660 and 1678. (A register of those omitted is to appear in a later volume of the series.) Most of the poems are arranged chronologically in three sections (political, ecclesiastical and literary), and those outside the main stream of events are included in the miscellaneous fourth section of "Portraits."

Over the years I have drawn extensively on the resources and knowledge of a great many institutions and individuals and have encountered the utmost generosity and helpfulness at every turn. Miss Marjorie Wynne, Librarian of the Rare Book Room at Yale, and her counterparts at the Folger Shakespeare Library, the British Museum, the Bodleian Library, and the Harvard University Library supplied me with innumerable manuscripts and books. I am also indebted to all those who have provided indispensable microfilms and photostats from these institutions, and also from the following: the Advocates' Library, Edinburgh; All Souls' College Library; Austrian National Library; Edinburgh University Library; Henry E. Huntington Library; Library Company of Philadelphia; National Library of Scotland; New York Public Library; Nottingham University Library; Ohio State University Library; and the Victoria and Albert Museum. I wish also to express my thanks to the following individuals for making available manuscripts in private collections: the Marquis of Bath and the librarian at Longleat, Dorothy Coates; the Earl of Jersey; the Earl of Leicester and the librarian at Holkham, W. O. Hassells; the Duke of Portland; Robert Taylor; and J. Harold Wilson. I owe a particular debt of gratitude to James M. Osborn for making available his large collection of seventeenth-century manuscripts and for his continuing interest in acquiring items of great value to this undertaking.

I have received much advice and information from my co-editors. James M. Osborn and Maynard Mack have made invaluable suggestions about procedure and style and Basil D. Henning has given help on numerous historical points. J. Max Patrick, in the course of his editorial labors on Marvell, has referred me to much important material and raised many vital questions. Herbert Davis was enormously helpful and kind when I was doing research at Oxford. Thomas H. Jackson has checked references throughout. Alvin Kernan made many useful critical comments on the Introduction. David M. Vieth read the manuscript in its entirety and gave freely of his extensive knowledge of Restoration literature. Anne M. Royer, Susan Greene, and Marilyn Riley have at various times provided indispensable assistance in research and in preparing the manuscript. Benjamin F. Houston has undertaken the difficult task of editing this manuscript for the Yale University Press, to the editors of which I am also greatly indebted. In the search for appropriate illustrations I have received much help from David Piper of the National Portrait Gallery, London. In Amsterdam Jonkheer W. van Andringa de Kempenaer most kindly helped my search for material in the Rijksmuseum. Specific debts to collectors and collections are acknowledged in the List of Illustrations. I wish to acknowledge a particular debt to Richard Vowles for his pioneering Yale Ph.D. dissertation, an edition of the

1689 *Poems on Affairs of State*. His work and the late H. M. Margoliouth's edition of Marvell have done much to make this volume possible.

Editorial procedure is explained in the Note on the Text. All dates, unless otherwise stated, are Old Style, except that the year has been regarded as beginning on January 1.

The date supplied after the title of a poem is either the year of composition or, where that is undetermined, the year of the latest event mentioned in the poem.

Unless otherwise noted, definitions in the notes are taken from the *Oxford English Dictionary*.

G. deF. L.

Yale University
March 1963

CONTENTS

LIST OF ILLUSTRATIONS

WORKS FREQUENTLY CITED

Manuscript Sources

Muddiman Newsletters: Manuscript volumes of newsletters compiled by Henry Muddiman et al., from 29 April 1667 to 28 March 1685. In the library of the Marquis of Bath at Longleat.

S. P. Dom. Chas. II: Domestic State Papers of Charles II. In the Public Record Office.

Thorn Drury: Manuscript notes upon various state poems by the late George Thorn Drury. In the Yale Library.

Abbreviations of Printed Sources

Case: Arthur E. Case, *A Bibliography of English Poetical Miscellanies, 1521–1750,* Oxford, The Bibliographical Society, 1935.

CJ: Journals of the House of Commons.

CSPD: Calendars of State Papers Domestic.

EB: Encyclopedia Britannica, 13th edition.

HMCR: Historical Manuscripts Commission Reports.

Other Printed Sources

Aitken, G. A., ed., *Satires of Andrew Marvell, Sometime Member of Parliament for Hull,* London, George Routledge & Sons; New York, E. P. Dutton, 1901.

Allin, Thomas, *Journals,* ed. R. C. Anderson, 2 vols. London, The Navy Records Society, 1939.

Angliae Notitia, or the Present State of England, together with Divers Reflections upon the Ancient State thereof, compiled and edited by Edward Chamberlayne, 2nd ed. London, 1669.

Aubrey, John, *Brief Lives,* ed. Andrew Clark, 2 vols. Oxford, 1898.

Banks, Theodore H., Jr., ed., *The Poetical Works of Sir John Denham,* New Haven, Yale University Press, 1928.

Barbour, Violet, *Henry Bennet, Earl of Arlington, Secretary of State to Charles II,* Washington, The American Historical Association; London, Humphrey Milford, 1914.

Bate, Frank, *The Declaration of Indulgence, 1672: A Study in the Rise of Organized Dissent,* London, 1908.

Bell, Walter G., *The Great Fire of London in 1666,* London, The Bodley Head, 1951.

——, *Unknown London,* London, The Bodley Head, 1951.

Brett-Smith, H. F. B., ed., *The Dramatic Works of Sir George Etherege,* Oxford, Basil Blackwell, 1927.

Brown, Louise Fargo, *The First Earl of Shaftesbury,* New York & London, D. Appleton-Century, 1933.

Browning, Andrew, *Thomas Osborne, Earl of Danby and Duke of Leeds, 1632–1712,* 3 vols. Glasgow, Jackson, 1951.

Burghclere, Lady Winifred, *George Villiers, Second Duke of Buckingham, 1628–1687: A Study in the History of the Restoration,* London, 1903.

Burnet. Osmund Airy, ed., *Burnet's History of My Own Time,* 2 vols. Oxford, 1897.

Carr, John Dickson, *The Murder of Sir Edmund Godfrey,* New York & London, Harper, 1936.

Charnock, J., *Biographia Navalis, or Impartial Memoirs of the Lives and Characters of Officers of the Navy . . . from . . . 1660 to the Present Time,* 6 vols. London, 1812–17.

Clarendon, Edward Hyde, Earl of, *The Life of Edward, Earl of Clarendon, Lord High Chancellor of England, and Chancellor of the University of Oxford in which is included a Continuation of his History of the Grand Rebellion,* 2 vols. Oxford, 1857.

Colenbrander, H. T., *Bescheiden uit vreemde archieven omtrent de groote Nederlandsche Zeeorlogen, 1652–1676,* 2 vols. The Hague, 1919.

Corbett, Sir Julian S., *England in the Mediterranean: A Study of the Rise and Influence of British Power within the Straits, 1603–1713,* 2 vols. London, 1904.

Craik, Sir Henry, *The Life of Edward, Earl of Clarendon,* 2 vols. London, 1911.

Dasent, Arthur I., *Nell Gwynne, 1650–1687,* London, Macmillan, 1924.

Davies, Godfrey, *The Restoration of Charles II, 1658–1660,* San Marino, Cal., The Huntington Library, 1955.

Davies, J. D. Griffith, *Honest George Monck,* London, The Bodley Head, 1936.

Dering. B. D. Henning, ed., *The Parliamentary Diary of Sir Edward Dering, 1670–1673*, New Haven, Yale University Press, 1940.

Downes, John, *Roscius Anglicanus*, ed. Montague Summers, London, The Fortune Press, 1928.

D'Oyley, Elizabeth, *James, Duke of Monmouth*, London, Geoffrey Bles, 1938.

Evelyn, John, *Diary*, ed. E. S. de Beer, 6 vols. Oxford, The Clarendon Press, 1955.

Feiling, Keith, *British Foreign Policy*, 1660–1672, London, Macmillan, 1930.

———, *A History of the Tory Party*, 1640–1714, Oxford, The Clarendon Press, 1924.

Flagellum Parliamentarium, being Sarcastic Notices of Nearly Two Hundred Members of the First Parliament after the Restoration (A.D. *1661* to A.D. *1678*), Aungervyle Society Reprints, Edinburgh, 1881.

Fraser, Peter, *The Intelligence of the Secretaries of State and Their Monopoly of Licensed News, 1660–1688*, Cambridge University Press, 1956.

Gillett, Charles R., *Burned Books: Neglected Chapters in British History and Literature*, 2 vols. New York, Columbia University Press, 1932.

Gilmour, Margaret, *The Great Lady: A Biography of Barbara Villiers, Mistress of Charles II*, New York, Knopf, 1941.

Gramont, Anthony, Count Hamilton, *Memoirs of Count Gramont*, ed. Allan Fea, London, 1906.

Grey, Anchitell, *Debates of the House of Commons from the Year 1667 to the Year 1694*, 10 vols. London, 1769.

Grosart, Alexander B., *The Complete Works in Verse and Prose of Andrew Marvell, M.P.*, 4 vols. London, The Fuller Worthies' Library, 1872–75.

Haley, K. H. D., *William of Orange and the English Opposition, 1672–4*, Oxford, The Clarendon Press, 1953.

Hannay, David, *A Short History of the Royal Navy, 1217 to 1688*, London, 1898.

Harrington, James, *Commonwealth of Oceana*, London, 1656.

Harris, F. R., *The Life of Edward Montagu, K. G., First Earl of Sandwich (1625–1672)*, 2 vols. London, John Murray, 1912.

Hartmann, Cyril Hughes, *Clifford of the Cabal: A Life of Thomas, First*

Lord Clifford of Chudleigh, Lord High Treasurer of England (1630–1673), London, William Heinemann, 1937.

Hatton Correspondence. *Correspondence of the Family of Hatton, being Letters chiefly addressed to Christopher, First Viscount Hatton, 1601–1704*, ed. E. M. Thompson, 2 vols. London, The Camden Society, 1878.

Hazlitt, W. Carew, *A Manual for the Collector and Amateur of Old English Plays*, London, 1892.

Hooker. Edward N. Hooker and H. T. Swedenberg, Jr., eds., *The Works of John Dryden*, Vol. 1: *Poems 1649–1680*, Berkeley & Los Angeles, University of California Press, 1956.

Jesse, John H., *Memoirs of the Court of England during the Reign of the Stuarts, including the Protectorate*, 4 vols. 2nd ed. London, 1846.

Lingard, John, *The History of England from the First Invasion by the Romans to the Accession of William and Mary in 1688*, 10 vols. Edinburgh, 1902.

Lodge, Richard, *The History of England from the Restoration to the Death of William III (1660–1702)*, London, 1910.

Mackay, Janet, *Catherine of Braganza*, London, J. Long, 1937.

Margoliouth, H. M., ed., *The Poems and Letters of Andrew Marvell*, 2 vols. 2nd ed. Oxford, The Clarendon Press, 1952.

Masson, David, *The Life of John Milton Narrated in Connection with the Political, Ecclesiastical, and Literary History of His Time*, 7 vols. London, 1859–94.

Milward, John, *The Diary of John Milward, Esq.: Member of Parliament for Derbyshire September 1666 to May 1668*, ed. Caroline Robbins, Cambridge University Press, 1938.

Muddiman, J. G., *The King's Journalist, 1659–1689: Studies in the Reign of Charles II*, London, The Bodley Head, 1923.

Neal, Daniel, *The History of the Puritans or Protestant Nonconformists from the Reformation, 1517, to the Revolution of 1688*, 4 vols. London, 1732–38.

Newton, Douglas, *London West of the Bars*, London, Robert Hale, 1951.

North, Roger, *The Life of the Right Hon. Francis North, Baron Guilford*, London, 1742.

Ogg, David, *England in the Reign of Charles II*, 2 vols. Oxford, The Clarendon Press, 1956.

Osborne, Mary Tom, *Advice-to-a-Painter Poems, 1633–1856. An Annotated Finding List,* Austin, University of Texas Press, 1949.

Oxford Companion to English Literature, compiled and edited by Sir Paul Harvey, Oxford, The Clarendon Press, 1934.

Partridge, Eric, *A Dictionary of Slang and Unconventional English,* 4th ed. London, Routledge & Kegan Paul, 1956.

Penn, Sir William, *Memorials of Sir William Penn, Admiral and General of the Fleet, 1644 to 1670,* 2 vols. London, 1833.

Pepys, Samuel, *Diary,* ed. Henry B. Wheatley, 10 vols. New York, Limited Editions Club, 1942.

Pinto, V. de Sola, *Enthusiast in Wit: A Portrait of John Wilmot, Earl of Rochester, 1647–1680,* Lincoln, University of Nebraska Press, 1962.

———, *Sir Charles Sedley, 1639–1701: A Study in the Life and Literature of the Restoration,* London, Constable, 1927.

Ranke, Leopold von, *A History of England Principally in the Seventeenth Century,* 6 vols. Oxford, 1875.

Reresby, Sir John, *Memoirs and Selected Letters,* ed. Andrew Browning, Glasgow, Jackson, 1936.

The Rochester-Savile Letters, 1671–1680, ed. J. Harold Wilson, Columbus, The Ohio State University Press, 1941.

Savile Correspondence. *Letters to and From Henry Savile Esq.,* ed. William D. Cooper, London, The Camden Society, 1878.

Scott, Eva, *Rupert, Prince Palatine,* London, 1904.

Sergeant, Philip W., *My Lady Castlemaine: Being a Life of Barbara Villiers, Countess of Castlemaine, afterwards Duchess of Cleveland,* Boston, Dana, Estes, 1911.

Stoughton, John, *The History of Religion in England, from the Opening of the Long Parliament to the End of the Eighteenth Century,* 4 vols. London, Hodder & Stoughton, 1881.

Tedder, Arthur W., *The Navy of the Restoration from the Death of Cromwell to the Treaty of Breda; Its Work, Growth, and Influence,* Cambridge University Press, 1916.

Thompson, Edward, *The Works of Andrew Marvell, Esq., Poetical, Controversial, and Political, containing Many Original Letters, Poems, and Tracts, never before Printed, with a New Life of the Author,* 3 vols. London, 1776.

Tilley, Morris P., *A Dictionary of the Proverbs in England in the Six-*

xxiiWORKS FREQUENTLY CITED

xxiiWORKS FREQUENTLY CITED

teenth and Seventeenth Centuries, Ann Arbor, University of Michigan Press, 1950.

Turner, F. C., *James II,* London, Eyre & Spottiswoode, 1948.

Van Doren, Mark, *John Dryden: A Study of his Poetry,* New York, Henry Holt, 1946.

Walpole, Horace, *A Catalogue of the Royal and Noble Authors of England, with Lists of Their Works,* 2 vols. London, 1759.

Walton, Clifford, *History of the British Standing Army, 1660–1700,* London, 1894.

Ward, Charles E., *The Life of John Dryden,* Chapel Hill, The University of North Carolina Press, 1961.

Wedgwood, C. V., *Poetry and Politics under the Stuarts,* Cambridge University Press, 1960.

Wilson, J. Harold, *All the King's Ladies: Actresses of the Restoration,* Chicago, University of Chicago Press, 1958.

———, *The Court Wits of the Restoration: An Introduction,* Princeton, Princeton University Press, 1948.

———, *A Rake and His Times: George Villiers, Second Duke of Buckingham,* New York, Farrar, Straus & Young, 1954.

Woodbridge, Homer E., *Sir William Temple, the Man and His Work,* New York, The Modern Language Association of America; Oxford, Oxford University Press, 1940.

COLLECTION

OF

POEMS

ON

Affairs of State;

Viz.

Advice to a Painter.
Hodge's *Vifion.*
Britain *and* Raleigh.
Statue at Stocks-M——
Young Statefman.
To the K——
Noftradamus *Prophecy.*

Sir Edmondbury God-
  frey's *Ghoft.*
On the King's *Voyage to*
  Chattam.
Poems on Oliver, *by Mr.*
  Driden, *Mr.* Sprat,
  and Mr. Waller.

BY

A— M—l Efq; and other Eminent Wits.

Moft whereof never before Printed.

L O N D O N,

Printed in the Year, MDCLXXXIX.

Title page of the first edition of *Poems on Affairs of State* (1689).

The letter **A** which originally appeared at the top of the page was cropped when the text was bound.

Introduction

INTRODUCTION

I. WHAT ARE THE *State Poems?*

THE RESTORATION, as we have often been told, was a great period of satire. Dryden, whose name provided a synonym for the age, has received more acclaim for *Absalom and Achitophel* than for any of his other works in verse or prose. The greatest English poem of its kind, *Absalom* unites two dominant interests of the Restoration period: politics and satire.

Absalom and two or three other poems by Dryden have virtually monopolized critical and historical accounts of Restoration satire. Literary historians, in attempting to show how Dryden the satirist typified his age, give passing notice to a few of his contemporaries. Usually they pay brief tribute to *Hudibras,* to the *Satire against Mankind,* to the *Satires against the Jesuits* (largely, one suspects, because Dryden praised Oldham), and to Marvell's political lampoons (almost invariably described as "rough" and "mordant"). There the typical account of Restoration satire usually ends.

Restoration satirists fare still worse at the hands of anthologists. The massive (1,356 pages) *Oxford Anthology of English Poetry* (second edition, 1956) prints only two Restoration satires, *Absalom* and *Mac Flecknoe. Poems for Study* (743 pages, 1953) includes only these two. *Treasury of Great Poems* (1,288 pages, 1942) contains only a short excerpt from *Mac Flecknoe* and a four-line squib of Rochester's on Charles II. I choose these anthologies at random, but such meager representation is, no doubt, typical. Individual satirists are equally neglected. One looks in vain for adequately edited and annotated texts of Butler, Rochester, Oldham, and others.

This customary emphasis on Dryden's pre-eminence coupled with a corresponding neglect of his contemporaries confronts us with a strange situation. Dryden towers over a void. The other satirists by virtue of whom he is affirmed to be typical and pre-eminent remain almost unknown.

Those who derive their impressions of the period from such sources may wonder at the fact that in quantity and popularity satire stood first among the various kinds of non-dramatic verse written between 1660 and 1714. More than 3,000 satirical pieces from this period survive in print. Of these approximately 1,200 were published in various collections between 1689 and 1716, the best known of which were entitled *Poems on Affairs of State*. *POAS* (also commonly called *State Poems*) was a leading poetical miscellany for thirty years. About thirty such volumes were printed. In addition some 2,500 poems on state affairs survive only in manuscript.

This mass of satirical verse is directed at every aspect of public affairs, from national issues of the greatest consequence down to the most trivial incidents of life at court. The early editors who named these *Poems on Affairs of State* had more in mind than we would ordinarily infer from the title. The "affairs of state" that these poems celebrate are as likely to be the love affairs of kings and courtiers as they are the matters of public policy that we normally associate with the term. While political or ecclesiastical matters may be their chief concern, many of the poems are devoted in whole or in part to literary battles and court gossip. Their focus is almost invariably personal and particular. Even where great historical events and issues are the basis of these poems—battles, treaties, plots, acts of Parliament—their ultimate emphasis is upon the men and women involved. Those who held power or aspired to it in this period of British history formed a compact and well-known group compared with the amorphous bureaucracies of our own day. Figures with no official position in the government also influenced public policy deeply. Aside from those of recognized importance in high offices of Church and State—kings, chief ministers, a few M.P.'s, judges, bishops, and courtiers—power was often centered in royal mistresses and favorites, in political careerists and adventurers. Some, like Louise de Kéroualle or John Ayloffe, were agents of other powers, who exerted a pro-French or pro-Dutch influence on King or Parliament. Others, like Father Patrick or Titus Oates, sought to bring corresponding influences to bear on ecclesiastical affairs. There were, in addition, those shadowy figures of the back stairs who ministered variously to the royal or ducal pleasures—the Chiffinches, Bab Mays, Killigrews, and Brounckers whose minor positions at court were by no means always commensurate with their true importance.

Influence radiated outward from the acknowledged and unac-

knowledged centers of power in Church and State, in Parliament
and the military services, to lend ephemeral importance to various
actors, spies, ladies-in-waiting, and adventurers. Beyond these, in
terms of influence, came some of the writers on public affairs. A
few, like the "Court Wits," had a certain standing at Whitehall.
Two or three were professional men of letters, like Dryden. Some
were dedicated amateurs, like Marvell. Many were denizens of Grub-
street or propagandists for outlawed political or religious sects who
shrouded themselves in anonymity. At the furthest range we en-
counter figures of the most marginal importance as far as state af-
fairs are concerned—bullies, fops, bawds, beaux-garçons and their
misses, green and gullible heirs of country squires. At this point
political satire merges with social satire.

This varied world centered on Whitehall and Westminster is
vividly reflected in the *State Poems* with a corresponding variety in
tone and technique. The poems range from the gravity and patriotic
fervor sometimes evident in Marvell, Dryden, or Oldham, through
the irreverent raillery of *The History of Insipids,* to ribald cata-
logues of court vices devised by anonymous hacks. In form they
range from sophisticated and complex mock-heroic poems to dog-
gerel sung in the streets by peddlers.

However crude or sophisticated, however trivial or grave its sub-
ject, Augustan satirical verse is remarkable for the freedom with
which it attacks public figures and institutions that would in other
ages have been immune from such attacks. Until the quarrel be-
tween Charles I and Parliament reaches its crisis in civil war there
is very little topical satire on affairs of Church and State. What lit-
tle there is usually shrouds itself in allegories and ambiguities like
Spenser's *Mother Hubbard's Tale* or Skelton's *Why come ye not to
Court?* Until the 1630s most English satire is typical rather than
topical. This is as true of Chaucer's arraignment of worldly ec-
clesiastics as it is of Langland's. It is also true of the Elizabethan
satirists of the 1590s, Donne, Marston, and Hall, the imitators of
Juvenal, Persius, Horace, and Martial, whose works attracted ec-
clesiastical censure in spite of their concern with types rather than
individuals.

Verse satire directed explicitly at public figures and institutions
first appears in England as the Civil War breaks out.

The ferment of political activity, the quarrels over methods
of government and religious dogma, the animosities which sep-
arated and the shifting alliances which united the peoples, their
fears, hopes, ideals and misunderstandings were reflected in the
varied literature of an immensely productive epoch. . . .
Writers of popular ballads were unceasingly prolific; in re-
sponse to a new demand the press was born—a noisy, pre-
cocious infant; political satire developed from clumsy adoles-
cence to ferocious maturity.[1]

The inauguration of this new literary epoch may be marked by the
invocation to his caustic muse of the Royalist poet, John Cleveland:

> Come, keen iambics with your badgers' feet,
> And badger-like bite till your teeth do meet!

For the next eighty years the political warfare of Cavalier and
Roundhead, of Court Party and Country Party, of Whig and Tory,
was to find increasingly uninhibited expression in satirical verse.

From 1640 to about 1720, then, one finds leading poets as well
as poetasters and ballad-makers increasingly concerned with politi-
cal and religious issues or with the underlying ideological and meta-
physical questions reflected in these issues. Public affairs become, ac-
cordingly, a leading subject for such writers as Cleveland, Wither,
Brome, Denham, Butler, Wild, Marvell, Rochester, Ayloffe, Old-
ham, Dryden, Garth, Pope, and Swift.

The outbreak of the Civil War stands as a watershed between
the old order and the new. The old order, with its mystique of
monarchy and its divinely-sanctioned hierarchies in Church and
State and Society so richly exemplified under Elizabeth, was shaken
under James and shattered under Charles. The death-blow was
struck on the scaffold outside Whitehall Palace on January 30, 1649,
and Marvell, the poet who was so diligently to undermine the au-
thority of Charles II, commemorated this occasion with extraor-
dinary percipience and judgment:

> *He* nothing common did or mean
> Upon that memorable Scene:
> But with his keener Eye

1. C. V. Wedgwood, *Poetry and Politics under the Stuarts* (Cambridge University
Press, 1960), pp. 1–2.

> The Axes edge did try:
> Nor call'd the *Gods* with vulgar spight
> To vindicate his helpless Right,
>   But bow'd his comely Head,
>   Down as upon a Bed.
> This was that memorable Hour
> Which first assur'd the forced Pow'r.[2]

The almost-paradoxical "helpless Right"—Divine Right without adequate temporal power to uphold the myth—exemplifies the Stuart dilemma from the reign of James I right up to the last vain Jacobite uprising. For the remainder of the century the underlying issue at stake between Cavalier and Roundhead or Tory and Whig may be regarded as a contest between a view of monarchy as divinely ordained and sanctioned and the opposing view of monarchical power as limited by certain inalienable rights of the subject. This metaphysical issue is reflected specifically in the period between the Restoration and the Revolution as a conflict between Royal prerogative and Parliamentary privilege.

The execution of Charles I simply demonstrated, as Marvell's *Ode* shows, that the theoretically unlimited Divine Right was in fact limited by the power opposed to it. When Englishmen found that they could pull down kings and set them up again, the myth of Divine Right became a polite fiction. Opposition writers of the Restoration were not slow to discover flaws in the "ancient rights" affirmed by Royalists and Anglicans, and they went back to Henry VIII to suggest that these had their real origin in purely human urgencies. As one satirist wrote of Charles II,

> The virtues in thee, Charles, inherent
>   (Although thy count'nance be an odd piece)
> Prove thee as true a God's vicegerent
>   As e'er was Harry with the codpiece.[3]

Once the divinity that doth hedge a king had been stripped away by events, political writers anxious to defend the liberties of the subject against the encroachments of royal power turned with alacrity to the task of exposing the human weaknesses of their

2. *An Horatian Ode upon Cromwell's Return from Ireland,* 57–66.
3. *The History of Insipids,* 7–10.

monarchs. From Rochester's attacks on Charles II to Pope's on
George II one finds a flood of trenchant, bitter, sometimes obscene
and sometimes witty verse purporting to expose every imaginable
weakness and folly in the reigning monarch. Satirical Roundheads
had confined themselves to attacks on Charles I's ministers and
officers, but from about 1670 on kings themselves were attacked as
freely as Old Nol or the Rump had been.

As dissatisfaction with the administration of Charles II grew, op-
position satirists exercised their utmost ingenuity in order to dis-
credit their rulers. For a while—in the 1660s, especially—the pre-
tense was maintained that Charles was a great king with misguided
counsellors, but about the time of the secret entente with France
and the Third Dutch War unmitigated personal abuse is directed
at him and at the whole Stuart dynasty. As the long-suffering Britan-
nia puts it, in John Ayloffe's *Britannia and Raleigh* (1674?),

> Raleigh, no more: too long in vain I've tri'd
> The Stuart from the tyrant to divide.
> As easily learn'd virtuosos may
> With the dog's blood his gentle kind convey
> Into the wolf and make him guardian turn
> To the bleating flock by him so lately torn.
> If this imperial oil once taint the blood,
> It's by no potent antidote withstood.
> Tyrants like lep'rous kings for public weal
> Must be immur'd, lest their contagion steal
> Over the whole: th' elect Jessean line
> To this firm law their scepter did resign;
> And shall this stinking Scottish brood evade
> Eternal laws by God for mankind made?

The satirist here entirely subverts the traditional sanctions of mon-
archy, transforming the sanctifying chrism from a symbol of divine
ordination into a mark of tyrannical power and affirming God-given
rights in the subject while denying them in the sovereign.

At a less abstruse and philosophical level this iconoclastic atti-
tude toward royalty appears in the casual and familiar treatment
of the King even in poems written by his friends. To the Court
Wits Charles was merely the first gentleman of England, with all
that the term implied, and his well-known gentlemanly vices did

nothing to maintain the myth that he was God's vicegerent and Defender of the Faith. A revealing anecdote touches on this last point. In the course of a theological debate concerning matters of faith Charles is reported to have observed to a court lady that all wise men were of one religion. When she asked him what religion that was he answered that wise men never tell.

The skepticism of the King was typical of the age. Violent political and ecclesiastical upheavals, sectarianism, the breakdown of even the appearance of conventional moral standards in the court, the efflorescence of empirical thinking about political institutions, exemplified in the works of Hobbes and Locke, and the growth in scientific experiment marked by the establishment of the Royal Society paralleled the widespread skepticism and libertinism in the seats of power and influence.

The apologists for Charles II and his brother could only help to delay—they could not arrest—the progressive disintegration of traditional attitudes toward monarchy. The greatest satirist of the period, who had represented Charles in *Annus Mirabilis* (1666) as a heroic figure like Aeneas, was obliged, fifteen years later, to make concessions to the well-established satirical image of the King in *Absalom's* opening lines. Dryden could only counter the *ad hominem* attacks of the Marvells and Rochesters by simultaneously conceding and belittling the King's human weaknesses while affirming the divine authority of his office. In this respect Dryden's conservative political poetry marks the end of the era of Divine Right. Parliamentary prerogative and the concept of inalienable rights in the subject were to win a decisive victory seven years later.

WHO WROTE THE *State Poems?*

The intense and widespread interest in politics and satire which dominated the half-century following Charles II's restoration is reflected in the large number of known literary men who produced these poems, such as Dryden, Marvell, Butler, Rochester, Oldham, Swift, and Pope. There were, in addition, many noblemen and gentlemen who wrote mainly on affairs at court and formed a clique of cognoscenti: the Duke of Buckingham, the Earl of Mulgrave, Henry Savile, Sir Fleetwood Sheppard, Sir George Etherege, Sir Charles Sedley, and others. The largest group, most of them unidentified, includes both the little-known patriots who wrote out of a deep con-

cern and the minor hacks who wrote for bread. Among the former
John Ayloffe, secret agent, propagandist, and friend of Marvell, is
an outstanding representative. One thinks also of the irrepressible
Stephen College who was executed for his satirical attacks on Charles
II. The commercial hacks are the hardest of all to identify, possibly
because there is little stylistic distinction or ideological consistency
in their works, or because their social insignificance prevented the
gossip that surrounded the literary activities of the others.

Since the government promulgated strong laws against "libels"
and attempted to enforce them rigorously, very few of these opposi-
tion poems were printed before the downfall of James II in 1688.
The few satires that were printed before the Revolution came from
unlicensed presses. The rest circulated only in manuscript. From
the Duke of Buckingham down to the poorest Grubstreet drudge,
the authors of attacks on the Establishment had strong reasons to
conceal their authorship. Almost without exception their satires
circulated anonymously. In 1689, when they could at last be legally
published, the editors of *POAS* and similiar collections ascribed
some of the pieces to various authors, usually on dubious grounds.
Fortunately, much effective scholarship has been devoted to expos-
ing these spurious attributions, but the passion for anonymity char-
acteristic of opposition satirists in this period necessarily means that
when the last shred of evidence has been sifted the authors must in
most cases remain unknown.

In other respects, as well, it seems as though circumstances had
conspired to make the *State Poems* inaccessible to modern readers.
Not only are the poems unrepresented in modern anthologies and
editions and their authors largely unknown, but their concentra-
tion on the topical requires much elucidation. The particularity
which made them popular in their own day helps make them teasing
and inscrutable in ours. It is hoped that the commentary in these
volumes together with the light which the poems arranged chrono-
logically shed on each other will help to eliminate the barriers.

II. Circulation

The great majority of these poems issued anonymously from the
author's hands, were copied by nameless scribes, and were dis-
tributed surreptitiously. In periods of strong censorship like that
which prevailed in 1660–79 a few pieces were printed from un-

licensed presses. Thus we find every stage of composition, transcription, and circulation marked by anonymity or illegality or both.

Most of the printed texts date from 1689 or after, when criticism of the old regime had become a sign of fidelity to the new. From the Revolution onwards, the presses poured forth collections of these poems as anti-Jacobite propaganda. When they were first written, however, almost all of them passed from hand to hand without benefit of either license or printing press.

The chief reason for the extraordinary traffic in manuscripts during the Restoration period was the government's strenuous effort to prevent the publication of anything that could be construed as critical of its policies or personnel. Satires which in any way reflected on Charles or James, their ministers or mistresses, were produced and circulated at the risk of severe penalties. A Treason Act was the first statute passed by the Cavalier Parliament. It included in the category of overt offenses "all printing, writing, preaching, or malicious and advised speaking calculated to compass or devise the death, destruction, injury, or restraint of the sovereign, or to deprive him of his style, honor, or kingly name." In 1683 Algernon Sidney was convicted and executed when the Act was interpreted to extend to unpublished and uncirculated writings. Thus circulation in manuscript, though it often mitigated the risks, could not always avoid penalties for treason.

The Licensing Act of 1662 extended the statutory basis for suppressing dissident literature. This Act prohibited "the printing or importing of any books or pamphlets containing doctrines contrary to the principles of the Christian faith or to the doctrine of government or of governors in Church or State." This Act lapsed with the dissolution of the Cavalier Parliament in 1679 and was followed by a royal proclamation ordering the seizure of "libels" and the arrest of their authors and printers, with a reward of £40 payable to informers.

The Licensing Act was rarely resorted to in practice, but it provided judges with justifications to proceed more rigorously under the Common Law. Its importance was principally due to the powers of search and seizure vested in the Crown, delegated to the Secretaries of State, and exercised by that watchdog of the press, Sir Roger L'Estrange. Armed with these powers, L'Estrange ferreted out the authors and publishers of seditious literature. A perennial culprit was Francis "Elephant" Smith, who was imprisoned from 1661 to 1663 for printing *Annus Mirabilis, the Year of Prodigies,* the first of those radical pamphlets to which Dryden's *Annus Mirabilis* (1666) was a rejoinder. L'Estrange was highly successful in discovering other inflammatory literature, such as the last speeches of the regicides executed in October 1660; or *Prelatic Preachers* (1663), an attack on episcopacy; or *A Treatise of the Execution of Justice* (1663), which advocated the assassination of King Charles.

At first sight it may seem strange, in view of the spate of radical prose pamphlets produced in the early 1660s, that there should have survived almost no verse satires attacking the government. Up to 1666 the output of such pieces is negligible. The earliest anti-government verse satires of any substance written in this period are the second and third *Advices to a Painter,* which deal with the Dutch War in the years 1665 and 1666. The explanation for the production in the early 1660s of so much opposition prose and so little verse may lie in the fact that the prose pamphleteers were violently radical and seditious and would have been at any time irreconcilable to the restored Stuart monarchy, while most of the verse satirists seem to have been more moderate and to have conceived of themselves as members of a loyal opposition. It is only in the disenchantment of the 1670s that attacks on monarchy begin. Before that time nearly all the verse satirists seem to have accepted, or to have made a pretense of accepting, the institution of monarchy.

From 1660 to 1666 both Charles and his ministers seem to have received nothing but panegyrics from the poets. Dryden set the pace with *Astræa Redux* and *To my Lord Chancellor.* Waller's eulogistic *Instructions to a Painter,* which celebrates the Duke of York's victory over the Dutch at Lowestoft in June 1665, brought the honeymoon to an end by providing the model for Marvell's parodic *Second Advice to a Painter,* the first substantial satiric attack in verse and the first of a series of important poems in the genre. *Second Advice* and *Third Advice,* which followed it a year later, are highly circumstantial narrative poems exposing the fiascos of the war against the Dutch in the summers of 1665 and 1666 and assigning blame with considerable satiric skill to York, various ministers of Charles, courtiers and court ladies, naval officers, and servile M.P.'s.

Although the two *Advices* specifically excluded the King from criticism and affirmed a deep loyalty to him, the government evidently regarded them with concern. Not only were they among the few opposition satires printed in the reign, but the large number of unlicensed editions (some with a false Breda imprint) testify to their popularity. They seem, furthermore, to have enjoyed an unusually wide circulation in manuscript before they were printed. Finally, copies reached the innermost recesses of the government at Whitehall and Westminster.

The government's efforts to suppress the *Advices* and ferret out the publisher, "Elephant" Smith, are a further indication of the concern with which they regarded them:

> Questions to be put to the Master and Wardens [of the Stationers' Company] relative to their late searches for unlicensed books; their seizure of other printers and presses, as well as Milburn's and Darby's; sale of a tract on the firing of the city, and of "Second and Third Advice to a Painter," offered by Fras. Smith.[4]

A few months later, in July 1667, we find another record of attempts to censor these satires:

> Declaration of William Burden. Fras. Smith of the Elephant and Castle, Strand, asked him to let Johnson, a printer living in his house, print two or three sheets of verse, called "The Second and Third Advice to a Painter." Asked if they reflected on Government, and Smith confessed that they reflected on the Lord Chancellor, Duchess of Albemarle, and others of the Court; refused either to allow it to be printed at his house, or to help him to a printer. Told Royston, a warden of the Stationers' Company, of this business, and advised him to look after it.[5]

According to a second entry of the same date, Smith was summoned before Lord Arlington, the Secretary of State. It must have been a stormy interview, since Arlington was the object of a devastating attack in *Third Advice* and was not a man known for his humor.

Despite the penalties which Smith presumably suffered on this occasion, he evidently continued to defy the law during the next

4. *CSPD, 1666–67*, p. 430. Cited by Margoliouth.
5. *CSPD, 1667*, p. 330. Cited by Margoliouth.

two decades. On 16 September 1670 he was "ordered to enter into a recognizance of £100 to appear at the next Quarter Sessions of Middlesex" for having "sold scandalous pamphlets." [6] On 11 June 1684 he was tried before Judge Jeffreys for "printing and publishing a scandalous libel called *The Raree Show*," the lampoon on Charles II which had been a contributory factor in the execution of its author, Stephen College, on a charge of high treason three years earlier. This time Smith was convicted and sentenced "to pay a fine of £500, to stand in the pillory at the Palace yard at Westminster, at the Temple, and at the Royal Exchange, and the libel to be burnt by the common hangman, and to have a paper set on him signifying his crime, to find sureties for his good behavior for life, and to be committed till all was done." [7]

"Elephant" Smith was merely the best-known and most persistent of the booksellers and publishers who attempted to defy the censorship and circulate satirical verse in print. On the same day that Smith received his sentence from Jeffreys one Jane Curtis was tried and convicted for publishing *Justice in Masquerade,* a lampoon on Jeffreys' friend and associate, Lord Chief Justice Scroggs. Sometimes attempts were made by the victims of the censorship to evade penalties by subornation. On 18 October 1683 a bookseller named John How admitted that he had bribed a member of the Stationers' Company to drop proceedings against him for publishing a poem attacking Scroggs, the Duke of York, and the Duchess of Portsmouth as Papists ("His Holiness has three grand friends").[8] The authors of these pieces were, of course, much harder to find than publishers and booksellers, unless, like the foolhardy College, they openly defied the authorities. Yet the government's agents seem to have conducted their search for satirical poets with some vigor, if not with much success. When Queen Mary's pregnancy in 1687 seemed to jeopardize hopes of a Protestant successor to the throne, one of the lampoons produced upon the occasion provoked an intense search for the culprit. The incident is reported in the blasé tones of a young scholar named Richard Lapthorne: "It seems there is some idle brain hath made a lampoon relating to the late thanksgiving

6. *HMCR*, 7, 517.
7. Luttrell, *A Brief Historical Relation* (Oxford, 1857), *1*, 311.
8. *CSPD, 1683–84*, p. 43.

and a strict inquiry is made after the author who, if he be discovered, will according to deserts be severely punished." [9]

CIRCULATION IN MANUSCRIPT

The Licensing Act of 1662 applied, of course, only to printed libels. In 1677, however, L'Estrange recommended to the Libels Committee of the House of Lords that the legal definition of "libel" be extended to include manuscript material, "because it is notorious that not one in forty libels ever comes to the press, though by the help of manuscripts they are well-nigh as public." Pepys, as we shall see, received the second, third, fourth, and fifth *Advices* one-by-one in manuscript form, before they were printed together in 1667.

The government's attempt to extend censorship to unpublished material led to extremes of injustice and brutality in the case of Algernon Sidney, the Whig politician. Judge Jeffreys sent Sidney to the scaffold for merely *possessing* the manuscript of a lampoon. Thus neither publication nor circulation needed to be proved. This travesty of the legal process became in its turn the subject of a telling satirical attack:

> Algernon Sidney,
> Of Commonwealth kidney,
> Compos'd a damn'd libel (ay, marry, was it!)
> Writ to occasion
> Ill blood in the nation,
> And therefore dispers'd it all over his closet. [10]

This spirited rejoinder to the tyrant Jeffreys shows, as does the great volume of other satires written in the cause of freedom, that neither fine nor prison nor pillory nor scaffold was adequate to deter the satirists.

The assumption that many such poems enjoyed a wide distribution in manuscript is further supported by the large number which has survived in this form. In the Osborn collection, for example, there are many satires copied out on single sheets or folios, folded as though for the pocket, and occasionally bearing an addressee's name on the outside.

9. *Portledge Papers*, ed. R. J. Kerr and Ida C. Duncan (London, 1928), p. 24.
10. *A New Song for the Times, 1683* (Case 189 [2], p. 12).

While many lampoons were passed around in manuscript among friends or tacked to the doors of enemies, there was a well-organized business in their commercial reproduction and sale. Robert Julian, facetiously known as the "secretary of the Muses," kept himself supplied with brandy for years through the proceeds from such a clandestine clearing-house. Julian was himself the subject of numerous lampoons, one of which describes his function in clear, if unflattering terms:

> Thou common shore of this poetic town,
> Where all our excrements of wit are thrown—
> For sonnet, satire, bawdry, blasphemy
> Are empti'd and disburden'd all on thee.[11]

On 12 November 1684 Julian was convicted of "making and publishing that scandalous libel, *Old Rowley the King*. For this and other items he was sentenced to pay a fine of 100 marks and stand in the pillory.[12] Julian had a successor in the business, one Capt. Warcup, addressed in the *Letter to C—— W——* as "thou second scandal-carrier of the town."

Coffee-houses must have been among Julian's best customers. North in the *Examen* notes that during the 1670s these establishments "began to be direct seminaries of sedition and offices for the dispatch of lying." [13] An order for their suppression was issued in 1675 but not enforced. In 1677 King Charles was reported to be highly incensed by those proprietors who, "to gain a little money had the impudence and folly to prostitute affairs of state indifferently to the views of those that frequent such houses, some of them of lewd principles, and some of mean birth and education." [14] In his expostulation Charles was merely reflecting the traditional idea that affairs of state were a mystery about which ordinary subjects should be kept ignorant. In 1616 Charles' grandfather had expressed more emphatically this traditional attitude toward the *arcana imperii:*

11. *A familiar Epistle to Mr. Julian, Secretary to the Muses,* 1–4.
12. Luttrell, *A Brief Historical Relation, 1,* 319–20. Cited by Brice Harris, "Captain Robert Julian, Secretary to the Muses," *ELH, 10* (1943), 301.
13. Roger North, *Examen* (1740), p. 139.
14. H. Thynne to T. Thynne, 19 Sept. 1677, in B.M. Add. MS. 32095, f. 38. Cited by Ogg, *England in the Reign of Charles II,* p. 102.

That which concerns the mystery of the King's power is not lawful to be disputed; for that is to wade into the weakness of princes, and to take away the mystical reverence that belongs unto them that sit in the throne of God. . . . As for the absolute prerogative of the Crown, that is no subject for the tongue of a lawyer, nor is lawful to be disputed. It is atheism and blasphemy to dispute what God can do; good Christians content themselves with his Will revealed in his Word: so it is presumption and high contempt in a subject to dispute what a King cannot do, or say that a King cannot do this or that, but rest with that which is the King's revealed will in his law.[15]

James I's statement enunciates a belief in Divine Right that was, as we have seen, increasingly discredited as the century wore on, but the quasi-religious instinct that affairs of state were not the concern of the subject lingered on in our period, especially in the writings of Dryden. The various ways in which the governments of Charles II and James II tried to embody this principle through censorship and suppression of all real news helped actually to induce the writing and circulation of satire. The outpouring of verse on public affairs during the Restoration showed a strong and widespread desire to penetrate the barrier of silence which the government and its monopoly *Gazettes* and *Intelligencers* maintained around national issues. Undoubtedly the "seditious" literature disseminated through the coffee-houses did much to educate, arouse, and—sometimes—to mislead Englishmen in this crucial period.

These political satires, whether printed or not, found their way also into the hands of the great and powerful. They circulated in the very citadels of government, in Whitehall and Westminster. There is, for instance, the well-known anecdote of Rochester's banishment from court for accidentally showing Charles II a lampoon on the King himself.[16] A large manuscript volume in the Osborn collection containing many satires on James II and bearing his arms testifies to the royal interest in this kind of literature.

The story of the circulation of the second and third *Advices* provides us with an unusually interesting and well-documented

15. James I, *Political Works*, ed. C. H. McIlwain (London, 1918), p. 62. Cited by J. R. Tanner, *English Constitutional Conflicts of the Seventeenth Century, 1603–1689* (Cambridge University Press, 1928), p. 20.
16. See *The Earl of Rochester's Verses for Which He was Banished.*

case. Here we have abundant evidence of the impact on a high government official of this kind of political verse, and, in addition, a strong presumption that the same pieces were employed in an attempt to influence the House of Commons.

The Second Advice to a Painter and its sequels, as we have seen, deal circumstantially with British naval fiascos in the Dutch War of 1665–67. Samuel Pepys, who was probably the most experienced and knowledgeable official in the Restoration navy, noted down in his diary his impressions of each of these satires as it came into his hands. Of *Second Advice,* which he received from his old friend, Sir H. Chumley, he wrote: "I am sorry for my Lord Sandwich's having so great a part in it." [17] Edward Montagu, Earl of Sandwich, had succeeded the Duke of York as Commander-in-Chief of the navy in the late summer of 1665. *Second Advice* attacks Sandwich, who was a close friend and patron of Pepys, for incompetence in general and especially for a flagrant breach of naval regulations and procedures in sharing a rich Dutch prize with his officers before the vessel had been through the prize court. In view both of his intimate knowledge of naval affairs and his close relation to Sandwich, Pepys' comment on *Second Advice* seems like an implicit acknowledgement of the poem's veracity.

Another friend of Pepys, Mr. Brisband ("a good scholar and a sober man") gave him at Whitehall a manuscript of *Third Advice to a Painter,* "a bitter satire upon the service of the Duke of Albemarle the last year." Again the future Secretary of the Admiralty seems to acknowledge the effectiveness and fidelity of the satire: "I took it home with me and will copy it, having the former, being also mightily pleased with it." [18]

The crowning disaster of the war occurred in the summer of 1667, when the Dutch fleet sailed almost unopposed up the Thames and Medway and destroyed or captured many English men-of-war. During an inspection of defensive installations in this third summer of the war, Pepys and some colleagues met with "the several *Advices to a Painter,* which made us good sport, and indeed are very witty" in exposing "the folly of our masters in the management of things at this day." [19] These may, of course, have been in one of the early

17. *Diary,* 14 Dec. 1666.
18. *Diary,* 20 Jan. 1667.
19. *Diary,* 1 July 1667.

printed editions, but there is no way of knowing. At the end of that summer Pepys found a manuscript of *Fourth Advice* at a friend's house and noted that it "made my heart ache, it being too sharp, and so true." [20]

Several significant conclusions may be drawn from all this. First of all, the fact that Samuel Pepys saw at least three of four important satires in manuscript is an indication of the effectiveness of this mode of circulation. In the second place, the fact that the future "savior of the navy" should have received these pieces from close friends in the government is an indication that Restoration political satire was by no means aimed only at the politically disaffected. In the third place, the fact that Pepys, who knew as much about naval affairs as anyone in England, should affirm the sharpness and truth of these satires amounts to an impressive testimonial to their importance.

The circulation of political lampoons in the centers of government was not limited, however, to such methods as we find in the case of Pepys. There is on record an attempt to influence the entire House of Commons by distributing copies of a verse lampoon to each member. The incident occurred in February 1668 during a debate on the naval miscarriages of the war just ended. On the 12th, "several small printed papers in rhythm [i.e. rhyme] were by a porter conveyed to the doorkeeper of the House of Commons under several coverts directed to the respective members of the House." [21] Our authority goes on to say that "the matter of them is libellous and the whole thing shows the author to be more fraught with malice than poetry." Henry Verney supplies additional details of the incident: "Yesterday a fellow brought a bag of about 400 letters for Parliament to the door and slunk away; they were printed books of verses, a downright libel, quite like Wither's *Abuses Whipped and Stripped*." [22] Two days later, we are told, "a libel was conveyed to the Speaker of the House of Commons of such a nature that it was not thought fit to be published even in that great Council." [23]

At this time the House was investigating the disastrous division of the fleet in 1666, when a large force under Prince Rupert was

20. *Diary,* 16 Sept. 1667.
21. Muddiman Newsletter, 13 Feb. 1668.
22. *HMCR*, 7, 486. Letter dated 13 Feb. 1668.
23. Muddiman Newsletter, 15 Feb. 1668.

detached to attack a French force wrongly reported to be in the Channel. The main fleet under the Duke of Albemarle encountered the Dutch shortly after and was saved from annihilation after a bloody three days' battle by Rupert's last-minute reappearance. The House was interested chiefly in two questions: who was responsible for the false report that the French were in the Channel; who was responsible for the decision to divide the fleet in the face of the imminent appearance of the Dutch? It is possible that the "printed books of verses" which Verney mentions bore upon these and other questions of naval mismanagement. At any rate Marvell, whose *Third Advice* arraigns Arlington for the intelligence failures, is quoted in Grey two days after the satires were delivered to the door-keeper to the same effect:

> Mr. Marvell, reflecting on Lord Arlington somewhat trans-
> portedly said: "We have had Bristols and Cecils Secretaries and
> by them knew the King of Spain's Junto and letters of the
> Pope's cabinet; and now such a strange account of things! The
> money allowed for intelligence so small, the intelligence was
> accordingly—a libidinous desire in men for places makes them
> think themselves fit for them—the place of Secretary ill gotten,
> when bought with £10,000 and a barony." He was called to ex-
> plain himself, but said the thing was so plain it needed it not.[24]

III. The *State Poems* and History

Political satire is related to historical events in two ways. It is a record of events, a "history," however distorted by partial views and private motives. It also exerts influence, however slight, upon the events themselves. The political verse of the Restoration played a considerable part in the determination of large issues in England: the question of a Protestant or a Catholic succession, for one, and the relative power of royal prerogative and Parliament for another. Viewed either as "history" or as an instrument of party warfare, Restoration political satire is marked by a circumstantial and highly personal approach to events. As history and as propaganda, it pur-ports to tell the real story, to set the record straight, and its prime method is to present the reader with a plausible body of purported fact. For us who are studying these events three hundred years after

24. *Debates*, 14 Feb. 1668.

they happened, two questions arise: How accurately do the *State Poems* reflect events? To what extent did they influence events?

From 1665 on, every aspect of public affairs in England was subjected to the satirist's increasingly minute and bitter scrutiny. Charles' personal faults, which might have been tolerated in a monarch whose political and religious inclinations were more congenial to his subjects, were magnified until he was depicted as another Sardanapalus. The mistresses, whose greed supposedly drained off vast sums appropriated for the national welfare and whose alien creeds threatened the liberties of Charles' subjects, were exposed to appalling, but sometimes justified, invective. Not a drunken frolic, nor a brawl at court, nor a bribe in Parliament, not an instance of cowardice or chicanery in the navy, nor one of hypocrisy or bigotry in the Church escaped satirical notice. The Restoration is a period unusually rich in detailed records: the diaries of Pepys, Evelyn, Dering, and Milward; the letters of Rochester and Savile, of Etherege, Marvell, and Henry Verney; the memoirs of Grammont, Barillon, North, Burnet, and Clarendon; the state papers and newsletters —all make it a richly-documented period. Nearly every item of even the slightest public interest in such sources is mentioned in the thousands of poems on public affairs which have survived. The most important of these, set in chronological order with their occasions and persons identified, comprise a priceless record. Their particularity and involvement and gossipy interest in everything that happened give them something of the appeal that we find in Pepys. The pictures they paint are always, to some extent, distorted. The mirror they hold up to flawed human nature is often flawed itself, but thanks to rebuttals and apologias and to the abundance of other dependable records in this period, the modern student of Restoration history and manners may still get at kinds of truth through this medium.

What, then, can be said of these poems as history? The writer of commendatory verse selects his details, softens his focus, and heightens his colors to produce an image heroic or benign of king, queen, or chancellor. *Second Advice* reveals, for example, the many unheroic realities that Waller omitted or glossed over in *Instructions to a Painter*. The satirist, on the other hand, despite the pretense of delivering unvarnished truth, distorts and colors realities for his own political and aesthetic purposes. Waller's panegyrical treatment of the war of 1665 reminds us that Marvell underrated the courage of James and the magnanimity of Clarendon.

In the preface to *Annus Mirabilis* Dryden implied, I believe, just such a discrepancy between the heroic or the satirical image and reality. In defending his adaptation of Virgilian tropes and phrases, he writes:

> Such descriptions or images, well wrought, which I promise not for mine, are, as I have said, the adequate delight of heroic poesy; for they beget admiration, which is its proper object; as the images of the burlesque, which is contrary to this, by the same reason beget laughter; for the one shows nature beautified, as in the picture of a fair woman, which we admire; the other shows her deformed, as in that of a lazar or of a fool with distorted face and antic gestures, at which we cannot forbear to laugh, because it is a deviation from nature.

We go a step beyond Dryden's explicit statement to say that the "fair woman" and the "lazar" are essentially images of the same person, but a comparison of Dryden's massive apologia for the regime of Charles II with, say, *Third Advice,* suggests that this is true. In *Annus Mirabilis* Dryden bent his energies on painting anew, with a palette of heroic colors, such figures as the King, the Duke of York, the Duke of Albemarle, whom the satirists depicted in livid colors and grotesque postures.

The juxtaposition of a heroic poem like Waller's *Instructions to a Painter* or *Annus Mirabilis* with satiric poems dealing with the same figures and events sheds new light not only upon the events themselves but on the techniques of the heroic and satiric modes in topical poetry. The poems of Waller and Dryden, of Marvell and Rochester, are mutually illuminating. In the first place the underlying aesthetic assumptions of both modes are thrown into relief by the comparison. The heroic mode, as Dryden's important comment suggests, is designed to "beget admiration" or wonder; the satiric (or "burlesque") to "beget laughter." The heroic mode aims at an imaginative identification of contemporary persons and events with the heroic tradition in epic or biblical accounts. The technique necessarily entails a careful selection from the available mass of fact, an idealizing or heightening of the details selected, and a cunning association of these details with mythic precedents. The

satiric artist also selects from the available mass of fact, but pays
particular regard to details which may appear as grotesque and in-
congruous. His technique depends upon a vivid and naturalistic
treatment of detail, and, if he employs heroic associations, he does
so in order to denigrate the present reality by contrast with an ideal
past. Thus Dryden, in *Annus Mirabilis,* projects upon Charles II
Aeneas' pious care for his people and his country's destiny, while
Marvell draws grotesque analogues between Ovid's fabulous artificer
and the cunning political architect he sees in Clarendon. An ex-
ample of the difference between the two modes is found in the ac-
counts of the wounding of the British Admiral Monck in the Three
Days' Battle. Monck's breeches were shot away, and he suffered a
minor wound in the buttock. Dryden permits himself a moment of
grave levity before reasserting the epic mood:

> Our dreaded Admiral from far they threat,
>   Whose batter'd rigging their whole war receives.
> All bare, like some old oak which tempests beat,
>   He stands, and sees below his scatter'd leaves.
>
> Heroes of old, when wounded, shelter sought,
>   But he, who meets all danger with disdain,
> Ev'n in their face his ship to anchor brought,
>   And steeple high stood propp'd upon the main.
>
> At this excess of courage all amaz'd,
>   The foremost of his foes a while withdraw:
> With such respect in enter'd Rome they gaz'd,
>   Who on high chairs the god-like fathers saw.

As Hooker judiciously remarks, "Dryden's raillery is admirable by
the best standards of his age: it is a gentle thrust, serving to reveal
or heighten certain admirable qualities in the object of raillery—
in this instance, the Duke's unshaken courage." In treating the same
incident Marvell employs mock-modesty and a Ciceronian dis-
claimer in advising his painter:

> But most with story of his hand or thumb,
> Conceal (as Honor would) his Grace's bum,
> When that rude bullet a large collop tore
> Out of that buttock never turn'd before.

> Fortune, it seem'd, would give him by that lash
> Gentle correction for his fight so rash,
> But should the Rump perceive't, they'd say that Mars
> Had now reveng'd them upon Aumarle's arse.

Here something like heroic dignity is momentarily assumed to emphasize by contrast the prevailing effect of broad humor. Heroic personifications of Honor and Fortune wage a vain struggle with low words like bum and arse. In the lines which follow this passage Marvell, like Dryden, brings in further analogues from the heroic tradition, but with an effect that is directly opposite to Dryden's:

> The long disaster better o'er to veil,
> Paint only Jonah three days in the whale,
> Then draw the youthful Perseus all in haste
> From a sea-beast to free the virgin chaste,
> (But neither riding Pegasus for speed,
> Nor with the Gorgon shielded at his need);
> For no less time did conqu'ring Ruyter chaw
> Our flying Gen'ral in his spongy jaw.
> So Rupert the sea dragon did invade,
> But to save George himself and not the maid,
> And so arriving late, he quickly miss'd
> E'en sails to fly, unable to resist.

In this account of Prince Rupert's attempt to rescue the beleaguered Monck the mythical allusions to Jonah, Perseus and Andromeda, and St. George have a discordant effect. They underscore by contrast the irrelevance of heroic attitudes to the present "long disaster." The effect of the passage runs counter to that which Dryden gains by his sonorous lines on Rome's "god-like fathers." It awakens the reader's skepticism whereas Dryden's weighty lines excite his awe.

These two passages represent a fundamental distinction between heroic and mock-heroic verse. The heroic poet attempts to draw over contemporary public affairs the sanctions of myth, of heroic values, of a conservative tradition. The satirist invokes the same sanctions to expose what he regards as instances of folly in contemporary affairs. One might add that the conflicting techniques and strategies of the two genres tend to illustrate the basic ideological oppositions of the century: on the one hand the appeal to faith

in traditional values, rituals, and myths, on the other the appeal
to empirical, skeptical, and critical attitudes toward experience.

As I have already suggested, circumstances conspired in this
period to arouse such skeptical and critical attitudes toward author-
ity. The actual character and conduct of great Restoration figures
often seem like those found in satires in other ages. The truth could
be stranger than fiction, and the Restoration satirist of court life
was rarely called upon to strain his powers of invention. As Roches-
ter wrote of his enemy, Sir Carr Scroope,

> in thy person we more clearly see
> That satire's of divine authority,
> For God made one on man when he made thee,
> To show there were some men as there are apes,
> Fram'd for mere sport, who differ but in shapes.

In his famous portrait of Zimri Dryden took few liberties with the
historical Duke of Buckingham. The wits and bravoes of this per-
iod, like Charles himself, were a self-conscious lot, and one suspects
them at times of trying to imitate hyperboles that imagination drew
of them. Sir Robert Howard sometimes seems to have modeled
his haughty demeanor on the heroes of his own dramas. One is
driven to wonder if Restoration life imitated art more than in other
periods. To what extent, for example, did Etherege invent Roches-
ter in creating Dorimant?

In matters of politics the same rule often applies. Marvell's satiri-
cal account of England's defeat by the Dutch in 1667 and the Par-
liamentary and diplomatic maneuvers which accompanied it is a
primary source for historians. In her scholarly edition of the Par-
liamentary diary of John Milward, Professor Caroline Robbins
draws upon *Last Instructions* continually for illustration and con-
firmation of her author. When Charles II, with the aid of Clifford,
"the mad Cethegus of the age," and Arlington, evolved in secret the
Grand Design of making England a dependency of Louis XIV and
the Catholic Church, the worst suspicions of the satirist fell short of
the truth.

If Charles, the ironist, "never said a foolish thing, nor ever did a
wise one," at least he managed to preserve the crown for his humor-
less brother James, who wore it with a difference and only for a
short time. Charles embodied the Restoration spirit of compromise,
whereas James was intractable and wrongheaded. The best that

could be said of Charles has been said by the great exponent of compromise, the Earl of Halifax:

> That *yieldingness*, whatever foundations it might lay to the disadvantage of posterity, was a specific to preserve us in peace for his own time. If he loved too much to lie upon his own down-bed of ease, his subjects had the pleasure, during his reign, of lolling and stretching upon theirs. As a sword is sooner broken upon a feather-bed than upon a table, so his pliantness broke the blow of a present mischief much better than a more immediate resistance would perhaps have done.
>
> Ruin saw this, and therefore removed him first to make way for further overturnings.[25]

James' Phaethon-like career as king is another chapter, but even in the satires of the 1670s we find him attacked for the stubbornness of his alien ideas, which most Englishmen regarded with dismay in an heir apparent. Depending on how one looks at it, his grim unyieldingness was a disaster or a godsend. The Popish and authoritarian tendencies of Charles crystallized early in James. His rock-hard bigotry and arrogance brought to a head anxieties which had plagued England for more than two decades and led to the Revolution of 1688.

SATIRICAL VERSE OF THE RESTORATION AS A POLITICAL INSTRUMENT

We come now to the second relationship between political satire and history. To what extent did the enormous output of the Restoration satirists influence the course of history? Some of the answers to this question have already been implied. Circulation of these pieces in defiance of severe legal penalties and a vigilant censorship raises a strong presumption in favor of their effectiveness. Obviously we are not likely to find well-documented instances of political conversion. Yet the testimony of a distinguished public servant, such as Pepys, in favor of the force and authenticity of some of these pieces is an indication of their impact. And the sheer volume of Restoration satire and its evidently wide circulation even in government circles are indications of its significance as a political instrument.

The implicit question with which this part of our discussion

25. *A Character of King Charles II.*

opened was what effect, if any, political verse had in contributing to the downfall of James II. As we have seen, the issues which led to the Revolution of 1688 had been alive in the 1660s. The Protestant, liberty-loving subjects of Charles had been alerted to the dangers of "Popery and arbitrary government" for many years, partly through the agency of surreptitiously-distributed satires. What made them revolt against James was not so much a change in royal policy on questions of religion and prerogative as it was the crystallization in James of tendencies long associated with both the brothers.

For twenty-five years before the Revolution the satirists had driven home again and again the dangers inherent in the authoritarian and Catholic proclivities of Charles and his brother. In 1688, then, the public had only to learn of a long-feared plot for their forced conversion to rise against James. Feeling against their Catholic ruler and his mercenary Irish soldiers found its most popular expression in Lord Wharton's famous ballad, *Lilliburlero,* which was directed, oddly enough, not against James, as almost everyone supposed, but against Lord Talbot.

The influence of *Lilliburlero* cannot, of course, be measured, but it seems to have provided James' outraged subjects with an intoxicating distillate of the rebellious feelings which had found expression in thousands of satirical songs and poems over the years. Bishop Percy went so far as to say that *Lilliburlero* "had once a more powerful effect than either the Philippics of Demosthenes or Cicero, and contributed not a little towards the great revolution of 1688." [26] Macaulay, on the other hand, regarded it as "the effect and not the cause of that excited state of public feeling which produced the Revolution." [27] David Hume was probably nearer the truth in saying that it "both discovered and served to increase the general discontent of the kingdom." [28]

IV. The *State Poems* as Literature

As we have seen, the poems in this collection are concerned in detail with the issues of the period. Judged as literature, topical satire so deeply embedded in historical fact seems to suffer from a double disability. In the first place, satire has often been granted

26. *Reliques of Ancient Poetry* (London, 1910), 2, 157.
27. *History, 3,* 1072.
28. *History of England, 5* (1762), 455.

only a grudging and precarious status as a literary genre. In the second place, satire directed at ephemeral issues and persons seems above all to lack the autonomy or universality of true poetry.

If satire has suffered as a literary genre, the satirist himself has often been to blame for this neglect. For the satirist disavows his art and pretends to give only a factual, artless account of things as they are. Taking him at his word, we all too often accept this pretense and confine ourselves to the historical circumstances of his work. Thus, as a recent writer has put it, "satire is denied the independence of artistic status and made a biographical and historical document, while the criticism of satire degenerates into discussion of an author's moral character and the economic and social conditions of his time." [29] Lytton Strachey's view of Pope's satires as boiling oil ladled out by an ape is typical of this approach.[30]

In our own time satire has begun to receive serious critical attention as literature. Northrop Frye has considered it as one of four basic literary "myths." [31] Mary Claire Randolph and Maynard Mack have explored in different ways the arts which the satirist pretends not to use.[32] Alvin Kernan and Robert C. Elliott have greatly advanced our understanding of satires as literary artifacts.[33] Several excellent critical studies, finally, have helped to rescue the Augustan satirists from an exclusively historical, biographical, or cultural approach.

As a consequence we are less inclined than former ages to treat satire only as a social document. This is especially true of the more obviously fictional satires in which the relation of the author to his characters or subject is remote, oblique, or impersonal. "Menippean" satire, which emphasizes the scene rather than the satirist, is perhaps more readily accepted as literature than formal satire in which the satirist plays a prominent part. In formal satire the temptation is especially strong to take "the satirist's word for it that he is a truthful, unskilled fellow driven to write by his indignation." [34]

29. Alvin Kernan, *The Cankered Muse: Satire of the English Renaissance* (New Haven, Yale University Press, 1959), p. 2.

30. *Pope. The Leslie Stephen Lecture for 1925* (New York, Harcourt Brace, 1926).

31. *Anatomy of Criticism* (Princeton University Press, 1957).

32. Randolph, "The Structural Design of Formal Verse Satire," *PQ, 21* (1942), 368–84. Mack, "The Muse of Satire," *Yale Review, 41* (1951–52), 80–92.

33. Kernan, *The Cankered Muse*. Elliott, *The Power of Satire: Magic, Ritual, Art* (Princeton University Press, 1960).

34. Kernan, p. 4.

Maynard Mack has shown, however, that even in those satires where Pope seems to speak *in propria persona* he in fact employs a variety of satiric masks. We should be alert, therefore, to the differences between the real author and the identities he assumes.

Many of the satires in these volumes are artless and direct attacks by one historical person on another, but there are many others which introduce fictional and poetic devices the great Augustans were to perfect.

The richest satire, as the example of the Augustans reminds us, is that which transmutes concrete historical realities into universals. Its fictions include but transcend historical fact. It employs freely any of the means by which poetry is made from the passing shows of our experience, but it recurs most frequently to a series of techniques which, though not necessarily peculiar to it, the great satirists have made their own. For convenience these may be categorized as the satirical *persona,* the satirical butt, the audience for whom the satire is written, the scene, and the action. The satirical *persona* includes such popular types as "the scourge of villainy," the naïf, the honest man, the cynic, and the patriot. He may be identified by the author's name, or by a pseudonym, or he may be nameless. The butt has a corresponding range of identities: the various types of folly, greed, and vice under the names of living persons, or in the guise of historical or legendary figures. The audience addressed is usually more shadowy than the two principals. Sometimes, of course, as in the simpler kinds of lampoon, it is the butt himself. Sometimes it is the sober, hard-headed *adversarius,* like Pope's Arbuthnot. Usually, it is not identified specifically, but its character is implied by the assumed identity of the satirist and the nature of the appeals and arguments he uses. In some cases the satirist addresses a figure representing the virtues and values he finds lacking around him: Queen Elizabeth, Sir Walter Raleigh, Shakespeare, Horace, and so forth. Wherever a specific auditor is addressed, we also find ourselves, of course, as members of an audience who are overhearing it all. The scene and action, especially in topical satires like those collected here, are usually contemporary places and events: a debate in the Commons, a council of war aboard the *Royal Charles,* dalliance at Whitehall. Frequently, however, a contemporary event is associated with some historical, biblical, or mythological incident or place: the court of Nero, the trials of David, the loves of Pasiphaë in Cretan legend.

There is a corresponding variety in the structural forms employed. The ballad is generally used to produce an effect of ironic naïveté. The satirical song often jars ironically with the associations of the familiar tune to which it is set. Even the mock-litany, the crudest and least successful of forms, shows an attempt to be indirect, oblique, and wry. Among the more sophisticated devices are the naïve confession, the dialogue, the dream, the vision, the beast fable, and the sessions of the poets. Among the more ambitious and technically complex we find the advice to the painter and the mock epic.

In painter poems the satirist adopts the mask of the patriotic ironist who in turn engages a painter to depict the satirical scene. This strategy serves to heighten the sense of realism, to justify the emphasis on quasi-visual detail, and to make us accept more readily a satiric revelation which does not seem to depend on the personal attitude of the satirist toward his material. There are many other ways, of course, for the satirist to feign objectivity, but this is one of the most effective because of his apparent disengagement and because of the authority with which we tend to endow what we seem to be *seeing*. The arrangement of narrative "instructions" with large tableaux interspersed with sketches or full-length portraits of the principal figures permits a great deal of structural and tonal variety. Occasionally, too, the figures themselves speak, heightening our sense of authenticity. Perhaps the peak of satirical indirection is to be found in Marvell's *Third Advice* where the poet describes the Duchess of Albemarle to the painter, who draws such a speaking likeness of her that she begins in fact to speak and delivers a satirical exposé of the administration, at the same time unconsciously revealing her own vulgarity. The rich irony of this is crowned in the solemn envoy to the King by the allusion to the Duchess' splenetic diatribe as "Cassandra's song" and by the concluding identification of this erstwhile seamstress with Philomela:

> So Philomel her sad embroid'ry strung,
> And vocal silks tun'd with her needle's tongue.
> The picture dumb in colors loud reveal'd
> The tragedies of Court so long conceal'd;
> But when restor'd to voice, increas'd with wings,
> To woods and groves, what once she painted, sings.

The tragic vision and the satiric vision are thus potently combined. Such vivid, quasi-pictorial effects as we have noted are of course not confined to this genre of satire. *Annus Mirabilis* employs such visual details without the painter machinery. As Jean Hagstrum observes, "in order to make us understand, Dryden wanted first to make us see," and, like the painter-poet, gives us "visual images that do not come directly from nature but from the canvases of baroque artists and emblematists." [35] In *Mac Flecknoe* and, above all, in *Absalom and Achitophel*, he brought the pictorial technique to its perfection in satiric modes by bringing together "images that beget admiration" and "images that beget laughter."

In relating Dryden's poetry on public affairs to that of his contemporaries we find, accordingly, new and unexplored areas of significance, both thematic and aesthetic. If we read *Annus Mirabilis* with the painter poems of the 1660s, or *Mac Flecknoe* with the literary satires of the next decade, or *Absalom and Achitophel* with the long series of lampoons on Charles II and Buckingham and Shaftesbury, the Age of Dryden takes on new life and meaning. An aspect of this is suggested by Hagstrum's remark "that in drawing the analogy between painting and satire, Dryden followed the example of Marvell and other seventeenth-century satirists, who had used this parallel frequently enough to make it a convention." [36]

The poetic images of great satire, as I have said, grow out of and supersede historical truth. The Duke of Buckingham, fixed for all time as Zimri, sadly acknowledged this principle in his unpublished poem, *To Dryden:*

> As witches images of man invent
> To torture those they're bid to represent,
> And as that true live substance does decay
> Whilst that slight idol melts in flames away,
> Such and no lesser witchcraft wounds my name,
> So thy ill-made resemblance wastes my fame.[37]

In this complaint the Duke unwittingly hit upon the primitive origins of satire in witchcraft, which Robert C. Elliott has recently described. The satirist's images may bear as little resemblance to the

35. *The Sister Arts. The Tradition of Literary Pictorialism in English Poetry from Dryden to Gray* (University of Chicago Press, 1958), pp. 179, 180.
36. Hagstrum, p. 180.
37. Commonplace book of George Villiers, second Duke of Buckingham, belonging to the Earl of Jersey. I am indebted to the Earl for permission to quote and to Professor J. Harold Wilson for lending a microfilm of the book.

living original as the magician's wax figures, but they can be equally destructive.

Dryden's Zimri is one of those satiric portraits that, like Pope's Sporus, supersedes by its vividness and life the historical person who served as its model. If we compare Dryden's creation with another sketch of Buckingham from an anonymous Restoration satire, we can see, finally, how closely Dryden's technique is related to that practiced by his contemporaries.

On the Prorogation attacks Buckingham for advising Charles to prorogue Parliament in 1671. The satirist adopts the character of a loyal M.P. who has faithfully represented the King's interests without reward and, usually, against the dictates of conscience:

> And must we, after all our service done
> In field for father and in House for son,
> Be thus cashier'd to please a pocky peer
> That neither Roundhead is nor Cavalier,
> But of some medley cut, some ill-shap'd brat,
> Would fain be something if he knew but what?
> A commonwealth's man he owns himself to be,
> And, by-and-by, for absolute monarchy,
> Then neither likes, but, some new knicknacks found,
> Nor fish nor flesh, nor square is nor yet round.
> Venetian model pleaseth him at night;
> Tomorrow, France is only in the right.
> Thus, like light butterflies, much flutter makes,
> Sleeps of one judgment, of another wakes.
> Zealous in morn, he doth a bishop make,
> Yet before night all bishops down he'd take.
> He all things is, but unto nothing true,
> All old things hates, but can abide no new.

This passage marks a great advance over the crude personal invectives of the Commonwealth period. In the first place it employs the occasion of the prorogation as an effective dramatic context for the outburst. In the second place, the satirist's mask as a Royalist appealing to the King against the King's evil adviser disarms any suspicion we might have that personal animus motivates the attack. In the third place, the details of the portrait are all integrated with the central animating principle of the character: his constant inconstancy.

The portrait moves through an accumulation of significant incidentals to final enunciation of a general truth in the last couplet. The apparently random character of the images—Buckingham is a shapeless piece of cloth, neither fish nor flesh, square nor round, a fluttering butterfly—is exactly appropriate to the erratic impulses of the character. Finally, even the rhetorical movement and rhythm are responsive to the tone and meaning, most obviously in the lines,

> Thus, like light butterflies, much flutter makes,
> Sleep'st of one judgment, of another wakes.

This portrait of Buckingham has the autonomous poetic life of true satire.

My own feeling, which I cannot prove, is that Dryden must have known this passage because his portrait shares with it central conceptions and techniques. Whether he knew it or not, the important point is that the anonymous passage exemplifies the formal and stylistic features by which satire can transmute history into poetry. Dryden's lines are more concentrated and fluent, but they are of the same creative kind:

> A man so various that he seemed to be
> Not one, but all mankind's epitome.
> Stiff in opinions, always in the wrong;
> Was everything by starts and nothing long:
> But, in the course of one revolving moon,
> Was chemist, fiddler, statesman, and buffoon:
> Then all for women, painting, rhyming, drinking;
> Besides ten thousand freaks that died in thinking.
> Blest madman, who could every hour employ
> With something new to wish, or to enjoy!

There is no need to multiply examples from the almost unknown works of minor Augustan satirists. Many such pieces fail to transmute history into poetry. On the other hand, here and there a passage or, sometimes, a whole poem will be touched by the true satiric art into poetry. In episode, description, or characterization, the critical question remains the same: has the satirist succeeded, by his masks, his indirections, his ironies and his myths, in freeing his poem from the trammels of historical circumstance and in bestow-

ing upon it the poetic autonomy of true satire? In a thousand un-
known examples, in a bewildering array of formal and satirical de-
vices, we can find topical verse struggling toward the condition of
an art which the great Augustans, profiting by these examples,
brought to perfection.

I. Political Affairs

ROBERT WILD

Iter Boreale
(*1660*)

"He is the very Wither of the city: they have bought more editions of his works than would serve to lay under all their pies at the Lord Mayor's Christmas. When his famous poem first came out in the year 1660, I have seen them reading it in the midst of 'Change time; nay so vehement they were at it, that they lost their bargain by the candles' ends." Thus Eugenius, in Dryden's *Essay of Dramatic Poesy*, testifies to the extraordinary impact of *Iter Boreale,* a poem that was not only the most popular of the innumerable lampoons upon the expelled Rump Parliament, but the most popular of the many effusions in verse which welcomed Charles Stuart back to his kingdom.

Dryden's discussion of popular occasional verse had begun with a reference to the English naval victory over the Dutch on 3 June 1665, the famous Battle of Lowestoft, which was to be an important motif in so much Restoration poetry. Wild, Crites says, is a poet who watches a battle "with more diligence than the ravens and birds of prey," one "whom this victory with both her wings will never be able to escape." Although Wild did not happen to celebrate this occasion in his verses, the spirit of Crites' prophecy is right—few important events, especially in the realm of ecclesiastical affairs, escaped Wild's vigilant pen, and he did turn out a panegyric upon a later engagement with the Dutch fleet. As a Puritan minister and a Royalist Wild was always trying to vindicate the loyalty of Charles II's Nonconformist subjects, while he derided both the jealousies and the forms of the Anglicans. In George Monck (1608–70), the great Presbyterian architect of Charles' restoration, he found a subject heaven-sent. *Iter Boreale* relates with gusto and with considerable historical detail the steps by which this shrewd and taciturn hero outmaneuvered both the Rump Parliament and the Army faction to engineer this bloodless revolution.

Iter Boreale illustrates clearly the peculiar appeal of minor politi-

3

cal verse—its intense contemporary interest, its vivid detail, and its occasional vitality of thought and style. In the person of Crites, the greatest of Restoration satirists remarks that Wild, who was probably the most popular, is addicted to "a certain clownish kind of raillery," and that he is "a very Leveler in poetry; he creeps along with ten little words in every line, and helps out his numbers with *for to* and *unto* and all the pretty expletives he can find." The remark is not exactly just, for *Iter Boreale* manages, in its intense Clevelandesque way, to convey some of the excitement and joy so deeply and widely felt on the eve of the Restoration, as well as some of the popular contempt for the regimes which immediately preceded it.

The text is based on the first edition (1660).

ITER BOREALE

Attempting Something upon the Successful
and Matchless March of the Lord General
George Monck from Scotland to London in
the Winter, 1659

1.

The day is broke! Melpomene, begone;
Hag of my fancy, let me now alone;
Nightmare my soul no more; go take thy flight
Where traitors' ghosts keep an eternal night;
Flee to Mount Caucasus and bear thy part   5
With the black fowl that tears Prometheus' heart
For his bold sacrilege; go fetch the groans
Of defunct tyrants, with them croak thy tones.
Go see Alecto with her flaming whip,
How she firks Nol and makes old Bradshaw skip.   10
Go make thyself away—thou shalt no more
Choke up my standish with the blood and gore
Of English tragedies: I now will choose
The merriest of the nine to be my Muse,

10. *firks:* Beats. *Nol:* Oliver Cromwell. *Bradshaw:* John Bradshaw (1602–59), President of the Commission that tried Charles I.
12. *standish:* Inkstand.

George Monck, Duke of Albemarle. From an engraving by Loggan.

And, come what will, I'll scribble once again.   15
The brutish sword hath cut the nobler vein
Of racy poetry; our small-drink times
Must be contented and take up with rhymes.
They're sorry toys from a poor Levite's pack,
Whose living and assessments drink no sack—   20
The subject will excuse the verse, I trow;
The venison's fat, although the crust be dough.

2.

I he who whilom sat and sung in cage
My King's and country's ruin by the rage
Of a rebellious rout; who weeping saw   25
Three goodly kingdoms, drunk with fury, draw
And sheathe their swords, like three enraged brothers,
In one another's sides, ripping their mother's
Belly, and tearing out her bleeding heart;
Then, jealous that their father fain would part   30
Their bloody fray and let them fight no more,
Fell foul on him and slew him at his door;
I that have only dar'd to whisper verses,
And drop a tear by stealth on loyal hearses;
I that enraged at the times and Rump,   35
Had gnaw'd my goose-quill to the very stump,
And flung that in the fire, no more to write,
But to sit down poor Britain's Heraclite,
Now sing the triumphs of the men of war,
The glorious rays of the bright Northern Star,   40
Created for the nonce by Heav'n to bring
The wise men of three nations to their King.
Monck! the great Monck! that syllable outshines
Plantagenet's bright name or Constantine's.
'Twas at his rising that our day begun;   45

17. *small-drink:* Trivial.
19. *Levite:* Priest.
23–42. While Wild was a Royalist throughout his life, there is no evidence that he wrote or suffered imprisonment in the cause of Charles I. The career here described sounds much like that of John Cleveland, whose influence is reflected in the style and opinions of *Iter Boreale.*
38. *Heraclite:* Heraclitus, the "weeping philosopher."

Be he the morning star to Charles our sun.
He took rebellion rampant by the throat,
And made the canting Quaker change his note.
His hand it was that wrote (we saw no more)
Exit tyrannus over Lambert's door.   50
Like to some subtle lightning, so his words
Dissolved in their scabbards rebels' swords.
He with success the sov'reign skill hath found
To dress the weapon and so heal the wound.
George and his boys, as spirits do, they say,   55
Only by walking scare our foes away.

3.

Old Holofernes was no sooner laid
Before the idol's funeral pomp was paid
(Nor shall a penny e'er be paid for me:
Let fools that trusted his true mourners be),   60
Richard the Fourth just peeping out of squire
(No fault so much as the old one was his sire,
For men believ'd, though all went in his name,
He'd be but tenant till the landlord came),
When on a sudden, all amaz'd, we found   65
The seven years' Babel tumbl'd to the ground,
And he, poor heart, thanks to his cunning kin,
Was soon in cuerpo honest Dick again.

50. *Lambert:* John Lambert (1619–83) commanded the army sent north in November 1659 to oppose Monck's entry into England. His soldiers deserted en masse.

54. A reference to the medical superstition that wounds could be healed by treating the weapon which had inflicted them.

57. *old Holofernes:* Wild refers to Oliver Cromwell by the name of Nebuchadnezzar's tyrannical general. See the Book of Judith in the Old Testament Apocrypha.

58. Cromwell died 3 Sept. 1658. His body lay in state at Somerset House "amid banners, escutcheons, black velvet draperies and all the sombre gorgeousness of the greatest royal funerals. . . and not until the 23rd of November was there an end to these ghastly splendors" (Masson, *Life of Milton*, 5, 415).

59. *for me:* On my behalf.

61. *Richard the Fourth:* Richard Cromwell, who succeeded his father as Lord Protector. *out of squire:* Out of square, out of proper order or rule.

67. *cunning kin:* Charles Fleetwood (d. 1692), Richard Cromwell's brother-in-law, a leader of the army or Wallingford House faction, whose ambition to be Commander-in-Chief released forces that were to topple the new Protector (Masson, *Life of Milton*, 5, 425).

68. *in cuerpo:* Naked.

Exit Protector. What comes next? I trow,
Let the state-huntsmen beat again. "So ho!"   70
Cries Lambert, Master of the Hounds, "Here sits
That lusty puss, the Good Old Cause, whose wits
Show'd Oliver such sport." "That! that!" cries Vane,
"Let's put her up, and run her once again!
She'll lead our dogs and followers up and down,   75
Whilst we match families and take the crown."
Enter the old Members. 'Twas the month of May
These maggots in the Rump began to play.
Wallingford anglers, though they stunk, yet thought
They would make baits by which fish might be caught,   80
And so it prov'd—they soon by taxes made
More money than the Holland fishing-trade.

4.

Now broke in Egypt's plagues all in a day
And one more, worse than theirs. We must not pray
To be deliver'd—their scabb'd folks were free   85
To scratch where it did itch—so might not we.
That meteor Cromwell, though he scar'd, gave light,
But we were now cover'd with horrid night.
Our magistracy was, like Moses' rod,
Turn'd to a serpent by the angry God.   90
Poor citizens when trading would not do
Made brick without straw and were basted too.
Struck with the botch of taxes and excise,

71–73. When Richard fell in April 1659, Lambert recovered his old position as chief representative of the army in the negotiations which preceded the restoration of the Rump Parliament. Though not a member of the Wallingford House party, Lambert joined with Fleetwood and John Desborough (1608–80), the leaders of this faction, in restoring the Rump to satisfy public clamor for the Good Old Cause (the pure Republican constitution).

73. *Vane:* Sir Henry Vane the younger (1613–62) played a leading part in the restoration of the Rump. After Charles II returned he was among those capitally excepted from pardon as too dangerous to live. He was executed 14 June 1662.

77–78. The Rump was restored on 7 May 1659.

79–80. This rather confusing passage means that the Wallingford House party hoped to enhance their own power by using the Rump to which they were really opposed.

90. See Exodus 3–4:5.

92. *basted:* Cudgelled.

93. *botch:* An eruptive disease.

Servants (our very dust) were turn'd to lice—
It was but turning soldiers, and they need   95
Not work at all, but on their masters feed.
Strange caterpillars ate our pleasant things,
And frogs croak'd in the chambers of our kings;
Black-bloody veins did in the Rump prevail,
Like the Philistines' emrods in the tail.   100
Lightning, hail, fire, and thunder Egypt had,
And England guns, shot, powder (that's as bad).
And that sea-monster Lawson, if withstood,
Threaten'd to turn our rivers into blood;
And—plague of all these plagues—all these plagues fell   105
Not on an Egypt, but our Israel.

5.

Sick as her heart can hold the nation lies,
Filling each corner with her hideous cries:
Sometimes rage, like a burning fever, heats,
Anon despair brings cold and clammy sweats;   110
She cannot sleep—or if she doth she dreams
Of rapes, thefts, burnings, blood, and direful themes;
Tosses from side to side, then by-and-by
Her feet are laid there where the head did lie.
None can come to her but bold empirics,   115
Who never meant to cure her but try tricks.
Those very doctors who should give her ease—
God help the patient!—were her worst disease.
The Italian mountebank Vane tells her sure
Jesuits' powder will effect the cure;   120
If grief but makes her swell, Marten and Neville

100. *emrods:* Hemorrhoids. For an account of the Philistines' afflictions see I Samuel 5.

103. *Lawson:* Sir John Lawson (d. 1665), Commander-in-Chief of the fleet in 1659. He finally favored the restoration of Charles II and his great influence helped bring the navy over to the King.

115. *empirics:* Quacks.

120. *Jesuits' powder:* A powdered Peruvian bark used in the treatment of fevers, with an allusion to Vane's eclectic religious views or to his tolerant attitude toward Catholics.

121. *Marten:* Henry Marten (1602–80), regicide and member of the Council of State (the assembly elected after Charles I's execution). *Neville:* Henry Neville (1620–94), member of the Council of State and doctrinaire Republican.

Conclude it is a spice of the king's evil.
"Bleed her again!" another cries, and Scot
Says he could cure her if 'twas—you know what,
But giddy Harrington a whimsey found   125
To make her head like to his brains run round.
Her old and wise physicians, who before
Had well-nigh cur'd her, came again to the door,
But were kept out, which made her cry the more
"Help, help, dear children! oh, some pity take   130
On her who bore you! help, for mercy sake!
Oh, heart! oh, head! oh, back! oh, bones! I feel
They've poison'd me with giving too much steel!
Oh, give me that for which I long and cry—
Something that's sovereign, or else I die!"   135

6.

Kind Cheshire heard and, like some son that stood
Upon the bank, straight jump'd into the flood,
Flings out his arms and strikes some strokes to swim.
Booth ventur'd first and Middleton with him;
Stout Mackworth, Egerton, and thousands more,   140

122. *spice:* Kind.

123. *Scot:* Thomas Scot, regicide and staunch Republican. Even after the secluded members returned in 1660 he affirmed the justice of Charles I's execution. He was condemned to death and executed on 17 Oct. 1660.

125–26. *Harrington:* James Harrington (1611–77), the well-known Republican political theorist. He is reported to have drunk such quantities of guaiac (a stimulating drug like cantharides) that it injured his brain.

127–28. An allusion to the secluded members of the Long Parliament, who were re-admitted by Monck's intervention.

133. *steel:* Medicine containing iron.

135. *something that's sovereign:* An especially efficacious remedy.

136ff. A general rising against the Rump occurred in Cheshire in 1659, but Lambert suppressed it.

139. *Booth:* George Booth, first Lord Delamere (1622–84), supported the Parliamentary party in Cheshire during the Civil War. Later he "became one of the leaders of the party of Cromwellian malcontents called 'the new Royalists,' who, with the Cavaliers, concocted the 'general plot' for the restoration of Charles II" (*DNB*). He led the Cheshire rising and after its defeat attempted to escape disguised as a woman, but was discovered and committed to the Tower. After the Restoration the House of Commons offered him a reward of £20,000 for his services. *Middleton:* Sir Thomas Middleton (1586–1666), a Parliamentary general during the Civil War. He took part in Booth's rising, was captured and imprisoned, and was later rewarded by Charles II.

140. *Mackworth:* Sir Francis Mackworth, another participant in the Cheshire rebellion. *Egerton:* Randolph Egerton, another major-general who took part in the rising.

Threw themselves in and left the safer shore;
Massey, that famous diver, and bold Browne
Forsook his wharf, resolving all to drown
Or save a sinking kingdom; but (O sad!)
Fearing to lose her prey, the sea grew mad,   145
Rais'd all her billows and resolv'd her waves
Should quickly be the bold adventurers' graves.
Out marches Lambert like an eastern wind
And with him all the mighty waters join'd.
The loyal swimmers bore up heads and breasts,   150
Scorning to think of life or interests.
They pli'd their arms and thighs, but all in vain:
The furious main beat them to shore again,
At which the floating island, looking back,
Spying her loyal lovers gone to wrack,   155
Shriek'd louder than before, and thus she cries:
"Can you, ye angry heav'ns and frowning skies,
Thus countenance rebellious mutineers,
Who, if they durst, would be about your ears?
That I should sink with justice may accord,   160
Who let my pilot be thrown overboard,
Yet 'twas not I, ye righteous heav'ns do know—
The soldiers in me needs would have it so—
And those who conjur'd up these storms themselves
And first engag'd me 'mongst these rocks and shelves,   165
Guilty of all my woes, have rais'd this weather,
Fearing to come to land and choosing rather
To sink me with themselves. O cease to frown!
In tears, just heav'ns, behold, myself I drown!
Let not these proud waves do it; prevent my fears   170
And let them fall together by the ears."

142. *Massey:* Sir Edward Massey (1619?–74?), Parliamentary major-general and states-man impeached by the army in 1647. He took service under Charles II as lieutenant-general in the invasion of England in 1651. After Worcester he was brought to Lon-don for trial, but he managed to escape to Holland. In 1659 he plotted a rising in Gloucestershire, but was betrayed and captured. *Browne:* Sir Richard Browne (d. 1669), Parliamentary general expelled by the army from the House of Commons. He joined Booth's rising.
148. Lambert defeated Booth's forces at Winnington (or Winwick) Bridge 19 August 1659.
154. *The floating island:* England. Cf. line 144.

7.

Heav'n heard and struck the insulting army mad;
Drunk with their Cheshire triumphs straight they had
New lights uprear'd, and new resolves they take,
A single person once again to make.   175
Who shall he be? Oh! Lambert, without rub,
The fittest de'il to be Beelzebub.
He, the fierce fiend cast out of the House before,
Return'd and threw the House now out of door;
A legion then he rais'd of armed sprites,   180
Elves, goblins, fairies, Quakers, and New Lights,
To be his under-devils; with this rest
He soul and body, Church and State, possess'd,
Who though they fill'd all countries, towns, and rooms,
Yet, like that fiend that did frequent the tombs,   185
Churches and sacred grounds they haunted most—
No chapel was at ease from some such ghost.
The priests ordain'd to exorcise those elves
Were voted devils and cast out themselves—
Bible, or Alcoran, all's one to them;   190
Religion serves but for a stratagem—
The holy charms these adders did not heed;
Churches themselves did sanctuary need.

8.

The Church's patrimony and rich store
Alas! was swallow'd many years before.   195
Bishops and deans we fed upon before
(They were the ribs and sirloins of the Whore);
Now let her legs, the priests, go to the pot
(They have the Pope's eye in them—spare them not!)

174. *New Lights:* Novel doctrines (esp. theological and ecclesiastical) the partisans of which lay claim to superior enlightenment. I have followed Wild's editor, Hunt, in emending the text's *appear'd* to *uprear'd.*

175ff. In the fall of 1659 Lambert blockaded Parliament and prevented members from entering. It was widely assumed that he intended to make himself Lord Protector.

197. *the Whore:* The Roman Catholic Church.

199. *the Pope's eye:* The lymphatic gland surrounded with fat in the middle of a leg of mutton; regarded by some as a tidbit.

We have fat benefices yet to eat—   200
Bel and our Dragon army must have meat.
Let us devour her limb-meal, great and small,
Tithe-calves, geese, pigs, the pettitoes and all.
A vicarage in sippets, though it be
But small, will serve a squeamish sectary.   205
Though universities we can't endure,
There's no false Latin in their lands, be sure.
Give Oxford to our Horse and let the Foot
Take Cambridge for their booty and fall to't.
"Christ Church I'll have," cries Vane; Desb'rough swops   210
At Trinity; King's is for Berry's chops;
Kelsey, take Corpus Christi; All Souls, Packer;
Carve Creed St. John's; New College leave to Hacker;
Fleetwood cries, "Weeping Magdalen shall be mine,
Her tears I'll drink instead of muscadine."   215
The smaller halls and houses scarce are big
Enough to make one dish for Hasilrig.
"We must be sure to stop his mouth, though wide,
Else all our fat will be in the fire," they cri'd,
"And when we have done these, we'll not be quiet—   220
Lordships' and landlords' rents shall be our diet."
Thus talk'd this jolly crew, but still mine host
Lambert resolves that he will rule the roast.

9.

But hark! methinks I hear old Boreas blow.
What mean the north winds that they bluster so?   225
More storms from that black nook? Forbear, bold Scot!
Let not Dunbar and Worcester be forgot.

201. Bel and the Dragon are voracious Babylonian idols in the apocryphal book
of that name. The sectaries wished the Apocrypha included in the authorized Bible.
202. *limb-meal:* Piecemeal, *obs.*
206–17. This plot to despoil the universities is a fiction. Desborough, James Berry
(fl. 1665), Thomas Kelsey (d. 1680?), John Creed, Francis Hacker (d. 1660), Charles
Fleetwood (d. 1692), and Sir Arthur Hasilrig (d. 1661) were among those senior of-
ficers who signed a petition at Derby demanding that Parliament grant vast powers to
the army. Monck did not sign the petition and was in consequence appointed Com-
mander-in-Chief of the Parliamentary forces.
210. *swops:* Strikes.
227. Cromwell defeated the Scots at Dunbar 3 Sept. 1650 and exactly one year later
routed the Scottish forces of Charles II at Worcester.

What! would you chaffer with us for one Charles more?
The price of kings is fallen, give the trade o'er.
"And is the price of kings and kingdoms too,   230
Of laws, lives, oaths, souls, grown so low with you?
Perfidious hypocrites! monsters of men!"
Cries the good Monck, "We'll raise their price again!"
Heav'n said Amen! and breath'd upon that spark;
That spark, preserv'd alive in the cold and dark,   235
First kindl'd and enflam'd the British Isle
And turn'd it all to bonfires in a while.
He and his fuel were so small no doubt
Proud Lambert thought to tread or piss them out.
But George was wary; his cause did require   240
A pillar of a cloud as well as fire:
'Twas not his safest course to flame but smoke—
His enemies he will not burn but choke.
Small fires must not blaze out, lest by their light
They show their weakness and their foes invite;   245
But furnaces the stoutest metals melt,
And so did he, by fire not seen but felt;
Dark-lantern language and his peep-bo play
Will-e-wisp'd Lambert's New Lights out of the way.
George and his boys those thousands (O strange thing!)   250
Of snipes and woodcocks took by lowbelling;
His few Scotch-coal kindl'd with English fire
Made Lambert's great Newcastle heaps expire.

10.

Scotland, though poor and peevish, was content
To keep the peace and (O rare!) money lent.   255
But yet the blessing of their Kirk was more—

240–51. Monck was extremely cautious in divulging his political intentions. In a
letter to Fleetwood 20 Oct. 1659 he merely declared his intention of upholding the
authority of Parliament (Godfrey Davies, *The Restoration of Charles II*, p. 164). Even
after he had entered London Monck remained noncommittal. "The ambiguity of his
utterances and the contradictions between his words and his actions puzzled the
shrewdest observers. Neither Hyde nor the Royalist agents in England could guess
whether he meant to serve the King or to maintain the Rump in power" (*DNB*).
248. *Dark-lantern:* Cryptic. *peep-bo:* Bo-beep, hidden and unpredictable.
251. *lowbelling:* Lowbells were bells used in fowling at night to stupefy birds.
253. *Newcastle:* The headquarters of Lambert's army.

George had that too—and with this slender store
He and his myrmidons advance. Kind Heaven
Prepar'd a frost to make their march more even,
Easy, and safe: it may be said, that year,   260
Of the highways Heav'n itself was overseer
And made November ground as hard as May.
White as their innocence, so was their way.
The clouds came down in feather-beds to greet
Him and his army and to kiss their feet.   265
The frost and foes both came and went together,
Both thaw'd away, and vanish'd God knows whither.
Whole countries crowded in to see this friend,
Ready to cast their bodies down to mend
His road to Westminster, and still they shout,   270
"Lay hold of the Rump and pull the monster out!
A new one or a whole one, good my Lord,"
And to this cry the island did accord.
The echo of the Irish hollow ground
Heard England and her language did rebound.   275

11.

Presto! Jack Lambert and his sprites are gone
To dance a jig with his brother Oberon.
George made him and his cut-throats of our lives
Swallow their swords as jugglers do their knives,
And Carter Desborough to wish in vain   280
He now were wagoner to Charles's Wain.
The conqueror's now come into the south,
Whose warm air is made hot by ev'ry mouth
Breathing his welcome and in spite of Scot
Crying "The whole child, sir, divide it not."   285

257–67. "The going was hard in the very wintry weather, with frost and snow so
continuous that, according to Price [Monck's chaplain and biographer], 'I do not re-
member that ever we trod upon plain earth from Edinburgh to London'" (Davies,
The Restoration of Charles II, pp. 265–66).

280. *Carter:* An allusion to Desborough's former occupation as a small farmer.
This term leads to a typical bit of Wild wordplay on *Charles's Wain* (the Big Dipper).

284. Scot was sent by the Rump to placate Monck, but his mission was unsuccessful.

285. This reference to Solomon's judgment alludes to Monck's insistence on the
readmission of the secluded members. Cf. I Kings 3:16–28.

The Rump begins to stink: "Alas!" cry they,
"We've rais'd a devil which we cannot lay;
I like him not." "His belly is so big,
There's a king in it!" cries furious Hasilrig.
"Let's bribe him," they cry all, "Carve him a share   290
Of our stol'n venison!" Varlets, forbear!
In vain you put your lime-twigs to his hands.
George Monck is for the King, not for his lands.
When fair means would not do, next foul they try:
"Vote him the City scavenger," they cry—   295
"Send him to scour their streets." "Well, let it be;
Your Rumpship wants a scouring too," thinks he,
"That foul house where your worships many years
Have laid your tail sure wants a scavenger.
I smell your fizzle though it make no crack.   300
You'd mount me on the City's galled back
In hopes she'd cast her rider. If I must
Upon some office in the town be thrust,
I'll be their sword-bearer, and to their dagger
I'll join my sword. Nay, good Rump, do not swagger;   305
The City feasts me, and as sure as gun
I'll mend all England's Commons ere I've done."

12.

And so he did. One morning next his heart
He went to Westminster and play'd his part.
He vamp'd their boots, which Hewson ne'er could do   310

292. *lime-twigs:* Twigs smeared with birdlime.

295–307. When it was believed that the City refused to pay taxes levied by the Rump, Monck was ordered at Scot's instigation to make the gates of the City indefensible and to arrest a number of leading citizens (9 Feb. 1660). By this device Scot hoped to inflame the citizens against Monck, who was becoming popular. Monck obeyed his orders but explained to the Corporation that he had undertaken this disagreeable duty so that it might not be performed more severely by his enemies. The attempt to discredit Monck miscarried and, in fact, led to his alliance with the citizens in a successful demand for the seating of the secluded members. By this stratagem the Rump paved the way for its own dissolution and the election of the Convention Parliament which restored Charles II.

307. *Commons:* 1. the Lower House; 2. daily fare.

310. *vamp'd:* Repaired.

310–11. On 5 Dec. 1659 some apprentices defiantly presented a petition to the Common Council. In the ensuing disorder a regiment of foot under the regicide Col. John

With better leather, made them go upright too.
The restor'd members, Cato-like, no doubt,
Did only enter that they might go out.
They did not mean within those walls to dwell,
Nor did they like their company so well,   315
Yet Heav'n so bless'd them that in three weeks' space
They gave both Church and State a better face.
They gave Booth, Massey, Browne, some kinder lots
(The last year's traitors, this year's patriots).
The Church's poor remainder they made good   320
And wash'd the nation's hands of royal blood;
And that a Parliament they did devise
From its own ashes, phoenix-like, might rise.
This done by act and deed that might not fail
They pass'd a fine and so cut off th' entail.   325

13.

Let the bells ring these changes now from Bow
Down to the country candlesticks below.
Ringers, hands off! The bells themselves will dance
In memory of their own deliverance.
Had not George show'd his metal and said nay,   330
Each sectary had borne the bell away.
"Down with them all, they're christen'd," cri'd that
    crew;

Hewson fired on the crowd and killed some apprentices. Hewson had been a shoe-maker.

312–15. "By the month of March 1660 the position was this—a decayed remnant of Parliament had been reinvigorated by a transfusion of Presbyterian blood in order to provide the energy to commit suicide" (Ogg, *England in the Reign of Charles II*, *I*, 25.

318. Booth was appointed a commissioner to settle the militia. Massey represented London in the Convention Parliament. Browne, a secluded member, was readmitted to his seat.

321. "Before the dissolution a disorderly and apparently irrelevant debate took place about the execution of Charles I. John Crew had moved that before they separated for the last time members should bear their witness against 'the horrid murder.' One after another rose to deny their concurrence in it. Then Scot bravely defended the execution and hoped he would never repent of it and desired that on his tombstone might be inscribed: 'Here lies Thomas Scot, who adjudged to death the late King'" (Davies, *The Restoration of Charles II*, p. 305).

327. *country candlesticks:* Country churches. Cf. Revelation 1:20: "the seven candlesticks which thou sawest are the seven Churches."

331. *had borne the bell away:* Had won.

"Tie up their clappers and the parsons too;
Turn them to guns, or sell them to the Dutch."
"Nay, hold," quoth George, "my masters, that's too
    much. 335
You will not leap o'er steeples thus I hope—
I'll save the bells, but you may take the rope."
Thus lay Religion panting for her life,
Like Isaac bound under the bloody knife;
George held the falling weapon, sav'd the lamb, 340
Let Lambert in the briars be the ram.
So lay the royal virgin, as 'tis told,
When brave St. George redeem'd her life of old.
Oh that the knaves that have consum'd our land,
Had but permitted wood enough to stand 345
To be his bonfires! We'd burn ev'ry stem
And leave no more but gallow-trees for them!

14.

March on, great hero! as thou hast begun,
And crown our happiness before thou'st done.
We have another Charles to fetch from Spain; 350
Be thou the George to bring him back again.
Then shalt thou be, what was deni'd that knight,
Thy Prince's and the people's favorite.
There is no danger of the winds at all,
Unless together by the ears they fall 355
Who shall the honor have to waft a king,
And they who gain it while they work shall sing.
Methinks I see how those triumphant gales,
Proud of their great employment, swell the sails;
The joyful ship shall dance, the sea shall laugh, 360
And loyal fish their master's health shall quaff.
See how the dolphins crowd and thrust their large
And scaly shoulders to assist the barge;

338–41. Cf. Genesis 22:1–14. Lambert was not destined to act the part of the sacrificial lamb, but died a prisoner in Guernsey in 1683.

350–53. Monck's journey to Breda to fetch Charles II is compared with that of George Villiers, first Duke of Buckingham, who accompanied Charles I, then Prince of Wales, to Spain in a vain attempt to make a match with the Infanta. This labored comparison contrasts the popularity of this George with the widespread hatred of Charles I's favorite.

The peaceful kingfishers are met together
About the decks and prophesy calm weather;   365
Poor crabs and lobsters have gone down to creep,
And search for pearls and jewels in the deep;
And when they have the booty, crawl before,
And leave them for his welcome to the shore.

15.

Methinks I see how throngs of people stand,   370
Scarce patient till the vessel come to land,
Ready to leap in, and, if need require,
With tears of joy to make the waters higher.
But what will London do? I doubt Old Paul
With bowing to his Sovereign will fall;   375
The royal lions from the Tower shall roar,
And though they see him not, yet shall adore;
The conduits will be ravish'd and combine
To turn their very water into wine,
And for the citizens, I only pray   380
They may not, overjoy'd, all die that day.
May we all live more loyal and more true,
To give to Caesar and to God their due.
We'll make his father's tomb with tears to swim,
And for the son, we'll shed our blood for him.   385
England her penitential song shall sing
And take heed how she quarrels with her King.
If for our sins our Prince shall be misled,
We'll bite our nails rather than scratch our head.

16.

One English George outweighs alone, by odds,   390
A whole committee of the heathens' gods;
Pronounce but Monck, and it is all his due:
He is our Mercury, Mars, and Neptune too.
Monck, what great Xerxes could not, prov'd the man
That with a word shackl'd the ocean;   395
He shall command Neptune himself to bring

378–79. When Charles arrived in London, public fountains did, in fact, flow with
wine. See Bryant, *Charles II*, p. 81.

His trident and present it to our King.
Oh, do it then, great Admiral! Away!
Let him be here against St. George's day,
That Charles may wear his *Dieu et mon droit,*   400
And thou the noble-garter'd *Honi soit.*
And when thy aged corpse shall yield to fate,
God save that soul that sav'd our Church and State.
There thou shalt have a glorious crown, I know,
Who crown'st our King and kingdoms here below.   405
But who shall find a pen fit for thy glory,
Or make posterity believe thy story?

Vive St. George!

399. *Iter Boreale* was published on St. George's day, 23 April. The King did not reach London until 29 May, his birthday.

400. *Dieu et mon Droit:* A motto of English kings.

401. *Honi soit [qui mal y pense]:* Motto of the Order of the Garter with which Monck was invested on the day after Charles landed.

EDMUND WALLER

Instructions to a Painter
(*1665*)

To judge from the poetry which celebrates them, the first five years of the Restoration were halcyon ones. Except for one or two inferior squibs on the plight of the Cavaliers, who were bitter about the Restoration settlement in general and felt that the Act of Indemnity and Oblivion in particular was "an act of indemnity for the King's enemies and oblivion for the King's friends," not a breath of criticism survives among all the commendatory verses on the royal family, on Lord Chancellor Hyde, or on Charles' reigning mistress, the Countess of Castlemaine.

Early in 1665 England managed to provoke a war with Holland, her commercial rival, after a sneak attack on Dutch merchantmen in the western Mediterranean. The high point of this Second Dutch War was the English victory off Lowestoft on 3 June 1665. That night, however, as the Dutch fled eastward, orders were given in the flagship of the Duke of York, Lord High Admiral, to call off pursuit, and the English missed their chance to destroy Dutch sea power. The Dutch fleet revived and in 1667 inflicted on the unprepared English navy the most humiliating defeat it has ever suffered.

The abortive victory of the Duke of York is the subject of this panegyric by Waller, whose zeal was intensified, no doubt, by uneasiness over his *Panegyric to my Lord Protector* (1655) and his elegy *Upon the Late Storm and of the Death of his Highness* (1658). Dryden was in a similar plight over his *Heroic Stanzas to the Glorious Memory of Cromwell* and had already paid court to the new regime in *Astræa Redux* (1660), *To his Sacred Majesty, a Panegyric upon his Coronation* (1661), and *To my Lord Chancellor, Presented on New Year's Day* (1662). The Duke of York at Lowestoft was to have his turn in the poem with which Dryden dedicated *Annus Mirabilis* (1666) to the Duchess.

Instructions to a Painter is modeled upon Giovanni Francesco Busenello's celebration of a Venetian naval victory over the Turks

An engagement between English and Dutch warships. From a painting by William Van de Velde the younger.

off Candy (Crete) in 1655. This poem (translated in 1658 as *A Pro-spective of the Naval Triumph of the Venetians*) introduced into English poetry an *ut pictura poesis* device in which the poet instructs the painter in detail how he is to depict the victory. Waller's tribute had a wholly unexpected effect because of the many unfavorable aspects of the engagement which had been excluded. In *The Second Advice to a Painter,* a mock imitation of his poem, some satirist (probably Marvell) hastened to supply the missing details and paint Lowestoft and English naval affairs in 1665 as a masterpiece of mismanagement, greed, and cowardice. *Second Advice* thus helped establish the painter convention in satirical poetry. It was followed by a *Third Advice* (probably also Marvell's), by the *Fourth* and *Fifth Advices* (printed in 1667 with the second and third under the name of Sir John Denham), by Marvell's *Last Instructions* and his *Further Instructions,* and by dozens of other pieces in the same form.* The concentration on visual detail which the painter convention demands made it a singularly effective technique for the satiric poet intent upon the grotesque.

Waller's *Instructions* appeared as a broadside in 1665. The folio, on which our text is based, appeared the following year.

INSTRUCTIONS TO A PAINTER

For the Drawing of the Posture and Progress of His Majesty's Forces at Sea, under the Command of His Highness-Royal; together with the Battle and Victory Obtained over the Dutch, June 3, 1665.

First draw the sea, that portion which between
The greater world and this of ours is seen;
Here place the British, there the Holland fleet,
Vast floating armies, both prepar'd to meet!

---

* The authorship of the second and third *Advices* is discussed in a series of articles in the *Bulletin of the New York Public Library:* George deF. Lord, "Two New Poems by Marvell?" *Bulletin, 62* (1958), 551–70; Ephim G. Fogel, "Salmons in Both, or Some Caveats for Canonical Scholars," *Bulletin, 63* (1959), 223–36, 292–308; and Lord, "Comments on the Canonical Caveat," *Bulletin, 63* (1959), 355–66. The inclusion of these two poems in Bod. MS. Eng. Poet. d. 49, presumably the manuscript prepared at the direction of William Popple, the poet's nephew, is further evidence in support of Marvell's authorship (see Margoliouth, ed., *The Poems and Letters of Andrew Marvell, 1,* xiv–xv).

Draw the whole world expecting who shall reign,   5
After this combat, o'er the conquer'd main.
Make Heav'n concern'd and an unusual star
Declare th' importance of th' approaching war.
Make the sea shine with gallantry and all
The English youth flock to their Admiral,   10
The valiant Duke, whose early deeds abroad
Such rage in fight and art in conduct show'd.
His bright sword now a dearer int'rest draws,
His brother's glory and his country's cause.
Let thy bold pencil hope and courage spread   15
Through the whole navy, by that hero led;
Make all appear, where such a prince is by,
Resolv'd to conquer or resolv'd to die.
With his extraction and his glorious mind
Make the proud sails swell more than with the wind;   20
Preventing cannon, make his louder fame
Check the Batavians and their fury tame.
So hungry wolves, though greedy of their prey,
Stop when they find a lion in their way.
Make him bestride the ocean and mankind   25

7. *unusual star:* Perhaps the comet reported by Pepys 6 April 1665: "great talk of a new comet, and it is certain one do now appear as bright as the late one at the best, but I have not seen it myself."

9. *gallantry:* Many shortcomings of the Restoration navy were attributed to gentlemen captains and noble volunteers. "The navy as a service was popular with the gentry. And James took steps to utilise that popularity in a regular and reliable manner" (Tedder, *The Navy of the Restoration,* p. 59). The failure of the English fleet to achieve a decisive victory over the Dutch after Lowestoft can be directly attributed to a gentleman volunteer aboard the Duke's flagship. While the Duke was sleeping Henry Brouncker "delivered an order purporting to come from James to slacken sail and thus allow the Dutch to escape" (*DNB,* James II). Pepys reports that the Duchess of Albermarle "cried mightily out against the having of gentleman captains with feathers and ribbands, and wished the King would send her husband to sea with the old plain sea captains, that he served with formerly, that would make their ships swim with blood, though they could not make legs as captains nowadays can" (10 Jan. 1666).

11. *The valiant Duke* is, of course, James Duke of York, Lord High Admiral. His *early deeds abroad* included service with Turenne against the Fronde in 1652, a second campaign with Turenne in 1653 against Spain and Lorraine, and further service with Turenne in 1654–55 as lieutenant-general. At the siege of Mousson in 1653 he was nearly killed, but received a hero's reception in Paris. In 1657 he joined the Spanish forces in Flanders. In the siege of Ardres James was criticized for exposing himself recklessly to enemy fire.

Ask his consent to use the sea and wind;
While his tall ships in the barr'd channel stand,
He grasps the Indies in his armed hand.
Paint an east wind and make it blow away
Th' excuse of Holland for their navy's stay;   30
Make them look pale and, the bold Prince to shun,
Through the cold north and rocky regions run.
To find the coast where morning first appears,
By the dark Pole the wary Belgian steers,
Confessing now he dreads the English more   35
Than all the dangers of a frozen shore,
While from our arms, security to find,
They fly so far they leave the day behind.
Describe their fleet abandoning the sea
And all their merchants left a wealthy prey.   40
Our first success in war make Bacchus crown
And half the vintage of the year our own.
The Dutch their wine and all their brandy lose,
Disarm'd of that from which their courage grows,
While the glad English, to relieve their toil,   45
In healths to their great leader drink the spoil.
His high command to Afric's coast extend

31–38. In July 1664 a fleet under the command of the Earl of Sandwich put to sea to act as a defense for the rest of the English navy, which was still being made ready for war. The Dutch were also taking defensive measures at this time and "warned their merchant shipping to sail round the north of Scotland rather than through the Channel" to avoid Sandwich (Tedder, p. 104).

34. *Belgian:* A citizen of the Low Countries

41–46. In Nov. 1664 "Tyddeman and his small squadron had opened the campaign of attacks on trade which formed the usual preliminaries of a naval war. He opened well on the 20th by capturing the greater part of the Dutch fleet from Bordeaux laden with French commodities" (Tedder, p. 111). Among several reports on Dutch prizes taken is the following (*CSPD*, 6 Dec. 1664): "Capt. Tobias Sackler to the Navy Commrs. Loss of his boat in chasing and capturing a Dutch prize from St. Martin's Island, laden with wine and brandy."

47. "The King and the Duke of York, when they found that war with the States would be popular, decided to follow Cromwell's example. A squadron was fitted out to attack the Dutch possessions on the West Coast of Africa, and was placed under the command of Sir Robert Holmes" (Hannay, *A Short History of the Royal Navy*, pp. 327–28). Holmes sailed from England in Oct. 1663. He took some prizes and occupied some minor Dutch posts. In Aug. 1664 "both England and Holland had a squadron preparing to go to Guinea, the latter ostensibly to convoy four West Indiamen there, the former to follow the latter, convoy some Guinea ships and

And make the Moors before the English bend:
Those barbarous pirates willingly receive
Conditions such as we are pleas'd to give.   50
Deserted by the Dutch, let nations know
We can our own and their great business do,
False friends chastise and common foes restrain,
Which, worse than tempests, did infest the main.
Within those straits make Holland's Smyrna fleet   55
With a small squadron of the English meet:
Like falcons these, those like a num'rous flock
Of fowl which scatter to avoid the shock.
There paint confusion in a various shape:
Some sink, some yield, and flying, some escape.   60
Europe and Africa, from either shore,
Spectators are and hear our cannon roar,
While the divided world in this agree,
Men that fight so deserve to rule the sea.
   But, nearer home, thy pencil use once more   65
And place our navy by the Holland shore.

---

presumably to protect Holmes's conquests" (Tedder, pp. 104–05). The English fleet suffered countless delays in preparation and never got further than Portsmouth, when winter set in.

48–50. These lines probably refer to a treaty negotiated by Sir Thomas Allin with the Algerines in Nov. 1664. If so, they present the treaty in a much too favorable light, although its terms for a while "strengthened English prestige in the Mediterranean, both by admitting to England the freedom of those seas, and by having a chastening effect on two other trade disturbers—Tripoli and Tunis" (Tedder, p. 94).

55–64. Waller tactfully omits all reference to Allin's first disastrous attempt on the Smyrna fleet (2 Dec. 1664) when, "owing to bad weather, bad piloting, and darkness, nearly every one of his nine ships ended the chase on shore; the *Nonsuch* and the *Phoenix* were lost, the *Bonaventure* more or less crippled by leaks, and some of the others damaged to a lesser degree" (Tedder, p. 95).

On 29 Dec. Allin actually encountered a much diminished Smyrna fleet and took two prizes. "Such was the somewhat ignominious action by which the English opened the Dutch War" (Tedder, p. 97). It should be remembered that England had not declared war, but managed by these hostilities to provoke the States into doing so on 14 Jan. 1665. As Hannay remarks, "Waller greatly exaggerated the British victory" (*Short History of the Royal Navy*, p. 337).

65–76. Waller's account is especially fanciful here. The British fleet sailed over to the Dutch coast in May 1665. The Dutch fleet was still divided between the harbors at Texel and Vlie. "It was obvious that so long as a united English fleet was cruising between those places the divided Dutch squadrons were not likely to come out to be attacked piecemeal" (Tedder, p. 116). For ten days the English fleet plied up and down the coast without attacking the Dutch. Finally the Duke of York was forced to return to port because of the shortage of provisions.

The world they compass'd while they fought with Spain,
But here already they resign the main.
Those greedy mariners, out of whose way
Diffusive Nature could no region lay,   70
At home, preserv'd from rocks and tempests, lie,
Compell'd, like others, in their beds to die.
Their single towns th' Iberian armies press'd;
We all their provinces at once invest,
And, in a month, ruin their traffic more   75
Than that long war could in an age before.
   But who can always on the billows lie?
The wat'ry wilderness yields no supply:
Spreading our sails, to Harwich we resort,
And meet the beauties of the British court.   80
Th' illustrious Duchess and her glorious train
(Like Thetis with her nymphs) adorn the main.
The gazing sea-gods, since the Paphian queen
Sprung from among them, no such sight had seen.
Charm'd with the graces of a troop so fair,   85
Those deathless powers for us themselves declare,
Resolv'd the aid of Neptune's court to bring
And help the nation where such beauties spring.
The soldier here his wasted store supplies
And takes new valor from the ladies' eyes.   90
   Meanwhile, like bees, when stormy winter's gone,
The Dutch (as if the sea were all their own)

70. *Diffusive:* Dispensing or shedding widely or bountifully.

77–90. The Duchess of York began her visit to the fleet at Harwich 16 May 1665.
"For the next fortnight the business of victualling was relieved by intervals of merry-
making. Many of the volunteers—Buckingham, Falmouth, and the like—left the fleet;
but they who remained were sufficient to entertain throngs of women. Night and day
were made merry by the sailors' wives and sweethearts. Countess, courtesan, and
country wench, jostled one another both in cabin and forecastle" (Harris, *Life of
Sandwich, 1,* 293). It was probably at the end of the Duchess' visit that Charles Sack-
ville, Lord Buckhurst (later the Earl of Dorset) composed his celebrated poem "To all
you ladies."

91–94. While the English fleet was victualling the Dutch came out. "They had
only been out of port six days when they fell in with a fleet which they at first mis-
took for the English fleet: it proved to be an English fleet of merchantmen from
Hamburg laden with the most valuable stores. The mistake concerning nationality
had been mutual, and the man-of-war convoy 'mistaking the Dutch fleet for the
English fell into it' (*CSPD,* 29 May 1665)" (Tedder, pp. 118–19). For further details
of this disaster see *Second Advice,* 49–50 and note.

Desert their ports, and, falling in their way,
Our Hamburg merchants are become their prey.
Thus flourish they before th' approaching fight,   95
As dying tapers give a blazing light.
To check their pride, our fleet half-victual'd goes,
Enough to serve us till we reach our foes,
Who now appear so numerous and bold,
The action worthy of our arms we hold.   100
A greater force than that which here we find
Ne'er press'd the ocean nor employ'd the wind.
Restrain'd a while by the unwelcome night,
Th'impatient English scarce attend the light.
But now the morning (Heav'n severely clear)   105
To the fierce work indulgent does appear,
And Phoebus lifts above the waves his light,
That he might see, and thus record, the fight.
As when loud winds from different quarters rush,
Vast clouds encount'ring, one another crush,   110
With swelling sails so, from their several coasts,
Join the Batavian and the British hosts.
For a less prize, with less concern and rage,
The Roman fleets at Actium did engage;
They, for the empire of the world they knew,   115
These for the old contend and for the new.
At the first shock, with blood and powder stain'd,
Nor heav'n nor sea their former face retain'd;
Fury and art produce effects so strange,
They trouble nature and her visage change.   120
Where burning ships the banish'd sun supply,
And no light shines but that by which men die,
There York appears, so prodigal is he

97. *our fleet half-victual'd goes:* Throughout the Second Dutch War the English fleet was perennially short of supplies and especially of food and drink. The provisioning was entirely entrusted to a single private contractor, Denis Gauden, but the shortages can be blamed on the system rather than on the man, for "no fleet was ever so ill supplied for quantities of provision, as, to do the victualler right, none ever better for the goodness, against which there is not one complaint" (*S.P. Dom. Chas. II,* cxxi, f. 128, cited by Tedder, p. 113). The difficulties of supplying the fleet were aggravated by the plague.

105. *severely:* With austere plainness or simplicity of style. Cf. *Annus Mirabilis,* 208.

Of royal blood as ancient as the sea,
Which down to him, so many ages told,   125
Has through the veins of mighty monarchs roll'd!
The great Achilles march'd not to the field
Till Vulcan that impenetrable shield
And arms had wrought, yet there no bullets flew,
But shafts and darts which the weak Phrygians threw.   130
Our bolder hero on the deck does stand
Expos'd, the bulwark of his native land:
Defensive arms laid by as useless here
Where massy balls the neighboring rocks do tear.
Some power unseen those princes does protect,   135
Who for their country thus themselves neglect.
   Against him first Opdam his squadron leads,
Proud of his late success against the Swedes,
Made by that action and his high command
Worthy to perish by a prince's hand.   140
The tall Batavian in a vast ship rides,
Bearing an army in her hollow sides,
Yet not inclin'd the English ship to board,
More on his guns relies than on his sword;
From whence a fatal volley we receiv'd: 145
It miss'd the Duke, but his great heart it griev'd;
Three worthy persons from his side it tore
And dy'd his garment with their scatter'd gore.

137. *Opdam:* Jacob Wassenaer, Baron von Opdam, Admiral of the Dutch Navy.
From 1657 to 1660 the Dutch interfered successfully in the Swedish-Danish War in
order to prevent the entrance of the Baltic from falling into exclusively Swedish con-
trol. Opdam took part in these encounters.

147. *Three worthy persons:* Charles Berkeley, Earl of Falmouth, better known as
Lord Fitzharding; Charles MacCarthy, Lord Muskerry (in the Irish peerage); and
Richard Boyle, second son of the Earl of Burlington, "a youth of great hope, who
came newly home from travel, where he had spent his time with singular advantage,
and took the first opportunity to lose his life in the King's service" (Clarendon, *Life*,
section 643; quoted by Wheatley, *Pepys' Diary*, 8 June 1665 n.). "Both Charles and
James were more genuinely affected by Falmouth's death than by any other bereave-
ment in either of their lives. James had a very high opinion of his abilities, particu-
larly as a soldier, and held that once he had shed the follies of youth—for he was a
notorious libertine—he would have developed all the qualities of a statesman"
(Turner, *James II*, p. 80).

148. Pepys mentions "their blood and brains flying in the Duke's face, and the head
of Mr. Boyle striking down the Duke, as some say" (8 June 1665).

Happy! to whom this glorious death arrives,
More to be valu'd than a thousand lives!   150
On such a theatre as this to die,
For such a cause, and such a witness by!
Who would not thus a sacrifice be made
To have his blood on such an altar laid?
The rest about him struck with horror stood,   155
To see their leader cover'd o'er with blood:
So trembl'd Jacob, when he thought the stains
Of his son's coat had issu'd from his veins.
He feels no wound but in his troubled thought:
Before for honor, now revenge, he fought.   160
His friends in pieces torn, the bitter news,
Not brought by fame, with his own eyes he views;
His mind at once reflecting on their youth,
Their worth, their love, their valor, and their truth;
The joys of court, their mothers, and their wives,   165
To follow him, abandon'd—and their lives!
He storms and shoots, but flying bullets now,
To execute his rage, appear too slow:
They miss, or sweep but common souls away,
For such a loss Opdam his life must pay!   170
Encouraging his men, he gives the word,
With fierce intent that hated ship to board
And make the guilty Dutch, with his own arm,
Wait on his friends, while yet their blood is warm.
His winged vessel like an eagle shows,   175
When through the clouds to truss a swan she goes:
The Belgian ship unmov'd, like some huge rock
Inhabiting the sea, expects the shock.
From both the fleets men's eyes are bent this way,
Neglecting all the business of the day.   180
Bullets their flight, and guns their noise, suspend;
The silent ocean does th' event attend
Which leader shall the doubtful vict'ry bless
And give an earnest of the war's success,
When Heav'n itself, for England to declare,   185

185–86. Opdam's ship, the *Eendracht,* blew up about 3:00 P.M. June 3rd. Opdam
had already died of wounds before the explosion and only five men escaped.

Turns ship and men and tackle into air.
Their new commander from his charge is toss'd,
Which that young Prince had so unjustly lost,
Whose great progenitors, with better fate
And better conduct, sway'd their infant state. 190
His flight tow'rds Heav'n th'aspiring Belgian took,
But fell, like Phaethon, with thunder strook;
From vaster hopes than this he seem'd to fall,
That durst attempt the British Admiral.
From her broadsides a ruder flame is thrown 195
Than from the fiery chariot of the sun,
That bears the radiant ensign of the day,
And she, the flag that governs in the sea.
    The Duke (ill-pleas'd that fire should thus prevent
The work which for his brighter sword he meant), 200
Anger still burning in his valiant breast,
Goes to complete revenge upon the rest:
So on the guardless herd, their keeper slain,
Rushes a tiger in the Lybian plain.
    The Dutch, accustom'd to the raging sea, 205
And in black storms the frowns of Heav'n to see,
Never met tempest which more urg'd their fears
Than that which in the Prince's look appears.
Fierce, goodly, young! Mars he resembles when
Jove sends him down to scourge perfidious men, 210
Such as with foul ingratitude have paid
Both those that led and those that gave them aid.
Where he gives on, disposing of their fates,

187–88. *that young Prince:* Evidently the young Prince of Orange, and the passage seems to refer to the rights and powers traditionally his which were withheld from him by the grand pensionary of Holland, John de Witt. William was proclaimed Stadholder, Captain- and Admiral-General in July 1672. At the time of the Battle of Lowestoft William would have been only fourteen.

213. *gives on:* Makes an assault. *Obs.*

213–20. Waller did not exaggerate York's violent encounters with the Dutch. One of the best accounts of the end of the action is in Harris' *Life of Sandwich*, pp. 304–05: "The *Oranje* meanwhile endeavored to board the Duke's flagship, but the *Mary* attacked her, and was reinforced by two ships from the Blue Squadron, the *Royal Catherine* and the *Essex*. The vessels were grappled and locked together; the fighting at close quarters was furious; man after man was cut down, or his brains were blown out by pistols held only a few feet away. . . . After an hour's desperate

Terror and death on his loud cannon waits,
With which he pleads his brother's cause so well,   215
He shakes the throne to which he does appeal.
The sea with spoil his angry bullets strow,
Widows and orphans making as they go;
Before his ship fragments of vessels torn,
Flags, arms, and Belgian carcasses are borne,   220
And his despairing foes, to flight inclin'd,
Spread all their canvas to invite the wind.
So the rude Boreas, where he lists to blow,
Makes clouds above and billows fly below,
Beating the shore, and, with a boist'rous rage,   225
Does Heav'n at once, and earth and sea, engage.
    The Dutch elsewhere did through the wat'ry field
Perform enough to have made others yield,
But English courage, growing as they fight,
In danger, noise, and slaughter takes delight: 230
Their bloody task, unweari'd still, they ply,
Only restrain'd by death, or victory.
Iron and lead, from earth's dark entrails torn,
Like show'rs of hail from either side are borne:
So high the rage of wretched mortals goes,   235
Hurling their mother's bowels at their foes!
Ingenious to their ruin, every age
Improves the arts and instruments of rage.
Death-hast'ning ills Nature enough has sent,
And yet men still a thousand more invent.   240
    But Bacchus now, which led the Belgians on
So fierce at first, to favor us begun;
Brandy and wine (their wonted friends) at length
Render them useless and betray their strength.
So corn in fields, and, in the garden, flowers   245
Revive and raise themselves with moderate showers,
But overcharg'd with never-ceasing rain,

---

struggle the *Oranje* was compeled to yield, her men were taken prisoners, and she was
set on fire."

    241–44. I have found no evidence that the Dutch were drunk, but Englishmen had
long tended to regard drunkenness as a Dutch characteristic. Cf. Donne's "spongy,
hydroptic Dutch" (Elegy XVI, *On his Mistress*).

Become too moist and bend their heads again.
Their reeling ships on one another fall,
Without a foe, enough to ruin all.   250
Of this disorder and the favoring wind
The watchful English such advantage find
Ships fraught with fire among the heap they throw
And up the so-entangled Belgians blow.
The flame invades the powder-rooms, and then,   255
Their guns shoot bullets, and their vessels, men.
The scorch'd Batavians on the billows float,
Sent from their own, to pass in Charon's boat.
    And now our royal Admiral success,
With all the marks of victory, does bless;   260
The burning ships, the taken, and the slain
Proclaim his triumph o'er the conquer'd main.
Nearer to Holland, as their hasty flight
Carries the noise and tumult of the fight,
His cannons' roar, forerunner of his fame,   265
Makes their Hague tremble, and their Amsterdam.
The British thunder does their houses rock,
And the Duke seems at ev'ry door to knock.
His dreadful streamer, like a comet's hair,
Threat'ning destruction, hastens their despair,   270
Makes them deplore their scatter'd fleet as lost
And fear our present landing on their coast.
The trembling Dutch th'approaching Prince behold,
As sheep a lion leaping tow'rds their fold.
Those piles which serve them to repel the main   275
They think too weak his fury to restrain.
What wonders may not English valor work,
Led by th'example of victorious York?
Or what defence against him can they make,
Who at such distance does their country shake?   280
His fatal hands their bulwarks will o'erthrow
And let in both the ocean and the foe!
Thus cry the people, and their land to keep,
Allow our title to command the deep,
Blaming their States' ill conduct to provoke   285
Those arms which freed them from the Spanish yoke.

    Painter, excuse me, if I have a while
Forgot thy art and us'd another style,
For, though you draw arm'd heroes as they sit,
The task in battle does the Muses fit.   290
They, in the dark confusion of a fight,
Discover all, instruct us how to write,
And light and honor to brave actions yield,
Hid in the smoke and tumult of the field.
Ages to come shall know that leader's toil   295
And his great name on whom the Muses smile.
Their dictates here let thy fam'd pencil trace,
And this relation with thy colors grace.
    Then draw the Parliament, the nobles met,
And our great Monarch high above them set.   300
Like young Augustus let his image be,
Triumphing for that victory at sea,
Where Egypt's queen and eastern kings o'erthrown
Made the possession of the world his own.
Last draw the Commons at his royal feet,   305
Pouring out treasure to supply his fleet;
They vow with lives and fortunes to maintain
Their King's eternal title to the main,
And with a present to the Duke approve
His valor, conduct, and his country's love.   310

To the King

Great Sir, disdain not in this piece to stand,
Supreme commander both of sea and land!
Those which inhabit the celestial bower
Painters express with emblems of their power:
His club Alcides, Phoebus has his bow,   315

299. Parliament met at Oxford (because of the plague) in Oct. 1665. They rejected
a French offer to mediate and thus provoked the threatened breach with France.
"The two Houses joined in an address in which they expressed to the King their
resolution to assist him with their lives and fortunes against the Dutch, or any
others that would assist them" (Ranke, 3, 433). The large sum of £1,250,000 was voted
for the next year.

305–10. For his heroic conduct Commons voted James £120,000 in Oct. 1665 "to
be paid him after the £1,250,000 is gathered upon the tax which they have now
given the King" (Pepys, 28 Oct. 1665).

Jove has his thunder, and your navy you.
But your great providence no colors here
Can represent, nor pencil draw that care
Which keeps you waking to secure our peace,
The nation's glory, and our trade's increase. 320
You for these ends whole days in council sit
And the diversions of your youth forget.
Small were the worth of valor and of force,
If your high wisdom govern'd not their course.
You as the soul, as the first mover, you, 325
Vigor and life on ev'ry part bestow:
How to build ships and dreadful ordnance cast,
Instruct the artists and reward their haste.
So Jove himself, when *Typhon Heav'n* does brave,
Descends to visit *Vulcan's* smoky cave, 330
Teaching the brawny *Cyclops* how to frame
His thunder mix'd with terror, wrath, and flame.
Had the old Greeks discover'd your abode,
Crete had not been the cradle of their god:
On that small island they had look'd with scorn 335
And in *Great Britain* thought the Thunderer born.

321–22. "Shipping and sea affairs . . . seemed to be so much his talent, both for knowledge as well as inclination, that a war of that kind was rather an entertainment than any disturbance to his thoughts. . . . 'Tis certain that no prince was ever more fitted by nature for his country's interest than he was in all his maritime inclinations" (Buckingham, cited by Bryant, *King Charles II*, p. 171).
333–34. Crete is the legendary birthplace of Zeus.

ANDREW MARVELL

The Second Advice to a Painter
(1666)

The Second Advice to a Painter mimics the structure, style, attitudes, and substance of Waller's *Instructions*. One finds here absurd similes that mock Waller's insipid analogies from natural history ("So the land crabs, at Nature's kindly call,/ Down to engender at the sea do crawl"), the interspersed mythological references ("One thrifty ferry-boat of mother-pearl/ Suffic'd of old the Cytherean girl"), and an envoy to the King alluding to Cretan legend. The poet of *Second Advice* is, if anything, more conscious than Waller of the convention he is using and comments repeatedly on painting techniques.

This satire extends the subject matter of Waller's poem to include the entire naval campaign of the first year of war, from Allin's disastrous attack on Dutch merchantmen in December 1664, through the equally disastrous attempt on Bergen in August 1665, to the disgraced Lord Sandwich's embassy to Spain the following spring. It deals in detail with the Battle of Lowestoft and dwells upon the Duke of York's failure to pursue the Dutch fleet, which became a subject for Parliamentary inquiry. Despite its caustic treatment of politicians and naval officers, *Second Advice* makes a careful distinction in the envoy between the King and his ministers.

Although *The Second Advice to a Painter,* unlike most satirical attacks on the government, was published soon after the event (with its sequel, in 1667), it circulated in manuscript before publication, as noted in the Introduction. On 14 December 1666 Pepys received "sealed up from Sir H. Chumley, the lampoon, or Mock Advice to a Painter, abusing the Duke of York and my Lord Sandwich, Penn, and everybody and the King himself, in all matters of the navy and the war." This lampoon was undoubtedly *The Second Advice.* As a Navy official and a close associate of some of the victims Pepys was deeply concerned: "I am sorry for my Lord Sandwich's having so great a part in it."

Since the question of the authorship of *Second Advice* is inextricably related to that of the third, fourth, and fifth *Advices* and *The Last Instructions to a Painter*, the reader is referred to the articles cited in the headnote to Waller's *Instructions to a Painter*. Suffice it to say here that the evidence for assigning the second and third *Advices* to Marvell seems more substantial than what is usually found in such cases of disputed authorship. The use of Denham's name as author in the printed texts and in line 336 ("Denham saith thus, though Waller always so") is clearly a blind to conceal the true author. Denham, a staunch Royalist who enjoyed the King's patronage as Surveyor-General, would not have put his name to such a piece; he would not have promised a satire on his wife ("Madam l'Édificatresse," line 340) who was the Duke of York's mistress; and he was known to be mad in 1666 (see *Divination*, line 61 n. and Samuel Butler's *Panegyric upon Sir John Denham's Recovery from his Madness*).

The text is based on Bod. MS. Eng. Poet. d. 49 (*R″*), which is described and discussed in Margoliouth's second edition of Marvell's *Poems and Letters* (1952), *1*, xiv–xv. As Margoliouth argues, this is probably the Marvell manuscript that Capt. Thompson refers to in his Preface as the compilation of William Popple, the poet's nephew (Marvell, *Works* [1776], *1*, xxviii–xxxix).

The epigraph from Persius is translated as follows in Dryden's version:

> The high-sho'd plowman, should he quit the land,
> To take the pilot's rudder in his hand,
> Artless of stars, and of the moving sand,
> The gods would leave him to the waves and wind
> And think all shame was lost in humankind.

This epigraph appears only in Bod. MS. Eng. Poet. d. 49.

The Second Advice to a Painter

for drawing the History of our naval Business

In Imitation of Mr. Waller.

navem si poscat sibi peronatus arator
luciferi rudis, exclamet Melicerta perisse
frontem de rebus.
—Persius, Satire 5, 102–04.

London, April 1666

Nay, Painter, if thou dar'st design that fight
Which Waller only courage had to write,
If thy bold hand can, without shaking, draw
What e'en the actors trembl'd when they saw
(Enough to make thy colors change like theirs   5
And all thy pencils bristle like their hairs)
First, in fit distance of the prospect main,
Paint Allin tilting at the coast of Spain:
Heroic act, and never heard till now,
Stemming of Herc'les' Pillars with his prow!   10
And how two ships he left the hills to waft,
And with new sea-marks Dover and Calais graft.
    Next, let the flaming *London* come in view,

3. *bold hand:* Cf. Waller, *Instructions,* 15: "Let thy bold pencil hope and courage spread."
    4. *trembl'd:* Trembled at, *obs. rare.* See *tremble* †3, *OED.*
    6. *pencils:* Brushes.
    8–12. For Allin's "tilting at the coast of Spain" see Waller, *Instructions,* 55–64 n.
    10. *Stemming:* Ramming, *obs.*
    11. *two ships:* The *Nonsuch* and the *Phoenix* ran aground on the eastern side of Gibraltar and had to be abandoned. *waft:* To convey safely by water; to carry over or across a river, sea, etc. (*OED*). It also could mean to convoy.
    12. The MSS. agree in reading *Calais* (instead of the printed texts' *Cadiz* or *Cales*). The somewhat laborious joke seems to be that Allin left the two ships in the Straits to convoy ("waft") the Pillars of Hercules to new positions in the English Channel in order to join Dover and Calais with new sea-marks.
    13–14. The frigate *London* blew up off the Nore 6 March 1665. It was reported rather cryptically that "the blowing up of the *London* was caused by Chapmen selling powder 20s. a barrel cheaper than in London" (*CSPD,* 9 March 1665). The ship was replaced voluntarily by the City: "the King has accepted the offer of the Lord Mayor and Aldermen to build him a ship instead of the *London,* adding that it is to be called the *Loyal London*" (*CSPD,* 17 March 1665).

Like Nero's Rome, burnt to rebuild it new:
What lesser sacrifice than this was meet   15
To offer for the safety of the fleet?
Blow one ship up, another thence does grow:
See what free cities and wise courts can do!
So some old merchant, to insure his name,
Marries afresh, and courtiers share the dame;   20
So whatsoe'er is broke, the servants pay 't,
And glasses prove more durable than plate.
No mayor till now so rich a pageant feign'd,
Nor one barge all the companies contain'd.

    Then, Painter, draw cerulean Coventry,   25
Keeper, or rather chanc'llor, of the sea;
Of whom the captain buys his leave to die,
And barters or for wounds or infamy;
And more exactly to express his hue,
Ultramarine must do 't, the richest blue.   30
To pay him fees, one's silver trumpet spends;
The boatswain's whistle on his place depends.
Pilots in vain repeat the compass o'er,

19–20. A difficult comparison. The old merchant corresponds to the mercantile City which "insures its name" by giving a new frigate, the *Loyal London*, to replace the lost one. Just as the old merchant must share his young wife with the courtiers, the City shares its ship with the gentlemen volunteers of the navy. The poet feels that the *Loyal London* will not be in good hands. At any rate, "the ship had a short life, being burned by the Dutch in the Thames the next year. She seemed ill-fated from the start. Pepys recorded (26 June 1666) that at the trial of her guns, all of them exploded" (Hooker, p. 299 n.).

21. The citizens are in the strange position of servants who must pay for the guests' breakage.

22. *And glasses prove more durable than plate,* because, unlike plate, glasses would not be subject to collection in drives for such "voluntary" contributions.

23–24. A reference to the floats of the various City companies (Goldsmiths', Fishmongers', etc.), which appeared in the Lord Mayor's show. All the companies contributed to this "barge."

25–40. *cerulean Coventry:* Sir William Coventry (1628–86), secretary to the Duke of York and one of the four Navy Commissioners. He was noted for venality: "reports were soon disseminated that Coventry was 'feathering his nest' by a sale of offices. He admitted subsequently that, like everybody else, he did make money by selling offices" (*DNB*). A *keeper* was one who kept a mistress. It was also, of course, a title of state.

31–32. Not even the lower ranks, such as boatswains and trumpeters, were, according to these lines, safe from Coventry's greed.

Until of him they learn that one point more:
The constant magnet to the pole does hold,   35
Steel to the magnet, Coventry to gold.
Muscovy sells us hemp and pitch and tar,
Iron and copper, Sweden; Münster, war;
Ashley, prize; Warwick, customs; Cart'ret, pay;
But Coventry sells the whole fleet away.   40
   Now let our navy stretch its canvas wings,
Swoll'n like his purse, with tackling like its strings,
By slow degrees of the increasing gale,
First under sale, and after under sail;
Then in kind visit unto Opdam's gout,   45
Hedge the Dutch in only to let them out.
So huntsmen fair unto the hares give law,
First find them and then civilly withdraw;
That the blind Archer, when they take the seas,

38. *Münster:* Christopher Bernhard von Galen, Bishop of Münster from 1650 to
1678. On 3 June 1665 his agent signed an offensive alliance with England by which
the Bishop undertook to invade Holland in return for certain Dutch territory to
which he had a dubious claim (Ogg, *England in the Reign of Charles II, 1,* 289).
"War was his hobby, bombs and siege artillery his specialized art, and this pillar of
the Church, whose Latin was as good as his shooting, was preceded by a guard of
'Heyducks' armed to the teeth with poleaxes and carbines" (Feiling, *British Foreign
Policy, 1660–72,* pp. 150–51).
   39. In this elliptical line *sells* is understood: Ashley sells positions in the Prize
Office, Warwick in the Customs, Carteret in the Paymaster's. *Ashley:* Antony Ashley
Cooper (1621–83), first Baron Ashley and later first Earl of Shaftesbury, appointed
Chancellor of the Exchequer in 1661. He was Treasurer of Prizes during the Second
Dutch War. *Warwick:* Sir Philip Warwick (1609–83), to whom the Earl of Southamp-
ton, Lord High Treasurer, largely left the business of his office. According to Burnet,
Warwick "was an incorrupt man, and during the seven years' management of the
Treasury he made but an ordinary fortune out of it" (Burnet, *History of My Own
Time, 1,* 171). *Cart'ret:* Sir George Carteret (d. 1680) was appointed Treasurer of
the Navy after the Restoration.
   41. Cf. the opening line of Waller's poem *To the King, on His Navy* (1627?):
     Where'er thy navy spreads her canvas wings.
   45–46. The sarcastic pretense here that the British failed to press their victory
against the Dutch out of consideration for Opdam's illness seems to echo the *News*
for 27 April 1665: "Unless his Royal Highness should take occasion to give the Heer
Opdam a visit (whose gout has effectually put him in condition to receive it)." When
York was forced to leave the Dutch coast to revictual, their fleet put out to sea
from the Texel and the Vlie. See Waller, *Instructions,* 77–90 and n.
   47. *give law:* Impose one's will.
   49–50. For the capture of the Hamburg convoy by the Dutch see Waller, *Instruc-
tions,* 91–94 and n. The "blindness" of Captain Archer is indicated in a newspaper

The Hamburg convoy may betray at ease.   50
So that the fish may more securely bite,
The fisher baits the river overnight.
    But, Painter, now prepare, t' enrich thy piece,
Pencil of ermines, oil of ambergris:
See where the Duchess, with triumphant tail   55
Of num'rous coaches, Harwich does assail!
So the land crabs, at Nature's kindly call,
Down to engender at the sea do crawl.
See then the Admiral, with navy whole,
To Harwich through the ocean caracole.   60
So swallows, buri'd in the sea, at spring
Return to land with summer on their wing.
One thifty ferry-boat of mother-pearl
Suffic'd of old the Cytherean girl;
Yet navies are but properties, when here   65
(A small sea-masque and built to court you, dear)
Three goddesses in one: Pallas for art,
Venus for sport, and Juno in your heart.
O Duchess! if thy nuptial pomp were mean,
'Tis paid with int'rest in this naval scene.   70
Never did Roman Mark within the Nile
So feast the fair Egyptian Crocodile,

---

report of his encounter with these enemy warships: "About seven in the afternoon, they spied some ships, and in a very little time made them to be a very great fleet. So soon as they discovered them, Captain Archer shot off a gun to command all the ships under his convoy to come up to him, and so sailed with them all towards the said fleet without taking the least stop for the discovery of what they should be, or giving the least notice or advertisement to the ships under his convoy, nor so much as fired one gun at his taking" (*The Intelligencer*, 19 June 1665).

55-58. The Duchess of York began her Harwich visit 16 May 1665. Compare Waller's adulatory account in *Instructions to a Painter*, 77-90.

60. *caracole:* Move in a zigzag course or, more loosely, caper.

61-62. An allusion to the discredited theory that swallows are torpid in the winter.

65. *properties:* Stage properties.

69. "The Duke of York had courted Anne Hyde, the Chancellor's daughter, when she was a Maid of Honor in attendance on the Princess of Orange. Her pregnancy compelled the Duke to admit a binding promise of marriage, and the ceremony was secretly performed in her father's house on September 3, 1660" (Lodge, *Political History of England, 1660–1702*, p. 3). Hence the meanness of her "nuptial pomp."

71-72. Cf. the refrain to Cleveland's *Mark Antony* (1647): "Never Mark Antony/Dalli'd more wantonly/With the fair Egyptian Queen."

Nor the Venetian Duke, with such a state,
The Adriatic marry at that rate.

Now, Painter, spare thy weaker art, forbear   75
To draw her parting passions and each tear;
For love, alas! has but a short delight:
The winds, the Dutch, the King, all call to fight.
She therefore the Duke's person recommends
To Brouncker, Penn, and Coventry, as friends: 80
Penn much, more Brouncker, most to Coventry;
For they, she knew, were all more 'fraid than she.
Of flying fishes one had sav'd the fin,
And hop'd with these he through the air might spin;
The other thought he might avoid his knell   85
In the invention of the diving bell;
The third had tri'd it, and affirm'd a cable,
Coil'd round about men, was impenetrable.
But these the Duke rejected, only chose
To keep far off and others interpose.   90
    Rupert, that knew not fear, but health did want,
Kept state suspended in a chaise-volante;
All save his head shut in that wooden case,

73–74. A Doge instituted the wedding of Venice to the sea, a magnificent ceremony
which still commemorates on Ascension Day that city's maritime importance.
    80. *Brouncker:* William, second Lord Brouncker (1620?–84), the first president of the
Royal Society and an extra Commissioner of the Navy during 1664–66. He was a
brother of Henry Brouncker. *Penn:* Sir William Penn (1621–70), a Commissioner of
the Navy. In the Second Dutch War he was second-in-command and Admiral of the
Duke's flagship.
    83. *Of flying fishes one had sav'd the fin:* A virtuoso habit. See Butler's satire on
Brouncker and other members of the Royal Society, *The Elephant in the Moon.*
    86. The diving bell was introduced into England from Sweden in 1661. See Evelyn,
19 July 1661 and *CSPD, 1660–61,* pp. 320, 490.
    87. *The third:* Sir William Penn, a highly experienced naval officer. Pepys heard
(9 Nov. 1663) that "there was a cruel articling against Penn after one fight, for cow-
ardice, in putting himself within a coil of cables, of which he had much ado to acquit
himself."
    91. *Rupert:* Prince Rupert (1619–82), Count Palatine of the Rhine and Duke of
Bavaria. He fought bravely in European campaigns and joined Charles I in 1642 as
General of the Horse. He was welcomed by Charles II at the Restoration, granted an
annuity of £4,000 a year, and admitted to the Privy Council.
    92. *chaise-volante:* Marvell's term for a sort of sedan chair. At this time Rupert was
suffering from a serious injury to his head. Pepys claims he had syphilis (15 Jan. 1665).
Cf. 99–100 below.

He show'd but like a broken weatherglass;
But, arm'd in a whole lion cap-a-chin,   95
Did represent the Hercules within.
Dear shall the Dutch his twinging anguish know,
And feel what valor whet with pain can do.
Curst in the meantime be the trait'ress Jael
That through his princely temples drove the nail!   100
Rupert resolv'd to fight it like a lion,
But Sandwich hop'd to fight it like Arion:
He, to prolong his life in the dispute
And charm the Holland pirates, tun'd his lute,
Till some judicious dolphin might approach   105
And land him safe and sound as any roach.
Hence by the gazetteer he was mistook,
As unconcern'd as if at Hinchingbrooke.
    Now, Painter, reassume thy pencil's care;
It hath but skirmish'd yet, now fight prepare   110
And draw the battle terribler to show
Than the Last Judgment was of Angelo.
    First, let our navy scour through silver froth,

95–96. The skin of the Nemean lion served Hercules as armor. The analogy is apt since the heraldic symbol of the Palatine was a golden lion. *Cap-a-chin* means head-to-chine (chine = backbone).

99–100. See Judges 4.

102. *Sandwich:* Edward Montagu (1625–72), Earl of Sandwich, served at Lowestoft as Admiral of the Blue, or rear, squadron. The White, or van, was commanded by Prince Rupert, and the Red by the Duke of York.

103–04. Sandwich's *lute* was a guitar: "and so followed my Lord Sandwich, who was gone a little before me on board the *Royal James*. And there spent an hour, my Lord playing upon the guitar, which he now commends above all music in the world, because it is bass enough for a single voice and is so portable and manageable without much trouble" (Pepys, 17 Nov. 1665).

107–08. After the Battle of Lowestoft Sandwich felt with some justice that he had been neglected in the published accounts: "That all the discourse of the town and the printed relation should not give him one word of honor my Lord thinks mighty strange" (Pepys, 23 June 1665). There is no mention of Sandwich in the very full newspaper accounts of the action until *The Intelligencer* for 15 June 1665, and the poem sarcastically echoes its phrasing: "It seems the Earl of Sandwich's vessel (the *Prince*) was much damnified in the battle, her hull, masts, and rigging being exceedingly shattered and torn, his Lordship showing himself aloft all the while, *as unconcerned as if he had been in his own parlor*. He had 14 men killed in this ship and 25 wounded" (italics mine). *Hinchingbrooke* was Sandwich's country seat near Huntingdon.

The ocean's burden and the kingdom's both,
Whose very bulk may represent its birth   115
From Hyde and Paston, burdens of the earth:
Hyde, whose transcendent paunch so swells of late
That he the rupture seems of law and state;
Paston, whose belly bears more millions
Than Indian carracks and contains more tuns.   120

  Let shoals of porpoises on ev'ry side
Wonder, in swimming by our oaks outvi'd,
And the sea fowl, at gaze, behold a thing
So vast, more strong and swift, than they of wing,
But, with presaging gorge, yet keep in sight   125
And follow for the relics of a fight.

  Then let the Dutch, with well-dissembl'd fear,
Or bold despair, more than we wish, draw near,
At which our gallants (to the sea but tender,
More to the fight) their queasy stomachs render,   130
With breasts so panting that at ev'ry stroke
You might have felt their hearts beat through the oak,
While one concern'd most, in the interval
Of straining choler, thus did cast his gall:

    "Noah be damn'd and all his race accurst,   135
    That in sea-brine did pickle timber first!
    What though he planted vines! He pines cut down—
    He taught us how to drink and how to drown.
    He first built ships and in that wooden wall,
    Saving but eight, e'er since endangers all.   140
    And thou Dutch necromantic friar, be damn'd,
    And in thine own first mortar-piece be ramm'd!
    Who first invented cannon in thy cell,

116. *Hyde:* Edward Hyde, Earl of Clarendon (1609–74), the Lord Chancellor. Con-
temporary portraits show him as a man of florid countenance and portly figure, but
the satirist exaggerates these signs of well-being into grossness. *Paston:* Sir Robert
Paston (1631–83), later Earl of Yarmouth, M.P. for Castle Rising in Norfolk, who moved
the unprecedented sum of £2,500,000 on 9 Feb. 1665 for the war. He was a close friend
of Charles II and was allegedly granted the imposition of deals coming to Yarmouth
(worth £3,000 a year) for this service to the King (George E. Cokayne, ed., *Complete
Peerage of England, Scotland, Ireland* . . . , *8* [1898], 210).

120. *carracks:* Large merchant ships.

141. *Dutch necromantic friar:* Berthold Schwartz, a fourteenth-century German who
helped to develop gunpowder and adapt it to military uses.

Nitre from earth and brimstone fetch'd from Hell.
But damn'd and treble damn'd be Clarendine,   145
Our seventh Edward, and his house and line!
Who, to divert the danger of the war
With Bristol, hounds us on the Hollander;
Fool-coated gownman! sells, to fight with Hans,
Dunkirk; dismantling Scotland, quarrels France;   150
And hopes he now hath bus'ness shap'd and pow'r
T' outlast his life or ours and 'scape the Tow'r;
And that he yet may see, ere he go down,
His dear Clarinda circl'd in a crown."

By this time both the fleets in wrath dispute,   155
And each the other mortally salute.
Draw pensive Neptune, biting of his thumbs,
To think himself a slave whos'e'er o'ercomes,
The frighted nymphs retreating to the rocks,
Beating their blue breasts, tearing their green locks.   160
Paint Echo slain: only th' alternate sound
From the repeating cannon does rebound.
    Opdam sails in, plac'd in his naval throne,
Assuming courage greater than his own,
Makes to the Duke and threatens him from far   165

146. The poet sarcastically places the Earl of Clarendon seventh in England's royal line of Edwards.

147–48. *war with Bristol:* George Digby, second Earl of Bristol (1612–77), brought a charge of high treason against Clarendon in the House of Lords on 10 July 1663. The charges were dismissed and Bristol's actions so displeased the King that he was obliged to live in seclusion for the next two years.

149. *gownman:* A civilian, in contradistinction to a soldier.

149–50. *sells . . . Dunkirk:* Late in October 1662 Clarendon negotiated the sale of Dunkirk to France for five million livres on the grounds that its continued possession might involve England in a continental war. Sandwich had already declared the harbor bad and scarcely worth its upkeep. Public opinion resented the sale, and Clarendon was often charged with enriching himself by it. *dismantling Scotland:* Clarendon instructed Lauderdale to sell the four forts in Scotland which Cromwell had built. *quarrels France:* In 1665 France attempted to mediate between England and Holland. Clarendon favored the rejection of French mediation, as did Parliament.

153–54. Clarendon's daughter, Anne Hyde, married the Duke of York (see note on line 69). Clarendon, by his own report, opposed the match and advised "that the King should immediately cause the woman to be sent to the Tower and to be cast into a dungeon under so strict a guard that no person living should be admitted to come to her and then that an act of Parliament should be immediately passed for the cutting off her head, to which he would not only give his consent, but would willingly be the first man that should propose it" (*Life, 1,* sec. 54).

To nail himself to 's board like a petar,
But in the vain attempt takes fire too soon
And flies up in his ship to catch the moon.
Monsieurs like rockets mount aloft and crack
In thousand sparks, then dancingly fall back.   170
Yet ere this happen'd, Destiny allow'd
Him his revenge, to make his death more proud:
A fatal bullet from his side did range
And batter'd Lawson—O too dear exchange!
He led our fleet that day too short a space,   175
But lost his knee, di'd since in Glory's race;
Lawson, whose valor beyond fate did go
And still fights Opdam through the lakes below.
    The Duke himself (though Penn did not forget)
Yet was not out of danger's random set.   180
Falmouth was there (I know not what to act—
Some say 'twas to grow duke, too, by contact);
An untaught bullet in its wanton scope
Quashes him all to pieces and his hope.
Such as his rise such was his fall, unprais'd: 185
A chance shot sooner took than chance him rais'd.
His shatter'd head the fearless Duke distains
And gave the last-first proof that he had brains.
    Berkeley had heard it soon and thought not good
To venture more of royal Harding's blood;   190

166. *petar:* More commonly spelled *petard*, a small engine of war used to blow in a wall or gate, or to make a breach in a wall, etc.

167–68. See Waller, *Instructions,* 185–86 and n.

169. The *OED* notes that *monsieur* was often used in speaking of (European) foreigners of other than French nationality.

174. *Lawson:* Sir John Lawson, Vice-Admiral of the Red, who died of wounds in the knee. Cf. *Iter Boreale,* 103

180. *random:* The range of a piece of ordnance.

181–88. For an account of Falmouth's death see Waller, *Instructions,* 147–48 and n.

189. *Berkeley:* William Berkeley (1639–66), second Viscount Fitzharding (Irish peerage) and younger brother to the Earl of Falmouth. Public opinion resented his behavior in the Battle of Lowestoft. "It is strange to see how people do already slight Sir William Berkeley, my Lord Fitzharding's brother, who three months since was the delight of the court" (16 June 1665). There is a very different account of Berkeley's conduct in *CSPD:* "nine Dutch ships ran away, Capt. Berkeley pursuing them with six; the rest made for the Texel, but our fleet forced them northward" (5 June 1665).

190. *royal Harding's blood:* A sardonic allusion to the "Harding" of whom "Fitzharding" is the son. Cf. note above. Surnames beginning in *Fitz* were sometimes used

610

Battaglia Navale tra' Inglesi, et Olandesi Succeßa
adi 13 di Giugno. 1665.

The Battle of Lowestoft, 3 June 1665. From an engraving by an unknown artist.

To be immortal he was not of age
And did e'en now the Indian prize presage,
But judg'd it safe and decent (cost what cost)
To lose the day, since his dear brother's lost.
With his whole squadron straight away he bore,   195
And, like good boy, promis'd to fight no more.
    The Dutch *Urania* fairly on us sail'd,
And promises to do what Opdam fail'd.
Smith to the Duke does intercept her way
And cleaves t' her closer than the remora.   200
The captain wonder'd and withal disdain'd,
So strongly by a thing so small detain'd,
And in a raging brav'ry to him runs;
They stab their ships with one another's guns;
They fight so near it seems to be on ground,   205
And e'en the bullets meeting bullets wound.
The noise, the smoke, the sweat, the fire, the blood,
Are not to be express'd nor understood.
Each captain from the quarter-deck commands;
They wave their bright swords glitt'ring in their
    hands.   210
All luxury of war, all man can do
In a sea-fight, did pass betwixt them two,
But one must conquer, whosoever fight:
Smith took the giant and is since made knight.
    Marlb'rough, that knew and dar'd, too, more than
      all,   215

---

to designate royal bastards, viz. Charles Fitzroy, the son of Charles II by the Duchess of Cleveland.

192. *Indian prize:* See below, lines 305ff.

197. *The Dutch Urania:* Capt. Sebastian Senten, commanding *Urania*, had "sworn to board the Duke" (Pepys, 8 June 1665). The *Mary*, commanded by Capt. Jeremy Smith, came between and took the *Urania* and 200 of her men. Smith was knighted for this action and in 1669 appointed to succeed Penn as Comptroller of the Victualling, an office which he held until Sept. 1675.

200. *remora:* The sucking-fish, believed anciently to have the power of staying the course of any ship to which it attached itself.

215. *Marlborough:* "James Ley, third Earl of Marlborough, born 1618, succeeded to the title 1 April 1638. It is said of him that 'none more prepared was to die' because of the strong presentiment of death which he had and which caused him to write his well-known letter to Sir Hugh Pollard from 'aboard the old *James* near the

Falls undistinguish'd by an iron ball:
Dear Lord! but born under a star ingrate,
No soul so clear, and no more gloomy fate.
Who would set up war's trade that meant to thrive?
Death picks the valiant out, the cow'rds survive.   220
What the brave merit th' impudent do vaunt,
And none's rewarded but the sycophant;
Hence all his life he against Fortune fenc'd,
Or not well known or not well recompens'd.
But envy not this praise to 's memory: 225
None more prepar'd was or less fit to die.
   Rupert did others, and himself, excel:
Holmes, Tyddiman, Myngs; bravely Sansum fell.
What others did let none omitted blame;
I shall record, whos'e'er brings in his name.   230
But (unless after stories disagree)
Nine only came to fight, the rest to see.
   Now all conspires unto the Dutchman's loss:
The wind, the fire, we, they themselves, do cross,
When a sweet sleep the Duke began to drown   235
And with soft diadem his temples crown.
But first he orders all beside to watch,
That they the foe (whilst he a nap) might catch.
But Brouncker, by a secreter instinct,

---

coast of Holland May 27th, 1665.' See *Fair Warnings to a Careless World* (4°, 1665)
where the letter is misdated April 24" (Thorn Drury).
   227–28. There is no completely satisfactory reading for this couplet. Since neither
Holmes, Myngs, nor Tyddiman was wounded at Lowestoft, it is probably best to take
Holmes, Tyddiman, and Myngs as the *others* whom Rupert *excelled*. Even so the con-
struction is awkward. Sir Robert Holmes (1622–92) was captain of the *Revenge* in
Rupert's squadron at the Battle of Lowestoft. Sir Thomas Tyddiman (d. 1668?) was
Rear Admiral of the Blue under the Earl of Sandwich. Sir Christopher Myngs (1625–66)
was Vice-Admiral of the White. Robert Sansum, Rear Admiral of the White under
Rupert, was killed in the battle
   239–42. Henry Brouncker, York's good-for-nothing confidant, pretended to come
from the Duke's cabin with an order to shorten sail. Though the English had the
upper hand, Capt. Harman did not question the order, and when the Duke arose the
next morning he discovered that the Dutch had made an unimpeded escape. Shortly
after Lowestoft Brouncker became an M.P., but in April 1668, after a lengthy parlia-
mentary investigation, he was expelled from the House. The essential facts of the
incident and the rôles of York and Brouncker in it have not been fully established.

Slept not, nor needs it; he all day had wink'd.   240
The Duke in bed, he then first draws his steel,
Whose virtue makes the misled compass wheel:
So ere he wak'd, both fleets were innocent,
And Brouncker member is of Parliament.
    And now, dear Painter, after pains like those,   245
'T were time that thou and I too should repose.
But all our navy 'scap'd so sound of limb
That a small space serv'd to refresh its trim,
And a tame fleet of theirs does convoy want,
Laden with both the Indies and Levant.   250
Paint but this one scene more, the world's our own;
The halcyon Sandwich does command alone.
    To Bergen now with better maw we haste,
And the sweet spoils in hope already taste,
Though Clifford in the character appears   255
Of supercargo to our fleet and theirs,
Wearing a signet ready to clap on

As Hannay says, "Brouncker, who was of infamous character, was capable of misusing the Duke's name, but it is strange that if he did he was not sooner punished. The explanation that he was valuable to his master for services it is not well to record [procuring], is as nearly discreditable to the Duke's character as want of firmness could have been in the reaction natural after such a terrible experience" (*Short History of the Royal Navy*, pp. 342–43).

247–48. The English fleet was prepared and provisioned four weeks after Lowestoft. Its twofold mission was to intercept Admiral de Ruyter's fleet, which was returning from Newfoundland via the north of Scotland, and to capture or destroy a rich fleet of Dutch merchantmen returning from the East Indies, the *tame fleet* of line 249.

252. After Lowestoft, under pressure from the King and Council (and perhaps the Queen Mother) the Duke of York was forced, for dynastic reasons, to withdraw from active service, and command of the Navy was entrusted to Sandwich, whom *Flagellum Parliamentarium* describes as "the halcyon [i.e. timorous] bulkbreaking Sandwich."

253. *Bergen:* Sir Gilbert Talbot, English envoy at Copenhagen, was conducting negotiations with the King of Denmark with an eye to a joint attack on the Dutch merchantmen that had taken shelter in neutral Danish harbors. *better maw:* Better appetite.

255. *Clifford:* Sir Thomas Clifford (1630–73), later Lord Clifford of Chudleigh, took a leading part in negotiations with Ahlefeldt, the governor of Bergen, which was then a Danish possession. Clifford had accompanied Tyddiman, commander of the squadron which Sandwich had detached to attack the Dutch ships at Bergen. Frequent reports from Clifford to Arlington indicate that he joined the fleet as Arlington's confidential agent. Late in June he had been rewarded with the prize ship *Patriarch Isaac* for his constant service in the disposal of ships, preventing embezzlement, etc.

And seize all for his master Arlington.
Ruyter, whose little squadron skimm'd the seas
And wasted our remotest colonies,   260
With ships all foul return'd upon our way.
Sandwich would not disperse, nor yet delay,
And therefore (like commander grave and wise)
To 'scape his sight and fight, shut both his eyes,
And, for more state and sureness, Cuttance true   265
The left eye closes, the right Montagu,
And even Clifford proffer'd (in his zeal
To make all safe) t'apply to both his seal.
Ulysses so, till he the Sirens pass'd,
Would by his mates be pinion'd to the mast.   270
Now may our navy view the wished port;
But there too (see the fortune!) was a fort.
Sandwich would not be beaten nor yet beat:
Fools only fight, the prudent use to treat.
His cousin Montagu (by Court disaster   275

259–70. Admiral Michael de Ruyter (1607–76) had been sent in Sept. 1664 to the Guinea coast with twelve men-of-war and instructions to harry the English and re-capture trading posts which they had taken. On 22 Dec. 1664 Pepys reports that the English had been "beaten to dirt at Guinea." By late July 1665 de Ruyter was off the Faroes on his return voyage from Newfoundland with English prize ships taken off the coast of America. Sandwich attempted to intercept de Ruyter between Dogger Bank and the Naze of Norway, but the Dutch fleet eluded him by hugging the Danish coast and safely reached the Ems on July 27th. De Ruyter's return greatly heartened the Dutch after their defeat and was a great blow to the English. It was some time before Sandwich heard of it.

265–66. The MSS. readings seem inferior. *Cuttance* [Cutten] *true* is preferable, since Capt. Roger Cuttance was Sandwich's captain. Even so the lines are confusing, al-though their general intention is clear enough. *Montagu:* Edward Montagu (1635–65), nephew of the Earl of Sandwich, who took a leading part in negotiations with the Danes at Bergen.

267–68. Clifford's biographer, Hartmann, gives a detailed account of the Bergen affair. He quotes lines 253–68 of this poem and comments: "there was no sort of foundation for the insinuations contained in Sir John Denham's attack. From the point of view of international law and morality the enterprise at Bergen was quite unwar-rantable, but there is no reason to believe that either Arlington or Clifford had a personal axe to grind in the matter. Nor can Sandwich justly be blamed for the fiasco; his plans had been laid with the utmost care" (*Clifford of the Cabal*, London, 1937, p. 79).

272. *fort:* The Danish fort overlooking Bergen harbor.

275–82. An unusually difficult passage. Edward Montagu, Sandwich's cousin, had been dismissed by the Queen from his post as her Master of the Horse for impertinent

Dwindl'd into the wooden horse's master)
To speak of peace seem'd among all most proper,
Had Talbot then treated of nought but copper,
For what are forts, when void of ammunition?
With friend or foe what would we more condition? 280
Yet we three days (till the Dutch furnish'd all—
Men, powder, cannon, money) treat with Wall.
Then Teddy, finding that the Dane would not,
Sends in six captains bravely to be shot,
And Montagu, though dress'd like any bride, 285
Though aboard him too, yet was reach'd and di'd.
    Sad was this chance, and yet a deeper care
Wrinkles our membranes under forehead fair:
The Dutch armada yet had th' impudence
To put to sea to waft their merchants hence; 290
For, as if all their ships of walnut were,
The more we beat them, still the more they bear;
But a good pilot and a fav'ring wind
Bring Sandwich back and once again did blind.
    Now, gentle Painter, ere we leap on shore, 295

behavior. Bod. MS. Eng. Poet. d. 49 has a note on the incident, probably written by
Marvell's editor, Edward Thompson: "Montagu was Master of the Horse to the Queen.
One day, as he led her, he tickled her palm. She asked the King what that meant. The
King by this means getting knowledge of it, turned Montagu out of his place."
    Now, in the scheme to seize the Dutch Indies fleet at Bergen with the connivance of
the Danes, Montagu has become master of a *wooden horse*. Had Sir Gilbert Talbot,
the envoy in charge of negotiations with the Danes, confined his demands to a re-
quest for guaranteed annual quotas of naval supplies like *copper*, Montagu would
have been well-fitted for his role, but Talbot included other provisions which would
have entailed Denmark's breaking off relations with the Dutch, chief among them a
declaration of war to be made when the East Indies convoy arrived in some Danish
port. The Danes refused to declare war, but agreed to give the British a free hand in
attacking the Indies convoy at the price of half the spoils. This scheme would have
secured for the British what they wanted, the satirist argues, when the Bergen fort
was without ammunition and therefore unable to make a show of defending the neu-
tral Dutch against English men-of-war, but the unnecessary protraction of negotiations
gave the Dutch the opportunity to supply and man the fort which then helped to
destroy the British squadron. *Wall* personifies Danish intransigeance.
    283. *Teddy:* Sir Thomas Tyddiman, Commander of the British squadron.
    291–92. According to the *Encyclopedia Britannica* (13th edition), "in some parts of
England the trees are thrashed with rods or poles to obtain the nuts, but this is not
a commendable mode of collecting them." Cf. the old saying (1639): "A woman, ass,
and walnut tree, the more you beat the better be" (M. P. Tilley, *Proverb in England*).
    295–304. "September came in like a lion; one after another their vessels were dis-

With thy last strokes ruffle a tempest o'er,
As if in our reproach the winds and seas
Would undertake the Dutch while we take ease.
The seas their spoils within our hatches throw,
The winds both fleets into our mouths do blow,   300
Strew all their ships along the coast by ours,
As easy to be gather'd up as flow'rs.
But Sandwich fears for merchants to mistake
A man of war, and among flow'rs a snake.
Two Indian ships, pregnant with eastern pearl   305
And diamonds, sate the officers and Earl.
Then warning of our fleet, he it divides
Into the ports, and he to Oxford rides,
While the Dutch, reuniting to our shames,
Ride all insulting o'er the Downs and Thames.   310
      Now treating Sandwich seems the fittest choice
For Spain, there to condole and to rejoice;
He meets the French, but, to avoid all harms,
Slips to the Groin (embassies bear not arms!)

---

persed, and the attempts to reassemble them were all in vain. Great East Indiamen, laden with riches, but foul after their long journey, broke away from their convoys, and rolled helplessly about in the North Sea, at the mercy of the tempest and the enemy" (Harris, *Life of Sandwich*, *1*, 341). Sandwich was widely criticized for not pursuing the Dutch squadron and securing a decisive victory, but this would have entailed the risk of a night battle in rough weather on a lee shore (Tedder, *The Navy of the Restoration*, p. 142).

305–06. "Sandwich assigned to the flag-officers a proportion of the silks and spices which were in the holds of the *Phoenix* and *Slothony*. Many a sailor has built the family fortune upon the goods seized at sea; but Sandwich made the greatest mistake of his life in allowing these goods to be earmarked for distribution before any warrants were issued. He allotted so much to Penn, so much to himself, and so much to each flag-officer. Their shares were worth the having" (Harris, *Sandwich*, *2*, 5).

308. Sandwich had second thoughts about the distribution of prizes which he had permitted and went off to Oxford to discuss the matter with the King. His absence from the fleet at this time was unfortunate for his reputation, because just then the Dutch appeared in English waters (see 309–10).

311–12. Sandwich was "kicked upstairs" for having broken bulk without warrant. Clarendon arranged for his appointment as Ambassador Extraordinary to Madrid, where he negotiated a commercial treaty with Spain. He was to *condole* over the death of Philip IV (7 Sept. 1665) and *rejoice* over the succession to the throne of the sickly infant, Charles II, Philip's son.

314. *Groin:* Sandwich sailed from Portsmouth 3 March 1666. En route to Spain a storm forced him into Corunna, that part of northwest Spain called "the Groin" by sailors. While in quarantine off Corunna Sandwich's ship seized a Dutch merchant-

There let him languish a long quarantine   315
And ne'er to England come till he be clean.
    Thus having fought we know not why, as yet,
We've done we know not what nor what we get:
If to espouse the ocean all the pains,
Princes unite and will forbid the bains;   320
If to discharge Fanatics, this makes more,
For all Fanatic turn when sick or poor;
Or if the House of Commons to repay,
Their prize commissions are transferr'd away;
But for triumphant checkstones, if, and shell   325
For Duchess' closet, 't has succeeded well.
If to make Parliaments all odious pass;
If to reserve a standing force, alas!
Or if, as just, Orange to reinstate,
Instead of that, he is regenerate;   330
And with four millions vainly giv'n as spent,
And with five millions more of detriment,
Our sum amounts yet only to have won
A bastard Orange for pimp Arlington!
    Now may historians argue con and pro: 335
Denham saith thus, though Waller always so;
But he, good man, in his long sheet and staff,
This penance did for Cromwell's epitaph.
And his next theme must be o' th' Duke's mistress:

---

man, a warlike act not appropriate to the ship's diplomatic mission. Hence the ironic "embassies bear not arms."

325–26. One of the few beneficiaries of the war, the poet says, is the Duchess of York. "Checkstones" are counters used in a children's game. "Shell" is cant for money. I have not found any evidence that the Duchess shared in the prizes.

330. Traditional authority was withheld from the Prince of Orange until he was made Stadholder in 1672. *Regenerate* has the obsolete sense of *degenerate*: as a result of the war the Prince of Orange's prospects have declined.

334. Henry Bennet, Earl of Arlington, was married to Isabel von Beverweert, daughter of Louis of Nassau, who was a natural son of Prince Maurice. They were married in April 1666. *pimp Arlington:* "In particular he shared with his intimate friend, Sir Charles Berkeley, the management of the King's mistresses (Burnet, *1*, 18, ed. 1833), and in Nov. 1663 we find him acting with Edward Montagu and Buckingham in the shameful scheme 'for getting Mrs. Stewart for the King' (Pepys, 6 Nov. 1663)" (*DNB*).

337–38. The *long sheet* alludes to an old custom of performing penance in this attire. Waller is depicted as writing his *Instructions* thus attired in penance for his elegy, *Upon the Late Storm and the Death of his Highness Ensuing the Same* (1659).

Advice to draw Madam l'Édificatresse.   340
    Henceforth, O Gemini! two Dukes command:
Castor and Pollux, Aumarle, Cumberland.
Since in one ship, it had been fit they went
In Petty's double-keel'd *Experiment*.

To the King

Imperial Prince, King of the seas and isles,   345
Dear object of our joys and Heaven's smiles:
What boots it that thy light does gild our days
And we lie basking in thy milder rays,
While swarms of insects, from thy warmth begun,
Our land devour and intercept our sun?   350
Thou, like Jove's Minos, rul'st a greater Crete
And for its hundred cities count'st thy fleet.
Why wilt thou that state-Daedalus allow,
Who builds thee but a lab'rinth and a cow?
If thou art Minos, be a judge severe   355
And in's own maze confine the engineer;
Or if our sun, since he so near presumes,
Melt the soft wax with which he imps his plumes
And let him, falling, leave his hated name
Unto those seas his war hath set on flame.   360
From that enchanter having clear'd thine eyes,
Thy native sight will pierce within the skies
And view those kingdoms calm of joy and light,
Where's universal triumph but no fight.

340. *Madam l'Édificatresse:* The bawdy pun refers to Lady Denham, wife of Sir John Denham, the poet, who was appointed Surveyor-General of the Works (i.e. royal architect) at the Restoration. Lady Denham became the Duke of York's mistress in 1666.

341–42. After Sandwich's removal theNavy was entrusted to the joint command of Rupert, who also held the title of Duke of Cumberland, and George Monck, Duke of Albemarle.

344. Sir William Petty (1623–87) designed a double-keeled ship, the *Experiment,* which was lost in a storm in the Irish Sea.

353–54. *State-Daedalus* refers to Clarendon, and the lines give a satiric twist to Waller's comparison of Charles to Minos in the envoy to *Instructions*. Where Daedalus built a contrivance to satisfy Pasiphäe with a bull, from which union the Minotaur was born, Clarendon has, by his evil policies, confined Charles himself in a labyrinth and provided him with a cow (the barren Queen?).

Since both from Heav'n thy race and pow'r descend,   365
Rule by its pattern, there to reascend:
Let justice only draw and battle cease;
Kings are in war but cards: they're gods in peace.

368. In war kings are but playing-cards, powerless instruments of their ministers.

CHRISTOPHER WASE

Divination
(1666)

Divination is a detailed rejoinder to *Second Advice* written by the headmaster of Tonbridge School, Christopher Wase (1625?–90), former Fellow of King's College, Cambridge, classical scholar, and later Printer to the University of Oxford. Wase was a friend of both Waller and Denham and wrote an elegy on the latter. In 1668 Evelyn proposed his appointment as historiographer royal, to write the official account of the Second Dutch War, but the King appointed Evelyn himself instead (Evelyn, *3*, 523 n.).

The animus for this counterattack stems from Wase's anger that *Second Advice* should have been attributed to his loyalist friend, Denham, and also from his abhorrence of what he considered a seditious attack on the Duke of York and the government of Clarendon.

The style of *Divination* is often elliptical to the point of incoherence, and in view of Wase's presumed erudition it looks as though he tried to attain the rugged, cryptic qualities which had been considered, especially in earlier Stuart and Elizabethan times, appropriate to the satiric mode. But though it has small literary merit, *Divination* deserves a place here for several reasons: it gives an early and unanswerable argument against Denham's authorship of *Second Advice;* it is one of the very few political satires which support the government in this period; and it makes some interesting points about the ethics of anonymous attacks on the administration.

Throughout his rejoinder Wase sardonically employs the assistance of the well-known astrologer, Lilly, who, throughout the political vicissitudes of Commonwealth, Oliver, Richard, Rump, and Charles, had sought to please those in power with his prophecies, in order to identify the true author of *Second Advice*. He absolves Davenant, Dryden, and Denham and seems to hint at the Duke of Buckingham as the culprit. While there is no other evidence, external or internal, that Buckingham had anything to do with *Sec-*

ond Advice, many signs both circumstantial and detailed point to
Marvell as the author (see headnote to Waller's *Instructions*). Of
course, the possibility of collaboration is not to be ruled out en-
tirely.

Divination, here printed for the first time, is ascribed to Christo-
pher Wase in Bod. MS. Eng. Poet. e. 4, where it appears between the
second and third *Advices.* The MS. includes some excerpts from
Buckingham's *Rehearsal* and an elegy on Denham and a panegyric
on Charles II, both by Wase. The panegyric ends in the following
manner:

> Let poet-painter prate
> (The saddest marks of an ill-govern'd state)
> You in your thankful subjects' heart shall stand
> Subscrib'd the father of his native land.

In some places the text seems corrupt, and the only other MS. I
have seen (B.M. Harl. 7649) provides little help.

DIVINATION

Tell me, thou confidant of what is done
Abroad ere it at Rome be but begun,
Inform'd by stars, whose influences fall
With sure effect upon the dark Cabal.
A well drawn picture! I would know what hand,   5
Envious of royal honor, late hath stain'd
Valor and beauty with lamp-black defac'd,
And what he ought to worship hath disgrac'd.
    Nor ask me where nor how long since this pass'd;
Bid me return; you will a figure cast.   10
You, Sir, who can a whole year antedate
Commissions not yet issu'd out by Fate,
From east to west your judgment can explain

---

4. *the dark Cabal: Second Advice* attacks two members of the Cabal, Arlington and
Clifford.

6–8. *Second Advice* impugns the valor of the Duke of York and the beauty of his
Duchess. *Lamp black* was used in making ink.

10. *a figure cast:* calculate astrologically.

What ominous sparkles in last comet's train
Portended plagues, what wars, what dismal times,   15
What conflagrations, what these evil rhymes:
Wildfire of wit, made up in a close cell,
Where only night and conscious horror dwell,
Thence flung like balls, which, wheresoe'er they take,
'Twixt prince and people new combustions make.   20
Resolve me where and when, since if you will,
Place can no more than time prescribe your skill,
Or earth or moon; men in your *Merlin* see
What is, what was, and what shall never be.
True, if in lust and wine he cares would drown,   25
He were the merry Laureate of the town,
Who, free from plots, with his own easy lays
Pleases himself nor labors for much praise.
These vapors of a spleen with guilt oppress'd,
Restless themselves, disturb the public rest,   30
Awake our fears and jealousies create
Enough to put a frenzy in the state.
Or else if love and honor crown each page,
You well had read the champion of the stage:
Here the kind Duchess is forbid to mourn   35
When her Lord parts, or joy at his return.
Such checks against less ministers of state,
As on the great, reflect a popular hate.
Or if abuses strip and whip and sing

14. *Last comet's train:* A comet appeared late in 1664 and was observed from south-
ern England throughout the winter.

18. *conscious:* Guilty.

21. *Resolve:* Answer.

22. *prescribe:* Limit, restrict, restrain; confine within bounds, *obs.*

23. *Merlin:* Lilly's almanacs entitled *Merlini Anglici Ephemeris* were published an-
nually over many years.

26. Will D'Avenant was Laureate until his death in 1668.

34. *the champion of the stage:* Presumably Dryden, who had produced, by the time
Divination was written, *The Wild Gallant, The Rival Ladies, The Indian Queen* (in
collaboration with Sir Robert Howard), and *The Indian Emperor.*

35-36. See *Second Advice,* 75ff.

39-40. The construction here is obscure. The idea seems to be that were the un-
known poet to castigate contemporary abuses and arraign his betters, he would be some
petty satirical poetaster, but, as the following lines point out, the author of *Second
Advice* is a more important figure. Wase probably alludes in line 39 to George Wither

And in mistaken zeal his betters bring   40
Under the petty lash of saucy rhymes,
He were the minor poet of the times.
Against the court this, with worse-meaning art,
Levels a polish'd but a poison'd dart.
Suggest the work of well-contriv'd and high,   45
A master-builder speaks in poetry.
Produce me in whose pressure sign'd by us,
Waller said always so, or Denham thus?
These credibilities lose credit: none
That treason speaks thus labors to be known.   50
Go, fond imposter! Cheat some ruder age!
This sober malice is not Denham's rage—
Denham, whose wit and candor stand alone,
Or brooking to be rival'd but by one.
Waller, thou art too patient; right thy friend!   55
So shall the present age thy worth defend.
If thou beest silent and his straying muse,
Careless of fame, self-pleasing errors choose,
Denham accus'd would make a statue speak,
And melting rocks into soft numbers break: 60
Whose brains, though strong, by stronger passions rack'd,
May yield, but 's loyalty was never crack'd.
Plead not both poets terse, both full and free,
When in the better part they disagree.
Deep is the stream, and broad, yet clear and still,   65

(1588–1667), the well-known author of *Abuses Stript and Whipt* (1613), whose outspoken writings after the Restoration, especially the unpublished *Vox Vulgi*, caused his imprisonment in the Marshalsea. See the account in *DNB*.

45–46. Another obscure construction, though it distinguishes clearly enough the skill and style of *Second Advice's* author from that of a minor poetaster.

48. See *Second Advice*, 340.

61. Denham went mad in 1666. Aubrey relates that he "went from London to see the famous free-stone quarries at Portland in Dorset, and when he came within a mile of it, turned back to London again and did not see it. He went to Hounslow and demanded rents of lands he had sold many years before; went to the King and told him he was the Holy Ghost." By the fall of 1666 he seems to have recovered his wits, since he served on several parliamentary committees. See *Poetical Works*, ed. Banks, pp. 22–23.

65–66. Denham's famous poem *Cooper's Hill* first appeared in 1642. Cf. lines 191–92:

Though deep, yet clear, though gentle, yet not dull,
Strong without rage, without o'erflowing full.

Nor chides aloud, that runs from *Cooper's Hill.*
So harmless fury, but how bold! how brave!
When he doth in his matchless *Sophy* rave.
This satirist in each insidious line
Declares no poet, but an assassine.   70
Poets to profit promise or delight:
This seeks to do you ruin, and despite
His master. Speak, with what religious fear
He chastely wont t'approach his sacred ear:
No subject blasted with a pleasing tale,   75
Nor fellow servant, when he smil'd, look'd pale.
This in soft accents steals the public breast
And kills some noble fame at every jest.
Thus when two gems their emulous light display,
That in a true, this in a glist'ring ray,   80
Vulgar spectators with distracted eyes
Gaze, or more highly the false jewel prize,
Till, to a skilful lapidary shown,
He parts the diamond from the Bristol stone.
Sage Merlin, I the face would fain descry,   85
That forehead, those pale cheeks, that hollow eye.
Then damp the windows, let no species pass,
Read a spell o'er thy necromantic glass.
For nonsense spare Albumazar and quack
Three lines of thy more pow'rful almanac.   90
    Wot ye the man that blemishes his friend,

68. *The Sophy,* an historical tragedy about the Turkish court, appeared in 1641.
74. *He:* Denham. *wont:* the past tense of the verb *won, obs.,* to be accustomed. *his sacred ear:* The King's.
84. *Bristol stone:* A kind of rock crystal. Supposing Buckingham to be the suspected author of *Second Advice,* the line may refer also to the alliance of Buckingham and George Digby, Earl of Bristol, in opposition to Clarendon.
87. *species:* An unreal or imaginary object of sight; a phantom or illusion, *obs.*
89. *Albumazar:* An Arabian astronomer (805–85), who appears as a rascally wizard in a play by that name written by Thomas Tomkis (fl. 1604–15). It was revived at Lincoln's Inn Fields, 21 Feb. 1667.
91. *his friend:* Edmund Waller was an old friend of Buckingham's. Sir John Clayton tells how "we dined at Uxbridge, and never in all my life did I pass my day with such gusto, our company being his Grace [Buckingham], Mr. Waller, Mr. Surveyor [Christopher] Wren, and myself; nothing but quintessence of wit and most excellent discourse" (quoted by Wilson, *A Rake and his Times,* p. 152). Wilson later describes Waller's returning home at 4:00 A.M. from a convivial supper with Buckingham and his mistress, the Countess of Shrewsbury (pp. 155–56).

Reviles his Prince, scarce any can commend?
Nothing his froward humor satisfies:
The Duke that conquers or the Earl that dies.
Fight Sandwich well, he is without dispute   95
A coward, for he brought aboard a lute.
The Lesbian lord no less on vocal string
The ills of sea, the ills of war did sing.
That lyre which grac'd his cabin, with him sent
Abroad, did ease the ills of banishment.   100
Yet, ere he go, a Duke and Prince must claim
Nothing yet acted to succeed in blame.
Who thus can at a venture hate, doth hate
Not this nor that commander but the State:
At variance with himself, whose youth and age   105

94. *The Duke that conquers or the Earl that dies:* The Duke of York, Lord High Admiral, and the Earl of Falmouth, whose death is related in lines 181–88 of *Second Advice.*

95–96. See *Second Advice,* 102–07.

97. *The Lesbian Lord:* Orpheus, who was torn to pieces by Thracian Maenads. His scattered limbs were buried by the Muses on Olympus, but his head and lyre floated down the Hebrus to the sea and across the sea to Lesbos, where they were buried.

100. *the ills of banishment:* Sandwich was sent to Spain on an embassy in May 1666. See *Second Advice,* 311–16.

101–02. The Duke and Prince are Albemarle and Rupert, who succeeded Sandwich as co-commanders of the fleet. I am not sure what these lines mean.

105–12. This description suggests a specific rather than a typical person as author of *Second Advice,* and most of the details are appropriate to Buckingham, who was continually involved in Court intrigues in the '60s and '70s. As early as 1645 he was regarded as an "evil counsellor" to the future Charles II, "having already got into all the impieties and vices of the age" (Burnet, *History, 1,* 183). An orthodox Anglican like Wase might well regard as a "soph divine" such an outspoken defender of liberty of conscience as Buckingham. Buckingham treated very lightly the points of dissension between the Establishment and the Nonconformists: "It is certainly a very uneasy kind of life to any man that has either Christian charity, humanity, or good nature, to see his fellow subjects daily abused, divested of their liberty and birthrights, and miserably thrown out of their possessions and freeholds, only because they cannot agree with others in some niceties of religion which their consciences will not give them leave to consent to, and which, even by the confession of those who would impose them upon them, are no ways necessary to salvation" (speech in the House of Lords, 16 Nov. 1667 in *Works* [1715], *2,* 202–03).

Buckingham was a "mock-philosopher" (i.e. a dilettante natural philosopher or scientist) par excellence. One of the outstanding amateur virtuosi of his time, he spent a fortune searching for the philosopher's stone and procured at considerable expense some powdered unicorn's horn which was employed by Lord Brouncker and other colleagues in the Royal Society to test the hypothesis that spiders could not walk out of a ring made of such powder (Wilson, *A Rake and his Times,* p. 22).

Confronted in a mortal feud engage,
A court-spy and an evil counsellor,
A soph-divine, a mock-philosopher,
Many in one, one from himself another,
Two States, two Churches in the same false brother.   110
For him saints, poets, princes to revile,
And wound their glories with unhallow'd style.
Prometheus, when he would dull clay inspire,
Mounts up aloft, brings down celestial fire;
This Angelo sticks not, that he may well   115
Limn a despair, to fetch a coal from Hell—
Ill scholars, that can speak in trope and scheme,
Methodically treason and blaspheme!
  Why at the Chancellor so much repine
As for his sake to curse the royal line?   120
When Turnus would the Phrygian leader wound,

Two States, two Churches, in the same false brother accurately describes the kind of political turncoat and religious eclectic that Buckingham seemed to be. Although he fought with Charles II at Worcester, in 1652 he was attempting to negotiate a settlement with Cromwell through Sir Ellis Leighton and was discussing simultaneously with John Lilburne the feasibility of restoring the King through the help of the Levellers! "These intrigues and Buckingham's policy of sacrificing the interests of the Church to the political exigencies of the moment deepened the breach between the Duke and the ministers of Charles II" (*DNB*).

The more general details of the description are equally appropriate to Buckingham. One of the most celebrated things about him was his inconsistency ("at variance with himself"), which was to be noted in Dryden's famous portrait:

> A man so various, that he seem'd to be
> Not one, but all mankind's epitome.
> (*Absalom and Achitophel,* 545–46)

Buckingham was thirty-eight at the time this poem was written, and his wildly eccentric behavior could quite rightly be seen as a "mortal feud" between youth and age, between frivolity and gravity.

110. *brother:* Member of a Nonconformist sect.

111–12. These lines make no sense as they stand, and there is probably something missing.

117–18. I take *scheme* as a noun (= rhetorical figure) and *treason* as the rare verb (= betray).

119. Buckingham's antipathy to the Chancellor, Lord Clarendon, was deep-seated. "It was to his influence that Buckingham attributed the conspicuous omission of his name from the list of the Privy Council, to which all the former members had been reappointed" (Burghclere, *Buckingham,* pp. 116–17).

120. For the curse on Clarendon and his line see *Second Advice,* 145–54.

121–24. See *Aeneid,* 12.897ff.

Heaving a mighty millstone from the ground,
Such as nine men of our degenerate world
Could scarce have mov'd, he at Aeneas hurl'd.
Our race, though lesser grown, doth louder roar,   125
Bombing out imprecations cannon-bore.
The sluggish rock fell at the hero's feet;
So words fall short, more angry than discreet.
Oh! at this commonplace he doth rehearse,
Imprimis, items, articles in verse: 130
For Scotland slighted, for a daughter marri'd,
For Dunkirk parted with, the Queen miscarri'd;
His person hates, nor his alliance spares,
Settles an execration on his heirs.
Look to your title ere you further rail: 135
That hero's faith shall cut off the entail.
Dear to his Prince, and with the senate fair,
Stands he absolved at Apollo's bar,
Nor by my lines but his best offspring prais'd,
Confutes that curse, above vain libels rais'd,   140
Sons bred like noblemen of old, whose care
Virtue and business was, and when to spare:
In these more than his envi'd charges great,
May he survive and calumny defeat,
Himself content this royal badge to bear,   145
Still well to act though still he worse should hear;
Whose loyal thoughts can hope nor joy alone,
But counts his master's welfare most his own;

129. *commonplace:* An exercise or thesis on some set theme, *obs.* *rehearse:* Perhaps
an allusion to Buckingham's well-known satirical play, *The Rehearsal,* which was said
to be ready for the stage in 1665.
131–32. For the "articling" of Clarendon for dismantling forts in Scotland, marrying
his daughter to the Duke of York, selling Dunkirk, and matching Charles II with the
barren Catherine de Braganza, see *Second Advice,* 150ff.
134. For the execration settled on Clarendon's heirs, see *Second Advice,* 145–46.
135–36. A difficult couplet. If the entail is taken to be the execration settled on
Clarendon's heirs, Clarendon's faithfulness will cut it off. If the entail is taken to mean
Buckingham's title, there is a threat that his heirs will not inherit it.
138. Apollo here is principally the embodiment of justice, but his other attributes,
as patron of divination and poetry, are relevant.
139ff. Henry, second Earl of Clarendon (1638–1709), and Laurence, Earl of Rochester
(1641–1711), were devoted sons and warmly defended their father on his impeachment
in 1667.

Next, lest his Royal Highness should be harm'd,
Regardless of himself, is most alarm'd.   150
Slanders at random flying don't impeach
That noble breast which Opdam could not reach.
What cares Detraction, planted in the dark,
Having selected out the fairest mark,
Whether it true or seeming crimes object?   155
Nor highest birth nor merit shall protect
Him that great James's courage dares deny;
The same may question his loyalty,
Then follow the Dutch justice with applause
And in the end revive the Good Old Cause.   160
What other in these realms an heart doth bear
So full of reverence and so void of fear?
Such one of us if our just Sovereign knew,
To make him next the greatest were his due,
One to fierce times a safe example shown,   165
Born to approach and stay a tott'ring throne.
If Nature's frame should start, Atlas might cease
To fear, assisted by this Hercules.
Though 'tis fit th' encroaching Dutchman be chastis'd,
England, of her late daring Prince advis'd,   170
Forbears too cheaply to expose her hope,
To storm a castle or a cannon stop.
At too great odds our danger we invited
Who ventur'd what no conquest had requited.
Let soaring pens those acts commit to fame;   175
His loyal zeal my duty shall inflame.
      Good Lilly, one thing more, for thou of face
As well as hands the crooked lines can'st trace,
What means his various count'nance? Does that smile
Relate t' his country or Sir William's Isle?   180
Which if it do, we rightly may infer,

149. *his Royal Highness:* The Duke of York.
159. For the suggestion that *Second Advice* regards the Dutch cause as just see lines 367–68.
160. *Good Old Cause:* The Commonwealth.
169–76. After Lowestoft the Duke of York withdrew from active service. See *Second Advice,* 252 n.
180. *Sir William's Isle:* I am unable to explain this allusion.

He is of France some secret pensioner.
Unfold those wrinkled membranes. Is that crease
Concern'd in a Dutch honorable peace?
You ill persuade me that his country's love   185
Doth knit those brows and twinkling eyelids move.
Go, tear thy trig, break thy ill-printed glass;
Right reason will a better judgment pass.
Who draws the landscape of our woes, our wracks,
Disasters, errors, aggravates our tax;   190
What every faithful subject ought to hide
(His country's shame) makes his delight and pride.
Words prove the man: Caesar could not have wrote
So well unless as well he could have fought.
He that dares with a flaming *London* sport,   195
If fear to act what fearless to report,
Would not perhaps the city wrap in flames,
Cover with flying boats the busy Thames,
Yet be content a town in ashes sit
To guide the pencil of his wanton wit.   200
Wisely that great metropolis thought meet
To be insur'd amidst the royal fleet
(Pledge that this pile, refin'd from dust and guilt,
Shall be by no less grateful Charles rebuilt).
Of war and peace he, wiser than the State   205
And juster than the King, dares arbitrate.
Knows he the Dutch, whose valor he does raise?
Or where they trade whose justice he doth praise?
Betwixt the Sluys and Ems is a short span;
Their greatest province is the ocean;   210
This cover'd with unnumber'd vessels groans,
From either pole to waft their galleons.
A nation seated where the Rhine doth fall,
The Rhine, the Maas, the Yssel, and the Waal—

183. Cf. *Second Advice,* 287–88.

187–88. The specific sense is not clear, though the poet is obviously dismissing the astrologer Lilly in favor of "right reason."

195–200. A man who could joke about the loss of the *London* by fire (cf. *Second Advice,* 13–18) would not, perhaps, go so far as to set fire to the City—fear would prevent him—yet he would be content to have the "town in ashes sit" as a subject for his satires. The Fire broke out 2 Sept. 1666.

Hides the robb'd world within her shelves and sands,   215
As Tunis safe behind the Sirte stands.
She from disfurnish'd realms her stores doth swell,
Can buy a famine and a famine sell,
Defective Nature hath suppli'd with art,
Though barren, yet the universal mart,   220
Whose thrifty prudence might of praise partake,
If she the sacred thirst of gold could slake.
Her infants thrown upon the falling Rhine
(Which doth a native Hollander define)
Born in a cabin, grow upon the main   225
And wander all about the liquid plain
In swimming wagons to th' Antipodes.
The Dutchman is the Tartar of the seas,
And no less cruel, if his gain command,
To sack a fleet or to unplant a land;   230
Old friendship slights, now rich and potent grown,
Nor bless'd enough till he be bless'd alone.
Their policies our naval force defy,
For whom they cannot conquer they outbuy.
The Portuguese their right resign, and we   235
More than their men of war their factors flee.
Did brave Emanuel, upon this design,
Double the Cape and first twice cut the Line?
Or bless'd Elizabeth open to the West
The untouch'd riches of the frozen East,   240
Venturing, like Jason for the golden ram,
Spices and furs to find for Amsterdam?
By force or fraud Lisbon and London, made
Brokers to carry on the Holland trade,
Are near excluded through expression: 245
That from the torrid, this the frigid zone.

216. *Sirte:* The Gran Sirte, a large gulf off the coast of Tunis.
219. *She* is the subject of *hath supplied.*
236. *factors:* Merchants.
237. *brave Emanuel:* Manuel I of Portugal (1495–1521). His reign marked the apogee of Portuguese power following the great discoveries of Vasco da Gama and Magellan.
239–40. The Muscovy Company was, in fact, chartered in 1555 before Elizabeth's accession, but she encouraged its activities.
245. *through expression:* Through being squeezed out.

  Thinks the deep Siren with one pleasing charm
The King and angry senate to disarm?
Since our discovering Monarch, whom he styles
Imperial Prince, King of the Seas and Isles,   250
Led by his counsel, he would but prefer
In his own island to be prisoner.
Great politician! Should our fleet at ease
Ride in vain triumph o'er the Narrow Seas,
Waiting our baffled carracks with half freight   255
Return'd from India, to convoy in state?
Or while their busses on our rifled shore
Be fully fraught, look on, and keep the door?
Such gilded pleasure-boats with pasteboard guns
Neptune ne'er saw, nor of so many tons.   260
  Then void the court and let thy painted muse
With flatt'ring strains some foreign prince abuse.
Our duller clime can never read aright
Thy grave advice nor on known worth requite.
Such wisdom slighted here would be address'd   265
To the puissant Monarch of the West
He would reward thee with fit title (thing)
And Counselor to the thrice Christian King,
Or, if a kindness where thou seem'st dost bear,
To thy beloved Hollander declare.   270
Though he a while himself absolved call
(Himself the judge, himself the criminal);
Though thousand ships from all the compass round
Sail, these for Holland, these for Zeeland bound;
France with the States, the States with Denmark join,   275
And all the world or stand neuter or combine;
Nay, England, too; the Belgic pride doth owe
To wrong'd mankind her sudden overthrow.
In vain they would by craft or wealth prevail:

---

247. *one pleasing charm:* The envoy to *Second Advice.*
250. This is the opening line of the envoy to *Second Advice,* 345.
264. *requite:* Avenge oneself, *obs. rare.*
266. *the puissant Monarch of the West:* Louis XIV.
271–78. This passage seems hopelessly corrupt.
277. *Belgic:* Dutch.

Not Fortune but Astræa holds the scale,   280
Who doth examine with impartial weights
The rise and fall of kingdoms and of states.
They levy soldiers, new alliance seek,
Equip armadas, block up every creek,
Securer, had they in this balance laid,   285
Arms set aside, the laws of peace and trade.

280. *Astræa:* Justice.

ANDREW MARVELL

The Third Advice to a Painter
(1666)

With the removal of Sandwich, command of the navy was vested jointly in the versatile Monck, now Duke of Albemarle, and the aging, ailing Prince Rupert. Late in May 1666 a squadron of twenty ships under Rupert was detached to attack some French warships under the duc de Beaufort reported to be near Belle-Île in the Bay of Biscay. With the remainder of the English fleet Albemarle encountered a superior Dutch force on 1 June 1666 between the North Foreland and Dunkirk. In the Four Days' Battle (1–4 June) Albemarle's ships were battered and total defeat was avoided only by Rupert's last-minute reunion with the main fleet.

The division of the fleet was investigated by Parliament in October 1667 just as the Commons were exploring methods of impeaching Clarendon. A recent study based upon new evidence (Fraser, *Intelligence of the Secretaries of State*, 1956) puts the chief blame on the joint commanders. It now appears that Albemarle and Rupert, after the miscarriage, fell in with Clarendon's desire to lay the blame on Sir William Coventry and the Earl of Arlington, who had initiated the movement to impeach the Chancellor. Rupert and Albemarle testified that Arlington's intelligence service had falsely reported Beaufort at Belle-Île when he was in the Mediterranean and had failed to learn of the advanced readiness of the Dutch fleet. They also testified that Coventry had failed to send the order recalling Rupert with due dispatch.

Fraser shows that these allegations are false and that Albemarle's engagement of the powerful Dutch fleet without Rupert's forces was intentional:

> Rupert sailed with the morning tide on the 29th. The same day Albemarle received advice from a ship that the Dutch fleet had sailed. He made no attempt to recall the Prince, who was then only ten miles distant, but was confident that he could en-

gage the Dutch alone. . . . On his way to the station he had
chosen between the Downs and the Gunfleet Albemarle ran
into the Dutch fleet. His note to Coventry, written at 11 A.M.
on I June reveals that he was neither surprised, nor disinclined
to a combat. (p. 83)

Though *Third Advice* implicates Arlington and Coventry as the
chief culprits, it assigns Albemarle a share of the blame:

> But let the Prince to fight with Rumor go;
> The General meets a more substantial foe:
> Ruyter he spies, and full of youthful heat,
> Though half their number, thinks the odds too great. (31–34)

Third Advice was first published without license in 1667 under a
Breda imprint together with *Second Advice* and some other items.
It was written after the outbreak of the Great Fire (2 Sept. 1666).
Pepys saw a manuscript in January 1667: "I took it home with me
and will copy it, having the former, being also mightily pleased with
it."

For a discussion of Marvell's authorship, see the articles referred
to in the headnote to Waller's *Instructions to a Painter*.

THE THIRD ADVICE TO A PAINTER

London, October 1st, 1666

Sandwich in Spain now, and the Duke in love,
Let's with new Gen'rals a new painter prove:
Lely's a Dutchman, danger in his art;

1. Sandwich was in Spain from May 1666 to September 1668. See *Second Advice*,
307–10 and n., concerning his mission. *the Duke in love:* With Lady Denham, née
Margaret Brooke, married to Sir John Denham 25 May 1665. On 10 June 1666 a friend
told Pepys "how the Duke of York is wholly given up to his new mistress, my Lady
Denham, going at noon-day with all his gentlemen to visit her in Scotland Yard; she
declaring she will not be his mistress, as Mrs. Price, to go up and down the Privy-
stairs, but will be owned publicly; and so she is."

2. *Gen'rals:* Commanding officers at sea were so designated.

3. *Lely:* Sir Peter Lely (1617–80), famous as a painter of court beauties. His real
name was Vander Vaas, and he is said to have obtained the name of Lely or du Lys
from the fact that his father was born at the Hague at a perfumer's shop which had
the sign of the Lily. Lely's appearance in the poem is ironically appropriate, since

His pencils may intelligence impart.
Thou, Gibson, that among thy navy small   5
Of marshall'd shells commandest admiral
(Thyself so slender that thou show'st no more
Than barnacle new-hatch'd of them before)
Come, mix thy water-colors and express,
Drawing in little, how we do yet less.   10
   First paint me George and Rupert, rattling far
Within one box, like the two dice of war,
And let the terror of their linked name
Fly through the air like chain-shot, tearing fame.
Jove in one cloud did scarcely ever wrap   15
Lightning so fierce, but never such a clap!
United Gen'rals! sure the only spell
Wherewith United Provinces to quell.
Alas, e'en they, though shell'd in treble oak,
Will prove an addle egg with double yolk.   20
And therefore next uncouple either hound
And loo them at two hares ere one be found.
Rupert to Beaufort hollo, "Ay there, Rupert!"
Like the fantastic hunting of St. Hubert
When he, with airy hounds and horn of air,   25
Pursues by Fontainebleau the witchy hare—
Deep providence of state that could so soon
Fight Beaufort here ere he had quit Toulon!
So have I seen, ere human quarrels rise,
Foreboding meteors combat with the skies.   30
   But let the Prince to fight with Rumor go;

---

early in 1666 York had commissioned him to paint the portraits of the admirals in the Lowestoft engagement (Pepys, 17 April 1666).

   5. *Gibson:* Richard Gibson (1615–90), a dwarf painter of miniatures, copied Lely's works. His wife was of the same size and Waller celebrated their marriage in verse.

   11. *George and Rupert:* Cf. *Second Advice,* 317–18 and n. In the St. James' Fight Albemarle and Rupert were both on the flagship *Royal Charles.*

   14. *chain shot:* A kind of shot formed of two half-balls, connected by a chain, used to destroy masts and rigging.

   16. *clap:* A punning reference to Rupert's alleged affliction. Pepys (15 Jan. 1665): "my Lord Fitzharding come thither, and fell to discourse of Prince Rupert, and made nothing to say that his disease was the pox and that he must be fluxed, telling the horrible degree of the disease upon him with its breaking out on his head."

   23–28. See headnote.

The Gen'ral meets a more substantial foe.
Ruyter he spies, and full of youthful heat,
Though half their number, thinks his odds too great.
The fowler, so, watches the wat'ry spot,   35
And more the fowl, hopes for the better shot.
Though such a limb were from his navy torn,
He found no weakness yet, like Sampson shorn.
But swoll'n with sense of former glory won,
Thought Monck must be by Albemarle outdone.   40
Little he knew, with the same arm and sword,
How far the gentleman outcuts the lord.
    Ruyter, inferior unto none for heart,
Superior now in number and in art,
Ask'd if he thought, as once our rebel nation,   45
To conquer theirs too by a declaration?
And threatens, though he now so proudly sail,
He shall tread back his *Iter Boreale.*
This said, he the short period, ere it ends,
With iron words from brazen mouths extends.   50
Monck yet prevents him ere the navies meet
And charges in, himself alone a fleet,
And with so quick and frequent motion wound
His murd'ring sides about, the ship seem'd round,
And the exchanges of his circling tire   55
Like whirling hoops show'd of triumphal fire.
Single he does at their whole navy aim
And shoots them through a porcupine of flame.
He plays with danger and his bullets trolls
(As 'twere at trou-madam) through all their holls.   60
In noise so regular his cannon met
You'd think that thunder were to music set.

33. *Ruyter:* See *Second Advice,* 259–70 n.
46. *declaration:* The Declaration of Breda, which preceded Charles II's restoration.
It was Hyde's handiwork, although Monck undoubtedly had a part in devising it.
48. *Iter Boreale:* The march by Monck and his army from Scotland to London. See
Wild, *Iter Boreale.*
55. *tire:* The simultaneous discharge of a battery of ordnance; a volley or broadside.
59. *trolls:* Trolls, or rolls, as with dice or balls.
60. *trou-madam:* A ladies' game in which metal balls were rolled down a table con-
taining eleven holes at the far end.   *holls: Obs.* form of hulls or holds.

Ah, had the rest but kept a time as true,
What age could such a martial consort shew?
The list'ning air unto the distant shore   65
Through secret pipes conveys the tuned roar,
Till, as the echoes vanishing abate,
Men feel a deaf sound like the pulse of Fate.
If Fate expire, let Monck her place supply:
His guns determine who shall live or die.   70
  But Victory does always hate a rant:
Valor her brave, but Skill is her gallant.
Ruyter no less with virtuous envy burns
And prodigies for miracles returns.
Yet she observ'd how still his iron balls   75
Bricol'd in vain against our oaken walls,
And the hard pellets fell away as dead,
Which our enchanted timber fillipped.
"Leave then," said he, "th' invulnerable keel;
We'll find their foible, like Achilles' heel."   80
  He, quickly taught, pours in continual clouds
Of chain'd dilemmas through our sinewy shrouds.
Forests of masts fall with their rude embrace;
Our stiff sails, mash'd, are netted into lace,
Till our whole navy lay their wanton mark,   85
Nor any ship could sail but as the ark.
Shot in the wing, so, at the powder's call
The disappointed bird does flutt'ring fall.
Yet Monck, disabl'd, still such courage shows
That none into his mortal gripe durst close.   90
So an old bustard, maim'd, yet loth to yield,
Duels the fowler in Newmarket field.
But soon he found 'twas now in vain to fight
And imps his plumes the best he may for flight.
  This, Painter, were a noble task, to tell   95
What indignation his great breast did swell.

64. *consort:* 1. A company of ships sailing together; 2. a concert.
76. *Bricol'd:* Recoiled.
78. *fillipped:* Struck.
82. *chain'd dilemmas:* The Dutch chain shot.
88. *disappointed:* Destroyed, *obs.*
94. *imps:* Engrafts feathers *upon.*

Not virtuous men unworthily abus'd,
Not constant lovers without cause refus'd,
Not honest merchant broke, not skilful play'r
Hiss'd off the stage, not sinner in despair,   100
Not losing rooks, not favorites disgrac'd,
Not Rump by Oliver or Monck displac'd,
Not kings depos'd, not prelates ere they die,
Feel half the rage of gen'rals when they fly.
    Ah, rather than transmit our scorn to fame,   105
Draw curtains, gentle artist, o'er this shame.
Cashier the mem'ry of Du Tell, rais'd up
To taste, instead of death's, his Highness' cup.
And if the thing were true, yet paint it not,
How Berkeley (as he long deserv'd) was shot,   110
Though others that survey'd the corpse so clear
Say he was only petrifi'd with fear;
And the hard statue, mummi'd without gum,
Might the Dutch balm have spar'd and English tomb.
Yet, if thou wilt, paint Myngs turn'd all to soul,   115
And the great Harman chark'd almost to coal,

97–104. Cf. *The Rape of the Lock*, IV.3–10.

101. *rooks:* Cheats, sharpers.

107. *Du Tell:* The Duchess of Albemarle complained to Pepys (4 April 1667) that the Duke of York had employed as cupbearer Du Tell, a Frenchman whom Albemarle and Rupert had dismissed because he "fired more shot into the Prince's ship and others of the King's ships than of the enemy." This may be the Sir John Du Tiel mentioned by Charnock as of French extraction and a Knight of Malta (Charnock, *Biographia Navalis*, p. 163).

110. *Berkeley:* William Berkeley (1639–66), younger brother of Charles, Earl of Falmouth, a favorite of the Duke of York. See *Second Advice*, 189–96 and notes for his part in the Battle of Lowestoft. After his death the Dutch at first treated his body with little respect, displaying it publicly in a sugar chest (Pepys, 16 June 1666), but later the government ordered it embalmed and held for English disposal (15 July 1666, *London Gazette*, no. 69).

115. *Myngs:* Sir Christopher Myngs (1625–66), leading the van in the *Victory*, was fatally wounded on the fourth day of battle. Though his throat was partly blown away he stopped the gap with his fingers and continued to give orders. He died some days later.

116. *Harman:* Sir John Harman (d. 1673), Rear Admiral of the White. In the Four Days' Battle, Harman's ship was set upon by three Dutch fire ships in quick succession. His ship, the *Henry*, was fired, many men deserted him, and a falling mast pinned his leg. Nevertheless he managed to extinguish the fire and take his ship to Harwich. Harman had the ship refitted during the night and rejoined the fleet the next day.

And Jordan old, thy pencil's worthy pain,
Who all the way held up the ducal train.
But in a dark cloud cover Ayscue when
He quit the *Prince* t' embark in Lowestein,   120
And wounded ships, which we immortal boast,
Now first led captive to a hostile coast.
But most with story of his hand or thumb
Conceal (as Honor would) his Grace's bum,
When the rude bullet a large collop tore   125
Out of that buttock never turn'd before.
Fortune, it seem'd, would give him by that lash
Gentle correction for his fight so rash,
But should the Rump perceiv 't, they'd say that Mars
Had now reveng'd them upon Aumarle's arse.   130
     The long disaster better o'er to veil,
Paint only Jonah three days in the whale,
Then draw the youthful Perseus all in haste
From a sea-beast to free the virgin chaste
(But neither riding Pegasus for speed,   135
Nor with the Gorgon shielded at his need);
For no less time did conqu'ring Ruyter chaw
Our flying Gen'ral in his spongy jaw.
So Rupert the sea dragon did invade,
But to save George himself and not the maid,   140
And so arriving late, he quickly miss'd

117. *Jordan:* Captain Joseph Jordan, knighted 1 July 1665 for his bravery at Lowe-stoft, where he replaced Sir John Lawson as commander of the *Royal Oak.* Jordan wrote to Sir William Penn, 5 June 1666: "It is believed, that if Prince Rupert had been with us the first day, the enemy could not have escaped. But we must submit to the all-seeing Providence, who knows what is best for us. It is my part to praise God that hath delivered me and this ship wonderfully, after so many days' battle; the greatest passes, I think, that ever was fought at sea" (*Memorials of Sir William Penn,* 2, 390).

119–22. *Ayscue:* Sir George Ayscue or Ayscough (1646–71), Admiral of the White in that part of the fleet that remained with Albemarle. On the third day of the battle he ran the *Royal Prince* aground on Galloper Sands as he was trying to join Rupert's squadron, and was captured. "The Hollanders' rejoicings were infamous; they painted Sir George Ayscough over with a long tail and train, and set fire to it and blew him up" (*CSPD,* 10 July 1666). He was afterwards imprisoned in the Castle of Lowestein.

123–30. "The Duke himself [Albemarle] had a little hurt in his thigh, but signified little" (Pepys, 4 June 1666).

133. *youthful:* Rupert was 47 in 1666.

E'en sails to fly, unable to resist.
  Not Greenland seamen, that survive the fright
Of the cold chaos and half-eternal night,
So gladly the returning sun adore   145
Or run to spy their next year's fleet from shore,
Hoping yet once within the oily side
Of the fat whale again their spears to hide,
As our glad fleet with universal shout
Salute the Prince and wish the second bout;   150
Nor winds, long pris'ners in earth's hollow vault,
The fallow seas so eagerly assault,
As fi'ry Rupert with revengeful joy
Does on the Dutch his hungry courage cloy,
But soon unrigg'd lay like a useless board   155
(As wounded in the wrist men drop the sword)
When a propitious cloud betwixt us stepp'd
And in our aid did Ruyter intercept.
Old Homer yet did never introduce,
To save his heroes, mist of better use.   160
Worship the sun who dwell where he does rise:
This mist does more deserve our sacrifice.
  Now joyful fires and the exalted bell
And court-gazettes our empty triumph tell.
Alas, the time draws near when overturn'd   165
The lying bells shall through the tongue be burn'd;
Paper shall want to print that lie of state,
And our false fires true fires shall expiate.

155–58. "At last the whole English fleet succeeded in running through the gauntlet
to the windward position, but by then there was complete disorder, and neither side
had enough strength to continue the contest, which had been fought until the ships
above water were badly mauled and tattered and the surviving crews completely ex-
hausted. According to the Dutch account, the English were saved from annihilation
by the sudden descent of a fog" (Ogg, *England in the Reign of Charles II, 1,* 301).

163–68. "The court gave out that it was victory and public thanksgivings were
ordered, which was horrid mocking of God and a lying to the world" (Burnet, *1,* 409).
London Gazette, 7 June, refers to the first day's battle as "a great victory."

166. "Forgery, cheating, libelling, false weights and measures, forestalling the mar-
ket, offences in baking and brewing, are commonly punished with standing in the
pillory and sometimes to have one or both ears nailed to the pillory and cut off or
there bored through the tongue with a hot iron" (Chamberlayne, *Angliae Notitia,*
1669, p. 76).

168. The line refers, of course, to the Great Fire, 2–9 Sept. 1666.

> Stay, Painter, here a while, and I will stay,
> Nor vex the future times with nice survey.   170
> Seest not the monkey Duchess all undress'd?
> Paint thou but her, and she will paint the rest.
>
>   The sad tale found her in her outer room,
> Nailing up hangings not of Persian loom,
> Like chaste Penelope that ne'er did roam,   175
> But made all fine against her George came home.
> Upon a ladder, in her coat much shorter,
> She stood with groom and porter for supporter,
> And careless what they saw or what they thought,
> With *Hony-pensy* honestly she wrought.   180
> For in the Gen'ral's breech none could, she knows,
> Carry away the piece with eyes or nose.
> One tenter drove, to lose no time nor place,
> At once the ladder they remove, and Grace.
> While thus they her translate from north to east   185
> In posture just of a four-footed beast,
> She heard the news, but alter'd yet no more
> Than that what was behind she turn'd before,
> Nor would come down, but with a handkercher
> (Which pocket foul did to her neck prefer)   190
> She dri'd no tears, for she was too viraginous,
> But only snuffling her trunk cartilaginous,
> From scaling ladder she began a story
> Worthy to be had it *memento mori,*
> Arraigning past, and present, and *futuri,*   195
> With a prophetic (if not spirit) fury.

171. *monkey Duchess:* The Duchess of Albemarle, formerly Ann Clarges, daughter of Monck's regimental farrier. She attended Monck as seamstress while he was confined in the Tower. "Nan Clarges was kind to him," writes Aubrey (2, 72–78), "in a double capacity." In 1654, she became his wife, although it was said that she had a husband named Radford living. Clarendon describes her as "a woman of the lowest extraction, the least wit, and less beauty" (Jesse, *Memoirs of the Court,* 1846, 3, 433). *all undress'd:* en déshabille. *and she will paint the rest:* i.e. with her needle. The Duchess does, in fact, "paint the rest," or most of it, except for the couplet dismissing Gibson at line 435 and the envoy.

180. *Hony-pensy:* An allusion to the Garter, whose motto is *Honi soit qui mal y pense,* of which order Albemarle was a member. Cf. *Iter Boreale,* 100 and n.

183. *tenter:* Tenter-hook, one of the hooks or bent nails by which the edges of the cloth are firmly held.

Her hair began to creep, her belly sound,
Her eyes to startle, and her udder bound.
Half witch, half prophet, thus she-Albemarle,
Like Presbyterian sibyl, out did snarl: 200
   "Traitors both to my Lord, and to the King!
Nay, now it grows beyond all suffering!
One valiant man on land, and he must be
Commanded out to stop their leaks at sea.
Yet send him Rupert as a helper meet,   205
First the command dividing ere the fleet!
One may, if they be beat, or both, be hit,
Or if they overcome, yet honor's split,
But reck'ning George already knock'd o'th' head,
They cut him out like beef ere he be dead.   210
Each for a quarter hopes: the first does skip,
But shall snap short, though at the gen'ralship;
Next, they for Master of the Horse agree;
A third the Cockpit begs, not any me.
But they shall know, ay, marry, shall they do,   215
That who the Cockpit has shall have me too.
   "I told George first, as Calamy did me,
If the King these brought over, how 'twould be:
Men that there pick'd his pocket to his face
To sell intelligence or buy a place,   220
That their religion pawn'd for clothes, nor care
('T has run so long) now to redeem 't, nor dare.
O what egregious loyalty to cheat!
O what fidelity it was to eat!

200. *Presbyterian sibyl:* "All the evidence tends to prove that Monck was at heart a moderate Presbyterian, just as his wife was a violent one" (*DNB*).

201 ff. See Pepys, 9 Dec. 1665: "At table the Duchess, a damned ill-looking woman, complaining of her Lord's going to sea the next year, said the cursed words: 'If my Lord had been a coward he had gone to sea no more: it may be that he might have been excused, and made an Ambassador' (meaning my Lord Sandwich)." See also the entry for 26 Feb. 1666. In her story the Duchess is addressing the four Navy commissioners, though she doubtless has the Duke of York in mind also.

213. Albemarle was appointed Master of the Horse to the King 26 May 1660.

214. *Cockpit:* The Duke of Albemarle's lodgings in Whitehall.

217. *Calamy:* Edmund Calamy (1600–66), celebrated Nonconformist divine, appointed chaplain to Charles II in 1660, a post which he quickly resigned.

While Langdales, Hoptons, Glenhams starv'd abroad,   225
And here true Roy'lists sunk beneath the load,
Men that did there affront, defame, betray
The King, and do so here, now who but they?
What, say I men? nay, rather monsters! men
Only in bed, nor to my knowledge then.   230
See how they home return in revel rout
With the same measures that they first went out:
Nor better grown, nor wiser all this while,
Renew the causes of their first exile,
As if (to show you fools what 'tis I mean)   235
I chose a foul smock when I might have clean.
    "First, they for fear disband the army tame,
And leave good George a gen'ral's empty name:
Then bishops must revive and all unfix
With discontents to content twenty-six.   240
The Lords' House drains the houses of the Lord,
For bishops' voices silencing the Word.
O Barthol'mew, saint of their calendar!

225. *Langdales, Hoptons, Glenhams:* Marmaduke, first Baron Langdale (1598?–1661); Ralph, Lord Hopton (1598–1652); and Sir Thomas Glenham (d. 1659?). In April 1660 Langdale left the Low Countries and retired to a monastery in Germany to live with more frugality. His extreme poverty prevented attendance at the King's coronation. Hopton, to live cheaper, retired to Wesel in 1650. He died at Bruges, September 1652. Little is known about Glenham's last years. All were active Royalists.

232. *measures:* 1. Policies or strategies; 2. dances.

236. Lady Carteret and Pepys agreed that the Duchess was "a filthy woman" (*Diary,* 26 Feb. 1666). Aubrey described her as "not at all handsome, nor cleanly" (2, 72–78).

237. Finances immediately after the Restoration necessitated the disbanding of the army. However, Monck's Life Guards and his regiments of horse remained on a permanent but somewhat informal basis (Walton, *History of the British Standing Army,* pp. 3ff.).

238. When war was declared on the French, 10 Feb. 1666, Monck was styled in the proclamation "General of His Majesty's forces by land," an empty name indeed (Charnock, *Biographia Navalis, 1,* 204 n.).

239. Seven new prelates were consecrated at Westminster 2 Dec. 1660.

240. *twenty-six:* A bill to modify the rigidity of the Anglican service and insure indulgences for Nonconformists was defeated by 26 votes in the House 28 Nov. 1660 (see *Commons' Journal* for that day and Stoughton, *History of Religion in England, 1,* 121–22).

241. The line refers to the return of the bishops to the House of Lords after the Restoration.

243–44. The Act of Uniformity, which received royal approval 19 May 1662, de-

What's worse, thy ejection or thy massacre?
Then Culp'per, Gloucester, ere the Princess, di'd: 245
Nothing can live that interrupts an Hyde.
O more than human Gloucester! Fate did shew
Thee but to earth, and back again withdrew.
Then the fat scriv'ner durst begin to think
'Twas time to mix the royal blood with ink.   250
Berkeley, that swore as oft as she had toes,
Does kneeling now her chastity depose,
Just as the first French Card'nal could restore
Maidenhead to his widow-niece and whore.
For portion, if she should prove light when weigh'd,   255
Four millions shall within three years be paid.

---

prived all clergy without episcopal ordination of their pulpits. This took effect on 24
Aug. 1662, the anniversary of the Bartholomew's Day Massacre (1572), which became
known as "Black Bartholomew."

245. *Culp'per:* John, first Lord Colepeper or Culpeper, Royalist policy maker, who
in 1659 suggested to Hyde that the King make overtures to Monck. He was returned
to England at the Restoration, but died that summer. Henry, Duke of Gloucester and
Princess Mary, brother and sister to Charles II, both died in 1660.

246. *an Hyde:* A punning reference to Anne Hyde, with the insinuation that she
tried to ensure her husband's succession to the throne by having possible claimants,
Mary and Gloucester, put out of the way. One version of *An Historical Poem,* 17–18
makes a similar accusation (see Case 189 [4], p. 17):

> But the best times have ever some allay,
> His younger brother di'd by treachery.

I have not seen the insinuation elsewhere, but the doctors were much blamed for both
deaths (Pepys, *1,* 222, 289 and n.).

249–50. See note on *Second Advice,* 153–54 for Clarendon's professed detestation of
the match between Anne and the Duke of York.

251–54. "Sir Charles Berkeley (afterwards Lord Falmouth), the same courtier whom
Clarendon charges with having originally sought to injure him by promoting this
match, induced the younger Henry Jermyn, Lord Arran, and others, 'all men of
honor' (Gramont, pp. 162ff.), to furnish the Duke with personal evidence of his
wife's misconduct with them before her marriage . . . , yet her worst enemy, the
Queen Mother [Henrietta Maria] was converted by an opportune letter from Cardi-
nal Mazarin. While she now very graciously received both the Chancellor and his
daughter, the latter accepted the submission of Berkeley and promised to forget his
offence" (*DNB*). I cannot shed light on the reference to the French cardinal, except to
note that the mistresses of Catholic clerics were often described as nieces.

255–56. Sir Robert Paston had suggested that Parliament "might give his Majesty
two million and a half, which would amount to five-and-twenty hundred thousand
pounds" to be raised in three years (Clarendon, *2,* 66). The grant was increased by
half the next year (Ranke, *3,* 433).

To raise it, we must have a naval war,
As if 'twere nothing but tara-tan-tar!
Abroad, all princes disobliging first,
At home, all parties but the very worst.   260
To tell of Ireland, Scotland, Dunkirk's sad,
Or the King's marriage, but he thinks I'm mad,
And sweeter creature never saw the sun,
If we the King wish'd monk, or Queen a nun.
But a Dutch war shall all these rumors still,   265
Bleed out those humors, and our purses spill.
Yet after one day's trembling fight they saw
'Twas too much danger for a son-in-law;
Hire him to leave with six-score thousand pound,
As with the King's drums men for sleep compound.   270
Then modest Sandwich thought it might agree
With the state prudence to do less than he,
And to excuse their tim'rousness and sloth,
They've found how George might now do less than both.
    "First, Smith must for Leghorn, with force enough   275

261. See *Second Advice*, 145–50 and n. The reference to Ireland has to do with the release of Irish Catholics "whom Cromwell had settled all in one corner" (Pepys, 15 Dec. 1665).

262. *but he thinks I'm mad:* The poet has momentarily forgotten that the Duchess, and not Denham, is speaking. In his madness Denham is supposed to have thought he was the Holy Ghost and confided this to Charles.

262–64. *the King's marriage:* The Duchess implies that Clarendon advocated the match with Catherine de Braganza because he had reason to think she would prove barren and thereby hoped to improve his chances of having a grandchild of his own inherit the throne. The marriage was also unpopular because of the Queen's religion.

267–69. Parliament voted James £120,000 " 'in token of the great sense they had of his conduct and bravery in the late engagement.' They followed up this vote, however, by a humble address to the King asking him not to allow James to risk his life again. To this appeal Charles readily acceded. . ." (Turner, *James II*, p. 82). See Pepys, 25 June 1665: "He [Coventry] did concur with me that, for the Duke's honor and safety, it were best, after so great a service and victory and danger, not to go again; and above all, that the life of the Duke cannot but be a security to the Crown."

270. *As with the King's drums men for sleep compound:* Perhaps by making payments to the press gang to avoid service?

275–80. Upon declaration of war with the French, in Feb. 1666, Sir Jeremy Smith was dispatched to the Straits of Gibraltar to protect the Levant trade. The move was brilliant in that Smith's position prevented the union of Beaufort's fleet at Toulon and the Atlantic squadron under Du Quesne. But the English were unaware of their

To venture back again, but not go through.
Beaufort is there, and to their dazzling eyes
The distance more the object magnifies.
Yet this they gain, that Smith his time shall lose,
And for my Duke, too, cannot interpose,   280
But fearing that our navy, George to break,
Might yet not be sufficiently weak,
The Secretary, that had never yet
Intelligence but from his own *Gazette,*
Discovers a great secret, fit to sell,   285
And pays himself for't ere he would it tell:
Beaufort is in the Channel! Hixy, here!
Doxy, Toulon! Beaufort is ev'rywhere!
Herewith assembles the Supreme Divan,
Where enters none but Devil, Ned, and Nan,   290
And upon this pretence they straight design'd
The fleet to sep'rate and the world to blind:
Monck to the Dutch, and Rupert (here the wench
Could not but smile) is destin'd to the French.
To write the order, Bristol's clerk they chose   295

---

strategic success; in fact they had little idea where Beaufort was, and they pulled
Smith out at a critical moment. Apparently the poet thought Beaufort frightened
Smith from the Mediterranean. (See Corbett, *England in the Mediterranean, 1603–
1713,* pp. 53–55, and Tedder, *The Navy of the Restoration,* pp. 100–01.)

281–87. The intelligence service was operated by the Secretary of State, who, in this
reference, would have been Arlington. The only licensed newspaper drew its news
from this source. The *London Gazette* for May 1666 carries repeated reports of an
expected union of Beaufort with the Dutch fleet. Cf. 23–28 n. above.

287. *Beaufort is in the Channel:* While Beaufort withdrew to the Tagus the British
intelligence service reported that he was at the mouth of the Channel. Cf. headnote.

287–88. *Hixy* and *doxy* are variants of the juggler's patter, *hixius-doxius,* which is
either a spurious Latin phrase (cf. *hocus-pocus*) or a corruption of *hicce est doctus*
(Partridge, *Dictionary of Slang*).

289. *Divan:* Council.

290. *Ned and Nan:* Clarendon and the Duchess of York.

294. Rupert was assigned to encounter the French, but Lady Albermarle is smiling
at her punning allusion to Rupert's alleged "French disease."

295. *Bristol's clerk:* Arlington, who began his career as secretary to Lord Bristol,
who was then Secretary of State. The Civil War left its mark on him in the form of a
saber cut on the bridge of his nose. Rather than attempt to conceal it, he accentuated
it with a strip of black plaster. Arlington announced on 13 May that the French
fleet had already left Brest (Allin, *Journals,* 2, xvii), but the *Gazette* reports on 14 May
that Beaufort was at Île de Thières, near Marseilles, so Arlington did have intelli-
gence sources other than "his own *Gazette.*"

(One slit in's pen, another in his nose)
For he first brought the news, and 't is his place;
He'll see the fleet divided like his face,
And through that cranny in his gristly part
To the Dutch chink intell'gence may start.   300
   "The plot succeeds; the Dutch in haste prepare,
And poor pilgarlic George's arse they share,
And now presuming of his certain wrack,
To help him late they write for Rupert back.
Officious Will seem'd fittest, as afraid   305
Lest George should look too far into his trade.
On the first draught they pause with statesmen's care;
They write it fair, then copy 't out as fair,
Then they compare them, when at last 'tis sign'd.
Will soon his purse-strings but no seal could find.   310
At night he sends it by the common post,

300. *chink: The female pudendum* (Partridge, *Dictionary of Slang*). Arlington had recently married the Dutch Isabel de Nassau. On 25 Oct. 1667 Pepys mentions that Parliament was investigating Lord Arlington's letters and their importance in "the business of the Dutch fleet's coming abroad."
Colenbrander prints an anonymous English report about these rumors of Arlington's treasonous correspondence with the enemy: "Some said that the Lord Chancellor, envying the glory of the General [Monck], had purposely devised this way to eclipse it. Others said that the Lord Arlington, having married a Dutch lady, she held private correspondence with some of her great kindred, who sate at the helm in Holland, and by that means, all the councils at Whitehall were discovered and betrayed; that the Dutch knew the English fleet was to be divided before we knew it ourselves, for which great sums of money were paid to I know not who [sic]. . . . But they who understood better knew there was no sense at all nor shadow of reason in these surmises. Yet since those who knew best where the fault lay were faulty themselves, it concerned them to let the truth be disguised at any rate, that the blame being so divided and dispersed might divert and not fall too heavy upon them" (Colenbrander, *Der Groote Nederlandsche Zeeorlagen, 1652–1676, 1, 339*).
302. *pilgarlic:* An appellation given first to a "pilled" or bald head ludicrously likened to a peeled head of garlic, and then to a bald-headed man. It is often used in a mock pitiful manner, as "poor creature."
304. On 1 June Albemarle wrote the Duke of York of his decision to attack the Dutch fleet. York "ordered Coventry to prepare orders for the return of Rupert. Coventry contented himself with sending the signed order to Arlington for his countersignature; but as Arlington was in bed when the missive arrived, and could not be disturbed until next morning, valuable time was lost" (Ogg, *England in the Reign of Charles II, 1, 298–99*).
305–06. *Will:* Sir William Coventry. See *Second Advice,* 25–40 n. *Trade* refers to his selling of offices in the navy.
311–12. Coventry's explanation is contained in a conversation with Pepys (*Diary,* 24 June 1666): "for sending them [the orders] by the post express, and not by gentle-

To save the King of an express the cost.
Lord, what ado to pack one letter hence!
Some patents pass with less circumference.
   "Well, George, in spite of them thou safe dost ride,   315
Lessen'd, I hope, in nought but thy backside,
For as to reputation, this retreat
Of thine exceeds their victories so great.
Nor shalt thou stir from thence by my consent,
Till thou hast made the Dutch and them repent.   320
'Tis true, I want so long the nuptial gift,
But (as I oft have done) I'll make a shift,
Nor with vain pomp will I accost the shore,
To try thy valor at the Buoy of the Nore.
Fall to thy work there, George, as I do here: 325
Cherish the valiant up, cowards cashier,
See that the men have pay and beef and beer,
Find out the cheats of the four millioneer.
Out of the very beer they steal the malt,
Powder of powder, from powder'd beef the salt.   330
Put thy hand to the tub; instead of ox,
They victual with French pork that has the pox:
Never such cotqueans by small arts to wring,

---

men on purpose, he made a sport of it, and said, I knew of none to send it with, but
would at least have lost more time in fitting themselves out, than any diligence of
theirs beyond that of the ordinary post would have recovered." Pepys adds that "this
was not so much the town talk as [was] the reason of dividing the fleet."

314. *circumference:* Roundabout process, ado *about* a thing. (*OED* cites this line.)

322. *make a shift:* A pun on the Duchess' former occupation of dressmaker.

323–24. The Duchess reflects sarcastically on the visit of the Duchess of York to
Harwich in May 1665. See *Second Advice*, 55–58.

324. *Buoy of the Nore:* The Nore is a sandbank at the mouth of the river Thames.
Its buoy was a major seamark and a base for victualing and reconnoitering.

328. *the cheats of the four millioneer:* The cheats who were misusing the four mil-
lion pounds appropriated for the war against the Dutch.

329–36. On 19 June a navy memorandum was addressed to Pepys asking him to
"take a survey of 12 tuns of stinking beer" (*CSPD, 1665–66*, p. 446). For complaints
about meat and "salt victuals" see *CSPD, 1665–66*, pp. 309, 314.

330. In the margin of his copy of the 1705 edition of *POAS*, Pope revises the sense
of this line to "Peter from Powder, from Beef the Salt."

331–32. *Tub* refers to the barrel of salt beef and is also a cant term for the Dis-
senters' pulpit. There is also a suggestion here of the powdering tubs used in the treat-
ment of venereal disease. For complaints about French pork see *CSPD*, 13 Nov. 1665.

333. *cotqueans:* Men that act the part of meddling, ill-mannered housewives.

Ne'er such ill housewives in the managing.
Pursers at sea know fewer cheats than they;   335
Mar'ners on shore less madly spend their pay.
See that thou hast new sails thyself and spoil
All their sea market and their cable-coil.
Tell the King all, how him they countermine;
Trust not, till done, him with thy own design.   340
Look that good chaplains on each ship do wait,
Nor the sea diocese be impropriate.
Look to the pris'ners, sick, and wounded: all
Is prize; they rob even the hospital.
Recover back the prizes, too: in vain   345
We fight, if all be taken that is ta'en.
        "Now by our coast the Dutchmen, like a flight
Of feeding ducks, morning and ev'ning light.
How our land-Hectors tremble, void of sense,
As if they came straight to transport them hence!   350
Some sheep are stol'n, the kingdom's all array'd,
And even Presbyt'ry's now call'd out for aid.
They wish e'en George divided to command,
One half of him the sea and one the land.
        "What's that I see? Ha, 'tis my George again!   355
It seems they in sev'n weeks have rigg'd him then.
The curious Heav'n with lightning him surrounds
To view him, and his name in thunder sounds,
But with the same shaft gores their navy near
(As, ere we hunt, the keeper shoots the deer).   360

338. *cable-coil:* An allusion to Sir William Penn's sheltering himself in a coil of
cable at the Battle of Lowestoft. See *Second Advice,* 87–88.

341–42. Albemarle was on intimate terms with his chaplains. Two of them, Gumble
and Price, wrote lives of him.

342. *impropriate:* Impropriated, annexed. Used particularly of ecclesiastical bene-
fices.

351. *some sheep are stol'n:* "The news for certain that the Dutch are come with
their fleet before Margate, and some men were endeavoring to come on shore when
the post come away, perhaps to steal some sheep" (Pepys, 16 Oct. 1665).

356. *in sev'n weeks:* The next encounter with the Dutch was St. James' Fight, 25,
July 1666 (see Tedder, pp. 171–75, for a full and accurate account).

360. *the keeper shoots the deer:* None of the known circumstances of the battle
shed light on the Duchess' veiled comment. It is possible that reference is made to
the separation of the Dutch commander, Tromp, from the body of the Dutch fleet in

Stay, Heav'n, a while, and thou shalt see him sail
And how George, too, can lighten, thunder, hail!
Happy the time that I thee wedded George,
The sword of England and of Holland scourge!
Avaunt, Rotterdam dog! Ruyter avaunt!   365
Thou water rat, thou shark, thou cormorant!
I'll teach thee to shoot scissors! I'll repair
Each rope thou losest, George, out of this hair.
Ere thou shalt lack a sail and lie adrift
('Tis strong and coarse enough) I'll cut this shift.   370
Bring home the old ones; I again will sew
And darn them up to be as good as new.
What, twice disabl'd? Never such a thing!
Now, Sov'reign, help him that brought in the King.
Guard thy posterior left, lest all be gone: 375
Though jury-masts, th' hast jury-buttocks none.
Courage! How bravely, whet with this disgrace,
He turns, and bullets spits in Ruyter's face!
They fly, they fly! Their fleet does now divide!
But they discard their Trump; our trump is Hyde.   380
     "Where are you now, De Ruyter, with your bears?
See how your merchants burn about your ears.
Fire out the wasps, George, from their hollow trees,
Cramm'd with the honey of our English bees.
Ay, now they're paid for Guinea: ere they steer   385
To the Gold Coast, they'll find it hotter here.

---

pursuit of Sir Jeremy Smith. In this respect the Dutch were largely responsible for
their loss (see Ogg, *1*, 302).

367. *scissors:* Chain shot, which cut rigging away.

376. Hooker quotes the *Gazette* for 4–7 June 1666: "The Duke had all his tackle
taken off by chain shot, and his breeches to his skin were shot off, but he rigged again
with jury masts, and fell into the whole body of the Dutch fleet, where he attacked
de Ruyter," and he observes that "the humor of the situation was widely recognized
by the coffeehouse wits of the time" (p. 290).

380. *they discard their Trump:* "As De Ruyter gave way further to the leeward the
struggle between Tromp and Smith became further and further separated until they
were lost sight of by the rest of the combatants" (Tedder, p. 173). *Our trump is
Hyde* means, perhaps, that we should follow suit and discard Clarendon.

382. See Ogg, *1*, 302–03 for the destruction of Dutch merchantmen and stores known
as "Holmes's bonfire."

385. *Guinea:* See *Second Advice*, 259–70 n.

Turn their ships all to stoves ere they set forth,
To warm their traffic in the frozen north.
Ah, Sandwich! had thy conduct been the same,
Bergen had seen a less but richer flame,   390
Nor Ruyter liv'd new battle to repeat
And oft'ner beaten be than we can beat.
    "Scarce has George leisure, after all this pain,
To tie his breeches: Ruyter's out again.
Thrice in one year! Why sure the man is wood: 395
Beat him like stockfish, or he'll ne'er be good.
I see them both prepar'd again to try:
They first shoot through each other with the eye,
Then—but that ruling Providence that must
With human projects play, as winds with dust,   400
Raises a storm (so constables a fray
Knock down) and sends them both well-cuff'd away.
Plant now Virginian firs in English oak;
Build your ship-ribs proof to the cannon's stroke;
To get a fleet to sea exhaust the land;   405
Let longing princes pine for the command.
Strong marchpanes! Wafers light! So thin a puff
Of angry air can ruin all that huff.
So champions, having shar'd the lists and sun,
The judge throws down his warder, and they've done.   410

389–90. See *Second Advice,* 253–94 and notes.

394–95. "Meanwhile the Dutch preparations were hastening towards completion, and on the 26th [of August] De Ruyter was at sea again and making for the Channel in order to effect the long-promised junction with de Beaufort and his fleet" (Tedder, p. 177).

Albemarle did not go to sea again this year according to Tedder: on 28 August "the English fleet, under sole command of Prince Rupert, set out to find de Ruyter and to prevent the junction" (p. 177). According to Monck's biographer, however, Monck and Rupert both set out on the 28th. "Next day they sighted the Dutchmen, but in their eagerness to come to grips the English ships fell foul of the Galloper shoal, and while they were getting their ships off De Ruyter slipped away towards the French coast. And then came the news that a great fire was raging in London and that Monck must return at once to assist the authorities to meet the catastrophe" (Davies, *Honest George Monck,* p. 268). That Monck did take part in the battle is indicated by a letter from him and Rupert to the King giving an account of the action, in *CSPD,* 2 Sept. 1666.

396. *stockfish:* A dried, salted fish which must be beaten before cooking.

407. *marchpanes:* Marzipan, a kind of confectionery, with the obsolete figurative sense here of something exquisite or dainty.

For shame, come home, George! 'Tis for thee too much
To fight at once with Heaven and the Dutch.
   "Woe's me! what see I next? Alas, the fate
I see of England and its utmost date!
Those flames of theirs at which we fondly smile,   415
Kindl'd like torches our sepulchral pile.
War, fire, and plague against us all conspire;
We the war, God the plague, who rais'd the fire?
See how men all like ghosts, while London burns,
Wander and each over his ashes mourns!   420
Dear George, sad fate, vain mind, that me didst please
To meet thine with far other flames than these!
Curs'd be the man that first begot this war,
In an ill hour, under a blazing star.
For others' sport two nations fight a prize;   425
Between them both religion wounded lies.
So of first Troy the angry gods unpaid
Raz'd the foundations which themselves had laid.
   "Welcome, though late, dear George! Here hadst
      thou been,
We'd scap'd. Let Rupert bring the navy in.   430
Thou still must help them out when in the mire,
Gen'ral at land, at sea, at plague, at fire.
Now thou art gone, see, Beaufort dares approach,
And our whole fleet angling has catch'd a roach."
   Gibson, farewell, till next we put to sea: 435
Faith thou hast drawn her in effigie.

413–20. Monck returned to London 7 September at the King's request. "Largely as a result of Charles's personal efforts the fire was held by the 8th, and although at first Monck was actively engaged in supervising the work of the fire-fighters he was soon given the more difficult task of bringing some sort of order out of chaos in a disorganized city. Half the population was homeless: to feed them alone meant a tremendous organization. . . . For the remainder of the year Monck was the mainstay of the government in this work of reorganization in London" (Davies, p. 270).

424. *under a blazing star:* Cf. *Instructions,* 7 and n.

427–28. Apollo and Poseidon had erected the walls of Troy for Laomedon, one of the early founders, who cheated them of their pay and thus exposed his city to their later act of vengeance. See *Iliad* 21.

433. "Part of Beaufort's fleet is at Rochelle, and part cruising off Ireland" (*CSPD,* 2 Sept. 1666).

434. *To catch a roach* seems to be a contemptuous expression for ineffectual action, but I have found no definition of the phrase.

To the King

Great Prince, and so much greater as more wise,
Sweet as our life, and dearer than our eyes,
What servants will conceal and couns'llors spare
To tell, the painter and the poet dare;   440
And the assistance of a heav'nly Muse
And pencil represents the crimes abstruse.
Here needs no sword, no fleet, no foreign foe:
Only let vice be damn'd and justice flow.
Shake but like Jove thy locks divine and frown—   445
Thy sceptre will suffice to guard thy crown.
Hark to Cassandra's song ere Fate destroy,
By thy own navy's wooden horse, thy Troy.
Us our Apollo from the tumult's wave
And gentle gales, though but in oars, will save.   450
  So Philomel her sad embroid'ry strung,
And vocal silks tun'd with her needle's tongue.
The picture dumb in colors loud reveal'd
The tragedies of court so long conceal'd;
But when restor'd to voice, increas'd with wings,   455
To woods and groves, what once she painted, sings.

449–50. Apollo was a patron deity of Troy. *Oars,* by transference, are small rowing-boats. The clause seems to mean: Apollo will save us in storms and calms even though we are embarked in little boats (rather than men-of-war).

ANDREW MARVELL

Clarendon's Housewarming
(1667)

From the Restoration to 1666 Clarendon had no proper house of his own but dwelt in a series of rented houses. "It was only after many changes that he ventured, in the full tide of his prosperity and with the encouragement of the King, to provide a house of his own; but his ignorance of architecture—and probably also his absorption in weightier affairs—made him the victim of the architect [Roger Pratt], who estimated the cost at less than one-third of what it came to, which was £50,000. He found himself not only involved in debt, but the mark of envious scandal for the pride and ostentation of his dwelling" (Craik, *Clarendon*, 2, 324). The year 1666, with its miscarriages in naval affairs, the plague, and the Great Fire, which broke out in September, was an inauspicious time to undertake what soon became widely known as Dunkirk House (on the assumption that the Chancellor was financing his new abode from the proceeds of the unpopular sale of Dunkirk to France several years earlier). In this clever and tightly-knit satire Marvell expresses the odium which Clarendon House drew down upon its unfortunate builder.

Clarendon's Housewarming, with its suggestion that the new residence of the Chancellor was "warmed" by the fires of afflicted London, was written some time between 25 June 1667, when Parliament was summoned by proclamation, and St. James' Day (25 July), when it convened. The text is from Bod. MS. Eng. Poet. d. 49.

CLARENDON'S HOUSEWARMING

1.

When Clarendon had discern'd beforehand
(As the cause can eas'ly foretell the effect)

Clarendon House. From an engraving after J. Spilbergh.

At once three deluges threat'ning our land,
  'Twas the season, he thought, to turn architect.

2.

Us Mars and Apollo and Vulcan consume,   5
  While he, the betrayer of England and Flanders,
Like the kingfisher chooseth to build in the brume,
  And nestles in flames like the salamanders.

3.

But observing that mortals run often behind
  (So unreasonable are the rates they buy at)   10
His Omnipotence therefore much rather design'd
  How he might create a house with a fiat.

4.

He had read of Rhodopis, a lady of Thrace,
  That was digg'd up so often ere she did marry,
And wish'd that his daughter had had as much grace   15
  To erect him a pyramid out of her quarry.

5.

But then recollecting how harper Amphion
  Made Thebes dance aloft while he fiddled and sung,
He thought (as an instrument he was most free on)
  To build with the jews' trump of his own tongue.   20

3. *three deluges:* War, plague, and fire; sent by Mars, Apollo, and Vulcan.
6. Clarendon is seen as the betrayer of Flanders because of the Dutch War, responsibility for which is falsely ascribed to him.
7. *brume:* Winter, a coinage from Latin *bruma.* According to legend the kingfisher builds its nest in the winter solstice.
13-16. *Rhodopis:* A courtesan celebrated for her beauty, who made a great deal of money out of her career and was supposed to have built a pyramid out of her earnings (see Herodotus, 2.134-35, cited by Margoliouth). This stanza compares her career with that of Anne Hyde and represents Clarendon as wishing his daughter had been equally resourceful. The comparison explains the witty indecencies of *digg'd up* and *quarry.* Marvell is alluding to the aspersions on the pre-nuptial chastity of the Duchess of York before her marriage. Cf. *Third Advice,* 251-54 and *Last Instructions,* 49-54.
17-18. Amphion with his twin brother Zethus constructed the walls of Thebes with stones miraculously fitted together by the music of his lyre.
20. *jews' trump:* Jews' harp, with a hit at Clarendon's acquisitiveness (Margoliouth).

6.

Yet a precedent fitter in Virgil he found
   Of African Poult'ney and Tyrian Dide,
That she begg'd for a palace so much of his ground
   As might carry the measure and name of an Hyde.

7.

Thus daily his gouty invention he pain'd,   25
   And all for to save the expence of brickbat,
That engine so fatal which Denham had brain'd,
   And too much resembled his wife's chocolate.

8.

But while these devices he all does compare,
   None solid enough seem'd for his thong-caster;   30
He himself would not dwell in a castle of air,
   Though he'd built full many a one for his master.

9.

Already he'd got all our money and cattle,
   To buy us for slaves and to purchase our lands;
What Joseph by famine, he wrought by sea-battle: 35

21–24. King Iarbas of Carthage granted Dido as much land as might be enclosed with the hide of an ox. Dido cut the hide into fine strips and thus acquired much more land than Iarbas had intended to give her. *Aeneid* 1.367.

22. *Poult'ney:* Sir William Poulteney was one of the original proprietors of the land granted to Clarendon (Margoliouth).

24. Cf. the play on Anne Hyde's name in *Third Advice,* 246.

25. On the eve of Clarendon's flight Evelyn "found him in his garden at his new-built palace, sitting in his gout wheel-chair, and seeing the gates towards the north and the fields setting up" (1 Dec. 1667). Clarendon had suffered from gout for a long time.

26. *brickbat:* bricks.

27–28. Sir John Denham was mad for a short time in 1666 (Cf. *Divination,* 61 n.). This line suggests that his madness was caused by the impact of a falling brick and alludes to his position as Surveyor-General of the Works (principal royal architect). Lady Denham, mistress of the Duke of York, died 6 Jan. 1667 under the mistaken belief that she had been poisoned by a cup of chocolate. Cf. *Last Instructions,* 65–68.

30. *thong:* The rawhide which was to be *cast* about the site of Clarendon's house.

35–36. During the famine Joseph bought up all the land of Egypt except for the priests' with corn which he had stored during the seven years of good harvests. Cf. Genesis 47:13–26.

Nay, scarce the priests' portion could 'scape from
  his hands.

10.

And henceforth like Pharaoh that Israel press'd
  To make mortar and brick, yet allow'd 'em no straw,
He car'd not though Egypt's ten plagues us infest,
  So he could but to build make that policy law. 40

11.

The Scotch forts and Dunkirk, but that they were sold,
  He would have demolish'd to raise up his walls,
Nay, even from Tangier sent back for the mold,
  But that he had nearer the stones of St. Paul's.

12.

His wood would come in at the easier rate, 45
  As long as the yards had a deal or a spar:
His friends in the navy would not be ingrate,
  To grudge him some timber, who fram'd 'em the war.

13.

To proceed on this model he call'd in his Allens—
  The two Allens when jovial that ply him with gallons, 50

40. Provided he could build his house, that is, he was willing to pass off his rapacious *policy* as a lawful one.

41. In Clarendon's administration four forts which Cromwell had built in Scotland were dismantled. *Dunkirk* was sold to France in 1662. Cf. *Second Advice,* 149–50 and n.

43. *Tangier* was part of Catherine of Braganza's dowry. England constructed a large mole (*mold*) there in the hope of making it a major port and naval station.

44. Old St. Paul's burned down in the Great Fire when Clarendon House was nearly finished. Clarendon bought the stones to use in completing his house.

49–52. *Allens:* Sir Allen Apsley (1616–83), Royalist officer and, after the Restoration, M.P. for Thetford; and Sir Allen Broderick, M.P. for Orford and Callington in Cornwall. Apsley was rewarded by Charles II for his loyalty by many lucrative positions and later became Treasurer of the Household to the Duke of York. *Flagellum Parliamentarium* (1678) describes him thus: "Treasurer to His Highness; Master to the King, and has had £40,000 in other things; not worth a penny before." Broderick is described as: "Bribe-broker for his master the Chancellor. Surveyor of Ireland. He got £30,000, but in keeping whores has spent most again." The two Allens were jovial companions, as Pepys reports (19 Dec. 1666): "Sir Allen Broderick and Sir Allen Apsley did come drunk the other day into the House and did both speak for half an hour together and could not be either laughed or pulled or bid to sit down and

The two Allens that serve his blind justice for balance,
The two Allens that serve his injustice for talons.

14.

They approv'd it thus far and said it was fine,
    Yet his Lordship to finish it would be unable,
Unless all abroad he divulg'd the design,   55
    But his house then would grow like a vegetable.

15.

His rent would no more in arrear run to Worcester,
    He should dwell more nobly and cheap, too, at home;
While into a fabric the presents would muster,
    As by hook and by crook the world cluster'd of atom.   60

16.

He lik'd the advice, and they soon it assay'd,
    And presents crowd headlong to give good example;
So the bribes overlaid her that Rome once betray'd:
    The tribes ne'er contributed so to the Temple.

17.

Straight judges, priests, bishops (true sons of the Seal)   65
    Summ'ners, governors, farmers, bankers, patentees,
Bring in the whole milk of a year at a meal,
    As all Cheddar dairies club to th'incorporate cheese.

---

hold their peace, to the great contempt of the King's service and cause; which I am
grieved at with all my heart."

52. That is, they serve as instruments of Clarendon's injustice in their exactions.

57. Before his own house was built Clarendon lived in Worcester House in the
Strand and paid £500 a year for it (Margoliouth).

60. According to Epicurean science the atoms clung together as if by hooks
(Margoliouth).

63. The daughter of Tarpeius, commander of a Roman citadel, offered to betray
the citadel to the Sabines in exchange for what they had on their left arms, meaning
their gold bracelets, but they crushed her to death under their shields. See Livy, 1.11.

65. *bishops, true sons of the Seal:* Clarendon was Keeper of the Great Seal and took
the lead in restoring episcopacy.

66. *farmers:* Tax-farmers. *patentees:* Holders of monopolies or members of trading
companies. See 74–76 below.

18.

Bulteel's, Bellings', Morley's, Wren's fingers with telling
   Were shrivel'd, and Clutterbuck's, Agar's, and Kipp's: 70
Since the Act of Oblivion was never such selling,
   As at this benevolence out of the snips.

19.

'Twas then that the chimney contractors he smok'd,
   Nor would take his beloved Canary in kind,

69–70. All these names clearly refer to underlings of Clarendon whom Marvell imagines to be employed in counting the "contributions." *John Bulteel* was Clarendon's secretary. *Bellings* is probably Sir Richard Bellings, the Queen's secretary, a friend of Clarendon's son, Lord Cornbury, and a secret agent for the government in France. Margoliouth suggests that *Morley* may be George Morley, Bishop of Winchester and a great friend of Clarendon. *Wren* is Matthew Wren, a cousin of Sir Christopher and also one of Clarendon's secretaries. *Clutterbuck, Agar,* and *Kipp* were all obscure functionaries of the Lord Chancellor.

71. *Act of Oblivion:* The Act of Pardon, Indemnity, and Oblivion, which provided *inter alia* that lands sold voluntarily during the Interregnum because of economic or other pressures should remain the property of the purchasers. This caused much distress to impoverished Royalists who had been obliged to sell their lands to pay fines levied by the Parliament. "At the very commencement of the civil troubles many Royalists disposed of a portion, or the whole, of their estates, that they might relieve the pecuniary wants of the King, or enable themselves to raise men and serve in the royal armies; and at its conclusion all of them were compelled to have recourse to similar measures, that they might discharge their debts and pay the heavy fines imposed on them by order of the revolutionary governments. That these men had strong claims on the gratitude and pity of the King and Parliament could not be denied; but these claims were neglected; the sales had been effected with their consent, they were bound by their own acts and consigned to murmur in penury and despair" (Lingard, *9,* 17–18). When the titles of purchasers of such lands had been confirmed by the act, many of the new owners must have sold out.

72. *benevolence:* A voluntary contribution to the revenue. *Snips:* Perquisites. The word occurs frequently in *Flagellum Parliamentarium* (Margoliouth).

73. *chimney-contractors:* Collectors of the Chimney Money or hearth tax, a form of revenue that was widely resented. *smok'd:* Took note of. Now archaic.

74. Clarendon is accused of insisting on money rather than wine from the investors in the Canary Patent. On 29 Oct. 1666 this charter granted to merchants trading with the Canaries was condemned by a Parliamentary committee as an illegal monopoly. Clarendon writes of his own part in the matter as follows: "And if the motives of state were not of weight enough to support the patent, more ought not to be objected to him than to every other counsellor, there having never been a more unanimous concurrence at that board in any advice they have given; and the delays he used in the passing the charter after it came to his hand, his giving so long time for the making objections against it . . . are no signs that he had such a mind to please them as a man would have who had been corrupted by them . . ." (*Life,* p. 630).

But he swore that the Patent should ne'er be revok'd—   75
No, would the whole Parliament kiss him behind!

20.

Like Jove under Aetna o'erwhelming the giant,
　For foundation he Bristol sunk in the earth's bowel,
And St. John must now for the leads be complaint,
　Or his right hand shall else be hack'd off with a trowel.   80

21.

For surveying the building, Pratt did the feat,
　But for the expense he reli'd upon Wolst'holm,
Who sat heretofore at the King's receipt,
　But receiv'd now and paid the Chancellor's custom.

22.

By subsidies thus both cleric and laic,   85
　And of matter profane cemented with holy,
He finish'd at last his palace mosaic
　By a model more excellent than Leslie's folly.

23.

And upon the tarras, to consummate all,
　A lantern like Faux's surveys the burnt town,   90
And shows on the top by the regal gold ball
　Where you are to expect the scepter and crown.

78. *Bristol:* See note on *Last Instructions,* 933. After his unsuccessful attempt to impeach Clarendon in 1663, Bristol went into hiding for two years to avoid arrest (Margoliouth).

79. *St. John:* Charles Paulet, Lord St. John of Basing, member of a group which contracted for the farming of the customs.

82. *Wolst'holm:* Sir John Wolstenholm, a farmer of the customs.

83–84. Wolstenholm is seen as collecting payments now for Clarendon's private benefit.

88. *Leslie's folly:* Dr. John Leslie, Bishop of Orkney, built a palace so strongly fortified that it long resisted Cromwell's arms (Aitken).

89. *tarras:* Terrace.

90. Guy Fawkes (1570–1606), the architect of the Gunpowder Plot, was captured in the cellar of the Parliament House and a dark-lantern, gunpowder, and matches were found in his possession.

24.

Fond city, its rubbish and ruins that builds,
  Like vain chemists, a flow'r from its ashes returning,
Your metropolis house is in St. James's fields,   95
  And till there you remove, you shall never leave burning.

25.

This temple of war and of peace is the shrine,
  Where our idol of state sits ador'd and accurs'd,
And to handsel his altar and nostrils divine,
  Great Buckingham's sacrifice must be the first.   100

26.

Now some (as all buildings must censure abide)
  Throw dust on its front and blame situation,
And others as much reprehend its backside,
  As too narrow by far for his expatiation,

27.

But do not consider in process of times   105
  That for namesake he may with Hyde Park it enlarge,
And with that convenience he hence for his crimes
  At Tyburn may land and spare the Tower barge.

94. Margoliouth cites Browne on palingenesis in plants in *Religio Medici, I,* 48.
99. *handsel:* Inaugurate the use of.
100. Buckingham had been a chief supporter of the Irish Cattle Bill in 1666–67, Clarendon opposing. He further alienated the King and his ministers by provoking a brawl with the Marquis of Dorchester in the House of Lords, for which both were confined in the Tower. While Buckingham was there, an unscrupulous servant named Braythwaite told the King that his master had been engaged in a mysterious conspiracy. Shortly afterwards Arlington unearthed among the Duke's papers a horoscope of the King's nativity cast by a fraudulent astrologer named Heydon at the Duke's request. Such a proceeding came within the statute of High Treason, and the charge was accordingly brought against Buckingham, but he evaded the King's Sergeant-at-Arms and went into hiding. He finally made his submission and was reconciled with the King.
104. *expatiation:* Expansion, with a reflection on Clarendon's corpulence.
108. *Tyburn,* with its celebrated gallows, was at the northeast corner of Hyde Park near the present Marble Arch. The western boundary of the land granted to Clarendon was "a little brook." Margoliouth conjectures that this joined the stream which gave its name to Tyburn and that this is the point of *land.*

28.

Or rather, how wisely his stall was built near,
    Lest with driving too far his tallow impair,   110
When like the whole ox, for public good cheer,
    He comes to be roasted next St. James's Fair.

112. *St. James's Fair:* That is, at the meeting of Parliament fixed for St. James' Day, 25 July 1667.

ANDREW MARVELL

The Last Instructions to a Painter
(*1667*)

The Last Instructions to a Painter is concerned with parliamentary, court, administrative and naval affairs between September 1666 and the downfall of Clarendon in the following autumn. The opening couplet links the poem explicitly to the two earlier *Advices,* and there are throughout numerous allusions to those satires and to Waller's encomiastic *Instructions* which serves them ironically as a model. This sequence of three satirical painter poems thus provides a complete and continuous record of England's part in the Second Dutch War. Although it amounts to a massive indictment of Clarendon's administration and the Court party in the House of Commons, the record is in the main remarkably faithful to the facts insofar as they can be determined from other sources.

No other Restoration poem is more comprehensive or specific in its treatment of public affairs. Not even the ubiquitous and omniscient Pepys is so accurate in recording the events of this crucial last year of the war. After a preliminary sketch of England's besotted pro-French envoy, the Earl of St. Albans, who was trying to procure Louis XIV's intervention as a peacemaker with the Low Countries, the satirist proceeds to attack with unrivaled bitterness that most unpopular member of Charles II's petticoat government, the Catholic Countess of Castlemaine. The poem is studded with vivid portraits of important public figures—with hated ones like Clarendon, Sir William Coventry and his brother Henry, York and his Duchess, the Earl of Arlington, and so forth—and with a smaller group of patriots ("the race of English gentry nobly born") like Strangeways, Tomkins, and the heroic warrior Douglas.

These portraits are, however, subordinate in interest to two long narrative sections: the first (lines 105–334) dealing principally with the momentous session of the House of Commons in 1666; the second (523–760) recounting the Dutch attack on the unprepared British ships in the Thames and the Medway the following summer. As

in the two earlier *Advices,* the chief naval action of the summer
(here, the most disgraceful maritime defeat in England's history)
is the climactic action of the poem, while the narrative of parlia-
mentary issues not only provides the background for this event but
provides a record of the partisan struggle over finances in the fall
of 1666 unequalled in other sources. The main work of that session
was to devise means to raise the royal supply of £1,800,000. The
Court party favored a general excise on domestic goods which the
Country party and some independent M.P.'s regarded as tyrannous
and inquisitional. This issue of the general excise (not to be con-
fused with the foreign excise) is scarcely mentioned in standard par-
liamentary records. The only adequate record outside this poem is
found in Milward's *Diary* edited by Caroline Robbins, who cites
Last Instructions to corroborate her author's account. The excise
was defeated 8 November 1666, and the supply was raised by a
hearth tax, a land tax (favored by the Country party), and a foreign
excise. But though the general excise was defeated and might there-
fore be well forgotten, it seems from the accounts of *Last Instruc-
tions* and Milward to have been the most important issue in crystal-
lizing the antagonists into embryonic political parties.

In one instance there are serious factual inaccuracies which *Last
Instructions* shares with almost all other contemporary records. A
parliamentary inquiry into the causes of the division of the fleet in
1666 laid the blame chiefly on Sir William Coventry and the intel-
ligence service of the Earl of Arlington. A recent study based on
newly-available sources (Fraser, *Intelligence of the Secretaries of
State*) has demonstrated, as was mentioned in the headnote to *Third
Advice,* that the joint commanders of the fleet, Prince Rupert and
the Duke of Albemarle, were themselves mainly responsible for this
unfortunate decision, and the Earl of Clarendon connived with
them to lay the blame on his two chief enemies.

Last Instructions culminates brilliantly in the night scene where
the King is visited by a visionary nude figure ("England or the
Peace") who tries to warn him about his evil counselors and favor-
ites. The warning is vain, however, for the Merry Monarch, failing
to recognize the lady's allegorical status, responds to her appeals
with misdirected but characteristic gallantry:

> The object strange in him no terror mov'd:
> He wonder'd first, then piti'd, then he lov'd,

And with kind hand does the coy vision press,
Whose beauty greater seem'd by her distress,
But soon shrunk back, chill'd with a touch so cold,
And th' airy picture vanish'd from his hold.

(899–904)

The poem abounds in such mixtures of the grave and the absurd. It displays a remarkably wide range of tones from the scurrilities on Birch and the excise (142–46), which gain force from the echoes of *Paradise Lost* (published a few months before *Last Instructions* was composed), to the pastoral beauty of De Ruyter's passage up the Thames (522–50) or the metaphysical fervor of the elegy on Douglas (649–96, which forms the nucleus of another poem, *The Loyal Scot*), with their overtones of Spenser, Shakespeare, and Marvell himself. Despite the exhaustive factual information which *Last Instructions* requires, it transmutes its facts into an outstanding satirical poem of great historical interest and considerable poetic force.

Possibly because of the government's strenuous efforts to apprehend the author and the printer of the second and third *Advices*, *Last Instructions* was not published until 1689. There is a manuscript in the Osborn collection and the poem is also included in a Marvell manuscript, Bod. MS. Eng. Poet. d. 49 (*R''*), the version printed here. As to authorship, I agree with Margoliouth's statement that "of all the satires attributed to Marvell there is none of which one can feel less doubt." Only an active M.P. versed in maritime affairs and a patriot of Marvell's political complexion possessing Marvell's poetic power could have written it.

The Last Instructions to a Painter

London, September 4th, 1667

After two sittings, now, our Lady State,
To end her picture, does the third time wait.
But ere thou fall'st to work, first, Painter, see
It be'nt too slight grown or too hard for thee.
Canst thou paint without colors? Then 'tis right: 5

1–2. Three sittings was the usual number for "limning" a portrait (Margoliouth). The first two, of course, were described in the second and third *Advices*.

For so we too without a fleet can fight.
Or canst thou daub a sign-post, and that ill?
'Twill suit our great debauch and little skill.
Or hast thou mark'd how antic masters limn
The aly-roof with snuff of candle dim,   10
Sketching in shady smoke prodigious tools?
'Twill serve this race of drunkards, pimps, and fools.
But if to match our crimes thy skill presumes,
As th' Indians, draw our luxury in plumes.
Or if to score out our compendious fame,   15
With Hooke, then, through the microscope take aim,
Where, like the new Comptroller, all men laugh
To see a tall louse brandish the white staff.
Else shalt thou oft thy guiltless pencil curse,
Stamp on thy palette, nor perhaps the worse.   20
The painter so long having vex'd his cloth,
Of his hound's mouth to feign the raging froth,
His desp'rate pencil at the work did dart:
His anger reach'd that rage which pass'd his art;
Chance finish'd that which art could but begin,   25
And he sat smiling how his dog did grin.
So may'st thou perfect by a lucky blow
What all thy softest touches cannot do.
        Paint then St. Albans full of soup and gold,

6. *without a fleet:* The fleet was laid up in May 1667.

9. *antic masters:* Masters of grotesque painting (Margoliouth).

10. *aly roof:* Ceiling of an alehouse or tavern.

14. The Indians of Florida and the Caribbean developed the art of "painting" by arranging various colors and sizes of feathers and gluing them together. Such paintings were necessarily on a large scale (Margoliouth). *Plumes* would also represent fittingly the *luxury* of the court.

15. *score out:* Sketch in outline. *compendious:* Minute (Margoliouth).

16–18. Robert Hooke (1635–1703) was an experimental philosopher and fellow of the Royal Society. In his *Micrographia* (1665) he depicted various objects seen under the microscope, among which was a louse climbing a human hair, which Marvell here compares to the new Comptroller of the Household, Lord Clifford of Chudleigh, who took office in November 1666. The Comptroller carried a white staff as the emblem of his office (Margoliouth).

21. Margoliouth identifies this painter as Protogenes in Pliny's *Nat. Hist.* 35.36.101–03.

29. *St. Albans:* Henry Jermyn, Earl of St. Albans (d. 1684), was ambassador at the French court at the beginning of Charles II's reign. He was sent to France in January 1667 to negotiate a treaty with Louis XIV. In his youth he acquired the reputation

The new court's pattern, stallion of the old.   30
Him neither wit nor courage did exalt,
But Fortune chose him for her pleasure salt.
Paint him with drayman's shoulders, butcher's mien,
Member'd like mules, with elephantine chine.
Well he the title of St. Albans bore,   35
For Bacon never studi'd nature more.
But age, allaying now that youthful heat,
Fits him in France to play at cards and treat.
Draw no commission, lest the Court should lie,
That, disavowing treaty, ask supply;   40
He needs no seal but to St. James's lease,
Whose breeches were the instrument of peace;
Who, if the French dispute his pow'r, from thence
Can straight produce them a plenipotence.
Nor fears he The Most Christian should trepan   45

---

of a rake and was once banished from court for seducing Eleanor Villiers, a Lady of Honor. He was rumored to have married Queen Henrietta Maria and devoted his old age to the pleasures of the table and to cards. Margoliouth cites the following comment of Evelyn (18 Sept. 1663): "He has lived a most easy life, in plenty even abroad, whilst his Majesty was a sufferer; he has lost immense sums at play, which yet, at about 80 years old, he continues, having one that sits by him to name the spots on the cards. He ate and drank with extraordinary appetite. He is a prudent old courtier and much enriched since his Majesty's return."

35–36. In this couplet Marvell wryly compares the lecherous Earl of St. Albans with the great exponent of the inductive approach to nature, Francis Bacon, first Baron Verulam and Viscount St. Albans (1561–1626).

38. *treat:* 1. to entertain; 2. to negotiate a treaty.

39. The negotiations undertaken by St. Albans were at first informal and unofficial (cf. Ranke, *3*, 441), and Marvell attributes this failure to send a duly-authorized ambassador with commission and seal to the Court's desire for a large grant from Parliament. Parliament did, in fact, vote £1,800,000, but there was much resentment about alleged waste in the expenditure of earlier grants.

41. *St. James's lease:* St. Albans obtained a large grant of land in Pall Mall and planned St. James' Square.

42. This line seems to refer somewhat obscurely to St. Albans' widely-rumored affair with Henrietta Maria. Whether or not such an affair took place, his influence with the Queen Mother was great, and it was through her that Louis XIV was persuaded to consider negotiations for peace between Holland and Britain.

43–44. These lines carry on the suggestion of line 42 about the source of St. Albans' authority to negotiate. "St. Albans' instructions, drafted by Clarendon, did not empower him even to sign preliminaries" (Feiling, *Foreign Policy*, p. 213).

45. *The Most Christian:* Louis XIV. *trepan:* Entrap.

45–48. St. Albans, who could "neither choose well, nor buy cheap," according to Charles, trusting in the efficacy of his mission, "sank cosily into the French atmosphere

Two saints at once, St. Germain, St. Alban,
But thought the Golden Age was now restor'd,
When men and women took each other's word.
  Paint then again her Highness to the life,
Philosopher beyond Newcastle's wife.   50
She naked can Arch'medes' self put down,
For an experiment upon the crown.
She perfected that engine, oft assay'd,

-----

in which he felt at home and staked his life on the pacifism of France" (Feiling, p. 214). His report led Charles to accept French terms which seemed to promise a peace with Holland.
  46. *St. Germain, St. Alban:* A play on the Ambassador's name and title and on the quarter of Paris in which he resided.
  49–78. Much popular gossip about Anne Hyde, Duchess of York, is assembled in this passage. She was secretly married to York on 3 Sept. 1660 and gave birth to the short-lived Charles, Duke of Cambridge, less than two months after the ceremony (55–56), which was performed by Dr. Joseph Crowther, the Duke's chaplain. Lines 49–58 refer to the allegations against her chastity made by two of the Duke's friends, Sir Charles Berkeley and Henry Jermyn (St. Albans' nephew), who wished to prevent the recognition of the marriage. For further details see *Third Advice,* 251–54 and n.
  Margaret Brooke, Lady Denham, became York's mistress in 1665, and Sir John's madness was widely attributed to grief at this development. She is the "Madam l'Edificatress" referred to in *Second Advice,* 242, and is mentioned in the opening line of *Third Advice.* Her sudden death on 6 Jan. 1667 was thought, without evidence, to be from poison introduced into her cocoa, and Denham and the Countess of Rochester were both blamed. Marvell, however, introduces the suggestion that the Duchess of York was the culprit, an idea that agrees with the attack on her in *Third Advice,* 245–46:

  Then Culp'per, Gloucester, and the Princess di'd:
  Nothing can live that interrupts an Hyde.

  53–54. The satirical pretence that the Duchess had discovered "how after childbirth to renew a maid" appears also in *Third Advice,* 253–54, where the renewal of lost virginity is attributed jointly to Berkeley's recantation and, ironically, to the intervention of Cardinal Mazarin, who prevailed on Henrietta Maria to drop her opposition to the marriage. Here Anne is presented as a *philosopher* (natural philosopher or scientist) and *inventress* whose *engine* (device) for restoring virginity makes her superior to her friend the famed bluestocking, Margaret, Duchess of *Newcastle,* and even to *Archimedes.* Archimedes founded the science of hydrostatics, as the well-known legend has it, by discovering the principle of displacement while taking a bath. He applied this principle in answering a question from a prince named Hiero, who feared that his gold crown might be alloyed with silver. In the same manner, Marvell suggests, the Duchess has devised some way of demonstrating that she is not a light woman and thereby could make *an experiment upon the crown,* i.e. an attempt upon it, either for herself (as future queen) or through her children. A similar ambitiousness in the Hyde family is attributed to her father in *Second Advice,* 153–54, and to Anne in *Third Advice,* 245–46, quoted in the preceding note.

How after childbirth to renew a maid,
And found how royal heirs might be matur'd   55
In fewer months than mothers once endur'd.
Hence Crowther made the rare inventress free
Of's Highness's Royal Society—
Happiest of women, if she were but able
To make her glassen Dukes once malleable!   60
Paint her with oyster lip and breath of fame,
Wide mouth that 'sparagus may well proclaim;
With Chanc'llor's belly and so large a rump,
There (not behind the coach) her pages jump.
Express her studying now if china clay   65
Can, without breaking, venom'd juice convey,
Or how a mortal poison she may draw
Out of the cordial meal of the cacao.
Witness, ye stars of night, and thou the pale
Moon, that o'ercome with the sick steam did'st fail;   70
Ye neighb'ring elms, that your green leaves did shed,
And fauns, that from the womb abortive fled!
Not unprovok'd, she tries forbidden arts,
But in her soft breast love's hid cancer smarts,
While she revolves at once Sidney's disgrace,   75

58. The Duke of York was a charter member of the Royal Society.
60. *glassen Dukes:* Margoliouth conjectures that this refers to the short-lived children of this marriage: James, Duke of Cambridge (born 12 July 1663, died 20 June 1667) and Charles, Duke of Kendal (born 4 July 1666, died 22 May 1667). Cf. Marvell's epigram,

> Kendal is dead and Cambridge riding post:
> What fitter sacrifice for Denham's ghost.

62. Like the mouth of a street-seller hawking asparagus (Margoliouth).
65–68. Margoliouth cites Browne, *Pseudodoxia Epidemica* (1646): "Surely the properties must be verified which by Scaliger and others are ascribed to china dishes, that they admit no poison, that they strike fire, . . . for such as pass amongst us . . . will only strike fire, but not discover aconite, mercury, nor arsenic. . . ." (II.5.sec. 7). Lady Denham died 6 Jan. 1667.
69–74. This description of the Duchess' black arts seems indebted in a general way to Ovid's account of Medea's trafficking in sorcery (*Metamorphoses* 7).
74. Aitken cites Burnet to the effect that when the Duchess died in 1671 she had cancer of the breast. Whether there was any evidence of the disease as early as 1667 is conjectural, but, according to the *DNB*, she had suffered from it for some time.
75. Henry Sidney (1636–1708), Groom of the Bedchamber to the Duke and Master of the Horse to the Duchess, was dismissed as a result of the Duke's jealousy. See

And her self scorn'd for emulous Denham's face,
And nightly hears the hated guards away
Galloping with the Duke to other prey.
    Paint Castlemaine in colors that will hold
(Her, not her picture, for she now grows old):   80
She through her lackey's drawers, as he ran,
Discern'd love's cause and a new flame began.
Her wonted joys thenceforth and court she shuns,
And still within her mind the footman runs:
His brazen calves, his brawny thighs (the face   85
She slights), his feet shap'd for a smoother race.
Poring within her glass she readjusts
Her looks and oft-tri'd beauty now distrusts;
Fears lest he scorn a woman once assay'd,
And now first wish'd she e'er had been a maid.   90
Great Love, how dost thou triumph and how reign,
That to a groom could'st humble her disdain!
Stripp'd to her skin, see how she stooping stands,
Nor scorns to rub him down with those fair hands,
And washing (lest the scent her crime disclose)   95
His sweaty hooves, tickles him 'twixt the toes.
    But envious Fame, too soon, began to note

Reresby, *Memoirs*, p. 55: "This Duchess was Chancellor Hyde's daughter. She was a very handsome woman, had a great deal of wit; therefore it was not without reason that Mr. Sidney, the handsomest youth of his time, . . . was so much in love with her, as appeared to us all, and the Duchess not unkind to him, but very innocently. He was afterwards banished the court for another reason, as was reported." But cf. Pepys (9 Jan. 1666): "After dinner Pierce and I up to my chamber, where he tells me how a great difference hath been between the Duke and Duchess, he suspecting her to be naught (i.e. wicked) with Mr. Sidney." See also Wheatley's reference to Spence's *Anecdotes* in a note on Pepys' entry.

79–104. Although most of Lady Castlemaine's many love affairs seem to be minutely and extensively recorded, this seems to be the only account of her alliance with the lackey. In July 1667 Pepys notes that she was in love with Henry Jermyn (1636–1708), who had the reputation of a court rake and buffoon. The King, according to Gramont, "did not think it consistent with his dignity that a mistress whom he had honored . . . should appear chained to the car of the most ridiculous conqueror that ever was. His majesty had frequently expostulated with the Countess upon the subject, but his expostulations were never attended to. It was in one of these differences that, when he advised her to bestow her favors upon Jacob Hall the rope-dancer, who was able to return them rather than lavish her money upon Jermyn to no purpose . . . she was not proof against his raillery. The impetuosity of her temper broke forth like lightning" (quoted by Sergeant, *My Lady Castlemaine*, pp. 176–77).

More gold in's fob, more lace upon his coat,
And he, unwary and of tongue too fleet,
No longer could conceal his fortune sweet. 100
Justly the rogue was whipp'd in porter's den,
And Jermyn straight has leave to come again.
Ah, Painter, now could Alexander live,
And this Campaspe thee, Apelles, give!
    Draw next a pair of tables op'ning, then 105
The House of Commons clatt'ring like the men.
Describe the Court and Country, both set right
On opposite points, the black against the white.
Those having lost the nation at trick-track,
These now advent'ring how to win it back. 110
The dice betwixt them must the fate divide
(As chance doth still in multitudes decide).
But here the Court does its advantage know,
For the cheat Turnor for them both must throw.
As some from boxes, he so from the chair 115
Can strike the die and still with them goes share.
    Here, Painter, rest a little, and survey
With what small arts the public game they play.
For so, too, Rubens, with affairs of state,
His lab'ring pencil oft would recreate. 120

104. Apelles was court painter to Alexander of Macedon. "Enamored of his Theban captive, Campaspe," Alexander "gives her freedom and engages Apelles to paint her portrait. Apelles and Campaspe fall in love with each other, and when the portrait is finished, Apelles spoils it so as to have occasion for further sittings." Alexander finally surrenders Campaspe to the painter (*Oxford Companion to Eng. Lit.* on Lyly's *Alexander and Campaspe*, 1584).

109. *trick-track:* A kind of backgammon played on *tables.* The players (*men*) represent the two Parliamentary parties: the Court party, whose chiefs are enumerated in 113–238, and the Country party who appear in 239–307. The battle, which is won by the Country party with which Marvell's sympathies obviously lie, is fought on the issue of a general excise which the Court wished to impose in order to raise the eighteen-hundred-thousand pounds (332) voted late in 1666 (Margoliouth). The general excise was defeated on 8 Nov. 1666.

114. *Turnor:* Sir Edward Turnor or Turner (1617–76), Speaker of the House of Commons, 1661–73. *Cheat* may refer simply to several large gifts bestowed on him from the treasury through royal favor, though he was later removed as Solicitor-General, according to Roger North, for having received a trifling gratuity from the East India Company.

116. *strike the die:* Throw in some particularly fraudulent manner.

120. *recreate:* Refresh (by a change of occupation). Rubens was occasionally sent on diplomatic missions (Margoliouth).

    The close Cabal mark'd how the navy eats,
And thought all lost that goes not to the cheats;
So therefore secretly for peace decrees,
Yet as for war the Parliament would squeeze,
And fix to the revenue such a sum   125
Should Goodrick silence and strike Paston dumb,
Should pay land armies, should dissolve the vain
Commons, and ever such a court maintain;
Hyde's avarice, Bennet's luxury should suffice,
And what can these defray but the excise?   130
Excise, a monster worse than e'er before
Frighted the midwife and the mother tore.
A thousand hands she has and thousand eyes,
Breaks into shops and into cellars pries,
With hundred rows of teeth the shark exceeds,   135
And on all trade like cassowar she feeds:
Chops off the piece where'er she close the jaw,
Else swallows all down her indented maw.
She stalks all day in streets conceal'd from sight
And flies, like bats with leathern wings, by night;   140
She wastes the country and on cities preys.
Her, of a female harpy, in dog days,
Black Birch, of all the earth-born race most hot
And most rapacious, like himself, begot;
And, of his brat enamour'd, as't increas'd,   145
Bugger'd in incest with the mongrel beast.
    Say, Muse, for nothing can escape thy sight

121. *cabal:* A committee for foreign affairs drawn from the Privy Council.

126. *Goodrick:* Sir John Goodrick, member for the county of York, who sometimes acted as teller for the Court party during this session (Margoliouth). Paston first moved the huge appropriation of 2½ million pounds for the war. See *Second Advice*, 119–20.

136. *cassowar:* The omnivorous cassowary (Margoliouth).

142–46. In matter and manner this passage seems to be a mock-epic imitation of the incestuous relationship of Satan to his daughter Sin, which produced Death. See *Paradise Lost*, II: 746–85.

143. *Birch:* John Birch (1616–91), excise official under the Protectorate and Auditor after the Restoration. "An old Rumper who formerly bought nails at Bristol where they were cheap and carried them into the west to sell at Exeter and other places, but marrying a rich widow, got into the House and is now a Commissioner in all excises and is one of the Council of Trade" (*Flagellum Parliamentarium*, cited in Margoliouth).

(And, Painter, wanting other, draw this fight),
Who, in an English senate, fierce debate
Could raise so long for this new whore of state.   150
    Of early wittals first the troop march'd in,
For diligence renown'd and discipline;
In loyal haste they left young wives in bed,
And Denham these by one consent did head.
Of the old courtiers next a squadron came,   155
That sold their master, led by Ashburnham.
To them succeeds a despicable rout,
But know the word and well could face about;
Expectants pale, with hopes of spoil allur'd,
Though yet but pioneers, and led by Stew'rd.   160
Then damning cowards rang'd the vocal plain,
Wood these commands, Knight of the Horn and Cane.
Still his hook-shoulder seems the blow to dread,
And under's armpit he defends his head.
The posture strange men laugh'd at, of his poll,   165
Hid with his elbow like the spice he stole.
Headless St. Dennis so his head does bear,
And both of them alike French martyrs were.
Court officers, as us'd, the next place took,

151. *wittals:* Cuckolds.

156. *Ashburnham:* John Ashburnham (1603–71), who, with Sir John Berkeley, arranged King Charles I's flight to the Isle of Wight. For a long time he was suspected of having betrayed the King to the Governor of the island. He sat in Parliament for Sussex and was expelled in November 1667 for taking a bribe from French merchants (Margoliouth).

160. *Stew'rd:* James Butler, Duke of Ormonde, Lord Steward of the Household (J. Max Patrick).

162. *Wood:* Sir Henry Wood (1597–1671), Clerk of the Spicery to Charles I, member for Hythe, a Clerk Comptroller of the Board of Green Cloth, in which capacity he was responsible for maintaining order in the palace and for examining the accounts. As to his appearance Evelyn (17 Nov. 1651) calls him "that odd person," and Pepys (26 Oct. 1663) quotes the Queen's remark that "she never saw such a man as this Sir H. Wood in her life." Pepys again (19 Sept. 1666) heard, with other examples of the violence of his tongue, "many profane stories of Sir Henry Wood damning the parsons for so much spending the wine at the sacrament" (Margoliouth). *Knight of the Horn and Cane:* J. Max Patrick suggests that this phrase alludes to the powers of the Clerks of the Green Cloth over the allowance of victuals granted to members of the royal household (cf. horn of plenty) and their right to judge offenses against the household, which presumably included the right to have offending servants caned.

And follow'd Fox, but with disdainful look.   170
His birth, his youth, his brokage all dispraise,
In vain, for always he commands that pays.
Then the procurers under Progers fil'd,
Gentlest of men, and his lieutenant mild,
Brouncker, Love's squire: through all the field array'd,   175
No troop was better clad nor so well paid.
Then march'd the troop of Clarendon, all full,
Haters of fowl, to teal preferring bull:
Gross bodies, grosser minds, and grossest cheats,
And bloated Wren conducts them to their seats.   180
Charlton advances next, whose coif does awe

170. *Fox:* Sir Stephen Fox (1627–1716), member for Salisbury and Paymaster-General. He came from a modest Wiltshire family, and after an early training in book-keeping was employed by the Percys. In 1654 he took charge of Charles II's house-hold. He made a large fortune, "honestly got and unenvied," computed at £200,000 (Evelyn, 6 Sept. 1680). He opposed Clarendon's impeachment (Margoliouth).

171. *brokage:* The premium or commission of a broker. Fox made a profit on money advanced to pay the soldiers.

173. *Progers:* Edward Progers, member for Brecon and one of the King's procurers.

175. *Brouncker:* Henry Brouncker, cofferer to Charles II and Gentleman of the Bed-chamber to the Duke of York, whom he served in the same capacity as Progers did Charles. He was dismissed from the court in August 1667 and expelled from Parlia-ment in April 1668 for "bringing pretended orders from the Duke for lowering the sails" of the *Royal Prince* and thereby breaking off the pursuit of the Dutch in the Battle of Lowestoft (Grey *1*, 144; Margoliouth). Cf. *Second Advice*, 81ff., 237ff.

178. A play on the name of John Bulteel, a member for Lostwithiel and secretary to the Earl of Clarendon.

180. *Wren:* Matthew Wren (1629–72), original member of the Royal Society and cousin of Christopher, member for St. Michael, secretary to Clarendon, 1660–67, and to York 1667–72 (Margoliouth). Pepys remarks (26 Feb. 1668): "I to Westminster Hall, where, it being now six o'clock, I find the House just risen; and met with Sir. W. Coventry and the Lieutenant of the Tower, they having sat all day; and with great difficulty have got a vote for giving the King £300,000, not to be raised by any land-tax. The sum is much smaller than I expected, and than the King needs; but is grounded upon Mr. Wren's reading our estimates the other day of £270,000 to keep the fleet abroad, wherein we demanded nothing for setting and fitting of them out, which will cost almost £200,000. I do verily believe and do believe [*sic*] that the King hath no cause to thank Wren for this motion. I home to Sir W. Coventry's lodgings, with him and the Lieutenant of the Tower, where also was Sir John Coventry, and Sir John Duncombe, and Sir Job Charlton. And here a great deal of good discourse, and they seem mighty glad to have this vote pass, which I do wonder at, to see them so well satisfied with so small a sum, Sir John Duncombe swearing, as I perceive he will freely do, that it was as much as the nation could bear."

181–82. *Charlton:* Sir Job Charlton (1614–97), member for Ludlow and Chief Justice of Chester. *The Mitre troop* presumably refers to a group of lawyers associated with

The Mitre troop, and with his looks gives law.
He march'd with beaver cock'd of bishop's brim,
And hid much fraud under an aspect grim.
Next the lawyers' mercenary band appear: 185
Finch in the front and Thurland in the rear.
The troop of privilege, a rabble bare
Of debtors deep, fell to Trelawny's care.
Their fortune's error they suppli'd in rage,
Nor any further would than these engage.   190
Then march'd the troop, whose valiant acts before
(Their public acts) oblig'd them still to more.
For chimney's sake they all Sir Pool obey'd,
Or, in his absence, him that first it laid.
Then comes the thrifty troop of privateers,   195
Whose horses each with other interferes.
Before them Higgons rides with brow compact,
Mourning his Countess, anxious for his Act.

Mitre Court, one of the Inns of Court since demolished. Charlton later became Speaker. Roger North described him as "an old Cavalier, loyal, learned, grave, and wise."

186. *Finch:* Heneage Finch (1621–82), Solicitor-General and member for Oxford University, who supported oppressive measures against Dissenters. Cf. line 256 n. *Thurland:* Sir Edward Thurland (1624–85), member for Reigate and solicitor to the Duke of York (Margoliouth).

187. *the troop of privilege:* Those who relied on the immunity of Parliamentary privilege to avoid arrest for debt.

188. *Trelawny:* Sir Jonathan Trelawny (1624–85) was ruined by sequestration but, according to *Flagellum Parliamentarium* (1677), later made a fortune as an informer (Margoliouth and Aitken).

193. Sir Courtenay Pool, member for Honiton, proposed the hearth tax (chimney money) of two shillings on every hearth in 1662. "Considering its small yield, it was probably the most unwise fiscal measure of the later Stuarts because of the inquisitorial system necessary for its enforcement, and also the great inequalities in its incidence" (Ogg, *England in the Reign of Charles II*, 2, 429).

194. *him:* Perhaps Sir John Bramston, Chairman of the Committee on hearth tax. *laid:* Assessed.

195. *thrifty troop of privateers:* Those who, like Higgons (see below, 197) sought to enrich themselves by the passage of private bills, and whose horses are therefore represented as overriding each other.

197. *Higgons:* Sir Thomas Higgons (1624–91), Court party member for New Windsor, who introduced a bill in the session of 1666–67 for the recovery of £4,500 (Margoliouth). Marvell reports the defeat of this bill on 12 Jan. 1667 (see Corporation Letter of that date). He married the widow of the Earl of Essex and published an oration delivered at her funeral in 1656.

Sir Fred'rick and Sir Salomon draw lots
For the command of politics or sots,   200
Thence fell to words, but, quarrel to adjourn,
Their friends agreed they should command by turn.
Cart'ret the rich did the accountants guide
And in ill English all the world defi'd.
The Papists—but of these the House had none;   205
Else Talbot offer'd to have led them on.
Bold Duncombe next, of the projectors chief,
And old Fitzhardinge of the Eaters Beef.
Late and disorder'd, out the drinkers drew;
Scarce them their leaders, they their leaders knew.   210
Before them enter'd, equal in command,
Apsley and Brod'rick, marching hand in hand.

199. *Sir Frederick and Sir Salomon:* Usually identified as Sir Frederick Hyde (Court party member for Haverfordwest) and Sir Salomon Swale (Court party member for Aldborough). Swale was a Roman Catholic and opposed the bill against recusants at this session.

200. *politics:* Politicians.

203. *Cart'ret:* Sir George Carteret (d. 1680), Treasurer of the Navy after the Restoration. He served in the navy from childhood (see Pepys, 4 July 1663 on his lack of education) and resigned his post while the Dutch were in the Medway. He was a rich man. He appeared in Parliament before the Committee on Accounts 26 Sept. 1666. "The persons principally aimed at [by the Committee] were Sir G. Carteret the Treasurer of the navy, through whom all that expense had passed, who had many enemies upon the opinion that his office was too great, and the more by the ill offices Sir Wm. Coventry was always ready to do him, and the Lord Ashley, who was Treasurer of all the money that had been raised upon prizes, which could not but be a great proportion."

206. There were three Talbots in the Commons at this time, and two of them appear in *Flagellum Parliamentarium:* Sir Gilbert Talbot, "the King's jeweller, a great cheat at bowls and cards, not born to a shilling," and Sir John Talbot, "Commissioner of Prizes and a great cheater therein." The Talbots were an Irish Roman Catholic family.

207. *Duncombe:* Sir John Duncombe, a Privy Councillor, once Commissioner of the Ordnance, now of the Treasury, and Baptist May's brother-in-law. *projectors:* Schemers, speculators, cheats.

208. *Fitzhardinge:* Sir Charles Berkeley (1600–68), second Viscount Fitzhardinge in the Irish peerage and Treasurer of the Household, in which capacity he was in charge of the yeomen of the guard. This is the first known instance of their being called beefeaters (Margoliouth).

212. *Apsley:* Sir Allen Apsley (1616–83), Treasurer of the Duke of York's household. *Brod'rick:* Sir Allen Broderick, member for both Orford and Callington (Cornwall). Cf. *Clarendon's Housewarming,* 49–52 n.

Last then but one, Powell, that could not ride,
Led the French standard, welt'ring in his stride.
He, to excuse his slowness, truth confess'd   215
That 'twas so long before he could be dress'd.
The lords' sons, last, all these did reinforce:
Cornb'ry before them manag'd hobby-horse.
　　Never before, nor since, an host so steel'd
Troop'd on to muster in the Tothill Field: 220
Not the first cock-horse, that with cork were shod
To rescue Albemarle from the sea-cod,
Nor the late feather-men, whom Tomkins fierce
Shall with one breath like thistledown disperse.
All the two Coventrys their gen'rals choose,   225
For one had much, the other nought to lose;
Nor better choice all accidents could hit,
While Hector Harry steers by Will the Wit.
They both accept the charge with merry glee,
To fight a battle from all gunshot free.   230
Pleas'd with their numbers, yet in valor wise,

213. *Powell:* Sir Richard Powell, Gentleman of the Horse to the Duchess of York. *French standard* is an allusion to the pox, which caused him to *welter in his stride*.

218. *Cornb'ry:* Henry Hyde, Lord Cornbury (1638–1709), Clarendon's eldest son, Chamberlain to the Queen. *hobby-horse:* Perhaps an allusion to his youth.

220. *Tothill Field:* Tothill Fields, Westminster, used for drilling troops.

221–22. This obscure couplet alludes to the rescue of Albemarle by Rupert in the Four Days' Fight (1–4 June 1666). *Sea-cod* represents De Ruyter, who was prevented from destroying Albemarle's ship by Rupert's intervention (cf. the sea-dragon in *Third Advice*, 135–42). *Cock-horse* shod with cork may refer obscurely to Rupert's career as a famous cavalry leader in the Civil wars. Margoliouth suggests that cock-horse alludes to Cocke, the naval contractor, and notes that "cork-heeled shoon" marked the gallant. The word-play turns on the similar pronunciation in the seventeenth century of *cock* and *cork*.

223–24. The *feather-men* are probably the standing army raised by the government in the spring of 1667 ostensibly to prevent an invasion, which Sir Thomas Tomkins spoke against in the abortive Parliamentary session of 25–29 July 1667 (Margoliouth).

225–34. The *two Coventrys* are Henry (1619–86) and Sir William (1628?–86), who "practically led the House" (*DNB*). Henry had "nought to lose," because, having concluded an embassy to Sweden, he was now without an appointment from the government, and Sir William much to lose, because he was Commissioner of the Treasury and of the Navy and could protect the large profits allegedly made from these posts by active leadership of the Court faction.

230. An allusion to Coventry's alleged cowardice at Lowestoft. See *Second Advice*, 79–82.

They feign a parley, better to surprise;
They that ere long shall the rude Dutch upbraid,
Who in a time of treaty durst invade.
   Thick was the morning, and the House was thin,   235
The Speaker early, when they all fell in.
Propitious heavens, had not you them cross'd,
Excise had got the day and all been lost!
For th' other side all in loose quarters lay,
Without intelligence, command, or pay: 240
A scatter'd body, which the foe ne'er tri'd,
But oft'ner did among themselves divide.
And some ran o'er each night, while others sleep,
And undescri'd return'd ere morning peep.
But Strangeways, that all night still walk'd the round   245
(For vigilance and courage both renown'd)
First spi'd the enemy and gave th' alarm,
Fighting it single till the rest might arm.
Such Roman Cocles strid before the foe,
The falling bridge behind, the stream below.   250
Each ran, as chance him guides, to sev'ral post,
And all to pattern his example boast.
Their former trophies they recall to mind
And to new edge their angry courage grind.
First enter'd forward Temple, conqueror   255

233–34. Henry Coventry was one of the ambassadors who negotiated the Dutch peace, and his brother is held chiefly responsible for having failed to prepare the fleet on the grounds that peace was expected.

235. The Court party members proposed the grant of £1,800,000 for the King before all the Country party members had assembled. On 12 Oct. "The Court party moved for a general excise of all things, which was no way pleasing" (Milward).

236. *Speaker:* Turnor.

239. *loose quarters:* The opposite of close quarters. Loose quarters are indefensible positions.

245. *Strangeways:* Sir John Strangeways, who acted as teller against the government in several divisions on finance during this session (Margoliouth).

249. *Cocles:* Publius Horatius Cocles (Macaulay's Horatius at the bridge), who defended single-handed a bridge leading into Rome against the army of Porsena, King of Etruria.

255. *Temple:* Sir Richard Temple, a leader of the Country party who supported the act against the importation of Irish cattle, a major issue in this session. The act passed in January 1667.

Of Irish cattle and Solicitor;
Then daring Seymour, that with spear and shield,
Had stretch'd the monster Patent on the field;
Keen Whorwood next, in aid of damsel frail
That pierc'd the giant Mordaunt through his mail,   260
And surly Williams, the accountants' bane,
And Lovelace young, of chimney-men the cane.
Old Waller, trumpet-gen'ral, swore he'd write
This combat truer than the naval fight.
Of birth, state, wit, strength, courage, How'rd presumes   265
And in his breast wears many Montezumes.
These and some more, with single valor, stay
The adverse troops and hold them all at bay.
Each thinks his person represents the whole
And with that thought does multiply his soul,   270
Believes himself an army, theirs one man

256. *Solicitor:* Sir Heneage Finch (1621–82), Solicitor-General, who spoke against the Irish Cattle Bill.

257. *Seymour:* Sir Edward Seymour (1633–1708), later Speaker of the House, who attacked the Canary Patent, a charter for merchants trading with the Canary Islands as "an illegal patent, a monopoly, and a grievance to the subject" (Margoliouth).

259. *Whorwood:* Brome Whorwood, member for the city of Oxford, who helped draw up an impeachment against John, Viscount *Mordaunt* (1627–75), Constable of Windsor Castle, who had allegedly imprisoned one William Tayleur because his daughter would not yield herself to him (Margoliouth). On 8 July the King granted Mordaunt a pardon.

261. *Williams:* A committee to investigate public accounts was appointed 26 Sept. 1666. Caroline Robbins identifies Williams as Col. Henry Williams (alias Cromwell), member for Huntingdon, but no one by this name is listed on the committee in *CJ.* See Milward, p.c.

262. *Lovelace:* John Lovelace (1638?–93), an opponent of the widely-hated hearth tax.

263–64. *Waller:* Waller was widely criticized as a political turncoat. "As far as his public utterances went," however, "the second half of his Parliamentary career was in every way creditable to him. He spoke with great courage against the dangers of a military despotism, and his voice was constantly raised in appeals for toleration for Dissenters . . ." (*DNB*). Cf. these lines with the opening couplet of *Second Advice. Trumpet-general* may allude to Waller's position as the poet who celebrates battles but does not participate in them.

265–66. *How'rd:* Sir Robert Howard (1626–98), member for Stockbridge and collaborator and brother-in-law of Dryden with whom he wrote *The Indian Queen* (1665), a drama whose hero is Montezuma. He was prominent in the proceedings against Clarendon. Evelyn described him as "pretending to all manner of arts and sciences . . . not ill-natured, but insufferably boasting" (16 Feb. 1685).

As eas'ly conquer'd; and, believing, can;
With heart of bees so full, and head of mites,
That each, though duelling, a battle fights.
Such once Orlando, famous in romance,   275
Broach'd whole brigades like larks upon his lance.
        But strength at last still under number bows,
And the faint sweat trickled down Temple's brows.
E'en iron Strangeways, chafing, yet gave back,
Spent with fatigue, to breathe a while toback,   280
When, marching in, a seas'nable recruit
Of citizens and merchants held dispute;
And, charging all their pikes, a sullen band
Of Presbyterian Switzers made a stand.
        Nor could all these the field have long maintain'd   285
But for th' unknown reserve that still remain'd,
A gross of English gentry, nobly born,
Of clear estates, and to no faction sworn;
Dear lovers of their King, and death to meet,
For country's cause, that glorious think and sweet;   290
To speak not forward, but in action brave,
In giving gen'rous, but in counsel grave;
Candidly credulous for once, nay twice,
But sure the Devil cannot cheat them thrice.
The van and battle, though retiring, falls   295
Without disorder in their intervals,
Then closing, all in equal front fall on,
        Led by great Garr'way and great Littleton.

275–76. The hero of *Orlando Furioso* spitted six enemies at once on his lance.
280. *toback:* Tobacco.
281. *recruit:* A fresh or auxiliary body of troops added as a reinforcement to an
army. *Obs.*
284. *Presbyterian Switzers:* Presumably a faction of Presbyterian members who
joined the opposition.
287–88. Margoliouth cites Pepys (5 November 1666): "all the country gentlemen are
publicly jealous of the courtiers in the Parliament, and they do doubt everything that
they propose, and . . . the true reason why the country gentlemen are for a land-tax
against a general excise is because they are fearful that if the latter be granted they
shall never get it down again, whereas the land-tax will be but for so much, and, when
the war ceases, there will be no ground got by the Court to keep it up."
298. *Garr'way:* William Garraway (Garway or Garroway), member for Chichester,
who examined Pepys' accounts 3 Oct. 1666. According to Pepys, Sir William Coventry
spoke of him as ill-used by the Court but staunchly loyal to the King (6 Oct. 1666). He

Lee, ready to obey or to command,
Adjutant-general, was still at hand. 300
The martial standard, Sandys displaying, shows
St. Dunstan in it, tweaking Satan's nose.
See sudden chance of war! To paint or write
Is longer work and harder than to fight.
At the first charge the enemy give out, 305
And the excise receives a total rout.
Broken in courage, yet the men the same,
Resolve henceforth upon their other game:
Where force had fail'd with stratagem to play
And what haste lost recover by delay. 310
St. Albans straight is sent to to forbear,
Lest the sure peace, forsooth, too soon appear.
The seamen's clamor to three ends they use:
To cheat their pay, feign want, the House accuse.
Each day they bring the tale, and that too true, 315

seconded Tomkins' motion against the standing army. *Littleton:* Sir Thomas Little-
ton (d. 1681), 2nd Bart., member for Great Wenlock, mentioned by Pepys as "one of
the greatest speakers in the House" (18 July 1666).

299. *Lee:* Sir Thomas Lee, member for Aylesbury. Pepys mentions him and Littleton
as "professed enemies to us and everybody else," when he was examined by the House
5 March 1668 (Margoliouth).

301. *Sandys:* Col. Samuel Sandys, member for Worcestershire.

302–03. "In art St. Dunstan is chiefly honored by a foolish representation of the
devil caught by the nose by a pair of blacksmith's pincers. The legend relates that
Satan tempted him as he was at work at his forge, by assuming the form of a beautiful
girl. Dunstan at once attacked him with his pincers and put him to flight" (S. Baring-
Gould, *The Lives of the Saints*, Edinburgh, 1914, 5, 288). Dunstan (924–88) was Bishop
of Worcester, hence the connection with Sandys.

305–06. The general excise was "routed" on 8 November 1666:

The rest of the day the Speaker kept his Chair and the debate was about rais-
ing the King's supply.
Secretary Morice declared to the House that the King would not part with the
chimney money.
Assurance being given in the House that the same excise would not be any
farther prosecuted, Mr. Garroway made this proposition to the House, that thir-
teen hundred and twenty thousand pounds of the £1,800,000 should be raised by
eleven months' tax at the rate of £120,000 per mensem and that the other four
hundred and fourscore thousand pounds should be raised by the poll bill, sealed
paper and excise of certain foreign commodities (Milward, *Diary*).

313–24. *seaman's clamor:* As Pepys reports (19 Dec. 1666), the seamen were begin-
ning to riot because they had not been paid for so long, and because the tickets they
received in lieu of cash were not being redeemed by the government.

How strong the Dutch their equipage renew.
Meantime through all the yards their orders run
To lay the ships up, cease the keels begun.
The timber rots, and useless axe doth rust,
Th' unpractic'd saw lies buri'd in its dust,   320
The busy hammer sleeps, the ropes untwine,
The stores and wages all are mine and thine.
Along the coast and harbors they take care
That money lack, nor forts be in repair.
Long thus they could against the House conspire,   325
Load them with envy, and with sitting tire,
And the lov'd King, and never yet deni'd,
Is brought to beg in public and to chide;
But when this fail'd, and months enough were spent,
They with the first day's proffer seem content,   330
And to land tax from the excise turn round,
Bought off with eighteen-hundred-thousand pound.
Thus, like fair thieves, the Commons' purse they share,
But all the members' lives, consulting, spare.
    Blither than hare that hath escap'd the hounds,   335
The House prorogu'd, the Chancellor rebounds.
Not so decrepit Aeson, hash'd and stew'd,
With bitter herbs, rose from the pot renew'd,
And with fresh age felt his glad limbs unite;
His gout (yet still he curs'd) had left him quite.   340
What frosts to fruit, what ars'nic to the rat,
What to fair Denham mortal chocolate,
What an account to Cart'ret, that, and more,
A Parliament is to the Chancellor.
So the sad tree shrinks from the morning's eye,   345
But blooms all night and shoots its branches high.
So, at the sun's recess, again returns

328. The King addressed an urgent demand for supply to the House on 18 January 1667.

331. The land tax, which was supported by the Country party against the general excise of the Court party, was passed on 8 November 1666.

336. *prorogu'd*: On 8 Feb. 1667 when the land tax bill received the royal assent.

337–39. See *Metamorphoses* 7.

345–46. *sad tree*: Nyctanthes Arbor-tristis, Night-Jasmine of India. During the day it loses its brightness (Margoliouth).

The comet dread and earth and heaven burns.
   Now Mordaunt may, within his castle tow'r,
Imprison parents and the child deflow'r.   350
The Irish herd is now let loose and comes
By millions over, not by hecatombs;
And now, now, the Canary patent may
Be broach'd again for the great holiday.
   See how he reigns in his new palace culminant   355
And sits in state divine like Jove the fulminant!
First Buckingham, that durst 'gainst him rebel,
Blasted with lightning, struck with thunder, fell.
Next the twelve Commons are condemn'd to groan
And roll in vain at Sisyphus's stone.   360
But still he car'd, while in revenge he brav'd,
That peace secur'd and money might be sav'd:
Gain and revenge, revenge and gain are sweet,
United most else when by turns they meet.
France had St. Albans promis'd (so they sing),   365
St. Albans promis'd him, and he the King:
The Count forthwith is order'd all to close,
To play for Flanders and the stake to lose,
While, chain'd together, two ambassadors
Like slaves shall beg for peace at Holland's doors.   370
This done, among his Cyclops he retires
To forge new thunder and inspect their fires.
   The Court as once of war, now fond of peace,
All to new sports their wanton fears release.
From Greenwich (where intelligence they hold)   375

349. See note on 259.
351. See note on 255.
357-58. Buckingham had been chief supporter of the Irish Cattle Bill in the House of Lords, 1666-67, Clarendon opposing. His arrest was ordered 25 Feb. 1667 for treasonable practices, one charge being that he obtained a cast of the King's horoscope. After some months he gave himself up and was sent to the Tower.
359-60. Twelve of the eighteen Commissioners for the Public Accounts, appointed 21 March 1667, were members of the House of Commons.
367. *Count:* i.e. the Earl of St. Albans; perhaps with a glance at his "Frenchiness."
368. The French aimed at peace with England in order to be free to carry out their designs on Flanders.
369. See note on 233-34.
375-96. These lines refer to the "Skimmington Ride," in which aggressive wives and timid husbands were ridiculed by their neighbors. Here France and Flanders are the

Comes news of pastime martial and old,
A punishment invented first to awe
Masculine wives transgressing Nature's law,
Where, when the brawny female disobeys
And beats the husband till for peace he prays,   380
No concern'd jury for him damage finds,
Nor partial justice her behavior binds,
But the just street does the next house invade,
Mounting the neighbor couple on lean jade,
The distaff knocks, the grains from kettle fly,   385
And boys and girls in troops run hooting by:
Prudent antiquity, that knew by shame
Better than law domestic crimes to tame,
And taught youth by spectacle innocent!
So thou and I, dear Painter, represent   390
In quick effigie, others' faults and feign,
By making them ridiculous, to restrain.
With homely sight they chose thus to relax
The joys of state for the new peace and tax.
So Holland with us had the mast'ry tri'd,   395
And our next neighbors, France and Flanders, ride.
   But a fresh news the great designment nips—
Off at the Isle of Candy Dutch and ships!
Bab May and Arlington did wisely scoff
And thought all safe, if they were so far off.   400
Modern geographers, 'twas there, they thought,
Where Venice twenty years the Turk had fought,
While the first year our navy is but shown,
The next divided, and the third we've none.
They by the name mistook it for that isle   405

---

neighbors while Holland is the masterful wife and England the beaten husband.
(Margoliouth).
   391. *Effigie,* Margoliouth notes, was pronounced as four syllables in the 17th cen-
tury. Cf. *Third Advice,* 436.
   398. *Candy:* 1. Candia Island, off the Essex coast; 2. an old name for Crete. Marvell
was probably also referring to the occasion for Busenello's *Prospective of the Naval
Triumph* (tr. Thomas Higgons, 1658) achieved by the Venetian navy over the Turks
near Crete. This poem was Waller's model.
   399. *Bab May:* Baptist May, Keeper of the Privy Purse.

Where Pilgrim Palmer travell'd in exile
With the bull's horn to measure his own head
And on Pasiphäe's tomb to drop a bead.
But Morice learn'd demonstrates, by the post,
This Isle of Candy was on Essex coast.   410
   Fresh messengers still the sad news assure;
More tim'rous now we are than first secure.
False terrors our believing fears devise,
And the French army one from Calais spies.
Bennet and May and those of shorter reach   415
Change all for guineas and a crown for each,
But wiser men and well foreseen in chance
In Holland theirs had lodg'd before, and France.
Whitehall's unsafe; the court all meditates
To fly to Windsor and mure up the gates.   420
Each does the other blame and all distrust,
But Mordaunt, new oblig'd, would sure be just.
Not such a fatal stupefaction reign'd
At London's flame, nor so the court complain'd.
The Bloodworth-Chanc'lor gives, then does recall,   425

406. *Pilgrim Palmer:* A punning reference to Roger Palmer, Earl of Castlemaine, a Roman Catholic. When his wife left him for Charles II he traveled to the Levant in 1664 with the Venetian admiral Andrea Cornaro (Margoliouth). In 1666 he published *An Account of the Present War between the Venetians and the Turks, with the State of Candy, in a Letter to the King* [Charles II].

408. *Pasiphäe* of Crete, wife of Minos, fell in love with a bull. The product of their union was the Minotaur, which Minos caused Daedalus to imprison in a labyrinth. See *Metamorphoses,* especially 8 and 9, and the reference to the myth in *Second Advice,* 349–58.

409. *Morice:* Sir William Morice (1602–76), joint Secretary of State with Arlington. Though a learned man, he was criticized as ignorant of languages and foreign affairs (Margoliouth). *by the post:* From his knowledge of postal matters he demonstrates to Arlington, the Postmaster-General, that this Candy is in Essex (Margoliouth).

415–18. Cf. Pepys, 13, 14, 15 June 1667: he could get no gold pieces on 13 June, "all being bought up last night that were to be had, and sold for 24s. and 25s. a piece" (Margoliouth).

419–20. "The gates of the court were shut up upon the first coming of the Dutch to us" (Pepys, 17 June 1667, cited by Margoliouth).

422. See note on 260. Mordaunt is "new oblig'd" because of the dropping of proceedings against him (Margoliouth).

425. *Bloodworth:* Sir Thomas Bloodworth was Mayor of London during the Great Fire and was noted for his fecklessness.

Orders; amaz'd at last gives none at all.
    St. Alban's writ to, that he may bewail
To master Louis and tell coward tale,
How yet the Hollanders do make a noise,
Threaten to beat us, and are naughty boys.   430
Now Dolman's disobedient and they still
Uncivil; his unkindness would us kill.
Tell him our ships unrigg'd, our forts unmann'd,
Our money spent; else 'twere at his command.
Summon him therefore of his word and prove   435
To move him out of pity, if not love;
Pray him to make De Witt and Ruyter cease
And whip the Dutch, unless they'll hold their peace.
But Louis was of memory but dull
And to St. Albans too undutiful;   440
Nor word, nor near relation, did revere,
But ask'd him bluntly for his character.
The gravell'd Count did with the answer faint
(His character was that which thou didst paint)
And so enforc'd, like enemy or spy,   445
Trusses his baggage and the camp does fly,
Yet Louis writes and, lest our heart should break,
Consoles us morally out of Seneque.
    Two letters next unto Breda are sent:
In cipher one to Harry Excellent;   450
The first instructs our (verse the name abhors)

427–28. An express with appeals for peace went to St. Albans on 15 June.
431. *Dolman's disobedient:* Col. Thomas Dolman, an English officer, commanded the Dutch troops in the invading fleet. An act was passed in October 1665 attainting him if he and others did not surrender by a certain day (Margoliouth).
435. *prove:* Attempt.
440. *undutiful:* As a nephew. Marvell assumes that St. Albans was married to Henrietta Maria, in which case he would have been Louis XIV's uncle.
442. *character:* Official rank or status.
446. See Pepys, 26 June 1667, on Louis' chastisement of St. Albans.
447–48. This consolatory letter from Louis XIV to Charles is undoubtedly a figment of the poet's imagination. Seneca was one of the classical writers whom Louis, as a young man, was made to read. There is a letter from Louis XIV congratulating Charles on the completion of the Treaty of Breda (See *Oeuvres,* 1806, *5,* 415–16).
451–56. " 'I look upon the peace as made' was the cue taken from St. Albans, and as May passed into June our blind dependence grew more marked" (Feiling, *Foreign Policy,* p. 218).

Plenipotentiary ambassadors
To prove by Scripture treaty does imply
Cessation, as the look adultery,
And that by law of arms, in martial strife,   455
Who yields his sword has title to his life.
Presbyter Holles the first point should clear,
The second Coventry the Cavalier;
But, would they not be argu'd back from sea,
Then to return home straight, *infecta re.*   460
But Harry's order'd, if they won't recall
Their fleet, to threaten we will grant them all.
The Dutch are then in proclamation shent
For sin against th' eleventh commandment.
Hyde's flippant style there pleasantly curvets,   465
Still his sharp wit on states and princes whets
(So Spain could not escape his laughter's spleen:
None but himself must choose the King a Queen),
But when he come the odious clause to pen
That summons up the Parliament again,   470
His writing master many a time he bann'd
And wish'd himself the gout to seize his hand.
Never old lecher more repugnance felt,
Consenting, for his rupture, to be gelt;
But still in hope he solac'd, ere they come,   475
To work the peace and so to send them home,
Or in their hasty call to find a flaw,
Their acts to vitiate and them overawe;

452. Coventry and Holles.

454. Cf. Matthew 5:27–28. "Whosoever looketh on a woman to lust after her hath committed adultery with her already in his heart."

459. *they:* The Dutch fleet.

460. *infecta re:* Without having accomplished the business.

464. *eleventh commandment:* See lines 453–54.

465–66. Clarendon's attitude toward Holland during preliminary negotiations was unyielding and contemptuous. See Feiling, *Foreign Policy,* p. 216.

467–68. Margoliouth notes that in the negotiations preceding the Portuguese marriage Clarendon may have been responsible for the sharp tone of the King's replies to the Spanish ambassador.

469–70. Clarendon repeatedly "told the King that Queen Elizabeth did all her business in '88 without calling a Parliament and so might he do" (Pepys, 25 June 1667), but a Parliament was summoned by proclamation on 25 June to meet 25 July.

471. *bann'd:* Cursed.

But most reli'd upon this Dutch pretense
To raise a two-edg'd army for's defense.   480
      First then he march'd our whole militia's force
(As if, indeed, we ships or Dutch had horse);
Then, from the usual commonplace, he blames
These, and in standing Army's praise declaims;
And the wise Court, that always lov'd it dear,   485
Now thinks all but too little for their fear.
Hyde stamps, and straight upon the ground the swarms
Of current Myrmidons appear in arms,
And for their pay he writes as from the King
With that curs'd quill pluck'd from a vulture's wing   490
Of the whole nation now to ask a loan
(The eighteen-hundred-thousand pound was gone).
This done, he pens a proclamation stout,
In rescue of the *banquiers banquerouts,*

480. After the naval disgrace an army of twelve new regiments under the command
of old Parliamentarians was raised "to conciliate popular opinion. . . . But this was
only adding fuel to the fire, since it raised the suspicion that a standing army was
intended" (Ogg, *England in the Reign of Charles II*, p. 313).

481–82. Earlier in the spring of 1667 when the government's economy drive was in
full swing, Arlington instructed the lords lieutenant of southeastern England "to
make the greatest show you can in numbers . . . more especially of horse, even
though it be of such as are otherwise wholly unfit; horse being the force that most
discourage the enemy from landing" (quoted in Ogg, p. 309). After the Dutch attacked,
the London train-bands were mustered and marched away, "which, considering the
soldiers drawn out to Chatham and elsewhere, looks as if they had a design to ruin
the City and give it up to be undone . . ." (Pepys, 11 June 1667).

484. *These:* The Dutch.

487–88. Marvell's account of the origins of the Myrmidons is not quite accurate.
When Aeacus, King of Aegina, had lost most of his army because of the plague, a
new army was miraculously created out of ants. See *Metamorphoses* 7, 615ff.

489–90. "When the Dutch fleet rode victorious in the mouth of the river he had ad-
vised the King to dissolve the Parliament and support the troops on the coast by
forced contributions from the neighboring counties, to be paid out of the next sup-
ply. This counsel was divulged by some of his enemies and represented as a plan to
govern the kingdom with a standing army in the place of the Parliament" (Lingard,
9, 149).

494. *banquiers banquerouts:* Ungrammatical; *banquiers en banqueroute* would be
correct. "Cocke says the bankers cannot, till peace returns, ever hope to have credit
again; so that they can pay no more money, but people must be contented to take
public security such as they can give them. . . . But the King's declaration in behalf
of the bankers, to make good their assignments for money, is very good, and will, I
hope, secure me" (Pepys, 23 June 1667).

His minion imps that in his secret part 495
Lie nuzzling at the sacramental wart,
Horse-leeches circling at the hem'rrhoid vein:
He sucks the King, they him, he them again.
The kingdom's farm he lets to them bid least
(Greater the bribe, and that's at interest). 500
Here men induc'd by safety, gain, and ease,
Their money lodge, confiscate when he please.
These can at need, at instant, with a scrip
(This lik'd him best) his cash beyond sea whip.
When Dutch invade, when Parliament prepare, 505
How can he engines so convenient spare?
Let no man touch them or demand his own,
Pain of displeasure of great Clarendon.
    The state affairs thus marshall'd, for the rest,
Monck in his shirt against the Dutch is press'd. 510
Often, dear Painter, have I sat and mus'd
Why he should still b'on all adventures us'd:
If they for nothing ill, like ashen-wood,
Or think him, like herb john, for nothing good?
Whether his valor they so much admire, 515
Or that for cowardice they all retire,
As Heav'n in storms, they call, in gusts of state,
On Monck and Parliament yet both do hate.

495–98. Cf. Cleveland, *Rebel Scot*, 83–85:

Sure, England hath the hemorrhoids, and these
On the north postern of the patient seize
Like leeches . . . .

496. *wart:* Nipple, *obs.*
499. *kingdom's farm:* The farming of taxes.
500. *That's* refers to *farm.*
502. *Confiscate* is an adjective.
503. *scrip:* Receipt for a portion of a loan subscribed.
512. Cf. *Third Advice*, 432, where the Duchess of Albemarle speaks of her husband as "Gen'ral at land, at sea, at plague, at fire."
513. *ashen-wood:* The ash is a tree second in value only to the oak, and its wood has a thousand uses. Margoliouth cites *Faerie Queene*, I.1.9: "the ash for nothing ill."
514. *herb john:* Properly St. John's wort, but also denoting "some tasteless herb of neutral qualities; hence applied, in proverbial phrases, to something inert or indifferent" (*OED*, cited by Margoliouth).

All causes sure concur, but most they think
Under Herculean labors he may sink.   520
Soon then the independent troops would close,
And Hyde's last project would his place dispose.
    Ruyter the while, that had our ocean curb'd,
Sail'd now among our rivers undisturb'd,
Survey'd their crystal streams and banks so green   525
And beauties ere this never naked seen.
Through the vain sedge the bashful nymphs he ey'd:
Bosoms and all which from themselves they hide.
The sun much brighter, and the skies more clear,
He finds the air and all things sweeter here.   530
The sudden change and such a tempting sight
Swells his old veins with fresh blood, fresh delight.
Like am'rous victors he begins to shave,
And his new face looks in the English wave.
His sporting navy all about him swim   535
And witness their complacence in their trim.
Their streaming silks play through the weather fair
And with inveigling colors court the air,
While the red flags breathe on their top-masts high
Terror and war but want an enemy.   540
Among the shrouds the seamen sit and sing,
And wanton boys on every rope do cling.
Old Neptune springs the tides and water lent
(The gods themselves do help the provident),
And, where the deep keel on the shallow cleaves,   545
With trident's lever and great shoulder heaves.
Aeolus their sails inspires with eastern wind,
Puffs them along, and breathes upon them kind.
With pearly shell the Tritons all the while

521–22. I agree with Margoliouth's suggestion that "independent troops" refers to
the projected standing army: "The point may be that, with Monck's death, the ob-
stacles to the consolidation of a standing army under Clarendon's control would dis-
appear."

532. *old:* De Ruyter was now sixty.

533–40. This passage seems to show a general indebtedness to Enobarbus' account
of the first meeting between Antony and Cleopatra in Shakespeare's play (II.2.193–
228).

543. Pepys notes (14 June) that the easterly winds and spring tides helped the
Dutch to go up the Thames and the Medway and to break the chain at Chatham.

Michael Adrian De Ruyter, Admiral General of Holland, after the Dutch victory at Chatham, 9 June 1667. From an engraving by an unknown artist.

Sound the sea-march and guide to Sheppey Isle.   550
So have I seen in April's bud arise
A fleet of clouds, sailing along the skies;
The liquid region with their squadrons fill'd,
Their airy sterns the sun behind does gild,
And gentle gales them steer, and Heaven drives,   555
When, all on sudden, their calm bosom rives
With thunder and lightning from each armed cloud;
Shepherds themselves in vain in bushes shroud.
Such up the stream the Belgic navy glides
And at Sheerness unloads its stormy sides.   560
    Spragge there, though practic'd in the sea command,
With panting heart lay like a fish on land
And quickly judg'd the fort was not tenable,
Which, if a house, yet were not tenantable.
No man can sit there safe: the canon pours   565
Thorough the walls untight and bullets show'rs,
The neighb'rhood ill and an unwholesome seat,
So at the first salute resolves retreat
And swore that he would never more dwell there
Until the City put it in repair;   570
So he in front, his garrison in rear,
March straight to Chatham to increase the fear.
    There our sick ships unrigg'd in summer lay
Like molting fowl, a weak and easy prey,
For whose strong bulk earth scarce could timber find,   575
The ocean water, or the heavens wind—
Those oaken giants of the ancient race,
That rul'd all seas and did our Channel grace.
The conscious stag, so, once the forest's dread,
Flies to the wood and hides his armless head.   580
Ruyter forthwith a squadron does untack;
They sail securely through the river's track.
An English pilot too (O shame, O sin!)
Cheated of pay, was he that show'd them in.

561. *Spragge*: Sir Edward Spragge (d. 1673), Vice-Admiral of the Blue, then com-
manding at Sheerness.
568–72. On the 10th the Dutch bombarded Sheerness and forced the evacuation of
Spragge and the garrison.

Our wretched ships, within, their fate attend,   585
And all our hopes now on frail chain depend:
Engine so slight to guard us from the sea,
It fitter seem'd to captivate a flea.
A skipper rude shocks it without respect,
Filling his sails, more force to recollect.   590
Th' English from shore the iron deaf invoke
For its last aid: "Hold chain, or we are broke!"
But with her sailing weight the Holland keel,
Snapping the brittle links, does thorough reel
And to the rest the open'd passage shew;   595
Monck from the bank the dismal sight does view.
Our feather'd gallants, which came down that day
To be spectators safe of the new play,
Leave him alone when first they hear the gun
(Cornb'ry the fleetest) and to London run.   600
Our seamen, whom no danger's shape could fright,
Unpaid refuse to mount our ships for spite,
Or to their fellows swim on board the Dutch,
Which show the tempting metal in their clutch.
Oft had he sent of Duncombe and of Legge   605
Cannon and powder, but in vain, to beg;
And Upnor Castle's ill-defended wall,
Now needful, does for ammunition call.
He finds, wheres'e'er he succor might expect,
Confusion, folly, treach'ry, fear, neglect.   610
But when the *Royal Charles* (what rage, what grief!)
He saw seiz'd and could give her no relief—
That sacred keel which had, as he, restor'd
His exil'd Sov'reign on its happy board,
And thence the British Admiral became,   615

597. *feather'd gallants:* On 10 June Pepys found "a great many idle lords and gen-
tlemen, with their pistols and fooleries" at Gravesend.

601–04. Pepys reports (14 June) that "Englishmen on board the Dutch ships . . .
did cry and say, 'We did heretofore fight for tickets; now we fight for dollars!' "

605. *Legge:* William Legge, Lieutenant-General of the Ordnance.

607. *Upnor Castle* was two miles below Chatham. It was inadequately supplied by
the ordnance office to withstand the Dutch attack.

613–14. The *Royal Charles,* formerly the *Naseby,* brought the King to Dover in 1660.

Crown'd, for that merit, with their master's name;
That pleasure-boat of war, in whose dear side
Secure so oft he had this foe defi'd,
Now a cheap spoil and the mean victor's slave,
Taught the Dutch colors from its top to wave—   620
Of former glories the reproachful thought,
With present shame compar'd, his mind distraught.
Such, from Euphrates' bank, a tigress fell
After the robber for her whelps doth yell;
But sees enrag'd the river flow between,   625
Frustrate revenge, and love, by loss more keen;
At her own breast her useless claws does arm:
She tears herself, since him she cannot harm.
    The guards, plac'd for the chain's and fleet's defence,
Long since were fled on many a feign'd pretence.   630
Daniel had there adventur'd, man of might;
Sweet Painter, draw his picture while I write.
Paint him of person tall and big of bone,
Large limbs, like ox, not to be kill'd but shown.
Scarce can burnt iv'ry feign an hair so black;   635
Or face so red, thine ochre and thy lac.
Mix a vain terror in his martial look,
And all those lines by which men are mistook;
But when, by shame constrain'd to go on board,
He heard how the wild cannon nearer roar'd   640
And saw himself confin'd like sheep in pen,
Daniel then thought he was in lion's den.
And when the frightful fireships he saw,
Pregnant with sulphur, to him nearer draw,
Captain, lieutenant, ensign, all make haste   645
Ere in the fi'ry furnace they be cast.
Three children tall, unsing'd, away they row,
Like Shadrack, Meshack, and Abednego.

631. *Daniel:* Probably Sir Thomas Daniel, who commanded a company of foot guards, who were supposed to defend the *Loyal London* or the *Royal James* (Margoliouth).
634. *shown:* Like a prize ox.
636. *lac:* A crimson pigment.
648. See the Bible, Daniel 3.

Not so brave Douglas, on whose lovely chin
The early down but newly did begin,   650
And modest beauty yet his sex did veil,
While envious virgins hope he is a male.
His yellow locks curl back themselves to seek,
Nor other courtship knew but to his cheek.
Oft as he in chill Esk or Seine by night   655
Harden'd and cool'd his limbs, so soft, so white,
Among the reeds, to be espi'd by him,
The nymphs would rustle; he would forward swim.
They sigh'd and said, "Fond boy, why so untame,
That fli'st love's fires, reserv'd for other flame?"   660
Fix'd on his ship, he fac'd that horrid day
And wonder'd much at those that run away.
Nor other fear himself could comprehend
Than lest Heav'n fall ere thither he ascend,
But entertains the while his time too short   665
With birding at the Dutch, as if in sport,
Or waves his sword, and could he them conjure
Within its circle, knows himself secure.
The fatal bark him boards with grappling fire,
And safely through its port the Dutch retire.   670
That precious life he yet disdains to save
Or with known art to try the gentle wave.
Much him the honors of his ancient race
Inspire, nor would he his own deeds deface,
And secret joy in his calm soul does rise   675
That Monck looks on to see how Douglas dies.
Like a glad lover the fierce flames he meets
And tries his first embraces in their sheets.
His shape exact, which the bright flames enfold,
Like the sun's statue stands of burnish'd gold.   680
Round the transparent fire about him glows,

649. *Douglas:* Archibald Douglas, who commanded a company of Scottish troops, died in defending the *Royal Oak,* which was fired by the Dutch.

673–74. When Douglas was advised to retire he refused, saying, "It shall never be told that a Douglas quitted his post without orders" (*DNB*).

678. Actually, Douglas left a widow, Frances, who petitioned for a prize ship as compensation (*CSPD, 1667,* p. 430, cited by Margoliouth).

As the clear amber on the bee does close,
And, as on angels' heads their glories shine,
His burning locks adorn his face divine.
But when in his immortal mind he felt   685
His alt'ring form and solder'd limbs to melt,
Down on the deck he laid himself and di'd,
With his dear sword reposing by his side
And on the flaming plank so rests his head
As one that's warm'd himself and gone to bed.   690
His ship burns down and with his relics sinks,
And the sad stream beneath his ashes drinks.
Fortunate boy! If either pencil's fame,
Or if my verse can propagate thy name,
When Oeta and Alcides are forgot,   695
Our English youth shall sing the valiant Scot.
    Each doleful day still with fresh loss returns:
The *Loyal London* now a third time burns,
And the true *Royal Oak* and *Royal James*,
Alli'd in fate, increase with theirs her flames.   700
Of all our navy none should now survive,
But that the ships themselves were taught to dive,
And the kind river in its creek them hides,
Fraughting their pierced keels with oozy tides.
    Up to the bridge contagious terror strook: 705
The Tow'r itself with the near danger shook,
And, were not Ruyter's maw with ravage cloy'd,
E'en London's ashes had been then destroy'd.
Officious fear, however, to prevent
Our loss does so much more our loss augment: 710
The Dutch had robb'd those jewels of the crown;

693. Cf. *The Loyal Scot,* 59–60:

Fortunate boy! if e'er my verse may claim
That matchless grace to propagate thy fame . . .

Margoliouth notes that the change makes the lines here appropriate to the "painter" convention.

695. Hercules (Alcides) was burned to death on Mt. Oeta.

698. The *London* was blown up in March 1665. Then the loyal City of London was burned by the Great Fire. Now the *Loyal London* (cf. *Second Advice,* 13–24) is burned. Cf. Evelyn, 28 June: "the *London* (now the third time burnt)" (Margoliouth).

702. Some ships were sunk to keep them from being burned.

Our merchantmen, lest they be burn'd, we drown.
So when the Fire did not enough devour,
The houses were demolish'd near the Tow'r.
Those ships that yearly from their teeming hole   715
Unloaded here the birth of either pole—
Furs from the north and silver from the west,
Wines from the south, and spices from the east;
From Gambo gold, and from the Ganges gems—
Take a short voyage underneath the Thames,   720
Once a deep river, now with timber floor'd,
And shrunk, least navigable, to a ford.
    Now (nothing more at Chatham left to burn),
The Holland squadron leisurely return,
And, spite of Ruperts and of Albemarles,   725
To Ruyter's triumph lead the captive *Charles.*
The pleasing sight he often does prolong:
Her masts erect, tough cordage, timbers strong,
Her moving shapes, all these he does survey,
And all admires, but most his easy prey.   730
The seamen search her all, within, without:
Viewing her strength, they yet their conquest doubt;
Then with rude shouts, secure, the air they vex,
With gamesome joy insulting on her decks.
Such the fear'd Hebrew, captive, blinded, shorn,   735
Was led about in sport, the public scorn.
    Black day accurs'd! on thee let no man hail
Out of the port, or dare to hoist a sail,
Nor row a boat in thy unlucky hour.
Thee, the year's monster, let thy dam devour,   740
And constant Time, to keep his course yet right,
Fill up thy space with a redoubled night.
When aged Thames was bound with fetters base,
And Medway chaste ravish'd before his face,
And their dear offspring murder'd in their sight,   745

712. Some merchantmen newly-laden with valuable cargo and newly-commissioned
fire ships were sunk in a panic below Woolwich to stop the Dutch (Pepys, 14 June
1667).
715. *hole:* Hold.
722. *least navigable:* At its least navigable point.
735–36. *the fear'd Hebrew:* Samson. See Judges 16.

Thou and thy fellows held'st the odious light.
Sad change since first that happy pair was wed,
When all the rivers grac'd their nuptial bed,
And father Neptune promis'd to resign
His empire old to their immortal line!   750
Now with vain grief their vainer hopes they rue,
Themselves dishonor'd, and the gods untrue,
And to each other, helpless couple, moan,
As the sad tortoise for the sea does groan.
But most they for their darling *Charles* complain,   755
And, were it burnt, yet less would be their pain.
To see that fatal pledge of sea command
Now in the ravisher De Ruyter's hand,
The Thames roar'd, swooning Medway turn'd her tide,
And, were they mortal, both for grief had di'd.   760
    The court in farthing yet itself does please,
And female Stuart there rules the four seas,
But Fate does still accumulate our woes,
And Richmond her commands, as Ruyter those.
    After this loss, to relish discontent,   765
Someone must be accus'd by punishment.
All our miscarriages on Pett must fall:
His name alone seems fit to answer all.
Whose counsel first did this mad war beget?
Who all commands sold through the navy? *Pett.*   770
Who would not follow when the Dutch were beat?
Who treated out the time at Bergen? *Pett.*

747–48. Cf. the marriage of the Thames and the Medway, *Faerie Queene*, IV.11.

762. Frances Stuart, on whom Charles had set his eye, married the Duke of Richmond in 1667. She was the model for Britannia on medals and coins. The farthings of Charles II bore the legend *Quatuor maria vindico* (Margoliouth).

765. *relish:* Make pleasant to the taste.

767. *Pett:* Peter Pett (1610–70?) superintended the dockyard at Chatham. Margoliouth quotes a letter from Henry Savile to his brother, George (18 June): "Commissioner Pett was sent for from Chatham and sent the last night to the Tower. He is most undoubtedly to be sacrificed; all that are greater lay the fault upon him in hopes that he is to bear all the blame; the town has no mind to be so satisfied." Pett was arraigned 31 Oct. and set free on bail of £5,000. Marvell spoke that day against sending him to the Tower (Milward, *Diary*). Impeachment proceedings were begun 19 Dec., but the matter was dropped.

771. On 3 June 1665. It was the Duke of York's flagship that "would not follow." See *Second Advice*, 233–42. *Beat* was pronounced *bet*.

772. Cf. *Second Advice*, 269–92.

Who the Dutch fleet with storms disabl'd met,
And, rifling prizes, them neglected? *Pett.*
Who with false news prevented the *Gazette,*   775
The fleet divided, writ for Rupert? *Pett.*
Who all our seamen cheated of their debt,
And all our prizes who did swallow? *Pett.*
Who did advise no navy out to set,
And who the forts left unrepaired? *Pett.*   780
Who to supply with powder did forget
Landguard, Sheerness, Gravesend and Upnor? *Pett.*
Who all our ships expos'd in Chatham's net?
Who should it be but the Fanatic *Pett?*
Pett, the sea-architect, in making ships,   785
Was the first cause of all these naval slips:
Had he not built, none of these faults had been;
If no creation, there had been no sin.
But, his great crime, one boat away he sent,
That lost our fleet and did our flight prevent.   790
      Then (that reward might in its turn take place,
And march with punishment in equal pace),
Southampton dead, much of the treasure's care
And place in council fell to Duncombe's share.
All men admir'd he to that pitch could fly: 795
Powder ne'er blew man up so soon so high,

773–74. Cf. *Second Advice,* 293–308.
775–76. Cf. *Third Advice,* 283–88, 291–94.
779–80. Sir William Coventry seems to have been most culpable for the failure to set out a fleet in 1667. "It is well known who of the Commissioners of the Treasury gave advice that the charge of setting forth a fleet this year might be spared, Sir W. C. by name" (Evelyn, 29 July 1667).
782. *Landguard:* A fort at Harwich attacked by the Dutch in June 1667.
784. *Fanatic:* Pett had served as a navy commissioner under the Commonwealth. In 1648 he was instrumental in preventing the ships at Chatham from joining the Royalists.
785–88. Cf. the curse on Noah as the first shipbuilder in *Second Advice,* 135–40.
789. The chief charges against Pett were "the not carrying up of the great ships and the using of the boats in carrying away his goods" (Pepys, 19 June 1667).
793. *Southampton:* Thomas Wriothesley, fourth Earl of Southampton (1607–67), Lord High Treasurer, had died in the spring, and the treasury was put in charge of a commission consisting of Albemarle, Ashley, Sir W. Coventry, Sir John Duncombe, and Sir Thomas Clifford. Duncombe was actually appointed to the commission three weeks before the Dutch attack (Margoliouth).
795. Pepys (31 May 1667): "I saw Duncombe look as big and take as much state on him as if he had been born a lord."

But sure his late good husbandry in petre
Show'd him to manage the Exchequer meeter;
And who the forts would not vouchsafe a corn,
To lavish the King's money more would scorn.   800
Who hath no chimneys, to give all is best,
And ablest Speaker, who of law has least;
Who less estate, for Treasurer most fit,
And for a couns'lor, he that has least wit.
But the true cause was that, in's brother May,   805
Th' Exchequer might the Privy-Purse obey.
    But now draws near the Parliament's return;
Hyde and the Court again begin to mourn:
Frequent in council, earnest in debate,
All arts they try how to prolong its date.   810
Grave primate Sheldon (much in preaching there)
Blames the last session and this more does fear:
With Boynton or with Middleton 'twere sweet,
But with a Parliament abhors to meet
And thinks 'twill ne'er be well within this nation,   815
Till it be govern'd by a Convocation.
But in the Thames' mouth still De Ruyter laid;
The peace not sure, new army must be paid.
Hyde saith he hourly waits for a dispatch;
Harry came post just as he show'd his watch,   820
All to agree the articles were clear,

797. *petre:* Saltpetre, an ingredient in gunpowder. Duncombe had been Master of the Ordnance, in which capacity he could have made illicit profits.

799. *corn:* A grain of gunpowder.

801–02. Margoliouth notes that Duncombe's poverty and political inexperience are the butt of these lines.

805. *brother May:* Baptist May, Keeper of the Privy Purse, Duncombe's brother-in-law.

811. *Sheldon:* Gilbert Sheldon (1598–1677), Archbishop of Canterbury, according to Pepys "as very a wencher as can be" (29 July 1667).

813. *Boynton and Middleton:* Katherine Boynton and Mrs. Charles Middleton were court beauties.

816. *Convocation:* i.e. of bishops.

820. *Harry:* Henry Coventry. On 8 July Pepys wrote: "Mr. Coventry is come from Breda, as was expected, but, contrary to expectation, brings with him two or three articles which do not please the King" (quoted by Margoliouth).

821–26. The idea here seems to be that Ambassador Coventry was eager to believe that the articles implied an early settlement because he was confronted by the double threat of the Dutch fleet and the approaching session of Parliament in which the war with Holland would be attacked as a grievance.

The Holland fleet and Parliament so near;
Yet Harry must job back and all mature,
Binding, ere th' Houses meet, the treaty sure,
And 'twixt necessity and spite, till then,   825
Let them come up so to go down again.
    Up ambles country justice on his pad
And vest bespeaks to be more seemly clad.
Plain gentlemen in stagecoach are o'erthrown
And deputy-lieutenants in their own.   830
The portly burgess through the weather hot
Does for his corporation sweat and trot;
And all with sun and choler come adust
And threaten Hyde to raise a greater dust.
But, fresh as from the mint, the courtiers fine   835
Salute them, smiling at their vain design,
And Turnor gay up to his perch does march
With face new bleach'd, smoothen'd and stiff with starch;
Tells them he at Whitehall had took a turn
And for three days thence moves them to adjourn.   840
"Not so!" quoth Tomkins, and straight drew his tongue,
Trusty as steel, that always ready hung;
And so, proceeding in his motion warm,
Th' army soon rais'd he doth as soon disarm.
True Trojan! While this town can girls afford,   845
And long as cider lasts in Hereford,
The girls shall always kiss thee, though grown old,
And in eternal healths thy name be troll'd.
    Meanwhile the certain news of peace arrives

826. The House met 25 July and was dismissed 29 July.

828. *vest:* A garment designed by Charles II to make English fashions independent of France. See Pepys, 15 Oct. 1666, for a description.

833. *adust:* Dried up with heat.

837. *Turnor:* The Speaker. See note on line 114.

839–40. "The Speaker told them, as soon as they were sat, that he was ordered by the King . . . to move that they would adjourn themselves till Monday next" (Pepys, 25 July, cited by Margoliouth).

841–44. See note on 233–34. "But before they would come to the question whether they would adjourn, Sir Thomas Tomkins steps up and tells them that all the country is grieved at the new-raised standing army; and that they thought themselves safe enough in their train-bands; and that, therefore, he desired the King might be moved to disband them" (Pepys, 25 July 1667).

846. *Hereford:* Tomkins' county.

At court and so reprieves their guilty lives. 850
Hyde orders Turnor that he should come late,
Lest some new Tomkins spring a fresh debate.
The King that day rais'd early from his rest,
Expects (as at a play) till Turnor's dress'd.
At last together Eaton come and he: 855
No dial more could with the sun agree.
The Speaker, summon'd, to the Lords repairs,
Nor gave the Commons leave to say their pray'rs,
But like his pris'ners to the bar them led,
Where mute they stand to hear their sentence read. 860
Trembling with joy and fear, Hyde them prorogues,
And had almost mistook and call'd them rogues.
　Dear Painter, draw this Speaker to the foot;
Where pencil cannot, there my pen shall do't:
That may his body, this his mind explain. 865
Paint him in golden gown, with mace's brain,
Bright hair, fair face, obscure and dull of head,
Like knife with iv'ry haft and edge of lead.
At pray'rs his eyes turn up the pious white,
But all the while his private bill's in sight. 870
In chair he smoking sits like master cook,
And a poll-bill does like his apron look.
Well was he skill'd to season any question
And make a sauce fit for Whitehall's digestion,
Whence ev'ry day, the palate more to tickle, 875
Court-mushrumps ready are sent in in pickle.

851–52. "The Speaker . . . was kept from coming in the morning to the House on purpose, till after the King was come to the House of Lords, for fear they should be doing anything in the House of Commons to the further dissatisfaction of the King and his courtiers" (Pepys, 29 July, quoted by Margoliouth).
855. *Eaton:* Sir John Eaton or Ayton, Usher of the Black Rod.
858. There is no mention of the customary morning prayers at the beginning of the session of 29 July in *CJ*. Cf. Milward (29 July 1667): "the Speaker came not until almost an hour after the King was come to the House of Lords; we had not time for prayers nor did I see the Chaplain."
870–72. The Speaker received large fees from the passage of private bills. Turnor sweats like a cook while the bill is being voted on, and a poll-bill such as that by which part of the supply was raised in 1666–67 might resemble his spotted apron because of various amendments attached to it.
874. As Margoliouth notes, Turnor was chiefly distinguished by the courtly style of his addresses to the throne.

When grievance urg'd, he swells like squatted toad,
Frisks like a frog to croak a tax's load;
His patient piss he could hold longer than
An urinal and sit like any hen;   880
At table jolly as a country host
And soaks his sack with Norfolk like a toast;
At night than Chanticleer more brisk and hot,
And Sergeant's wife serves him for Pertelotte.

Paint last the King and a dead shade of night,   885
Only dispers'd by a weak taper's light,
And those bright gleams that dart along and glare
From his clear eyes (yet these too dark with care).
There, as in th' calm horror all alone
He wakes and muses of th' uneasy throne,   890
Raise up a sudden shape with virgin's face,
(Though ill agree her posture, hour, or place),
Naked as born, and her round arms behind
With her own tresses interwove and twin'd;
Her mouth lock'd up, a blind before her eyes,   895
Yet from beneath the veil her blushes rise,
And silent tears her secret anguish speak;
Her heart throbs and with very shame would break.
The object strange in him no terror mov'd:
He wonder'd first, then piti'd, then he lov'd   900
And with kind hand does the coy vision press
(Whose beauty greater seem'd by her distress),
But soon shrunk back, chill'd with her touch so cold,
And th' airy picture vanish'd from his hold.
In his deep thoughts the wonder did increase,   905
And he divin'd 'twas England or the Peace.
Express him startling next with list'ning ear,

882. *Norfolk:* James Norfolk, Sergeant-at-Arms.
884. Cf. Marvell, *Further Advice to a Painter,* 13–16:

> draw Sir Edward mounted on his throne,
> Whose life does scarce one generous action own,
> Unless it be his late assumed grief
> To keep his own and lose his Sergeant's wife.

The *Sergeant* is Norfolk.
907. *startling:* Starting.

As one that some unusual noise does hear.
With cannon, trumpets, drums, his door surround,
But let some other painter draw the sound.   910
Thrice did he rise, thrice the vain tumult fled,
But again thunders when he lies in bed.
His mind secure does the known stroke repeat
And finds the drums Louis's march did beat.
Shake then the room and all his curtains tear   915
And with blue streaks infect the taper clear,
While the pale ghosts his eye does fix'd admire
Of grandsire Harry and of Charles his sire.
Harry sits down, and in his open side
The grisly wound reveals of which he di'd,   920
And ghastly Charles, turning his collar low,
The purple thread about his neck does show,
Then, whisp'ring to his son in words unheard,
Through the lock'd door both of them disappear'd.
The wondrous night the pensive King revolves,   925
And rising straight on Hyde's disgrace resolves.
At his first step he Castlemaine does find,
Bennet, and Coventry, as't were design'd;
And they, not knowing, the same thing propose
Which his hid mind did in its depths enclose.   930
Through their feign'd speech their secret hearts he knew:
To her own husband, Castlemaine untrue;
False to his master Bristol, Arlington;
And Coventry, falser than anyone,
Who to the brother, brother would betray,   935

913. *secure:* Careless, overconfident. Now *arch.*

918. *grandsire Harry:* Henry IV of France, father of Henrietta Maria. He was assassinated by Ravaillac in 1610.

927–28. Lady Castlemaine, Bennet, and Sir William Coventry were Clarendon's worst enemies at Court.

933. *Bristol:* George Digby, second Earl of Bristol (1612–77), a Roman Catholic, had attempted to impeach Clarendon in 1663 (cf. *Second Advice,* 147–48) and renewed his attack on 29 July 1667. Bennet had been in Bristol's employ as early as 1643, but they quarreled on the advisability of Charles II declaring his conversion to Catholicism (Margoliouth).

934–36. Presumably an allusion to Sir William Coventry's position as the Duke of York's secretary, in which capacity, Marvell implies, he acted against the King's interests.

Nor therefore trusts himself to such as they.
His father's ghost too whisper'd him one note,
That who does cut his purse will cut his throat,
But in wise anger he their crimes forbears,
As thieves repriev'd for executioners;   940
While Hyde, provok'd, his foaming tusk does whet,
To prove them traitors and himself the Pett.
    Painter, adieu! How well our arts agree,
Poetic picture, painted poetry;
But this great work is for our Monarch fit,   945
And henceforth Charles only to Charles shall sit.
His master-hand the ancients shall outdo,
Himself the painter and the poet too.

To the King

    So his bold tube man to the sun appli'd
And spots unknown to the bright star descri'd,   950
Show'd they obscure him while too near they prease,
And seem his courtiers, are but his disease.
Through optic trunk the planet seem'd to hear,
And hurls them off e'er since in his career.
    And you, great Sir, that with him empire share,   955
Sun of our world, as he the Charles is there,
Blame not the Muse that brought those spots to sight,
Which, in your splendor hid, corrode your light:
Kings in the country oft have gone astray
Nor of a peasant scorn'd to learn the way.   960
Would she the unattended throne reduce,
Banishing love, trust, ornament, and use,
Better it were to live in cloister's lock,
Or in fair fields to rule the easy flock.
She blames them only who the Court restrain   965
And, where all England serves, themselves would reign.
    Bold and accurs'd are they that all this while
Have strove to isle our Monarch from his isle,
And to improve themselves, on false pretence,
About the common Prince have rais'd a fence;   970
The kingdom from the crown distinct would see

951. *prease:* Press.

And peel the bark to burn at last the tree.
But Ceres corn, and Flora is the spring,
Bacchus is wine, the country is the king.
Not so does rust insinuating wear,   975
Nor powder so the vaulted bastion tear,
Nor earthquakes so an hollow isle o'erwhelm,
As scratching courtiers undermine a realm
And through the palace's foundations bore,
Burr'wing themselves to hoard their guilty store.   980
The smallest vermin make the greatest waste,
And a poor warren once a city ras'd.
But they whom, born to virtue and to wealth,
Nor guilt to flatt'ry binds, nor want to stealth;
Whose gen'rous conscience and whose courage high   985
Does with clear counsels their large souls supply;
That serve the King with their estates and care,
And as in love on Parliaments can stare,
Where few the number, choice is there less hard:
Give us this Court and rule without a guard.   990

982. See Pliny, *Nat. Hist.* 8.43 (Margoliouth).

The Fourth and Fifth Advices to a Painter
(*1667*)

Together these satires recount events between the parliamentary session which began in September 1666 and the flight of Clarendon on 29 November 1667. They traverse most of the same ground covered by *Last Instructions,* which is one reason, as Margoliouth points out, for not ascribing them to the same author.

Although the fourth and fifth *Advices* share the basic political views of the earlier mock *Advices* and *Last Instructions,* their technique is much less circumstantial. The painter convention is used perfunctorily, and the vivid pictorial effects of the others are lacking. In their outspoken attacks on Charles II as a latter-day Nero and an effeminate monarch, these two poems also are to be distinguished from the others, which all have envoys (lacking here) carefully distinguishing the King from his ministers.

In poetical technique the fourth and fifth *Advices* are clearly inferior to the other three poems. Differences in attitude and style indicate that they did not issue from the same hand or hands as the others. Nevertheless the author or an unidentified publisher printed all four *Advices* in 1667, presumably in the hope of capitalizing on the popularity of the first two, which had been published together earlier in the year. This small octavo volume, which also prints *Clarendon's Housewarming* as the work of an unknown author, identifies the four *Advices* as "the Last Works of Sir John Denham." The ascription of these satires to Denham was clearly a blind to conceal the true authors, who would have been prosecuted if known. There seems little hope of discovering the real identity of the author of the fourth and fifth *Advices,* but the Latin epigram on King Charles with which the latter poem concludes has been attributed to Rochester, according to Margoliouth, upon what evidence he does not say.

THE FOURTH ADVICE TO A PAINTER

Draw England ruin'd by what was giv'n before,
And draw the Commons slow in giving more.
Too late grown wiser, they their treasure see
Consum'd by fraud or lost by treachery,
And vainly now would some account receive   5
Of those vast sums which they so idly gave
And trusted to the management of such
As Dunkirk sold to make war with the Dutch—
Dunkirk, once destin'd for a nobler use
Than to erect a petty lawyer's house.   10
But what account could they from those expect
Who, to grow rich themselves, the state neglect?
Men who in England have no other lot
Than what they by betraying it have got;
Who can pretend to nothing but disgrace   15
Where either birth or merit find a place.
Plague, fire, and war have been the nation's curse,
But to have these our rulers is a worse.
Yet draw these causers of our kingdom's woe
Still urging danger from our growing foe,   20
Asking new aid for war with the same face
As if, when giv'n, they meant not to make peace.
Meanwhile they cheat the public with such haste
They will have nothing that may ease it pass'd.

1–8. £1,800,000 was voted in September 1666 before the lower House was all as-sembled. Once the Country members had taken their seats, it became evident that they suspected a mishandling of the previous appropriation. A proviso was inserted into the Poll Tax Bill by which the new appropriation was to be raised directing a Parlia-mentary commission to investigate the accounts of the officers involved. Cf. Pepys (8 Dec. 1666): "there shall be a committee of nine persons that shall have the inspection upon oath . . . of all the accounts of the money given and spent for this war. This hath a most sad face and will breed ill blood."

8. Cf. *Second Advice*, note on lines 149–50.

9–10. Bristol had accused Clarendon of making £100,000 for himself on the sale of Dunkirk, and the eleventh article of impeachment later blamed him for the sale, though there is reason to believe he was acting at Charles' behest. The Clarendon profits were popularly thought to have built Hyde's pretentious house near St. James, and so it came to be known as "Dunkirk House" (Pepys, 20 Feb. 1665). Cf. *Clarendon's Housewarming*.

The law 'gainst Irish cattle they condemn   25
As showing distrust o'th' King, that is, of them.
Yet they must now swallow this bitter pill
Or money want, which were the greater ill,
And then the King to Westminster is brought
Imperfectly to speak the Chanc'llor's thought,   30
In which, as if no age could parallel
A prince and council that had rul'd so well,
He tells the Parliament he cannot brook
Whate'er in them like jealousy doth look;
Adds that no grievances the nation load,   35
While we're undone at home, despis'd abroad.
Thus pass'd the Irish with the Money Bill,
The first not half so good as th'other ill.
With these new millions might we not expect
Our foes to vanquish and ourselves protect?   40
If not to beat them off usurped seas,
At least to force an honorable peace?
But though the angry fate (or folly, rather)
Of our perverted state allow us neither,
Could we hope less than to defend our shores,   45
Than guard our harbors, forts, our ships and stores?
We hop'd in vain—of those remaining are,
Not what we sav'd, but what the Dutch did spare.
Such was our rulers' gen'rous stratagem,

25. *Irish cattle:* On 18 Jan. 1667 the Poll Tax and the Irish Bill were passed, the
latter being "An Act Prohibiting the Importation of Cattle from Ireland," a pro-
tectionist measure. Clarendon was violently opposed to the bill on the grounds that
it deprived the King of his dispensing power.

29–42. "The eighth of February the King came to the Parliament, and the Speaker
of the House presented the Bill to the King, who gave his royal assent to it and
thanked them for it, with his assurance 'that the money should be laid out for the
ends it was given [for].' He told them, 'the season of the year was very far spent, in
which the enemy had got great advantage, but, by the help of God, he would make
all the preparations he could, and as fast as he could: and yet he would tell them
that if any good overtures were made for an honorable peace, he would not reject
them. . . .'

'He did pray them,' and said, 'he did expect it from them that they would use
their utmost endeavors to remove all those false imaginations out of the hearts of
the people, which the malice of ill men had industriously infused into them of he
knew not what jealousies and grievances: for he must tell them again, and he was
sure he was in the right, that the people had never so little cause to complain of
oppression and grievances as they had since his return to them" (Clarendon, *Life*,
sections 1012, 1013).

A policy worthy of none but them.   50
   After two millions more laid on the nation,
The Parliament grows ripe for prorogation:
They rise, and now a treaty is confess'd,
'Gainst which before those state cheats did protest,
A treaty which too well makes it appear   55
Theirs, not the kingdom's int'rest, is their care.
Statesmen of old thought arms the way to peace:
Ours scorn such threadbare policies as these.
All that was given for the state's defense
These think too little for their own expense;   60
Or if from that they anything can spare,
It is to buy peace, not maintain a war,
For which great work ambassadors must go
With base submissions to our arming foe.
These, leaving a defenseless state behind,   65
Vasts fleets preparing by the Belgians find,
Against whose fury what can us defend,
Whilst our great politicians here depend
Upon the Dutch good nature? For when peace
(Say they) is making, acts of war must cease.   70
Thus were we by the name of truce betray'd,
Though by the Dutch nothing like it was made.
   Here, Painter, let thine art describe a story,
Shaming our warlike island's ancient glory:

53. After Charles prorogued Parliament on 8 Feb., Breda was agreed on as a location for peace negotiations with the Dutch, although the Dutch were known to be preparing their fleet for a campaign. As the preceding note shows, Charles was quite open in advocating an "honorable peace," and neither Parliament nor people was deceived on this score.

63–66. "On the same day [7 June] that Henry Coventry landed at Dover bearing the preliminary articles of peace from Breda, a fleet of 50–70 Dutch ships was sighted off the North Foreland, and at 8 p.m. it was seen to anchor in the Gunfleet" (Ogg, *England in the Reign of Charles II, 1,* 309).

71–72. Tedder, the naval historian, concurs in the poet's opinion. The ill-judged policy of retrenchment began with the decommissioning of first- and second-line ships in October 1666. "Months later, when this policy had borne its inevitable fruit, much complaint was made from English sources of the 'perfidy' of the Dutch, who, under cover of the peace negotiations, had made so base and dishonorable an attack on England. But really it is difficult to see much deeper grounds for these assertions than those of injured pride and dignity. It is obvious that the continuance of the war in the meantime was a fact perfectly understood and accepted by the English authorities, and measures were taken all along the coast for the fortification of important posts against possible Dutch attacks" (*The Navy of the Restoration,* p. 181).

A scene which never on our seas appear'd,   75
Since our first ships were on the ocean steer'd.
Make the Dutch fleet, while we supinely sleep,
Without opposers, masters of the deep.
Make them securely the Thames' mouth invade,
At once depriving us of that and trade.   80
Draw thunder from their floating castles sent
Against our forts, weak as our government.
Draw Woolwich, Deptford, London, and the Tow'r
Meanly abandon'd to a foreign pow'r.
Yet turn their first attempts another way,   85
And let their cannons upon Sheerness play,
Which soon destroy'd, their lofty vessels ride
Big with the hope of the approaching tide.
Make them more help from our remissness find
Than from the tide, or from the eastern wind.   90
Their canvas swelling with a prosp'rous gale,
Swift as our fears, make them to Chatham sail;
Through our weak chain their fireships break the way
And our great ships unmann'd become their prey.

79. The Dutch fleet entered the Thames on the evening of June 7th and remained anchored in some part of the river for more than a month, "a dreadful spectacle as ever any Englishman saw, and a dishonor never to be wiped off" (Evelyn, 28 June 1667).

83. *Woolwich:* The chief dockyard of the Restoration navy, nine miles east of St. Paul's. To prevent Dutch seizure, Prince Rupert hastened there and sank several loaded supply ships in the harbor (Evelyn, 14 June 1667). *Deptford:* A navy dockyard on the right bank of the Thames, three miles southeast of London Bridge. The immense victualing yard is still in use.

86. *Sheerness:* A naval seaport and garrison town on the Isle of Sheppey, off the right bank of the Medway at its junction with the Thames. "The Dutch, after easily beating off Sir Edward Spragge from Sheerness Fort, which was not in a posture of defense (for which Sir Edward is much blamed), forced the chain, which some say was fastened with cable yarn, and came up" (*CSPD*, 15 June 1667).

87. *lofty vessels:* Cf. *Annus Mirabilis*, 233–34:

> On high-rais'd decks the haughty Belgians ride,
> Beneath whose shade our humble frigates go.

92. *Chatham:* A Kentish seaport on the right bank of the Medway, 34 miles E.S.E. of London. In Charles' time it became the chief naval station of England.

93. The chain was broken about noon, 12 June 1667.

94. *unmann'd:* Of 1100 Chatham yard employees, unpaid for months, only three could be persuaded to attend the Duke of Albemarle. Cf. *Last Instructions*, 601–02.

Then draw the fruit of our ill-manag'd cost,   95
At once our honor and our safety lost.
Bury those bulwarks of our isle in smoke,
While their thick flames the neighb'ring country choke.
The *Charles* escapes the raging element
To be with triumph into Holland sent,   100
Where the glad people to the shore resort
To see their terror now become their sport.
    But, Painter, fill not up thy piece before
Thou paint'st confusion on our troubl'd shore:
Instruct then thy bold pencil to relate   105
The saddest marks of an ill-govern'd state.
Draw th'injur'd seamen deaf to all command,
While some with horror and amazement stand.
Others will know no enemy but they
Who have unjustly robb'd them of their pay,   110
Boldly refusing to oppose a fire
To kindle which our errors did conspire.
Some, though but few, persuaded to obey,
Useless for want of ammunition stay.
The forts design'd to guard our ships of war   115
Void both of powder and of bullets are,
And what past reigns in peace did ne'er omit
The present, whilst invaded, doth forget.
    Surpassing Chatham, make Whitehall appear,
If not in danger, yet at least in fear.   120
Make our dejection, if thou canst, seem more
Than our pride, sloth, and ign'rance did before.
The King of danger now shows far more fear
Than he did ever, to prevent it, care;

97. The Dutch fired the *Unity, Amity, Charles V, Monmouth*, and *Matthias*. Later they reached three ships half-sunk, the *Royal Oak, Loyal London*, and *James*, which they also fired.

99. The *Royal Charles*, formerly the *Naseby*, had brought Charles II to Dover in May 1660. An unpaid, mutinous crew did nothing to prevent the Dutch from seizing it and towing it home. Its stern-piece is today displayed in an Amsterdam museum.

109–18. "In the Medway the fireships were unmanned, the guardships half manned, the forts without guns, and according to some accounts even the chain was not yet in place. Not merely was the work not done, but there were no men to do it when Albemarle arrived. Men who had not been paid for months refused to work in this emergency" (Tedder, p. 183).

Yet to the city doth himself convey,   125
Bravely to show he was not run away,
Whilst the Black Prince and our fifth Henry's wars
Are only acted on our theaters.
    As Nero once, with harp in hand, survey'd
His flaming Rome and, as that burn'd, he play'd,   130
So our great Prince, when the Dutch fleet arriv'd,
Saw his ships burn'd and, as they burn'd, he swiv'd.
So kind he was in our extremest need,
He would those flames extinguish with his seed.
But against Fate all human aid is vain: 135
His pr— then prov'd as useless as his chain.
    Our statesmen, finding no expedient,
I'th' fear of danger, but a Parliament,
Twice would avoid by clapping up a peace:
The cure's to them as bad as the disease.   140
But, Painter, end here till it doth appear
Which most, the Dutch or Parliament, they fear.

THE FIFTH ADVICE TO A PAINTER

Painter, where was't thy former work did cease?
Oh, 'twas at Parliament and the brave peace!

125–26. Cf. Burnet, *History, 1,* 448: The King "was intending to retire to Windsor, but that looked so like a flying from danger, that he was prevailed on to stay. And it was given out that he was cheerful that night at supper with his mistress, which drew many libels upon him that were writ with as much wit as malice and brought him under a general contempt. He was compared to Nero, who sung while Rome was burning." Cf. lines 135–38.

127. *The Black Prince* and *Henry V* are rhymed tragedies by Roger Boyle, first Earl of Orrery. Pepys saw the first-night performance of *The Black Prince* 19 Oct. 1667, and in his entry refers to Orrery's earlier play, which was first performed 13 Aug. 1664.

129–36. "Sir H. Chumley come to me this day, and tells me the Court is as mad as ever and that the night the Dutch burned our ships the King did sup with my Lady Castlemaine at the Duchess of Monmouth's and they were all mad in hunting a poor moth" (Pepys, 21 June 1667).

139. Parliament was prorogued to October 10th, but the pressure of events led to Charles' summoning it by proclamation to meet July 25th. He then adjourned it to July 29th, announced the conclusion of the Peace, and prorogued it to October 10th, thereby *twice avoiding* sessions which would have dwelt on grievances arising from the War.

Now for a cornucopia: peace, you know,
Brings plenty with it; wish it be not woe!
Draw coats of pageantry and proclamations   5
Of peace concluded with one, two, three nations.
Canst thou not on the 'Change make merchants grin,
Like outward smiles while vexing thought's within?
Thou art no artist, if thou canst not feign
And counterfeit the counterfeit disdain.   10
   Draw a brave standard, ruffling at a rate
Much other than it did for Chatham's fate.
The Tow'r guns too, thund'ring their joys, that they
Have 'scap'd the danger of being ta'en away.
These, as now mann'd, for triumph are, not fight,   15
As painted fire for show, not heat or light.
   Amongst the roar of these and the mad shout
Of a poor nothing-understanding rout,
That think the on-and-off-peace now is true,
Thou might'st draw mourners for black Barthol'mew: 20
Mourners in Sion! Oh 'tis not to be
Discover'd! Draw a curtain courteously
To hide them. Now proceed to draw at night
A bonfire here and there, but none too bright
Nor lasting, for 'twas brushwood, as they say,   25
Which they that hop'd for coals now flung away.
   But stay, I had forgot my mother! Draw

5–6. The Treaty of Breda was signed 21 July 1667 and proclaimed 24 August (St. Bartholomew's Day). There were three separate instruments with Holland, France, and Denmark.

7. "At the office all morning and at noon to the 'Change, where I met Fenn; and he tells me that Sir John Coventry do bring the confirmation of the peace; but I do not find the 'Change at all glad of it, but rather the worse, they looking upon it as a peace made only to preserve the King for a time in his lusts and ease, and to sacrifice trade and his kingdoms only to his own pleasures" (Pepys, 27 July 1667).

19. on-and-off-peace: So called because the English had retrenched their naval expenses during the preceding winter in expectation of the peace and because the Dutch attacked Sheerness just as the English ambassador was returning from Breda with the preliminary articles.

20. black Barthol'mew: 24 August 1662, the day on which Nonconformist ministers were ejected from their livings under the Act of Uniformity.

23–26. Because of Dutch attacks on the collier fleets, coal was "very dear, viz. 27s. per chaldron" (CSPD, 12 Sept. 1667).

27. mother: Mother Church.

The Church of England 'mongst thy *opera,*
To play their part too, or the Dutch will say
In war and peace they've borne the bell away.   30
At this end then, two or three steeples ringing,
At th' other end draw choirs *Te Deum* singing;
Between them leave a space for tears: remember
That 'tis not long to th' second of September.
    Now if thou skill'st prospective landscape, draw   35
At distance what perhaps thine eyes ne'er saw:
Pularoon, Spicy Islands, Kitts, or Guinea;
Surinam, Nova Scotia, or Virginia.
No, no! I mean not these, pray hold your laughter:
These things are far off, not worth looking after.   40
Give not a hint of these: draw highland, lowland,
Mountains and flats; draw Scotland first, then Holland.
See, canst thou ken the Scots' frowns? Then draw those
That something had to get but nought to lose.
Canst thou through fogs discern the Dutchmen drink?   45
Buss-skippers, lately capers, stamp to think
Their catching craft is over; some have ta'en,
To eke the war, a warrant from the Dane.
But passing these, their statesmen view a while,
In ev'ry graver countenance a smile: 50
Copy the piece there done, wherein you'll see
One laughing out, "I told you how 'twould be!"
    Draw next a pompous interchange of seals;
But curs'd be he that articles reveals
Before he knows them! Now for this take light   55

30. A pun on the phrase *to bear away the bell,* to carry off the prize.
34. The Great Fire broke out 2 Sept. 1666.
37–38. Except for Virginia all these places were involved in the Peace of Breda. Holland retained the Spice Islands, including Pularoon. England lost Surinam and most of her holdings in Guinea. She regained her share of St. Christopher at the cost of yielding part of Nova Scotia to France. Virginia had suffered much by the war. As Lodge observes, however, "the annexation of New York and New Jersey was worth infinitely more than anything which was lost elsewhere" (*Political History,* p. 80).
43. The Scots frown because peace has put an end to their profitable privateering.
46–48. Dutch privateersmen are annoyed with peace for the same reason that the Scots are (see note above). *Busses* are herring-boats, *capers* privateers. According to the poet some Dutch skippers continued privateering under Danish letters of marque.

From him that did describe Sir Edward's fight:
You may perhaps the truth of 't doubt—what though?
You'll have it then *cum privilegio.*
Then draw our Lords Commissioners' advance,
Not Romewards, but for Flanders, or for France;   60
There to parlier a while, until they see
How things in Parliament resented be.
    So much for peace. Now for a Parliament:
A petty session draw, with what content
Guess by their countenance who came up post,   65
And quickly saw they had their labor lost,
Like the small merchants when they bargains sell:
"Come hither Jack! What say? Come kiss, farewell."
But 'twas abortive, born before its day;
No wonder then it di'd so soon away.   70
Yet breath'd it once, and that with such a force,
It blasted thirty-thousand foot and horse.
As once Prometheus' man did sneeze so hard,
As routed all that new-rais'd standing guard

56. *The London Gazette* gave some highly laudatory accounts of Sir Edward Spragge's activities against the Dutch as Vice-Admiral of the Blue, commanding at Sheerness. There is a most glowing account of his skill and courage in the action of 23 July (no. 177), but, as the next issue points out, Sir Edward was not aboard his ship at the time.

58. *cum privilegio* [*ad imprimendum solum*]: A sardonic reference to the *Gazette*, the official and only licensed newspaper, which carried the words "published with authority" on its masthead.

59. *Lords Commissioners:* Ambassadors Coventry and Holles.

61. *parlier:* To speak French, the only instance given in *OED*.

64. *petty session:* Parliament met on 29 July. The King announced the conclusion of peace and dismissed them. "Some of them had come from a great distance, travelling under the difficulties of that time in the heat of summer, when they would have been more useful at home; they were dismissed without anything having been transacted, without thanks for their trouble" (Ranke, *3*, 454).

67. To sell a bargain is to make a fool of a person.

71–76. "The King put off the opening a few days to allow the still missing members time to arrive; but that did not hinder those who were present from proceeding to discuss the principal grievance of the day, the maintenance of the standing army. . . . The proposal was made that the express wish of the House for the disbanding of the army immediately on the conclusion of peace should be carried to the King by those members of the Privy Council who were also members of the House" (Ranke, *3*, 453).

73–75. This seems to be a garbled version of the story of Cadmus and the dragon's teeth in *Metamorphoses* 3.

Of teeth, to keep the tongue in order—so   75
Down fall our new gallants without a foe.
But if this little one could do so much,
What will the next? Give a prophetic touch,
If thou know'st how; if not, leave a great space
For great things to be portray'd in their place.   80
   Now draw the shadow of a Parliament,
As if to scare the upper world 'twere sent.
Cross yourselves, gentlemen, for shades will fright,
Especially if it be an English sprite!
Vermilion this man's guilt, ceruse his fears,   85
Sink th'other's eyes deep in his head with cares.
Another thought some on accounts to see
How his disbursement with receipts agree.
Peep into coaches, see periwigs neglected,
Cross'd arms and legs of such as are suspected,   90
Or do suspect what's coming, and foresee
Themselves must share in this polytrophy.
   Painter, hast travell'd? Didst thou e'er see Rome?
That fam'd piece there, Angelo's day of doom?
Horrors and anguish of descenders there,   95
May teach thee how to paint descenders here.
Canst thou describe the empty shifts are made,
Like that which dealers call forcing a trade?
Some shift their crimes, some places, and, among
The rest, some will their countries too, ere long.   100
Draw in a corner gamesters, shuffling, cutting,
Their little crafts, no wit, together putting:
How to pack knaves, 'mongst kings and queens, to make
A saving game, whilst heads are at the stake.
But cross their cards, until it be confess'd   105

81–92. Parliament met again October 10th and began an investigation of corruption and mismanagement in the navy.

85. *ceruse:* To paint the face with ceruse, a white cosmetic.

92. *polytrophy:* Abundant or excessive nutrition. The word was probably confused with *polytropy.*

94. *Angelo's day of doom:* The frescoes on the ceiling of the Sistine Chapel. Cf. *Second Advice,* 112.

95. *descenders:* The damned descending to Hell.

104. *a saving game:* Neither winning nor losing.

105. *cross:* Thwart.

Of all the play fair dealing is the best.
Draw a veil of displeasure, one to Hyde,
And some prepar'd to strike a blow on's side.
Let him that built high now creep low to shelter,
When potentates must tumble helter-skelter.   110
The purse, seal, mace are gone, as it was fit:
Such marks as these could not choose but be hit.
The purse, seal, mace are gone: Barthol'mew day,
Of all the days i'th' year, they're ta'en away.
The purse, seal, mace are gone, but to another   115
Mitre, I wish not so, though to my brother.
I care not for translation to a see,
Unless they would translate to Italy.
   Now draw a sail playing before the wind
From the northwest; that which it leaves behind,   120
Curses or outcries, mind them not, till when
They do appear realities, and then
Spare not to paint them in their colors, though
Crimes of a viceroy: deputies have so
Been serv'd ere now. But if the man prove true,   125
Let him, with Pharaoh's butler, have his due.
Make the same wind blow strong against the shore
Of France, to hinder some from coming o'er.
And rather draw the golden vessel burning,
E'en there, than hither with her freight returning.   130
'Tis true, the noble Treasurer is gone,
Wise, faithful, loyal, some say th'only one.
Yet I will hope we've pilots left behind
Can steer our vessel without southern wind.

107. There seems to be a rather feeble pun here on *Hyde-hide*.

111–14. *The purse, seal, mace are gone:* Clarendon was removed from the offices of Commissioner of the Exchequer, Keeper of the Great Seal, and Lord Chancellor on 30 August and not, as the poem says, on St. Bartholomew's Day, 24 August.

115–18. Clarendon had been a member of the Middle Temple, but the poet may have thought he was a member of Mitre Court. Perhaps he is using *mitre* in the sense of barrister.

126. See Genesis 11.

129. *the golden vessel:* The ship which took Clarendon to France.

131. *noble Treasurer:* Thomas Wriothesley, fourth Earl of Southampton, who was Treasurer from the Restoration until his death on 16 May 1667.

134. *without southern wind:* Without Catholic influences.

Women have grossly snar'd the wisest prince   135
That ever was before, or hath been since:
And grandam Athaliah in that nation
Was a great hinderer of reformation.
Paint in a new piece painted Jezebel;
Give't to adorn the dining room of Hell.   140
Hang by her others of the gang, for more
Deserve a place with Rosamond, Jane Shore.
    Stay, Painter! now look, here's below a space;
I'th' bottom of all this, what shall we place?
Shall it be Pope, or Turk, or prince, or nun?   145
Let the resolve write *nescio*. So have done.
Expose thy piece now to the world to see,
Perhaps they'll say of it, of thee, of me,
Poems and paints can speak sometimes bold truths,
Poets and painters are licentious youths.   150

*Quae sequuntur, in limine thalami regii, a nescio
quo nebulone scripta, reperibantur:*

Bella fugis, bellas sequeris, belloque repugnas,
    et bellatori sunt tibi bella tori;
imbelles imbellis amas, audaxque videris   155
Mars ad opus Veneris, Martis ad arma Venus.

137. The pro-Catholic contrivances of the Queen Mother, Henrietta Maria, are here
glanced at. *Athaliah* tried to secure the throne of Judah for herself by killing all the
members of the royal family she could find, but a priest named Jehoida organized a
revolution in which she was slain and the dynasty of David restored (2 David 11, 12).
    139. *painted Jezebel:* Probably the Duchess of Castlemaine, Charles II's mistress
since 1660.
    142. *Rosamond:* Mistress of Henry II. *Jane Shore:* Mistress of Edward IV.
    146. *resolve:* Answer. *nescio:* I do not know.
    151–56. This Latin apostrophe to Charles II has been attributed to Rochester and
appears as a separate item in some MSS.

The following lines, written by some unknown idle rascal, were found on the
threshold of the royal bedchamber:
    You shun battles and chase beauties, hate what is warlike and make your wars
    in bed. Being fond of peace you love the weak. You seem like bold Mars only
    in the works of Venus, but like Venus in the arms of Mars."

The Answer of Mr. Waller's Painter to
his Many New Advisers
(1667)

The series of mock *Advices* and *Instructions* provoked some loyal soul to assume the role of the harrassed painter in this witty rejoinder published as a pamphlet in 1667. His protest against satirical painter poems was vain, however, for the convention continued in popularity well into the following century (see Mary Tom Osborne's *Advice-to-a-Painter Poems,* 1949).

My text follows the 1667 edition, the only known version.

THE ANSWER OF MR. WALLER'S PAINTER TO HIS MANY NEW ADVISERS

Good sirs, be civil, can one man, d'ye think,
As fast lay colors as you all spill ink?
At what a pass am I! A thousand hands
I need, if I must be at all commands.
Thy sparkling fancy, Waller, first design'd   5
A stately piece, true picture of thy mind.
But (how conceits engender!) on thy wit
Each scribbler new *Advices* doth beget;
And so the breed's embas'd, that now 'tis grown
Like royal blood when mixed with the clown.   10
'Twas racy wine ran from thy loyal quill,
But these their brandy from its dregs distill,
Or, like false vintners, they adulterate
Thy nectar with a poisonous sublimate.
Without thy muse thy fancy they purloin,   15
And bastard scions to thy stock they join.

9. *embas'd:* Debased, *obs.*

Thus in dead bodies Satan acts a soul,
And Virgil's self's travesti'd to a droll.
    I shall forswear my art if I must be
Thus school'd by bunglers, whilst I paint for thee;   20
Or if I must each new adviser please,
Jumble our world with the Antipodes,
And mix the firmament and Stygian Lake,
A chaos, not a picture, I shall make.
And then (as he that marr'd a noble draught   25
By alt'ring it as each spectator taught)
I shall forswear the piece, too, and write by:
This monster my advisers made, not I.
    However, sirs, my colors will not do,
And therefore I must be suppli'd by you.   30
I have no mixtures to paint treason's face
So fair, for loyalty to make it pass,
None that will blemish princes on report,
Which none dares own, to make the rabble sport.
Besides, slander's a fading color: though   35
It stick a while, it will not long do so.
If I make use of that, this I shall have,
When it decays, my work will prove me knave.
    Yea princes, sirs, are gods, as they're above,
Though as men in a mortal sphere they move.   40
As gods, 'tis sacrilegious to present
Them in such shapes as may bespeak contempt,
And who allows 'em men does therewithal
Allow 'em possibility to fall.
Yet paint not their infirmities. Would you   45
In each foul posture be expos'd to view?
Baulk not the noble rule and let them have
The charity, at least, that you would crave.
    My colors will not alter forms of state
After the whimsies of each crowing pate.   50
What paint will draw utopias, or where
Shall the groundwork be for castles in the air?
What colors wears the man i'the moon? Who can

18. Several burlesques of various books of the *Aeneid*, entitled *Scarronides*, appeared
in 1664 and 1665. One was written by R. Monsey and others by Charles Cotton.

Limn an *Oceana* or *Leviathan?*
Rob the chameleon, sirs, or polypus   55
For colors, if you mean t'employ me thus.
   Fie, at the old play still! what have we got
By Rotas, ballots, and I know not what?
Who cheats me once, he fools me, but 'tis plain
I fool myself to deal with him again.   60
Bought wit is best, 'tis said, but who buys oft
Shall never sell it at the rates he bought.
Cast up your books, sirs, and I dare engage
Creditor's falls short of the debtor's page.
Unhinge not governments except you could   65
Supply us better ere you change the old.
You would have all amended. So would I,
Yet not deface each piece where faults I spy.
'Tis true I could find colors to expose
Faulty grandees and over-paint a rose,   70
But this checks me, that whatsoe'er is aim'd,
Few such are mended by being proclaim'd.
Public disgrace oft smaller sinners scares,
But vice with greatness arm'd no colors fears.
Besides, the rout grows insolent hereby,   75
And slights the once disgrac'd authority,
Whence, to paint all our betters' faults would be
To hang up order in effigie.
Leave such, then, to their masters and the laws;
Who play with lions at last feel their paws.   80
   But one word more, sirs: grant I yield to you,
Am I secure I have no more to do?
If thus *Advices* spawn, your three or four
May shortly propagate to half a score,

54. *Oceana:* The model commonwealth described by the Republican political theo-
rist James Harrington in *The Commonwealth of Oceana* (1656). *Leviathan* refers, of
course, to Thomas Hobbes' famous anatomy of political power published in 1651.

58. The *Rota* was a club formed by Harrington ust before the Restoration to dis-
cuss his political schemes, which included elaborate systems for balloting and for
rotating representatives.

61. See Aphra Behn, *Sir Patient Fancy* (1678), II.1, p. 38; " 'Twas a saying of my
grandmother's . . . that bought wit was best" (quoted in Tilley, *The Proverb in Eng-
land*).

78. *effigie:* Pronounced as four syllables.

And those, by hundreds multipli'd, may make   85
A task Briareus would not undertake,
Besides the clash—"Dash out that line!" says one;
Another, "Alter this, let that alone!"
So Babel's builders marr'd their tow'r and made
An heap unlike the project that they laid.   90
    Pray leave advising then, for (never crave it)
No art can paint a world as all would have it,
Or, if you're set upon't, to fit your mind,
I'll tell you where a painter you may find.
Look out some canvas-stainer, whose cheap skill   95
With rhythms and stories alehouse-walls doth fill.
Such men will do your work best—sorry elves—
They paint all kings and princes like themselves.
So, with jack-wheels upon their heads, they slander
Arthur and Godfrey and great Alexander.   100
Here David stands with's harp of whipcord-strings,
And Solomon's wives who, sure, lov'd no such things,
Yea, Ahab and Queen Jezebel, who ne'er
Painted herself as she is painted there.
Thus th' Royal Oak in country signs is found   105
In a park copi'd from the neighbor pound,
And royal Charles's head looks peeping through,
Much in the posture that's the dauber's due.
Employ these, then, not me, except you please
To use my art on your own visages.   110
Those I know who would thank me for't, and then
Your faces might be famous as your pen.
And, lastly, that done, three large dashes by
I doubt would serve to paint your destiny.

86. *Briareus:* One of three Hecatoncheires (hundred-handed giants).
95–96. Cf. *Last Instructions,* 7–11.
99. *jack-wheels:* Wheels from roasting-spits.
105. *Royal Oak:* The tree at Boscobel in which Charles II was concealed after the
Battle of Worcester.
106. *neighbor:* Neighboring.

The Downfall of the Chancellor
(*1667*)

As the preceding painter poems show, opposition to Clarendon in-
creased steadily from the time of the Uniformity Act (1662). Non-
conformists held him responsible for the hated Conventicle Act
(1664) and the Five Mile Act (1665). Old Cavaliers blamed him for
the government's failure to reward them with places in the new ad-
ministration. He was condemned, unjustifiably, for promulgating
the King's marriage to a barren and Catholic queen and for contriv-
ing the Dutch War, which ended in the humiliating defeats of the
summer of 1667. While Parliament bitterly resented his efforts to
curb its increasing encroachments on the royal prerogative, the King
grew steadily more restive under the Chancellor's uncompromising
disapproval of his personal conduct. When a rumor sprang up after
the prorogation of 9 July 1667 tht Clarendon was urging the King
to rule without Parliament by means of a standing army, Charles
refused to clear his minister of a charge which he privately conceded
was groundless.

For personal reasons, and as a gesture of appeasement to the
House of Commons, Charles removed Clarendon from office on Au-
gust 30th. When Parliament met in October, the Chancellor's ene-
mies, still unsatisfied, trumped up several charges against him, in-
cluding the accusation that Clarendon had treasonously betrayed
the King's counsels to his enemies. When Clarendon finally realized
that the King would do nothing in his defense, but was indeed
through intermediaries urging him to flee, he left England on No-
vember 29th for exile in France.

The Downfall of the Chancellor sums up most of the allegations
against Clarendon and gives voice to the widespread hatred which
he incurred.

The Downfall of the Chancellor

Pride, lust, ambition, and the people's hate,
The kingdom's broker, ruin of the state,
Dunkirk's sad loss, divider of the fleet,
Tangier's compounder for a barren sheet,
This shrub of gentry, marri'd to the Crown   5
(His daughter to the heir), is tumbl'd down.
The grand affronter of the nobles lies,
Grov'ling in dust, as a just sacrifice
T'appease the injur'd King and abus'd nation.
Who could expect this sudden alteration?   10
God is reveng'd too for the stones he took
From aged Paul's to make a nest for th' rook.
More cormorants of state as well as he
We shortly hope in the same plight to see.
Go on, great Prince! the people to rejoice: 15
Methinks I hear the nation's total voice
Applauding this day's action to be such
As roasting Rump or beating of the Dutch.
Now look upon the wither'd Cavaliers,
Who for reward have nothing had but tears,   20
Thanks to this Wiltshire hog, son of the spittle—
Had they been look'd on, he had had but little.
Break up the coffers of this hoarding thief:
There millions will be found for their relief.
I've said enough of linsey-woolsey Hyde—   25
His sacrilege, ambition, lust, and pride.

3. For Clarendon's reluctant part in the sale of Dunkirk see *Second Advice,* 150 n.
For the disastrous division of the fleet in May 1666 see *Third Advice,* 21–8 and n.
   4. *Tangier* was part of the Queen's dowry.
   5. *shrub:* A mean, inferior, insignificant person, *obs.*
   11–12. When old St. Paul's was demolished Clarendon bought the stones to finish
his house. See *Clarendon's Housewarming,* 44.
   12. *rook:* Cheat.
   21. Hyde was born in Dinton, Wiltshire. *spittle:* A house for the indigent or
diseased.
   25. *linsey-woolsey:* Being neither one thing nor the other, also with an allusion,
perhaps, to Hyde's allegedly humble origins

Edward Hyde, Earl of Clarendon. From an engraving by R. White after the portrait by Lely.

The King's Vows
(*1670*)

The King's Vows, in which Charles II jauntily recites the chief misdemeanors with which he was charged during the first decade of his reign, appears in the manuscript of Marvell's poems that was presumably compiled by the poet's nephew (Bod. MS. Eng. Poet. d. 49). Another manuscript ascribes it to Buckingham and a third to Buckhurst (see textual notes), and, in the absence of further evidence, Marvell's authorship seems doubtful. Although it is printed as Marvell's in the 1707 volume of *POAS,* such late attributions in printed texts are unreliable, and it is quite possible that *The King's Vows,* like the poems by Ayloffe included in MS. Eng. Poet, d. 49, was copied off by Marvell and found with the authentic pieces among his papers after his death.

B.M. Add. MS. 18220 supplies, under the text of the poem, the note: "Communicat fr: T. W. May 20:1670." The lines on Sir John Coventry (40–42) were added in a later version, and four more stanzas on Danby were added still later (see textual notes).

THE KING'S VOWS

When the plate was at pawn and the fob at low ebb,
And the spider might weave in our stomach its web,
Our pockets as empty as brain,
   Then Charles without acre
   Made these vows to his Maker: 5
   If e'er I see England again:

1.

I will have a religion then all of my own,
Where Papist from Protestant shall not be known,
But if it grow troublesome, I will have none.

1. *fob:* Purse.

2.

I will have a fine Parliament always to friend   10
That shall furnish me treasure as fast as I spend,
But when they will not, they shall be at an end.

3.

I will have as fine bishops as were e'er made with hands,
With consciences flexible to my commands,
But if they displease me, I will have all their lands.   15

4.

I will have my Chancellor bear all the sway,
Yet if men should clamor, I'll pack him away,
And yet call him home again, soon as I may.

5.

I will have a fine navy to conquer the seas,
And the Dutch shall give caution for their provinces,   20
But if they should beat me, I will do what they please.

6.

I will have a new London instead of the old
With wide streets and uniform of my own mold,
But if they build it too fast, I'll soon make them hold.

7.

I will have a fine son (in making though marr'd)   25
If not o'er a kingdom, to reign o'er my Guard,
And successor, if not to me, to Gerrard.

8.

I will have a fine court with ne'er an old face,
And always who beards me shall have the next grace,
And I either will vacate or buy him a place.   30

20. *caution:* Security given for the performance of some engagement.

22–24. According to Bell (*The Great Fire of London,* p. 263), the rebuilding of London after the Fire was chiefly due to the energy and imagination of the King.

25–27. The Duke of Monmouth succeeded Lord Gerrard as commander of the King's Lifeguards 16 Sept. 1668. *In making though marr'd* refers to his illegitimacy.

9.

I will have a Privy Purse without a control,
I will wink all the while my revenue is stole,
And if any be question'd, I'll answer the whole.

10.

I will have a Privy Council to sit always still,
I will have a fine junto to do what I will, 35
I will have two fine Secret'ries piss through one quill.

11.

But whatever it cost I will have a fine whore,
As bold as Al'ce Pierce and as fair as Jane Shore,
And when I am weary of her I'll have more,

12.

Which if any bold commoner dare to oppose, 40
I'll order my bravoes to cut off his nose,
Though for't I a branch of prerogative lose.

13.

My bawd shall ambassadors send far and near,
Of my pimp I shall make my minister premier,

33. After Charles had prorogued Parliament in Dec. 1669, he himself examined the war accounts and the Commissioners of the Navy and satisfied himself that there had been no default. Accordingly he addressed Parliament at its next session (Feb. 1670) as follows: "that no misapprehensions or mistakes touching the expenses of the last war may remain with you, I think fit to let you know that I have fully informed myself in that matter, and do affirm to you that no part of those moneys that you gave to me for that war have been diverted to other uses, but on the contrary, besides all those supplies, a very great sum has been raised out of my standing revenue and credit, and a very great debt contracted, and all for the war" (Bryant, *Charles II*, pp. 208–09).

35. *junto:* The Cabal.
36. There were two Secretaries of State from 1660 onwards.
38. Alice Perrers was mistress of Edward III and Jane Shore of Edward IV. In Sept. 1664 Lady Castlemaine was rebuked in St. James' Park as a Jane Shore (*DNB*; Gilmour, *The Great Lady*, pp. 177–78).
40. *bold commoner:* Sir John Coventry. See below, *A Ballad called the Haymarket Hectors.*
43. *My bawd:* Arlington, presumably, who helped to overcome Louise de Kéroualle's resistance to the King in 1670.
44. *my pimp:* Probably Buckingham, who had formed a plan to make Frances Teresa Stuart Charles' mistress and to govern the King through her. The plan failed

And my wench shall dispose of the *congé d'élire*.   45

14.

If this please not, I'll reign upon any condition:
Miss and I'll both learn to live on exhibition,
And I'll first put the Church, then my crown in
     commission.

15.

I will have a fine tunic, a sash, and a vest,
Though not rule like the Turk, yet I will be so dress'd,   50
And who knows but the mode may soon bring in the rest?

16.

I will have a fine pond and a pretty decoy
Where the ducks and the drakes may their freedoms enjoy
And quack in their language still, "Vive le Roy!"

---

when "la Belle Stuart" married the Duke of Richmond in 1667. See *Last Instructions*, 762 and n.

45. *congé d'élire:* Royal permission to a monastic body or cathedral chapter to fill up a vacant see or abbacy by election. In this line it seems to mean only the power of appointment.

47. *on exhibition:* On a fixed allowance, *obs.*

48. The model for this suggestion seems to have been the putting of the Treasury into commission in 1670.

49. *vest:* Evelyn (18 Oct. 1666) describes the King for the first time "putting himself solemnly into the eastern fashion of vest, changing doublet, stiff collar, bands, and cloak, etc. into a comely vest, after the Persian mode, with girdle or sash and shoe-strings and garters into buckles, of which some were set with precious stones, resolving never to alter it and to leave the French mode, which had hitherto obtained to our great expense and reproach."

52–54. "The King, who loved all animals, made his park [St. James'] a home for them. Evelyn thought it a strange and wonderful thing to see the wildfowl breeding so near a great city. Beyond the lake were deer of all kinds: antelopes, an elk, guinea goats, and Arabian sheep. And everywhere Charles planted flowers and walks of trees, making a green paradise for old age and coming generations" (Bryant, *Charles II*, p. 107).

52. *decoy:* A pond out of which run narrow arms covered with network (Margo-liouth).

ANDREW MARVELL

Further Advice to a Painter
(*1671*)

Further Advice to a Painter marks a change in Marvell's attitude toward Charles II. In the second and third *Advices* and *Last Instructions* he had treated the King with respect, while laying the blame for administrative malfeasance and misfeasance on his ministers and other officials. Near the end of *Last Instructions,* to be sure, there is some implied criticism of Charles' relations with Lady Castlemaine, but the hortatory envoy expresses the theme of the preceding *Advices* in urging Charles to dispense with evil counselors. *Further Advice,* however, makes a direct attack on the King for his "degenerate" habits and accuses him of neglecting state business for his affair with Nell Gwynne. In comparing Charles to Commodus, Marvell expresses the disillusionment with the King that characterizes his latter satires.

Among other reasons for this change of views—Charles' involvement with Nell Gwynne, his assumed share in the responsibility for the attack on Sir John Coventry, the bribing of the parliamentary opposition, and the farming of taxes—one stands out. This was the King's apparent indifference to the threat to English liberties posed by Louis XIV's growing military power:

> Thus whilst the King of France with pow'rful arms
> Frightens all Christendom with fresh alarms,
> We in our glorious bacchanals dispose
> The humble fate of a plebeian nose.   (35–38)

The conclusion of the bogus treaty with France in December 1670 which reversed the anti-French policy incorporated in the Triple Alliance of January 1668 no doubt had a deep effect on Marvell.

Further Advice was written some time after the assault on Coventry in December 1670 and in the end of the parliamentary session in April. Margoliouth notes that on 15 March 1671 a bookseller named Palmer was fined and pilloried for "circulating a scandalous

pamphlet in MS. called the *Advice to the Painter,* in which their
Majesties and many of the nobility were maligned" (*HMCR,*
XII.vii.76). The poem is ascribed to Marvell in the Scottish Na-
tional Library MS. Advocate 19.1.12 and in the *State Poems.* It is
dated 1670 in several texts. Margoliouth compares its remarks on
"the five recanters of the House" with Marvell's letter to Popple of
28 November 1670.

FURTHER ADVICE TO A PAINTER

Painter, once more thy pencil reassume,
And draw me in one scene London and Rome.
There holy Charles, here good Aurelius sate,
Weeping to see their sons degenerate:
The Roman taking up the fencer's trade,   5
The Briton jigging it in masquerade,
Whilst the brave youths, tir'd with the work of state,
Their weari'd limbs and minds to recreate,
Do to their more belov'd delights repair,
One to his pathic, the other to his play'r.   10
    Then change the scene and let the next present
A landskip of our motley Parliament,
Where draw Sir Edward mounted on his throne,
Whose life does scarce one gen'rous action own,
Unless it be his late assumed grief   15
To keep his own and lose his Sergeant's wife,
And place me by the bar on the left hand
Circean Clifford with his charming wand;
Our pig-ey'd Duncombe with his Dover fashion

3. *sate:* An old form of *set.*
4. *their sons:* Charles II and Commodus.
10. *play'r:* Nell Gwynne.
13. Sir Edward Turnor, Speaker of the House of Commons, 1661–73, kept as his
mistress the wife of James Norfolk, Sergeant-at-Arms of the House.
18–19. Marvell pretends that Clifford with his white staff of office as Controller of
the Household possessed a Circe-like power of transforming men into beasts—hence
"pig-ey'd Duncombe." Cf. *Last Instructions,* 17 and n. After Coventry's retirement in
1669 and Albemarle's death in 1670 Clifford, Duncombe, and Shaftesbury were the
only members of the Treasury Commission. I can shed no light on Duncombe's "Dover
fashion."

Set by the worst attorney of the nation—   20
This great triumvirate that can divide
The spoils of England—and along that side
Place Falstaff's regiment of threadbare coats,
All looking this way how to give their votes,
Their new-made band of pensioneers,   25
That give their votes more by their eyes than ears;
And of his dear reward let none despair,
For money comes when Seymour leaves the chair.
    Change once again and let the next afford
The figure of a drunken council board   30
At Arlington's, and round about it sate
Our mighty masters in a warm debate:
Capacious bowls with lusty wine replete
To make them th' other council board forget.
Thus whilst the King of France with pow'rful arms   35
Frightens all Christendom with fresh alarms,
We in our glorious bacchanals dispose
The humble fate of a plebeian nose;
Which to effect when thus it was decreed
Draw me a champion mounted on his steed,   40

20. *Attorney* here carries the obsolete sense of "one appointed or ordained to act for another; an agent, deputy, commissioner" (*OED*). Shaftesbury was not a lawyer.

25–26. Presumably the "pensioneers" voted according to visual signals from their leaders instead of pondering the issues raised in debate, hence the pun on *eyes-ayes*.

28. *Seymour:* Sir Edward Seymour (1633–1708) was chairman of the Committee of Supply in 1670–71. Feiling notes that he was "foremost in serving the royal supply" in this session (*History of the Tory Party*, p. 142).

29–34. I have no evidence that Arlington was privy to the plot against Sir John Coventry. "Th' other council board" (34) probably refers to the Cabal which is rightly suspected of furthering a dangerous liaison with Louis XIV. "It began to be noticed that although France was arming for some large undertaking that fact seemed to be causing no uneasiness to the English ministers" (Barbour, *The Earl of Arlington*, p. 175). Arlington did try to suppress a speech by Bridgeman extolling the Triple Alliance "so flagrant was the contradiction in this speech to the actual designs of the government" (ibid.).

Evelyn bears witness to the splendor of Arlington's hospitality in his account of a visit to Euston (16 Oct. 1671): "such a furnished table had I seldom seen, nor anything more splendid and free."

36. Louis XIV's occupation of Lorraine in Sept. 1670 caused widespread concern in England.

38. *nose:* Sir John Coventry's.

40. *champion:* Sir Thomas Sandys, Lieutenant of the Guard.

And after him a brave brigade of horse,
Arm'd at all points, ready to reinforce
The body of foot that was to have the van
In this assault upon a single man.
'Tis this must make O'Brien great in story   45
And add new beams to Sandys's former glory.
    Draw our Olimpia next in council sate
With Cupid Seymour and the tool of state,
Two of the five recanters of the House
That aim at mountains and bring forth a mouse,   50
Who make it by their mean retreat appear
Five members need not to be demanded here.
These must assist her in her countermines
To overthrow the Derby House designs,
Whilst Positive walks Woodcock in the dark,   55
Contriving projects with a brewer's clerk.
Thus all employ themselves and without pity

47. *Olimpia:* Donna Olimpia Maidalchini was the notorious sister-in-law of Innocent X and controlled his policy. Here the Duchess of York is intended. For Seymour's relationship with her cf. the following extract from *Flagellum Parliamentarium*, p. 20: "the Duchess's convert, who, by agreement, lost £1,500 at cards to him, and promised if he would vote for her he should be a rich man" (Margoliouth).

48–49. *F'* glosses *tool of state* as Lord Hollis, but Sir Frescheville Holles is probably intended. Marvell wrote Popple (*Letters*, p. 305) how, in a debate on supply, "Sir R. Howard, Seymour, Temple, Carr, and Holles openly took leave of their former party and fell to head the King's business" (28 Nov. 1670; Margoliouth).

54. *Derby House designs:* Republican designs. The Committee of Derby House succeeded the Committee of Both Kingdoms in January 1648 as the governing council of the nation. It helped bring about the establishment of a republic (Margoliouth).

55. *F'* glosses *Positive* and *Woodcock* as Sir Robert Howard and Lord St. John. Margoliouth notes that Sir Positive-at-All in Shadwell's *Sullen Lovers* considers himself omniscient on all subjects and that Woodcock is "a familiar loving coxcomb." St. John is Charles Paulet, Lord St. John of Basing (1625?–99), described by Burnet as a splenetic, extravagant, and avaricious man. These two gentlemen and Sir William Bucknall were members of a group which contracted for the farming of the customs in Nov. 1670. Cf. Marvell, *Letters*, p. 116: "Those that took the customs etc. at £600,000 are now struck off again and Sir R. Howard, Bucknall, and the brewers have them as formerly projected." Bucknall was a leading member of a syndicate of London brewers which had for some time farmed the liquor taxes in London and the neighboring counties (Margoliouth). *walks:* *L'* reads *leads*, and this lends weight to Margoliouth's conjecture that Howard was leading St. John by the nose.

58–64. *Temple:* Sir Richard Temple (1634–97), M.P. for Buckingham, one of the "five recanters." Until this session he had been a strong opponent of government policy. He was in trouble with the King in 1663, opposed the repeal of the Triennial Act in 1664, attacked the mismanagement of the Second Dutch War, and was a fore-

Leave Temple single to debate the City.
What scandal's this! Temple, the wise, the brave,
To be reproach'd with term of turncoat knave,   60
Whom France esteem'd our chief in Parliament,
To be at home made such a precedent!
'Tis hard, yet this he has for safe retreat:
'Tis by afflictions passive men grow great.

---

most supporter of Clarendon's impeachment. Mr. L. Naylor, the parliamentary historian, has written me that he considers Temple "one of the greatest Parliamentarians of the later Seventeenth Century." Temple was essentially a "Trimmer" and, as Godfrey Davies observes, may have hoped "to make himself so prominent as an opponent of the Court that the King would mitigate or even silence his opposition by the grant of a lucrative position." On 30 May 1671 he was appointed to the Council of Foreign Plantations, and other lucrative positions followed ("Sir Richard Temple's Political Career," *HLQ, 4* [1940–41], 58–59).

Marvell's notion that Sir Richard was regarded by the French as their foremost opponent in Parliament is borne out by Homer Woodbridge's conjecture that he, rather than Sir William, was the "chevalier Temple" described by Cominges in a letter to Louis XIV (25 June 1663) as "un homme d'autant plus dangereux qu'il a beaucoup d'esprit et de credit" (*Sir William Temple,* p. 60). After his defection from the Country party Temple took a leading part, along with Sir William Coventry, Clifford, and others of the Court party, in opposing the high interest on government loans from the City bankers (Grey, *Debates, 1,* 351). The four other "recanters" are not reported as having taken part in these debates, hence the line, "Leave Temple single to debate the City," in which I follow *L'* in preference to the hypermetric reading of the other texts, "Leave Temple single to be beat in the City."

A Ballad called the Haymarket Hectors
(*1671*)

On 21 December 1670, when Sir John Coventry proposed a tax on theaters in the House of Commons, Sir John Birkenhead objected that the players were the King's servants and a part of his pleasure. Thinking of Nell Gwynne and Moll Davis, each of whom had recently borne the King a bastard, Coventry recklessly asked whether his Majesty's pleasure lay among the men or women players?

That night twenty Life Guards, under the command of Sir Thomas Sandys and Captain O'Brien, lay in wait for Coventry, who had been visiting a tavern in Suffolk Street, near the Haymarket. Although he defended himself vigorously, Coventry's nose was slit to the bone. Though Monmouth took no hand in the assault, as captain of the King's Life Guard of Horse he was responsible for giving the orders.

When Parliament reassembled on 10 January, many members expressed indignation and horror at the act. Sandys and O'Brien were banished, and a special "Act to Prevent Malicious Mischief and Maiming" was passed before the debate on supply was resumed. Edmund Waller remarked: "When the Greeks and Romans had slaves disfigured and marked, it was a dishonor to the master, but that a free man, an ambassador of the people, should be thus marked is much more horrible" (Grey, *Debates, 1,* 338–39).

The poem appears in Bod. MS. Eng. Poet. d. 49, the Marvell manuscript, and was printed in Capt. Thompson's edition (1776). Grosart includes it among unauthenticated poems, and Margoliouth does not print it. Without further supporting evidence, ascription to Marvell seems questionable.

Nell Gwynne. From a painting by Simon Verelst.

A Ballad called the Haymarket Hectors

1.

I sing a woeful ditty
Of a wound that long will smart-a,
  Giv'n, the more's the pity,
In the realm of Magna Charta.
Youth, youth, should'st better be slain by thy foes 5
Than live to be hang'd for cutting a nose.

2.

Our good King Charles the Second,
Too flippant of treasure and moisture,
  Stoop'd from the Queen infecund
To a wench of orange and oyster. 10
Consulting his cazzo, he found it expedient
To engender Don Johns on Nell the comedian.

3.

The lecherous vainglory
Of being lim'd with majesty
  Mounts up to such a story 15
This Bitchington travesty,
That to equal her lover, the baggage must dare
To be Helen the Second and cause of a war.

4.

And he, our amorous Jove,
Whilst she lay dry-bobb'd under, 20
  To repair the defects of his love,
Must lend her his lightning and thunder;
And for one night prostitutes to her commands
Monmouth, his Life Guards, O'Brien, and Sandys.

5. This line mimics the words of a well-known song, "Youth, youth, thou hadst better been starv'd at nurse."
11. *cazzo:* It. *membrum virile.*
14. *lim'd:* Coupled.
16. *Bitchington travesty:* Nell Gwynne.
20. *dry-bobb'd:* A dry bob is coition without emission.

5.

And now all the fears of the French   25
And pressing need of navy
    Are dwindl'd into a salt wench
And *amo, amas, amavi.*
Nay he'll venture his subsidy so she cloven may see,
In female revenge, the nostrils of Coventry.   30

6.

O ye Haymarket Hectors,
How came ye thus charm'd
    To be the dissectors
Of one poor nose unarm'd,
Unfit to wear sword or follow a trumpet,   35
That would brandish your knives at the word of a
    strumpet?

7.

But was it not ungrateful
In Monmouth, ap Sidney, ap Carlo,
    To contrive an act so hateful,
O Prince of Wales by Barlow?   40
Since the kind world had dispens'd with his mother,
Might not he well have spar'd the nose of John Brother?

8.

Beware, all ye parliamenteers,
How each of his voice disposes;
    Bab May in the Commons, C. Rex in the Peers,   45

29. As the suspension of work on supply until the Coventry Act was passed later proved, this form of revenge did venture Charles' subsidy.

38. *Monmouth, ap Sidney, ap Carlo:* There was some question as to Monmouth's parentage, and Col. Robert Sidney was reputed to be his father. *Ap* is a Welsh form of *of,* and there is a play on the Welsh associations of the Duke's title.

40. *Barlow:* Lucy Walters, Monmouth's mother, adopted the name of Barlow.

42. *John Brother:* Facetious reference to Sir John Coventry.

45. May's "duties as chief bribery agent of the Court had long previously familiarized him with the usages of the House of Commons" (*DNB*). Charles made a practice of attending debates in the House of Lords on the bill for Lord Roos' divorce in 1670. At first this embarrassed and angered some of the peers, but the King behaved discreetly and found this spectacle "better than going to a play" (Marvell, letter to Popple, 14 April 1670).

Sit telling your fates on your noses,
And decree, at the mention of every slut,
Whose nose shall continue and whose shall be cut.

9.

   If the sister of Rose
Be a whore so anointed
    That the Parliament's nose
Must for her be disjointed,
Should you but name the prerogative whore,
How the bullets would whistle, the cannon would roar!

50

49. Nell Gwynne had an elder sister named Rose.
53. *the prerogative whore:* The Duchess of Cleveland.

On the Three Dukes Killing the Beadle
and
Upon the Beadle
(*1671*)

Unchastened by the outraged public reaction to the attack on Sir John Coventry in December, Monmouth took part in a brawl inside a brothel in Whetstone's Park a few weeks later in which a beadle named Peter Vernell was murdered, "praying for his life upon his knees" (Marvell, letter to Mayor Ackham, 28 February 1671). Monmouth's cohorts were Robert Constable, Viscount Dunbar; Christopher Monck, Duke of Albemarle; and, according to some versions of the poem, the young Duke of Somerset; together with some other gentlemen of spirit. The culprits all received pardons, but as Marvell wrote, it was "an act of great scandal." Dryden may have been referring to Monmouth's part in the affair in his allusion to "Amnon's murther" in *Absalom and Achitophel*, 39.

ON THE THREE DUKES KILLING THE BEADLE
ON SUNDAY MORNING, FEB. THE 26TH, 1671

Near Holborn lies a Park of great renown—
The place, I do suppose, is not unknown—
For brevity's sake the name I shall not tell,
Because most gentle readers know it well.
(Since Middle Park near Charing Cross was made,   5

1. *Park:* Whetstone Park, a narrow lane between Lincoln's Inn Fields and Holborn. Monmouth had earlier been at revels in Lincoln's Inn Hall, where he, together with the King, the Duke of York, and Prince Rupert, had been admitted to the Honorable Society (D'Oyley, *James Duke of Monmouth,* p. 77).

5. *Middle Park:* Probably St. James' Park (see *m.n.* in textual notes). "Charles II delighted in the Park, adding to its acreage and calling in Le Nôtre, the deviser of the grottoes and groves of Versailles, to mould it into brilliant formality" (Douglas Newton, *London West of the Bars,* p. 156).

172

They say there is a great decay of trade).
'Twas here a gleek of dukes, by fury brought,
With bloody mind a sickly damsel sought
And against law her castle did invade
To take from her her instrument of trade.   10
'Tis strange (but sure they thought not on't before)
Three bastard dukes should go t'undo a whore.
Murder was cri'd (truth is, her case was sad,
When she was like to lose e'en all she had);
In came the watch, disturb'd from sleep and ale   15
By the shrill noise, but they could not prevail
T'appease their Graces; straight rose mortal jars
Between the night's black guard and silver stars.
Then fell the beadle by a ducal hand
For daring to pronounce the saucy *stand!*   20
(The way in blood certain renown to win
Is first with bloody noses to begin).
The high-born youths their hasty errand tell,
"Damn you, you rogue, we'll send your soul to Hell!"
They need not send a messenger before—   25
They're too well known there to stand long at door.
See what mishaps dare e'en invade Whitehall!
This silly fellow's death puts off the ball

7. *gleek:* A set of three court cards of the same rank in one hand in the game of gleek, obs.

12. *Three bastard dukes:* D reads *two,* and only two dukes are named in the pardons, Monmouth and Albemarle. See *CSPD, 1671,* pp. 142, 183. *Bastard* seems to be poetic license, since Monmouth was the only illegitimate child of the three.

18. *silver stars:* The stars of the Order of the Garter worn by the dukes.

22. *bloody noses:* An allusion to the maiming of Sir John Coventry.

28–29. Lady Mary Bertie describes a number of masked balls at Whitehall at this time in letters to her niece, Katherine Noel. On 4 March 1671 she writes: "I doubt not but you have heard of the watchman that was killed. They say that the gentlemen that were in it are fled, and 'tis believed the two Dukes will also be tried by their peers. They say the King hath put out a proclamation to forbid masquerades and to command those who were concerned in killing the man to come to their trial" (*HMCR, 12, 5, 23*). The King's reaction to the outrage is described in a newsletter on 7 March 1671:

> 1st, His Majesty, considering the late sad accident of killing the beadle near Holborn, has changed the ballet, intended to have been continued till Shrovetide, into common dancing; they therefore were this evening at Clarendon House. 2nd, His Majesty, in detestation of the late horrid barbarous fact, has called a council, commanded the Chief Justice to attend him there to give him an account of the

And disappoints the Queen, poor little chuck
(I warrant would have danc'd like any duck):   30
The fiddlers, voices, entries, all the sport,
And the gay show put off, where the brisk Court
Anticipates in rich subsidy-coats
All that is got by mercenary votes.
Yet shall Whitehall, the innocent, the good,   35
See these men dance, all daub'd with lace and blood.
Near t'other Park there stands an aged tree,
As fit as if't were made o'the nonce for three,
Where, that no ceremony may be lost,
Each duke for state may have a several post.   40
What storms may rise out of so black a cause,
If such turd-flies shall break through cobweb laws!

UPON THE BEADLE

Assist me, some auspicious muse, to tell
The great adventures that of late befell
Near to that street one side whereof does show
As lofty buildings as the other low;
Where the fierce Albemarle with stout Dunbar,   5
Savage, and Fenwick, mighty men in war,
By spritely Monmouth led with sword in hand,
Resolve to conquer all that shall withstand

---

matter, and considering the many mischiefs that may arise and have lately by
persons under pretence of masquerade, intended, it is said, to have strictly pro-
hibited the same, but after consideration it was thought fit to certify the Justice
of the Peace that the Guards have orders upon all occasions to assist the watch
in any part of the town, against all persons of whatsoever quality they be.

(*HMCR*, *12*, 7, 76)

31. *entries:* Ceremonial entrances.
33. *subsidy-coats:* Coats paid for out of bribes given for passing subsidies.
37. *aged tree:* The gallows at Tyburn, near the northeast corner of Hyde Park.
38. *o'the nonce for:* Expressly for.
5–6. "Grants of pardons to the Duke of Monmouth and Edward Griffin respectively
in the same words, *mutatis mutandis*, as that to the Duke of Albemarle of 23 March.
"Warrant for a similar pardon to Robert Constable, Viscount Dunbar in Scotland,
Peter Savage, and John Fennicke, adding that they stand indicted of the felonious
murder of the said Peter Virnill by inquisition taken before the coroner of Middle-
sex" (*CSPD*, 11 Apr. 1671).

Their gen'rous fury, sprung from this just ground,
Because a nun of Whetstone prov'd unsound.   10
Whetstone's the place where many a duke and lord
Have on bare knees the Queen of Love ador'd.
These more especially in this amorous grove
Full oft have panted in successful love,
That 'twas an injury beyond repair   15
To clap a king's son and a great duke's heir.
And therefore in their fury 'tis decreed
This Jezebel must fall as th' other did;
Which fatal resolution to perform
The Cyprian convent they attempt by storm,   20
Which yet held out some little time, 'tis said,
Though kept but by the abbess and one maid.
But all in vain they do resistance make
When Albemarle and Monmouth once attack,
Brothers in arms, two more of Mars's sons,   25
And both begot on Cytherean nuns,
That from their promising youth like feats may come
As from the brothers that first founded Rome.
The next occasion that they have for fight
Is with the peaceful captain of the night,   30
The Constable, whose presence straight diverts
The former purpose of their wrathful hearts.
They who assailants were not long ago
Must now defendants be against this foe;
Which they perform with that undaunted heat,   35
They put the bold attackers to retreat,
And, having Hannibal's great fate in view,
They wisely do their victory pursue,
When an old beadle, vers'd i'th' English law,
Seeing his mates so shamefully withdraw,   40
Faces about when all the rest were gone
And the pursuants dares oppose alone;
Which put the gallant Monmouth in such flame
That thus he seems against the law t' exclaim:
"Curs'd be their politic heads that first began   45

26. *Cytherean nuns:* Prostitutes. Ann Clarges was reputed to have been George
Monck's mistress long before he married her in 1653.

To circumscribe the liberties of man,
Man that was truli'st happy when of old
His actions, like his will, were uncontroll'd,
Till he submitted his great soul to awe
And suffer'd fear to fetter him with law—   50
This law that animates with partial looks
One saucy watchman to oppose two dukes,
Though back'd with four or five brave youths beside
That only sought to have their courage tri'd."
This fir'd their indignation so that all   55
Upon the poor old man with fury fall,
Who begs in vain that they his life would spare.
"No mercy!" cries our late great Gen'ral's heir,
Who presses on more boldly when he sees
The wretched beadle sinking on his knees,   60
And leaps upon him with that active force
(His father ne'er slew Scot with less remorse)
And does resolve to give him one death more,
Though the poor wretch was slain three times before.
This act their youthful thoughts with glory fill'd,   65
That Pyrrhus-like each had old Priam kill'd,
And to the world by this achievement show
What to their arms posterity must owe,
That without any more assistance can
Subdue the prowess of one poor old man.   70

58. *late great Gen'ral:* George Monck, Duke of Albemarle (1608–70).
62. In 1654 Cromwell had commissioned Monck as Commander-in-Chief of the
Commonwealth armies for the pacification of Scotland.

ANDREW MARVELL

Upon Blood's Attempt to Steal the Crown
(*1671*)

Colonel Thomas Blood (1618?–80) was one of the more spectacular adventurers of the period. For his activities on the Parliamentary side in the Civil War he was rewarded by Henry Cromwell with gifts of land in Ireland which were confiscated by the government after the Restoration. He twice attempted to kidnap the Duke of Ormonde, once in 1663 when Ormonde was Lord-Lieutenant of Ireland, and again in 1670 when Ormonde was in London. The second attempt is recorded in a number of political satires. In both cases his purpose seems to have been to compel Ormonde to restore his lands. "Six months later Blood made his great attempt to seize the crown jewels, on 9 May 1671, and this ultimately led to his regaining the Irish estates" (*DNB*).

Blood, in the guise of a parson, managed to ingratiate himself with Talbot Edwards, the Keeper of the crown jewels in the Tower. On the pretext of making a match between a nephew of his and Mrs. Edward's daughter, and after disarming the Keeper by buying his pistols as a pretended present for a young nobleman, Blood appeared at Edward's house early on the morning of 9 May 1671 with three well-armed friends. When he had persuaded Edwards to show the crown jewels to his companions, the conspirators gagged and bound the Keeper. One put the orb in his breeches, another tried to file the sceptre in two and carry it off in a bag, while Blood crushed the crown and hid it under his parson's cloak. Just as the robbers were making their escape in good order, the Keeper's son happened to return from Flanders on leave, found his father bound and wounded, and spread the alarm which led to their capture. Blood refused to talk about his plot before the examining magistrates and insisted on seeing the King, who pardoned him and restored his forfeited lands. Buckingham, who had been his protector, later sued him for slander, claiming £10,000 damages. He seems to have held Blood to blame for the recurrent charge that he had committed sodomy.

Charles II's surprising action in pardoning Blood may be attributable to Blood's usefulness as an intelligence agent and informer.

The poem appears as lines 178–85 of *The Loyal Scot,* which has been attributed to Marvell, but appears separately in various MSS. and editions of *State Poems.* There is a Latin version by Marvell, *Bludius et Corona. A New Collection of Poems Relating to State Affairs* (1705) notes in the title that this poem was "written in Latin by Andrew Marvell Esq. and translated by Fleet Shepherd."

Epigram

UPON BLOOD'S ATTEMPT TO STEAL THE CROWN

When daring Blood, his rents to have regain'd,
Upon the English diadem distrain'd,
He chose the cassock, surcingle, and gown
(No mask so fit for one that robs a crown),
But his lay-pity underneath prevail'd,
And while he spar'd the Keeper's life, he fail'd.
With the priest's vestments had he but put on
A bishop's cruelty, the crown was gone.

Colonel Thomas Blood. From a drawing by William Faithorne.

On the Prorogation
(1671)

During the evolution of the grand design for a French alliance and war with the Dutch, Parliament was not permitted to meet. On 22 April 1671 it was prorogued to 16 April 1672, then to 30 October 1672, and finally to 4 February 1673. This poem refers to the second of these prorogations, which was proclaimed in September 1671, seven months before the expiration of the first (see lines 94–95). A generous grant of £1,200,000 in the last session together with grants to Charles from Louis made the King financially independent of Parliament, and the government could thus silence Parliamentary critics of its policy by a succession of prorogations.

ON THE PROROGATION

Prorogu'd on prorogation—damn'd rogues and whores!
Our pockets pick'd and we turn'd out of doors!
Have we our country plagu'd, our trust betray'd,
Giv'n polls, loans, subsidies, and royal aid,
Hearth money, imposts, and the lawyers' fees,   5
Ruin'd all trades, tormented all degrees,
Crush'd poor Fanatics and broke through all laws
Of Magna Charta and the Good Old Cause,
                         to be thus fobb'd at last?
Have we more millions giv'n in ten years' space   10
Than Norman bastard had and all his race,
Hurri'd up money bills 'gainst Dutch and French,
But see all spent upon a dunghill wench?
Were we content the kingdom to undo

11. *Norman bastard:* William the Conqueror was the natural son of Robert II, Duke of Normandy, by Arlette, daughter of a Falaise tanner named Fulbert.
13. *dunghill wench:* Nell Gwynne.

T' enrich an overridden whore or two,   15
                                 and all for this?
With plague, war, fire was the kingdom curs'd,
But of all plagues were we ourselves the worst,
Who just elections null'd and took much pain
To make the Parliament a rogue in grain;   20
Had Coventry's nose slit, and, through our fears,
Stood to be piss'd on by the House of Peers;
Unworthy gentlemen, like servants base,
Run to our master's cellar to fox our Mace,
And hundred yet more humble acts than these,   25
That we might not his Majesty displease,
                                 to be thus serv'd?
Welfare! true Vaughan, Howard, Osborne, Carr,

19. *just elections null'd:* A few of the returns were disputed in the session of
1670–71.
20. *rogue in grain:* Thorough rogue.
21. See *The Haymarket Hectors.*
22. On 10 Jan. 1671 the Commons voted to suspend all debate on supply until a
bill to banish Coventry's attackers had been passed. Dering observed in his diary that
many considered this "as great a breach of privilege upon the Lords as this affront
done to Sir John Coventry was of ours" (pp. 46–47).
24. *fox:* To intoxicate, befuddle. *Mace* here refers to the Speaker of the House, Sir
Edward Turnor (1617–76). The mace which lies on the table in the House of Com-
mons when the Speaker is in the chair is viewed as a symbol of the authority of the
House.
In a letter to William Popple (21 March 1670) Marvell writes: "the King sent
for us alone, and recommended a rasure of all proceedings [in the investigation of
naval accounts]. The same thing you know that we proposed at first. We presently
ordered it, and went to tell him so the same day, and to thank him. At coming
down (a pretty ridiculous thing!), Sir Thomas Clifford carried Speaker, and Mace,
and all members there, into the King's cellar, to drink his health" (*Letters,* p. 301).
28. *Welfare:* Obsolete verbal phrase here employed ironically: "good luck to."
28–35. Roger Vaughan, Sir Robert Howard, Sir Thomas Osborne, Robert Carr, Sir
Thomas Littleton, Sir Edward Seymour, and William Garraway had all been members
of the opposition, but they appear in the Court party lists printed by Browning
(*Danby, 3,* 37–43), for the sessions of 1669–71. When Buckingham's group threw in its
lot with the Court in the autumn of 1670, "Seymour, Howard, and others among
Buckingham's satellites became extremely active on behalf of the government"
(Browning, *Danby, 1,* 83). Marvell comments on these and other defections in a letter
to William Popple (28 Nov. 1670): "The House was thin and obsequious. They voted
at first they would supply him [the King] according to his occasions, *nemine,* as it
was remarked, *contradicente;* but few affirmatives, rather a silence as of men ashamed
and unwilling. Sir R. Howard, Seymour, Temple, Carr, and Hollis openly took leave
of their former party to head the King's business" (*Letters,* p. 305). Seymour had been

Littleton, Seymour, and our great man of war,
Will Garraway, the Hector of the House,   30
Who always fetch'd his blow to kill a louse.
These patriots malcontent did plot
Their country's good, till they had places got,
Bluster'd and huff'd till they were officer'd,
But then o'th'country more the Devil a word.   35
    Damn'd Buckingham, of a false sire the son,
Did we for this dismount old Clarendon
And set thee up, thou mighty man of state,
And in thy hands put the whole kingdom's fate?
Did we forget thy former treachery,   40
When, false, our King thou left'st in misery,
Turn'd kneeling renegade to what was trump,
And pay'd allegiance to the rotten Rump?
Did we free thee when Chancellor thee mumbl'd
And wast by him from post to pillar tumbl'd?   45
Did we connive at spilling Shrewsbury's life,
That with more freedom thou might'st whore his wife?
And all for this return? Ungrateful wretch,
May pox and plague and Devil hence thee fetch!
Or some prorogu'd, incensed Felton, rather,   50
Send this curs'd son to find his guilty father!
No other way could'st find t' attain thy ends

---

for removal of evil ministers and redress of grievances before supply in 1668, but in 1670 was foremost in urging the granting of a supply before all other questions. He, Littleton, and Howard took the same position in Jan. 1671, and Garraway spoke against a proviso specifying that any supply granted should be used to maintain the Triple League (Dering, *Parliamentary Diary*, pp. 45, 76).

40–43. Buckingham left the exiled King in 1657 to marry Fairfax's only daughter, regain thereby part of his estates, and, through Fairfax's influence, obtain the Protector's pardon. He was imprisoned by Cromwell, but on the death of the Lord Protector was released on his word of honor not to abet the enemies of the Commonwealth.

44–45. Buckingham was sent to the Tower in June 1667 on a charge of treason. Regarding Clarendon as the author of his late eclipse, he took an energetic part in the prosecution of the Chancellor.

46–47. The Earl of Shrewsbury died of wounds inflicted by Buckingham in a duel fought on 16 Jan. 1668. His wife was reported to have held Buckingham's horse during the encounter.

50. John Felton, a discharged officer, assassinated the first Duke of Buckingham as a tyrant on 23 Aug. 1628.

Than by disgusting the King and his best friends,
Turn off the Parliament that ne'er king before
Had such a one, nor never will have more?   55
What gave thee cause to fear we should not do
Whate'er the King or thou commanded 's to?
If standing army 'twas thou would'st been at,
As well as others we would have raised that.
We could have made, as well as any other,   60
The bastard's right legitimate as brother,
Turn'd Kate a-grazing, the infecund Queen,
And newer issue had, had the humor been.
League Tripartite we could have broke and dance
Fram'd to the measure and the pipe of France,   65
Look'd through our fingers and laugh'd to behold
New London flaming, as we did the old.
We could have yielded to raise citadel
More our own city than the Dutch to quell.
We could plots make, as Oliver on Hewit,   70
And make them guilty on't that never knew it.
And must we, after all our service done
In field for father and in House for son,
Be thus cashier'd to please a pocky peer
That neither Roundhead is nor Cavalier,   75
But of some medley cut, some ill-shap'd brat,
Would fain be something if he knew but what?
A commonwealth's man he owns himself to be,
And, by and by, for absolute monarchy,

54–55. The further prolongation of Parliament's prorogation to Oct. 1672 was at-
tributed by the French to York and Buckingham (Feiling, *Foreign Policy*, p. 329).

60–63. There had been many rumors that the King intended to legitimize Mon-
mouth as early as 1663 (see Pepys, 15 May). Buckingham took a leading part in get-
ting a bill passed to permit Lord Roos to divorce his adulterous wife and remarry,
hoping thereby to establish a precedent for Charles to follow in divorcing Catherine
and marrying again. At the last minute, however, the King refused to allow a mo-
tion for the dissolution of his marriage to be introduced. There is no evidence that
Buckingham was championing Monmouth as heir to the throne as early as 1670, when
the Roos bill came up.

64–65. Buckingham, of course, was a leader in establishing a pro-French policy.

70. Dr. John Hewit, Anglican priest and ardent loyalist, was executed on charges
provided by Cromwell's *agents provocateurs* in 1658.

76. *brat:* A cloth used as an overgarment, generally of a makeshift character.

Then neither likes, but, some new knicknacks found,   80
Nor fish nor flesh, nor square is nor yet round.
Venetian model pleaseth him at night;
Tomorrow, France is only in the right.
Thus, like light butterflies, much flutter makes,
Sleeps of one judgment, and of another wakes.   85
Zealous in morn, he doth a bishop make,
Yet before night all bishops down he'd take.
He all things is, but unto nothing true,
All old things hates, but can abide no new.
But please your pocky Grace to give me leave   90
To ask why thus you do our Prince deceive?
Your first prorogue might sure have stood, for then
'Twas time enough for to prorogue again,
And not all in a hurry, sev'n months before
Our former was expir'd, to add six more.   95
                                        Was fob so full?
Nell's in again, we hear, though we are out.
Methinks we might have met to give a clout
And then prorogue again: our wont hath been
Never to miss a session 'gainst lying in.   100
For always 'gainst the time, the French invades,
'Gainst when we money raise to keep the jades,
And twenty to one, before next spring is over,
March'd must our horse again be unto Dover
To guard the shore against the Dutch and French,   105
When all this means but new supply for wench.
The curs'd Cabal saw 'twas in vain to move
For dissolution (we had too much love
To be dissolv'd), which put thee to find out
This damn'd side wind to bring thy ends about.   110

82. *Venetian model:* A republic like Venice.
94–95. The proclamation further proroguing Parliament was issued 22 Sept. 1671.
96. *fob:* Fob-pocket, the Treasury.
98. Nell Gwynne's second son, James, was born on Christmas Day, 1671. This line
facetiously suggests that Parliament should have been permitted to meet in order to
vote the new baby a diaper (*clout*).
108–09. *we had too much love/To be dissolv'd:* We were too obliging to deserve
dissolution. The government felt with some reason that a new Parliament would be
less co-operative than the old.

For now the sacred codpiece must keep Lent,
Unless some kind supplies from France be sent.
Our first prorogue had many an ostent plain,
Enough to show we ne'er should sit again.
Had we but hearken'd and the foregame play'd,   115
We had prevented our being thus betray'd.
For had we observation made, we might
'Fore morn have known the fate we found at night.
For Caesar more presages never had
Of falling greatness than to us was made.   120
Though Heav'n for us no comets kindly show'd,
Yet we had portents which were all as good:
A crow cross'd Speaker's coach, as to th'House he came;
On crutches that day went the cripple lame;
The Thames at our proroguing backward run;   125
Moon shone at midnight and at noon the sun;
A hollow, earthy voice in the House was heard,
Which made the Speaker of Guy Fawkes afear'd;
Owen's pease pottage unkindly boil'd that day;
Foul handkerchief in pocket had Bab May;   130
That day our clock, too, was upon his tricks:
'Twould not go right, struck five when 'twas near six.
But since there's no resisting of our fate,
We hope we may have leave to invocate:
Oh sweet Revenge! let us but live to see   135
Such rogues to be prorogu'd as well as we;
Indulge our envy but to see the day,
Though we be ruin'd all, as well as they.
We tyrants love, if we can tyrants be;
If not, next wish is we may all be free.   140

113. *ostent:* Portent.
129. An allusion, perhaps, to Sir Arthur Owen or Sir Hugh Owen, both M.P.'s.
130. Bab May's dirty handkerchief is one of several commonplace phenomena
which the satirist pretends to regard as portentous.

Nostradamus' Prophecy
(1672)

This poem, as Margoliouth notes, is based on the prophetic qua-
trains of the famous Michel de Nôtredame, which were published in
1555 and recollected by Londoners after the Great Fire of 1666.
Nostradamus' verses are sufficiently interesting to quote in full:

> Le sang du juste à Londres fera faute,
> Brulez par foudres de vingt trois les six;
> Le dame antique cherra de place haute,
> De mesme secte plusieurs seront occis.

> Dans plusieurs nuits la terre tremblera:
> Sur le printemps deux effors suite:
> Corinthe, Ephèse aux deux mers nagera,
> Guerre s'esmeut par deux vaillains de luite.

> La grand peste de cité maritime
> Ne cessera, que mort ne soit vengée
> De juste sang par pris damné sans crime,
> De la grand dame par feincte n'outragée.

(The blood of the just shall be required of London,
burnt by fireballs in thrice twenty and six; the old Cathe-
dral shall fall from its high place, and many [edifices] of
the same sort shall be destroyed.

Through many nights the earth shall tremble; in the
spring two shocks follow each other; Corinth and Ephesus
shall swim in the two seas, war arising between two com-
batants strong in battle.

The great Plague of the maritime city shall not diminish
till death is sated for the just blood, basely sold, and con-

demned for no fault. The great Cathedral outraged by feigning.)

(From Charles A. Ward, *The Oracles of Nostradamus,* New York, 1940, pp. 187–88.)

Londoners who put their faith in prophecy saw anticipated in these verses the Fire of London, the destruction of St. Paul's, the naval war with Holland, and the Great Plague.

I follow Margoliouth in dating *Nostradamus' Prophecy* after 1 January 1672, when the Exchequer was closed (see line 14), and I agree with him that the attribution of this poem to Marvell is exceedingly doubtful, both because of its low literary calibre and because only the *State Poems,* whose attributions are quite unreliable, make the ascription. On the basis of internal evidence I would ascribe it tentatively to John Ayloffe (see my forthcoming study of Ayloffe). The anti-monarchical and republican viewpoint, the comparison of the King to decadent Roman tyrants, and the violent personal attack on Buckingham are among my reasons for doing so.

Nostradamus' Prophecy

Her faults and follies London's doom shall fix,
And she must sink in flames in sixty-six.
Fire-balls shall fly, but few shall see the train,
As far as from Whitehall to Pudding Lane,
To burn that City, which again shall rise,   5
Beyond all hopes, aspiring towards the skies
Where Vengeance dwells. But there is one thing more,
Though its walls stand, will bring that City low'r.
When legislators shall their trust betray,
Hir'd for their share, to give the rest away,   10
And those false men, by th' easy people sent,
Give taxes to the King and Parliament;
When barefac'd Villainy shan't blush to cheat,

4. *Whitehall:* As the Roman Catholics were accused of firing the city, the charge was naturally fastened later on the Duke of York, when it became known that he was one of them. *Pudding Lane:* Where the fire began.

9–12. A reference to the five deserters from the Country party in the last session of Parliament (24 Oct. 1670 to 22 April 1671). Cf. *On the Prorogation,* 28–35 and n.

And 'Chequer doors shall shut up Lombard Street;
When players come to act the part of queens   15
Within the curtains and behind the scenes;
When sodomy is the Prime Minister's sport,
And whoring shall be the least crime at court;
When a boy shall take his sister to his mate,
And practice incest betwixt seven and eight;   20
When no man knows in whom to put his trust,
When e'en to rob th' Exchequer shall be just;
When declarations lie, and ev'ry oath
Shall be in use at court, but faith and troth;
When two good kings shall be at Brentford town,   25
And when at London there shall not be one;

14. For the closing of the Exchequer on 1 Jan. 1672 see Ranke, 3, 526–27: "The greatest excitement was caused by a measure which was adopted in the Treasury. The bills for the repayment of advances made by the bankers upon the revenues of the year 1672 were not to be honored in the course of that year, but the total sums that came in from the taxes were to be used solely for the necessities of the war. . . . Not only the banks which had provided the advances but also the private persons who had placed their money in them, amongst whom were many who possessed nothing besides, were most seriously affected. Against their claims, which might be pursued at law, the bankers demanded security; that the Lord Keeper Bridgeman refused to put the seal to a declaration for this purpose was the reason of his fall. It is a disputed point which of the two, Clifford or Ashley Cooper, had the greater share in the measure; both were impelled by personal ambition as well; Clifford, who arranged it, was raised to be Treasurer; Ashley, Earl of Shaftesbury, for he appears now with this title, to be Chancellor of the kingdom" (cited by Margoliouth). Lombard Street and the adjacent area, then as now, were the center of banking in the City.

15–16. An allusion to the role of actresses in heroic dramas and as royal mistresses ("within the curtains"), among them Elizabeth Farley, Moll Davis, and Nell Gwynne. See J. H. Wilson, *All the King's Ladies,* passim.

17. The charge of sodomy was repeatedly brought against the Duke of Buckingham in libels and lampoons. The notorious Col. Thomas Blood was later found guilty of conspiring to defame the Duke by such a report and £10,000 damages were awarded his victim. This judgment proved a crushing blow to Blood, who died soon after on 24 Aug. 1680.

19–20. D. M. Vieth suggests that these lines refer to *Sodom,* an obscene play attributed (probably wrongly) to Rochester.

23. As Margoliouth notes, *declarations* may apply generally to Charles' protestations of good intentions made at the opening of Parliamentary sessions or to his Declaration of Breda (1660) and his Declaration of Indulgence (1662).

25. The two kings of Brentford are characters in Buckingham's *Rehearsal,* first acted on 7 Dec. 1671.

26. I have followed MS. Codrington 116 (*L'*) and the printed texts in omitting six lines found in the other MSS. (see textual notes) which follow at this point, because they repeat in idea and phrasing other passages in the poem. Note especially "And

When the seal's given to a talking fool,
Whom wise men laugh at and whom women rule,
A minister able only in his tongue
To make starch'd empty speeches two hours long;   30
When an old Scotch Covenanter shall be
The champion for th' English hierarchy;
When bishops shall lay all religion by
And strive by law t' establish tyranny;
When a lean Treasurer shall in one year   35
Make himself rich, his King and people bare;
When the English Prince shall Englishmen despise,
And think French only loyal, Irish wise;
Then wooden shoes shall be the English wear,
And Magna Charta shall no more appear;   40
Then th' English shall a greater tyrant know
Than either Greek or Gallic stories show.
Their wives to lust expos'd, their wealth to spoil,
With groans to fill his treasury they must toil,
But like the Belides shall toil in vain,   45
For that still fill'd runs out as fast again.
Then they with envious eyes shall Belgium see,
And wish in vain Venetian liberty.

---

wooden shoes shall come to be the wear," the third line of the omitted passage, which
appears in substantially the same form as line 41 of my text.

27. *a talking fool:* Probably Sir Orlando Bridgeman who held the seals from 1667
until they were turned over to Shaftesbury 17 Nov. 1672. According to North (*Life
of Guilford*) he was a failure and his lady "a most violent intriguess in business"
(Margoliouth).

31. *an old Scotch Covenanter:* Lauderdale.

33–34. A probable reference to the second Conventicle Act (1670), for the supres-
sion of Dissenters. See Lodge, *Political History*, p. 94.

35. Clifford, one of the three Commissioners of the Treasury, the "tall louse" of
Last Instructions, 18.

37–38. During his exile on the continent the Duke of York distinguished himself
as a commander of French troops. Only the Irish among his future subjects flocked
to his colors when he was raising a force under the auspices of Spain in 1655 (Burnet,
I, 132).

39. *wooden shoes:* An emblem of tyrannized and impoverished subjects, as the
French were popularly regarded in England.

45. *Belides:* The fifty daughters of Danaus, compelled in Hades to pour water
perpetually into sieves.

48. *Venetian liberty:* See Harrington's *Oceana*.

Too late the frogs, grown weary of their crane,
Shall beg of Jove to take him back again. 50

49–50. See Aesop's third Fable. The frogs, tired of their easy life, petitioned Jupiter for a king. He good-humoredly obliged them by throwing a log into their pond. At first they were terrified by the splash, but in the course of time grew accustomed to and then contemptuous of the log. Then they petitioned Jupiter a second time, and he sent them a stork who proceeded to devour them. When they appealed to Jupiter a third time, he refused to remove the stork, since they suffered for their own folly.

A Litany
(1672)

This poem, here published for the first time, appears in only one
MS. where it has no title but is headed by the line "These were writ
in Lincoln's Inn Boghouse/1672" (a boghouse is a privy). This de-
tail indicates the ubiquitousness of political expression during these
trying times.

A LITANY

From peace with the French and war with the Dutch,
From a new mouth which will cost us as much,
And from councils of wits which advise us to such,
    Libera nos, Domine.

From Pope and from priests which lead men astray,   5
From fools that by cheats will be so led away,
From saints that "Go to the Devil" will pray,
    Libera nos, Domine.

From Parliament-sellers elected for ale,
Who sell the weal public to get themselves bail,   10
And if e'er it be dissolv'd will die in a jail,
    Libera nos, Domine.

---

2. *a new mouth:* This phrase may refer to a specific person, but most likely the
writer is thinking of any Court spokesman in the House of Commons.
11. M.P.'s were immune to actions for debt while Parliament was in session.

The Dream of the Cabal
(1672)

The poem describes an imaginary meeting of the Cabal, Charles'
informal cabinet, in 1672. The King himself is present, as is the
Duke of Ormonde, who alone attempts to defend the liberties of
the subject against the tyrannous incitations of the other ministers.
Although the episode is fictitious, it succeeds in capturing the politi-
cal attitudes and manners of the various speakers. Parliament had
been prorogued since April 1671 and was not to meet until February
1673 (see *On the Prorogation*). In this long interval Charles planned
to execute the great stroke of making war against Holland in al-
liance with France and declaring his adherence to Roman Catholi-
cism. The Cabal met regularly with Charles to take measures for
carrying out the French treaty. Parliament and people were largely
opposed to an alliance with France, and Louis' military preparations
in the beginning of the year made, in the words of the Puritan
divine, Richard Baxter, "the Protestant hearts to tremble."

The members of the Cabal were all "agreed in wishing to
strengthen the royal prerogative by moderating the uniformity laws,
with the help of France, and during the excitement caused by a
foreign war" (Ranke, *3*, 520), but only two of them, Clifford and
Arlington, knew of the secret Treaty of Dover and of its provision
that Charles should proclaim himself a Catholic in return for an ad-
ditional subsidy from Louis. The debate that the poem pretends to
report centers mainly on ways and means for Charles to extend his
prerogative and govern without Parliament.

No attributions are made in any of the texts I have seen. In
subject matter, ideas, and the convention of the dream or vision,
this poem resembles two satires ascribed to John Ayloffe, *Britannia
and Raleigh* and *Marvell's Ghost*. For a detailed discussion of the
evidence see my forthcoming study on Ayloffe.

The Dream of the Cabal: A Prophetical Satire
Anno 1672

As t'other night in bed I thinking lay
How I my rent should to my landlord pay,
Since corn, nor wool, nor beast would money make,
Tumbling perplex'd, these thoughts kept me awake:
"What will become of this mad world?" quoth I.   5
What's its disease? What is its remedy?
Where will it issue? Whereto does it tend?
Some ease to misery 'tis to know its end."
Till servants dreaming, as they us'd to do,
Snor'd me asleep. I fell a-dreaming too.   10
    Methought there met the grand Cabal of seven
(Odd numbers, some men say, do best please Heaven).
When sat they were and doors were all fast shut,
I secret was behind the hangings put.
Both hear and see I could, but he that there   15
Had plac'd me bade me have as great a care
Of stirring as my life, and, ere that out
From thence I came, resolv'd should be my doubt:
What would become of this mad world, unless
Present designs were cross'd with ill success?   20
    An awful silence there was held some space,
Till, trembling, thus began one call'd his Grace:
"Great Sir, your government for first twelve years
Has spoil'd the monarchy and made our fears
So potent on us that we must change quite   25
The old foundations and make new, wrong or right.
For too great mixture of democracy
Within this government allay'd must be,
And no allay like nulling parliaments,
O'th' people's pride and arrogance the vents,   30
Factious and saucy, disputing royal pleasure,

    11. *grand Cabal of seven:* Clifford, Ashley, Buckingham, Arlington, Lauderdale, plus
Ormonde and King Charles.
    22. *his Grace:* Buckingham.

THE DREAM OF THE CABAL

Who your commands by their own humors measure.
For king in barnacles and to th'rack-staves ti'd
You must remain, if these you will abide."
    So spake the long blue ribbon; then a second,   35
Though not so tall, yet quite as wise is reckon'd,
Did thus begin: "Great Sir, you are now on
A tender point much to be thought upon,
And thought on only, for by ancient law
'Tis death to mention what my Lord foresaw.   40
His trembling show'd it, wherefore I'm so bold
To advise its standing, lest it should be told
We did attempt to change it; for so much
Our ancestors secur'd it, that to touch,
Like sacred Mount, 'tis death, and such a trick   45
I no ways like to make tongue break my neck."
    Thus said, he sat. Then Lord of northern tone,
In gall and guile a second unto none,
Enraged rose, and, chol'ric, thus began:
"Dread Majesty, male beam of fame, a son   50
Of th' hundred-and-tenth monarch of the nore,
De'il split the weam of th'lowne that spoke afore!
Shame faw the crag of that ill-manner'd Lord
That 'nent his King durst speak so faw a word!
And aw my saul right weel the first man meant,   55
De'il hoop his lugs that loves a parliament!
Twa houses aw my saul are twa too mickle.
They'll gar the laird shall ne'er have more a prickle,

33. *barnacles:* Instruments of torture. *rack-staves:* The upright arms of a rack.
    35. *long blue ribbon:* Buckingham received the Garter in 1649. *a second:* The Duke of Ormonde.
    39. *ancient law:* Presumably Magna Charta. I cannot, however, find any reference there to capital punishment for those who advocate the nullification of parliaments.
    45. *sacred Mount:* Sinai. See Exodus 19:12: "whosoever toucheth the Mount shall be surely put to death."
    47. *Lord of northern tone:* Lauderdale.
    51. *nore:* The north, i.e. Scotland.
    52. *weam:* Belly. *lowne:* Rogue.
    53. *faw:* Fall upon. *crag:* Neck.
    54. *'nent:* Anent or against. *faw:* False dialect for "foul."
    56. *hoop his lugs:* Box his ears.
    58. *gar:* Cause. *laird:* A landed proprietor in Scotland, but here referring to Charles II. *prickle:* Penis.

194 POLITICAL AFFAIRS

Na siller get to gie the bonny lass:
But full as good be born without a tarse. 60
Ten thousand plagues light on his crag that 'gin
To make you be but third part of a king.
De'il take my saul, I'll ne'er the matter mince,
I'd rather subject be than sike a prince.
To hang and burn and slay and draw and kill 65
And measure aw things by my own guid will
Is gay dominion; a checkmate I hate
Of men or laws, it looks so like a state."
    This eager, well-meant zeal some laughter stirr'd,
Till, nose half-plush, half-flesh, the inkhorn Lord 70
Crav'd audience thus: "Grave Majesty divine
(Pardon that Cambridge title I make mine),
We now are enter'd on the great'st debate
That can concern your throne and royal state.
His Grace hath so spoke all, that we who next 75
Speak after can but comment on his text.
Only 'tis wonder at this sacred board
Should sit 'mongst us a Magna Charta lord,
A peer of old rebellious barons' breed,
Worst and great'st enemies to royal seed. 80
But to proceed: well was it urg'd by's Grace
Such liberty was giv'n for twelve years' space
That are by pass'd; there's now necessity
Of new foundations, if safe you'll be.
What travail, charge, and art (before was set 85
This Parliament) we had, you can't forget;
How forc'd to court, cajole, and bribe, for fear
They wrong should run, e'er since they have been here;

59. *gie:* Give.
65–68. In 1673 Lauderdale, according to Burnet, offered to overawe Parliament with Scottish forces (*History of My Own Time,* 2, 11).
68. *state:* Non-monarchical commonwealth.
70. *inkhorn lord:* Arlington, who had been the Earl of Bristol's clerk.
72. An allusion, no doubt, to the formal oratory with which Charles would have been greeted on visits to Cambridge University. On such occasions Charles desired that speeches might be "few and short, or none" (Bryant, *Charles II,* p. 219).
78. Ormonde was descended from Theobald Butler (d. 1206), who had opposed King John.
85. *set:* Sat.

What diligence, what study day and night,
Was on us, and what care to keep them right!   90
Wherefore, if good you can't make Parliament,
On whom such costs, such art and pains were spent,
And moneys, all we had for them to do,
Since we miss that, 'tis best dismiss them too.
'Tis true, this House the best is you can call,   95
But, in my judgment, best is none at all."
    "Well mov'd!" the whole Cabal cri'd, "Parliaments
Are clogs to princes and their brave intents."
One did object, 'twas against majesty
T'obey the people's pleasure. Another he   100
Their inconvenience argues, and that neither
Close their designs were, nor yet speedy either.
    Whilst thus confused chatter'd the Cabal,
And many mov'd, none heard, but speak did all,
A little bobtail'd Lord, urchin of state,   105
A Praisegod-Barebones-peer whom all men hate,
Amphibious animal, half fool, half knave,
Begg'd silence and this purblind counsel gave:
"Blest and best Monarch that e'er scepter bore,
Renown'd for virtue, but for honor more,   110
That Lord spake last has well and wisely shown
That parliaments, nor new, nor old, nor none,
Can well be trusted longer, for the state
And glory of the crown hate all checkmate.
That monarchy may from its childhood grow   115
To man's estate, France has taught us how.
Monarchy's divine: divinity it shows
That he goes backward that not forward goes.
Therefore go on, let other kingdoms see
Your will's your law: that's absolute monarchy.   120
A mix'd hodge-podge will now no longer do;

93–94. *Moneys* is appositive to *all* and antecedent to *that.*
105. *a little bobtail'd Lord:* Shaftesbury.
106. Shaftesbury was one of the few gentlemen in the Barebones Parliament (4 July–12 Dec. 1653). This Parliament was named for Praisegod Barebones, a London leather-seller who took a prominent part in it.
115–16. Some of Charles' close advisers at this time were urging him to extend his prerogative after the pattern of Louis XIV.

Caesar or nothing you are brought unto.
Strike then, great Sir, 'fore these debates take wind;
Remember that Occasion's bald behind.
Our game is sure in this, if wisely play'd,   125
And sacred votes to the vulgar not betray'd.
But if the rumour should once get on wing
That we consult to make you abs'lute King,
The plebeians' head, the gentry forsooth,
They straight would snort and have an aching tooth.   130
Lest they, I say, should your great secrets scent,
And you oppose in nulling Parliament,
I think it safer and a greater skill
To obviate than to o'ercome an ill.
For those that head the herd are full as rude,   135
When th' humor takes, as the following multitude.
Therefore be quick in your resolves, and when
Resolv'd you have, execute quicker then.
Remember your great father lost the game
By slow proceedings. Mayn't you do the same?   140
An unexpected, unregarded blow
Wounds more than ten made by an open foe.
Delays do dangers breed; the sword is yours,
By law declar'd, what need of other pow'rs?
We may unpolitic be judg'd, or worse,   145
If we can't make the sword command the purse.
No art or courtship can the rule so shape
Without a force: it must be done by rape,
And when 'tis done, to say you cannot help
Will satisfy enough the gentle whelp.   150
Fanatics they'll to Providence impute
Their thraldom and immediately grow mute,
For they, poor pious fools, think the decree
Of Heav'n falls on them, though from Hell it be;
And when their reason is abas'd to it,   155
They forthwith think't religion to submit,
And vainly glorying in a passive shame,
They'll put off man to wear the Christian name.

124. *Occasion:* Traditionally personified as a woman bald except for a forelock.

Wherefore to lull 'em, do their hopes fulfill
With liberty; they're halter'd at your will.   160
Give them but conventicle-room, and they
Will let you steal the Englishman away,
And heedless be, till you your nets have spread,
And pull'd down conventicles on their head.
Militia, then, and parliaments, cashier;   165
A formidable standing army rear;
They'll mount you up, and up you soon will be.
They'll fear, who ne'er did love, your monarchy,
And if they fear, no matter for their hate:
To rule by law becomes a sneaking state.   170
Lay by all fear, care not what people say,
Regard to them will your designs betray.
When bite they can't, what hurt can barking do?
And, Sir, in time we'll spoil their barking too,
Make coffee-clubs talk of more humble things   175
Than state affairs and interest of kings."
    Thus spake the rigling Peer, when one more grave,
That had much less of fool but more of knave,
Began: "Great Sir, it gives no small content
To hear such zeal for you 'gainst Parliament;   180
Wherefore, though I an enemy no less
To parliaments than you yourselves profess,
Yet I must also enter my protest
'Gainst these rude rumbling counsels indigest,
And, great Sir, tell you, 'tis an harder thing   185
Than they suggest to make you abs'lute king.
Old buildings to pull down, believe it true,
More danger in it hath than building new,
And what shall prop your superstructure till
Another you have built that suits your will?   190
An army shall, say they. Content. But stay,

159–64. These lines refer to Charles' Declaration of Indulgence, which suspended the penal laws against Nonconformists in 1672. Under pressure from Parliament it was withdrawn in 1673.

161. The assemblies of Nonconformists were known as *conventicles*.

177. *rigling:* Northern dialectal variant of ridgeling, a male animal with only one testicle. *one more grave:* Clifford.

From whence shall this new army have its pay?
For easy, gentle, government a while
Appear must to this kingdom, to beguile
The people's minds and make them cry up you,   195
For rasing old and making better new.
For taxes with new government all will blame
And put the kingdom soon into a flame,
For tyranny has no such lovely look
To catch men with unless you hide the hook,   200
And no bait hides it more than present ease.
Ease but their taxes, then do what you please.
Wherefore, all wild debates laid by, from whence
Shall money rise to bear this vast expense?
For our first thoughts thus well resolved, we   205
In other things much sooner shall agree.
Join then with Mother Church, whose bosom stands
Ope to receive us, stretching forth her hands.
Close but this breach, and she will let you see
Her purse as open as her arms shall be;   210
For, sacred Sir (by guess I do not speak),
Of poor she'll make you rich, and strong of weak.
At home, abroad, no money, no, nor men
She'll let you lack; turn but to her again."
    The Scot could here no longer hold, but cri'd: 215
"De'il take the Pape and all that's on his side,
The whore of Rome, that mickle man of sin,
Plague take the mother, bairns, and aw the kin!
What racks my saul? Must we the holy rood
Place in God's Kirk again? Troth, 'tis not guid.   220
I defy the lowne, the De'il, and aw his work!
The Pape shall lig no mare in God's guid Kirk."
    The Scot with laughter check'd, they all agreed
The Lord spake last should in his speech proceed,
Which thus he did: "Great Sir, you know 'tis season   225
Salts all the motions that we make with reason,
And now a season is afforded us,
The best e'er came, and most propitious.
Besides the sum the Cath'lics will advance,

207. Clifford was the soul of the Catholic project in the secret Treaty of Dover.

You know the offers we are made from France,   230
And to have money and no Parliament
Must fully answer your design'd intent.
And thus without tumultuous noise or huff
Of parliaments, you may have money enough,
Which, if neglected now, there's none knows when   235
Like opportunities may be had again;
For all t'extirpate now combined be
Both civil and religious liberty.
Thus money you'll have to exalt the Crown,
Without stooping majesty to country clown.   240
The Triple League, I know, will be objected,
As if that ought by us to be respected!
But who to heretics or rebel pay'th
The truth engaged to by solemn faith
Debaucheth virtue: by those very things,   245
The Church profaneth and debaseth kings,
As you yourself have admirably shown
By burning Solemn Cov'nant, though your own.
Faith, justice, truth, plebian virtues be,
Look well in them but not in majesty.   250
For public faith is but a public thief,
The greatest cheat in Nature's vain belief."
    The second Lord, though check'd, yet did not fear,
Impatient grew and could no longer bear,
But rose in heat, and that a little rude;   255
The Lord's voice interrupts and for audience su'd:
"Great Majesty, authentic authors say,
When hand was lifted up Croesus to slay,
The father's danger on the dumb son did make
Such deep impressions that he forthwith spake.   260
Pardon, great Sir, if I, in imitation,

230. The secret Treaty provided a grant of two million livres to aid Charles in suppressing any insurrection which might arise from his public conversion to Catholicism, and further annual grants of three million livres to support the naval war against the Dutch (Lingard, 9, 183).

248. The Solemn League and Covenant was burned by order of Parliament on 29 May 1661, the King's birthday.

253. *The second lord:* Ormonde.

258. *Croesus:* See Herodotus, *History* 1.85.

Seeing the danger to yourself and nation,
Do my resolv'd-on silence also break,
Although I see the matter I shall speak
Under such disadvantages will lie,   265
It shall exploded be as well as I.
But vainly do they boast they loyal are
That can't for princes' good reflections bear,
Nor will I call compurgators to prove
What honor to the crown I've borne with love.   270
My acts have spoken and sufficient are
Above whate'er detractors did or dare.
Wherefore, great Sir, 'tis ignorance or hate
Dictates these counsels you to precipitate.
For say 't again I will, not eat my word,   275
No council's power, no, nor yet the sword
Can old foundations alter or make new:
Let time interpret who hath spoken true.
Those country gentry with their beef and bacon
Will show how much you courtiers are mistaken.   280
For parliaments are not of that cheap rate
That they will down without a broken pate.
And then I doubt you'll find those worthy lords
More braves and champions with their tongue than
     swords.
Wherefore, dread Sir, incline not royal ear   285
To their advice, but safer counsels hear.
Stay till these lords have got a crown to lose.
And then consult with them which way they'll choose.
Will you all hazard for their humor's sake,
Who nothing have to lose, nothing at stake,   290
And at one game your royal crown expose
To gratify the foolish lusts of those
Who hardly have subsistence how to live
But what your crown and grace to them does give?
And one of those bagpudding gentlemen   295

269–70. In the court of Charles II Ormonde "was almost the sole representative of
the high-toned virtues of a nobler generation" (*DNB*).
269. *compurgators:* Character witnesses.
295. *bagpudding:* Clownish.

(Except their places) would buy nine or ten.
Then why they should thus slight the gentleman,
I see no reason, nor think how they can.
For had not gentleman done more than lord
(I'll boldly say 't) you ne'er had been restor'd.   300
But why of armies now, great Sir, must we
So fond just now all on the sudden be?
What faithful guardians have they been to pow'rs
That have employ'd them that you'd make 'em yours?
Enough our age, we need not seek the glory   305
Of armies' faith in old or doubtful story.
Your father 'gainst the Scots an army rear'd,
But soon that army more than Scot he fear'd.
He was in haste to raise them, as we are,
But to disband them was far more his care.   310
How Scottish army after did betray
His trust and person both, I need not say.
Rump-Parliament an army rear'd, and they
The Parliament that rais'd them did betray.
The Lord Protector they set up one hour,   315
The next pull'd down the protectorian pow'r.
Your father's block and judges the same troops
Did guard; same tongues at death of both made whoops.
And will you suffer armies to beguile
And give your crown and you to cross and pile?   320
What if a Monck should both swear, lie, and feign,

296. *Except their places:* Except for what the noble members of the Cabal make from their offices at court.

305–06. i.e. we are old enough to have seen for ourselves how unfaithful armies can be.

307–12. In 1639 Charles I attempted with soldiers to enforce the use of the Anglican prayer book in Scotland. His troops were undisciplined, however, and he was obliged to suspend the attempt, fearing they might revolt for want of pay. In 1648 a secret treaty was signed between Charles and the Scots by which they engaged to restore him with an army in return for concessions to Presbyterianism. This army was defeated by Parliamentary forces under Cromwell and Fairfax.

313–14. The Parliamentary army under Monck forced the Rump to dissolve itself in 1660.

315–16. i.e. in deposing Richard Cromwell.

320. *cross and pile:* The toss of a coin. Cf. *Hudibras*, pt. 3, canto 3, 689: "cross, I win, and pile, you lose." Were Charles to attempt to secure his power with an army he would lose his crown, whatever happened.

Till he does both your trust and army gain,
And you believe his oath and faith is true,
But serves himself instead of serving you?
Pardon, great Sir, if zeal transports my tongue   325
T'express what e'en your greatness don't become.
Expose I can't your crown and sacred throat
To the false faith of a common redcoat.
Your law your all does fence secure from fears:
That kept, what trouble needs of bandoleers?   330
Consider, Sir, 'tis law that makes you King.
The sword another to the crown may bring,
For force knows no distinction: longest sword
Makes peasant prince, lackey above his lord.
If that be all that we must have for laws,   335
Your will inferior may be to Jack Straw's,
If greater force him follow: there's no right
Where law is failing and for will men fight.
Best man is he alone whose steel's most strong;
Where no law is, there's neither right nor wrong.   340
That fence broke down and all in common laid,
Subjects may prince and prince may them invade.
See, greatest Sir, how these your throne lay down
Instead of making great your royal crown,
How they divest you of your majesty,   345
For, law destroy'd, you are no more than we.
And very vain would be the plea of crown,
When statute laws and parliaments are down."
    This Peer proceeded on to show how vain
An holy league would be with Rome again,   350
And what dishonor 'twould be to our crowns
If we to France give cautionary towns.
He's interrupted and bid speak no more
By's enraged Majesty, who deeply swore
His tongue had so run o'er that he'd take   355

330. *bandoleers:* Boxes containing charges for muskets. The sense seems to be that
the King need not use force to keep his subjects in order if he is faithful to law.
    336. *Jack Straw:* A leader in the Peasant's Revolt, 1381.
    352. *cautionary towns:* Towns given as pledges for performance of a treaty. There
was no such provision in the secret Treaty of Dover, although Charles was to be
granted Walcheren, Sluys, and the island of Cadsand out of the anticipated conquests.

Such vengeance on him and example make
To after ages, all which heard should fear
To speak what would displease the royal ear,
And bid the Lord that spoke before go on,
And silence all should keep till he had done;   360
Who thus his speech resum'd: "If Lord spake last
To interrupt me had not made such haste,
I soon had done, for I was come, great Sir,
T'advise your sending Dutch ambassador;
But much it does concern you whom to trust   365
With this embassy, for none true nor just,
Wise, stout, or honorable, nor a friend
Should you in any wise resolve to send,
Lest any unseen or unlucky chance
Should in this war befall to us or France.   370
We may that loathed wretch give to the hate
Of the people's fury, them to satiate.
And when all's done that can be done by man,
Much must be left to chance, do what you can.
And if you'll make all Christendom your friend,   375
And put to Dutch Land League an utter end,
Then surely you may have of men and treasure
Enough of both to execute your pleasure."
    This speech being ended, six of seven agree
France shall be lov'd and Holland hated be.   380
All gone, I wak'd and wonder'd what should mean
All I had heard; methought 'twas more than dream.
And if Cabal thus serve us Englishmen,
'Tis ten to one but I shall dream again.

363–70. Sir George Downing was sent as ambassador to The Hague in Dec. 1672 to provoke a rupture with the Dutch. He was well-endowed for the task, for his impertinence so incensed the Dutch that he fled before his mission was completed and was sent to the Tower on his return to England (Feiling, *Foreign Policy*, p. 112).
  376. *Dutch Land League:* Presumably the Triple Alliance.

The Banished Priests' Farewell to the House of Commons
(*1673*)

When Parliament opened 4 February 1673 after a series of prorogations extending over almost two years (see *On the Prorogation*), Charles demanded supply for the increasingly unpopular Dutch War, declaring at the same time his intention of adhering to the Declaration of Indulgence by which he had suspended penal laws against Catholics and Nonconformists since 15 March 1672. The Commons presented the King with an address declaring that these laws could only be suspended by Parliament, and massive opposition in both houses forced Charles on 8 March to cancel the Declaration, "a step," Ogg says, "which no other male Stuart would have taken." On 29 March Charles gave his assent to the Test Act which confined the privileges of full citizenship to communicants of the Anglican Church who renounced under oath the doctrine of transubstantiation.

The title of this poem probably relates to a joint address that Charles received on 7 March desiring him to issue a royal proclamation commanding all foreign-born Jesuits except those attendant upon the Queen to leave the kingdom within thirty days (Bate, *The Declaration of Indulgence*, p. 123). This proclamation was never issued.

The Banished Priests' Farewell is a rare pro-Catholic satire and is published here for the first time.

THE BANISHED PRIESTS' FAREWELL TO THE HOUSE OF COMMONS

Go! sots, home to your gammons, go! and boast
The speeches you have made to every host,
And o'er the bacon and bagpudding tell

3. *bagpudding:* A boiled pudding.

Your fellow high-shod clowns how wond'rous well
In Parliament you did yourselves behave.   5
Set arms akimbo, swear you'll be no slave;
Crack how you sweat to set the people free,
Secure religion and their liberty;
Tell how Tom Lee, Jack Hotham, Powell spake,
How Country huff'd, and how the Court did quake.   10
Tell all the clownish jokes and silly jeers
Were said or done by Garraway or Meers.
Vaunt the proud motion that Lord Cavendish start,
But also tell, it was not worth a fart.
Boast old Strangeways and Sacheverell   15
(That cramp a tongue would to pronounce it well)
How well the Western, Welsh, and Yorkshire Tike
Did run this time; boast, none e'er saw the like.
If wit and courage 'mongst you had been seen,
You sure enough had Rump the Second been.   20
     Alas! poor fools, for you to imitate
The acts done by that great and proudest State,
Who neither principle nor valor have,

7. *crack:* Brag.

9. *Tom Lee:* One of the leaders of the Country party in this session. See *Britannia and Raleigh*, 17. *Jack Hotham:* Sir John Hotham, a Yorkshireman involved in the Republican rising of 1663. *Powell:* Henry Powell, who spoke much against the dangers of Popery in the debates on the royal Declaration.

12. *Garraway:* William Garraway, another anti-Catholic, who feared that the bill against "Romanists" might drive them underground. According to Grey (14 Feb.) he "would have them publicly in all their robes, and if you might see them in all their frippery, believes you would not have so many of them." *Meers:* Sir Thomas Meers. Grey reports him as follows (14 Feb.): "Let us take care that, whilst we dispute the indulging the Protestant subjects, the third dog [the Catholics] does not take the bone from us both."

13. *Cavendish:* William Cavendish, fourth Earl and first Duke of Devonshire (1640–1707). On 10 Feb. he moved "that the votes of the House in 1662 and 1663 may be read and the reasons against Toleration read" (Grey). In 1675 he was to draw up, with Littleton, Powell, Meers, and Sir John Coventry, the articles of impeachment against Danby.

15. *Boast:* i.e. let them boast. *Strangeways:* Sir John Strangeways. In a speech against the Declaration (Grey, 10 Feb.) he remarked: "We own the King's power to dispense with the punishment, by pardon; but the King cannot dispense with a man to be a Papist or Nonconformist." *Sacheverell.* William Sacheverell. On 28 Feb. he made a motion for the removal of all Popish recusants from military office.

17. The reference is obscure.

22. *that great and proudest State:* The Commonwealth.

Nor faith, nor anything above a slave,
Makes but your folly to appear the more,   25
Which known enough in conscience was before.
In rebellion only your talent would afford
To follow them, nor that neither with your sword.
For fifteen fields they with their Sovereign fought;
You fifteen times would sneaking peace have sought,   30
In ten of which, I dare be bold to say,
Your credit was for the King to run away.
And now so cowardly to fall on those
Who best did fight! More savage than our foes!
For they the liberty of worship gave us,   35
Although in all things else they did enslave us.
     Ungrateful wretches! Did we for you fight,
That you should spoil us of our natural right?
Did we contend for you with blood and treasure,
That you should plague and banish us at pleasure?   40
Did Worcester, Winchester, and Bellasis,
Bristol, Carnarvon, all engage for this?
Nay the whole Catholic nobility

35–36. Catholics were granted freedom of worship under the Commonwealth.
   41. *Worcester:* Edward Somerset, 6th Earl and 2nd Marquis of Worcester (1601–77),
Royalist officer. In 1644 he was chosen to retrieve Charles I's fortunes by calling in
Irish rebels and foreign Catholic troops, "marked out for this delicate and dangerous
enterprise by his wealth, by his intimate connection with the Irish nobility, and by
his devotion to the Roman Catholic religion" (*DNB*). *Winchester:* John Paulet, fifth
Marquis of Winchester (1598–1675), Catholic Royalist who "became at the outbreak
of the Civil War the great resort of the Queen's friends in southwest England." With a
force of 150 men he defended his seat, Basing House, for three months against the
"continued attack of the combined Parliamentary troops of Hampshire and Sussex."
On account of this he was called "the great loyalist" (*DNB*). *Bellasis:* John, Baron
Bellasis (1614–89), Catholic Royalist who joined Charles I at Oxford on the outbreak
of the Civil War. He raised six regiments at his own expense, was present at Edgehill,
Brentford, Newbury, Reading, Bristol, Newark, and Naseby. Marvell knew him as
Governor of Hull. At the time of the Popish Plot Oates charged falsely that Bellasis
had been designated leader of the Catholic army which Oates pretended was in the
course of formation.
   42. *Bristol:* George Digby, second Earl of Bristol (1612–77), and ardent Royalist
plotter during the Commonwealth, distinguished for gallantry at the capture of
Lichfield. He became a Catholic at Ghent in 1657. For his attack on Clarendon see
Second Advice, 148 n. *Carnarvon:* Robert Dormer, Earl of Carnarvon (d. 1643). He
appears to have been brought up as a Catholic. He fought many battles for Charles I
and died in action at Newbury.

(For, whoe'er were, we could not neuters be).
'Twere endless here to call upon the stage 45
Our Legge, our Langdale, Goring, and our Gage,
Our Winter, Talbot, Cansfield, Vavasour,
Our Lunsford, Slingsby, and ten thousand more.
For where's the Catholic was not engag'd
In person or in purse, though ne'er so ag'd? 50
And must we now be run upon by you
Worse than we were by that rebellious crew?
Are you, poor drunken noddies, fit to define
God's sacred worship and things most divine,
Which learned councils trembl'd how to do, 55
Though God and Church have call'd them thereunto?
You! Transubstantiate a wench! What, you

46. *Legge:* William Legge (1609?–70), Royalist officer, often imprisoned during the war by Parliament. Clarendon extols his integrity and fidelity to Charles I. *Langdale:* Marmaduke, first Baron Langdale (1598–1661). "When the Civil War began, Langdale, no doubt because of the severity of the Parliament against Catholics, adopted the King's cause with the greatest devotion." He was captured in the second Civil War but escaped to the continent where he lived in great poverty. See *Third Advice,* 225 and n. *Goring:* George, Baron Goring (1608–57), distinguished Royalist general and notorious debauchee. According to Clarendon "his ambition was unlimited and he was unrestrained by any respect to justice or good nature from pursuing the satisfaction thereof." His plots to supplant Hopton as lieutenant-general in 1645 paralyzed the western army. He is reported to have assumed the habit of a Dominican friar in his last days. *Gage:* Sir Henry Gage (1597–1654), Catholic member of Charles I's military council, a brave and distinguished officer, who died in a skirmish at Abingdon. "A man of great wisdom and temper and amongst the very few soldiers who made himself to be universally loved and esteemed" (Clarendon, quoted in *DNB*).
47. *Winter:* Sir John Winter (1600?–73), secretary to Queen Henrietta Maria, addicted to Roman Catholic ideas. In 1642 he joined Sir Ralph Hopton in the western campaign, and later harassed Parliamentary forces by guerilla tactics. *Talbot:* Richard Talbot, Earl and titular Duke of Tyrconnel (1630–91), Roman Catholic officer who became a Gentleman of the Bedchamber to the Duke of York at the Restoration. He was one of those who tried to defame Anne Hyde's character (see *Third Advice,* 249–52 and n.). In 1678 he was arrested in Ireland for supposed complicity in the Popish Plot. *Cansfield:* I have been unable to identify this figure. *Vavasour:* Probably the Col. William Vavasour mentioned by Clarendon as having, by the commission of Prince Charles, mustered some infantry at Flushing for the invasion of England in 1648.
48 *Lunsford:* Probably Sir Thomas Lunsford (1610?–53?), a colonel in the army of Charles I. He was of savage disposition and was rumored to be a cannibal and in the habit of eating children. Butler alludes to this baseless libel in *Hudibras,* pt. 3, canto 2, 1111–12. *Slingsby:* Sir Henry Slingsby (1602–58), soldier and conspirator executed for taking part in a projected Royalist rising in Yorkshire.

That to the empty altar make your bow,
Deny the Real Presence, yet adore
The very place on which it stood before?   60
Must the yea's and no's of such a pitiful crew
Give or deny our worship, as are you?
Must we be forc'd th' religion to defile
Of your great grandsires on your cross and pile?
T'other day you damn'd all conventicles; now   65
The humor's alter'd, you can them allow
And lastly vent your rage on us, whose blood
Against the common enemies ever stood.
And this change now gives us a lusty hope,
Since you Fanatics love no more than Pope,   70
That if his Majesty would kindly please
To give us liberty, you'd give us ease,
For you have given us measure good enough
How poor and insignificant is this huff.
The War and standing army you'd have down,   75
And Cabal's heads, as enemies to the Crown,
Or you'd no moneys raise, no, that you'd not—
One would have thought this was a goodly plot—
But war, cabals, and armies still, poor mome,
Yet money's rais'd, and you're gone sneaking home,   80
So that if his Majesty would please to be
As good t' his friends as to his enemy,
We doubt not your good nature would comply
With Turk or Pope without a reason why.
For all that reason which the rabble knows   85
Lies in the majority of yea's and no's,
Which shrinks all births to tympanies i'th' House,

63–64. *Cross and pile* here means "heads and tails." In other words the question
means "Must we surrender our religion because of your arbitrary votes (*yea's and
no's*)?"
65–66. An allusion to the legislation which was being prepared in this session to
extend toleration to some Protestants.
74. *huff:* Bluster.
79. *Are* is understood in this line, i.e. wars, cabals, and standing armies, the griev-
ances which you protested, are still in existence. *mome:* Blockhead or carping critic.
80. Parliament supplied £1,200,000 for the continuation of the war. See 107–09 be-
low.
87. *tympanies:* A tympany is a morbid swelling or tumor, figuratively "something

Like mountains pregnant, to bring forth a mouse.
Thick, clumsy wits, whetted with muddy ale,
Like froth, falls of itself and proves a stale.   90
On with your blue coats, your true ancient weed,
Which liv'ry shows you're of the vulgar breed.
To talk of hogs and oxen you are fitted;
They subjects are for brutes no better witted.
You talk of holy mysteries divine,   95
Whose conversation is scarce fit for wine.
Go, get you home, you rustics! *You* dictate
T' his Majesty the great intrigues of state?
Must your hodge-podge, piss'd-upon religion be
The standard of all worship, and must we   100
To that bald bawdy stuff submit, who name
The codpiece can, and cause from whence it came?
Go, silly fops, assure yourselves that we
To any sect will turn, before yours we'll be.
Go, get you home, you bumpkins, tell your maid   105
And she's in th' parish what i'th' House you said.
Crack how you'd have wonders done had not false Lee,

---

big or pretentious, but empty or vain" (*OED*). Here it carries a suggestion of false pregnancy.

91. *blue coats:* Formerly the dress of servants and the lower orders.

100–02. An oblique insult at the Anglican Church, tracing its establishment to Henry VIII's polygamous propensities. Cf. *The History of Insipids,* 7–10:

> The virtues in thee, Charles, inherent
>   (Although thy countenance be an odd piece)
> Prove thee as true a God's vicegerent
>   As e'er was Harry with the codpiece.

106. *she's:* Girls.

107–08. The allegation of treachery is based on the fact that at the beginning of this session the majority of the opposition were inclined to grant the government £600,000—enough to procure a peace but not enough to continue the war. Garraway and Lee, as leaders of the opposition, were to name this sum, "but Garraway named £1,200,000 and was seconded in it by Lee. So this surprise gained the great sum which enabled the Court to carry on the war. When their party reproached these persons for it, they said they had tried some of the Court on the head, who had assured them the whole agreement [to cancel the Declaration of Indulgence] would be broke if they offered so small a sum, and this made them venture on it. They had good rewards from the Court and continued still voting on the other side" (Burnet, 2, 15–16; an editorial note, 2, 92, describes how Lee was bribed with £6,000. Cf. *Britannia and Raleigh*, 17: "Till Lee and Garraway shall bribes reject." I can find no mention of Meers' alleged part in this stratagem.

Garraway, and Meers been traitors to ye,
That all may know the House affords no tools
But what divide themselves 'twixt knaves and fools.   110
Be gone, you sots, run to your powder'd beef!
Learn next to bite before you show your teeth,
But if your teeth should chance to prove too keen,
A med'cine may be found to cure your spleen.

His Highness' Conversion by Father Patrick
(*1673*)

The Duke of York's conversion to the Catholic faith became public knowledge when he resigned the Admiralty after the passage of the Test Act in March 1673. Father Patrick was a member of the Queen's entourage and appears frequently in anti-Catholic literature of this period. On 15 March 1673 he was named in the House of Commons, with Lord Arundell of Wardour and Colonel Richard Talbot, as "particularly active on behalf of Roman Catholics in Ireland and unfit to be near the King" (Grey's *Debates*).

His Highness's Conversion is ascribed to "E. of R." in the various editions of *State Poems*. A National Library of Scotland MS. (Adv. 19.1.12) ascribes it to Rochester, but most ascriptions in this MS. are unreliable. Lucyle Hook quotes a letter written 15 April 1673 which refers to the poem as follows:

> I have been in quest of some more of my Lord Rochester's ingenuity but cannot as yet accomplish my desires, but in the meantime I present you with a copy that is stolen from one to another about town and fortunately this morning came to my hands.
>
> ("Something More about Rochester," *MLN*, 75 [1960], 482)

Whether Thacker, the author of the letter, is assigning the poem to Rochester depends, as she observes, upon the interpretation of "ingenuity." In my opinion Thacker was indicating that the poem was not Rochester's.

His Highness' Conversion by Father Patrick

Between Father Patrick and's Highness of late
There happen'd a strong and weighty debate,
And religion the theme—'tis strange that they two
Should dispute about that which neither of 'em knew!

For I dare boldly say, had his Highness but known   5
The weakness of Patrick's and the strength of his own,
He'd have call'd it a madness and much like a curse
To change from a true one to one that's much worse.
For if it be true (as some wags make us think)
That a Papist of all his five senses must wink,   10
A man's no more a man when waking than sleeping,
As long as Father Patrick has his senses in keeping.
And sure it's not so, we must all be mistaken
And have liv'd in a dream and are just now awaken:
For the Father was mighty in word and in reason,   15
He urg'd not a syllable, but came so in season
That ev'ry argument was stronger and stronger,
So the Duke cri'd at last, "I can hold out no longer!"
The reason that mov'd most his Highness to yield
And so willingly quit to the Father the field,   20
Was, first, that they cheated and left you in the lurch
That told you there could be any more than one Church;
And next, he averr'd to the Duke for a certain
No footsteps of ours could be found before Martin.
At these two great reasons so full and profound   25
The Duke had much ado not to fall in a swound;
And straight he cri'd out, "Father Patrick, I find,
By a sudden conversion and change of my mind,
That neither your learning nor wit could afford
Such strength to your cause—'twas the finger o'th' Lord: 30
For now I remember that somewhere 'tis said
That from babes and from sucklings his truth is convey'd;
And therefore I submit, for my conscience's ease,
To be led by the nose as your fathership please."

So ended the matter 'twixt the priest and the knight,   35
In which (to speak truth and to do all sides right)
He manag'd this matter as he did his sea-fight.

32. See Luke 10:21: "Thou hast hid these things from the wise and prudent and hast revealed them unto babes."

37. *his sea-fight:* A reference, perhaps, to the Battle of Sole Bay (28 May 1672). James had permitted his fleet to be surprised by the Dutch, and the English had the worst of the fierce engagement which ensued. James was also criticized, perhaps unjustly, for having been "too careful of his own life in leaving ships that were sorely pressed by the enemy" (Turner, *James II,* p. 104).

Advice to a Painter to Draw the Duke by
(1673)

This anti-Catholic satire on the Duke of York and his circle was written, Margoliouth has shown, in the late summer of 1673, but it was not printed until the height of the public uproar over the Popish Plot in 1679. The occasion for the attack was the assembling on Blackheath of an army which the government pretended was designed for the invasion of Holland upon the anticipated defeat of De Ruyter's forces at sea. "De Ruyter, however, held his own, and the muster served only to inspire the suspicion that it aimed at the subjection of London to 'Popery and arbitrary government' " (Margoliouth). Other factors contributed to the aggravation of these anxieties: the ascendancy of Charles' French Catholic mistress, Louise de Kéroualle; England's alliance with Catholic, despotic France against Protestant Holland; the Test Act, which revealed York and Clifford as Catholics; and the Duke's declared intention of marrying the Catholic Mary of Modena.

The publication of the poem caused some excitement, possibly because of the aroused state of public feeling on the issues it dealt with. 1200 copies were seized by the government and burned on 20 February 1680 (see Charles R. Gillett, *Burned Books*, 2, 491–93). Letters exchanged by Henry Savile and his brother Halifax in July 1679 are a further indication of the impact of this *Advice*. On 17 July Halifax writes: "Here is lately come out in print, amongst other libels, an *Advice to a Painter*, which was written some years since and went about, but now by the liberty of the press is made public, which for many reasons I am sorry for." Savile attempts to reassure his brother in his answer of 22 July: "As for your concern for a certain printed paper, the greatest grief I have is that it is very falsely printed, for as to all other considerations such old stuff is so long forgot that I do not think it will have any effect to the prejudice of those you are concerned for."

From the Savile-Halifax exchange and an attribution in a later

hand in B. M. Harl. 7315 Margoliouth concluded that Savile was
the author. In a letter to his brother Charles dated 25 May 1676
Christopher Hatton reports that Savile was banished the court for a
sarcastic comment on the Duke of York's failure to attend Anglican
services. "After the Duke discoursing of the necessity to have guards
and soldiers to prevent tumults, H. S. told him that an army had
turned out Richard and he feared might turn out others, and that
he hoped to see England governed without soldiers" (*Hatton Cor-
respondence, 1,* 129). The tone and substance of the *Advice* are con-
sistent with these remarks. Against this evidence two other ascrip-
tions must be considered. The National Library of Scotland Advo-
cate MS. 19.1.12 identifies the poem as Marvell's, but its attributions
are generally unreliable. A more authoritative ascription to "Mr.
Aylof" occurs in Thompson's note in the Bodley Marvell MS. (Eng.
Poet. d. 49). Presumably Thompson, who edited Marvell's works in
1776, based his ascription on information not available to us. Al-
though the *Advice* in some respects resembles other satires which I
feel are probably by Ayloffe, the respectful envoy to Charles II is
not consistent with the contempt for Charles, for the Stuarts, and
for monarchy itself expressed in these other pieces. David Vieth has
mentioned to me, however, that this envoy appears alone, with an
ascription to Rochester, in B.M. Add. MS. 34109. In the present state
of the evidence I am inclined to accept Thompson's ascription of
the poem to Ayloffe.

ADVICE TO A PAINTER TO DRAW THE DUKE BY

Spread a large canvas, Painter, to contain
The great assembly and the num'rous train,
Who all in triumph shall about him sit,
Abhorring wisdom, and despising wit,
Hating all justice, and resolv'd to fight   5
To rob his native country of her right.
    First draw him falling prostrate to the south,
Adoring Rome, this label in his mouth:
"Most Holy Father, being join'd in league
With Father Patrick, Derby, and with Teague,   10

---

10. *Father Patrick:* A Catholic priest, named in the House of Commons 15 March
1673 with Lord Arundell of Wardour and Col. Richard Talbot as particularly active

Thrown at your sacred feet I humbly bow,
I, and the wise associates of my vow—
A vow nor fire nor sword shall ever end,
Till all this nation to your footstool bend.
Arm'd with bold zeal and blessings from your hands,   15
I'll raise my Papists and my Irish bands,
And by a noble, well-contrived plot,
Manag'd by wise Fitzgerald and by Scott,
Prove to the world I'll have old England know
That common sense is my eternal foe.   20
I ne'er can fight in a more glorious cause
Than to destroy their liberty and laws,
Their House of Commons and their House of Lords,
Their parchment precedents and dull records.
Shall these men dare to contradict my will   25
And think a prince o'th' blood can e'er do ill?

---

on behalf of Roman Catholics in Ireland and unfit to be near the King. It was through the upsetting of the closed coach in which he was driving with Clifford from Somerset House on 17 May 1673 that Clifford's recusancy became known (Margoliouth). Savile mentions Father Patrick sardonically in a letter to Halifax dated 22 July 1679 (*Saville Correspondence*, p. 109). *Derby:* I cannot find any individual by this name who makes a plausible identification. Grosart suggests that Derby refers to "Derby-House designs"—a Republican conspiracy (see Marvell, *Further Advice*, 54 and n.). The line would then point to a coalition against the government of three groups: the Catholics, the Republicans, and the Irish.

18. *Fitzgerald:* Col. John Fitzgerald or Fitzgerard, Irish Catholic soldier. Referring to the summer of 1673 Marvell writes: "Monsieur Schomberg, a French Protestant, has been made General and Col. Fitzgerald, an Irish Papist, Major General, as more proper for the secret: the first of advancing the French government, the second of promoting the Irish religion" (*Growth of Popery and Arbitrary Government, Works*, ed. Grosart, *4*, 293). *Scott:* Grosart's "infamous Col. John Scott" seems an unlikely identification in the absence of corroborating evidence. It seems to me that Sir Edward Scott has a strong claim to be the man in question. In a letter dated 18 Feb. 1673 the Lord Lieutenant of Ireland writes Arlington of "irregular actions of some of the Roman persuasion," among them "one Power, who has sent to Sir Edward Scott to represent his case" (*CSPD 1672–73*, p. 581). Scott had recently been replaced as Lieutenant-Colonel of Buckingham's regiment. In Nov. 1680 the Earl of Longford wrote Ormonde how "at Limerick, when the Plot [the Popish Plot] was in agitation there, there was a meeting in Dublin in order to it by Col. Talbot, Col. Fitzpatrick, Sir Edward Scott, Col. Dempsey, Peter Talbot, and Plunkett" (*HMCR, Ormonde* n.s., *5*, 480). At the time of the Revolution Sir Edward was Governor of Portsmouth and alarmed the citizens with the Irish troops loyal to James II under his command. He is reported to have sworn "that if the Prince of Orange's army ever appeared before the garrison, he would cut the throats of all the Corporation" (*HMCR, Dartmouth, 1*, 231–32).

It is our birthright to have power to kill.
Shall these men dare to think, or these decide
The way to Heaven and who shall be my guide?
Shall these pretend to say that bread is bread,   30
If we affirm it is a god indeed?
Or that there's not a Purgat'ry for the dead?
That extreme unction is but common oil,
And not infallible the Roman soil?
I'll have those villains in our notions rest;   35
And I do say it, therefore 'tis the best."
    Next, Painter, draw his Mordaunt by his side,
Conveying his religion, and his bride:
He who long since abjur'd the royal line
Does now in Popery with his master join.   40
Then draw the Princess with her golden locks,
Hast'ning to be envenom'd with the pox,
And in her youthful veins receive the wound
That sent Nan Hyde before her under ground;
That wound wherewith the tainted Churchill fades,   45
Preserv'd in store for a new set of Maids.
Poor Princess, born under a sullen star,
To find this welcome when you're come so far!

37–38. *Mordaunt:* Henry Mordaunt (1624?–97), second Earl of Peterborough, negotiated the marriage between the Duke of York and Mary of Modena. The marriage took place 30 Sept. 1673 with Mordaunt standing proxy for the Duke. He then accompanied Mary to England where she arrived 12 Nov. 1673. *Conveying* has here the obsolete sense of "carrying off clandestinely" (*OED*). By "conveying" to James a Roman Catholic bride, the Catholic Earl of Peterborough is seen as making away with the Duke's attachment to the Anglican faith. Actually James had revealed his conversion to Catholicism months before by not complying with the provisions of the Test Act.

39. Mordaunt fought for Parliament until 1643 (Margoliouth).

41. *golden locks:* Margoliouth quotes Ranke on the Princess' "dark eyes and raven hair." In *R"* *golden* is altered to *chestnut.*

44. The first Duchess died not of pox but of cancer of the breast.

45. *Churchill:* Arabella Churchill (1648–1730), daughter of the loyalist Sir Winston Churchill and sister of the famous first Duke of Marlborough. Sir Winston's fidelity to the Stuarts during the Civil War and Interregnum marked his family out for royal favor and Arabella was accordingly appointed Maid of Honor to the first Duchess of York. She soon won the affection of the Duke and became his mistress between 1665 and 1667. If Arabella was "fading," as the poet alleges, the wasting process was remarkably slow, since she lasted for almost sixty years after he wrote the poem.

46. *Maids:* Maids of Honor.

Better some jealous neighbor of your own
Had call'd you to some sound though petty throne,   50
Where 'twixt a wholesome husband and a page
You might have linger'd out a lazy age,
Than in false hopes of being once a queen
Die before twenty, rot before sixteen.
    Now, Painter, show us in thy blackest dye   55
The counsellors of all his villainy:
Clifford, who first appear'd in humble guise,
Was thought to be so meek and yet so wise,
But when he came to act upon the stage,
He prov'd the mad Cethegus of our age.   60
He and his Duke had each too great a mind
To be by justice or by law confin'd.
Their boiling heads can hear no other sounds
Than fleets and armies, battles, blood, and wounds;
And to destroy our liberties they hope   65
By Irish fools and by a doting Pope.
    Next, Talbot must by his great master stand,
Laden with folly, flesh, and ill-got land:
He's of a size indeed to fill a porch,

54. Mary of Modena, born 5 Oct. 1658, was just fifteen when she reached England. She died 7 May 1718.

60. *Cethegus:* The most outrageous of Catiline's fellow conspirators. During a debate on the Test Act in the House of Lords Clifford was the only peer "who had the courage to attack the Bill root and branch. With more zeal than discretion he launched into an impassioned harangue, which Colbert de Croissy described as resembling a sermon more than a speech" in the course of which he described the Bill as the *"monstrum horrendum* of Virgil" (Hartmann, *Clifford of the Cabal,* p. 261).

66. *doting Pope:* Clement X (1590–1676) was nearly eighty when he became Pope in 1670.

67. *Talbot:* Richard Talbot (1630–91), Gentleman of the Bedchamber to the Duke of York, afterwards Earl and titular Duke of Tyrconnel and Viceroy of Ireland. He was a man of commanding stature but corpulent and unwieldy. He received grants of land in Ireland at the Restoration. His brother, Peter Talbot (1620–80), was the titular Roman Catholic Archbishop of Dublin and a close friend of the Duke of York. For the alleged involvement of the two brothers in a Catholic plot see note on line 18. In a House of Commons debate of 17 March 1673 much agitation is expressed about Col. Richard Talbot and his troop of horse (see Grey's *Debates*). Richard Talbot "was a duellist, like his brother Gilbert, and ready to fight on the slightest provocation" (*DNB*). When he was made commander of the army in Ireland on the accession of James II, Talbot put into operation a scheme dating from 1671 to disband the Protestant militia in order to neutralize the Act of Settlement.

But ne'er can make the pillar of a Church.   70
His sword is all his argument and his book.
Although no scholar, he may act the cook,
And will cut throats again, if he be paid:
In th' Irish shambles he first learn'd that trade.
    Then, Painter, show thy skill, and in fit place   75
Let's see the nuncio Arundell's sweet face;
Let the beholders by thy art descry
His sense and soul, as squinting as his eye.
    Let Bellasis' autumnal face be seen,
Rich with the spoils of a poor Algerine,   80
Who trusting in him, was by him betray'd,
And so should we were his advice obey'd.
That hero once won honor by the sword;
He got his wealth by breaking of his word;
And now has got his daughter got with child,   85
And pimp'd to have his family defil'd.
    Next, Painter, draw the rabble of the plot:
Jermyn, Fitzgerald, Loftus, Porter, Scott.

76. *Arundell:* Henry Arundell (1606?–94), third Baron Arundell of Wardour, was one of the Roman Catholic peers sent by Charles II in 1669 on a secret mission to inform Louis XIV of the King's desire to be reconciled to Rome. See note on line 10.

79. *Bellasis:* John Lord Bellasis or Belasyse (1614–89), with Arundell of Wardour, Powis, Stafford, and Petre was committed to the Tower in 1678 for complicity in the Popish Plot on the information of Titus Oates. He was a noted soldier.

80–82. As Governor of Tangier Bellasis had made a fortune out of prizes. Pepys writes how he "told me the whole story of his gains by the Turkey prizes, which he owns he hath got about £5,000 by. Promised me the same profits Povy was to have had, and in fine I find him a pretty subtle man" (*Diary,* 23 May 1666).

85. *daughter:* Daughter-in-law, widow of Sir Henry Bellasis. "She was a zealous Protestant, though she was married into a Popish family. She was a woman of much life and great vivacity, but of a very small proportion of beauty, as the Duke was often observed to be led by his amours to objects that had no extraordinary charms. Lady Bellasis gained so much on the Duke that he gave her a promise under his hand to marry her; and he sent Coleman to her to draw her over to Popery, but in that she could not be moved" (Burnet, *2,* 19). Far from promoting a match of any sort between the Duke and this lady, Sir Henry engaged the King to separate the two lest Lady Bellasis wreck the design for bringing in Roman Catholicism. Soon after James married Mary of Modena.

88. *Jermyn:* Henry Jermyn, a Roman Catholic and Master of the Horse to the Duke of York. See *Last Instructions,* 102 n. *Loftus:* Dudley Loftus (1619–95), Irish jurist and oriental scholar, the holder of judicial posts under Cromwell and Charles II. *Porter:* Probably Charles Porter, who became Lord Chancellor of Ireland under James II.

These are fit heads indeed to turn a state,
And change the order of a nation's fate;   90
Ten thousand such as these can ne'er control
The smallest atom of an English soul!
Old England on her strong foundations stands,
Defying all their heads and all their hands.
Its steady basis never could be shook,   95
When wiser men its ruin undertook:
And can her guardian angel let her stoop
At last to madmen, fools, and to the Pope?
No, Painter, no; close up thy piece, and see
This crowd of traitors hang in effigy!   100

To the King

Great Charles, who full of mercy wouldst command
In peace and pleasure this thy native land,
At last take pity of thy tott'ring throne,
Shook by the faults of others, not thine own.
Let not thy life and crown together end,   105
Betray'd by a false brother and false friend.
Observe the danger that appears so near
And all your subjects do each minute fear:
A drop of poison or a Popish knife
Ends all the joys of England with thy life.   110
Brothers, 'tis true, by nature should be kind,
But to a zealous and ambitious mind,
Brib'd with a crown on earth and one above,
There's no more friendship, tenderness, or love.
See in all ages what examples are   115
Of monarchs murder'd by an impatient heir;
Hard fate of princes, who will ne'er believe
Till the stroke's struck which they can ne'er retrieve.

A Charge to the Grand Inquest of England
(1674)

The sessions of Parliament from February 1673 to February 1674 decisively defeated the attempts of Charles and some of his ministers to maintain the French alliance and the war against Holland, to suspend the penal laws against Dissenters and Catholics, and to extend the royal prerogative and reduce the King's financial dependence upon Parliament. These sessions struck mighty blows for freedom from "Popery and arbitrary government" by judiciously withholding the royal supply until grievances had been redressed. Among these grievances were violations of Parliamentary privilege, the maintenance of a standing army (purportedly for use against the Dutch), which was widely feared as an instrument to awe the uncooperative Commons, the alliance with Popish France against Protestant Holland, the presence of Catholics in high office (especially Clifford and York), the appointment of a foreigner to command the English army, and the high-handed policies of the three remaining members of the Cabal, Arlington, Buckingham, and Lauderdale. Although Charles was forced to make peace with the Dutch in 1674 as a result of opposition pressure, the Commons, now fully aroused to the threatened liberties of Englishmen, continued to vote address after address on various grievances until they were prorogued on 24 February 1674. So high did anti-Catholic feelings rise that measures were undertaken, though not completed before the prorogation, to exclude Catholic heirs from succeeding to the throne, and even the estimable Pepys was summoned to the bar of the House because the Earl of Shaftesbury was reported to have seen an altar and a crucifix in his house at Seething Lane. Pepys was cleared, but Parliament was later to return to the project of the Exclusion Bill in 1679.

A Charge to the Grand Inquest of England attacks the opposition in the House of Commons for abusing Parliamentary privilege and for encroaching on the royal prerogative. To judge from the almost unanimous hostility to the government's policies at this time, these sentiments make the satire a rare piece of pro-government propaganda, like *The Banished Priests' Farewell*. The poem singles out for attack the M.P.'s who took a leading part in pressing for the redress of grievances: Howard, Powell, Garraway, Meers, Temple, Marvell, Cavendish, and Whorwood. One version substitutes Birch, Lee, and Coventry for Powell and Garraway. In any event all the persons named were unrelenting in their efforts to oppose the French and Catholic bias of the administration, and their names appear on almost every page of Grey's *Debates* or on the committee lists in the *Commons Journals*. Both Sir John Coventry and his cousin, Sir William, were vigorous members of the opposition, while even Sir William's brother Henry, a Secretary of State, was lukewarm in his defense of his master's policies.

None of the texts of this poem is very satisfactory, since each has obvious errors and lacunae. The version here printed is based on the first edition with many emendations from the three MSS.

A CHARGE TO THE GRAND INQUEST OF ENGLAND, 1674

Room for the Bedlam Commons, hell and fury!
Room for the gentlemen of our grand jury,
Led by no conjuring bailiff with white wand,
But stately mace in stalking giant's hand.
Call them o'er, Cryer, swear them ev'ry man,   5
And let an oath fetter 'em if it can.
The Foreman first, preferr'd before the rest,
'Cause he has learn'd the art of prating best,

Title. "The House of Commons is the grand inquest of the realm, summoned from all parts, to present public grievances" (*Angliae Notitia, 1674*, Part II, 61).

1. *Room for:* Make way for.

4. After the ceremonious opening of Parliament in the Lords' chamber, the Sergeant-at-Arms of the Commons led them back to their chamber, carrying the mace.

5. *Cryer:* The clerk or assistant clerk who administers the oath of allegiance and supervises the signing of the roll.

6. *oath:* "I, —— ——, swear by Almighty God that I will be faithful and bear true allegiance to his Majesty King Charles, his heirs and successors, according to law. So help me God."

7. *Foreman:* Presumably the Speaker, who would now have been Sir Edward Seymour (1633–1708), well known for his eloquence. Seymour took a leading part in the unsuccessful impeachment proceedings against Arlington in 1674.

Then Howard, Powell, Garraway, and Meers,
Temple and Marvell, who yet wears his ears,   10
Cav'ndish the fop, Whorwood that senior soph,
Some fresh come on, some lately taken off.
When these have kiss'd the book, swear all the rest,
The numerous swarm of this too grand inquest,
Five hundred strong, a formidable crew   15

9. *Howard:* Sir Robert Howard (1626–98), dramatist, future Whig leader, and member for Castle Rising in Norfolk. Although critical of the King's ministers, Howard urged the House to vote supply (Grey, 2, 234). He was on the Committee of Elections and Privileges during this session. *Powell:* Henry Powell (1630–92), member for Cirencester, attacked Shaftesbury for issuing writs for by-elections during the recess without the Speaker's warrant. He opposed the Declaration of Indulgence, supported the Test Act, and attacked the proposed match between the Duke of York and Maria d'Este. Unlike Howard, he urged the House to withold supply until the King had redressed grievances connected with Roman Catholic favorites and with the standing army. On 13 Jan. 1674 he attacked the King's ministers vehemently and said: "every man is sensible of a pernicious design to alter the government, and these counsellors have brought us to the brink of destruction" (Grey, 2, 239). *Garraway:* William Garraway (Chichester, Country party), a severe critic of the conduct of the Third Dutch War. On 12 Jan. 1674 he is reported as speaking against the sneak attack on the Dutch Smyrna fleet as follows: "Did our ambassadors give Holland no security by the Triple League and Breda, that we would not fall on them? . . . War is a subtle thing; lose a correspondence in trade and you know not how to get it again" (Grey, 2, 231). *Meers:* Sir Thomas Meers (1635–1715), M.P. for Lincoln, Country party. On 12 Jan. 1674 he proposed a resolution to the effect that "the lieutenancy in London and Westminster and in the country may be ready to secure the nation from Popish and other tumultuous designs against the King and government" (Grey, 2, 235).

10. *Temple:* Sir Richard Temple (1634–97), member of the Country party for Buckingham. His zeal for the Exclusion Bill earned him the name of "the Stowe Monster" from the adherents of the Duke of York. *Marvell:* All three MSS. agree in this reading, although the first edition gives S——. *Marvell* is, of course, a likely reading. He was a well-known member of the Parliamentary opposition and probably the most famous satirist of the period. He was a member of the Committee of Privileges appointed 7 Feb. 1673.

11. *Cav'ndish:* William Cavendish, later first Duke of Devonshire (1640–1707), M.P. for Derby. On 12 Jan. he spoke against the King's ministers (Grey, 2, 233). *Whorwood:* Brome Whorwood, Country party member for Oxford. In 1673 he supported the Test Act (Dering, *Parliamentary Diary,* p. 136) and spoke against the bill excusing the Queen's servants from its provisions (pp. 146–47). *soph* (sophister): A student in his second or third year at Cambridge.

12. *Some fresh come on, some lately taken off:* Some having newly joined the opposition, some having recently been bought off. *take off.* To remove the opposition of by bribery or corruption, *obs.*

13. Members were required to kiss the Bible after taking the oath of allegiance.

15. *five hundred strong:* "The total number of the House of Commons is a little above 500 persons, whereof commonly near 200 are absent upon business, sickness, etc." (*Angliae Notitia, 1674,* Part II, 73).

(Would you could say of half, good men and true).
Stand close together, sirs, and hear your charge
In brief, which lawyers use to give at large:
  Imprimis, as to treason, let that pass,
Since to talk treason boldly long since was
A privilege of your House, and shortly you
Will privileg'd be to plot and act it too.
  For sacrilege, thefts, robberies, and rapes,
Murders, cheats, perjuries, with such petty scapes
Of which yourselves you too well guilty know,
Transmit these trifles to the courts below.
But if a member chance to get a scar
For the Cause, or by *fortune de la guerre,*
You of the inquest strictly must explore
Whether the wound were given by rogue or whore;
Vote it a breach of privilege, then pass
An act Sir John's nose is as whole as 'twas.
  If a blunt porter justle from the wall,
Or knavish boy at football give a fall
To one o' your House, let boys and porters be
Sent to the Tower or brought upon their knee.
  But above all beat boldly everywhere
For your just rights and privileges here;
Find them out all, and more than ever were.
Search the repositories of the Tower
And your own brains to stretch your lawless power.
Ransack your writers, Milton, Needham, Prynne;

19. *Imprimis:* In the first place.
27–32. These lines allude to the celebrated attack on Sir John Coventry (Dec. 1670) and to the special act passed by the Commons declaring mayhem committed upon a member to be felony without benefit of clergy. See *The Haymarket Hectors.*
28. *the Cause:* The Good Old Cause.
36. Offenders against the privileges or dignities of the House were required to present their apologies kneeling at the bar.
40. Many court records were preserved in the Tower.
42. *Needham:* Marchamount Needham or Nedham (1620–78), scurrilous political journalist. "Never has such a turncoat been seen. He had written against Charles I in *Mercurius Britannicus* from 1644 to 1646; for the King in *Mercurius Pragmaticus* from 1648 to 1649; for the Rump Parliament in *Mercurius Politicus* from 1650 onwards, and for Cromwell and his son in the same periodical and its supplement, the *Publick Intelligencer* (1655 to 1659)" (Muddiman, *The King's Journalist,* p. 14). At

Rather than fail, bring the sly Jesuit in,
Then swoll'n with pride and poison suck'd from these,
Vote your own privilege is what you please.   45
    Thus fortifi'd, each member is supreme:
What court of justice dare touch one of them?
The King disdains not to submit his cause
To the known course and trial of the laws.
Each subject may his King with safety sue,   50
But King nor subject can have right from you,
Who are lawgivers, judge, and party too.
With what distemper'd counsels are we fed,
When such convulsions are in England bred?
The very arse is hoisted o'er the head: 55
Well may you sitting love with all your heart;
It is a posture proper to those parts:
Humble as spiders while you crawl below,
Despis'd, afraid of ev'ry spurn and blow,
Crept in your hole once, you imperious grow: 60
Spread laws, oaths, snares for other men to fall,
And you yourselves may trample on them all.
    From privilege of sov'reign Parliament
(If you have any breath and time unspent)
In the next place to grievances proceed,   65
Such grievances as make the subject bleed.
What we nam'd last before, may here stand first,
For of all plagues with which this nation's curs'd
The privilege of Parliament is worst.
    Then with full throats and empty brains let fly   70
Against the rise and growth of Popery,
Pow'r arbitrary and the prerogative regal,
Monopolies and imprisonments illegal,
Offices set to sale, and scarce a clause

---

the Restoration he fled to Holland, but later obtained his pardon under the great
seal. *Prynne:* William Prynne (1600–69), the famous Puritan pamphleteer.
    43. *the sly Jesuit:* No particular Jesuit seems to be intended.
    60. *your hole:* The House of Commons.
    70–75. In the sessions of 1673–74 there were many addresses and bills against Popery,
against the Duke's marriage to Maria d'Este, against the use of the royal prerogative
to suspend the penal laws, and against arbitrary imprisonments (whence arose the
Habeas Corpus Act, which the prorogation of 24 Feb. prevented from becoming law).

Well executed of the cobweb laws; 75
But, though corrupt enough, touch not th' arcana
Of your dread idol, Law, your great Diana.
'Twill make the nation of lawyers rave
With tongue and pen, nonsense and noise, who have
By this false oracle heap'd up more gold 80
Than e'er that goddess's high-priest of old.
'Twould kindle 'mongst yourselves a civil war,
For those gallants, though not the greatest, are,
Of your whole House, the loudest half by far.
If ten or twelve create us such vexation, 85
What do ten thousand of them in the nation?
Then thunder out against supplies misspent,
The customs wasted through ill management;
Curse the commissioners to the pit of Hell,
Till some of you creep in, then all is well. 90
But pass not o'er the grievances before
You have, with all your might, knock'd down one more,
A grievance your design may ruinate,
As a Welsh knight gravely observ'd of late:
    Resolv'd the boys and footmen shall no more 95
Attend their lordships at the lobby door:
For should the Commons pass some wholesome votes
In their own House, to cut their lordships' throats,
Those rascals might, with their short clubs and swords,
Dare impudently to protect their lords, 100
And by endeavoring their preservation,
Highly oppose the safety of the nation.
    Impeachment on impeachment next renew
With impudent address against all who

94. The Welsh knight may be Sir Henry Vaughan the younger (1613–76), whose Royalist father was noted for his gravity, but I cannot find any record of this observation.

95–102. "Ordered that the Sergeant-at-Arms do take care to keep the stairs and passage to the House free from the disturbance of lackeys and footmen; and that no footman or lackey stand or remain upon the stairs, wherein if any of them shall transgress, that then the Sergeant shall take them into custody, and the officers belonging to the Knight Marshal are to assist him herein" (*CJ*, 7 Feb. 1673).

103. Impeachment proceedings were initiated against Lauderdale, Buckingham, and Arlington in Jan. 1673.

Have better heads or truer hearts than you.   105
On numerous articles let each charge run,
But, when it comes to th' upshot, prove not one.
   In the last place, though least of all you mind it
(Yet you must pull a crow where'er you find it)
With a seeming diligence bravely take in hand   110
The strength, defense, and honor of the land.
But then in this be sure you do no more
Than just spoil what was well begun before.
Your fatal policy too well does show,
Those lofty cares do not belong to you.   115
   When the proud Belgic lion stood at bay,
At once the easier and the nobler prey,
When he for fear more than for rage did roar,
His arse so lash'd as it ne'er was before;
When such a friendly chance kind Fortune threw,   120
No more expected than deserv'd by you,
Who but a parliament could slight it when
We might have drown'd that lion in his den,
Or beat him to a fawning whelp again?
You kindly spar'd your money and your foe: 125
Ere you much older or much wiser grow,
You may expect with interest from these
The timely fruits of your untimely peace.
Let the French proudly brave us on the main,
The Dutch our trade, the seas and Indies gain.   130

109. *pull a crow:* Find fault.

110. *seeming diligence:* "To prove their loyalty and patriotism, the Commons accepted a bill to grant £1,238,750. But its progress was suspended until the House had dealt with the Declaration of Indulgence" (Lodge, *Political History,* p. 115).

122–24. The failure to secure a decisive victory over the Dutch fleet was not the fault of Parliament. After the encounter in Sole Bay (May 1672), "James might still have crippled the enemy if he had been allowed to follow him into his own waters, but Charles and Shaftesbury were imperative that he should lay wait for the merchant ships for the Indies, whose cargoes were valued at millions. Such a prize would have freed the King from dependence either upon Parliament or upon France" (Lodge, p. 111).

128. While Parliament was arraigning the King's ministers early in 1674 "no notice whatever was taken of the King's demand for supplies." Realizing that the continuance of the war was hopeless, Charles appealed to Parliament and was urged to accept the unexpectedly favorable terms of peace offered by the Dutch. The Treaty of Westminister was signed 9 Feb. 1674 (Lodge, p. 124).

Let all the world appear concern'd so far
As to be party in this general war.
Though loud our honor, as our int'rest, calls,
You'll have no swords drawn but within your walls.
When thus, to your no little shame at last,   135
You've many months in doing nothing pass'd,
As curs have shown your teeth, but durst not bite,
As fops have drawn your swords, but dare not fight,
A private bill or two, rather than none,
Get pass'd, then bravely vote a session.   140
   Thus when your pow'r, though not your pride, abates,
Your purses grown as empty as your pates,
'Tis time to send you home to your estates,
Where your wives, who may be understood
T'have been more active for the public good   145
In their low spheres than you, to crown the plot,
Present you pretty babes you ne'er begot.

JOHN AYLOFFE

Britannia and Raleigh
(1674–5)

Britannia and Raleigh is one of several saturnine "visions" or "prophecies" exposing the Popish and authoritarian leanings of Charles II and his court. These poems, such as *The Dream of the Cabal, Nostradamus' Prophecy, Oceana and Britannia,* and *Marvell's Ghost,* were written in the 1670s and early 1680s. They are characterized by a grim, humorless tone, employ analogies from Roman history to underscore the decadence and tyranny of the Stuarts, and uphold republican ideals. *Britannia and Raleigh* is ascribed to "Mr. Ayloff" in Bod. MS. Eng. Poet. d. 49 by Capt. Thompson, who edited Marvell in 1776. Although there are ascriptions to Marvell in two other MSS., I think it likely that this poem, as well as the others I have mentioned, was written by John Ayloffe, but I would not rule out the possibility of collaboration with his close friend, Marvell. For a discussion of the evidence for attribution see my forthcoming study on Ayloffe.

I follow Margoliouth in dating *Britannia and Raleigh* after Henriette de Kéroualle married Philip Herbert Earl of Pembroke on 17 December 1674 (see line 170). It probably was written during the long period of prorogation between February 1674 and April 1675, as "long-scorn'd Parliament" suggests (line 135).

BRITANNIA AND RALEIGH

Brit.   Ah Raleigh, when thy breath thou didst resign
        To trembling James, would I had yielded mine!
        Cubs didst thou call 'em? Hadst thou seen this brood

---

3. Raleigh appears as an opponent of the succession of James I. He was condemned in 1603 for complicity in a plot to kill "the old fox and his cubs" and to put Arabella Stuart on the throne (Margoliouth).

Satyres

Britania
and
Rawleigh, by Mr Aylof

Br: Ah! Rawleigh, when thou didst thy breath resign
To trembling James, would I had yeilded mine:
Cubbs didst thou cal them? hadst thou seen this brood
Of Earls, of Dukes, of Princes of the blood,
No more of Scottish Race thou wouldst complain:
Those would be blessings in this suprious Reign.
Awake, arise from thy long blest repose:
Once more with me partake of mortal Woes.

Ra: What mighty Pow'r hath forc't me from my rest?
Ah! mighty Queen, why so untimely drest?

Br: Favour'd by night, conceal'd by this disguise,
Whilst the lewd Court in drunken slumber lys,
I stole away: and never wil return
Til England knows who did her City burn;
Til Cavaliers shall Favorites be deem'd,
And loyal Suff'rers by the Court esteem'd;

Of earls, of dukes, and princes of the blood,
No more of Scottish race thou wouldst complain;   5
Those would be blessings in this spurious reign.
Awake, arise from thy long-blest repose!
Once more with me partake of mortal woes.

Ral.   What mighty pow'r has forc'd me from my rest?
Ah, mighty Queen, why so unseemly dress'd?   10

Brit.   Favor'd by night, conceal'd by this disguise,
Whilst the lewd court in drunken slumber lies,
I stole away and never will return,
Till England knows who did her city burn,
Till Cavaliers shall favorites be deem'd   15
And loyal sufferings by the Court esteem'd,
Till Howard and Garr'way shall a bribe reject,
Till golden Osborne cheating shall detect,
Till atheist Lauderdale shall leave this land,
Till Commons' votes shall cut-nose guards disband,   20
Till Kate a happy mother shall become,

4. Charles II's bastard princes in 1675 included James, Duke of Monmouth, son of Lucy Walters or Barlow; Charles Fitzroy, Earl of Southampton and Henry Fitzroy, Earl of Euston, both sons of the Duchess of Cleveland; and Charles Lennox, Duke of Richmond, son of the Duchess of Portsmouth.

17. Some versions read *Leigh* (or *Lee*) and *Garraway*. Sir Robert Howard, according to a letter from Marvell to William Popple (28 Nov. 1670), was one of five members of the Country party "who openly took leave of their former party and fell to head the King's business" (*Letters*, p. 305). Howard's dishonesty is indicated by the following account (Browning, *Danby*, *1*, 245–46): "In September 1677 Danby revived the scheme he had first meditated nearly three years earlier and delivered his long-expected attack upon Sir Robert Howard, formally accusing him in council of conniving at the misuse of government funds by the tellers of the Exchequer, employing his knowledge of their irregularities to compel them to lend him money, and trying to defeat an investigation by exhibiting false bags, in which were lead blanks or pieces of iron with only a little silver on top. The charge appears to have been substantially true, and the best Howard could do in his defence was to interpose one delay after another." For *Garraway*, see *On the Prorogation*, line 30 and n. For Sir Thomas *Lee*, see Burnet's account (*The Banished Priests' Farewell*, 107–08 n.).

18. As the first minister to practice systematic bribery in Parliament, Osborne (the Earl of Danby) would have been the last person to expose venality.

19. *atheist:* Lauderdale, originally a Covenanter, turned his coat at the Restoration. In 1663 he declared himself ready to take a cart-load of oaths and to turn Turk to keep his place. (Margoliouth).

20. Another allusion to the maiming of Sir John Coventry. See *The Haymarket Hectors.*

21. *Kate:* Queen Catherine.

Till Charles loves Parliaments, till James hates Rome.

Ral.   What fatal crimes make you forever fly
Your own lov'd court and master's progeny?

Brit.   A colony of French possess the court;   25
Pimps, priests, buffoons i'th' privy-chamber sport.
Such slimy monsters ne'er approach'd a throne
Since Pharaoh's reign, nor so defil'd a crown.
I'th' sacred ear tyrannic arts they croak,
Pervert his mind, his good intentions choke,   30
Tell him of golden Indies, fairy lands,
Leviathans, and absolute commands.
Thus fairy-like the King they steal away,
And in his place a Louis changeling lay.
How oft have I him to himself restor'd,   35
In's left the scales, in's right hand plac'd the sword?
Taught him their use, what dangers would ensue
To those that tri'd to separate these two?
The bloody Scottish chronicle turn'd o'er,
Show'd him how many kings in purple gore   40
Were hurl'd to Hell by learning tyrants' lore.
        The other day fam'd Spenser I did bring,

25. Louise de Kéroualle was then at the height of her power.

27–28. See Exodus 8:4: "Their land brought forth frogs: yea, even in the king's chambers."

32. *Leviathans:* Charles II had been a pupil of Hobbes in Paris in 1646. *Leviathan* was first published in 1651. Ogg comments as follows on the relevance of Hobbes to the policies of Charles II: "In mentality the philosopher of Malmesbury was un-English; but his theories were to find their most complete vindication in Restoration England; and if he was not the inspiration of later Stuart absolutism, he was its prophet. Charles was restored without condition; he was protected against seditious talk by a special treason act; he was given absolute control over all the armed forces; his judges often considered themselves merely the mouthpieces of the royal will; he was empowered by statute to remodel corporations, and so was enabled to destroy those 'worms' which, according to Hobbes, consumed the entrails of the body politic. Each of these things had been advocated as a principle in the *Leviathan*. Still more, the Test Act of 1673 and the Act of 1678 imposed a state religion, for a political purpose and by secular penalties; with this cement Charles established an impregnable power, whereas James transferred his foundations to the shifting sands of compromise and toleration" (*England in the Reign of Charles II*, 2, 745–46).

39–41. The first four Jameses all died violent deaths, James I and James III at the hands of rebellious subjects (Margoliouth).

42–43. These lines allude to Spenser's praise of "great Gloriana" (Queen Elizabeth) in the *Faerie Queene*.

In lofty notes Tudor's blest reign to sing:
How Spain's proud pow'r her virgin arms controll'd
And golden days in peaceful order roll'd,   45
How like ripe fruit she dropp'd from off the throne,
Full of grey hairs, good deeds, endless renown.
As the Jessean hero did appease
Saul's stormy rage and check'd his black disease,
So the learn'd bard with artful songs suppress'd   50
The swelling passions of his canker'd breast
And in his heart kind influences shed
Of country's love, by truth and justice bred.
Then to confirm the cure so well begun,
To him I show'd this glorious setting sun: 55
How by her people's looks pursu'd from far,
She mounted up on a triumphal car,
Outshining Virgo and the Julian star.
Whilst in Truth's mirror this glad scene he spi'd,
Enter'd a dame bedeck'd with spotted pride,   60
Fair flower-de-luces within an azure field;
Her left arm bears the ancient Gallic shield,
By her usurp'd, her right a bloody sword,
Inscrib'd *Leviathan the Sov'reign Lord.*
Her tow'ry front a fiery meteor bears,   65
From exhalation bred of blood and tears.
Around her Jove's loud rav'nous curs complain.

48. *Jessean:* "And it came to pass, when the evil spirit from God was upon Saul, that David [the son of Jesse] took an harp, and played with his hand: so Saul was refreshed, and was well, and the evil spirit departed from him" (I Samuel 16:23).

58. *Julian star:* The comet which appeared at the time of Caesar's assassination.

60. This figure represents the regime of Louis XIV.

63. *usurp'd:* The King of England was still *Rex Angliae et Franciae* and quartered the lilies with the leopards (Margoliouth).

67. *Jove's curs:* Cerberus and the hounds which girdled Scylla, with, perhaps an allusion to Milton's Sin, who "seem'd woman to the waist, and fair," but

> about her middle round
> A cry of hell hounds never ceasing bark'd
> With wide Cerberean mouths full loud, and rung
> A hideous peal: yet, when they list, would creep,
> If aught disturb'd their noise, into her womb,
> And kennel there, yet there still bark'd and howl'd
> Within unseen.

> (*Paradise Lost,* II.652–58)

Pale Death, Lusts, Horror, fill her pompous train.
From th' easy King she Truth's bright mirror took,
And on the ground in spiteful rage it broke,   70
And frowning, thus, with proud disdain, she spoke:
    "Are threadbare virtues ornaments for kings?
Such poor pedantic toys teach underlings!
Do monarchs rise by virtue or the sword?
Whoe'er grew great by keeping of his word?   75
Virtue's a faint greensickness of the souls;
Dastards the hearts and active heat controls.
The rival gods, monarchs of th' other world,
This mortal poison amongst princes hurl'd,
Fearing the mighty projects of the great   80
Should drive them from their proud celestial seat
If not o'er-aw'd by new-found holy cheat.
These pious frauds, too slight t' ensnare the brave,
Are proper arts the long-ear'd rout t' enslave.
Bribe hungry priests to deify your might,   85
To teach your will's the only rule of right,
And sound damnation to those dare deny't.
Thus Heaven's designs against Heaven's self you'll turn,
And they will fear those powers they once did scorn.
When all their goblin interest in mankind,   90
By hirelings sold, to you shall be resign'd,
And by impostors God and man betray'd,
The Church and State you safely may invade.
So boundless Louis in full glory shines,
Whilst your starv'd pow'r in legal fetters pines.   95
Shake off those baby-bonds from your strong arms;
Henceforth be deaf to that old witch's charms.
Taste the delicious sweets of sov'reign power;
'Tis royal game whole kingdoms to deflower.
Three spotless virgins to your bed I bring,   100
A sacrifice to you, their god and King:
As these grow stale we'll harass humankind,
Rack nature, till new pleasures she shall find,

84. *long-ear'd rout:* The stupid mob.
90. *their:* The priests'.
100. *three spotless virgins:* England, Scotland, Ireland.

Strong as your reign, and beauteous as your mind."
When she had spoke a confus'd murmur rose   105
Of French, Scotch, Irish, all my mortal foes;
Some English too, disguis'd (oh shame!) I spi'd,
Led up by the wise son-in-law of Hyde.
With fury drunk, like Bacchanals, they roar,
"Down with that common Magna Charta whore!"   110
With joint consent on helpless me they flew,
And from my Charles to a base jail me drew,
My rev'rend head expos'd to scorn and shame,
To boys, bawds, whores, and made a public game.
Frequent addresses to my Charles I send,   115
And to his care did my sad state commend,
But his fair soul, transform'd by that French dame,
Had lost all sense of honor, justice, fame.
Like a tame spinster in's seragl' he sits,
Besieg'd by whores, buffoons, and bastard chits;   120
Lull'd in security, rolling in lust,
Resigns his crown to angel Carwell's trust.
Her creature Osborne the revenue steals,
False Finch, knave Anglesey misguide the seals,
Mac James the Irish pagod does adore: 125
His French and Teagues command on sea and shore.

108. *son-in-law of Hyde:* The Duke of York.

115–22. Britannia is here associated with Parliament, and she accuses Charles of abandoning her for a pro-French policy.

122. *Carwell:* The common Anglicized version of Kéroualle.

123. Osborn stabilized his high position by forming an alliance with the Duchess of Portsmouth in 1674 (Browning, *Danby, 1,* 129).

124. *Finch:* Heneage Finch (1621–82) became Lord Keeper 9 Nov. 1673. *Anglesey:* Arthur Annesley, first Earl of Anglesey (1614–86), became Lord Privy Seal 22 April 1673.

125. *Mac James:* An allusion to James' suspected reliance upon Irish soldiers to carry out his authoritarian and pro-Catholic policies. *pagod:* Idol, i.e. Roman Catholicism.

126. *His French and Teagues:* Margoliouth quotes Marvell's *Growth of Popery and Arbitrary Government:* "Monsieur Schomberg, a French Protestant, had been made general and Colonel Fitzgerald, an Irish Papist, major-general, as more proper for the secret; the first of advancing the French government, the second of promoting the Irish religion. And therefore the dark hovering of that army so long at Blackheath might not improbably seem the gatherings of a storm to fall upon London; but the ill successes which our fleet met withal this year [1673], also at sea, were sufficient, had there been any such design at home, to have quashed it: for such gallantries are not

The Scotch scabbado of one court, two isles,
Fiend Lauderdale, with ordure all defiles.
Thus the state's nightmar'd by this hellish rout,
And none are left these furies to cast out.   130
Ah Vindex, come, and purge the poison'd state!
Descend, descend, ere the cure's desperate.

Ral.   Once more, great Queen, thy darling try to save,
Rescue him again from scandal and the grave.
Present to his thought his long-scorn'd Parliament,   135
The basis of his throne and government.
In his deaf ear sound his dead father's name;
Perhaps that spell may's erring soul reclaim.
Who knows what good effects from thence may spring?
'Tis godlike good to save a falling king.   140

Brit.   Raleigh, no more; too long in vain I've tri'd
The Stuart from the tyrant to divide.
As easily learn'd virtuosos may
With the dog's blood his gentle kind convey
Into the wolf and make him guardian turn   145
To th' bleating flock, by him so lately torn.
If this imperial oil once taint the blood,
It's by no potent antidote withstood.
Tyrants, like lep'rous kings, for public weal
Must be immur'd, lest their contagion steal   150
Over the whole. Th' elect of Jessean line
To this firm law their scepter did resign.
And shall this stinking Scottish brood evade
Eternal laws, by God for mankind made?

---

to be attempted but in the highest raptures of fortune." At sea Rupert had suc-
ceeded James as Admiral on his refusal to take the test, but as Burnet observes
(*History*, 2, 17): "the captains were the Duke's creatures, so they crossed him all they
could and complained of everything he did."

127. *scabbado:* The pox.

131. *Vindex:* The governor of Gaul who started the revolt against Nero but failed
and committed suicide. See the references to Nero in line 171. Vindex here may only
stand for the avenger in general (Margoliouth).

147. *oil:* That with which kings are consecrated.

149–52. See II Chron. 26:21 for an account of the quarantining of the leperous
King Uzziah.

No!

To the serene Venetian state I'll go,   155
From her sage mouth fam'd principles to know;
With her the prudence of the ancients read,
To teach my people in their steps to tread.
By those great patterns such a state I'll frame   160
Shall darken story, engross loud-mouth'd Fame.
Till then, my Raleigh, teach our noble youth
To love sobriety and holy truth.
Watch and preside over their tender age,
Lest court corruptions should their souls engage.   165
Tell 'em how arts and arms in thy young days
Employ'd the youth, not taverns, stews and plays.
Tell 'em the gen'rous scorn their rise to owe
To flatt'ry, pimping, and a gaudy show.
Teach 'em to scorn the Carwells, Pembrokes, Nells,   170
The Clevelands, Osbornes, Berties, Lauderdales:
Poppea, Messaline, and Acte's name

162–63. An allusion to Raleigh's *Instructions to his Son and to Posterity*, of which a new edition appeared in 1656.

170. *Pembrokes:* This appears in *State Poems* 1689 as P——s and in some copies has been completed in pen as "Portsmouths." Since Portsmouth and Carwell are the same person, this is clearly wrong, and the reference to the Duchess of Portsmouth's sister, Henriette de Kéroualle, who married the Earl of Pembroke on 17 Dec. 1674, is clearly right. Philip Herbert, seventh Earl of Pembroke (1653–83), was a brutal profligate, who is thought by some historians to have murdered Sir Edmund Berry Godfrey by stomping him to death.

171. This line continues the list of promiscuous or politically powerful court ladies. *Osbornes* refers to Bridget Bertie, Osborne's wife, and *Berties* to her influential sisters. Bridget Osborne was reputed to exercise great influence upon her husband's policies and to have received many bribes. *Lauderdales* alludes to Elizabeth, Countess of Dysart and afterwards Duchess of Lauderdale (d. 1697), whose liason with Lauderdale while her first husband was still alive "scandalized even the court of Charles II" (*DNB*). She was rumored to have been the mistress of Oliver Cromwell and to have thereby secured immunity from the Protector's exactions for herself and her family. She was immensely powerful and controlled a great deal of patronage.

172. *Poppea:* Mistress and afterwards wife of Nero. *Messaline:* This reading is supplied from MS. Bod. Don. b. 8 (*D*). Most other versions have *Tegoline* or *Tegeline*, which Margoliouth supposes to be meant for Tigellinus, commander of Nero's Praetorian Guard, but since all the other names in this and the preceding lines are those of women, Messaline seems more appropriate. She was the third wife of the emperor Claudius, well-known for her profligacy and avarice. *Acte:* One of Nero's mistresses.

Yield to all those in lewdness, lust, and shame.
Make 'em admire the Sidneys, Talbots, Veres,
Blake, Cav'ndish, Drake, men void of slavish fears,   175
True sons of glory, pillars of the state,
On whose fam'd deeds all tongues, all writers, wait.
When with fierce ardor their brave souls do burn,
Back to my dearest country I'll return.
Tarquin's just judge and Caesar's equal peers   180
With me I'll bring to dry my people's tears.
Publicola with healing hands shall pour
Balm in their wounds, will fleeting life restore:
Greek arts and Roman arms, in her conjoin'd,
Shall England raise, relieve oppress'd mankind.   185
As Jove's great son th' infested globe did free
From noxious monsters, hell-born tyranny,
So shall my England, by a holy war,
In triumph lead chain'd tyrants from afar.
Her true crusado shall at last pull down   190
The Turkish crescent and the Persian sun.
Freed by thy labors, fortunate, blest isle,
The earth shall rest, the heaven shall on thee smile,
And this kind secret for reward shall give:
No pois'nous tyrant on thy ground shall live.   195

174. *Talbots:* The Earls of Shrewsbury, many of whom had distinguished themselves by military service to the Crown. *Veres:* Sir Francis and Sir Howard Vere, who distinguished themselves in Queen Elizabeth's wars in the Low Countries.

175. *Cav'ndish:* Sir Thomas Cavendish, who circumnavigated the globe.

178. *their:* Our youths'. See line 161.

180. *Tarquin's just judge:* Lucius Junius Brutus. *Caesar's equal peers:* Brutus, Cassius, and the others who killed Caesar.

182. *Publicola:* Publius Valerius, Consul in the first year of the Republic, who earned this cognomen through his respect for the people (Margoliouth).

186. *Jove's great son:* Hercules.

ANDREW MARVELL

Upon his Majesty's being made Free of the City
(1674)

On 29 October 1674 Charles II attended the installation of Sir Robert Viner as Lord Mayor of London. In token of their gratitude for this favor, the Lord Mayor and Aldermen presented a gold box containing the freedom of the City to the King in a ceremony at the Banqueting House on 18 December.

Marvell's poem, as Margoliouth notes, parodies the doggerel stanza used in songs for the Lord Mayor's show.

This poem is included in the Bodleian MS. of Marvell's poems (MS. Eng. Poet. d. 49).

UPON HIS MAJESTY'S BEING MADE FREE OF THE CITY

1.

The Londoners gent
To the King do present
In a box the City maggot;
'Tis a thing sure of weight,
That requires the might
Of the whole Guildhall team to drag it.

5

2.

Whilst the churches unbuilt
And the houses undwelt

---

1. *gent:* Well-bred, polite.
1–6. Cf. below, *History of Insipids,* 115–18:

> By the Lord Mayor and his grave coxcombs
>   Freeman of London Charles is made;
> Then to Whitehall a rich gold box comes,
>   Which is bestow'd on the French jade.

3. *maggot:* Whimsy.

And the orphans want bread to feed 'em,
In a golden box   10
Set with stones of both rocks
You in chains offer your freedom.

3.

Oh you addle-brain'd cits,
Who henceforth in their wits
Would entrust their youth to your heeding?   15
When in diamonds and gold
You have him thus enroll'd,
Yet know both his friends and his breeding.

4.

Beyond sea he began,
Where such riot he ran,   20
That all the world there did leave him;
And now he's come o'er,
Much worse than before,
Oh what fools were you to receive him!

5.

He ne'er knew, not he,   25
How to serve or be free,
Though he's pass'd through so many adventures;
But e'er since he was bound
('Tis the same to be crown'd)
Has ev'ry day broke his indentures.   30

6.

He spends all his days
In running to plays,
When in his shop he should be poring;
And wastes all his nights

11. *both rocks:* Two qualities of precious stones (Margoliouth).
12. *chains:* The Lord Mayor and those aldermen who had been Lord Mayors wore gold chains with their ceremonial robes.
25–30. The institution of apprenticeship was an essential feature of the City's business life, and Marvell compares Charles at length to an unruly apprentice.

In his constant delights   35
Of revelling, drinking, and whoring.

7.

When his masters too rash
Entrusted him with cash,
He us'd as his own to spend on't;
And amongst his wild crew   40
The money he threw,
As if he should ne'er see an end on't.

8.

Throughout Lombard Street
Each one he could meet
He would run on the score and borrow;   45
But when they ask'd for their own,
He was broken and gone
And his creditors all left to sorrow.

9.

Though oft bound to the peace,
He never would cease,
But molested the neighbors with quarrels;   50
And when he was beat,
He still made a retreat
To his Clevelands, his Nells, and his Carwells.

10.

Nay, his company lewd   55
Were thrice grown so rude,
But he chanc'd to have more sobriety,

46–48. An allusion to the stop of the Exchequer of January 1672, which suspended
payments on government loans and caused financial distress among the bankers of
the City.

49. *bound to the peace:* Probably an allusion to the Triple Alliance and the treaties
which ended the two Dutch wars (Margoliouth).

55–60. An allusion to three main attempts of Charles' counselors to extend the
royal prerogative: the Treaty of Dover, 1670; the Declaration of Indulgence, 1672; and
the suspected plot to establish a military dictatorship with the Blackheath army 1673
(Margoliouth).

And the House was well barr'd,
Else with guard upon guard
He had burglar'd all your propriety.   60

11.

The plot was so laid,
Had it not been betray'd,
As had cancell'd all former disasters;
All your wives had been strumpets
To his Highness's trumpets,   65
And the soldiers had all been your masters.

12.

So many are the debts
And the bastards he gets,
Which must all be defray'd by London,
That notwithstanding the care   70
Of Sir Thomas Play'r,
Your Chamber must needs be undone.

13.

His word nor his oath
Cannot bind him to troth,
He values not credit nor history;   75
And though he has serv'd now
Two 'prenticeships through,
He knows not his trade nor mystery.

14.

Then, O London, rejoice
In thy fortunate choice   80
To have made this freeman of spices;

60. *propriety:* Property.
62. Shaftesbury refused to support the King's policy and was dismissed 9 Nov. 1673.
He was reported to have said that it was only laying down his gown and girding on
his sword (Brown, *Shaftesbury*, p. 216).
65. *trumpets:* Trumpeters.
71. *Sir Thomas Play'r:* Chamberlain of the City, who presented the freedom to
Charles II. He was in charge of the Chamber, the Corporation Treasury.
77. *Two 'prenticeships:* i.e. twice seven years, 1660–74 (Margoliouth).
81. *spices:* Charles was an honorary member of the Company of Grocers.

Yet I do not distrust
But he may prove more just,
For his virtues exceed all his vices.

15.

But what little thing   85
Is that which you bring
To the Duke, the kingdom's darling?
How you hug it and draw,
Like ants at a straw,
Though too small for the carriage of Starling!   90

16.

If a box of pills
To cure the Duke's ills,
He is too far gone to begin it;
Or does your Grace trow
A-processioning go
With the pyx and the Host within it?   95

17.

You durst not, I find,
Leave this freedom behind,
And in this box you have sent it;
But if ever he get   100
For himself up to set,
The whole nation may chance to repent it.

18.

And yet if your toy
You would wisely employ,
It might deserve a box, and a gold one;   105
In balloting it use
A new duke to choose,
For we've had too much of the old one.

87. The Duke of York also received the freedom of the City, and, according to a letter of Marvell's, would later receive a proportionately smaller gold box (Margoliouth).

90. *Starling:* Probably a reference to Sir Samuel Starling, Lord Mayor 1669–70, who enforced the penalties of the Conventicle Act very severely.

92. The Duke was reputed to have syphilis.

19.

The very first head
Of the oath to him read   110
Shows how fit he is to govern;
When in heart you all knew
He could never be true
To Charles, our King and Sov'reign.

20.

And how could he swear   115
That he would forbear
To color the goods of an alien,
Who still doth advance
The government of France
With a wife and religion Italian?   120

21.

But all ye blind apes,
Bred in Hell by the papes,
Never think in England to swagger;
He will find who unlocks
The bottom of the box   125
London bears the cross with the dagger.

22.

And now, worshipful sirs,
Go and fold up your furs:
Turn again, Viner, turn again.
I see, whoe'er's freed,   130
You for slaves are decreed,
Until you all burn again, burn again.

110. *oath:* That prescribed by the Test Act of 1673. The Duke would not take this
oath and was obliged under the Act to surrender the office of Lord High Admiral.

117. To color a stranger's goods is to enter them at the custom-house under a citi-
zen's name (Margoliouth).

120. The Duke took Maria d'Este as his second wife in 1673.

126. *cross with the dagger:* The arms of the city of London.

The History of Insipids
(1674)

The History of Insipids (insipids are persons deficient in sense, spirit, or taste) recapitulates many of the events which grieved King Charles' subjects: the Declaration of Indulgence, Blood's favor at court after his attempt to steal the crown, the establishment of systematic bribery in Parliament, naval disasters in the two wars with Holland, the stop of the Exchequer, and the King's receiving the freedom of the City in December 1674.

The poem is ascribed to Rochester in Douce MS. 357 and in *State Poems*. (The text and ascription in Rawl. MS. Poet. 173 are derived from a printed text.) It was reprinted with *Rochester's Farewell* (not by Rochester) and *Marvell's Ghost* (by Ayloffe) in a small octavo in 1709.

Despite these indications, Rochester's authorship remains open to question. In style, tone, and substance, *The History of Insipids* is unlike any other work of Rochester's, while it recapitulates in detail many of the points made in some of Marvell's satires, especially *Second Advice* and *Upon His Majesty's Being Made Free of the City*. On the basis of internal evidence I am inclined to believe that Marvell wrote it, although the condemnation of Blood as a traitor (lines 43–48) conflicts with the attitude expressed in Marvell's epigram, *Upon Blood's Attempt to Steal the Crown*. As matters stand, there is not sufficient evidence for making a firm ascription.

THE HISTORY OF INSIPIDS

1.

Chaste, pious, prudent Charles the Second,
    The miracle of thy restoration
May like to that of quails be reckon'd,

3–6. See Exodus 16.

Rain'd on the Israelitish nation;
The wish'd-for blessing which Heaven sent   5
Became their curse and punishment.

2.

The virtues in thee, Charles, inherent
    (Although thy countenance be an odd piece)
Prove thee as true a God's vicegerent
    As e'er was Harry with the codpiece;   10
For chastity and pious deeds,
His grandsire Harry Charles exceeds.

3.

Our Romish bondage-breaker Harry
    Espoused half a dozen wives;
Charles only one resolves to marry,   15
    And other men's he never swives.
Yet hath he sons and daughters more
Than e'er had Harry by threescore.

4.

Never was such a Faith's Defender:
    He, like a politic prince and pious,   20
Gives liberty to conscience tender
    And doth to no religion tie us:
Jews, Christians, Turks, Papists, he'll please us,
With Moses, Mahomet, Pope, and Jesus.

5.

In all affairs of Church and State   25
    He very zealous is and able,
Devout at prayer and sits up late
    At the Cabal and council-table;

8. "The Prince . . . was no beauty. Unlike his parents he was swarthy and big—
a reversion to some far Provençal or Medici ancestor. 'He is so ugly,' wrote his mother,
'that I am ashamed of him' " (Bryant, *Charles II*, pp. 4–5).

10. *Harry:* Henry VIII.

12. *grandsire Harry:* The Saintly Henri IV of France.

21. Charles published a Declaration of Indulgence to Tender Consciences at Christ-
mas 1662 and another in 1672.

His very dogs at council-board
Sit grave and wise like any lord.   30

6.

Let Charles's policy no man flout—
   The wisest kings have all some folly—
Nor let his piety any doubt;
   Charles, like a sovereign wise and holy,
Makes young men judges of the bench   35
And bishops those that love a wench.

7.

His father's foes he doth reward,
   Preferring those cut off his head;
Old Cavaliers, the Crown's best guard,
   He leaves to starve for want of bread.   40
Never was any prince endu'd
With so much grace and gratitude.

8.

Blood that wears treason in his face,
   Villain complete, in parson's gown,

29. "He took delight to have a number of little spaniels follow him and lie in his bedchamber, where often times he suffered the bitches to puppy and give suck, which rendered it very offensive and, indeed, made the whole court nasty and stinking" (Evelyn, 6 Feb. 1685).

35. Though I can find no trace of Charles' appointing young men to the bench, the King was guilty of selecting judges of inferior ability who would bend their consciences to fit his policies: "As the King's policy developed, it became increasingly difficult to find an able lawyer who would adopt the King's views as to the relation of the prerogative to the law and to Parliament. No doubt, able lawyers could be found who honestly thought that the prerogative had a greater weight in the constitution than Hale, and those who thought with him, admitted. Finch, afterwards Lord Chancellor Nottingham, is the most eminent example; and another is Francis North, Chief Justice of the Common Pleas and afterwards Lord Keeper. But the reasoned Royalist views of such men did not meet the needs of the Court in cases of political importance. The Court could never be quite sure that they would not allow their judicial qualities to get the upper hand. It wanted men of whom it could be sure" (W. S. Holdsworth, *A History of English Law*, 6 [1924], 502–03) .

36. Pepys' cousin Roger told him that Gilbert Sheldon, Archbishop of Canterbury, "do keep a wench, and that he is as very a wencher as can be" (*Diary*, 29 July 1667).

43. The notorious Col. Thomas Blood (1618?–80) attempted, one night in Nov. 1670, to waylay the Duke of Ormonde in St. James' Street and hang him at Tyburn. The

How much is he at court in grace   45
   For stealing Ormonde and the crown?
Since loyalty doth no man good,
Let's seize the King and outdo Blood.

9.

A Parliament of knaves and sots
   (Members by name we must not mention)   50
He keeps in pay and buys their votes,
   Here with a place, there with a pension.
When to give money he can't collogue them
He doth with scorn prorogue, prorogue them.

10.

But they long since, by too much giving,   55
   Undid, betray'd, and sold the nation,
Making their memberships a living
   Better than e'er was sequestration.
God give thee, Charles, a resolution
To damn them all by dissolution.   60

11.

Fame is not founded on success:
   Though victories were Caesar's glory,
Lost battles made not Pompey less,
   But left him styled great in story.
Malicious Fate doth oft devise   65
To beat the brave and fool the wise.

Duke fought his way clear, and his son, Lord Ossory, charged Blood's protector, Buckingham, in the King's presence with instigating the attack. Six months later Blood attempted to steal the crown jewels from the Tower (see *On Blood's Stealing the Crown*). Charles himself questioned Blood but did not punish him, and the ruffian was often seen in the presence-chamber thereafter.

49–54. Under the administration of Danby (1673–79) opposition members of Parliament were systematically bribed into compliance with Court policy.

53. *collogue:* To prevail upon or influence by blandishment, *obs.*

58. *sequestration:* Under the Commonwealth the livings of Royalist ministers were sequestrated on various grounds and bestowed on pro-government clerics.

12.

Charles in the first Dutch War stood fair
  To have been master of the deep,
When Opdam blew up in the air,
  Had not his Highness gone to sleep.
Our fleet slack'd sails, fearing his waking;
The Dutch else had been in sad taking.

13.

The Bergen business was well laid,
  Though we paid dear for that design,
Had we not three days parling stay'd,
  The Dutch fleet there, Charles, had been thine:
Though the false Dane agreed to sell 'um,
He cheated us and saved Skellum.

14.

Had not Charles sweetly chous'd the States,
  By Bergen baffle grown more wise,
And made them shit as small as rats,
  By their rich Smyrna fleet's surprise,
Had haughty Holmes but call'd in Spragge,
Hans had been put into a bag.

70

75

80

69. Cf. *Second Advice*, 167ff.
70. Cf. *Second Advice*, 231ff.
73–78. For the attempt on the Dutch fleet at Bergen see *Second Advice*, 251ff.
78. *Skellum:* Cant term here used for the Dutch East Indies fleet: a thief, rogue.
79. *chous'd:* Tricked.
82. Several Dutch merchantmen were surprised and captured by Sandwich after the Bergen fiasco.
83–84. When England had determined on another war with Holland in 1672, a squadron under the command of Sir Robert Holmes (1622–92) was set out to surprise the Dutch Smyrna fleet in the Channel. Holmes, not wishing to share the glory, failed to signal a passing squadron under the command of Sir Edward Spragge for help, and his ships were severely mauled by the Dutch. Marvell described Holmes in *A Seasonable Argument* (1677) as "first an Irish livery boy, then a highwayman (a pirate would be nearer the mark), now Bashaw of the Isle of Wight, the cursed beginner of the two Dutch wars" (quoted in Eva Scott, *Rupert Prince Palatine*, p. 323).
84. *Hans:* The Dutch.

15.

Mists, storms, short victuals, adverse winds,   85
    And once the navy's wise division,
Defeated Charles's best designs,
    Till he became the foe's derision.
But he had swing'd the Dutch at Chatham,
Had he had ships but to come at 'em.   90

16.

Our Blackheath host without dispute
    (Rais'd, put on board, why, no man knows)
Must Charles have render'd absolute
    Over his subjects or his foes;
Had not the French King made us fools   95
By taking Maastricht with our tools.

17.

But Charles, what could thy policy be,
    To run so many sad disasters,
Joining thy fleet with false d'Estrées,
    To make the French of Holland masters?   100
Was't Carwell, brother James, or Teague
That made thee break the Triple League?

86. For the disastrous division of the English fleet in 1666 see *Third Advice*, 292ff.
89. For the Dutch attack on English ships and shore stations at Chatham in 1667 see *Last Instructions*, passim.
91. *Blackheath host:* In 1673, "the army, assembled on Blackheath, and later at Yarmouth, for the invasion of Holland—and so frequently inspected by the King—was said to be full of Papists, hired for the overthrow of English liberties" (Bryant, *Charles II*, p. 228).
96. English troops under the Duke of Monmouth played a crucial part in the seizure of Maastricht by the French army on 2 July 1673.
99. *false d'Estrées:* A squadron under Vice-Admiral d'Estrées was to cooperate with the English fleet but failed to participate actively in the various encounters of the war. In a naval battle off Scheveringen on 10 Aug. 1673 Prince Rupert charged d'Estrées with deliberately ignoring his signals to engage the enemy: "It was the plainest and greatest opportunity ever lost at sea" (Ogg, *England in the Reign of Charles II, 1*, 376).
101–02. The Duchess of Portsmouth (*Carwell*) was instrumental in persuading Charles to form an Anglo-French alliance. *Teague,* a cant term for an Irish Roman Catholic, does not here specify a particular person.
102. *The Triple League:* A defensive alliance formed in 1667 with Holland and Sweden, which was highly popular in England, especially with Nonconformists who

18.

Could Robin Viner have foreseen
   The glorious triumphs of his master,
The Woolchurch statue gold had been,   105
   Which now is only alabaster:
But wise men think, had it been wood,
'Twere for a bankrupt King too good.

19.

Those that the fabric well consider,
   Do of it diversely discourse;   110
Some pass their censure on the rider,
   Others their judgments on the horse.
Most say the steed's a goodly thing,
But all agree 'tis a lewd King.

20.

By the Lord Mayor and his wise coxcombs,   115
   Freeman of London Charles is made;
Then to Whitehall a rich gold box comes,
   Which is bestow'd on the French jade.
But wonder not it should be so, sirs,
When monarchs rank themselves with grocers.   120

21.

Cringe, scrape no more, you City fops,
   Leave off your feasting and fine speeches,

---

saw in Louis XIV's growing might a threat to religious and civil liberties. It was broken by the alliance with France.

103. *Robert Viner:* Sir Robert Viner (1631–88), a goldsmith who was elected Lord Mayor of London in 1674, set up an equestrian statue of Charles II in the Stocks Market. It was the object of other lampoons. See *A Dialogue between the Two Horses* and *On the Statue in Stocks Market.*

108. *bankrupt King:* In order to finance naval preparations the administration announced in Jan. 1672 that the principal of loans made to the government by City merchants would not be repaid. Many merchants went bankrupt, and Viner was ruined.

115–18. See headnote to *Upon his Majesty's being Made Free of the City.*

118. *the French jade:* The Duchess of Portsmouth.

120. Charles was an honorary Grocer. Cf. *Upon his Majesty's being Made Free of the City,* 81 n.

Beat up your drums, shut up your shops,
   The courtiers then may kiss your breeches.
Arm, tell that Romish Duke that rules,   125
You're free-born subjects, no French mules.

22.

New upstarts, pimps, bastards, whores,
   That locust-like devour the land,
By shutting up th' Exchequer doors
   When thither our money was trepann'd,   130
Have render'd, Charles, thy restoration
A curse and plague unto the nation.

23.

Then, Charles, beware thy brother York,
   Who to thy government gives law;
If once we fall to the old work,   135
   You must again both to Breda,
Where, spite of all that would restore you,
Turn'd commonwealth, we will abhor you.

24.

If of all Christian blood the guilt
   Cry loud for vengeance unto Heaven,   140
That sea by Charles and Louis spilt
   Can never be by God forgiven:
Worse scourges to their subjects, Lord,
Than pestilence, famine, fire, and sword.

25.

The wolf of France and British goat,   145
   One Europe's scorn, t'other her curse
(This fool, that knave, by public vote,
   Yet hard to say which is the worse),
To think such kings, Lord, reign by thee
Were most prodigious blasphemy.   150

129. Clifford was chiefly responsible for the stop of the Exchequer. See note on line 108.

26.

They know no law but their own lust:
   Their subjects' substance and their blood
They count a tribute due and just,
   Still spent and spilt for public good.
If such kings be by God appointed,   155
The Devil is then the Lord's anointed.

27.

Of kings curs'd be the power and name,
   Let all the earth henceforth abhor 'em;
Monsters which knaves sacred proclaim
   And then like slaves fall down before 'em.   160
What can there be in kings divine?
The most are wolves, goats, sheep, or swine.

28.

Then farewell, sacred Majesty,
   Let's pull all brutish tyrants down!
Where men are born and still live free,   165
   There ev'ry head doth wear a crown.
Mankind, like miserable frogs,
Is wretched, king'd by storks or logs.

168. In Aesop's fable, the frogs, "living an easy, free, life everywhere among the lakes and ponds," petitioned Jupiter for a king. Jupiter threw a log into their pool. Terrified by the splash, the frogs treated their king with fear and respect, but after a while they grew tired of the log through familiarity with it and wished a substitute. Jupiter obliged by sending a stork, who devoured them all.

The Chequer Inn
and
The Answer
(*1675*)

The Chequer Inn is a parody of Suckling's well-known *Ballad of a Wedding*. Its popularity, attested by many surviving manuscripts, was due in part to its model, in part to the mounting unpopularity of Thomas Osborne, Earl of Danby, who had become Lord High Treasurer in 1673.

The poem describes an imaginary banquet tendered by the Earl and Countess at Wallingford House, the official residence, to M.P.'s allegedly bribed to defeat the impeachment proceedings instigated against Danby by Arlington in April 1675. (The Chequer Inn stood nearby, on the southwest corner of St. Martin's Lane.) Among other articles, Danby was charged with "having violated and overthrown the ancient course and constitution of the Exchequer"; with assuming the management of Irish affairs, "which were in precedent times dispatched always by the Secretaries and passed in council"; and with being responsible for the continued stop of the Exchequer (the suspension of repayments by the government on loans from private individuals). The charges were quickly dismissed for lack of substance, but the poem pretends that Danby's supporters in the Commons sold their votes.

Although Danby did not need to use bribery in this case, the poem names more than twenty M.P.'s who appear in various lists which he compiled of members whose support the government could rely on because of pensions, jobs, or other material favors which they had received. The lists are printed in Browning's *Danby*, Vol. 1.

On the basis of evidence presently available the authorship of *The Chequer Inn* is open to question. Three manuscripts (Folger m.b. 12, Taylor MS. 2, and Bod Firth c. 15) attribute it to Henry Savile, but the appearance of Savile's name in Danby's lists of supporters for this period seems to discredit the attributions. Two manuscripts, furthermore, attribute the poem to Marvell (B.M. Harl. 7319 and Bod. MS. Eng. Poet. d. 49). *The Chequer Inn* does not resemble any other satires ascribed to Marvell, but it may be that the parody has obscured Marvell's usual marks of style.

The Answer, a brief sequel, is printed as Buckingham's in *Works,* Vol. 2 (3rd ed., 1715).

THE CHEQUER INN

A Supper given by the Treasurer to the Parliament Men, 1675.

1.

I'll tell thee, Dick, where I have been,
Where I the Parliament have seen,
 The choice of ale and beer;
But such a choice as ne'er was found
At any time on English ground,   5
 In borough or in sheere.

2.

At Charing Cross, there, by the way
Where all the Berties make their hay,
 There stands a house new painted;
Where I could see them crowding in,   10
But sure they often there had been,
 They seem'd so well acquainted.

1–6. Danby's feast is compared to the entertaining which accompanied parliamentary elections.

7–8. In 1653, after being refused by his cousin, Dorothy Osborne, Thomas married Lady Bridget Bertie, second daughter of the Royalist leader, Montague, Earl of Lindsey. The Berties were rich and powerful, and through his marriage Danby acquired many useful political and social connections, including the support of in-laws who were members of Parliament. The Exchequer office was on the north side of Charing Cross and Wallingford House just off Charing Cross on the present site of the Admiralty. The Haymarket also leads into Charing Cross, and the Berties lived in the vicinity.

9. *house:* Some MSS. note "Wallingford House, over against Whitehall, let by the Duke of Buckingham to the Earl of Danby, then Lord Treasurer, who treated the Commons there."

3.

The host that dwells in that same house
Is now a man, but was a mouse
    Till he was burgess chosen;   15
And for his country first began,
But quickly turned cat in pan,
    The way they all have rosen.

4.

And ever since he did so wex
That now he money tells by pecks,   20
    And hoards up all our treasure.
Thou'lt ken him out by a white wand
He dandles always in his hand,
    With which he strikes the measure.

5.

But though he now do look so big,   25
And bear himself on such a twig,
    'Twill fail him in a year.
And O! how I could claw him off,
For all that slender quarter-staff,
    And here have him, and there!   30

6.

He is as stiff as any stake,
And leaner, Dick, than any rake;
    Envy is not so pale.
And though by selling of us all,
He wrought himself into Whitehall,   35
    Looks like a bird of jail.

15. Osborne was elected M.P. for York in 1665.
17. To turn the cat in the pan is to change one's position or change sides out of
motives of interest.
18. *rosen:* Risen.
22. A white wand was an emblem of the Lord High Treasurer's office.
29. *quarter-staff:* A stout, iron-tipped staff; here the Treasurer's white staff.

7.

And there he might ere now have laid,
Had not the members most been made,
   For some had him indicted.
But even they that 'peach him durst   40
To clear him would have been the first,
   Had they too been requited.

8.

But he had men enough to spare
Beside a good friend in the chair,
   Though all men blush'd that heard it.   45
And (for I needs must tell my mind)
They all deserv'd to have been fin'd
   For such a shameful verdict.

9.

And now they marched tag and rag,
Each of his handiwork to brag,
   Over a gallant supper.   50
On backside of their letters some
For sureness summon'd were to come;
   The rest were bid by Cooper.

10.

They stood, when enter'd in the hall,   55
Mannerly rear'd against the wall,
   Till to sit down desir'd;
And simper'd (justly to compare)
Like maidens at our statute-fair.
   None went away unhir'd.   60

38. *made:* Had their prosperity assured by bribes. See *made* a.7, **OED**.

43. *a good friend in the chair:* Sir Edward Seymour, Speaker of the House. In 1673 "a definite alliance was struck between them which was to be an important factor in the political situation for the next five years" (Browning, *Danby, 1,* 119).

48. *shameful verdict:* The vote on the articles of impeachment.

54. One MS. (*T*) identifies Cooper as a doorkeeper of the House of Commons.

59. *statute-fair:* A fair or gathering held annually in certain towns and villages for the hiring of servants.

11.

The lady, dress'd like any bride,
Her forehead-cloth had laid aside,
　　And smiling through did sail;
Though they had dirted so her room
That she was fain to call her groom   65
　　To carry up her tail.

12.

Wheeler at board she next her set
And if it had been nearer yet,
　　She might it well afford;
For e'en at bed the time had been   70
When no man could see sky between
　　His lady and her lord.

13.

The knight was sent t'America,
And was as soon sent for away,
　　But not for his good deeds.   75
And since the soil whither he went
Would not bear his wild government
　　Here now he plants the seeds.

14.

Anent him sat George Montague,
The foreman of the British crew,   80
　　(His cup he never fails).
Mansel and Morgan and the rest,
All of'm of the grand inquest
　　(A right jury of Wales).

67. *Wheeler*: Sir Charles Wheeler, close friend and supporter of Danby. *Flagellum Parliamentarium* describes him as "a foot captain, once flattered with the hopes of being Master of the Rolls, now Governor of Nevis: privy chamber man."

73–78. Wheeler had been appointed Governor of the Leeward Islands in 1666.

79. George Montague's name appears in a list, probably drawn up by Williamson, of the King's dependents in the Parliament of 1675. (See Browning, *Danby*, 3, 65.)

82. Sir Edward Mansel's name and that of William Morgan appear in a list of the government whip in 1675. (See Browning, *Danby, 3,* 59, 60).

15.

The western glory, Henry Ford,   85
His landlord Bales outeat, outroar'd,
   And did the trenchers lick.
What pity 'tis a wit so great
Should live to sell himself for meat;
   But who can help it, Dick?   90

16.

Yet, wot'st thou, he was none of those,
But would as well as meat have clothes,
   Before he'd sell the nation;
And, wisely lodging at next door,
Was oft'ner served than the poor   95
   With his whole generation.

17.

Sir Courtney Poole and he contend
Which should the other most commend
   For what that day they spoke:
The man that gave that woeful tax,   100
And sweeping all our chimney-stacks,
   Excis'd us for our smoke.

18.

Wild with his tongue did all outrun,
And popping like an elder-gun,
   Both words and meat did utter.   105
The pellets that his chops did dart

85. Sir Henry Ford appears in a list of Excise Pensioners for 1674–77. He was to receive £300 p.a. (See Browning, *Danby, 3*, 46). *Flagellum Parliamentarium* describes him as "so much in debt he cannot help his taking his bribe and promise of employment" (p. 12).

97. Sir Courtney Poole is frequently mentioned in the lists of Court supporters and dependents. *Flagellum Parliamentarium* describes him as "the first mover for chimney money, for which he had the Court thanks but no snip" (p. 12). He had "snip" on many other occasions, however, and received four large payments out of secret service funds in 1677 and 1678 (Browning, *Danby, 3*, 53). Cf. *Last Instructions*, 193 and n.

103. *Wild:* Probably George Wild "who is taken into pay under the bribe-master, and has already had £800" (*Flagellum Parliamentarium*, p. 17).

Did feed his neighbor overthwart,
That gap'd to hear him sputter.

19.

But King, God save him, though so cramm'd,
The cheer into his breeches ramm'd,   110
  That butt'ry were and larder;
And of more provand to dispose,
Had sew'd on, too, his double hose,
  For times, thou know'st, grow harder.

20.

Holt, out of linen as of land,   115
Had mortgag'd of his two one band,
  To have the other wash'd,
And though his sweat, the while he ate,
With his own gravy fill'd his plate,
  That band with sauce too dash'd.   120

21.

His brain and face Tredenham wrung,
For words not to be said but sung;
  His neck it turn'd on wire.
And Birkenhead—in all that rout
There was but one could be chose out   125
  That was a greater liar.

109. *King:* Two Kings appear in lists of government pensioners, John and Thomas. The emphasis on King's extreme penury makes it likely that the reference concerns Thomas, whom *Flagellum Parliamentarium* describes as "a poor beggarly fellow, who sold his voice to the Treasurer for £50 bribe" (p. 13).

112. *provand:* Provender.

115. Sir Robert Holt appears both as an excise pensioner, 1674–77, and as a recipient of secret service payments in 1677.

116. *band:* Collar.

121. Sir Joseph Tredenham (d. 1707) appears frequently in various lists of government adherents printed by Browning. He was Sir Edward Seymour's son-in-law.

124. Sir John Birkenhead (1616–79), poet and satirist, published a Royalist newspaper, *Mercurius Aulicus,* during the Civil War. He appears among "the King's servants and dependents" in Browning.

22.

Old Hoby's brother Cheyne there,
Throckmorton, Neville, Doleman were,
  And Lawley, knight of Shropshire;
Nay, Portman, though men all cri'd shame,   130
And Cholm'ley of Vale Royal came
  For somewhat more than chop-cheer.

23.

The Hanmers, Harbords, Sandys, Musgraves,
Fathers and sons, like coupl'd slaves,
  They were not to be sunder'd;   135
The tale of all that there did sup
On 'Chequer tally was scor'd up,
  And came above a hundred.

127. Peregrine Hoby appears in a list of Court party members in 1669–71. Charles Cheyne (1624?–98), later Viscount Newhaven, appears in the same list (see Browning, *Danby, 3,* 37). Cheyne succeeded Hoby as M.P. for Great Marlow and is therefore called "old Hoby's brother."

128. *Throckmorton:* Sir Baynham Throckmorton appears in the list of Excise Pensioners, 1674–77, in the Government Whip of 1675, as one of the King's servants in 1675–78, and as a government supporter in 1676. *Flagellum Parliamentarium* reports that he has "£300 per annum in land given him" (p. 13). *Neville:* Probably Richard Neville, another supporter of Danby frequently mentioned in Court lists. He may be the Mr. Neville of Berkshire described in *Flagellum Parliamentarium* as a "court cully" (p. 8). *Doleman:* Sir Thomas Doleman also appears frequently in the lists of government supporters. *Flagellum Parliamentarium* describes him as "flattered with the belief of being made Secretary of State" (p. 8).

129. *Lawley:* Sir Francis Lawley, a faithful follower of Danby.

130. *Portman:* Sir William Portman appears as a government supporter in the Working Lists, 1675–78.

131. *Cholm'ley:* Thomas Cholmondeley, "a court cully" (*Flagellum Parliamentarium,* p. 9).

133. *Hanmers:* Sir Thomas and his son, Sir John, who frequently appear in the Court lists. *Flagellum Parliamentarium* describes Sir John Hanmer as "a privy-chamberman much in debt; had £500 given him to follow his election" (p. 21). *Harbords:* Sir Charles Harbord and William Harbord, both supporters of the government. William Harbord, however, took a prominent part in the impeachment of Danby. *Flagellum Parliamentarium* describes Sir Charles as "first, a poor solicitor, now His Majesty's Surveyor-General and a commissioner for the sale of fee-farm rents" (p. 10). *Sandys:* Samuel and his son, Samuel. Of the elder *Flagellum Parliamentarium* notes: "At the beginning of the sessions had £1,000 lick out of the bribe-pot; has £15,000 given him in the excise farm of Devon" (p. 20). *Musgraves:* Sir Philip Musgrave (1607–78) and his son Christopher (1632?–1704), both staunch Royalists.

24.

Our greatest barn could not have held
The belly-timber that they fell'd,   140
    But mess was rick'd on mess.
'Twas such a feast that I'm afraid
The reck'ning never will be paid
    Without another sess.

25.

They talk'd about and made such din   145
That scarce the lady could edge in
    The Papists and the Frenches.
On them she was allow'd to rail,
But (and thereby does hang a tale)
    Not a word of the wenches.   150

26.

The host plac'd at the lower end
The healths in order up did send,
    Nor of his own took care;
But down his physic bottle threw,
And took his wine when it was due,   155
    In spite of 'pothecare.

27.

They drunk, I know not who had most,
Till King both hostess kiss'd and host,
    Then clapp'd him on the back,
"And prithee why so pale?" Then swore   160
Should they indict him o'er and o'er,
    He'd bring him off i'fack.

144. *sess:* Assessment.
147. Danby and his wife were fervently anti-French and anti-Catholic.
150. In 1674 Danby formed an alliance with the Duchess of Portsmouth and was rumored to be her lover.
151–56. From the time that he had smallpox as a youth, Danby's health was very poor.

28.

They all said ay, that had said no,
And now, who could, 'twas time to go:
   For grace they would not stay;   165
And for to save the serving-men
The pains of coming in again,
   The guests took all away.

29.

Candlesticks, forks, salts, plates, spoons, knives
(Like sweetmeats for their girls and wives)   170
   And table-linen went.
I saw no more, but hither ran,
Lest some should take me for the man,
   And I for them be shent.

THE ANSWER

1.

"Curse on such representatives,
They sell us all, our barns and wives,"
   Quoth Dick, with indignation.
They are but engines to raise tax,
And the whole business of their acts   5
   Is to undo the nation.

2.

Just like our rotten pump at home,
We pour in water when 't won't come,
   And that way get more out.
So when mine host does money lack,   10
He money gives among the pack,
   And then it runs full spout.

3.

By wise volk I have oft been told,
Parliaments grow naught as they grow old:

We groan'd under the Rump,   15
But sure this is a heavier curse,
That sucks and drains thus ev'ry purse
   By this old Whitehall pump.

The Royal Buss
(*1675*)

The Royal Buss gives vent to the widely-felt indignation at Charles' prorogation of Parliament on 22 November 1675. In the words of Keith Feiling, "this doomed autumn session of 1675 marked a further stage in Danby's failure to get the co-operation of King and Parliament" and "indicated more sharply than ever the growing consolidation of party." By Charles' secret agreement with France, this session had been allowed only on probation, and the Commons' continued hostility to France was grounds for dissolution. Although Charles did not dissolve his stubborn Parliament, it did not sit again until February 1677. Charles' dependence on Louis XIV and such instruments of French policy as Louise de Kéroualle (Carwell) are here bitterly attacked.

The Royal Buss is dated 22 November 1675 in a lost manuscript endorsed as a "seditious and traitorous libel" by Secretary Williamson (*CSPD*, 3 May 1676).

Harvard MS. Eng. 636F ascribes the poem to Rochester, but the ascription seems doubtful in view of its prosodic awkwardness.

THE ROYAL BUSS

As in the days of yore was odds
Between the giants and the gods,
So now is rife a fearful brawl
Between the Parliament and Whitehall.
But, bless'd be Jove, the gods of ours   5
Are greater in their guilt than pow'rs.
Though then the heathens were such fools,
Yet they made gods of better tools.
No altars then to plackets were,
No majesty by puss would swear.   10

They'd hang a tippet at his door
Should break a Parliament to please a whore,
And, further to oblige them to it,
Would swear by Carwell's c—— he'd do it,
And by the contents of th' oath he took,   15
Kneel down in zeal and kiss the book.
They'd think the faith too much amiss
That such defenders had as this;
And that religion look'd too poor,
Whose head of Church kiss'd arse of whore.   20
But this he did, much good may't do him,
And then this quean held forth unto him.
The Devil take her for a whore!
Would he had kiss'd ten years before,
Before our city had been burn'd,   25
And all our wealth to plagues had turn'd;
Before she'd ruin'd (pox upon her!)
Our English name, blood, wealth, and honor.
Whilst Parliament too flippant gave,
And courtiers could but ask and have,   30
Whilst they were making English French,
And money'd vote to keep a wench,
And the buffoons and pimps to pay,
The devil a bit prorogu'd were they.
The kiss of t—— instead had stood,   35
And might have done three nations good.
But when the Parliament would no more
 Raise taxes to maintain the whore,
When they would not abide the awe
Of standing force instead of law,   40
When law, religion, property
They'd fence 'gainst will and Popery,
When they'd provide that all shall be
From slav'ry and oppression free,
That a writ of habeas corpus come,   45
And none in prison be undone,
That Englishmen should not, like beast,
To war by sea or land be press'd,
That peace with Holland should be made

When war had spoil'd our men and trade,   50
That treason it should be for any
Without Parliament to raise a penny,
That no courtier should be sent
To sit and vote in Parliament,
That when an end to this was gave,   55
A yearly Parliament we should have
According to the ancient law,
That mighty knaves might live in awe,
That King nor council should commit
An Englishman for wealth or wit,   60
Prerogative being ti'd thus tight
That it could neither scratch nor bite,
When whores began to be afear'd
Like armies they should be cashier'd,
Then Carwell, that incestuous punk,   65
Made our most gracious Sovereign drunk,
And drunk she let him give that buss
Which all the kingdom's bound to curse;
And so, red hot with wine and whore,
He kick'd the Parliament out of door.   70

ANDREW MARVELL

On the Statue Erected by Sir Robert Viner
(*1675*)

On 29 May 1672 Sir Robert Viner, a rich goldsmith, unveiled an equestrian statue in marble of Charles II in Stocks Market. The statue had originally represented a King of Poland with the figure of a Turk beneath his horse's feet, but Viner had the horseman changed into Charles and the prostrate figure into Cromwell. Viner erected this monument at his own expense, but the conversion had been so badly done that the statue was criticized: "When we enquire into the history of it the farce improves upon our hands, and what was before contemptible grows entertaining. This statue was originally made for Jan Sobieski, King of Poland, but, by some accident, was left upon the workman's hands, and about the same time the City was loyal enough to pay their devoirs to King Charles, and, finding the statue ready made to their hands, resolved to do it the cheapest way and convert the Polander into a Briton and the Turk underneath the horse into Oliver Cromwell to make their compliment complete. In this very manner it appears at present, and the turban upon the last mentioned figure is yet an undeniable proof of the story" (James Ralph, *A Critical View of the Public Buildings of London,* 1734, p. 12; cited by Margoliouth).

Margoliouth dates the poem in 1675. He suggests that the statue may have been covered up again for alterations (see lines 35 and 54) and calls attention to *"restore* us our King" (line 57) and the reference to the sculptor's *reforming* the equestrian figure in support of his opinion.

I am inclined to accept this poem as Marvell's on the basis of its inclusion in Bodley's Marvell Manuscript (MS. Eng. Poet. d. 49).

On the Statue Erected by Sir Robert Viner

1.

As cities that to the fierce conquerors yield
Do at their own charges their citadel build,
So Sir Robert advanc'd the King's statue in token
Of bankers defeated and Lombard Street broken.

2.

Some thought it a knightly and generous deed,   5
Obliging the City with a king and a steed,
Where with honor he might from his word have gone back:
He that vows in a calm is absolv'd in a wrack.

3.

But now it appears from the first to the last
To be all revenge and malice forecast,   10
Upon the King's birthday to set up a thing
That shows him a monster more like than a king.

4.

When each one that passes finds fault with the horse,
Yet all do affirm that the King is much worse,
And some by the likeness Sir Robert suspect   15
That he did for the King his own statue erect.

5.

To see him so disguis'd the herbwomen chide,
Who upon their panniers more decently ride,
And so loose is his seat that all men agree
That Sir William Peake sits much firmer than he.   20

3. *advanc'd:* 1. erected; 2. promoted, i.e. from King of Poland to King of England;
and 3. loaned on security. Sir Robert had loaned much money to the King and suf-
fered severe losses when the Exchequer was closed in 1672. See 1. 4. Goldsmiths often
acted as bankers.
    4. *Lombard Street:* The center of banking in the City.
    17–18. Herbwomen sold their produce in the Stocks Market and rode to market on
the panniers of their horses.
    20. *Sir William Peake:* Lord Mayor in 1667.

6.

But a market, they say, does suit the King well,
Who the Parliament buys and revenues does sell,
And others, to make the similitude hold,
Say his Majesty himself is bought too and sold.

7.

This statue is sure more scandalous far   25
Than all the Dutch pictures that caused the war,
And what the Exchequer for that took on trust
May be henceforth confiscate for reason more just.

8.

But Sir Robert, to take the scandal away,
Does the fault upon the artificer lay,   30
And allegeth the workmanship was not his own,
For he counterfeits only in gold, not in stone.

9.

But, Sir Knight of the Vine, how came't in your thought
That when to the scaffold your liege you had brought,
With canvas and deal you e'er since do him cloud,   35
As if you it meant for his coffin and shroud?

10.

Has Blood him away, as his crown once, convey'd,
Or is he to Clayton's gone in masquerade,
Or is in cabal in this cabinet set,
Or have you to the Counter remov'd him for debt?   40

22. For bribery and farming of taxes see *Further Advice to the Painter*.
24. An allusion to Charles' subventions from Louis XIV under the secret Treaty of Dover.
26. One of Charles' pretexts for declaring war on the Dutch in 1672 was the alleged circulation of abusive pictures in Holland.
37. See *On Blood's Stealing the Crown*.
38. Sir Robert Clayton (1629–1707) was a poor boy who became one of the richest men in London. Charles, who enjoyed making impromptu visits masked, would have gone to him for a loan.
40. *Counter:* A debtor's prison. On the closing of the Exchequer the King's debt to Viner was £416,274 (Margoliouth).

The Statue of Charles II in Stocks Market. From an engraving by an unknown artist.

11.

Methinks by the equipage of this vile scene
To change him into a jack-pudding you mean,
Or else to expose him to popular flouts,
As if we'd as good have a king made of clouts.

12.

Or do you his beams out of modesty veil 45
With three shatter'd planks and the rag of a sail,
To express how his navy was tatter'd and torn,
The day that he was both restored and born?

13.

Sure the King will ne'er think of repaying the bankers,
Whose loyalties all expire with their spankers; 50
Now the Indies and Smyrna do not him enrich,
They will scarce afford him a rag for his breech.

14.

But Sir Robert affirms that they do him much wrong,
For the graver's at work to reform him thus long;
But alas! he will never arrive at his end, 55
For 'tis such a king as a chisel can't mend.

15.

But with all his faults pray restore us our King,
If ever you hope in December for spring;
For though the whole world can't show such another,
Yet we'd better by far have him than his brother. 60

42. *jack-pudding:* A mountebank.

47–48. Probably an allusion to the Battle of Sole Bay, 28 May 1672, when the Royal James blew up with Sandwich on board. The *London Gazette* recorded the battle and the following day's unveiling and other birthday celebrations in the same number (Margoliouth).

50. *spankers:* Gold coins.

51. In March 1672, before the declaration of war, a squadron under Sir Robert Holmes made a piratical attack on the Dutch Smyrna fleet in the Channel. The attempt failed ignominiously.

ANDREW MARVELL

The Statue at Charing Cross
(1675)

As part of a program "that might unite and best pacify the minds of the people against the next session of Parliament," Danby sought to appeal to popular sentiment in 1675 by erecting a bronze statue of Charles I on horseback which had been cast by Le Sueur in 1633, but the long delay in carrying out the project laid it open to ridicule.

The Statue at Charing Cross is included in Bodley's Marvell manuscript (MS. Eng. Poet. d. 49).

THE STATUE AT CHARING CROSS

1.

What can be the mystery why Charing Cross
This five months continues still blinded with board?
Dear Wheeler, impart, for we're all at a loss
Unless Punchinello is to be restor'd.

2.

'Twere to Scaramuchio too great disrespect   5
To limit his troupe to this theater small,
Besides the injustice it were to eject
The mimic so legally seiz'd of Whitehall.

3. *Wheeler:* Sir Charles Wheeler, close friend and supporter of Danby. See *The Chequer Inn*, 67ff.

4. *Punchinello:* Puppet-shows had been presented in a booth in Charing Cross in the 1660s, but in 1675 the Italian *commedia dell' arte,* in which Punchinello and Scaramuccio are important characters, was being performed by living actors at Whitehall (Margoliouth).

8. Marvell to William Popple, 24 July 1675: "Scaramuccio acting daily in the hall of Whitehall and all sorts of people flocking thither and paying their money as at a common playhouse" (Margoliouth, 2, 320). The line identifies Charles II with the mimic who plays Scaramuccio.

3.

For a dial the place is too unsecure,
Since the privy garden could not it defend,
And so near to the Court they will never endure
Any monument how their time they misspend.

4.

Were these deals kept in store for sheathing our fleet,
When the King in armado to Portsmouth should sail,
Or the bishops and Treasurer, did they agree't,
To repair with such riffraff our Church's old pale?

5.

No, to comfort the hearts of the poor Cavalier,
The late King on horseback is here to be shown.
What ado with the kings and the statues is here!
Have we not had enough already of one?

6.

Does the Treasurer think men so loyally tame,
When their pensions are stopp'd, to be fool'd with a sight?
And 'tis forty to one, if he play the old game,
He'll reduce us ere long to forty and eight.

9. *dial:* "In the privy garden at Whitehall stood a sundial, 'the rarest in Europe,' an elaborate structure of glass spheres grouped in the form of an erect cone. Late on a June night in 1675, a gang of riotous courtiers, including the Earl of Rochester, Lord Buckhurst, and Fleetwood Shepherd, came back to Whitehall from their revels and passed through the privy garden. Inspired by wine, Rochester suddenly perceived the phallic significance of the dial in relation to a feminine personification of time." The revelers smashed the dial with their swords (Wilson, *The Court Wits*, pp. 37–38).

13–14. In July 1675 the King sailed from Gravesend to Portsmouth and back in very bad weather and was feared lost (Margoliouth, 2, 318).

15–16. In the parliamentary session which ended 9 June 1675 the bishops had supported Danby in promoting the bill for a non-resistance test (Margoliouth). This was part of Danby's project for a firm alliance of Anglicans and Royalists against Catholics, Dissenters, and all opponents of the prerogative.

20. *one:* Viner's equestrian statue in the Stocks Market. See *A Dialogue between the Two Horses.*

22. In order to raise the money necessary to pay off the fleet and reduce naval expenditures Danby, in 1674, put a temporary stop "to all salaries and pensions, even the secret service money" (Browning, *Danby, 1,* 130).

24. *forty and eight:* The year in which the Second Civil War began. Charles I was executed on 30 Jan. 1648 (o.s.).

7.

The Trojan Horse, though not of brass but of wood,   25
Had within it an army that burn'd up the town.
However, 'tis ominous if understood,
For the old King on horseback is but an half-crown.

8.

But his brother-in-law's horse had gain'd such repute
That the Treasurer thought prudent to try it again,   30
And instead of that market of herbs and of fruit,
He will here keep a market of Parliament men.

9.

But why is the work then so long at a stand?
Such things you should never, or suddenly, do.
As the Parliament twice was prorogu'd by your hand,   35
Will you venture so far to prorogue the King too?

10.

Let's have a King then, be he new, be he old,
Not Viner delay'd us so, though he was broken,
Though the King be of copper and Danby of gold,
Shall a Treasurer of guineas a prince grudge of token?   40

11.

The housewifely Treasuress sure is grown nice,
That so liberally treated the members at supper.

25–6. An oblique suggestion that Catholics set the Great Fire of 1666.
28. Margoliouth suggests that the half-crown was the only coin still circulating extensively which represented the late King on horseback.
29. *brother-in-law:* Sometimes applied humorously to the fathers of a young couple. Viner's stepdaughter was affianced to Danby's son.
31. Herbwomen conducted a market here.
35. Actually there were three prorogations between Danby's appointment as Treasurer in June 1673 and July 1675: 4 Nov. 1673, 24 Feb. 1674, and 9 June 1675 (Margoliouth).
38. Viner suffered heavy financial losses from the stop of the Exchequer in Jan. 1672.
40. An allusion to Danby's wealth and the King's poverty.
41–2. *Treasuress:* Formerly Lady Bridget Bertie. She "was reported to encourage" Danby "in his love of money, and soon drove, with 'his participation and concurrence,' a private trade in offices" (*DNB*, quoted in Margoliouth). Cf. *The Chequer Inn.*

She thinks not convenient to go to the price,
And we've lost both our King, our horse, and our crupper;

12.

Where for so many Berties there are to provide,   45
To buy a king is not so wise as to sell,
And however she said, it could not be deni'd
That a monarch of gingerbread would do as well;

13.

But the Treasurer told her he thought she was mad
And his Parliament-list withal did produce,   50
Where he show'd her that so many voters he had
As would the next tax reimburse them with use.

14.

So the statue will up after all this delay,
But to turn the face to Whitehall you must shun;
Though of brass, yet with grief it would melt him away,   55
To behold ev'ry day such a court, such a son.

44. *Crupper:* Buttocks.
48. *gingerbread:* Something showy and unsubstantial, *obs.*
50. Browning prints Danby's lists in vol. 3 of his biography.

A Dialogue between the Two Horses
(1676)

In this satire the marble and bronze horses of the two preceding poems engage in a debate on the faults of their masters, Charles I and Charles II. Where its predecessors are impudently jocose, however, *A Dialogue between the Two Horses* is bitter and harsh. *The Statue at Charing Cross* is directed at the faults and follies of Charles II and his Treasurer, Danby. It does not criticize Charles I, but depicts him rather as a virtuous foil to his son:

> So the statue will up after all this delay,
> But to turn the face to Whitehall you must shun;
> Though of brass, yet with grief it would melt him away,
> To behold ev'ry day such a Court, such a son.

A Dialogue, on the other hand, attacks both Charles I and Charles II:

> Though the father and son be different rods,
> Between the two scourges we find little odds.
> Both infamous stand in three kingdoms' votes:
> This for picking our pockets, that for cutting our throats.

It then proceeds to compare father and son, in their cruelty and debauchery, to Nero and Sardanapalus, attacks "all that shall reign of the false Scottish race," and proclaims a commonwealth (line 161) as a release from Stuart tyranny.

It seems unlikely that the poet who depicted a virtuous Charles I grieving over the follies of his son in *The Statue at Charing Cross* should have represented him as a Nero a few months later. It is almost as unlikely that Marvell, whose admiration and respect for Charles I are so clear in *An Horatian Ode,* could have written such a violent attack on him as we find here. The unmitigated hatred and contempt toward both kings, the disparagement not only of the Stuart dynasty but of monarchy itself, and the allusions to cruel and decadent Roman emperors all suggest another satirist, possibly John Ayloffe.

A Dialogue between the Two Horses is ascribed to Marvell only in the *State Poems*. In the absence of corroborative evidence such attributions have no authority. The poem does not appear in the Bodleian Marvell manuscript (MS. Eng. Poet. d. 49), which does include the two satires on the statues at Woolchurch and Charing Cross.

As Margoliouth has shown, the poem can be dated precisely between 29 December 1675 and 10 January 1676, the dates when the coffee-houses were closed and reopened by royal proclamation (see lines 187–88).

A DIALOGUE BETWEEN THE TWO HORSES

The Introduction

We read in profane and sacred records
Of beasts that have utter'd articulate words;
When magpies and parrots cry, "Walk, knave,
    walk,"
It is a clear proof that birds, too, can talk.
Nay, statues without either windpipe or lungs   5
Have spoken as plainly as men do with tongues.
Livy tells a strange story can hardly be fellow'd,
That a sacrific'd ox, when his guts were out, bel-
    low'd.
Phalaris had a bull which, grave authors tell ye,
Would roar like a devil with a man in his belly.   10
Friar Bacon had a head that spake, made of brass,
And Balaam the prophet was reprov'd by his ass.

3. *Walk, knave, walk:* A phrase taught to parrots.

8. Margoliouth notes that Livy mentions many talking cattle, but he cannot trace this particular episode.

9. *Phalaris:* The infamous tyrant of Agrigentum, notorious for his cruelty, who died in 549 B.C.

11. *Friar Bacon:* Roger Bacon (1214?–94), the founder of English philosophy. He was regarded as a necromancer by his contemporaries, and was believed to have constructed a brazen head capable of speaking. The brazen head appears in Greene's comedy, *Friar Bacon and Friar Bungay.*

12. See Numbers 22:28. Because the path was blocked by the angel of the Lord, who was invisible to Balaam, the ass turned aside into a field, crushing her rider's foot against a wall. Balaam struck the ass repeatedly and the poor beast finally said, "What have I done unto thee, that thou hast smitten me these three times?"

At Delphos and Rome stocks and stones now and
    then, sirs,
Have to questions return'd oracular answers.
All Popish believers think something divine,   15
When images speak, possesses the shrine;
But they that faith Catholic ne'er understood,
When shrines give answers, say a knave's i'the
    rood.
These idols ne'er spoke, but the miracle's done
By the Devil, a priest, a friar, or nun.   20
If the Roman Church, good Christians, oblige ye
To believe man and beast have spake in effigie,
Why should we not credit the public discourses
Of a dialogue lately between the two horses?
The horses, I mean, of Woolchurch and Charing,   25
Who have told many truths well worth a man's
    hearing,
Since Viner and Osborne did buy and provide 'em
For the two mighty monarchs that now do
    bestride 'em.
The stately brass stallion and the white marble
    steed
One night came together, by all is agreed,   30
When both the kings, weary of sitting all day,
Were stol'n off incognito, each his own way;
And that the two jades, after mutual salutes,
Not only discours'd, but fell to disputes.

22. *effigie:* Probably still a Latin word; here it still bears the Latin stress-accent, so rhyming with *oblige* [obleege] *ye* (Margoliouth).

25. The bronze statue of Charles I, cast by Le Sueur in 1633, was erected by Danby at Charing Cross in 1675, where it still stands. The statue of Charles II in marble was erected by Sir Robert Viner at his own expense in the Stocks Market on 29 May 1672. Its projected removal, finally carried out in 1738 when the Stocks Market was closed and land cleared for the Mansion House, was celebrated in a lampoon which begins:

    Ye whimsical people of London's fair town,
    Who one year put up what the next you pull down;
    Full sixty-one years have I stood in this place,
    And never till now met with any disgrace.
    What affront to crown'd heads could you offer more bare
    Than to pull down a king to make room for a mayor?

The statue was finally re-erected in 1883 at Newby Hall, the Yorkshire seat of the Vyner family (W. G. Bell, *Unknown London,* p. 120).

The Dialogue

W.   Quoth the marble white horse, " 'Twould make a   35
    stone speak
    To see a Lord Mayor and Lombard Street break:
    Thy founder and mine to cheat one another,
    When both knaves agreed to be each other's
    brother."

C.   Here Charing broke silence, and thus he went on:
    "My brass is provok'd as much as thy stone   40
    To see Church and State bow down to a whore,
    And the King's chief minister holding the door;

W.   To see *Dei Gratia* writ on the Throne,
    And the King's wicked life say, God there is none;

C.   That he should be styl'd Defender o'th' Faith,   45
    Who believes not a word the word of God saith;

W.   That the Duke should turn Papist and that
    Church defy
    For which his own father a martyr did die.

C.   Though he hath chang'd his religion, I hope he's
    so civil
    Not to think his own father is gone to the Devil.   50

W.   That bondage and beggary should be brought on
    a nation
    By a curs'd House of Commons and a bless'd
    Restoration;

C.   To see a white staff make a beggar a lord,
    And scarce a wise man at a long council-board;

W.   That the bank should be seiz'd, yet the Chequer   55
    so poor
    Lord have mercy and a cross may be set on the
    door;

35–36. Another reference to losses suffered by merchants like Viner after the closing of the Exchequer in 1672. Viner was Lord Mayor in 1674–75.

38. A match was made between Viner's stepdaughter and Danby's son in which, according to Margoliouth, Viner cheated Danby.

41. *whore:* The Duchess of Portsmouth. Danby made a point of getting on well with her.

53. *white staff:* Borne by Danby as Lord High Treasurer.

56. The usual signs that plague was within (Margoliouth).

C.   That a million and half should be the revenue,
     Yet the King of his debts pay no man a penny;
W.   That a King should consume three kingdoms'
         estates,
     And yet all his court be as poor as church rats;   60
C.   That of the four seas' dominion and guarding
     No token should appear but a poor copper
         farthing.
W.   Our worm-eaten navy may be laid up at Chatham,
     Not trade to secure, but for foes to come at 'em.
C.   And our few ships abroad to become Tripoli's   65
         scorn
     By pawning for victuals their guns at Leghorn;
W.   That making us slaves by Horse and Foot Guards
     For restoring the King should be our rewards—
C.   The basest ingratitude ever was heard,
     But tyrants ungrateful are always afear'd.   70
W.   On seventh Harry's head he that placed the crown
     Was after rewarded with losing his own.
C.   That Parliament-men should rail at the Court
     And get good preferment immediately for't;
W.   To the bold-talking members if the bastards you   75
         add,
     What a rabble of rascally Lords have been made!
C.   That traitors to their country in a brib'd House
         of Commons

57. Margoliouth cites Sacheverell's estimate in 1675 of taxes and customs as amounting annually to this sum.

62. The farthings of Charles II bore the legend *Quatuor maria vindico* (Margoliouth).

65–66. I have not been able to discover anything about this incident.

67. *Horse and Foot Guards:* Both date from the reign of Charles II (Margoliouth). This line seems to allude to the "Blackheath host."

71–72. Thomas Stanley picked up the crown on Bosworth Field and put it on Henry Tudor's head; but it was his younger brother William who turned the scale in Henry's favor at Bosworth and was afterwards executed for complicity in Perkin Warbeck's rebellion. Grosart sees an allusion to Argyle, who crowned Charles II at Scone, 1 Jan. 1651, and was beheaded at Edinburgh 27 May 1661 (Margoliouth).

75. *bastards:* Charles II's illegitimate princes in 1675 included James, Duke of Monmouth; Charles Fitzroy, Earl of Southampton and Henry Fitzroy, Earl of Euston (afterwards Duke of Grafton), both sons of the Duchess of Cleveland; and Charles Lennox, Duke of Richmond, son of the Duchess of Portsmouth.

> Should give away millions at every summons;
>
> *W.* Yet some of those givers such beggarly villains
> As not to be trusted for twice fifty shillin's; 80
>
> *C.* No wonder that beggars should still be for giving
> Who out of what's given do get a good living.
>
> *W.* Four knights and a knave, who were publicans
> made,
> For selling their conscience were lib'rally paid.
>
> *C.* Then baser the souls of the low-prized sinners, 85
> Who vote with the Court for drink and for
> dinners!
>
> *W.* 'Tis they that brought on us this scandalous yoke
> Of excising our cups and taxing our smoke.
>
> *C.* But, thanks to the whores who have made the
> King dogged,
> For giving no more the rogues are prorogued. 90
>
> *W.* That a King should endeavor to make a war cease,
> Which augments and secures his own profit and
> peace;
>
> *C.* And plenipotentiaries send into France
> With an addle-headed knight and a lord without
> brains.
>
> *W.* That the King should send for another French 95
> whore,

83. *publicans:* Farmers of excise. See *Further Advice,* 55 n.

85–86. See *The Chequer Inn.*

88. *excising:* See *Last Instructions,* 130–306 and notes. "Taxing our smoke" refers to the hearth tax or chimney money; see *Last Instructions,* 193 n.

90. Parliament was prorogued 16 Nov. 1675 and did not meet again for fifteen months.

93–94. English plenipotentiaries had been appointed to assist (probably in the French interest) at the negotiations for a peace between Holland and France which would in effect release the French for a possible attack on England. The plenipotentiaries were Sir Leoline Jenkins, who left England 20 Dec. 1675, and John Lord Berkeley (or Barclay) (l.94); "Jenkins lacked resource and independence of mind, was a great stickler for forms, and, according to Temple, was in an agony when left alone at Nymwegen" (*DNB*). Berkeley, Lord Lieutenant of Ireland in 1670 ("a man unthought of": Marvell, *Miscellaneous Letters,* 10), sailed 14 Nov. 1675, accompanied by Evelyn's son, and leaving his affairs in Evelyn's hands; he went first to Paris, and only reached Nymwegen twelve months later. Clarendon gives an unfavorable estimate of his brains (Margoliouth).

95. *another French whore:* Hortensia Mancini, Duchesse Mazarin, came to England at the end of November and first appeared at court 8 Dec. 1675. The following

When one already has made him so poor.

C.   Enough, dear brother! Although we have reason,
Yet, truth many times being punish'd for treason,
We ought to be wary and bridle our tongue:
Bold speaking hath done both man and beast   100
     wrong.
When the ass too boldly rebuked the prophet,
Thou knowest what danger was like to come of it:
Though the beast gave his master ne'er an ill word,
Instead of a cudgel Balaam wish'd for a sword.

W.   Truth's as bold as a lion. I am not afraid.   105
I'll prove ev'ry tittle of what I have said.
Our riders are absent; who is't that can hear?
Let's be true to ourselves; who then need we fear?
Where is thy King gone?   C. To see Bishop Laud.

W.   To cuckold a scriv'ner mine's in masquerade.   110
On such occasion he oft steals away,
And returns to remount about break of day.
In ev'ry dark night you are sure to find him
With a harlot got up on my crupper behind him.

C.   Peace, brother, a while, and calmly consider,   115
What hast thou to say against my royal rider?

W.   Thy priest-ridden King turn'd desperate fighter
For the surplice, lawn sleeves, the cross, and the
     mitre,
Till at last on a scaffold he was left in the lurch
By knaves that cri'd up themselves for the Church,   120
Archbishops and bishops, archdeacons and deans—

C.   Thy King will ne'er fight unless't be for queans!

W.   He that dies for ceremonies dies like a fool!

C.   The King on thy back's a lamentable tool!

W.   The goat and the lion I equally hate,   125

---

months were to witness her vain struggle with Portsmouth for ascendancy (Margo-
liouth).

   109. *Laud:* Charles I's famous high-church archbishop.

   110. *scriv'ner:* Margoliouth identifies the scrivener as Sir Richard Clayton, evidently
meaning the immensely rich London businessman, Sir Robert Clayton. This identifi-
cation is not supported by the accounts of Clayton's life which I have seen, and the
anecdote seems to refer to a typical rather than a specific action.

   125. *The goat and the lion:* Charles II and Louis XIV.

And free men alike value life and estate.
Though the father and son be different rods,
Between the two scourges we find little odds.
Both infamous stand in three kingdoms' votes:
This for picking our pockets, that for cutting our 130
    throats.

C. More tolerable are the lion king's slaughters
Than the goat's making whores of our wives and
    our daughters.
The debauch'd and the cruel, sith they equally
    gall us,
I had rather bear Nero than Sardanapalus.

W. One of the two tyrants must still be our case 135
Under all that shall reign of the false Scottish
    race.

C. De Witt and Cromwell had each a brave soul:
W. I freely declare, I am for old Noll.
Though his government did a tyrant's resemble,
He made England great and its enemies tremble. 140

C. Thy rider puts no man to death in his wrath,
W. But he's buri'd alive in lust and in sloth.
C. What is thy opinion of James Duke of York?
W. The same that the frogs had of Jupiter's stork:
With the Turk in his head and the Pope in his 145
    heart.
Father Patrick's disciple will make England smart.
If e'er he be King, I know Britain's doom:
We must all to the stake, or be converts to Rome.
A Tudor! a Tudor! We've had Stuarts enough.
None ever reign'd like old Bess in her ruff. 150

C. Her Walsingham could dark counsels unriddle,
W. And our Sir Joseph write newsbooks and fiddle.
C. Troth, brother, well said, but that's somewhat
    bitter.

---

133. *Sardanapalus:* Most effeminate and corrupt of Assyrian kings. Cf. *Marvell's Ghost,* 46 n.

144. See *Nostradamus' Prophecy,* 33–34.

152. *Sir Joseph:* Sir Joseph Williamson (1633–1701), Secretary of State and editor of *The London Gazette.*

W.	His perfum'd predecessor was never much fitter;
C.	Yet we have one Secret'ry honest and wise, 155
W.	For that very reason he's never to rise.
C.	But can'st thou divine when things will be mended?
W.	When the reign of the line of the Stuarts is ended.
C.	Then England rejoice, thy redemption draws nigh:
	Thy oppression together with kingship shall die! 160
Chorus.	A commonwealth! a commonwealth! we proclaim to the nation,
	For the gods have repented the King's Restoration.

Conclusion

If speech of brute animals in Rome's first age
Prodigious events did surely presage,
Then shall come to pass, all mankind may swear,   165
What two inanimate horses declare.
But I should have told you, before the jades
   parted,
Both gallop'd to Whitehall and there horribly
   farted,
Which monarchy's downfall portendeth much
   more
Than all that the beasts had spoken before.   170
If the Delphic Sibyls' oracular speeches
(As learned men say) came out of their breeches,
Why might not the horses, since words are but
   wind,
Have the spirt of prophecy likewise behind?

154. *predecessor:* Arlington, who resigned the secretaryship to Williamson 11 Sept. 1674 (Margoliouth).

155. *one Secret'ry:* Margoliouth identifies this person as Henry Coventry, who was one of the two Secretaries of State from 1671 to 1679.

163–64. See 7–10 above.

169. Margoliouth draws attention to the way the editors toned down the republican violence of this line by changing *monarchy's* to *tyranny's.*

172. *breeches:* Perhaps a reference to the sacred breach or cleft at Delphi; see Strabo ix.c.419 (Margoliouth).

Though tyrants make laws which they strictly   175
    proclaim,
To conceal their own crimes and cover their
    shame,
Yet the beasts in the field or the stones in the
    wall
Will publish their faults and proph'sy their fall.
When they take from the people the freedom of
    words,
They teach them the sooner to fall to their   180
    swords.
Let the City drink coffee and quietly groan;
They that conquer'd the father won't be slaves
    to the son.
It is wine and strong drink make tumults in-
    crease;
Choc'late, tea, and coffee are liquors of peace:
No quarrels nor oaths amongst those that drink   185
    'em;
'Tis Bacchus and brewers swear, damn 'em, and
    sink 'em!
Then, Charles, thy edicts against coffee recall:
There's ten times more treason in brandy and ale.

175–78. Margoliouth takes these lines as referring to the closing of coffee-houses by royal edict on 29 Dec. 1675. Another proclamation on the following 10 Jan. permitted them to reopen provided that no anti-government propaganda was circulated in them.

JOHN AYLOFFE

Marvell's Ghost
(*1678*)

Marvell's death in August 1678 marks the end of the period covered
by this volume. In the following month the authoritarian and pro-
Catholic tendencies of Charles II's policy, which Marvell had ex-
posed in his satires, were to provoke the explosive reaction of the
Popish Plot.

From 1665 to his death Marvell had defended English liberties
in Parliament, in his political verse and pamphlets, and, it now ap-
pears, as a member of an anti-French, anti-Catholic organization
aimed at alerting the House of Commons to the dangers of Charles'
policy. This organization, described by Haley in *William of Orange
and the English Opposition, 1672-4,* was directed by William's sec-
retary, Peter du Moulin. While some of the members seem to have
been mere adventurers, Marvell and his friend, John Ayloffe, were
clearly involved in this dangerous enterprise from the highest patri-
otic motives.

Ayloffe's career is marked by daring gestures and actions in sup-
port of freedom. During the crucial debates on foreign policy in
1673 he placed a wooden shoe (for Englishmen, an emblem of
slavery) beside the chair of the Speaker, Sir Edward Seymour, who
was subservient to the Court. The shoe bore the arms of England
and France and the motto, *Utrum horum mavis accipe* ("Choose
whichever of these you prefer"). He was also charged with printing
anti-government literature, including *England's Appeal from the
Private Cabal at Whitehall . . . to the Great Council of the Nation*
(1673) and was exiled for two years. He was outlawed for involve-
ment in the Rye House Plot (1683) and fled to Scotland with the
Earl of Argyle, where he was seized. He was executed before the gate
of the Inner Temple on 30 October 1685. Ayloffe was a member of
the Green Ribbon Club, and Macaulay describes him as belonging
to "that section of Whigs which sought for models rather among the
patriots of Greece and Rome than among the prophets and judges

of Israel" (*1, 560*). Grosart, with some exaggeration, calls *Marvell's Ghost* "one of the most drastic and powerful satires against the Stuarts, as burning and passionate in its invective as any of Marvell's own."

Marvell's Ghost is ascribed to Ayloffe in *State Poems* and appears under his name together with *The History of Insipids* in a small pamphlet (1709). I have not seen any manuscript attributions. There is another poem, *Marvell's Ghost: Being a True Copy of a Letter sent to the A. Bp. of Cant. upon his Sudden Sickness at the Prince of Orange's First Arrival into London, 1688/9,* which appears in Case 211(4)(a).

MARVELL'S GHOST

From the dark Stygian banks I come
T' acquaint poor England with her doom,
Which, as th' infernal Sisters sate,
I copi'd from the Book of Fate;
And though the sense may seem disguis'd,   5
'Tis in these following lines compris'd:
   When England does forsake the broom,
And takes a thistle in its room,
A wanton fiddler shall be led
By Fate to stain his master's bed,   10
From whence a spurious race shall grow
Design'd for Britain's overthrow.
These, while they do possess her throne,
Shall serve all int'rests but their own;
And shall be, both in peace and war,   15
Scourges unto themselves and her.
   A brace of exil'd youths, whose fates

7. *broom:* The emblem of the Plantagenets, the great house which occupied the English throne from 1154 to 1485. The name Plantagenet (originally Plante-geneste) was a personal nickname of Geoffrey, Count of Anjou, father of Henry II, and it is traditionally derived from Geoffrey's habit of adorning his cap with a sprig of broom or *planta genista (DNB,* under Plantagenet, family of).

8. *thistle:* The heraldic emblem of Scotland, standing here for the Stuarts.

9. *a wanton fiddler:* David Riccio or Rizzio (1533?–1566), a musician born in Turin, who became the chief counselor and, perhaps, lover of Mary Queen of Scots.

17. *A brace of exil'd youths:* Charles II and James, Duke of York.

Shall pull down vengeance on those states
That harbor'd them abroad, must come
Well-skill'd in foreign vices home,   20
And shall (their dark designs to hide)
With two contesting Churches side,
Till, with cross-persecuting zeal,
They have laid waste the commonweal.
Then incest, murder, perjury   25
Shall fashionable virtues be,
And villainies infest this isle
Would make the son of Claudius smile;
No oaths, no sacraments hold good
But what are seal'd with lust or blood—   30
Lusts that cold exile could not tame,
Nor plague, nor fire at home reclaim.
For this she shall in ashes mourn,
From Europe's envy turn'd her scorn,
And curse the days that first gave birth   35
To a Cecil or a Monck on earth.

But as I onwards strove to look,
The angry Sister shut the book
And said, "No more! That fickle state
Shall know no further of her fate;   40
Her future fortunes must lie hid
Till her known ills be remedi'd,
And she to those resentments come
That drove the Tarquins out of Rome,
Or such as did in fury turn   45
Th' Assyrian's palace to his urn."

28. *son of Claudius:* Nero, stepson of Claudius and son of his fourth wife, Aggripina.

36. *Cecil:* Robert Cecil, first Earl of Salisbury (1563?–1612), who was instrumental in bringing James I to the throne of England. *Monck:* George Monck, first Duke of Albemarle (1608–70), who played a major role in the restoration of Charles II.

44. *Tarquins:* Tarquinius Superbus, a king of Rome noted for his arrogance and tyranny, and his son, Tarquinius Sextus, who raped the virtuous Lucretia. They were expelled from Rome in a popular uprising.

46. *Th' Assyrian:* "Sardanapalus, the last king of the Assyrian monarchy, so excessively effeminate and luxurious that his captains conspired to kill him, but he made a pile of all his precious things and burned himself in his palace" (Shadwell's note to his *Tenth Satire of Juvenal*).

II. *Ecclesiastical Affairs*

ROBERT WILD

A Poem upon the Imprisonment of Mr. Calamy in Newgate (*1662*)

Edmund Calamy (1600–66), Nonconformist divine, a co-author of *Smectymnuus,* and member of the Savoy Conference for the composition of religious differences, was widely admired for his piety and moderation. After the Restoration he was appointed one of Charles II's chaplains. He was a noted preacher and was offered the bishopric of Coventry and Lichfield, which he refused. Calamy was one of some 2,000 Nonconformist ministers ejected from their churches on St. Bartholomew's Day (17 August 1662) under the provisions of the Act of Uniformity. This Act required all the clergy to sign a declaration repudiating the Solemn League and Covenant, denying the right to take up arms against the King, undertaking to adopt the liturgy of the Church of England, and prescribing episcopal ordination. The great majority of Nonconformist ministers felt they could not subscribe to all these provisions, especially since the newly-authorized Book of Common Prayer was not printed and distributed in time for most of them to familiarize themselves with provisions which they were nevertheless required to accept. After being ejected from St. Mary Aldermanbury in London, Calamy continued to attend this church. On 28 December 1662, when the regular minister failed to appear for the service, Calamy was prevailed upon to enter the pulpit and preached a fervent sermon. For this he was sent to Newgate on 6 January 1663, but was released soon after through the King's intervention.

The text is based on the 1662 broadside. There are no significant variants in the 1671 edition of *Iter Boreale with Other Select Poems.*

A Poem upon the Imprisonment of Mr. Calamy in Newgate

This page I send you, sir, your Newgate fate
Not to condole but to congratulate.

I envy not our miter'd men their places,
Their rich preferments, nor their richer faces:
To see them steeple upon steeple set,   5
As if they meant that way to Heaven to get.
I can behold them take into their gills
A dose of churches, as men swallow pills,
And never grieve at it: let them swim in wine
While others drown in tears, I'll not repine!   10
But my heart truly grudges, I confess,
That you thus loaded are with happiness;
For so it is, and you more blessed are
In Peter's chain than if you sat in's chair.
One sermon hath preferr'd you so much honor   15
A man could scarce have had from Bishop Bonner.
Whilst we, your brethren, poor erratics be,
You are a glorious fixed star we see.
Hundreds of us turn out of house and home;
To a safe habitation you are come.   20
What though it be a jail? Shame and disgrace
Rise only from the crime, not from the place.
Who thinks reproach or injury is done
By an eclipse to the unspotted sun?
He only by that black upon his brow   25
Allures spectators more, and so do you.
Let me find honey though upon a rod
And prize the prison where my keeper's God.

5–9. A reference to the pluralism practiced by many Anglican bishops.

14. *Peter's chain:* St. Peter was imprisoned under heavy guard by Herod after the crucifixion and, as an extra precaution, was chained to his two cell-mates. See Acts 12:1–6.

15. *one sermon:* Calamy preached on Eli's concern for the Ark of God. See *A Sermon Preached at Aldermanbury Church, Dec. 28 1662*, Oxford, 1663.

16. *Bishop Bonner:* Edmund Bonner or Boner (1500?–69), Bishop of London, an arch-persecutor of Puritans under Henry VIII.

17. *erratics:* Erratic stars or planets, *obs.*

27. Jonathan unwittingly violated an edict of his father, Saul, that no Israelite should partake of food during an engagement with the Philistines, by dipping up some honey with his staff and eating it. The food strengthened him after his long fast and he won a great victory. After the battle his violation of the edict was reported to Saul, who was prevented from carrying out a sentence of death by the intervention of the Israelites. See I Samuel 14:24–46. Wild seems to have distorted the meaning of the episode in his application of it.

The Reverend Dr. Edmund Calamy. From an engraving by R. White.

Newgate or Hell were Heav'n if Christ were there;
He made the stable so and sepulcher.   30
Indeed the place did for your presence call;
Prisons do want perfuming most of all.
Thanks to the Bishop and his good Lord Mayor,
Who turn'd the den of thieves into a house of prayer:
And may some thief by you converted be,   35
Like him who suffer'd in Christ's company.
    Now would I had sight of your *mittimus;*
Fain would I know why you are dealt with thus.
Jailer, set forth your prisoner at the bar:
Sir, you shall hear what your offences are.   40
    First, it is prov'd that you being dead in law,
As if you car'd not for that death a straw,
Did walk and haunt your church, as if you'd scare
Away the reader and his Common Prayer.
Nay, 'twill be prov'd you did not only walk,   45
But like a Puritan your ghost did talk.
Dead, and yet preach! these Presbyterian slaves
Will not give over preaching in their graves.
    Item, you play'd the thief, and if 't be so,
Good reason, sir, to Newgate you should go: 50
And now you're there, some dare to swear you are
The greatest pickpocket that e'er came there.
Your wife, too, little better than yourself you make:
She is the receiver of each purse you take.
But your great theft you act it in your church   55
(I do not mean you did your sermon lurch;
That's crime canonical) but you did pray
And preach, so that you stole men's hearts away;
So that good man to whom your place doth fall
Will find they have no heart for him at all.   60
This felony deserv'd imprisonment.
What, can't you Nonconformists be content

33. Calamy was imprisoned under the Lord Mayor's warrant or *mittimus* (see line
37).
    44. The *reader* is the Anglican minister. The Presbyterians and other sects, because
they disliked set forms of worship, objected to the Book of Common Prayer.
    56. *lurch:* Pilfer.

Sermons to make, except you preach them too?
They that your places have this work can do.
   Thirdly, 'tis prov'd when you pray most devout   65
For all good men, you leave the bishops out.
This makes seer Sheldon by his powerful spell
Conjure and lay you safe in Newgate-hell.
Would I were there too, I should like it well.
I would you durst swap punishment with me.   70
Pain makes me fitter for the company
Of roaring boys, and you may lie a-bed.
Now your name's up, pray do it in my stead,
And if it be deni'd us to change places,
Let us for sympathy compare our cases,   75
For if in suffering we both agree,
Sir, I may challenge you to pity me.
I am the older jail-bird; my hard fate
Hath kept me twenty years in Cripplegate.
Old Bishop Gout, that lordly proud disease,   80
Took my fat body for his diocese,
Where he keeps court, there visits every limb,
And makes them (Levite-like) conform to him.
Severely he doth article each joint,
And makes enquiry into every point.   85
A bitter enemy to preaching, he
Hath half a year sometimes suspended me,
And if he find me painful in my station,
Down I am sure to go next visitation.
He binds up, looseth, sets up and pulls down;   90
Pretends he draws ill humors from the crown.
But I am sure he maketh such ado,
His humors trouble head and members too.
He hath me now in hand and ere he goes,

65–66. Most Nonconformists objected to the Anglican institution of bishops because they felt that episcopal ordination and the doctrine of apostolic succession were papistical superstitions which gave the bishops unwarranted authority.

72. *roaring boys:* Riotous fellows.

79. *Cripplegate:* One of the posterns in the old City wall.

83. Wild's limbs, like parish priests (Levites), are compelled to conform to Bishop Gout.

84. *article:* Indict.

I fear for heretics he'll burn my toes.
Oh! I would give all I am worth, a fee,   95
That from his jurisdiction I were free.
    Now, sir, you find our sufferings do agree;
One bishop clapp'd up you, another me.
But oh! the difference, too, is very great;   100
You are allow'd to walk, to drink and eat:
I want them all and never a penny get,
And though you be debarr'd your liberty,
Yet all your visitors, I hope, are free.
Good men, good women, and good angels come   105
And makes your prison better than your home.
Now may it be so till your foes repent
They gave you such a rich imprisonment.
May, for the greater comfort of your lives,
Your lying in be better than your wive's.   110
May you a thousand friendly papers see,
And none prove empty except this from me.
And if you stay, may I come keep your door;
Then farewell parsonage! I shall ne'er be poor.

104. *all your visitors:* "Newgate Street was blocked by the coaches of his visitors. 'A certain popish lady' (apparently the King's mistress), detained on her way through the city, represented to the King the disturbed state of popular feeling. Calamy was set free by the King's express order, but it was stated that the act had not provided for his longer restraint. The Commons on 19 Feb. referred it to a committee to inquire into this defect, and addressed the King against toleration" (*DNB,* s.v. Robert Wild).

113–14. It was customary for visitors to tip doorkeepers.

"HUDIBRAS"

On Calamy's Imprisonment and Wild's Poetry
(*1663*)

Wild's poem on the imprisonment of Calamy brought a flood of re-buttals and counter-rebuttals, most of them devoid of substance and wit. The following attack is attributed by the *DNB* in its article on Calamy to George Sacheverell, presumably because it is found in Sacheverell's commonplace book (B.M. Add. MS. 28758). The poem is attributed to Butler in MS. Rawlinson Poet. 173 and in Bucking-ham's *Works* (1704), and to "Hudibras" in the broadside version (1663), which is the text followed here.

As René Lamar points out, the attribution to Butler is denied in a broadside attacking this poem (*On the Answer to Dr. Wild's Poem* . . . 1663):

> But oh! bold bard with brazen front,
> That durst put Hudibras upon't.
> And filch away that author's fame
> By counterfeiting of his name,
> Not as Bathillus did, who put
> His name to Virgil's verses, but,
> With far more impudence and shame,
> Thou hast to thine put Virgil's name.

(See Samuel Butler, *Satires and Miscellaneous Poetry and Prose,* Cambridge, 1928, pp. xiv–xv.) The contradictory evidence leaves the authorship of the poem in doubt.

The satirist adopts an extreme attitude toward Nonconformists as seditious and unjustly accuses Wild of having helped to instigate the execution of Charles I. He also fails to recognize, behind Wild's bantering tone, the deep admiration Wild felt for Calamy.

On Calamy's Imprisonment and Wild's Poetry

To the Bishops:

Most reverend Lords, the Church's joy and wonder,
Whose lives are lightning, and whose doctrine thunder,
The rare effects of both in this are found:
Ye break men's hearts, yet leave their bodies sound,
And from the court (as David did, they say)   *5*
Do with your organs fright the Devil away.
Awake! for though you think the day's your own,
The cage is open, and the bird is flown,
That bird (whom though your Lordships do despise)
May shit in Paul's and pick out Sheldon's eyes.   *10*
'Tis he who taught the pulpit and the press
To mask rebellion in a gospel dress;
He who blew up the coals of England's wrath,
And pick'd men's pockets by the public faith;
He who the melting sister's bounty tri'd,   *15*
And preach'd their bodkins into Caesar's side;
That crocodile of state, who wept a flood
When he was maudlin drunk with Charles's blood,
Is by the sisters' gold and brethren's prayer
Become a tenant to the open air,   *20*
For some were griev'd to see that light expire

5–6. With his lyre David exorcised the evil spirit which was tormenting Saul. See I Samuel 16:14–23. The Nonconformists had banned organs from the churches, but they were introduced again with the return of the Anglican clergy.

8. Calamy was released from Newgate at the King's order early in 1663.

10. There seems to be a reference here to the desecration of St. Paul's by Commonwealth soldiers, who stabled their horses there. Calamy was not involved. *Sheldon:* Gilbert Sheldon (1598–1671), Archbishop of Canterbury.

11–18. "Though he was a 'bitter enemy to all mobs' and a resolute opponent of the rising sectaries, his expressions on public affairs were quoted as countenancing 'incendiary' measures. The trial and execution of Charles he did what he could to oppose: his name is attached to the 'Vindication' of the London ministers' conduct in this affair drawn up by Christopher Burges" (*DNB*).

14. *the public faith:* "Jokes about the public faith were frequent in the Civil War. Parliament constantly borrowed money 'on the public faith' which meant that there was no guarantee at all of repayment" (C. V. Wedgwood, *Poetry and Politics under the Stuarts*, p. 84).

That lately help'd to set the Church on fire,
And when their ghostly father was perplex'd,
Could wrest an act, as he had done a text.
    Now enter Wild, who merrily lets fly   25
The fragments of his pulpit drollery.
Though his seditious ballad pleas'd the rout,
The verses, like the author, had the gout.
Yet he proclaims the show, invites the crew
(The Presbyters have their Jack-puddings too).   30
He tells you of a beast had lately been
Within the walls of Newgate to be seen,
That with a throat wide as the way to Hell
Could swallow oaths would choke the idol Bel
And burst the dragon, yet he could not swear   35
Obedience to the King and House of Pray'r.
    Ingenious Wild, 'tis thy unhappy fate
That *Iter Boreale*'s out of date;
Love's Tragedy's forgot, for (oh disgrace!)
Peters succeeds him in his martyr's place.   40
Publish the legend of that reverend brother,
And act the one, as thou hast writ the other;
For when St. Hugh did mount the fatal tree,
He left his coat a legacy to thee.
Oh may the gout no more disturb thy ease,   45

23. *perplex'd:* Entangled.
24. The poet charges Calamy's supporters with dishonesty in evading penalties of
the Act of Uniformity, but Calamy was released, according to the *DNB,* at the instiga-
tion of the King.
30. *Jack-puddings:* Buffoons in street shows.
34–35. *oaths:* Probably a reference to the Solemn League and Covenant. *Bel and
the dragon:* Babylonian idols in the apocryphal book of that name who devoured
huge sacrifices. The inclusion of this book in the Bible was insisted upon by the
Anglicans and opposed by the Nonconformists. The idea is that Calamy would strain
at a gnat but swallow a camel.
38. *Iter Boreale:* Wild's popular poem celebrating Monck's march from Scotland to
London.
39–44. Wild's *Tragedy of Christopher Love* (1660) celebrates the martyrdom of a
fiery Puritan minister executed in 1651 for plotting the restoration of Charles II.
Hugh Peters (1598–1660), an independent chaplain in the Parliamentary army, was
executed 16 Oct. 1660 for his alleged part in the death of Charles I, "which he denied
himself in his post-Restoration apologies; but his sermons during the trial, as was
proved by several witnesses, justified the sentence of the court" (*DNB*).

But Bishop Halter take his diocese,
And now th'art dead in law, though zealots laugh,
Impartial truth shall write this epitaph:
   This Presbyterian brat was born and cri'd,
Spat in his mother's face, and so he di'd.
He di'd, yet lives, and the unhappy elf   50
Divides Beelzebub against himself,
Abuses Calamy, that tail of Smec,
And shoots the prelates through his brother's neck.
   Bishops awake! and see a holy cheat:
The enemy sows tares among your wheat.   55
Do ye not hear the sons of Edom cry,
"Down with the Act of Uniformity!
We will compound and worship God by th'halves:
Take you the temples and give us the calves?"
Thus you behold the schismatic bravadoes—   60
Wild speaks in squibs, but Calamy granadoes.
Kirk, still these bairns, lest under Tyburn hedge,
The squire of Newgate rock them on a sledge.

52–54. Wild's poem, strangely enough, is mistaken as an attack on Calamy, and hence Beelzebub is divided against himself when Presbyterians fall out. Calamy is derided as the tail of another devil, Smec, his initials forming the last two letters of this abbreviation for *Smectymnuus.*

56. See Matthew 13:24: "The kingdom of Heaven is likened unto a man which sowed good seed in his field: But while men slept, his enemy came and sowed tares among the wheat and went his way."

57. *sons of Edom:* The descendants of Esau or Edom, who lived by the sword and slaughtered the Israelites in a long succession of battles. Here, the Nonconformists.

59. *compound:* To come to terms and pay for an offence or injury with special reference to the "compounding" of Cavaliers and malignants with the government during the interregnum.

60. The ejected ministers are shown slyly bargaining with the Anglicans for the calves (tithes?). In fact, however, the terms under which they were ejected were more severe than those inflicted earlier on the Anglican ministers, who had been permitted a small share in tithes to help support themselves.

A Pulpit to be Let
(*1665*)

A Pulpit to be Let attacks the Anglican ministers who fled London after the plague broke out in 1665. According to Neal, "some few of the established clergy, with a commendable zeal, ventured to continue in their stations and preach to their parishioners throughout the course of the plague . . . , but most of them fled and deserted their parishes at a time when their assistance was most wanted" (*The History of the Puritans, 4,* 398). Many Nonconformist clergy, who had been ejected under the Act of Uniformity in 1662, ventured to fill these places in violation of the Act. As a result, according to Neal, they incurred the wrath of Clarendon, who maintained that the Nonconformists "were ready, if any misfortune had befallen the King's fleet, to have brought the war into our fields and houses" (ibid., p. 399).

A Pulpit to be Let appeared as a broadside in 1665.

A Pulpit to be Let

Woe to the idle Shepherd that leaveth his Flock. Zechariah 11:7.
With a Just Applause of those Worthy Divines that Stay with us,
1665.

Beloved, and he sweetly thus goes on;
Now, where's Beloved? Why, Beloved's gone!
No morning matins now, nor evening song;
Alas! The parson cannot stay so long.
With Clerkenwell it fares as most in town,   5
The light-heel'd Levite's broke and the spark flown.

1. *Beloved:* The satirist wrily refers to the unfaithful minister by the term he used in addressing his congregation.
5. *Clerkenwell:* At the time a northern suburb of London.
6. *Levite:* A minister.

Broke did I say? They ne'er had quit the place
Had they but set up with a spark of grace!
They did the pulpit as a coffin greet
And took the surplice for a winding-sheet.
Had that so scar'd them? At the bells' sad tolls
They might have laid them by and learn'd of Paul's.
But for their parts, who will come in their rooms?
They are not mad to live among the tombs.
See how they choose three months to fly the rod
And dare not fall into the hands of God.
For God of persons no respecter is,
Then to respect themselves (pray) is't amiss?
They that should stay and teach us to reform
Gird up their loins and run to 'scape the storm,
And wing'd with fear, they flee to save their lives
Like Lot, from Sodom, with their brats and wives.
This is a tribe that for His punishments
Fear God, but keep not His Commandments.
They dread the plague and dare not stand its shock,
Let wolves or lions feed the fainting flock;
They made the sheep the subject now, men say,
Not so much of their prayer, as their prey.
But they are gone to have (it now appears)
The country hear them with their harvest-ears,
Whilst here at home we find Christ's saying true,
The harvest great is, but the lab'rers few.
Yet, like enough, the heat o'th' day being o'er,
You'll have them here again at the 'leventh hour.
Think you these men believe with holy Paul
For them to be dissolv'd is best of all?
Then, their own bodies they would never mind
More than the souls of those they left behind.
Who now, those sons of Aaron being fled,

22. See Genesis 19:1–29.
32. "The harvest truly is plenteous, but the laborers are few" (Luke 10:2).
33–34. An allusion to the parable of the laborers in the vineyard in Matthew 20.
35–36. An allusion, perhaps, to Romans 6:4: "Therefore we are buried with him by baptism into death: that like as Christ was raised up from the dead by the glory of the Father, even so we also should walk in newness of life."
39. *sons of Aaron:* Ministers.

Shall stand between the living and the dead?   40
We have at home the plague, abroad the sword,
And will they add the famine of the word?
But 'tis no matter, let what will befall,
A recantation sermon pays for all.
                        Ne saevi, magne Sacerdos!   45
    For you that stay, I have another sense;
These I revile, but you I reverence.
You have stood firm and God of mercy crav'd,
And holding out unto the end are sav'd.
You the true shepherds are, that would not keep   50
Your lives a minute, would they save the sheep.
Not hirelings, that away in peril sneak,
And leave the stones out of the wall to speak.
Whose heinous guilt is of a dye so deep,
It makes the dead even through the marble weep.   55
You, you have stood to't, as unmov'd as rocks,
And prov'd yourselves the only orthodox.
You have at Christ's command handed your lives
Without excuse of oxen, farms, or wives.
To you shall therefore glorious crowns be given,   60
And you shall shine bright as the stars in heaven.
Of life and death before you, well you choose,
For who will lose shall save, will save shall lose.
With reverence to the sacred word I shall
My theme an emblem of the Bible call: 65
For the canonical are those that stay,
They that obscure are the Apocrypha,
Of whom a man shall make (nay e'en St. John)
No revelation till the plague be gone.
Well, let them march; we have the better bread: 70
The wheat's the purer, now the chaff is fled.
Farewell wild grapes! For my part let 'em pass:
The gleanings better than the vintage was,

---

45. *Ne saevi, magne Sacerdos!:* Do not be angry, great priest!
51–52. Cf. John 10:11–15.

63. Cf. Matthew 10:39: "He that findeth his life shall lose it: and he that loseth his life for my sake shall find it."

72. The rebellious people of Israel are compared to wild grapes in Isaiah 5:1–7.

And let apostates ramble where they will,
The Church reserves her better angels still   75
Which she embraces, for in vain she cares
For wand'ring planets that has fixed stars.

Praelucendo pereo.

78. *Praelucendo pereo:* Though I bear a great light I perish.

ROBERT WILD

The Loyal Nonconformist
(*1666*)

Wild wrote this poem (first published as a broadside in 1666) in response to new measures against Nonconformists in what was commonly called the Five Mile Act of 1665. The Act forbade all in holy orders who refused to take the oaths prescribed by the Act of Uniformity (1662) to come within five miles of any corporate town or within five miles of any parish where they had served. The Act further forbade such persons to teach or to serve as private tutors and thus deprived ejected ministers of their commonest means of livelihood.

The Loyal Nonconformist attacks such requirements of the Established Church as the abjuring of the Solemn League and Covenant, the use of the Book of Common Prayer, and the wearing of surplices, either on the grounds of conscience or because there was no scriptural warrant for them, but its main point is that Nonconformity is no obstacle to loyalty, as the behavior of most Nonconformists under these persecutions abundantly showed.

The text is taken from *Iter Boreale with Other Select Poems* (1671) and has no substantive variants from the 1670 broadside. I have not seen the 1666 broadside.

THE LOYAL NONCONFORMIST

or An Account of What He Dare Swear and What He Dare not Swear.
Published in the year 1666.

1.

I fear an oath, before I swear to take it,
  And well I may, for 'tis the oath of God;
I fear an oath, when I have sworn, to break it,
  And well I may, for vengeance hath a rod.

2.

And yet I may swear and must, too: 'tis due   5
    Both to my heavenly and my earthly King.
If I assent, it must be full and true,
    And if I promise, I must do the thing.

3.

I am no Quaker, not at all to swear,
    Nor Papist, to swear east and mean the west;   10
But am a Protestant and shall declare
    What I cannot, and what I can, protest:

4.

I never will endeavor alteration
    Of monarchy nor of that royal name
Which God hath chosen to command this nation,   15
    But will maintain his person, crown, and fame.

5.

What he commands, if Conscience say not nay
    (For conscience is a greater king than he)
For Conscience' sake, not fear, I will obey,
    And if not active, passive I will be.   20

6.

I'll pray that all his subjects may agree
    And never more be crumbl'd into parts;
I will endeavor that his Majesty
    May not be King of Clubs but King of Hearts.

7.

The Royal Oak I swear I will defend,   25
    But for ivy which doth hug it so,
I swear that is a thief and not a friend
    And about steeples fitter far to grow.

8.

The civil government I will obey,
    But for Church policy I swear I doubt it,   30
And if my Bible want th' Apocrypha,
    I'll swear my book may be complete without it.

9.

I dare not swear Church government is right
    As it should be, but this I dare to swear
(If they should put me to't): the bishops might   35
    Do better and be better than they are.

10.

Nor will I swear, for all that they are worth,
    That bishoprics will stand and doomsday see,
And yet I'll swear the Gospel holdeth forth
    Christ with His ministers till then will be.   40

11.

That Peter was a prelate they aver,
    But I'll not swear't when all is said and done;
But I dare swear and hope I shall not err,
    He preached a hundred sermons to their one.

12.

Peter a fisher was, and he caught men,   45
    And they have nets and in them catch men too;
Yet I'll not swear they are alike, for them
    He caught he saved—these catch, and them undo.

13.

I dare not swear that courts ecclesiastic
    Do in their laws make just and gentle votes,   50
But I'll be sworn that Burton, Prynne, and Bastwick
    Were once ear-witnesses of harsher notes.

51–52. Henry Burton (1578–1648), William Prynne (1600–69), and John Bastwick, M.D. (1593–1654), Puritan controversialists, were sentenced in 1637 by the Star Chamber to lose their ears in the pillory for sermons and writings regarded as seditious by the government.

14.

Archdeacons, deans, and chapters are brave men,
    By canon, not by Scripture; but to this,
If I be called, I'll swear and swear again,   55
    That no such chapter in my Bible is.

15.

I'll not condemn those Presbyterians who
    Refused bishoprics and might have had 'em,
But Mistress Calamy I'll swear doth do
    As well as if she were a spiritual madam.   60

16.

I will not swear that they who this oath take
    Will for religion e'er lay down their lives,
But I will swear they will good jugglers make,
    Who can already swallow down such knives.

17.

For holy vestments I'll not take an oath   65
    Which linen most canonical may be;
Some are for lawn, some holland, some Scots cloth,
    And hemp, for some, is fitter than all three.

18.

Paul had a cloak, and books and parchments too,
    But that he wore a surplice I'll not swear,   70
Nor that his parchments did his orders show,
    Or in his books there was a Common Prayer.

19.

I owe assistance to the King by oath,
    And if he please to put the bishops down—
As who knows what may be?—I should be loath   75
    To see Tom Becket's miter push the crown.

60. *spiritual madam:* The wife of a bishop.

20.

And yet Church government I do allow,
   And am contented bishops be the men,
And that I speak in earnest, here I vow
   Where we have one, I wish we might have ten.   80

21.

In fine, the civil power I'll obey,
   And seek the peace and welfare of the nation;
If this won't do, I know not what to say,
   But farewell London, farewell Corporation.

Swearing and Lying
(*1666*)

Wild's poems on ecclesiastical issues upheld a moderate and tolerant Nonconformist position, but they elicited nonetheless a great many attacks. In its allegations that Wild's Nonconformist position is merely a cloak for heresy and treason, this anonymous Anglican satire is typical of many others.

Swearing and Lying, a rejoinder to *The Loyal Nonconformist,* was published as a broadside in 1666.

SWEARING AND LYING

or an
Answer to the Swearing Pamphlet
1666

1.

That you do fear an oath I dare not swear,
   Especially if it the Cause advance,
And yet I dare swear that one oath you fear,
   And that the oath is of allegiance.

2.

To God yet you will swear, and to your King,   5
   Provided that the oath be mystical.
You promise, and you must perform the thing,
   Though with the Forty 'tis to kill St. Paul.

2. *Cause:* Good Old Cause.
6. *mystical:* Secret, conspiratorial.
8. The Jews attacked St. Paul as a heretic, and more than forty of them swore to fast until they had killed him. See Acts 23:12–13.

3.

You are, you say, no Quaker to protest
    Against all swearing; that indeed I grant.   10
But if with Rome you swore not east and west,
    How a pox gulp'd ye down that Covenant?

4.

But what an alteration here is made?
    What subjects on a sudden ye commence!
Maintain the Crown and yet the Church invade—   15
    Come, ye'll yield all things but obedience.

5.

But if that great King Conscience says not nay,
    You to the King's commands will freely yield,
But is not this that Conscience, Sir, I pray
    That has our land with blood and rapine fill'd?   20

6.

What splay-mouth'd wish is this? Let all agree
    When you the concord crumble into parts,
But, Knaves of Clubs, maugre your villainy,
    His Majesty shall still be King of Hearts.

7.

You swear forsooth you will the Crown defend   25
    And all the dignity of the Royal Oak,
But here the thief usurps the name of friend,
    The Kirk the ivy is of which you spoke.

8.

With the Apochrypha you cannot bear,
    And your devotion stumbles at this log,   30
And what's the reason? 'Tis because you are
    Like Tobit blind and madder than his dog.

21. *splay-mouth'd:* Wide-mouthed, equivocating, *obs.*

32. For the blindness Tobit suffered as a test of his patience under divine affliction, see Tobit 2. His sight was later restored. A dog appears briefly in Tobit 11, but he is not mad.

9.

But we are got to my Lord Bishop now,
   Whose government you dare not say is right, sir.
But shall I tell you why your teeth you show?   35
   Jack has a peek at Aaron for his miter.

10.

I'll swear and venture all that I am worth,
   That bishops last as long as king and queen.
You have already, as the Act holds forth,
   Like baffled Henderson your doomsday seen.   40

11.

That Peter was a prelate I'll maintain,
   But that he preach'd so oft I doubt it greatly,
But by your leave, what Peters do you mean—
   Peters that preach'd at Charing Cross so lately?

12.

Peter a fisher was, and so are they: 45
   Would you be caught you might salvation get.
Their sacred nets they cast out day by day,
   But it seems all's not fish that comes to th' net.

13.

As for the court, that court ecclesiastic,
   As it is just, it merciful appears: 50
To waive all others, let me instance Bastwick,
   Whose head being forfeit could compound for's ears.

36. i.e., Jack Presbyter envies the miter of Aaron (the type of a bishop).

40. *Henderson*: Alexander Henderson (1583?–1646), Scottish divine, who drew up the Covenant and tried in vain to induce Charles I to take it.

44. *Peters*: Hugh Peters or Peter (1598–1660), Independent divine, was convicted as a regicide and executed at Charing Cross on 16 October 1660. On the 14th he had preached a farewell sermon to his fellow prisoners, which was published.

51. *Bastwick*: John Bastwick, M.D. (1593–1654), physician and ecclesiastical controversialist, wrote a pamphlet in 1637 denouncing bishops as enemies of God. The Star Chamber sentenced him to lose his ears in the pillory, to pay a fine of £5,000, and to be imprisoned for life.

14.

Archdeacons, deans, and chapters are the men
   Have honor, and your envy would implead it.
Turn over therefore, pray, your book again,   55
   'Tis a hard chapter, and you cannot read it.

15.

Spiritual Madam? Pray what madam's that?
   Heralds would swear you here false doctrine teach.
You refuse bishoprics?—away, ye prate!
   But foxes scorn the grapes they cannot reach.   60

16.

For holy vestments holland's fit, and lawn,
   But as for naisty Scotch cloth we'll have none.
And if the Kirkists won't to this be drawn,
   Then give 'em hemp as long as 'twill hang on.

17.

That Paul, because here's mention of a cloak,   65
   A Presbyterian was I cannot swear;
But this upon my oath may well be spoke,
   All he converted were by common prayer.

18.

You owe allegiance to the King, God save him!
   (But on condition bishops may go down),   70
But if he will not do as you would have him,
   You neither value miter, nor yet crown.

19.

And yet you seem to like of miter'd men,
   O Conscience! see what interest can do.
For if instead of one we should have ten,   75
   'Tis ten to one, but one might fall to you.

20.

In fine you must not sever Church and State;
  If you not both obey, you both provoke.
But if you will not? Porter, ope the gate,
  And farewell, Presbyter, farewell, long cloak!   80

A Character of the Church of Chichester
(1673)

Peter Gunning, Bishop of Chichester in 1670–75, "set himself with very great zeal to clear the Church of Rome of idolatry" in the hope of reconciling the Anglican Church with Catholicism on certain points (Burnet, *History, 1,* 321). Gunning "did his best to re-establish the authority of the Church in Sussex and probably encountered a good deal of resistance, for there was a large and powerful Puritan and Calvinistic element in the diocese" (W. R. W. Stephens, *The South Saxon Diocese, Selsey-Chichester,* 1881, p. 231). The Bishop's tolerant policies are derided in this squib which is found in the Osborn MS. entitled *Wit and Learning (D″).*

A CHARACTER OF THE CHURCH OF CHICHESTER, 1673

Is any church more catholic than we?
Two prebends apostate Puritans there be,
One perjur'd Protestant, the dean an atheist,
And Peter the head thereof an arrant Papist.
What a prodigious unity is here!   5
Calvinist, Arminian, Roundhead, Cavalier,
Protestant, Papist, atheist, devil and all,
Tim, Tom, and Tidy—isn't this catholical?
Had it but in it one poor Turk and Jew,
Hell would be hard put to't to match the crew.   10

The Geneva Ballad
(*1674*)

The Geneva Ballad, first published as a broadside in 1674, must have been unusually popular, because it appeared in a second broadside edition in 1678. Although it repeats all the usual clichés found in such literary attacks on Nonconformists, it succeeded in infusing some life into the caricature, partly, perhaps, because some of the details in the portrait seem to have been modeled after that strange divine, Thomas Goodwin.

The Geneva Ballad with the *Answer* is printed in *Bagford Ballads*. It has been popularly ascribed to Samuel Butler, but there is no firm evidence for the ascription.

THE GENEVA BALLAD
TO THE TUNE OF FORTY-EIGHT

1.

Of all the factions in the town
Mov'd by French springs or Flemish wheels,
None treads religion upside down,
Or tears pretences out at heels
Like Splay-mouth with his brace of caps,   5

1–2. Factions influenced by sectarian movements in France or the Low Countries.
4. *pretences out at heels:* Worn-out pretenses.
5. *Splay-mouth:* Wide-mouth, an equivocator. This satirical portrait is probably modeled in part on Thomas Goodwin D.D. (1600–80), Independent divine and President of Magdalen College, Oxford, 1650–60. Goodwin was noted for his peculiar habit of wearing two or more caps at one time. In an engraving in Calamy's *Nonconformists' Memorial* (1802) he is shown wearing two. Addison in *Spectator*, no. 494, relates how an undergraduate was summoned into Goodwin's austere presence and found him "with half-a-dozen nightcaps upon his head and religious horror in his countenance." Goodwin was dismissed from his presidentship after the Restoration and moved to London, "whither many of his church followed him, and he continued in the faithful discharge of his ministry there till his death" (Calamy).

Whose conscience might be scann'd, perhaps,
By the dimensions of his chaps.

2.

He whom the sisters so adore,
Counting his actions all divine,
Who, when the spirit hints, can roar,   10
And if occasion serves can whine—
Nay, he can bellow, bray, or bark—
Was ever sike a beuk-larn'd clerk
That speaks all linguas of the Ark?

3.

To draw in proselytes like bees,   15
With pleasing twang he tones his prose.
He gives his handkerchief a squeeze,
And draws John Calvin through his nose.
Motive on motive he obtrudes
With slip-stocking similitudes,   20
Eight uses more, and so concludes.

4.

When monarchy began to bleed
And treason had a fine new name,
When Thames was balderdash'd with Tweed,
And pulpits did like beacons flame,   25
When Jeroboam's calves were rear'd,
And Laud was neither lov'd nor fear'd,
This Gospel-comet first appear'd.

18. An allusion to the nasal twang supposed to be in vogue among Puritan preachers.
20. *slip-stocking:* Slipshod.
21. *Eight uses more:* An allusion to the manifold analyses of texts practised by Dissenting preachers.
24. When Anglicanism was adulterated with Scottish Presbyterianism.
26. *Jeroboam's calves:* Sectarian heresies. When Jeroboam led the ten tribes in revolt against Jerusalem he set up golden calves in Bethel and Dan (I Kings 12:28–29).
27. *Laud:* William Laud (1573–1645), Archbishop of Canterbury, the champion of episcopacy and high church liturgy, executed by Parliament.

5.

Soon his unhallow'd fingers stripp'd
His sov'reign Liege of pow'r and land,   30
  And having smote his master, slipp'd
His sword into his fellow's hand,
    But he that wears his eyes may note
    Oft-times the butcher binds a goat
    And leaves his boy to cut her throat.   35

6.

Poor England felt his fury then
Outweigh'd Queen Mary's many grains,
  His very preaching slew more men
Than Bonner's faggots, stakes, and chains.
    With Dog-star zeal and lungs like Boreas,   40
    He fought and taught and (what's notorious)
    Destroy'd his Lord to make him glorious,

7.

Yet drew for King and Parliament,
As if the wind could stand north-south,
  Broke Moses' Law with blest intent,   45
Murder'd, and then he wip'd his mouth;
    Oblivion alters not his case,
    Nor clemency nor acts of grace
    Can blanch an Ethiopian's face.

8.

Ripe for rebellion he begins   50
To rally up the saints in swarms.
  He bawls aloud, "Sirs, leave your sins!"
But whispers, "Boys, stand to your arms!"
    Thus he's grown insolently rude,

37. *grains:* Rosary beads, *obs.*

39. *Edmund Bonner* (1500?–69), Bishop of London, took a leading part in the per-
secution of Puritans under Henry VIII.

42. An allusion to the claim, often made by the Parliamentary party, that they were
fighting to rescue Charles I from the evil counselors who had misled him into war.

47. *Oblivion:* The Bill of General Pardon, Indemnity, and Oblivion (1660).

Thinking his gods can't be subdu'd—   55
Money, I mean, and multitude.

9.

Magistrates he regards no more
Than St. George or the kings of Colen,
Vowing he'll not conform before
The old wives wind their dead in woolen.   60
    He calls the Bishop Greybeard Goff
    And makes his power as mere a scoff
    As Dagon when his hands were off.

10.

Hark! How he opens with full cry:
"Halloo my hearts, beware of Rome!"   65
    Cowards that are afraid to die
Thus make domestic broils at home.
    How quietly great Charles might reign
    Would all these Hotspurs cross the Main
    And preach down Popery in Spain.   70

11.

The starry rule of Heaven is fix'd—
There's no dissension in the sky,
    And can there be a mean betwixt
Confusion and Conformity?
    A place divided never thrives;   75
    'Tis bad where hornets dwell in hives,
    But worse where children play with knives.

58. *St. George:* According to tradition, St. George displayed a courageous indifference to tyrannical authority by destroying in public an anti-Christian edict of the Emperor Diocletian. *kings of Colen:* The Archbishop-electors of the Empire were in perpetual feuds with the free imperial city of Cologne throughout the later Middle Ages.

60. To protect the English woolen industry the law required that shrouds be made of wool. There was much opposition to this act.

61. *Goff:* A stupid person.

63. *Dagon:* When the Philistines set the captured ark in the house of their god, Dagon, Dagon was found with his head and hands cut off (1 Samuel 5:1–4).

12.

I would as soon turn back to mass,
Or change my phrase to thee and thou,
Let the Pope ride me like an ass
And his priests milk me like a cow,
    As buckle to Smectymnuan laws
    The bad effects o'th' Good Old Cause,
    That have doves' plumes, but vultures' claws.

80

13.

For 'twas the Haly Kirk that nurs'd
The Brownists and the Ranters' crew;
Foul error's motley vesture first
Was oaded in a northern blue;
    And what's the enthusiastic breed
    Or men of Knipperdolling's creed
    But Cov'nanters run up to seed?

85

90

14.

Yet (they all cry) they love the King
And make boast of their innocence;
There cannot be so vile a thing
But may be color'd with pretence;
    Yet when all's said, one thing I'll swear,
    No subject like th' old Cavalier,
    No traitor like Jack Presbyter.

95

79. Like a Quaker.

82. *Smectymnuan laws:* Laws favoring dissent.

86. *Brownists:* A narrow and exclusive sect named after Richard Browne (1550?–1633?), the earliest separatist from the Church of England after the Reformation. Congregationalists regard him as the first enunciator of their principles. *Ranters:* "An antinomian and spiritualistic English sect in the time of the Commonwealth, who [*sic*] may be described as the dregs of the Seeker Movement" (*EB*).

88. *oaded:* Woaded, dyed, *obs.*

90. *Knipperdolling:* Bernard Knipperdolling (c. 1490–1536), a fanatical leader of the Münster Anabaptists in 1535–36.

An Answer to The Geneva Ballad
(1674)

An Answer to The Geneva Ballad incorporates most of the commonplaces of anti-Anglican propaganda and is thus exactly suited to the satire it answers. It was printed as a broadside in 1674. No other texts have been found.

AN ANSWER TO THE GENEVA BALLAD

1.

Of all the drollsters in the town
Of Popish or of Hobbian race,
  None drags religion up and down,
Or doth the Gospel such disgrace
    As Spruce with coat canonical   5
    Whose conscience echoes, "Have at all!"
    Would a fat benefice but fall.

2.

He whom the ruder wits adore,
And count his vile lampoons divine;
  Who pimps in rhyme for the Old Whore,   10
And fain would patch up Dagon's shrine,
    A sacred Proteus, one that can
    Blend Gospel with the Alcoran,
    And takes texts from *Leviathan*.

1. *drollsters:* Buffoons.
2. *Hobbian:* In *Leviathan* (1651) Thomas Hobbes proposed the subordination of the ecclesiastical to the secular authority. He was widely denounced as an atheist, materialist, and political absolutist.
6. *have at all:* A desperate risk, a phrase taken from the practice of gamblers.

3.

Yet if he list, this motley clerk, 15
Himself as loud as Smec can bray,
The Church he slanders in the dark,
But hectors for her in the day.
Of late he scoff'd at miter'd peers,
Pull'd the old graybeards by the ears, 20
And call'd them Heaven's overseers.

4.

Yet now he fawns on them again,
And grins in rage his foaming chaps,
Wishes poor Presbyter in Spain,
And tears his edifying caps. 25
So cowards kill where heroes spare,
And renegadoes always are
More fierce than native Turks by far.

5.

Thus with each heifer he can plow,
A Papist or an Independent: 30
What point the gales of profit blow
He always steers, and there's an end on't.
Was ever syke a priest among
All Gloucester cobblers' fulsome throng,
To pawn his conscience for a song? 35

6.

Whilst Presbyter with active fist
Makes it his work to preach and pray,
This modifi'd Episcopist
Shows 'tis to Heaven a jollier way:
With organs and with violin 40
And ballad new on merry pin,
He means to wheedle souls from sin.

16. *Smec:* Smectymnuus.
40. Presbyterians objected to the use of organs and other musical instruments in Anglican services.

7.

Geneva in a huff he kicks,
And swears by's reverend cassock-coat.
   The Leman Lake's a second Styx   45
Where none but damned souls do float,
     Though wise men think its water be
     From all such secret venom free,
     Nor half so brackish as Rome's sea.

8.

Perhaps the man has cause to stickle,   50
Since int'rest leads him to complain,
   Fearing some neighboring conventicle
His incomes to low ebb should drain.
     But be not, friend, at that dismay'd:
     Should preaching prove a sorry trade,
     Ballading is not quite decay'd.

9.

He varnishes his envious hate
With a pretended loyal zeal,
   But would in truth subvert the State,
And all embroil the Commonweal.   60
     His business is but to divide,
     Wound Protestants through Calvin's side,
     That Popelings once more might us ride.

10.

See how he slyly acts his part,
Commends Queen Mary's bloody days;   65
   And doubtless should we sound his heart,
Such bonfires here afresh would raise.
     But Heav'n defend those sad extremes,
     We hope to keep unfilled Thames
     Free both from Tweed's and Tiber's streams.   70

11.

Cease then impertinently to rant,
We understand the stale intrigue;
  Remember the Scotch Covenant
Was copi'd from your Gallic league.
    Against Bluebonnet swagger not,   75
    We know who hatch'd the Powder Plot,
    Nor yet is Ireland's blood forgot.

12.

Our Sovereign's pleasure we'll obey,
But scorn to truckle unto thine;
  Since Charles does liberty display,   80
How dare such pamphleteers repine?
    Peace, Becket Junior, know your place,
    Let no oblivion reach your case,
    Who cyphers make of Acts of Grace.

13.

The constant rules of Heaven we know   85
Whose stars in various orbs do move,
  Which we may copy here below,
Whilst several parties live in love.
    Without yoke of Conformity,
    We can keep Christian unity   90
    As different notes make harmony.

14.

Yet well may each good shepherd cry
Unto his flocks, "Beware of Rome!"
  When foreign wolves so oft we spy,
Making domestic broils at home.   95
    And in each corner of the land,
    Perceive those sly sheep-stealers stand
    To give them the red-letters brand.

74. Ebsworth emends *gall* to *gallant* league in *Bagford Ballads*. *Gallic* (refering
to the Huguenots) seems a more likely guess.
  98. To convert them to Catholicism.

15.

With holy beads they teach to chant
Their *ave's* and their unknown prayers,   100
   And all the while to Heav'n they mount,
Take special care to tell the stairs.
     The kitchen-wench comes into matin,
     And lines her soul with shreds of Latin,
     Like greasy fustian fac'd with satin.   105

16.

Their whole religion is so odd,
It seems a dark mysterious trade
   To disturb kings and worship God
Only in show and masquerade.
     A chaos of deformity   110
     Made up of blood, hypocrisy,
     Fraud, treason, and idolatry.

17.

Yet you as soon to mass would gad,
Alas! It is all one to thee—
   He that religion never had   115
May easily a Papist be:
     Where purchas'd pardons set him free
     Beyond a Ranter's liberty
     To wallow in debauchery.

18.

Though he contrive to hide his plot,   120
We yet can apprehend the snare,
   Through the sheep's clothing he has got
His fox's ears do plain appear.
     Protestant drones, look to your lives!
     He'd fain be burning of your hives,   125
     And counts the Scriptures dangerous knives.

104. *Latin:* The language of the Catholic mass.

19.

We'll not recriminate the case,
Nor make boast of our loyalty,
   But still with thankful hearts embrace
Our gracious Prince's clemency.   130
      Yet hope to prove our innocence,
      And actions void of just offence
      Against this slanderous pretence.

20.

When surplice was an useless thing,
And miter a poor relic lay,   135
     The preaching cloak brought back the King
And turn'd our dismal night to day.
      Mun Calamy, and a few more,
      Did then more on their Sov'reign's score
      Then troops of raillerists before.   140

138. *Mun Calamy:* The Rev. Edmund Calamy.

III. Literary Affairs

The Session of the Poets
(1668)

The "session" poem, in which poets, playwrights, court ladies, or beaux were summoned to derisive judgment, was a popular satirical form in the Augustan period. Suckling's *Session of the Poets* (1637?) was a model for the poem here printed and for several others which followed. (See Hugh Macdonald, *A Journal from Parnassus*, London, P. J. Dobell, 1937.)

The author of this *Session* comments adversely on the poets, playwrights, and poetasters of the age and retails a good deal of gossip about most of them. Neither MSS. nor printed texts make any attributions, nor does the style give any clues to his identity. Since almost every known poet of the period is attacked, the poem is presumably the work of an obscure writer.

This satire is dated 1666 in the copy-text (Bod. MS. Don b. 8), but allusions to later events (Shadwell's first play, for instance, was produced in 1668) implies a later date of composition or later additions.

THE SESSION OF THE POETS

1.

Apollo, concern'd to see the transgressions
   Our paltry poets did daily commit,
Gave order once more to summon a sessions
   Severely to punish the abuses of wit.

2.

Will D'Avenant would fain have been steward o'th' court,   5
   To have fin'd and amerc'd each man at his will,

---

5. *D'Avenant:* Sir William D'Avenant (1606–68), dramatist, Poet Laureate, and Master of the Duke's Company.

But Apollo had heard, it seems, a report
    That his choice of new plays did show he had no skill.

3.

Besides, some critics that ow'd him a spite
    A little before had made the god fret   10
By letting him know the Laureate did write
    That damnable farce, *The House to be Let.*

4.

Intell'gence was brought, the court being sat,
    That a play tripartite was very near made,
Where malicious Matt Clifford and spiritual Sprat   15
    Were join'd with their Duke, a peer of the trade.

5.

Apollo rejoic'd, and hop'd for amends,
    Because he knew it was the first case
The Duke e're did ask the advice of his friends,
    And so wish'd his play as well clapp'd as his Grace.   20

6.

Oyez being made and silence proclaim'd,
    Apollo began to read the suit-roll,
When as soon as he saw Frank Berkeley was nam'd,
    He scarce could forbear from tearing the scroll.

7.

But Berkeley, to make his int'rests the greater,   25
    Suspecting before what would come to pass,
Procur'd his cousin Fitzharding's letter,
    With which Apollo wiped his arse.

---

12. D'Avenant's *The Playhouse to be Let* (1663) "is nothing but a set of farces and burlesques loosely pinned together in one framework" (Allardyce Nicoll, *History of English Drama, I,* 248).

14. *play tripartite: The Rehearsal,* a comedy ridiculing D'Avenant and Dryden, was written in the 1660s by the Duke of Buckingham with the assistance of Martin Clifford (d. 1677), and Thomas Sprat (1635–1713), a founder of the Royal Society and later Bishop of Rochester. *The Rehearsal* was produced in 1671.

23. I cannot identify Frank Berkeley nor his "cousin Fitzharding" (line 27).

8.

Guy with his pastoral next went to pot;
   At first in a doleful study he stood,
Then show'd a certificate which he had got   30
   From the Maids of Honor, but it did no good.

9.

A number of other small poets appear'd
   With whom for a time Apollo made sport;
Gifford and Flecknoe were very well jeer'd,   35
   And in the conclusion whipp'd out of the court.

10.

Tom Killigrew boldly came up to the bar,
   Thinking his gibing would get him the bays,
But Apollo was angry and bid him beware
   That he caught him no more a-printing his plays.   40

11.

With ill luck in battle but worse in wit,
   George Porter began for the laurel to bawl,

29. *Guy:* Henry Guy, financier, politician, and a member of the court wits. His claim to literary fame rests upon a *Pastoral* now lost (J. H. Wilson, *The Court Wits,* passim).

35. *Gifford:* I am unable to trace any poet of this name. The variant Clifford found in some texts is unacceptable because Martin Clifford is the only playwright of that name, his output was confined to a share in *The Rehearsal,* and he has already been mentioned in the poem (line 15). *Flecknoe:* Richard Flecknoe (d. 1678), thought to be a Roman Catholic priest, was satirized by Marvell in *Flecknoe, an English Priest at Rome.* He wrote poems, which he was fond of reciting, and numerous plays, only one of which was produced. He lives chiefly in Dryden's lines:

In prose and verse was owned, without dispute,
Through all the realms of nonsense, absolute.

37. Thomas Killigrew (1612–83), dramatist and patentee of the King's Playhouse, of whom Denham wrote:

Had Cowley ne'er spoke, Killigrew ne'er writ,
Combin'd in one, they'd made a matchless wit.

42. *George Porter:* "An exceedingly quarrelsome fellow and quite sufficiently dissipated" (*Rochester-Savile Letters,* p. 52 n.). I cannot trace his literary productions.

But Apollo did think such impudence fit
  To be thrust out o'th' court as he's out of Whitehall.

12.

Savoy-missing Cowley came into the court,   45
  Making apologies for a bad play;
Ev'ryone gave him so good a report
  That Apollo gave heed to all he could say.

13.

Nor would he have had, as 'tis thought, a rebuke,
  Unless he had done some notable folly,   50
Writ verses unjustly in praise of Sam Tuke,
  Or printed his pitiful "Melancholy."

14.

Cotton did next to the bays pretend,
  But Apollo told him it was not fit:
Though his Virgil was well, yet it made but amends   55
  For the worst panegyric that ever was writ.

45. *Cowley:* Abraham Cowley (1618–67), the famous poet, wrote only two plays: *The Guardian* (1650) and *Cutter of Coleman Street,* which Pepys saw on its opening and pronounced "a very good play" (16 Dec. 1661). In his *Verses upon Several Occasions* (1663) Cowley lamented his failure to secure the Mastership of the Savoy. The poem, entitled *The Complaint,* begins:

> In a deep vision's intellectual scene,
>   Beneath a bower for sorrow made,
>   Th' uncomfortable shade
>   Of the black yew's unlucky green,
> Mix'd with the mourning willow's careful gray,
> Where rev'rend Cham cuts out his famous way,
>   The melancholy Cowley lay.

51. *Tuke:* Sir Samuel Tuke (d. 1674), Royalist officer and playwright. Cowley wrote commendatory verses on his tragicomedy, *The Adventures of Five Hours* (1663).
52. *"Melancholy":* The Complaint (see line 45 n.).
53. *Cotton:* Charles Cotton (1630–87), poet and translator of Montaigne. In 1664 he published anonymously a burlesque of the *Aeneid* entitled *Scarronides, or the First Book of Virgil Travestie.* A parody of the fourth book was added in 1670, and the work went through many editions
56. An allusion, presumably, to Cotton's prose panegyric on Charles II (1660).

15.

Old Shirley stood up and made an excuse,
  Because many young men before him were got,
He vow'd he had switch'd and spur-gall'd his muse,
  But still the dull jade kept to her old trot.   60

16.

Sir Robert Howard, call'd for over and over,
  At last sent in Teague with a packet of news,
Wherein the sad Knight, to his grief, did discover
  How Dryden had lately robb'd him of his muse.

17.

Each man in the court was pleas'd with the theft,   65
  Which made the whole family swear and rant,
Desiring, their Robin i'th' lurch being left,
  The thief might be fin'd for his *Wild Gallant*.

18.

Dryden, whom one would have thought had more wit,
  The censure of every man did disdain,   70
Pleading some pitiful rhymes he had writ,
  In praise of the Countess of Castlemaine.

19.

Ned Howard, in whom great nature is found,
  Though never took notice of till that day,

57. *Shirley:* James Shirley (1596–1666), dramatist. "No sneer could have been more unjust than that of the ribald *Session of the Poets* implying that after the Restoration Shirley engaged in futile attempts to equal the performances of younger men, while nothing is known as to the truth or falsehood of the assertion in the same poem that he 'owned' a play printed under the name of Edward Howard" (*DNB*).

61. *Howard:* Sir Robert Howard (1626–98), a dramatist described by Evelyn as "insufferably boasting" and as "that universal pretender." In his play *The Committee* (produced 1662) there is an Irish footman named Teague. Howard was assisted by Dryden, his brother-in-law, in writing *The Indian Queen,* a tragedy (produced 1664). Although Howard did not acknowledge Dryden's help, Dryden proclaimed his part in *The Indian Queen* in the preface to a sequel, *The Indian Emperor* (published 1667).

68–72. *The Wild Gallant:* Dryden's first acted play (1663). It was a failure despite the support of Lady Castlemaine, which Dryden acknowledged in the prologue.

73–80. *Howard:* Edward Howard (fl. 1669), brother of Sir Robert and James (see line 81 n.), was a dramatist and the author of the widely-satirized heroic poem *The*

Impatiently sat till it came to his round,   75
   Then rose and commended the plot of his play.

20.

Such arrogance made Apollo stark mad,
   But Shirley endeavors t'appease his choler
By owning the play and swearing the lad
   In poetry was a very pert scholar.   80

21.

James Howard being call'd for out of the throng,
   Booted and spurr'd to the bar did advance,
Where singing a damn'd nonsensical song,
   The youth and his muse were sent into France.

22.

Newcastle on's horse for entrance next strives,   85
   Well stuff'd was his cloakbag and so were his breeches,
And unbutt'ning the place where Nature's posset-maker lives,
   Pulls out his wife's poems, plays, essays, and speeches.

British Princes. His tragedy *The Usurper* (performed 2 Jan. 1664, published 1668) had an extremely complicated plot. It is in blank verse, which Howard defends in the preface as more "natural" than rhyme to a play "that should most nearly imitate in some cases our familiar converse." F. S. Boas notes that Howard was a great admirer of Shirley, but cannot find any grounds for the allegation that Shirley fathered this play (*The Change of Crownes*, London, 1949, p. 3). Cf. line 57 n.

81. *James Howard* (fl. 1674), brother of Sir Robert and Edward, was also a dramatist. In his comedy, *The English Monsieur*, one of the characters falls in love while pulling on his boots.

85. *Newcastle:* William Cavendish, Duke of Newcastle (1592–1676), a famous horseman who wrote two treatises on the subject. He took so much delight in his Barbary horses that nothing could part him from them. Newcastle wrote numerous plays and poems, and Pepys considered his *Humorous Lovers* "the most silly thing that ever came upon the stage" (30 March 1667).

87. *Nature's posset-maker: Membrum virile.* Two MSS. note that the phrase occurs in the Duchess' poems.

87–92. The Duchess, Margaret Cavendish (1624?–74), was a prolific writer of poems, plays, and philosophical treatises. In her plays common sense "is buried in an avalanche of ignorance and extravagance. . . . Her occasional appearance in theatrical costume and her reputation for purity of life, together with her vanity and affectation, contributed to gain her a reputation for madness" (*DNB*).

23.

"Whoop!" quoth Apollo, "What the de'il have we here?
  Put up thy wife's trumpery, good noble Marquis,   90
And home again, home again take thy career,
  To provide her fresh straw and a chamber that dark is."

24.

Sam Tuke sat and formally smil'd at the rest,
  But Apollo, who well did his vanity know,
Call'd him to the bar to put him to the test,   95
  But his muse was so stiff she scarcely could bow.

25.

She pleaded her labor deserv'd a reward;
  It seems in her age she doted on praise,
But Apollo resolv'd that such a bald bard
  Should never be grac'd with a perr'wig of bays.   100

26.

Stapleton stood up and had nothing to say,
  But Apollo forbids the old Knight to despair,
Commanding him once more to write a new play
  To be danc'd by the puppets in Barthol'mew Fair.

27.

Sir William Killigrew doubting his plays,   105
  Before he was call'd crept up to the bench,

93–100. See line 51 n.
101. *Stapleton:* Sir Robert Stapleton (d. 1669), dramatist and translator.
104. The repertory of the puppet theatre at Bartholomew Fair consisted in the main of old favorites such as *The Sorrows of Griselda, Dick Whittington, The Vagaries of Merry Andrew,* etc. It is not known that any of Stapleton's plays were performed there. On 4 Sept. 1668 Pepys attended a performance of Jonson's play and commented as follows: "At noon my wife and Deb. and Mercer and W. Hewer and I to the Fair, and there at the old house did eat a pig and was pretty merry, but saw no sights, my wife having in mind to see the play *Bartholomew Fair* with puppets. Which we did, and it is an excellent play; the more I see it, the more I love the wit of it."
105. *Sir William Killigrew* (1606–95), dramatist, Gentleman-Usher of the Privy Chamber to Charles II. In 1665 he published three plays, *Selindra, Pandora,* and *Ormasdes.*

And whisper'd Apollo, in case he would praise
   Selindra, he should have a bout with the wench.

28.

Buckhurst and Sedley with two or three more
   Translators of *Pompey* put in their claim,   110
But Apollo made them be turn'd out of door,
   And bade them be gone like fools as they came.

29.

Old Waller heard this and was sneaking away,
   But somebody spi'd him out in the crowd;
Apollo, though he'd not seen him many a day,   115
   Knew him full well and call'd to him aloud:

30.

"My old friend, Mr. Waller, and what make you there,
   Among these young fellows that spoil the French plays?"
Then beck'ning him to him, he whisper'd in's ear,
   And gave him good counsel instead of the bays.   120

31.

Then in came Denham, that limping old bard,
   Whose fame on *The Sophy* and *Cooper's Hill* stands,
And brought many stationers who swore very hard
   That nothing sold better unless 'twere his lands.

32.

But Apollo advis'd him to write something more,   125
   To clear a suspicion which possess'd the court
That *Cooper's Hill,* so much bragg'd on before,
   Was writ by a vicar who had forty pounds for't.

109–110. *Pompey the Great* (1664), a translation of Corneille's *Pompée,* was the joint work of Buckhurst, Sedley, Waller, and Sidney Godolphin. Another translation by Katherine Philips was first produced in Dublin in February 1663 and published in 1667.

121–28. *Cooper's Hill,* first published in 1640, was reissued in a revised version in 1655. *The Sophy,* a Senecan tragedy, was published in 1642 and 1667. In both works Denham was accused of plagiarizing, though the charges seem baseless. Cf. Butler's al-

33.

Then Hudibras boldly demanded the bay,
  But Apollo bid him not be too fierce,
And advis'd him to lay aside making his play,
  Since already he began to write worse and worse.   130

34.

Tom Porter came into the court in a huff,
  Swearing God damn him he'd writ the best plays,
But Apollo, it seems, knew his way well enough,
  And would not be hector'd out of the bays.   135

35.

Ellis in great discontent went away,
  Whilst D'Av'nant against Apollo did rage,
Because he declar'd *The Secret* a play
  Fitting for none but a mountebank's stage.   140

36.

John Wilson stood up and wildly did stare,
  When on the sudden stepp'd in a bold Scot
And offer'd Apollo he freely would swear
  The said Mr. Wilson might pass for a wott.

37.

But all was in vain, for Apollo, 'tis said,   145
  Would in no ways allow of any Scotch wit,
Then Wilson in spite made his plays to be read,
  Swearing he'd answer for all he had writ.

---

lusion to "the bought *Cooper's Hill* or borrowed *Sophy*" (*A Panegyric upon Sir John Denham's Recovery from his Madness*).

129–32. In a manuscript note on this passage Thorn-Drury mentions an unfinished tragedy, in Samuel Butler's commonplace book, entitled *Hero*, which is mentioned in W. C. Hazlitt's *Manual for the Collector and Amateur of the Old English Plays* (1892).

133–36. Pepys describes a drunken duel between Porter, a dramatist, and his close friend Sir Henry Belassis as a result of which Belassis later died (29 July 1667).

137–40. I have been unable to find any record of a dramatist named Ellis nor of a play called *The Secret*.

141. *John Wilson:* A minor dramatist of Scottish origins.

144. *wott:* Scottish dialectal form for wit (*OED*).

38.

Clarges stood up and laid claim to the bays,
    But Apollo rebuk'd that arrogant fool,   150
Swearing if e'er he translated more plays,
    He'd crown him Sir Reverence with a close stool.

39.

Damn'd Holden with's dull *German Princes* appear'd,
    Whom if D'Avenant had help'd, as some did suppose,
Apollo said the pill'ry should crop off his ears   155
    And make them more suitable unto his nose.

40.

Rhodes stood up and play'd at bo-peep in the door,
    But Apollo, instead of a Spanish plot,
On condition the varlet would never write more,
    Gave him threepence to pay for a pipe and a pot.   160

41.

Eth'rege and Shadwell and the rabble appeal'd
    To Apollo himself in a very great rage,
Because their best friends so freely had deal'd
    As to tell their plays were not fit for the stage.

42.

Then seeing a crowd in a tumult resort,   .   165
    Well furnish'd with verses, but loaded with plays,
It forc'd poor Apollo to adjourn the new court,
    And leave them together by th' ears for the bays.

149. Burney MS. 390 identifies *Clarges* as Sir Thomas Clarges, Monck's brother-in-law. No trace of his translations survives.

153. According to Allardyce Nicoll, this line is the only evidence for ascribing *The German Princess* to John Holden. W. C. Hazlitt suggests that it is the same play as Thomas Porter's *A Witty Combat, or the Female Victor* (1663).

157–58. *Rhodes:* Richard Rhodes' play *Flora's Vagaries* was acted at Christ Church, Oxford in 1663 and later in London. Pepys called it "as pretty a pleasant play as ever I saw" (8 Aug. 1664). Rhodes had traveled much in Spain, but the plot was taken from Boccaccio (Thorn Drury).

161. Shadwell's first play, *The Sullen Lovers*, was produced in May 1668.

43.

But when Apollo was quite withdrawn,
The wits, for fear of the critics' scoff,   170
The laurel on Lacy and Harris put on,
Because they alone made the plays go off.

171. *Lacy:* John Lacy, an actor and playwright, who once told Edward Howard he was "more a fool than a poet" (J. H. Wilson, *All the King's Ladies*, p. 29). *Harris:* Henry Harris, an actor in the Duke's Company.

Satires on Edward Howard
(1669–71)

The three pieces which follow are the best of the many discommendatory verses written on the poet and dramatist, Edward Howard. The first two ridicule Howard's heroic poem, *The British Princes* (1669), and the authors seem to have followed the example of Denham and others who published in 1651 a group of derisive verses on *Gondibert*. The third piece attacks Howard's comedy, *The Six Days' Adventure, or The New Utopia* (1671).

The first poem is attributed to Charles Sackville, Lord Buckhurst in three MSS. and to "B" or "Ld B" in two others. The second is ascribed to "E." in one MS. and to Major Aston (probably Edmund Aston or Ashton, a courtier and poetaster) in the Yale Rochester MS. The third poem is attributed to Dorset in two MSS., to Henry Savile in the Yale Rochester MS., and to "Witherley" (Wycherley?) in Harvard MS. Eng. 636F. I feel that the first poem may be regarded with some assurance as Buckhurst's and the second as Ashton's, but the evidence in the case of the third is indeterminate.

CHARLES SACKVILLE, LORD BUCKHURST

ON MR. EDWARD HOWARD
UPON HIS *British Princes*

Come on, ye critics! Find one fault who dare,
For, read it backward like a witch's prayer,
'Twill do as well; throw not away your jests
On solid nonsense that abides all tests.
Wit, like terse claret, when't begins to pall,　　　　　5
Neglected lies and's of no use at all;
But in its full perfection of decay,

---

5. *terse claret:* Claret in barrels.

Turns vinegar and comes again in play.
This simile shall stand in thy defence
'Gainst such dull rogues as now and then write sense.   10
He lies, dear Ned, who says thy brain is barren,
Where deep conceits, like vermin, breed in carrin;
Thou hast a brain (such as thou hast) indeed—
On what else should thy worm of fancy feed?
Yet in a filbert I have often known   15
Maggots survive when all the kernel's gone.
Thy style's the same whatever be the theme,
As some digestions turn all meat to phlegm:
Thy stumbling, founder'd jade can trot as high
As any other Pegasus can fly.   20
As skillful divers to the bottom fall
Sooner than those that cannot swim at all,
So in this way of writing without thinking
Thou hast a strange alacrity in sinking:
Thou writ'st below e'en thy own nat'ral parts   25
And with acquir'd dullness and new arts
Of studi'd nonsense tak'st kind readers' hearts.
So the dull eel moves nimbler in the mud
Than all the swift-finn'd racers of the flood.
Therefore, dear Ned, at my advice forbear   30
Such loud complaints 'gainst critics to prefer,
Since thou art turn'd an arrant libeller:
Thou sett'st thy name to what thyself dost write;
Did ever libel yet so sharply bite?

EDMUND ASHTON

On the Same Author upon his *British Princes*

As when a bully draws his sword,
Though no man gives him a cross word,
And all persuasions are in vain
To make him put it up again,
Each man draws too and falls upon him,   5

12. *carrin:* Carrion.

To take the wicked weapon from him,
E'en so, dear Ned, thy desp'rate pen,
No less disturbs all witty men,
And makes 'em wonder what a devil
Provokes thee to be so uncivil;   10
When thou and all thy friends must know 'em,
Thou yet wilt dare to print thy poem.
That poor cur's fate and thine are one,
Who has his tail pegg'd in a bone;
About he runs—nobody'll own him—   15
Men, boys, and dogs are all upon him;
And first the greater wits were at thee—
Now ev'ry little fool will pat thee.
Fellows that ne'er were heard or read of
(If thou writ'st on) will write thy head off.   20
Thus mastiffs only have a knack
To cast the bear upon his back,
But when th'unwieldy beast is thrown,
Mongrels will serve to keep him down.

ON THE SAME AUTHOR UPON HIS *New Utopia*

Thou damn'd antipodes to common sense!
Thou foil to Flecknoe! Prithee tell from whence
Does all this mighty stock of dullness spring,
Which in such loads thou to the stage dost bring?
Is 't all thy own, or hast thou from Snow Hill   5
Th' assistance of some ballad-making quill?
No, they fly higher yet; thy plays are such,
I'd swear they were translated out of Dutch:

    2. *Flecknoe:* Richard Flecknoe (d. 1678), Catholic priest and poet, was the object of
a satire written by Marvell in the late 1640s, in which the experience of hearing
Flecknoe read his verse is described thus:

        Straight without further information
        In hideous verse, he, and a dismal tone,
        Begins to exorcise, as if I were
        Possest, and, sure, the Devil brought me there.

    5. *Snow Hill:* An area near Newgate inhabited by ballad-makers and printers.

And who the devil was e'er yet so drunk
To own the volumes of Mynheer Van Dunk?   10
Fain would I know what diet thou dost keep:
If thou dost always or dost never sleep.
Sure, hasty-pudding is thy chiefest dish;
With lights and livers and with stinking fish,
Ox-cheek, tripe, garbage, thou dost treat thy brain,   15
Which nobly pays this tribute back again.
With daisy-roots thy dwarfish muse is fed:
A giant's body with a pigmy's head.
Canst thou not find 'mongst all thy num'rous race
One friend so kind to tell thee that thy play's   20
Laugh'd at by box, pit, gallery, nay stage
And grown the nauseous grievance of this age!
Think on't a while, and thou wilt quickly find
Thy body made for labor, not thy mind.
No other use of paper thou shouldst make   25
But carrying loads of reams upon thy back.
Carry vast burdens 'till thy shoulders shrink,
But curs'd be he that gives thee pen or ink:
Those dang'rous weapons should be kept from fools,
As nurses from their children keep edge-tools.   30
For thy dull muse a muckender were fit
To wipe the slav'rings of her infant wit,
Which, though 'tis late (if justice could be found)
Should, like blind, new-born puppies, yet be drown'd.
For were it not we must respect afford   35
To any muse that's grandchild to a Lord,
Thine in the ducking-stool should take her seat,
Drench'd like herself in a great chair of state,
Where like a muse of quality she'll die,
And thou thyself shalt make her elegy   40
In the same strain thou writ'st thy comedy.

10. *Mynheer Van Dunk:* The fictitious name of a dull Dutch writer.

17. *daisy-roots:* Touching a daisy was supposed to stunt the growth of nursing children (*Funk & Wagnalls Standard Dictionary of Folklore,* New York, 1949).

31. *muckender:* Handkerchief.

36. *grandchild to a Lord:* Howard was the fifth son of Thomas Howard, first Earl of Berkshire.

SIR GEORGE ETHEREGE

Ephelia to Bajazet
(1675)

Bajazet, the great Turkish emperor defeated by Tamerlaine, was ae-graded by Marlowe into an arrogant, self-indulgent brute. Bajazet was to suffer an even greater degradation, however, in being identified with the Earl of Mulgrave in this poem and the one that follows it. Ephelia, who does not appear either in historical accounts of Bajazet or in Marlowe's play, is probably a fiction fashioned by the satirist to reflect Mulgrave's complacent view of himself as the irresistible lover. This view Mulgrave reveals in *An Essay upon Satire*.

Ephelia to Bajazet is attributed to Sir George Etherege in the following lines from *A Familiar Epistle to Mr. Julian:*

> Poor George grows old, his muse worn out of fashion:
> Hoarsely she sung Ephelia's lamentation.

Ebsworth assigns it to him *(Roxburghe Ballads, 4,* 560–64), and it is included in Verity's edition of Etherege.

Rochester's satirical sequel, *A Very Heroical Epistle in Answer to Ephelia,* alludes (line 53) to a duel between Mulgrave and Percy Kirke on 4 July 1675, which was occasioned by Mulgrave's affair with Percy's sister Mall. Both poems were probably written later in that summer.

EPHELIA TO BAJAZET

How far are they deceiv'd who hope in vain
A lasting lease of joys from love t'obtain!
All the dear sweets we promise or expect,
After enjoyment, turn to cold neglect.
Could love a constant happiness have known,   5
The mighty wonder had in me been shown.
Our passions were so favored by Fate,

As if she meant 'em an eternal date;
So kind he look'd, such tender words he spoke,
'Twas past belief such vows should e'er be broke.   10
Fix'd on my eyes, how often would he say
He could with pleasure gaze an age away!
When thoughts too great for words had made him
    mute,
In kisses he would tell my hand his suit.
So great his passion was, so far above   15
The common gallantries that pass for love,
At worst I thought if he unkind should prove,
His ebbing passion would be kinder far
Than the first transports of all others are.
Nor was my love or fondness less than his: 20
In him I center'd all my hopes of bliss!
For him my duty to my friends forgot,
For him I lost . . . alas! What lost I not?
Fame, all the valuable things of life,
To meet his love by a less name than wife.   25
How happy was I then, how dearly bless'd,
When this great man lay panting on my breast,
Looking such things as ne'er can be express'd!
Thousand fresh looks he gave me ev'ry hour,
Whilst greedily I did his looks devour,   30
Till quite o'ercome with charms I trembling lay,
At ev'ry look he gave, melted away!
I was so highly happy in his love,
Methought I piti'd them that dwelt above!
Think then, thou greatest, loveliest, falsest man,   35
How you have vow'd, how I have lov'd, and then,
My faithless dear, be cruel if you can!
How I have lov'd, I cannot, need not, tell;
No, ev'ry act has shown I lov'd too well.
Since first I saw you I ne'er had a thought   40
Was not entirely yours. To you I brought
My virgin innocence and freely made
My love an off'ring to your noble bed;
Since when you've been the star by which I steer'd,
And nothing else but you I lov'd or fear'd.   45

Your smiles I only live by, and I must,
Whene'er you frown, be shatter'd into dust.
Oh! can the coldness that you show me now
Suit with the gen'rous heat you once did show?
I cannot live on pity or respect: 50
A thought so mean would my whole love infect.
Less than your love I scorn, sir, to expect.
Let me not live in dull indiff'rency,
But give me rage enough to make me die,
For if from you I needs must meet my fate,   55
Before your pity I would choose your hate.

JOHN WILMOT, EARL OF ROCHESTER

A Very Heroical Epistle in Answer to Ephelia
(1676)

In this "heroical epistle" (in imitation of Ovid's *Heroides*) Rochester employs the oblique device of the candid declaration to satirize the complacency and arrogance of the Earl of Mulgrave (Bajazet in the preceding epistle). The satire is heroical in another sense, too, for it upholds ironically as an heroic standard a besotted and inhuman self-centeredness:

> In my dear self I center ev'rything—
> My servants, friends, my mistress, and my King;
> Nay, heav'n and earth to that one point I bring.

The irony has for some reason eluded most of Rochester's critics, and even the knowledgeable V. de Sola Pinto declares that here the poet's "complete egoism . . . is stated frankly and with a boldness that must have shocked many who practised it in their lives, but who never had the courage to admit such principles openly" (*Enthusiast in Wit*, p. 148). Nor have the critics detected a second object of Rochester's satire in John Dryden, who, in the preface to *Aureng-Zebe* (1676), served up to his patron the adulatory concept of heroic greatness which the *Epistle* parodies:

> True greatness, if it be anywhere on earth, is in a
> private virtue removed from the notion of pomp
> and vanity, confined to a contemplation of itself,
> and centering on itself.

After misquoting lines from Lucretius, Dryden goes on to say, "If this be not the life of a deity, because it cannot consist with Providence, it is, at least, a god-like life." It is hard to tell where the Laureate's tongue was when he composed this tribute, but there is no doubt that his noble patron's boundless complacency would have accepted any such gift horses without inspecting their mouths.

A Very Heroical Epistle was published with *My Lord All-Pride*, another of Rochester's anti-Mulgrave pieces, in 1679.

A VERY HEROICAL EPISTLE IN ANSWER TO EPHELIA

Madam,
   If you're deceiv'd, it is not by my cheat,
For all disguises are below the great.
What man or woman upon earth can say
I ever us'd 'em well above a day?
How is it, then, that I inconstant am?   5
He changes not who always is the same.
In my dear self I center ev'rything—
My servants, friends, my mistress, and my King;
Nay, heav'n and earth to that one point I bring.
Well-manner'd, honest, generous, and stout   10
(Names by dull fools, to plague mankind, found out)
Should I regard, I must myself constrain,
And 'tis my maxim to avoid all pain.
You fondly look for what none e'er could find,
Deceive yourself, and then call me unkind,   15
And by false reasons would my falsehood prove,
For 'tis as natural to change as love.
You may as justly at the sun repine,
Because alike it does not always shine.
No glorious thing was ever made to stay: 20
My blazing star but visits and away.
As fatal, too, it shines as those i'th' skies:
'Tis never seen but some great lady dies.
The boasted favor you so precious hold
To me's no more than changing of my gold.   25
Whate'er you gave I paid you back in bliss;
Then where's the obligation, pray, of this?
If, heretofore, you found grace in my eyes,
Be thankful for it and let that suffice.
But women, beggar-like, still haunt the door   30
Where they've receiv'd a charity before.
Oh happy sultan, whom we barb'rous call,
How much refin'd art thou above us all!
Who envies not the joys of thy serail?
Thee, like some god, the trembling crowd adore: 35

Each man's thy slave and womankind thy whore.
Methinks I see thee underneath the shade
Of golden canopy, supinely laid,
Thy crowding slaves all silent as the night,
But, at thy nod, all active as the light.   40
Secure in solid sloth thou there dost reign,
And feel'st the joys of love without the pain.
Each female courts thee with a wishing eye,
While thou with awful pride walk'st careless by,
Till thy kind pledge, at last, marks out the dame   45
Thou fanci'st most, to quench thy present flame.
Then from thy bed submissive she retires,
And thankful for the grace no more requires.
No loud reproach nor fond unwelcome sound
Of women's tongues thy sacred ear dares wound.   50
If any do, a nimble mute straight ties
The true-love's-knot and stops her foolish cries.
Thou fear'st no injur'd kinsman's threat'ning blade,
Nor midnight ambushes by rivals laid,
While here with aching hearts our joys we taste,   55
Disturb'd by swords, like Damocles's feast.

JOHN WILMOT, EARL OF ROCHESTER

An Epistolary Essay from M.G. to O.B.
upon their Mutual Poems
(1676)

In a recently-published study, *Attribution in Restoration Poetry*, David Vieth show that the *Epistolary Essay* purports to be written by the Earl of Mulgrave to his poetic collaborator, Dryden (Old Bays). The identification had eluded previous critics of Rochester and the *Essay*, like the *Very Heroical Epistle in Answer to Ephelia*, had been regarded as Rochester's personal declaration. Like the *Heroical Epistle*, however, this satire employs a satirical persona to castigate Mulgrave for his arrogant disregard of rational human standards. The earlier poem devotes itself to Mulgrave's moral egotism, and this one exposes the false literary standards that grow out of such moral egotism:

> Which way soe'er desire and fancy lead,
> Contemning fame, that way I'll boldly tread,
> And, if exposing what I take for wit,
> To my dear self a pleasure I beget,
> No matter though the cens'ring critics fret.

Like its companion piece, the *Epistolary Essay* also attacks Dryden with a pervasive parody of his preface to *Aureng-Zebe* (1676) which, incidentally, had struck a glancing blow at Rochester's *Satire against Mankind*. What Rochester chiefly attacks here is Mulgrave's complacent disregard for critical standards other than his own, which Dryden describes in the following flattering terms:

> How much more great and manly than Cicero in your
> Lordship is your contempt of popular applause and your
> retired virtue, which shines only to a few.

The only known "mutual poem" of Mulgrave and Dryden is *An Essay upon Satire*. I assume that a draft of this poem was known by Rochester to be in existence as early as 1675 (see headnote), although the version we know, with its violent attack on Rochester, was not circulating until late 1679.

An Epistolary Essay from M.G. to O.B. upon their Mutual Poems

Dear Friend,
I hear this town does so abound
With saucy censurers that faults are found
With what of late we in poetic rage
Bestowing threw away on the dull age.
But howsoe'er envy their spleens may raise   5
To rob my brows of the deserved bays,
Their thanks at least I merit, since through me
They are partakers of your poetry;
And this is all I'll say in my defence:
T' obtain one line of your well-worded sense   10
I'd be content t' have writ the *British Prince*.
I'm none of those who think themselves inspir'd
Nor write with the vain hope to be admir'd,
But from a rule I have upon long trial
T' avoid with care all sort of self-denial.   15
Which way soe'er desire and fancy lead,
Contemning fame, that path I boldly tread,
And, if exposing what I take for wit,
To my dear self a pleasure I beget,
No matter though the cens'ring critics fret.   20
These whom my muse displeases are at strife
With equal spleen against my course of life,
The least delight of which I'll not forego
For all the flatt'ring praise man can bestow.
If I design'd to please, the way were then   25
To mend my manners rather than my pen:
The first's unnatural, therefore unfit,
And for the second I despair of it.
Since grace is not so hard to get as wit,
Perhaps ill verses ought to be confin'd   30
(In mere good breeding) like unsav'ry wind.

Were reading forc'd, I should be apt to think
Men might no more write scurvily than stink,
But 'tis your choice whether you'll read or no.
If likewise of your smelling it were so,   35
I'd fart just as I write for my own ease,
Nor should you be concern'd unless you please.
I'll own that you write better than I do,
But I have as much need to write as you.
What though the excrement of my dull brain   40
Flows in a harsh, insipid strain,
Whilst your rich head eases itself of wit?
Must none but civet cats have leave to shit?
In all I write should sense and wit and rhyme
Fail me at once, yet something so sublime   45
Shall stamp my poem that the world may see
It could have been produc'd by none but me;
And that's my end, for man can wish no more
Than so to write as none e'er writ before.
Yet why am I no poet of the times?   50
I have allusions, similes, and rhymes
And wit, or else 'tis hard that I alone
Of the whole race of mankind should have none.
Unequally the partial hand of Heav'n
Has all but this one only blessing giv'n.   55
The world appears like a great family
Whose lord, oppress'd with pride and poverty,
That to a few great bounty he may show,
Is fain to starve the num'rous train below.
Just so seems Providence, as poor and vain,   60
Keeping more creatures than it can maintain.
Here 'tis profuse, and there it meanly saves,
And for one prince it makes ten thousand slaves.
In wit alone 't has been magnificent,
Of which so just a share to each is sent   65
That the most avaricious is content;
For none e'er thought the due divisions such,
His own too little or his friends' too much.
Yet most men show or find great want of wit,
Writing themselves or judging what is writ,   70

But I, who am of spritely vigor full,
Look on mankind as envious and dull.
Born to my self, my self I like alone
And must conclude my judgment good or none.
For could my sense be naught, how should I know   75
Whether another mans were good or no?
Thus I resolve of my own poetry
That 'tis the best, and there's a fame for me.
If then I'm happy, what does it advance
Whether to merit due or arrogance?   80
Oh, but the world will take offence hereby!
Why then, the world shall suffer for 't, not I.
Did e'er this saucy world and I agree
To let it have its beastly will on me?
Why should my prostituted sense be drawn   85
To ev'ry rule their musty customs spawn?
But men will censure, yet 'tis ten to one
Whene'er they censure they'll be in the wrong.
There's not a thing on earth that I can name
So foolish and so false as common fame.   90
It calls the courtier knave, the plain man rude,
Haughty the grave, and the delightful lewd,
Impertinent the brisk, morose the sad,
Mean the familiar, the reserv'd one mad.
Poor, helpless woman is not favor'd more: 95
She's a sly hypocrite or public whore.
Then who the devil would give this—to be free
From th' innocent reproach of infamy?
These things consider'd make me, in despite
Of idle rumor, keep at home and write.   100

A Session of the Poets
(1676)

On the basis of available evidence the authorship of this piece is uncertain. It has been attributed to Elkanah Settle, to Rochester, and to Buckingham. It was included in Rochester's *Poems* (1680) and is ascribed to Rochester and Buckingham jointly in the 1715 edition of the latter's *Works*. J. H. Wilson summarizes and analyzes the evidence for authorship in *RES*, 22 (1946), 109–16, and concludes that "until further evidence appears (or better arguments) I suggest that the poem be allowed to rest quietly in the Rochester canon." Thorpe, in his edition of Rochester (1950), puts it among the doubtful poems and considers it "probably at least in large part Rochester's composition." However, in *Attribution in Restoration Poetry*, a recent study of the Rochester canon, David Vieth finds the evidence of authorship indeterminate.

There are two manuscript attributions which Wilson had apparently not seen when he wrote his article. Rawlinson Poet. MS. 173 gives it to Buckingham, although the ascription may be derived from a printed text. The Yale Rochester MS. notes that the poem was "supposed to be written by Elk. Settle." The scornful treatment of Settle (lines 45ff.) makes this ascription suspect.

Professor Wilson has established the date of the poem as November or December 1676.

A SESSION OF THE POETS

Since the sons of the Muses grow num'rous and loud,
For th' appeasing so clam'rous and factious a crowd,
Apollo thought fit in so weighty a cause
To establish a government, leader, and laws.
The hopes of the bays, at this summoning call,   5
Had drawn 'em together, the Devil and all.

All thronging and list'ning, they gap'd for the blessing;
No Presbyter sermon had more crowding and pressing.
   In the head of the gang John Dryden appear'd,
That ancient grave wit so long lov'd and fear'd,   10
But Apollo had heard a story i'the town
Of his quitting the Muses to wear the black gown,
And so gave him leave, now his poetry's done,
To let him turn priest, when Reeves is turn'd nun.
   This reverend author was no sooner set by,   15
But Apollo had got gentle George in his eye,
And frankly confess'd of all men that writ
There's none had more fancy, sense, judgment, and wit.
But i'th' crying sin idleness he was so harden'd,
That his long sev'n years' silence was not to be pardon'd.   20
   Brawny Wycherley was the next man show'd his face,
But Apollo e'en thought him too good for the place.
No gentleman writer that office should bear:
'Twas a trader in wit the laurel should wear,
As none but a cit e'er makes a Lord Mayor.   25
   Next into the crowd Tom Shadwell does wallow
And swears by his guts, his paunch, and his tallow
That 'tis he alone best pleases the age:
Himself and his wife have supported the stage.
Apollo, well pleas'd with so bonny a lad,   30
To oblige him he told him he should be huge glad
Had he half so much wit as he fanci'd he had.
However, to please so jovial a wit,
And to keep him in humor, Apollo thought fit
To bid him drink on and keep his old trick   35

12. i.e. to change the vocation of poet for that of priest. E. S. de Beer has advanced the theory that in 1676 Dryden was seeking a post at Oxford which would have required his taking orders ("Dryden's Anti-Clericalism," N&Q, 179 [1940], 254–57).

14. *Ann Reeves* was an actress in the King's Company, reputed to be Dryden's mistress. She was thought to have entered a convent abroad some time after 1672.

16. *gentle George:* Sir George Etherege, whose third and last comedy, *The Man of Mode,* was produced in March 1676.

26. This line seems to echo Settle's description of Shadwell in the preface to *Ibrahim, the Illustrious Bassa,* produced in June 1676: "No sooner comes a play upon the stage, but the first day 'tis acted he wallows into the pit like a porpoise before a storm" (Pinto, *Poems of Rochester*).

29. Shadwell's wife, Anne Gibbs, was an actress in the Duke's Company.

Of railing at poets and showing his p———.
  Nat Lee stepp'd in next in hopes of a prize;
Apollo remember'd he had hit once in thrice.
By the rubies in's face he could not deny
He had as much wit as wine could supply,   40
Confess'd that indeed he'd a musical note,
But sometimes strain'd so hard that he rattl'd i'the throat.
Yet owning he had sense, to encourage him for't,
He made him his Ovid in Augustus's court.
  Poet Settle his trial was the next came about;   45
He brought him an *Ibrahim* with the preface torn out,
And humbly desir'd he might give no offence.
"Damn him!" cries Shadwell, "He cannot write sense."
And "Ballocks!" cries Newport, "I hate that dull rogue."
Apollo, consid'ring he was not in vogue,   50
Would not trust his dear bays with so modest a fool
And bid the great boy should be sent back to school.
  Tom Otway came next, Tom Shadwell's dear zany,
And swears for heroics he writes best of any.
Don Carlos his pockets so amply had fill'd,   55
That his mange was quite cur'd, and his lice were all kill'd.
But Apollo had seen his face on the stage,
And prudently did not think fit to engage

38. Lee's first three plays were tragedies: *The Tragedy of Nero, Emperor of Rome* (acted May 1674); *Sophonisba, or Hannibal's Overthrow* (acted April 1675); and *Gloriana, or the Court of Augustus Caesar* (acted Jan. 1676). Sophonisba was "a decided success, not only in its own time, but through at least the first half of the eighteenth century" (Nicoll, p. 122).
44. An allusion to Lee's *Gloriana, or the Court of Augustus Caesar*, produced in Jan. 1676.
45-46. See note on line 26 above. The preface appeared in only a few copies of *Ibrahim*.
48. This line echoes Settle's complaint in the preface to *Ibrahim* that Shadwell attacked his plays sight unseen "and long before they are acted . . . cries *God damme I* [i.e. Settle] *can't write sense nor grammar*" (J. H. Wilson, "Rochester's 'A Session of the Poets,'" *RES*, 22 [1946], 113).
49. *Newport:* According to Wilson (ibid., p. 116) this is Francis ("Frank") Newport, a profane wit, a minor courtier, and a member, with Savile, Sedley, Rochester, and other Court Wits of the "Ballers" mentioned by Pepys (30 May 1668).
52. In the preface to *Notes and Observations on the Empress of Morocco* (1674), Dryden addressed Settle as "great boy" (Wilson, p. 112).
55. *Don Carlos:* Otway's heroic tragedy, produced with great success in June 1676.
57. Otway had failed as an actor before turning playwright.

The scum of a playhouse for the prop of an age.
    In the numerous herd that encompass'd him 'round
Little starch'd Johnny Crowne at his elbow he found.
His cravat-string new iron'd, he gently did stretch
His lily-white hand out the laurel to reach,
Alleging that he had most right to the bays,
For writing romances and shiting of plays.
Apollo rose up and gravely confess'd
Of all men that writ his talent was best:
For since pain and dishonor man's life only damn,
The greatest felicity mankind can claim
Is to want sense of smart and be past sense of shame,
And to perfect his bliss in poetical rapture,
He bade him be dull to the end of the chapter.
    The poetess Aphra next show'd her sweet face
And swore by her poetry and her black ace
The laurel by a double right was her own
For the plays she had writ and the conquests she'd won.
Apollo acknowledg'd 'twas hard to deny her,
But to deal frankly and ingeniously by her,
He told her, were conquests and charms her pretence,
She ought to have pleaded a dozen years since.
    At last *Mamamouchi* came in for a share,

60

65

70

75

80

61. Crowne was the author of a romance, *Pandion and Amphigenia* (1665), in addition to his other plays and poems.

73. *Aphra:* Aphra Behn (1640–89), the well-known writer and woman-about-town.

74. *black ace:* Cf. *the Man of Mode,* II.1.108ff.:

Medley. Indeed I had my belly full of that termagant, Lady Dealer, there never was so unsatiable a carder; an old gleeker never loved to sit to't like her; I have played with her now at least a dozen times, till she has worn out all her fine complexion, and her tour would keep in curl no longer.

Townley. Blame her not, poor woman, she loves nothing so well as a black ace.

Medley. The pleasure I have seen her in when she has had hope in drawing for a matador!

As Brett-Smith notes, "contemporary vulgar slang gave the word another meaning, of which however no hint is to be found in the *NED*" (Etherege, *Plays*, 2, 150, line 47 n.).

81. *Mamamouchi:* A reference to Edward Ravenscroft's adaptation of Molière's *Le Bourgeois Gentilhomme*, published as *The Citizen Turned Gentleman* (1672) and reissued in 1675 as *Mamamouchi* (Pinto). The meaningless "Anababalathou," which occurs here in some texts, seems to derive from the nonsense incantation sung by Turks in V. 1, "Hula baba la chou."

And little *Tom Essence's* author was there,
Nor could Durfey forbear for the laurel to stickle,
Protesting he had had the honor to tickle
The ears of the town with his dear *Madam Fickle*,   85
With other pretenders, whose names I'd rehearse,
But that they're too long to stand in my verse.
Apollo quite tir'd with their tedious harangue,
Finds at last Tom Betterton's face in the gang,
And since poets without the kind players may hang,   90
By his own sacred light he solemnly swore,
That in search of a laureate he'd look out no more.
A general murmur ran quite through the hall,
To think that the bays to an actor should fall;
But Apollo, to quiet and pacify all,   95
E'en told 'em, to put his desert to the test,
That he had made plays as well as the best,
And was the great'st wonder the age ever bore,
For of all the play scribblers that e'er writ before
His wit had most worth and most modesty in't,   100
For he had writ plays, yet ne'er came in print.

82. This line refers to Thomas Rawlins' play, *Tom Essence, or the Modish Wife*,
produced in November 1676 (Pinto).
85. Durfey's *Madame Fickle, or the Witty False One*, was produced in November
1676 (Pinto).
89. Thomas Betterton (1635–1710), the famous actor, author of several plays adapted
from Shakespeare, Molière, Fletcher, Webster, and Massinger (Pinto).
100. Betterton's life was "distinguished not only by integrity, respectability, and
prudence, but by that last of virtues to be expected in an actor, modesty" (*DNB*).
101. Betterton's adaptations were published after this poem was written, between
1679 and 1719.

JOHN WILMOT, EARL OF ROCHESTER

An Allusion to Horace
(*1675*)

Rochester's *Allusion* follows its Horatian model quite closely, as a comparison with the opening lines of Creech's version (1684) indicates:

> Well, Sir, I granted I said Lucilius' muse
> Is incorrect, his way of writing loose,
> And who admires him so, what friend of his
> So blindly partial to deny me this?

For Lucilius Rochester substitutes Dryden; for the farces of Laberius, the plays of John Crowne; for Horace's approving friends, Shadwell, Sheppard, Wycherley, and the rest. Although, from the allusions to contemporary events, Rochester probably wrote the satire late in 1675, Dryden did not reply until 1678, in his preface to *All for Love*. There he excoriated the "ignorant little zanies . . . , persecutors even of Horace himself . . . by their ignorant and vile imitations of him," who make "an unjust use of his authority" and turn "his artillery against his friends." Pretending ignorance of Rochester's authorship, Dryden went on to invite "this rhyming judge of the twelvepenny gallery, this legitimate son of Sternhold" to "subscribe his name to his censure, or (not to tax him beyond his learning) set his mark" and finished with detailed criticisms of the *Allusion* as untrue to its original and inaccurate in its judgment of contemporary poets.

Rochester's brief attack on his former friend, Sir Carr Scroope, immediately touched off a bitter feud recorded in the three satires which follow this one and in *On Poet Ninny,* but there is at present no trace of the censures with which Rochester charges Scroope (lines 115ff.). Although Rochester seems to have fired the last shot (in *On Poet Ninny*), victory, perhaps, ultimately belongs to Scroope for his penetrating attack on his adversary's character in *In Defence of Satire*. In his final salvo of abuse Rochester seems to have violated the principle here enunciated that "A jest in scorn points out and hits the thing/ More home than the morosest satire's sting."

AN ALLUSION TO HORACE

The 10th Satyr of the 1st Book
Nempe incomposito dixi pede, etc.

Well, Sir, 'tis granted I said Dryden's rhymes
Were stol'n, unequal, nay dull, many times.
What foolish patron is there found of his
So blindly partial to deny me this?
But that his plays, embroider'd up and down,   5
With wit and learning justly pleas'd the town,
In the same paper I as freely own.
Yet having this allow'd, the heavy mass
That stuffs up his loose volumes must not pass.
For by that rule I might as well admit   10
Crowne's tedious scenes for poetry and wit.
    'Tis therefore not enough when your false sense
Hits the false judgment of an audience
Of clapping fools, assembling a vast crowd,
Till the throng'd playhouse crack with the dull load.   15
Though e'en that talent merits in some sort
That can divert the rabble and the court,
Which blund'ring Settle never could attain,

11. *Crowne:* John Crowne (d. 1703?), a playwright who dedicated his *History of Charles VIII* (1672), a rhyming tragedy, to Rochester. Rochester contrived to have Crowne commissioned in Dryden's place to write a court masque, *Calisto, or the Chaste Nymph* (1675). According to St. Évremond, Rochester withdrew his patronage out of envy for Crowne's success as a writer of heroic dramas and afterwards lampooned him in this poem and in *The Session of Poets* (1676).

18. *Settle:* Elkanah Settle (1648–1724), the "City Poet," for a time surpassed Dryden in popularity as a writer of heroic tragedies. Until Rochester transferred his patronage to Crowne, Settle had enjoyed the Earl's favor. Dryden, Crowne, and Shadwell attacked Settle in *Notes and Observations on the Empress of Morocco,* and Settle appeared as Doeg in *Absalom and Achitophel,* Part II:

> Free from all meaning, whether good or bad,
> And, in one word, heroically mad.

And puzzling Otway labors at in vain.
But within due proportion circumscribe
Whate'er you write, that with a flowing tide   20
The style may rise, yet in its rise forbear
With useless words t' oppress the weari'd ear.
Here be your language lofty, there more light;
Your rhetoric with your poetry unite.   25
For elegance' sake sometimes allay the force
Of epithets: 'twill soften the discourse.
A jest in scorn points out and hits the thing
More home than the morosest satire's sting.
Shakespeare and Jonson did herein excell   30
And might in this be imitated well,
Whom refin'd Eth'rege copies not at all,
But is himself a sheer original,
Nor that slow drudge in swift Pindaric strains,
Flatman, who Cowley imitates with pains,   35
And rides a jaded Muse, whipp'd with loose reins.
When Lee makes temp'rate Scipio fret and rave,

19. *Otway:* Thomas Otway (1652–85), produced his first heroic tragedy, *Alcibiades,* in 1675. Rochester commended the piece and drew the attention of the Duke of York to the author. The female lead in this and in Otway's subsequent plays was taken by Mrs. Barry, who, about this time, became the mistress of Rochester, to whom she bore a son in December 1677. Otway for years was passionately in love with her, but she spurned his passion (*DNB;* J. H. Wilson, *All the King's Ladies,* p. 111). His *Titus and Berenice* (1677) is dedicated to Rochester. *Puzzling Otway,* Hayward suggests, refers to Otway's inability to write successful comedies.

32. *Eth'rege:* Sir George Etherege (1635?–91), one of the best Restoration comic dramatists. He was a close friend of Rochester and took part with him in the notorious Epsom brawl of 1676. Etherege modeled his nonchalant and witty Dorimant (*The Man of Mode, or Sir Fopling Flutter* [1676]) on Rochester.

35. *Flatman:* Thomas Flatman (1637–88), poet and miniature painter. His Pindarics, according to *DNB,* deserved the derision of Rochester. *Cowley:* Abraham Cowley (1618–67). His reputation with Dryden and other contemporary critics rested largely on his Pindaric odes.

37–40. *Lee:* Nathaniel Lee (1635?–92), son of Richard Lee, D.D. (cf. Wild's *Recantation of a Penitent Proteus,* 1664). He was patronized spasmodically by Buckingham and Rochester and "lost no time in imitating their vices, to the permanent injury of his health" (*DNB*). Lee had dedicated his heroic tragedy, *Nero* (1674), to Rochester. In April 1675 his second play, *Sophonisba,* was produced, in which the *temp'rate Scipio* raves as follows:

> My yet unshaken soul with virtue bound,
> No force of war or love could ever wound,

And Hannibal a whining, am'rous slave,
I laugh and wish the hot-brain'd fustian fool
In Busby's hands, to be well lash'd at school.   40
    Of all our modern wits none seems to me
Once to have touch'd upon true comedy
But hasty Shadwell and slow Wycherley.
Shadwell's unfinish'd works do yet impart
Great proofs of force of nature, none of art.   45
With just, bold strokes he dashes here and there,
Showing great mastery with little care,
And scorns to varnish his good touches o'er

But Mars and Cupid now at once appear,
And strike me with an object fierce and fair.
How her eyes shine! What killing fires they dart!
And all within I feel the fatal smart.
                                        (III.1.28–33).

In the same play Hannibal becomes the infatuated slave of Rosalinda and justifies his love by mythological precedents:

Since gods themselves and godlike men have lov'd,
Why should not I with beauty's charms be mov'd?
The highest power has love's blind mazes trod,
Then Hannibal love on, and imitate a god.
                                        (II.2.18–21)

40. Lee had attended Westminster School, the stern headmaster of which was the famous Richard Busby (1606–95).

43. *Shadwell:* Thomas Shadwell (1642?–92), dramatist, and, after the Revolution, poet laureate. Dryden attacked him for his bad poetry and whiggish views in *The Medal* (1682), and made him the butt of *Mac Flecknoe* in which Shadwell is tasked, *inter alia*, with being a *slow* writer:

Success let others teach, learn thou from me
Pangs without birth and fruitless industry.
Let *Virtuoso's* in five years be writ,
Yet not one thought accuse thy soul of wit.

Shadwell wrote *The Libertine* in five weeks, however, and often boasted of his speed in composition. *Wycherley:* William Wycherley (1640?–1716), one of the greatest Restoration dramatists, wrote only four plays, his last, *The Plain Dealer,* appearing in 1677. Dryden later attacked Rochester in the preface to *All for Love* (1678) and alluded to this line as follows: "If he have a friend whose hastiness in writing is his greatest fault, Horace would have taught him to have minced the matter, and to have called it readiness of thought and a flowing fancy . . . , but he would never have allowed him to have called a slow man hasty, or a hasty writer a slow drudge." Pope, according to Spence, said that Wycherley was far from being slow and that he wrote *The Plain Dealer* in three weeks.

To make the fools and women praise 'em more.
But Wycherley earns hard what e'er he gains. 50
He wants no judgment nor he spares no pains.
He frequently excels, and at the least
Makes fewer faults than any of the best.
　　Waller, by nature for the bays design'd,
With force and fire and fancy unconfin'd, 55
In panegyrics does excel mankind.
He best can turn, enforce, and soften things
To praise great conquerors or to flatter kings.
　　For pointed satires I would Buckhurst choose,
The best good man with the worst-natur'd muse, 60
For songs and verses mannerly obscene
That can stir nature up by springs unseen
And without forcing blushes warm the Queen.
　　Sedley has that prevailing gentle art
That can with a resistless charm impart 65
The loosest wishes to the chastest heart,
Raise such a conflict, kindle such a fire,
Betwixt declining virtue and desire,
Till the poor vanquish'd maid dissolves away
In dreams all night, in sighs and tears all day. 70
　　Dryden in vain tri'd this nice way of wit,
For he to be a tearing blade thought fit,
But when he would be sharp he still was blunt,

54–58. *Waller:* Edmund Waller (1606–87), a poet admired by Rochester (Etherege's Dorimant, modeled on Rochester, quotes Waller continually). Rochester alludes very tactfully ("To praise great conquerors, or to flatter kings") to Waller's change of political sympathies as reflected in the famous *Panegyric to My Lord Protector* (1655); *Three Poems upon the Death of the Late Usurper, Oliver Cromwell; To the King upon his Majesty's Happy Return;* and *Instructions to a Painter.*

59–63. *Buckhurst:* Charles Sackville, Lord Buckhurst, later sixth Earl of Dorset and Earl of Middlesex (1638–1706), one of the court wits and a rake. He was involved with Sedley and Sir Thomas Ogle in a notorious brawl at the Cock Tavern in Bow Street (see J. H. Wilson, *The Court Wits,* p. 40). A generous patron of letters, he gave material assistance to Dryden, Butler, and Wycherley. According to Walpole, Buckhurst was the finest gentleman of Charles II's court: "he had as much wit as his master or his contemporaries, Buckingham and Rochester, without the royal want of feeling, the Duke's want of principle, or the Earl's want of thought" (*Noble Authors,* 2, 96).

64–70. *Sedley:* Sir Charles Sedley (1639?–1701), minor poet, wit, and rake. His literary output consists mainly of a few plays, some translations, and some commonplace love poems.

To frisk his frolic fancy he'd cry "c——!"
Would give the ladies a dry, bawdy bob,   75
And thus he got the name of Poet Squab.
But to be just, 'twill to his praise be found,
His excellencies more than faults abound,
Nor dare I from his sacred temples tear
That laurel which he best deserves to wear.   80
But does not Dryden find e'en Jonson dull,
Fletcher and Beaumont incorrect and full
Of lewd lines (as he call them); Shakespeare's style
Stiff and affected, to his own the while
Allowing all the justness that his pride   85
So arrogantly had to these deni'd?
And may not I have leave impartially
To search and censure Dryden's works and try
If those gross faults his choice pen does commit
Proceed from want of judgment or of wit;   90
Or if his lumpish fancy does refuse
Spirit and grace to his loose slattern muse?
Five hundred verses every morning writ
Prove you no more a poet than a wit.
Such scribbling authors have been seen before: 95
Mustapha, The English Princes, forty more,
Were things perhaps compos'd in half an hour.
   To write what may securely stand the test
Of being well read over, thrice at least
Compare each phrase, examine ev'ry line,   100
Weigh ev'ry word, and ev'ry thought refine.

75–76. *Dry bob:* coition without emission. *Squab,* next to *Bays,* was Dryden's most popular nickname. It referred usually to his short, fat stature, but here the primary reference is to callow inexperience.

81–86. This arraignment of Dryden's critical opinions seems largely impressionistic; at any rate not many of the judgments Rochester attributes to him are to be found in Ker's edition of the essays. Dryden does express strong dislike for Jonson's clenches, "the lowest and most grovelling kind of wit" (*Defense of the Epilogue,* Ker, *1,* 173), and mentions the irregularity of structure in certain plays of Beaumont and Fletcher (*Essay of Dramatic Poesy,* Ker, *1,* 79). I have not been able to find references in Dryden's critical writing to Shakespeare's stiffness nor to Beaumont and Fletcher's "lewd lines." Dryden's long quarrel with Shadwell on whether Jonson had "wit" culminated in his writing *Mac Flecknoe* (see headnote to that poem).

96. *Mustapha:* A heroic play written in 1665 by Roger Boyle, Baron Broghill and first Earl of Orrery (1621–79). *The English Princes, or the Death of Richard III* (acted 1667) is a tragedy by John Caryll (1625–1711).

Scorn all applause the vile rout can bestow
And be content to please those few who know.
Canst thou be such a vain, mistaken thing
To wish thy works might make a playhouse ring 105
With the unthinking laughter and poor praise
Of fops and ladies, factious for thy plays?
Then send a cunning friend to learn thy doom
From the shrewd judges in the drawing room.

    I've no ambition on that idle score, 110
But say with Betty Morrice, heretofore,
When a court lady call'd her Bulkeley's whore,
"I please one man of wit, am proud on 't, too!
Let all the coxcombs dance to bed to you."
Should I be troubl'd when the purblind knight, 115
Who squints more in his judgment than his sight,
Picks silly faults and censures what I write?
Or when the poor-fed poets of the town,
For scraps and coachroom cry my verses down?
I lothe the rabble: 'tis enough for me 120
If Sedley, Shadwell, Sheppard, Wycherley,
Godolphin, Butler, Buckhurst, Buckingham,
And some few more, whom I omit to name,
Approve my sense. I count their censure fame.

111–12. *Betty Morrice* is probably Buckhurst's "black Bess" celebrated in "Methinks the poor town has been troubled too long." Rochester apparently alludes to her again in *A Letter from Artemisa in the Town to Cloe in the Country:*

F[oster] could make an Irish lord a nokes,
And B[etty] M[orrice] had her City cokes.
(183–84)

Bulkeley is probably Henry Bulkeley, Master of the Household to Charles II and James II.

121. *Sheppard:* Sir Fleetwood Sheppard (1634–98), a fashionable rake and wit who, according to Wood, after the Restoration "retired to London, hanged on the court, became a debauchee and an atheist, a grand companion with Lord Buckhurst, Henry Savile, and others" (quoted in *DNB*). Sheppard was a patron of poets, among them Prior, whom he discovered, and he himself wrote fugitive verse and lampoons.

122. *Godolphin:* Sidney Godolphin, Earl of Godolphin (1645–1712), Page of Honor, Groom of the Bedchamber, and Master of the Robes. He became one of the Chits, the group which formed an administration after the fall of Danby in 1679. *Butler:* Probably Lord John Butler, a son of the Duke of Ormonde, who had been one of several unsuccessful contenders for the hand of Elizabeth Mallett, the Countess of Rochester. See Pepys, 4 Feb. 1667.

SIR CARR SCROOPE

In Defense of Satire
(*1677*)

Scroope's *In Defense of Satire*, like its precursor, has a Horatian model, the fourth satire of the first book, but it is a much freer imitation than Rochester's.

The poem is attributed to Scroope in one manuscript (Osborn chest II #14), and Anthony Wood's circumstantial account of his authorship together with Rochester's reply, *On the Supposed Author*, leave no question that he wrote it.

In Defense of Satire was written after the death of Capt. Downs, Rochester's "brave companion" identified in most of the manuscripts, who was wounded in a "midnight frolic" at Epsom (see lines 53–55) and died at the end of June 1676. It is dated 1677 in two MSS.

IN DEFENSE OF SATIRE

When Shakespeare, Jonson, Fletcher rul'd the stage,
They took so bold a freedom with the age
That there was scarce a knave or fool in town
Of any note but had his picture shown.
And without doubt, though some it may offend,   5
Nothing helps more than satire to amend
Ill manners, or is trulier virtue's friend.
Princes may laws ordain, priests gravely preach,
But poets most successfully will teach.
For as a passing bell frights from his meat   10
The greedy sick man that too much would eat,
So when a vice ridiculous is made,
Our neighbor's shame keeps us from growing bad.
But wholesome remedies few palates please:
Men rather love what flatters their disease.   15
Pimps, parasites, buffoons, and all the crew
That under friendship's name weak man undo,

Find their false service kindlier understood
Than such as tell's bold truths to do us good.
   Look where you will and you shall hardly find   20
A man without some sickness of the mind.
In vain we wise would seem, while ev'ry lust
Whisks us about, as whirlwind doth the dust.
Here for some needless gain a wretch is hurl'd
From pole to pole and slav'd about the world,   25
While the reward of all his pains and care
Ends in that despicable thing, his heir.
There a vain fop mortgages all his land
To buy that gaudy plaything, a command,
To ride on cockhorse, wear a scarf at's arse,   30
And play Jack-pudding in a May-day farce.
Here one whom God to make a fool thought fit,
In spite of providence will be a wit,
But wanting strength t'uphold his ill-made choice,
Sets up with lewdness, blasphemy, and noise.   35

28. *D"* supplies the marginal note *Capt. Aston.* Probably the Edmund Aston or Ashton who bought a captaincy in Sir Allen Apsley's regiment in 1667. Maurice Irvine ("Identification of Characters in Mulgrave's 'Essay upon Satyr,'" *SP, 34* [1937], 533–51) says he was "popular in the satires of the day whenever his puny size or his vanity suggested him for comparison with the typical Restoration fops, Sir George Hewitt or Sir Carr Scroope." He fought a duel with Etherege, and the prologue, "Gentle reproofs have long been tri'd in vain," was credited to him as well as to Rochester. See his satire on Edward Howard ("As when a bully draws his sword").

29. *D"*: *Sir Edward Bash.* I have not found any significant information on this note.

35. *D"*: *Philip E. Pembroke.* Philip Herbert, seventh Earl of Pembroke (1653–83) was notorious for his coarseness and brutality. He fought several duels, including one with Sir George Hewitt in 1676, and he killed a good many men, either in duels or in drunken brawls. He was tried by a jury of his peers in the House of Lords in 1678 for killing a Mr. Carey, but was not convicted.

Pembroke married Henriette de Kéroualle, sister of the Duchess of Portsmouth. An instance of his "wit" is found in a letter of John Verney to his brother, Ralph:

> 1 Sept. 1675. The Duchess of Portsmouth told my Lord Pembroke that if he did not make some extraordinary provisions against her sister's lying in, as became a person of her quality, and deliver her a sum of money to lay out, she would complain of him to the King and make known her sister's grievances, to which he replied that if she did he would put her upon her head, and show his family the grievance of the nation.

> (*HMCR* 7, 466)

There is, of course, no way of knowing whether Scroope's rather general and mild portrait was really meant for Pembroke.

There at his mistress' feet a lover lies,
And for a tawdry painted baby dies,
Falls on his knees, adores, and is afraid
Of the vain idol he himself has made.
These and a thousand fools unmention'd here   40
Hate poets all because they poets fear.
"Take heed!" they cry, "Yonder mad dog will bite.
He cares not whom he falls on in his fit.
Come but in's way, and straight a new lampoon
Shall spread your mangl'd fame about the town."   45
    But why am I this bugbear to you all?
My pen is dipp'd in no such bitter gall.
He that can rail at one he calls his friend,
Or hear him absent wrong'd, and not defend,

37. *D"*: *Charles Ld Cornwallis.* The third Baron Cornwallis (bap. 1655), a fortune-hunter who married Elizabeth, daughter of Sir Stephen Fox. He was tried for murder in 1673 and acquitted. According to Gramont (*Memoirs*, p. 223), he "was very extravagant, loved gaming, lost as much as anyone would trust him, but was not quite so ready at paying. His father-in-law disapproved of his conduct, paid his debts, and gave him a lecture at the same time. The Chevalier de Gramont had won of him a thousand or twelve hundred guineas, which he heard no tidings of, although he was upon the eve of his departure, and he had taken leave of Cornwallis in a more particular manner than any other person. This obliged the Chevalier to write him a billet which was rather laconic. It was this:

> 'My Lord,
>   Pray remember the Count de Gramont, and
> do not forget Sir Stephen Fox.'"

I have not been able to find any anecdotes of Cornwallis as a lover, either in Gramont or elsewhere.

38–39. *D"*: *Sir George Hewet and Mrs. Marshall.* Sir George Hewet was a coxcomb and reputedly the model for Etherege's Sir Fopling Flutter.

48–59. This portrait, much the most specific in the poem, is unquestionably a sketch of Rochester, and is identified as such in the marginal notes of three MSS. (*D"*, *N*, *EE'*). The incident referred to in lines 52–54 is described by Christopher Hatton on 29 June 1676 as follows:

> Mr. Downs is dead. The Lord Rochester doth abscond, and so doth Etherege and Capt. Bridges, who occasioned the riot Sunday sennight. They were tossing some fiddlers in a blanket for refusing to play, and a barber, upon the noise, going to see what the matter, they seized upon him, and, to free himself from them, he offered to carry them to the handsomest woman in Epsom, and directed them to the constable's house, who demanding what they came for, they told him a whore, and, he refusing to let them in, they broke open his doors and broke his head and beat him very severely. At last he made his escape, called his watch, and Etherege made a submissive oration to them and so far appeased them that the constable dismissed his watch. But presently after, the

Who for the sake of some ill-natur'd jest 50
Tells what he should conceal, invents the rest,
To fatal midnight frolics can betray
His brave companion and then run away,
Leaving him to be murder'd in the street,
Then put it off with some buffoon conceit, 55
This, this is he you should beware of all,
Yet him a witty, pleasant man you call.
To whet your dull debauches up and down,
You seek him as top fiddler of the town.
But if I laugh, when the court coxcombs show, 60
To see that booby Sotus dance provoe,
Or chatt'ring Porus from the side box grin,
Trick'd like a lady's monkey new made clean,
To me the name of railer straight you give,
Call me a man that knows not how to live. 65
But wenches to their keepers true shall turn,
Stale maids of honor proffer'd husbands scorn,
Great statesmen flattery and clinches hate,
And, long in office, die without estate,

Lord Rochester drew upon the constable. Mr. Downs, to prevent his pass, seized on him, the constable cried out, "murther!" and the watch, returning, one came behind Mr. Downs and with a sprittle staff cleft his skull. The Lord Rochester and the rest run away, and Downs, having no sword, snatched up a stick and striking at them, they run him into the side with a half pike, and so bruised his arm that he was never able to stir it after.

(*Hatton Correspondence, 1*, 133–34).

61. *Sotus:* Probably pseudo-Latin for "sot." Two MSS. identify him as "Mr. Griffin," probably Edward Griffin, a Groom of the Bedchamber to the Duke of York and a familiar of Charles II. "On Tuesday the King and the jockeys met at supper at Ned Griffin's, where were made six hare matches for £500, a match to be run at Newmarket next meeting" (John Verney to Sir Ralph Verney, 23 Nov. 1676; *HMCR, 7*, 467b). An unpublished satire in Phillips MS. 7440, pp. 132–33, describes Griffin as follows:

> The world shall think clown Griffin just and brave,
> Griffin with whom even Killigrew durst fight,
> Whose horses lose their fellow-servants' right,
> Griffin the falsest that e'er friend deceiv'd,
> Yet by the best of friends too well believ'd.

Provoe or *provost* is an assistant fencing-master.

62. *Porus:* The Latin *porus* means a passage of the body and the English noun *pore* is derived from it. The name seems to suggest a sort of sponge-like creature. *D"* glosses Porus as Henry Jermyn, Earl of St. Albans (d. 1684), a famous courtier of whom Marvell draws a satiric portrait in *Last Instructions*.

Against a bribe Court-judges shall decide,   70
The City knavery want, the clergy pride,
E'er that black malice in my rhymes you find
That wrongs a worthy man or hurts his friend.
But then perhaps you'll say, "Why do you write?
What you call harmless mirth the world calls spite.   75
Why should your fingers itch to have a lash
At Simius the buffoon, or Cully bash?
What is't to you if Alidore's fine whore
F—— with some fop while he's shut out of door?
Consider, pray, that dang'rous weapon, wit,   80
Frightens a million where a few you hit.
Whip but a cur as you ride through a town,
And straight his fellow curs his quarrel own.
Each knave or fool that's conscious of a crime,
Though he 'scapes now, looks for't another time."   85
    "Sir, I confess all you have said is true,
But who has not some folly to pursue?
Milo turn'd Quixote fanci'd battles fights,
When the fifth bottle has increas'd the heights.
Warlike, dirt pies our hero Paris forms,   90

77. *Simius:* Ape (L.), glossed in *D"* as Frank Newport, Francis Viscount Newport of Bradford (1619–1708), Treasurer of the Household and Privy Counsellor. *Cully:* Dupe. Cf. Etherege's gullible Sir Nicholas Cully in *Love in a Tub.*

78. *Alidore's: D"* reads *Abdy's* and supplies in the margin *Sir John Abdy: Mrs. Michell Michell.* All other texts read *Alidore's,* which satisfies the metrical requirements of the line. I suspect the scribe of *D"* unintentionally substituted *Abdy's* from his gloss. There seems to be a cryptic allusion to this triangle in a letter from Margaret Bedingfield to Lady Paston (25 July 1675): "Mrs. Michell is in the height of her progress at the two Sir Johns' houses (*HMCR,* 7, 532a).

79. *D"* supplies in the margin "Ld Cornw: Ld Culpepr's issue: Willis Churchill Brouncker." Presumably this identifies Mrs. Michell's other lovers: Lord Cornwallis (cf. line 37), the son of John Lord Colepeper (d. 1660); John Churchill, first Duke of Marlborough (1650–1722); and Henry Brouncker (d. 1688), Cofferer to Charles II and Gentleman of the Bedchamber to the Duke of York. Willis is probably the noted prostitute, Sue Willis: "My Lord Culpeper is also returned from Paris with Mrs. Willis, whom he carried thither to buy whatsoever pleased her there and this nation could afford" (*Savile Correspondence,* p. 62).

88. *Milo:* A celebrated athlete killed by wild beasts while attempting to tear down a tree.

90. *Paris:* James Scott, Duke of Monmouth and Buccleuch (1649–85). One August night in 1674 he fought the battle of Maastricht over again in the meadows below Windsor Castle. Cf. Elizabeth D'Oyley, *Monmouth,* p. 97.

Which desp'rate Bessus without armor storms.
Cornus, the kindest husband e'er was born,
Still courts the spark that does his brows adorn,
Invites him home to dine and fills his veins
With the hot blood which his dear doxy drains.   95
Grandio thinks himself a beau garçon,
Goggles his eyes, writes letters up and down,
And with his saucy love plagues all the town,
Whilst pleas'd to have his vanity thus fed,
He's caught with Gosnell, that old hag, abed.   100
But why should I the crying follies tell
That rouse the sleeping satyr from his cell,
I to my reader should as tedious prove
As that old spark Albanus making love,
Or florid Roscius, when with some smooth flam   105

91. *Bessus:* A cowardly braggart in Beaumont and Fletcher's *A King and No King.* A marginal note in *D″* identifies him as Sir Thomas Armstrong (1624?–84), an intimate friend of Monmouth executed for complicity in the Rye House Plot. According to Sprat, Armstrong was "a debauch'd atheistical bravo," and Scroope may have attacked him here because Armstrong had killed his brother in a playhouse brawl in 1675. The *EE′* identification of Bessus with Rupert is unconvincing.

92. *Cornus:* Another pseudo-Latin name—the horned one. *D″* identifies him as Lord Grey [of Werk]. In Jan. 1680, according to the Dowager Lady Sunderland, Monmouth's attentions to Lady Grey caused her husband to remove her from London to Northumberland. If the report was true, "it made no difference to her husband's friendship with Monmouth" (D'Oyley, *Monmouth,* p. 162), hence Dryden represents him as "cold Caleb" in *Absalom and Achitophel,* 574.

96. *Grandio: D″* identifies this haughty, amorous fop as *Mulgrave* (John Sheffield, third Earl of Mulgrave and afterwards first Duke of Buckingham and Normanby [1648–1721]), the author of *An Essay upon Satire* (1679), which attacked Scroope, possibly in revenge for these lines.

100. *Gosnell:* Winifred Gosnell, an actress in the Duke's Company. She was at one time Mrs. Pepys' lady's-maid and Pepys thought highly of her singing and dancing, but when he saw her in Stapylton's *The Slighted Maid* in 1668 he wrote that she "is become very homely, and sings meanly, I think, to what I thought she did" (J. H. Wilson, *All the King's Ladies,* pp. 145–46).

104. *Albanus: D″* identifies him as *Col. Russell,* probably John Russell, third son of Francis, fourth Earl of Bedford. He was colonel of the first regiment of Foot Guards and died in 1681. He was one of Miss Hamilton's suitors and Gramont ridicules him for "a certain mixture of avarice and liberality, constantly at war with each other, ever since he had entered the lists with love" (*Memoirs,* ed. Fea, p. 143). *EE′* identifies him as the Earl of St. Albans, the aging and lecherous courtier whom Marvell satirizes in *Last Instructions.*

105. *Roscius:* Quintus Roscius Gallus (d. 62 B.C.), the most celebrated of Roman comic actors. Here *D″* identifies him as Heneage Finch, Baron Finch of Daventry

He gravely on the public tries to sham.
Hold then, my muse, 'tis time to make an end,
Lest taxing others thou thyself offend.
The world's a wood in which all lose their way,
Though by a diff'rent path each goes astray."   110

(1621–82), appointed Lord Chancellor in 1674. Finch was noted for his eloquence as "the English Roscius and the English Cicero." Roger North wrote that his love of "a handsome turn of expression gave him a character of a trifler which he did not so much deserve" (*DNB*). *flam:* A sham story, a fabrication.

106. *sham:* Obsolete verb meaning to impose or attempt to pass off (something) upon (a person) by deceit; to palm off.

JOHN WILMOT, EARL OF ROCHESTER

On the Supposed Author of a Late Poem
"In Defense of Satire"
(*1677*)

To rack and torture thy unmeaning brain
In satire's praise to a low untuned strain
In thee was most impertinent and vain,
When in thy person we more clearly see
That satire's of divine authority,   5
For God made one on man when he made thee,
To show there are some men as there are apes,
Fram'd for mere sport, who differ but in shapes.
In thee are all those contradictions join'd
That make an ass prodigious and refin'd.   10
A lump deform'd and shapeless wert thou born,
Begot in love's despite and nature's scorn,
And art grown up the most ungraceful wight,
Harsh to the ear and hideous to the sight;
Yet love's thy business, beauty thy delight.   15
Curse on that silly hour that first inspir'd
Thy madness to pretend to be admir'd,
To paint thy grisly face, to dance, to dress,
And all those awkward follies that express
Thy loathsome love and filthy daintiness;   20
Who needs will be an ugly *beau garçon*,
Spit at and shunn'd by ev'ry girl in town,
Where dreadfully love's scarecrow thou art plac'd
To fright the tender flock that long to taste;
While ev'ry coming maid, when you appear,   25
Starts back for shame and straight turns chaste for fear,
For none so poor or prostitute have prov'd,
Where you made love, t'endure to be belov'd.
'Twere labor lost, or else I would advise,
But thy half wit will ne'er let thee be wise.   30

371

Half witty and half mad and scarce half brave,
Half honest (which is very much a knave)—
Made up of all these halves, thou canst not pass
For anything entirely but an ass!

SIR CARR SCROOPE

The Author's Reply
(1677)

Rail on, poor feeble scribbler, speak of me
In as ill terms as the world speaks of thee.
Sit swelling in thy hole like a vex'd toad,
And all thy pox and malice spit abroad.
Thou canst blast no man's name by thy ill word: 5
Thy pen is full as harmless as thy sword.

6. An allusion to the abortive duel between Rochester and Mulgrave (Nov. 1669), in which Rochester reportedly demanded an unfair advantage over his opponent because of his allegedly weak condition.

JOHN WILMOT, EARL OF ROCHESTER

On Poet Ninny
(*1677*)

On Poet Ninny appears without ascription in the Yale Rochester MS. David Vieth regards it as probably Rochester's (see "Order of Contents as Evidence of Authorship: Rochester's *Poems* of 1680," *Publications of the Bibliographical Society of America*, 53 [1959], 293–308). Poet Ninny's ugliness, foppishness, melancholy, and "head romancy" all accord in detail with Rochester's other attacks on Scroope and leave little doubt of the author's identity or that of his victim.

As Pinto notes, Ninny, a character in Shadwell's comedy, *The Sullen Lovers*, is "a conceited poet always troubling men with impertinent discourses of poetry and the repetition of his own verses."

On Poet Ninny seems to be a rejoinder to Scroope's *The Author's Reply* and was probably written in 1677.

On Poet Ninny

Crush'd by that just contempt his follies bring
On his craz'd head, the vermin fain would sting.
But never satire did so softly bite,
Or gentle George himself more gently write.
Born to no other but thy own disgrace,   5
Thou art a thing so wretched and so base,
Thou canst not e'en offend but with thy face,
And dost at once a sad example prove
Of harmless malice and of hopeless love,
All pride and ugliness—Oh how we loathe   10
A nauseous creature so compos'd of both!
How oft have we thy cap'ring person seen

3. Cf. the last line of Buckhurst's satire on Edward Howard ("Come on, ye critics, find one fault who dare"): "Did ever libel yet so sharply bite?"

With dismal look and melancholy mien,
The just reverse of Nokes when he would be
Some mighty hero and makes love like thee. 15
Thou art below being laugh'd at out of spite:
Men gaze upon thee as a hideous sight
And cry, "There goes the melancholy knight!"
There are some modish fools we daily see,
Modest and dull; why they are wits to thee! 20
For of all folly sure the very top
Is a conceited ninny and a fop.
With face of farce join'd to a head romancy
There's no such coxcomb as your fool of fancy.
But 'tis too much on so despis'd a theme: 25
No man would dabble in a dirty stream.
The worst that I could write would be no more
Than what thy very friends have said before.

14. *Nokes:* James Nokes, a well-known comic actor.

JOHN DRYDEN

Mac Flecknoe
(*1676–77*)

Until quite recently *Mac Flecknoe* was thought to have been composed in 1682, the year in which the first, unauthorized, edition appeared. More recently, evidence that the poem was circulating in manuscript in 1678 has led Dryden's editors to assign it to that year. In a forthcoming study J. M. Osborn and David Vieth argue persuasively that the poem was written even earlier, in response to Shadwell's slighting remarks on Dryden in the dedication to *The Virtuoso* (published in July 1676), and before the production of Shadwell's *Timon* in January 1678. An apparent allusion to *Mac Flecknoe* in the satirical *Advice to Apollo* (probably written in October 1677) seems to assign Dryden's satire to the period of his "retirement" from the stage between the production of *Aureng-Zebe* (17 November 1675) and that of *All for Love* (12 December 1677). Dryden probably wrote *Mac Flecknoe*, then, between July 1676 and December 1677.

Through the preceding decade, Dryden and Shadwell had engaged in a long debate on the theory and practice of comedy. Shadwell had repeatedly upheld the Jonsonian "humors" against Dryden's emphasis on wit. "Dryden's *Essay of Dramatic Poesy* and *Defence of the Essay* (1668), his preface to *An Evening's Love* (1671), his epilogue to the second part of *The Conquest of Granada* and his *Defence of the Epilogue* (1672) had been answered by Shadwell's prefaces to *The Sullen Lovers* (1668), *The Royal Shepherdess* (1669), and *The Humorists* (1671), and by the dedication of *The Virtuoso* (1676)" (Van Doren, *Dryden,* p. 274). In his *Defence of the Epilogue* Dryden tried to end the argument with Shadwell by the conciliatory statement that

> for Ben Jonson, the most judicious of poets, he always writ properly and as the character required, and I will not contest farther with my friends who call that wit; it being very cer-

tain that even folly itself, well represented, is wit in a larger signification. . . .

He then proceeded, nonetheless, to underscore his main criticism of Jonson:

> In these low characters of vice and folly lay the excellency of that inimitable writer who, when at any time he aimed at wit in the stricter sense (that is, sharpness of conceit) was forced either to borrow from the ancients . . . , or, when he trusted himself alone, often fell into meanness of expression. Nay, he was not free from the lowest and most grovelling kind of wit, which we call clenches. . . .

Dryden goes on to make a good deal of "the last and greatest advantage of our writing, which proceeds from *conversation*," and which makes the wit of his age "much more courtly" than that of Jonson's.

Dryden's conciliatory gesture was not enough to appease his opponent, whose idol was Jonson. Shadwell renewed the battle in his dedication of *The Virtuoso,* his next play, with jibing allusions to Dryden's ideas about conversation, humor, and wit and Dryden's celebrated pension:

> Nor do I hear of any professed enemies to the play but some women and some men of feminine understanding who like slight plays only, that represent a tittle-tattle sort of conversation like their own, but true humor is not liked or understood by them. But the same people, to my great comfort, damn all Mr. Jonson's plays, who was the best dramatic poet that ever was. . . . That there are a great many faults in the conduct of this play I am not ignorant. But I (having no pension but from the theatre, which is either unwilling or unable to reward a man sufficiently for so much pains as correct comedies require) cannot allot my whole time to the writing of plays, but am forced to mind some other business of advantage.

To top this off, Shadwell damned heroic drama, of which Dryden was the leading practitioner, in his epilogue.

These were the provocations, then, which stung Dryden into celebrating Shadwell as the son of Flecknoe, the new dunce laureate. The dispute about wit and humor provided Dryden with the leit-

motiv of his satire: Mac Flecknoe is "to wage immortal war with
wit"; he has sworn "Ne'er to make peace with wit, nor truce with
sense"; "not one thought" can "accuse his toil of wit." His throne
is to be established among those who practice what Dryden called
"the lowest and most grovelling kind of wit," where

> Pure clinches the suburbian Muse affords,
> And Panton waging harmless war with words.

Shadwell had aimed at satire in *The Virtuoso*, but is told, "Thy in-
offensive satires never bite." He had proclaimed Jonson as his ideal,
but Flecknoe tells him, "Thou art my blood, where Jonson has no
part." In its subtle and apparently random fashion Dryden's great
mock-heroic poem thus manages to attack Shadwell on most of the
points which had been debated by them for almost ten years.

Mac Flecknoe is also a retort to Rochester's praise of Shadwell in
An Allusion to Horace (1675):

> Shadwell's unfinish'd works do yet impart
> Great proofs of force of nature, none of art;
> With just, bold strokes he dashes here and there,
> Showing great mastery with little care.

Dryden's Flecknoe disclaims the tribute both for himself and his son
in the rhetorical question, "What share have we in nature, or in
art?"

The text is from the first authorized edition, in *Miscellany Poems*
(1684).

MAC FLECKNOE

All human things are subject to decay,
And when fate summons, monarchs must obey.
This Flecknoe found, who, like Augustus, young
Was call'd to empire, and had govern'd long;
In prose and verse was own'd, without dispute,   5

---

3. *Flecknoe:* Richard Flecknoe (d. 1678?), dramatist and poet, satirized for his
"hideous verse" declaimed in a "dismal tone" by Marvell in *Flecknoe, an English
Priest at Rome*. Kinsley cites J. H. Smith's suggestion that Dryden might have been
offended by Flecknoe's general criticism of dramatists in the Prologue to *Emilia* (1672).

Through all the realms of Nonsense, absolute.
This aged Prince, now flourishing in peace,
And blest with issue of a large increase,
Worn out with business, did at length debate
To settle the succession of the State;   10
And, pond'ring which of all his sons was fit
To reign and wage immortal war with wit,
Cried, " 'Tis resolv'd; for nature pleads that he
Should only rule who most resembles me.
Sh—— alone my perfect image bears,   15
Mature in dulness from his tender years:
Sh—— alone, of all my sons, is he
Who stands confirm'd in full stupidity.
The rest to some faint meaning make pretense,
But Sh—— never deviates into sense.   20
Some beams of wit on other souls may fall,
Strike through, and make a lucid interval,
But Sh——'s genuine might admits no ray,
His rising fogs prevail upon the day.
Besides, his goodly fabric fills the eye,   25
And seems design'd for thoughtless majesty;
Thoughtless as monarch oaks that shade the plain,
And, spread in solemn state, supinely reign.
Heywood and Shirley were but types of thee,
Thou last great prophet of tautology.   30
Even I, a dunce of more renown than they,
Was sent before but to prepare the way;
And, coarsely clad in Norwich drugget, came
To teach the nations in thy greater name.
My warbling lute, the lute I whilom strung   35
When to King John of Portugal I sung,
Was but the prelude to that glorious day,
When thou on silver Thames didst cut thy way

29. *Heywood and Shirley:* Thomas Heywood (c. 1574–1641) and James Shirley (1596–1666), dramatists.
31–32. See Matt. 3:3–4.
33. *Norwich drugget:* A coarse woolen cloth. Shadwell was from Norfolk.
35–36. In the Preface to *Psyche: A Tragedy* (1675) Shadwell claims "some little knowledge" of music both as connoisseur and performer (Kinsley). Flecknoe had visited Portugal and boasted of being patronized by the King (Noyes).

With well-tim'd oars before the royal barge,
Swell'd with the pride of thy celestial charge,   40
And big with hymn, commander of a host,
The like was ne'er in Epsom blankets toss'd.
Methinks I see the new Arion sail,
The lute still trembling underneath thy nail.
At thy well-sharpen'd thumb from shore to shore   45
The treble squeaks for fear, the basses roar;
Echoes from Pissing Alley Sh——— call,
And Sh——— they resound from A——— Hall.
About thy boat the little fishes throng,
As at the morning toast that floats along.   50
Sometimes, as prince of thy harmonious band,
Thou wield'st thy papers in thy threshing hand.
St. André's feet ne'er kept more equal time,
Not e'en the feet of thy own *Psyche's* rhyme;
Though they in number as in sense excel: 55
So just, so like tautology, they fell,
That, pale with envy, Singleton forswore
The lute and sword, which he in triumph bore,

42. A reference to the fate of Sir Samuel Hearty in Shadwell's *The Virtuoso*
(1676). There is also an allusion to the title of Shadwell's play *Epsom Wells* (1672)
and probably also to the fate of the fiddler in the notorious Epsom affair, in which
Rochester, Etherege, Bridges, and others were involved. See *In Defense of Satire*, 52ff.
and n.

47. *Pissing Alley:* One of several by that name, this linked Friday Street and Bread
Street in the City.

48. *A——— Hall:* The unauthorized 1682 edition gives *Aston Hall*. This may be a refer-
ence to Edmund Ashton or Aston, an officer in the Life Guards and author of one of
the satires on Edward Howard. He is satirized in *A Familiar Epistle to Mr. Julian*,
13:

And little Ashton offers to the bum.

53. *St. André:* A French dancing-master.

54. *Psyche:* Shadwell's "long-expected opera . . . came forth in all her ornaments:
new scenes, new machines, new clothes, new French dances" at Dorset Garden in
February 1675 (Downes, *Roscius Anglicanus*, p. 35; cited by Kinsley).

57-59. *Singleton:* John Singleton (d. 1686), one of the King's musicians, often em-
ployed in the theatre. Villerius, the Grand Master of Rhodes, is a leading character
in Davenant's *Siege of Rhodes*, where much of the dialogue is in a sort of lyrical
recitative. In Buckingham's *Rehearsal* (Act V) two generals are made to fight a battle
"in *recitativo*," in parody of passages in Davenant's play, hence the allusion to *the
lute and sword* (Scott).

And vow'd he ne'er would act Villerius more."
Here stopp'd the good old sire and wept for joy   60
In silent raptures of the hopeful boy.
All arguments, but most his plays, persuade,
That for anointed dulness he was made.
    Close to the walls which fair Augusta bind
(The fair Augusta much to fears inclin'd)   65
An ancient fabric rais'd t'inform the sight
There stood of yore, and Barbican it hight:
A watchtower once; but now, so fate ordains,
Of all the pile an empty name remains.
From its old ruins brothel-houses rise,   70
Scenes of lewd loves and of polluted joys,
Where their vast courts the mother-strumpets keep,
And, undisturb'd by watch, in silence sleep.
Near these a Nursery erects its head,
Where queens are form'd and future heroes bred;   75
Where unfledg'd actors learn to laugh and cry,
Where infant punks their tender voices try,
And little Maximins the gods defy.
Great Fletcher never treads in buskins here,
Nor greater Jonson dares in socks appear;   80
But gentle Simkin just reception finds
Amidst this monument of vanish'd minds:
Pure clinches the suburbian Muse affords,

64-65. *Augusta*: London, "much to fears inclin'd" by suspected Popish intrigues.
74. *a Nursery*: One of two theatres established after the Restoration for the train-
ing of young actors. I am indebted to William J. Cameron for the following notes of
Secretary Williamson:

> The Nursery in London. Pull down that and coffee-houses, and nothing can
> be more to the establishment of the government. The City government is too lax
> already. The citizens already, even those that are of the Church of England,
> prefer to have fanatic children, rather than those bred in their own way. If the
> two nurseries in Barbican and Bunhill be not taken away in a year, expect a
> disorder.

(CSPD, 23 Nov. 1671)

78. *Maximins*: Maximin is the tyrant of Rome in *Tyrannic Love* (1670) whose rant-
ing manner Dryden repented of in his Epistle Dedicatory to *The Spanish Friar*
(1681).
81. *Simkin*: A stupid clown in a farce entitled *The Humors of Simkin*, collected
with other such pieces by Francis Kirkman in 1673 (Noyes).

And Panton waging harmless war with words.
Here Flecknoe, as a place to fame well known,   85
Ambitiously design'd his Sh——'s throne;
For ancient Dekker prophesi'd long since,
That in this pile should reign a mighty prince,
Born for the scourge of wit and flail of sense;
To whom true dulness should some *Psyches* owe,   90
But worlds of *Misers* from his pen should flow;
Humorists and *Hypocrites* it should produce,
Whole Raymond families, and tribes of Bruce.
   Now Empress Fame had publish'd the renown
Of Sh——'s coronation through the town.   95
Rous'd by report of Fame, the nations meet,
From near Bunhill and distant Watling Street.
No Persian carpets spread th' imperial way,
But scatter'd limbs of mangl'd poets lay;
From dusty shops neglected authors come,   100
Martyrs of pies and relics of the bum.
Much Heywood, Shirley, Ogleby there lay,
But loads of Sh—— almost chok'd the way.
Bilk'd stationers for yeomen stood prepar'd,
And H—— was captain of the guard.   105
The hoary Prince in majesty appear'd,
High on a throne of his own labors rear'd.
At his right hand our young Ascanius sate,

84. *Panton:* Apparently another character in a farce, although there may be an allusion here to the famous gambler, Thomas Panton (d. 1685).

87. *Dekker:* Noyes quotes Dryden's preface to *Notes and Observations on the Empress of Morocco,* in which he expresses the fear that by attacking Settle he might do him too much honor and then says: "but I considered Ben Jonson had done it before to Dekker, our author's predecessor, whom he chastiz'd in his *Poetaster* under the character of Crispinus, and brought him in vomiting up his fustian and nonsense."

91–93. Allusions to Shadwell's early plays. Kinsley quotes Settle's reference in the Preface to *Ibrahim* (1677) to "the humbler and modester days" of *The Humorists* (1671), *The Miser* (1672), and *The Hypocrite* (otherwise unknown), "three as silly plays as a man would wish to see." Raymond and Bruce are wits in *The Humorists* and *The Virtuoso* (1676) respectively.

102. *Ogleby:* John Ogleby (1600–76), translator of Virgil (1649), the *Iliad* (1660), and the *Odyssey* (1665).

105. *H——:* Herringman, Dryden's publisher until 1678, and the publisher of all Shadwell's plays from *Epsom Wells* (1673) to *Timon of Athens* (1678). The reason for Dryden's break with him is not known (Kinsley).

108–11. Kinsley points out that these lines parody the *Aeneid* 2.682–84.

Rome's other hope and pillar of the State.
His brows thick fogs, instead of glories, grace,   110
And lambent dulness play'd around his face.
As Hannibal did to the altars come,
Sworn by his sire a mortal foe to Rome;
So Sh—— swore, nor should his vow be vain,
That he till death true dulness would maintain,   115
And, in his father's right and realm's defense,
Ne'er to have peace with wit nor truce with sense.
The King himself the sacred unction made,
As king by office and as priest by trade.
In his sinister hand, instead of ball,   120
He plac'd a mighty mug of potent ale;
Love's Kingdom to his right he did convey,
At once his scepter and his rule of sway;
Whose righteous lore the Prince had practic'd young,
And from whose loins recorded Psyche sprung.   125
His temples, last, with poppies were o'erspread,
That nodding seem'd to consecrate his head.
Just at that point of time, if fame not lie,
On his left hand twelve rev'rend owls did fly.
So Romulus, 'tis sung, by Tiber's brook,   130
Presage of sway from twice six vultures took.
Th'admiring throng loud acclamations make,
And omens of his future empire take.
The sire then shook the honors of his head,
And from his brows damps of oblivion shed   135
Full on the filial dulness: long he stood,
Repelling from his breast the raging god;
At length burst out in this prophetic mood:
    "Heavens bless my son, from Ireland let him reign
To far Barbadoes on the western main;   140
Of his dominion may no end be known,
And greater than his father's be his throne;
Beyond Love's Kingdom let him stretch his pen!"
He paus'd, and all the people cri'd, "Amen."
Then thus continu'd he, "My son, advance   145
Still in new impudence, new ignorance.

122. Love's Kingdom: Flecknoe's tragicomedy (1664).

Success let others teach, learn thou from me
Pangs without birth, and fruitless industry.
Let *Virtuosos* in five years be writ,
Yet not one thought accuse thy toil of wit.   150
Let gentle George in triumph tread the stage,
Make Dorimant betray, and Loveit rage;
Let Cully, Cockwood, Fopling charm the pit,
And in their folly show the writer's wit.
Yet still thy fools shall stand in thy defense,   155
And justify their author's want of sense.
Let 'em be all by thy own model made
Of dulness, and desire no foreign aid;
That they to future ages may be known,
Not copies drawn, but issue of thy own.   160
Nay, let thy men of wit too be the same,
All full of thee, and differing but in name.
But let no alien S-dl-y interpose
To lard with wit thy hungry *Epsom* prose.
And when false flowers of rhetoric thou wouldst cull,   165
Trust nature, do not labor to be dull;
But write thy best and top, and in each line
Sir Formal's oratory will be thine:
Sir Formal, though unsought, attends thy quill,
And does thy northern dedications fill.   170
Nor let false friends seduce thy mind to fame
By arrogating Jonson's hostile name.
Let father Flecknoe fire thy mind with praise,
And uncle Ogleby thy envy raise.
Thou art my blood, where Jonson has no part: 175
What share have we in nature, or in art?
Where did his wit on learning fix a brand,

149. In the Prologue to *The Virtuoso* Shadwell declares that "Wit, like china, should long buri'd lie."
151. *gentle George:* Sir George Etherege. The allusions that follow are to characters in Etherege's comedies.
163–64. *S-dl-y:* Sedley wrote a prologue for *Epsom Wells* and was thought to have helped in its composition.
168. Sir Formal Trifle in *The Virtuoso* "never speaks without flowers of rhetoric."
170. *northern dedications:* Shadwell dedicated five plays to the Duke or Duchess of Newcastle.

And rail at arts he did not understand?
Where made he love in Prince Nicander's vein,
Or swept the dust in *Psyche's* humble strain?   180
Where sold he bargains, 'whip-stitch, kiss my arse,'
Promis'd a play and dwindl'd to a farce?
When did his muse from Fletcher scenes purloin,
As thou whole Eth'rege dost transfuse to thine?
But so transfus'd as oil on water's flow: 185
His always floats above, thine sinks below.
This is thy province, this thy wondrous way,
New humors to invent for each new play:
This is that boasted bias of thy mind,
By which one way, to dulness, 'tis inclin'd;   190
Which makes thy writings lean on one side still,
And, in all changes, that way bends thy will.
Nor let thy mountain-belly make pretense
Of likeness; thine's a tympany of sense.
A tun of man in thy large bulk is writ,   195
But sure thou'rt but a kilderkin of wit.
Like mine, thy gentle numbers feebly creep;
Thy tragic muse gives smiles, thy comic sleep.

179. *Prince Nicander:* A character in *Psyche*. Shadwell says in the Prologue:

> You must not here expect exalted thought,
> Nor lofty verse, nor scenes with labor wrought:
> His subject's humble, and his verse is so.

181. As Kinsley notes, to *sell bargains* commonly meant to overreach, make a fool of, but Dryden's use has the special meaning of prurient remarks, such as Sir Samuel Hearty's "Prithee, Longvil, hold thy peace, with a whipstitch, your nose in my breech" (*The Virtuoso*).

182. Cf. Dedication of *The Virtuoso:* "I say nothing of impossible, unnatural farce fools, which some intend for comical, who think it the easiest thing in the world to write a comedy, and yet will sooner grow rich upon their ill plays than write a good one."

184. Noyes investigates this charge and concludes that, except for superficial resemblances in plot and situation between *Epsom Wells* and Etherege's *She Would if She Could* and *Comical Revenge*, it is baseless.

189–92. A parody of lines in the Epilogue to Shadwell's *The Humorists:*

> A humor is the bias of the mind,
> By which with violence 'tis one way inclin'd:
> It makes our actions lean on one side still,
> And in all changes that way bends the will.
>
> (Noyes)

With whate'er gall thou sett'st thyself to write,
Thy inoffensive satires never bite.   200
In thy felonious heart though venom lies,
It does but touch thy Irish pen and dies.
Thy genius calls thee not to purchase fame
In keen iambics, but mild anagram.
Leave writing plays, and choose for thy command   205
Some peaceful province in acrostic land;
There thou may'st wings display and altars raise,
And torture one poor word ten thousand ways;
Or, if thou wouldst thy diff'rent talents suit,
Set thy own songs, and sing them to thy lute."   210
    He said: but his last words were scarcely heard;
For Bruce and Longvil had a trap prepar'd,
And down they sent the yet declaiming bard.
Sinking he left his drugget robe behind,
Borne upwards by a subterranean wind.   215
The mantle fell to the young prophet's part,
With double portion of his father's art.

202. Shadwell protested against Dryden's "giving me the Irish name of Mack, when
he knows I never saw Ireland till I was three-and-twenty years old and was there
but four months" (Dedication of *The Tenth Satire of Juvenal*, 1687).
    207. A reference to poems whose shapes represent their subjects, such as George
Herbert's *The Altar* and *Easter Wings* (1633).
    212–13. In *The Virtuoso*, III, Bruce and Longvil drop Sir Formal through a trap
door in the middle of one of his declamatory speeches.
    214–17. Cf. 2 Kings 2:9–13, in which Elijah is translated to heaven and his mantle
falls upon Elisha. As Kinsley points out, Flecknoe's mantle is returned from below.

GEORGE VILLIERS, DUKE OF BUCKINGHAM

A Familiar Epistle to Mr. Julian, Secretary
to the Muses
(1677)

Robert Julian, "Secretary to the Muses," operated a kind of clearing-house for collecting, copying, and distributing verse in manuscript. The chief product of this factory seems to have been satires and personal lampoons which could not be printed legally because of the licensing laws and the laws against libel. Undoubtedly Julian's scribes produced some of the manuscripts used in this volume.

A Familiar Epistle is printed as Buckingham's in the 1705 edition of his *Works* and is dated 1677 in Harleian MS. 7319 (Z). Its circumstantial and unflattering description of Sir Carr Scroope agrees in detail with other lampoons by the Rochester circle on the Knight with the "hard-favored face" (cf. especially *An Allusion to Horace* and *On the Supposed Author of "In Defence of Satire"*). Undoubtedly it is one of the pieces, like *Advice to Apollo*, which was composed when Buckingham and other members of "the merry gang" visited Rochester at Woodstock in October 1677.

Four manuscripts attribute the lampoon to Dryden, but the attribution is clearly wrong in view of the insulting reference to the Laureate's "bedrid age" in lines 18–19. This reference to Dryden's inactivity may be compared with that about his "quitting the stage" in *Advice to Apollo*.

A Familiar Epistle was first published as *An Exclamation against Julian, Secretary to the Muses; with the Character of a Libeller. By a Person of Quality*. Luttrell's copy is dated 1679.

Professor David Vieth has contributed much helpful information used in the notes.

A FAMILIAR EPISTLE TO MR. JULIAN, SECRETARY TO THE MUSES

Thou common shore of this poetic town,
Where all our excrements of wit are thrown—
For sonnet, satire, bawdry, blasphemy
Are empti'd and disburden'd all on thee:
The choleric wight, untrussing in a rage,   5
Finds thee and leaves his load upon thy page—
Thou Julian, O thou wise Vespasian, rather,
Dost from this dung thy well-pick'd guineas gather.
All mischief's thine; transcribing, thou dost stoop
From lofty Middlesex to lowly Scroope.   10
What times are these, when in that hero's room
Bow-bending Cupid does with ballads come,
And little Ashton offers to the bum!
Can two such pigmies such a weight support,
Two such Tom Thumbs of satire in a court?   15
Poor George grows old, his muse worn out of fashion:
Hoarsely he sung Ephelia's lamentation.
Less art thou help'd by Dryden's bedrid age:
That drone has left his sting upon the stage.
Resolve me, poor apostate, this main doubt: 20
What hope hast thou to rub this winter out?

1. *common shore:* Common sewer.

7. *Julian:* An allusion to the Emperor Julian the Apostate (331–63), born Christian but converted to paganism. *Vespasian:* Roman emperor (70–79), reputed to be avaricious.

10. *Middlesex:* Charles Sackville (1638–1706), poet and courtier, created Baron Cranfield and Earl of Middlesex 4 April 1675. He succeeded to his father's title of Earl of Dorset in 1677.

13. *Ashton:* Edmund Ashton, a poetaster and officer in the Life Guards. According to J. H. Wilson (*The Court Wits,* p. 210), he fought with Etherege in the summer of 1671. Cf. *Mac Flecknoe,* 48 n.

16. *George:* George Etherege (1635?–91), according to a marginal note in Taylor MS. 1 (*A*), the well-known dramatist and poet.

17. *Ephelia's lamentation:* See *Ephelia to Bajazet,* the verse epistle attacking the Earl of Mulgrave, probably written by Etherege in 1675.

18–19. These lines allude to Dryden's "retirement" from the stage between the production of *Aureng-Zebe* (Nov. 1675) and that of *All for Love* (Dec. 1677).

21. *rub out:* Contrive to get through.

Know and be thankful, then, for Providence
By me has sent thee this intelligence.
   A Knight there is, if thou canst gain his grace,
Known by the name of the hard-favor'd face.   25
For prowess of the pen renown'd is he,
From Don Quixote descended lineally,
And though like him unfortunate he prove,
Undaunted in attempts of wit and love.
Of his unfinish'd face what shall I say,   30
But that 'twas made of Adam's own red clay,
That much, much ochre was on it bestow'd:
God's image 'tis not, but some Indian god.
Our Christian earth can no resemblance bring
But ware of Portugal for such a thing.   35
Such carbuncles his fiery cheeks confess
As no Hungarian water can redress,
A face should he but see (but Heav'n was kind
And to indulge his self-love made him blind)
He dare not stir abroad for fear he meet   40
Curses of teeming women in the street.
The least could happen from this hideous sight
Is that they should miscarry with the fright.
Heav'n guard 'em from the likeness of the Knight!
   Such is our charming Strephon's outward man;   45
His inward parts let those describe who can.
But, by his monthly flow'rs discharg'd abroad,
'Tis full, brim-full, of pastoral and ode.

24. *A Knight:* Sir Carr Scroope.

25-44. The alleged ugliness of Scroope's face is a familiar detail in the many satirical attacks upon him. Cf. Rochester's *On Poet Ninny:*

Thou art a thing so wretched and so base
Thou canst not ev'n offend, but with thy face.

35. *ware of Portugal:* Unglazed Portuguese vessels called *buccaros,* made from red clay and widely used from 1500 to 1700.

37. *Hungarian water:* A distilled and perfumed alcoholic preparation used on the skin.

39. Scroope was extremely myopic. Cf. "the purblind knight" in Rochester's *Allusion to Horace.*

45. *Strephon:* Common name for a pastoral swain, applied to Rochester by Scroope in a song written for Etherege's *The Man of Mode.*

Erewhile he honor'd Bertha with his flame,
And now he chants no less Louisa's name,   50
For when his passion has been bubbling long,
The scum at last boils up into a song,
And sure no mortal creature at one time
Was e'er so far o'ergone with love and rhyme.
To his dear self of poetry he talks: 55
His hands and feet are scanning as he walks.
His squinting looks his pangs of wit accuse,
The very symptoms of a breeding muse,
And all to gain the great Louisa's grace,
But never pen did pimp for such a face.   60
There's not a nymph in city, town, or Court,
But Strephon's billets-doux have made 'em sport.
Still he loves on, yet still as sure to miss,
As they who wash an Ethiop's face, or his.
What fate unhappy Strephon does attend,   65
Never to get a mistress or a friend?
Strephon alike both wits and fools detest,
Because, like Aesop's bat, half bird, half beast.
For fools to poetry have no pretence,
And common wit supposes common sense.   70
Not quite so low as fool, nor quite atop,
He hangs between 'em both and is a fop.
    His morals like his wit are motley too:
He keeps from arrant knave with much ado,
But vanity and lying so prevail,   75
That one more grain of each would turn the scale.
He would be more a villain had he time,
But he's so wholly taken up with rhyme,
That he mistakes his talent; all his care
Is to be thought a poet fine and fair.   80
    Small beer and gruel are his meat and drink,
The diet he prescribes himself to think.
Rhyme next his heart he takes at morning peep,
Some love epistles at his hour of sleep.

49. *Bertha:* Perhaps Cary Frazier, daughter of Sir Alexander Frazier, the King's physician, whom he wooed unsuccessfully in the winter of 1676–77 (Vieth).
50. *Louisa:* Louise de Kéroualle, Duchess of Portsmouth.

So, between elegy and ode, we see   85
Strephon is in a course of poetry.
   This is the man ordain'd to do thee good,
The pelican to feed thee with his blood,
Thy wit, thy poet, nay thy friend! for he
Is fit to be a friend to none but thee.   90
Make sure of him and of his muse betimes,
For all his study is hung 'round with rhymes.
Laugh at him, justle him, yet still he writes:
In rhyme he challenges, in rhyme he fights.
Charg'd with the last and basest infamy,   95
His business is to think what rhymes to lie,
Which found in fury he retorts again.
Strephon's a very dragon at his pen:
His brother murder'd and his mother whor'd,
His mistress lost, yet still his pen's his sword.   100

99. *brother murder'd:* Scroope's younger brother was reportedly killed by Sir Thomas
Armstrong in a quarrel over an actress, at the Duke's Theatre in August 1675. *mother
whor'd:* Scroope's mother was the mistress of Henry Savile (Vieth).
   100. *mistress:* Cary Frazier. *and yet his pen's his sword:* The satirist retorts on
Scroope the charge of cowardice Scroope made against Rochester ("Thy pen is full as
harmless as thy sword") in *The Author's Reply.*

Advice to Apollo
(*1677*)

Advice to Apollo, J. H. Wilson shows, was probably produced by
Rochester and his fellow wits who assembled at Woodstock in mid-
October 1677 (*The Court Wits,* p. 195). The attack on Sir Carr
Scroope resembles in detail a larger passage in *A Familiar Epistle to
Mr. Julian,* composed earlier in the year and attributed to Bucking-
ham, while Mulgrave and Dryden were also at odds with Rochester
at this time. Fleetwood Sheppard, on the other hand, was probably
included among those satirized for failing to show up at the gather-
ing. The fact that the poem singles out Rochester and Dorset for
praise is a further indication that it probably emanated from Roches-
ter's circle.

Advice to Apollo is dated 1678 in *POAS* 1697 (*m*), but no date is
given in the manuscripts I have seen. The dates in *POAS* are gen-
erally as unreliable as the ascriptions, and Henry Savile may have
been referring to this poem in a letter to Rochester written on 1
November 1677:

> and now I am upon poetry I must tell you that the whole tribe
> are alarmed at a libel against them lately sent by the post to
> Will's coffee house. I am not happy enough to have seen it, but
> I hear it commended and therefore the more probably to have
> been composed at Woodstock, especially considering what an
> assembly is yet or at least has been there, to whom my most
> humble service, if they are yet with you.

Will's, of course, was the coffee-house which Dryden frequented.

The poem's chief interest, however, lies in its apparent allusions
to *Mac Flecknoe* and to Mulgrave's and Dryden's *Essay upon Satire.*
Dryden's satire is known to have been circulating in manuscript in
1678 and Mulgrave's in the fall of 1679, but the author of *Advice
to Apollo* seems to have known—or known of—versions of both
poems in the fall of 1677. He chides Dryden for having quit the

stage to seek a satirist's renown by "lashing the witty follies of the age," referring evidently to Dryden's "retirement" from writing plays between *Aureng-Zebe* (first acted 17 November 1675) and *All for Love* (first acted 12 December 1677). *Mac Flecknoe* is Dryden's only work which seems to fit this description and these circumstances. The idea gains further support from a new study by David Vieth and J. M. Osborn which finds the occasion for *Mac Flecknoe* in Shadwell's attack on Dryden in his dedicatory epistle to *The Virtuoso* (published 6 July 1676). (See my headnote to *Mac Flecknoe*.)

The allusion to the *Essay upon Satire* is more specific. Mulgrave is attacked vigorously as one who

> Ne'er saw thy light, yet would usurp thy pow'r,
> Would govern wit, and be its emperor,
> In fee with Dryden to be counted wise,
> Who tells the world he has both wit and eyes.

Mulgrave spoke of satire as a shining light (11), laid down the law in his haughty fashion, was helped by Dryden in this satire, and credited himself with wit (32) and "sharp eyes" for discerning "nicer faults" (33).

An Essay upon Satire, as we know it, could not, however, have been written before the summer of 1679. It has many topical allusions to that time and was reported circulating in manuscript at Whitehall in November 1679. Another version, much revised by Pope for his edition of Mulgrave's (Buckingham's) works in 1723, is similarly tied to the year 1679. Yet Pope has given us reason to suppose that Mulgrave had written an earlier version of the *Essay* by printing "written in the year 1675" on the half-title page. We know that Mulgrave repeatedly revised his chief poetical work, the *Essay on Poetry*, and it seems that he did the same with his *Essay upon Satire*.

ADVICE TO APOLLO

I've heard the Muses were still soft and kind,
To malice foes, to gentle love inclin'd,
And that Parnassus Hill was fresh and gay,

Crown'd still with flowers as in the fairest May;
That Helicon with pleasure charm'd the soul,   5
Could anger tame and restless care control;
That bright Apollo still delights in mirth,
Cheering, each welcome day, the drowsy earth.
Then whence comes satire—is it poetry?
O great Apollo, God of Harmony,   10
Far be't from thee this cruel art t'inspire!
Then strike these wretches who thus dare aspire
To tax thy gentleness, making thee seem
Malicious as their thoughts, harsh as their theme.
    First, strike Sir Carr, that Knight o'th' wither'd face,   15
Who, for th' reversion of a poet's place,
Waits on Melpomene and soothes her Grace.
That angry miss alone he strives to please
For fear the rest should teach him wit and ease,
And make him quit his lov'd laborious walks,   20
When sad and silent o'er the room he stalks
And strives to write as wisely as he talks.
    Next with a gentle dart strike Dryden down,
Who but begins to aim at the renown
Bestow'd on satirists, and quits the stage   25
To lash the witty follies of our age.
Strike him but gently that he may return,
Write plays again, and his past follies mourn.
He'd better make Almanzor give offence
In fifty lines without one word of sense   30
Than thus offend and wittily deserve
What will ensue, with his lov'd muse to starve.
    Dorset writes satire too, but writes so well,
O great Apollo, let him still rebel!
Pardon a muse which does so far excel,   35

15. *Sir Carr:* Sir Carr Scroope. Cf. *A Familiar Epistle to Mr. Julian,* 24ff.
17. *her Grace:* Melpomene.
29. *Almanzor:* The bombastic hero of *The Conquest of Granada,* produced in 1670.
33. *Dorset:* Charles Sackville, 6th Earl of Dorset, a member of the Court Wits.
Chief among his satires are "Tell me, Dorinda, why so gay" (on Katherine Sedley),
The Duel of the Crabs, A Faithful Catalogue of Our Most Eminent Ninnies, and the
attack on Edward Howard ("Come on, ye critics, find one fault who dare") included
in this volume.

Pardon a muse which does with art support
Some drowsy wit in our unthinking court.
  But Mulgrave strike with many angry darts;
He who profanes thy name, offends thy arts,
Ne'er saw thy light, yet would usurp thy pow'r,   40
Would govern wit, and be its emperor,
In fee with Dryden to be counted wise,
Who tells the world he has both wit and eyes.
  Rochester's easy muse does so improve
Each hour thy little wealthy world of Love   45
(That world in which thy pow'r is clearest seen,
That world in which each muse is thought a queen)
That he must be forgiv'n in charity—
Though his sharp satires have offended thee—
In charity to Love, who will decay   50
When his delightful muse (its only stay)
Is by thy power severly ta'en away.
Forbear, then, civil wars, and strike not down
Love, who alone supports thy tott'ring crown.
  But saucy Sheppard, with the affected train   55
Who satires write, yet scarce can spell their name,
Blast, great Apollo, with perpetual shame!

38–43. Cf. *An Essay upon Satire*, 33–42.

55. *Sheppard:* Fleetwood Sheppard. As we learn from a letter of Buckingham to
Rochester on 11 August 1677, he and Sheppard "are resolved to wait upon you at
Woodstock" to discuss "a new treasonable lampoon," which was being attributed
to Rochester at court. Sheppard failed to make the trip, apparently (Burghclere,
Buckingham, p. 331).

JOHN SHEFFIELD, EARL OF MULGRAVE
AND JOHN DRYDEN

An Essay upon Satire
(1679)

This is the famous "Rose Alley satire" written by Mulgrave and circulated in manuscript in 1679. It was attributed at the time, however, chiefly to Dryden, and has long been thought to have provoked the beating he suffered at the hands of three ruffians in Rose Street, Covent Garden, on the night of 18 December 1679, as he was returning home from Will's. Certainly no omnibus satire of the period could have been more offensive to more powerful people, all of whom were in a position to retaliate forcefully, the King, the Duchess of Portsmouth, Rochester, Shaftesbury, and the brutal Philip, Earl of Pembroke being chief among them.

If we assume that *An Essay upon Satire* was the cause of the Laureate's beating, the Duchess of Portsmouth and Rochester are the leading suspects. Portsmouth had been very roughly handled, and there was a precedent for this kind of retaliation against those who reflected on the King's mistresses in the maiming of Sir John Coventry nine years earlier (see *The Haymarket Hectors*). Agitated by her declining influence over the King and well known for her vindictive temper, Louise might well have taken such revenge on the satirist who had supposedly described her as "False, foolish, old, ill-natur'd and ill-bred." The case for the Duchess of Portsmouth's involvement is ably summed up by J. H. Wilson in "Rochester, Dryden, and the Rose-Street Affair," *RES, 15* (1939), 294–301.

In Wood's life of George Villiers, second Duke of Buckingham (*Athenae Oxoniensis, 4,* 210), cited by Wilson, we have a roughly contemporary account of the incident, which distributes the blame fairly vaguely between the Duchess and Rochester:

> In Nov. (or before) an. 1679, there being *An Essay upon Satire* spread about the city in MS. wherein many gross reflections were made on Ludovisa Duchess of Portsmouth and John

Wilmot Earl of Rochester, they therefore took it for a truth that Dryden was the author; whereupon one or both hiring three men to cudgel him, they effected their business in the said coffee-house at 8 of the clock at night on the 16th of Dec. 1679.

Wood, as Wilson points out, gets time and place wrong, and is apparently relying on hearsay, for in another entry (*Athenae, 1, lxxxvii*) he notes that Dryden was cudgelled "because he had reflected on certain persons in *Absalom and Achitophel.*"

Aside from such vague contemporary accounts of the affair, the case for Rochester's instigation of the attack has rested on a letter to Savile long thought to have been written shortly before, but which Wilson has incontrovertibly dated in the spring or summer of 1676. The following section of the letter clearly pertains to Dryden's reported reaction to Rochester's criticism in *An Allusion to Horace*, written earlier in the year:

> You write me word that I'm out of favor with a certain Poet, whom I have ever admired for the disproportion of him and his attributes. He is a rarity which I cannot but be fond of, as one would be of a hog that could fiddle or a singing owl. If he fall upon me at the blunt, which is his very good weapon in wit, I will forgive him, if you please, and leave the repartee to *Black Will*, with a cudgel.

As Wilson argues, "we cannot accept as evidence of guilt a vague and careless threat uttered nearly four years before the crime was committed. Rochester failed to carry out his threat in the spring of 1677/8 when Dryden did indeed fall upon him 'at the blunt' in his preface to *All for Love;* I contend that he did not fulfil it in December 1679."

Rochester's letter to Savile about the *Essay upon Satire* (21 Nov. 1679) shows a dégagé attitude toward the gross personal insult which had been offered him, subordinating it to a disgusted survey of the folly of the times, exemplified chiefly by the madness of the Popish Plot. The letter is worth quoting in full:

> The lousiness of affairs in this place is such (forgive the unmannerly phrase! Expressions must descend to the nature of things expressed) 'tis not fit to entertain a private gentleman,

much less one of a public character, with the retail of them.
The general heads under which this whole island may be con-
sidered are spies, beggars, and rebels. The transpositions and
mixtures of these make an agreeable variety; busy fools and
cautious knaves are bred out of 'em and set off wonderfully,
though of this latter sort we have fewer now than ever: hypoc-
risy being the only vice in decay amongst us, few men here
dissemble their being rascals, and no woman disowns being a
whore. Mr. O[ates] was tried two days ago for buggery and
cleared; the next day he brought his action to the King's Bench
against his accuser, being attended by the Earl of Shaftesbury
and other peers to the number of seven, for the honor of the
Protestant Cause. I have sent you herewith a libel, in which
my own share is not the least. The King having perused it is
no ways dissatisfied with his. The author is apparently Mr.
D[ryden], his patron my [Lord Mulgrave] having a panegyric
in the midst, upon which happened a handsome quarrel be-
tween his L[ordship] and Mrs. B[ulkeley] at the Duchess of
P[ortsmouth's]. She called him the Hero of the Libel and com-
plimented him upon having made more cuckolds than any man
alive, to which he answered, she very well knew one he never
made, nor never cared to be employed in making. —— Rogue
and Bitch ensued, till the King, taking his grandfather's charac-
ter upon him, became the peacemaker. I will not trouble you
any longer but beg you still to love

> Your faithful,
> humble servant,
> Rochester.

My text of this letter is based on the first edition (*Familiar Let-
ters . . .* 1697) and incorporates the change from Mr. T. B—— to
Mrs. B—— in the erratum slip prefaced to that edition. Undoubt-
edly Wilson is right in identifying Mr. —— as Dryden and his pa-
tron as my Lord Mulgrave. Initial letters were supplied in the first
collected edition of Rochester's works (1714). Circumstances show,
then, that Rochester considered *An Essay upon Satire* as *apparently*
(i.e. manifestly) the work of a Mr. ——, whose patron, Lord Mul-
grave is treated to a "panegyric" in lines 194–209. Rochester had
long known of the close association between Dryden and Mulgrave,

which dated from 1675. When the two men with whom he had been
at odds for years on literary and personal grounds joined forces to
make a violent invective deriding his wit and aspersing his honor,
Rochester must have been sufficiently exasperated to let Black Will
deal with one of them. In his relations with Dryden, Rochester's
gentle reproofs had long been tried in vain. His censures of Dryden's
excessive concern with audience reaction and "boffo" wit in *An
Allusion to Horace* (1675–76) had been more than balanced by a
generous tribute to his "excellencies." *Advice to Apollo* (1677) had
been both temperate and tactful. Between these Rochesterian pieces
Dryden had ridiculed Shadwell and, by implication, the Earl's
praise of Shadwell's "nature" and "wit" in *Mac Flecknoe* and had
collaborated with Rochester's loathed enemy, Mulgrave on *An Essay
upon Satire*. Then, in 1678, the Laureate had compounded his of-
fense and rejected the proffered olive branch, by an unjust and
insolent attack on Rochester as man and poet in the preface to *All
for Love*. As if this were not enough, Dryden, as Rochester had every
reason to suppose, had composed (or helped Mulgrave to compose)
the draft of *An Essay upon Satire* circulated in November 1679,
which contained a thirty-five line invective against the Earl of un-
surpassed virulence.

The quarrel between the Laureate and the Earl, which probably
culminated in Rose Alley, may be clearly traced in the following
recapitulation:

1. Rochester's criticism of Dryden in *An Allusion to Horace* (late
   1675 or early 1676).
2. Rochester's letter to Savile about Dryden's reported resentment
   and his decision to "leave the repartee to Black Will with a
   cudgel" (summer, 1676).
3. Dryden's attack on Shadwell (whom Rochester had praised in
   An Allusion) in *Mac Flecknoe* (written between July 1676 and
   mid-October 1677, when Rochester [et al.?] wrote *Advice to
   Apollo*).
4. An early draft of the Mulgrave-Dryden *Essay upon Satire* (sum-
   mer, 1677).
5. *Advice to Apollo,* censuring Dryden for leaving the stage "to lash
   the witty follies of the age" and echoing the *Essay* (composed at
   Woodstock in mid-October 1677).

6. Dryden's preface to *All for Love* (pub. 1678), calling Rochester "an ignorant little zany," a vile imitator of Horace, and "a legitimate son of Sternhold."

7. Circulation of *An Essay upon Satire* (revised and augmented version) with extended attack on Rochester (lines 230–69), referred to in Rochester's letter to Savile (21 Nov. 1679).

Perhaps the *Essay* unluckily provided a cue for the repartee which broke upon its supposed author's head in these lines on Rochester:

> To ev'ry face he cringes while he speaks,
> But when the back is turn'd the head he breaks.

At any rate, the available evidence still leaves Rochester very much in the running as instigator of the famous Rose Alley ambuscade. A satire so offensive to so many would, however, bring forth other contenders. Charles Ward reminds us that Dryden's beating need not have been connected with this poem and suggests Shaftesbury as a possible instigator (*Life of Dryden*, pp. 143–44). He had abundant provocation whether or not he knew of the attack upon him in the *Essay*. With less conviction, V. de Sola Pinto advances the candidacy of Philip Herbert, the mad and brutal Earl of Pembroke, briefly glanced at in the *Essay* (line 183), and suggests that "Black Will" in Rochester's letter should be emended to "Black Phill." (*Enthusiast in Wit*, p. 101). This idea has the merit of pinning upon Pembroke a second unsolved crime of the period, John Dickson Carr having built up a case against him as the murderer of Justice Godfrey (*The Murder of Sir Edmund Berry Godfrey*).

The unspeakable Mulgrave escaped almost scot-free. In his *Essay upon Poetry*, first published in 1682, he denied Dryden's authorship. In the second edition (1691), as Noyes points out, "he made the denial more emphatic by adding sidenotes":

> The Laureate here may justly claim our praise,
> Crown'd by *Mac Flecknoe* with immortal bays;
> Though prais'd and punish'd for another's rhymes,
> His own deserve as great applause sometimes.

Not the least of the tribulations which Dryden had to bear in this period must have been such patronage as this. We need not attach much credit to Mulgrave's sidenote to *An Essay upon Satire* claiming that Dryden was "not only innocent but ignorant of the whole matter." Mulgrave's vanity, as Noyes observes, would have made him minimize any aid he had received. If Rochester did retaliate against Mulgrave, it was in *My Lord All-Pride,* which echoes (or is echoed by) *An Essay upon Satire.* On available evidence it is not possible to decide which poem preceded the other, although the greater intensity of the corresponding passages in the Rochester piece suggest that it did follow the Mulgrave-Dryden poem.

Never has an indifferent poem had two such godfathers as this. Pope revised it extensively in his sumptuous edition of the *Works* (1723), and his note on the half-title page that it was written in 1675 lends some slight further support to my contention that a version of the poem was in being at least two years before the Rose Alley affair. It may be, however, that Pope was misled by another so-called *Essay upon Satire* published by Thomas Dring in 1680, essentially a reprint of a Royalist pamphlet originally published as *The Four Ages of England: or, the Iron Age* in 1648 and republished in 1675 under the same title (see Noyes and Mead, *U. Cal. Pub. Eng., 7* [1948], 139–56). On the other hand, Pope had access to all Mulgrave's papers and may have had manuscript evidence for assigning such an early date to the *Essay.* The structureless nature of the piece shows that it could easily have developed by stages over a considerable period of time. In any event, the version here printed could not have been written before July 17, 1679 when George Savile was created Earl of Halifax (see line 122 and note).

An Essay Upon Satire

How dull and how insensible a beast
Is man, who yet would lord it o'er the rest!
Philosophers and poets vainly strove

1–2. Cf. the opening of Rochester's *Satire against Mankind:*

Were I (who to my cost already am
One of those strange prodigious creatures man)
A spirit free, to choose for my own share,
What case of flesh and blood I pleas'd to wear,
I'd be a dog, a monkey, or a bear;
Or anything but that vain animal
Who is so proud of being rational.

In ev'ry age the lumpish mass to move,
But those were pedants when compar'd with these   5
Who knew not only to instruct but please.
Poets alone found that delightful way
Mysterious morals gently to convey
In charming numbers, so that as men grew
Pleas'd with their poems, they grew wiser too.   10
Satire has always shin'd amongst the rest,
And is the boldest way, if not the best,
To tell men freely of their foulest faults,
To laugh at their vain deeds and vainer thoughts.
In satire too the wise took diff'rent ways,   15
Though each deserving its peculiar praise:
Some did all follies with just sharpness blame,
While others laugh'd and scorn'd them into shame;
But of these two the last succeeded best,
As men aim rightest when they shoot in jest.   20
Yet if we may presume to blame our guides
And censure those who censur'd all besides,
In other things they justly are preferr'd;
In this alone methinks the ancients err'd.
Against the grossest follies they declaim;   25
Hard they pursue, but hunt ignoble game.
Nothing is easier than such blots to hit,
And 'tis the talent of each vulgar wit;
Besides, 'tis labor lost, for who would preach
Morals to Armstrong, or dull Asston teach?   30
'Tis being devout at play, wise at a ball,
Or bringing wit and friendship to Whitehall.

6. *not only to instruct, but please:* A critical commonplace of the time, Horace's
aut prodesse, . . . aut delectare. In his *Essay on Satire* Dryden speaks of "profit and
delight, which are the two ends of poetry in general."

19–20. Dryden makes the same observation in the *Discourse Covering the Original
and Progress of Satire* (1692): "the best and finest manner of satire . . . is that sharp,
well-mannered way of laughing a folly out of countenance." Mulgrave expressed the
same thought in his *Essay on Poetry* (1682): "A satyr's smile is sharper than his
frown."

30. *Armstrong:* Sir Thomas Armstrong (1624?–84), who was executed for his share
in the Rye House Plot. He was an intimate of the Duke of Monmouth, and led a
"very vicious life" (Burnet). Sprat says he "became a debauched atheistical bravo"
(*DNB*). *Asston:* Probably the Colonel Edmund Ashton or Aston who was Mulgrave's

But with sharp eyes those nicer faults to find
Which lie obscurely in the wisest mind,
That little speck which all the rest does spoil,   35
To wash off that would be a noble toil
Beyond the loose-writ libels of the age,
Or the forc'd scenes of our declining stage.
Above all censure too, each little wit
Will be so glad to see the greater hit,   40
Who judging better, though concern'd the most,
Of such correction will have cause to boast.
In such a satire all would seek a share,
And ev'ry fool will fancy he is there.
Old story tellers, too, must pine and die   45
To see their antiquated wit laid by,
Like her who miss'd her name in a lampoon
And griev'd to see herself decay'd so soon.
No common coxcomb must be mention'd here,
Nor the dull trains of dancing sparks appear,   50
Nor flutt'ring officers who never fight,
Of such a wretched rabble who would write?
Much less half-wits, that's more against our rules;

---

second in the abortive duel with Rochester (see lines 248–49). He (or another of that name) is mentioned in *A Familiar Epistle, to Mr. Julian, Secretary of the Muses*:

> Bow-bending Cupid doth with ballads come,
> And little Aston offers to the bum.

Maurice Irvine in "Identification of Characters in Mulgrave's *Essay upon Satyr*" (*SP*, 34 [1937], 533–51) provides further information about Aston (541–42): he was "popular in the satires of the day whenever his puny size or his vanity suggested him for comparison with the typical Restoration fops, Sir George Hewitt and Sir Carr Scroope. He was the Edmund Aston or Ashton who bought a captaincy in Sir Allen Apsley's regiment in 1667 and of whom Sir Carr Scroope wrote in his *Defence of Satire*:

> There a vain fop mortgages all his land,
> To buy that gaudy thing call'd a command.

He was Mulgrave's contemporary almost to the year and he later rose to be a major and colonel in the King's Own Troop of Guards and the Horse Guards. He fought a duel with Etherege and wrote scraps of verse. The Prologue, "Gentle reproofs have long been tri'd in vain," was credited to him as well as to Rochester, and in Etherege's letter-book are some lines on the joys of retirement described as 'Colonel Ashton's.' " I am indebted to David Vieth for the further information that Armstrong and Ashton received their commissions in the Life Guards the same day.

For they are fops, the others are but fools.
Who would not be as silly as Dunbar,   55
Or dull as Monmouth, rather than Sir Carr?
The cunning courtier should be slighted, too,
Who with dull knav'ry makes so much ado,
Till the shrewd fool, by thriving so too fast,
Like Aesop's fox, becomes a prey at last.   60
Nor shall the royal mistresses be nam'd,
Too ugly and too easy to be blam'd;
With whom each rhyming fool keeps such a pother,
They are as common that way as the other.
Yet saunt'ring Charles, between his beastly brace,   65

55. *Dunbar:* The Scott-Saintsbury edition identifies him as Robert Constable, third Viscount of Dunbar. On 25 March 1673 a duel between Rochester and Lord Dunbar, who was a notorious bully, was narrowly averted by the Earl-Marshall's intervention (V. de Sola Pinto, *Poems by Rochester,* Intro., xxiii).

56. *As dull as Monmouth:* A frequently repeated charge in the lampoons of the day:

> He, with his thick impenetrable skull,
> The solid harden'd armor of a fool,
> Well might himself to all war's ill expose,
> Who, come what will, yet had no brains to lose.
> *Rochester's Farewell*

Sir Carr: Sir Carr Scroope.

60. *Aesop's fox:* See the fable of the fox and the wolf.

65. *Yet saunt'ring Charles between his breastly brace:* In *A Character of King Charles II,* printed in Mulgrave's works, 1723, there is the following observation: "I am of the opinion also, that in his [Charles'] latter times there were as much of laziness, as of love, in all those hours he passed among his mistresses; who after all, served only to fill up his seraglio; while a bewitching kind of pleasure called saunt'ring, and talking without any constraint, was the true sultana queen he delighted in." Halifax, in his own character of Charles II, observes: "The thing called sauntering is a stronger temptation to princes than it is to others." According to Irvine, the beastly brace is Nell Gwynne and the Duchess of Portsmouth: Nell jilts him and affects to laugh, Portsmouth sells him and affects to weep. There is a specific allusion to these lines in *Satyr Quem Natura negat facit Indignatio versum, POAS* (1704), *3, 123;*

> Let Dryden's pen indulgent David blame,
> And brand his friends with hated rebels' name.
> He that could once call Charles a saunt'ring cully,
> By Portsmouth sold, and jilted by bitch Nelly.

This poem is attributed to a Mr. Allen and dated 1682 in BM Harl. 7319, f. 114 (Maurice Irvine, "Identification of Characters in Mulgrave's *Essay upon Satyr," SP, 34* [1931], 540 and n. 15). J. H. Wilson, however, disagrees with Irvine's identification:

Meets with dissembling still in either place,
Affected humor or a painted face.
In loyal libels we have often told him
How one has jilted him, the other sold him;
How that affects to laugh and this to weep;   70
But who can rail so long as he can keep?
Was ever prince by two at once misled,
False, foolish, old, ill-natur'd and ill-bred?
Earnely and Ailesbury with all that race
Of busy blockheads shall have here no place;   75
At council set as foils on Danby's score
To make that great false jewel shine the more,
Who all the while was thought exceeding wise
Only for taking pains and telling lies.
But there's no meddling with such nauseous men,   80
Their very names have tir'd my lazy pen;
'Tis time to quit their company and choose
Some fitter subject for a sharper muse.
　　First, let's behold the merriest man alive
Against his careless genius vainly strive;   85
Quit his dear ease some deep design to lay
'Gainst a set time, and then forget the day.
Yet he will laugh at his best friends and be

"The antitheses between the two are clear: Cleveland, notorious for her infidelity, has jilted Charles; Portsmouth, known to be strong for the French interest, has sold him; Cleveland, a brazen creature, affects to laugh; Portsmouth, a lachrymose lady, affects to weep. Neither description fits Gwynne" (*Court Wits*, p. 235).

74. *Earnely:* Sir John Earnely was bred to the law, but became distinguished as a second-rate statesman. He was Chancellor of the Exchequer in 1686 and was made one of the Commissioners of Treasury, in the room of the Earl of Rochester (Scott-Saintsbury). *Ailesbury:* Robert Bruce, second Earl of Elgin, in Scotland, created after the Restoration an English peer, by the titles of Baron and Viscount Bruce, Earl of Ailesbury. In 1678 he was of the Privy Council to his Majesty and Gentleman of the Bedchamber. In the reign of James II the Earl of Ailesbury succeeded to the office of Lord Chamberlain upon the death of the Earl of Arlington in July 1685, an office which he held only two months, as he died in October following (Scott-Saintsbury). Irvine adds the following details: "Ailesbury and Earnely had been appointed to the Council in 1678 and 1679 respectively and continued to support Danby, their benefactor, even after he was, in March, 1679, indicted for high treason and had lost the favor of both political parties (p. 542)."

84. *the merriest man alive:* The Duke of Buckingham. Cf. Dryden's characterization of him as Zimri in *Absalom and Achitophel.*

Just as good company as Nokes or Lee.
But when he aims at reason or at rule   90
He turns himself the best in ridicule;
Let him at business ne'er so earnest sit,
Show him but mirth, and bait that mirth with wit,
That shadow of a jest shall be enjoy'd
Though he left all mankind to be destroy'd: 95
So cat transform'd sat gravely and demure
Till mouse appear'd and thought himself secure;
But soon the lady had him in her eye
And from her friends did just as oddly fly.
Reaching above our nature does no good,   100
We must fall back to our own flesh and blood.
As by our little Machiavel we find
(That nimblest creature of the busy kind)
His limbs are crippl'd and his body shakes,
Yet his hard mind, which all this bustle makes,   105
No pity of his poor companion takes.
What gravity can hold from laughing out
To see that drag his feeble legs about
Like hounds ill coupl'd; Jowler lugs him still
Through hedges, ditches, and through all that's ill.   110
'Twere crime in any man but him alone

89. *Nokes or Lee:* James Nokes and Anthony Lee (or Leigh) were the most noted comic actors of the day. Colley Cibber in his *Apology* wrote of them: "In Sir Jolly, he [Lee] was all life and laughing humor, and when Nokes acted with him in the same play, they returned the ball so dexterously upon one another, that every scene between them seemed but one continued rest of excellence" (Irvine, p. 544).

96. *cat transform'd:* Derrick, in his edition of Dryden published in 1757 by Tonson, explained that the "cat transform'd" was a cat turnd into a grave and demure lady but still in her nature a cat. At dinner she was unable to resist the lure of a passing mouse, and, when she pounced upon it, she regained her old form (Irvine, p. 544). Mulgrave may have had in mind Aesop's fable of the young man and his cat. A certain youth fell in love with his cat whereupon he prayed to Venus to relieve him of his pain. The goddess accordingly changed the cat into a beautiful young girl whom the youth immediately married. On their wedding night the bride, hearing a mouse behind a hanging, sprang from her husband's arms to pursue it. Venus, enraged at having her rites thus profaned, and seeing that the bride though a woman in appearance was a cat at heart, changed her back to her original form.

102. *our little Machiavel:* Anthony Ashley Cooper, first Earl of Shaftesbury. Cf. this portrait with Dryden's Achitophel.

109. *Jowler:* A heavy-jawed dog. Used also as quasi-proper name for a dog of this kind.

To use his body so, though 'tis his own;
Yet this false comfort never gives him o'er,
That whilst he creeps his vig'rous thoughts can soar.
Alas! that soaring to those few that know 115
Is but a busy grov'ling here below.
So men in raptures think they mount the sky,
Whilst on the ground th' entranced wretches lie;
So modern fops have fanci'd they should fly,
Whilst 'tis their heads alone are in the air, 120
And for the most part building castles there.
As the new Earl, with parts deserving praise
And wit enough to laugh at his own ways,
Yet loses all soft days and sensual nights,
Kind nature checks, and kinder fortune slights; 125
Striving against his quiet all he can,
For the fine notion of a busy man;
And what is that at best but one whose mind
Is made to tire himself and all mankind?
To Ireland he would go—faith, let him reign, 130
For if some odd fantastic lord would fain
Carry my trunks and all my drudg'ry do,
I'll not pay only, I'll admire him too.
But is there any other beast that lives
Who his own harm so wittily contrives? 135
Will any dog that hath his teeth and stones

122. *the new Earl:* George Savile, created Earl of Halifax in July 1679.
130. In April 1679 a successor to the Duke of Ormonde was being considered and Essex, Robertes (Earl of Falmouth and Radnor), and Halifax were frequently mentioned for his post. Algernon Sydney wrote at this time: "but if a lieutenant be sent, I believe it will be Essex or Halifax." Burnet states that Halifax was suspected of aspiring to the post: "Some gave it out that he had pretended to be Lord Lieutenant of Ireland, and was uneasy when that was denied him: but he said to me that it was offered him and he had refused it" (Irvine, p. 548).
136–39. Taking this as a libel on the countess of Halifax, Irvine (p. 549) quotes a passage from the reply to this satire, called *The Cabal* or *In Opposition to Mr. Dryden's Essay on Satire:*

> Halif[ax] for empire has as great an itch
> As ever dog had for his salt swoln bitch
> His plumes impt with ambition, up he flies,
> And, to be something melts e'en in the skies:
> While th' humble wretch at home lies prostrate down
> To all the barking beagles of the town.

Refin'dly leave his bitches and his bones
To turn a wheel and bark to be employ'd
While Venus is by rival dogs enjoy'd?
Yet this fond man, to get a statesman's name,   140
Forfeits his friends, his freedom, and his fame.
    Though satire nicely writ no humor stings
But theirs who merit praise in other things,
Yet we must needs this one exception make,
And break one rule for Polytropos' sake,   145
Who was too much despis'd to be accus'd,
And therefore scarce deserves to be abus'd;
Rais'd only by his mercenary tongue
For railing smoothly and for reas'ning wrong:
As boys on holidays let loose to play   150
Lay waggish traps for girls who pass that way,
Then shout to see in dirt and deep distress
Some silly chit in her flow'r'd foolish dress;
So have I mighty satisfaction found
To see his tinsell'd reasons on the ground;   155
To see the florid fool despis'd (and know it)
By some who scarce have words enough to show it

    138. *to turn a wheel:* To be a turnspit, a dog kept to turn the roasting-spit by running within a kind of tread-wheel connected with it.

    145. *Polytropos:* This is Heneage Finch, Lord Chancellor. Polytropos is the epithet of Ulysses in the *Odyssey:* turning many ways, versatile, etc. (*OED*). There is undoubtedly an added hint to be found in another sense of the term: Finch, in his florid orations, used many tropes or figures of speech.

    146. *Who was too much despis'd to be accus'd:* This probably refers to the matter of Danby's impeachment in March 1679. Charles, to the great anger of the Commons, had given Danby a pardon in bar of the impeachment. The House appointed a committee, who demanded from Finch an explanation of the fact that the pardon bore the great seal. Finch's statement was that he neither advised, drew, nor altered it; that the King commanded him to bring the seal from Whitehall, and being there he laid it upon the table; thereupon his Majesty commanded the seal to be taken out of the bag, which it was not in his power to hinder; and the King wrote his name on the top of the parchment, and then directed to have it sealed, whereupon the person who usually carried the purse affixed the seal to it. He added that at the time he did not regard himself as having the custody of the seal (*DNB*).

    148. *his mercenary tongue:* Finch's forensic eloquence is testified to on all hands; though Burnet says he was too eloquent on the bench, in the Lords, and in the Commons, and calls his speaking labored and affected. Roger North in his autobiography confirms this view, saying that his love of "a handsome turn of expression gave him a character of a trifler which he did not so much deserve" (*DNB*).

(For sense sits silent and condemns for weaker
The finer, nay sometimes the wittier, speaker).
But 'tis prodigious so much eloquence   160
Should be acquir'd by such a little sense;
For words and wit did anciently agree,
And Tully was no fool though this man be.
At bar abusive, at the bench unable,
Knave on the woolsack, fop at council table,   165
These are the grievances: such fools as would
Be rather wise than honest, great than good.
    Another kind of wits must be made known,
Whose harmless errors hurt themselves alone:
Excess of luxury they think can please,   170
And laziness call loving of their ease.
To live dissolv'd in pleasure still they feign,
Though their whole life's but intermitting pain;
So much of surfeit, headache, claps are seen,
We scarce perceive the little time between.   175
Well-meaning men who make this gross mistake,
And pleasure lose only for pleasure's sake;
Each pleasure hath its price, and when we pay
So much of pain we squander life away.
Thus Dorset, purring like a thoughtful cat,   180
Marri'd (but wiser Puss ne'er thought of that)
And first he worri'd her with railing rhyme,
Like Pembroke's mastiff at his kindest time;
Then, for one night, sold all his slavish life

163. *Tully:* Finch was called the English Cicero by his contemporaries.
164-65. The author of *Advice to the Satirical Poets* ("Satire's despotic, now none can withstand") quotes this couplet as proof of the writer's wit:

> Save but his bones, he's well secur'd of fame,
> The Chancellor's epitaph must preserve his name.

180. *Dorset:* Charles Sackville, sixth Earl of Dorset and Earl of Middlesex. His first wife, Mary Bagot, widow of Charles Berkeley, Earl of Falmouth (line 185, "A teeming widow"), died 12 September 1679 without issue, and Dorset did not remarry until 1685.
183. *Pembroke's mastiff:* "This present Earl of Pembroke [Philip Herbert, 1653-83, seventh Earl of Pembroke] has at Wilton 52 mastiffs and 30 greyhounds, some bears, and a lion, and a matter of 60 fellows more bestial than they" (MS. Aubr. 6, a note on fol. 80ᵛ) in Aubrey's *Brief Lives*, ed. Andrew Clark, *I*, 317 (*under* William Herbert, first Earl of Pembroke).

T'a teeming widow but a barren wife.   185
Swell'd by contact of such a fulsome toad,
He lugg'd about the matrimonial load,
Till fortune, blindly kind as well as he,
Hath ill restor'd him to his liberty,
Which he will use in his old sneaking way,   190
Drinking all night and dozing all the day;
Dull as Ned Howard, whom his brisker time
Had fam'd for dulness in malicious rhyme.
   Mulgrave had much ado to 'scape the snare,
Though learn'd in those ill arts that cheat the fair: 195
For, after all his vulgar marriage mocks,
With beauty dazzl'd, Numps was in the stocks.
Deluded parents dri'd their weeping eyes
To see him catch his Tartar for his prize;
Th' impatient town waited the wish'd-for change,   200
And cuckolds smil'd in hopes of a revenge;
Till Petworth plot made us with sorrow see
As his estate his person too was free.
Him no soft thoughts, no gratitude could move;
To gold he fled from beauty and from love,   205

192–93. This is an allusion to Dorset's verses to the Honorable Edward Howard, *To a Person of Honor, upon his Incomparable, Incomprehensible Poem called "The British Princes."*

194–209. This passage on himself, in which the notoriously vain Mulgrave is represented as *l'homme fatale*, was a clue to his authorship as can be seen in a letter from Colonel Edward Cooke to the Duke of Ormonde (quoted by Irvine, p. 534):

> 22 November 1679. If I may be permitted to play at small game I shall repeat a particular that I was informed part [*sic*] this week at the Duchess of Portsmouth's, where just before the King came in a most scurrilous, libellous copy of verse was read, severe upon almost all the courtiers save my Lord Mulgrave, whose sole accusation was that he was a cuckold-maker. This brought him under suspicion to be (if not guilty of the making, yet) guilty of being privy to the making of them, who just coming in with the King, Mrs. Buckley saluted him (in raillery) by the name of cuckold-maker, who taking it in earnest replied she knew one cuckold he never made, which she took for so great an affront that it seems her husband was entitled to the revenge. But the King, it seems, came to the knowledge of it, and interfered his authority to antidote bloodshed.

Mulgrave's first marriage took place in March 1686. I have not found any other mention of the Petworth plot.

197. J. H. Wilson quotes Etherege on the occasion of Mulgrave's marriage: "Numps [a silly or stupid person, the nickname given him by the wits] is now in the stocks in earnest" (*Court Wits*, p. 77).

Yet failing there he keeps his freedom still,
Forc'd to live happily against his will.
'Tis not his fault if too much wealth and pow'r
Break not his boasted quiet ev'ry hour.
And little Sid, for simile renown'd,   210
Pleasure hath always sought but never found:
Though all his thoughts on wine and woman fall,
His are so bad, sure, he ne'er thinks at all.
The flesh he lives upon is rank and strong,
His meat and mistresses are kept too long;   215
But sure we all mistake this pious man,
Who mortifies his person all he can:
What we uncharitably take for sin,
Are only rules of this odd Capuchin;
For never hermit under grave pretence   220
Has liv'd more contrary to common sense,
And 'tis a miracle, we may suppose,
No nastiness offends his skillful nose
Which from all stinks can with peculiar art
Extract perfume, and essence from a fart.   225
Expecting supper is his great delight,
He toils all day but to be drunk at night;
Then o'er his cups this chirping nightbird sits
Till he takes Hewitt and Jack Howe for wits.

210. *And little Sid, for simile renown'd:* Sir Charles Sedley or Sidley. In the 1723 edition of Sheffield's works there is a note on this line: "Remarkable for making pleasant and proper similes on all occasions." In a draft of a satire on Sedley in the handwriting of Charles Montague, afterwards Earl of Halifax, there is the following line: "And pretty similes sprinkled here and there" (Pinto, *Sedley*, p. 313). The Scott-Saintsbury edition quotes a couplet from a poem in *BOAS, 3* (Case 211):

> To a soul so mean e'en Shadwell is a stranger;
> Nay, little Sid, it seems, less values danger.

In Pope's copy of the 1705 *POAS* the name is expanded in MS. to "Sidney," an obvious error. Pinto comments on this portrait: "What we know of Sedley enables us to annotate this brutal passage. The statement that his 'mistresses are kept too long' is certaily a reference to his connection with Miss [Ann] Ayscough, with whom he had now lived for seven years, which must have seemed a miracle of constancy to Mulgrave. The comment on Sedley's 'piety' is doubtless a sneer at the reformation in his manners which was now in progress" (Pinto, *Sedley*, p. 145).

229. *Hewitt:* Sir George Hewitt was a coxcomb of the period, after whom Etherege is said to have modeled Sir Fopling Flutter's character. *Jack Howe:* The reading of *F'* supports Noyes' conjecture that the usual reading, *Jack Hall,* is an error for Jack Howe, "a dissolute scribbler and politician" (*Poems of Dryden,* 1950 ed., p. 1042).

Rochester I despise for his mere want of wit   230
(Though thought to have a tail and cloven feet)
For while he mischief means to all mankind,
Himself alone the ill effect does find,
And so like witches justly suffers shame,
Whose harmless malice is so much the same.   235
False are his words, affected as his wit,
So often he does aim, so seldom hit;
To ev'ry face he cringes whilst he speaks,
But when the back is turn'd the head he breaks.
Mean in each motion, lewd in ev'ry limb,   240
Manners themselves are mischievous in him;
A proof that chance alone makes ev'ry creature,
A very Killigrew without good nature.
For what a Bessus hath he always liv'd,
And his own kicking notably contriv'd?   245
For there's the folly that's still mix'd with fear:
Cowards more blows than any hero bear.
Of fighting sparks some may their pleasure say,
But 'tis a bolder thing to run away.
The world may well forgive him all his ill,   250
For ev'ry fault does prove his penance still;
Falsely he falls into some dang'rous noose,

243. *Killigrew:* Either Thomas Killigrew the elder, dramatist, whom Oldys called the King's jester and Pepys "a merry droll" (*DNB*), or, more probably, Henry Killigrew, son of the former by his first wife, a wild wit whom Henry Savile in a letter addressed as "sweet namesake of mine, happy-humored Killigrew, soul of mirth and all delight" (Wilson, *Court Wits*, p. 84)

244. *Bessus:* A cowardly braggadocio character in Beaumont and Fletcher's *King and No King.*

248–49. Mulgrave and Rochester had been good friends until November 1669 when Mulgrave heard that Rochester had said something malicious of him. Mulgrave felt obliged to challenge Rochester but the latter, pleading illness, failed to appear on the field of honor. According to Mulgrave in his *Memoirs*, Colonel Ashton, Mulgrave's second, "thought himself obliged to write down every word and circumstance of this whole matter, in order to spread everywhere the true reason of our returning without having fought; which being never in the least either contradicted or resented by the Lord Rochester, entirely ruined his reputation as to courage (of which I was really sorry to be the occasion), though nobody had still a greater as to wit." J. H. Wilson, however, cites the report in the *House of Lords Journal* for 23 November 1669 and comments: "Evidently Rochester had been so eager to keep his appointment with Mulgrave that he had broken his parole to an officer of the House rather than risk losing his honor as a duelist" (*Court Wits*, p. 234).

And then as meanly labors to get loose;
A life so infamous it's better quitting,
Spent in base injuring and low submitting. 255
I'd like to have left out his poetry,
Forgot almost by all as well as me:
Sometimes he hath some humor, never wit,
And if it ever (very rarely) hit,
'Tis under so much nasty rubbish laid, 260
To find it out's the cinder-woman's trade,
Who for the wretched remnants of a fire,
Must toil all day in ashes and in mire.
So lewdly dull his idle works appear,
The wretched text deserves no comment here, 265
Where one poor thought's sometimes left all alone
For a whole page of dulness to atone.
'Mongst forty bad's one tolerable line,
Without expression, fancy, or design.
   How vain a thing is man and how unwise 270
E'en he who would himself the most despise!
I, who so wise and humble seem to be,
Now my own vanity and pride can see.
Whilst the world's nonsense is so sharply shown,
We pull down others but to raise our own: 275
That we may angels seem we paint them elves,
And are but satyrs to set up ourselves.
I, who have all this while been finding fault
E'en with my masters who first satire taught,
And did by that describe the task so hard 280
It seems stupendous and above reward,
Now labor with unequal force to climb
That lofty hill unreach'd by former time.
'Tis just that I should to the bottom fall:
Learn to write well, or not to write at all. 285

277. *satyrs:* A satyr or satire in Mulgrave's time could mean a satirist. The confusion between the words "satiric" and "satyric" gave rise to the notion that the satyrs who formed the chorus of Greek satyric drama had to deliver "satirical" speeches. Hence in the 16–17th centuries satyrs were thought censorious (*OED*).

JOHN WILMOT, EARL OF ROCHESTER

My Lord All-Pride
(1679)

My Lord All-Pride was published with *A Very Heroical Epistle in Answer to Ephelia* in a broadside in 1679. There is some question as to whether it preceded or followed *An Essay upon Satire,* but lines 7–10 seem to be modeled upon lines 258–63 of Mulgrave's poem and create a strong presupposition in favor of Rochester's authorship.

MY LORD ALL-PRIDE

Bursting with pride the loath'd impostume swells;
Prick him, he sheds his venom straight and smells;
But 'tis so lewd a scribbler that he writes
With as much force to nature as he fights.
Harden'd in shame, 'tis such a baffl'd fop   5
That ev'ry schoolboy whips him like a top,
And, with his arm and head, his brain's so weak
That his starv'd fancy is compell'd to rake
Among the excrements of others' wit,
To make a stinking meal of what they s——.   10
So swine for nasty meat to dunghill run,
And toss their gruntling snouts up when they've done.
Against his stars the coxcomb ever strives,
And to be something they forbid, contrives.
With a red nose, splay foot, and goggle eye,   15
A ploughman's looby mien, face all awry,
With stinking breath and every loathsome mark,
The Punchinello sets up for a spark.
With equal self-conceit, too, he bears arms,
But with that vile success his part performs   20
That he burlesques his trade, and what is best
In others turns, like Harlequin, to jest.

John Sheffield, Earl of Mulgrave. From an engraving by J. Smith after the portrait by Kneller.

So have I seen, at Smithfield's wond'rous fair,
When all his brother-monsters flourish there,
A lubbard elephant divert the town   25
With making legs and shooting off a gun.
Go where he will, he never finds a friend:
Shame and derision all his steps attend.
Alike abroad, at home, i'th' camp and court,
This Knight o'th' Burning Pestle make us sport.   30

IV. Portraits

J'ai vendu Dunkerque
(1666)

This amusing little poem presents Chancellor Clarendon as boasting of just those events for which he was most bitterly (though perhaps unjustly) condemned: the sale of Dunkirk, Charles II's marriage to the barren Catherine of Braganza, and the marriage of Ann Hyde to the Duke of York. These are commonplaces of anti-Clarendonian satire: compare *Second Advice to a Painter* and *Clarendon's Housewarming.*

The poem exists in only one manuscript, B.M. Harleian 6914 (*V*).

J'AI VENDU DUNKERQUE

J'ai vendu Dunkerque,
J'ai pillié l'Église,
J'ai dérobé mon maître
Jusqu'au chemise.
J'ai donné au Roi   5
Une femme stérile
Et à son frère unique
Ma putaine de fille.
N'est-ce pas agir
En ministre habile?   10

Nell Gwynne
(1669)

In 1669 Nell Gwynne left the stage to become Charles' mistress. She was the most popular of the King's ladies because, unlike Lady Castlemaine and the Duchess of Portsmouth, she was not a Roman Catholic and she did not attempt to exercise political influence. Once when she was mistaken for Portsmouth by a hostile crowd at Oxford she is reported to have made the well-known quip, "Pray, good people, be civil—I am the *Protestant* whore."

NELL GWYNNE

Hard by Pall Mall lives a wench call'd Nell.
  King Charles the Second he kept her.
She hath got a trick to handle his p——,
  But never lays hands on his sceptre.
All matters of state from her soul she does hate,   5
  And leave to the politic bitches.
The whore's in the right, for 'tis her delight
  To be scratching just where it itches.

Madame Ellen Groinn and her troo sons, Charles Earl of Beaufort and James LORD Beauclaire

Henry Gascar Pinxit

Nell Gwynne. From an engraving by Henry Gascar.

The Queen's Ball
(*1670*)

Except for *The Queen's Ball,* the unfortunate Queen Catherine is hardly mentioned in Restoration satire, but this ill-natured attack seems to illustrate Hamlet's observation to Ophelia: "Be thou as chaste as ice, as pure as snow, thou shalt not escape calumny." When the Queen found that her consort took pleasure in dancing with partners like Lady Castlemaine, she took up dancing with zeal if not with much success. "She made her chaplains and even the Abbé d'Aubigny join in country dances in her bedchamber. She had, indeed, begun to play like other ladies. And to play so unrestrainedly as to invite fresh criticism from the Puritans" (Janet Mackay, *Catherine of Braganza,* London, 1937, p. 112).

The Queen's Ball must have been written after Blood's attempt on the Duke of Ormonde (see lines 31–32) in December 1670. Janet Mackay attributes the poem to Marvell, but there is no evidence that he wrote it.

THE QUEEN'S BALL

Reform, great Queen, the errors of your youth,
And hear a thing you never heard, call'd truth:
Poor private balls content the Fairy Queen;
You must dance, and dance damnably, to be seen.
Ill-natur'd little goblin, and design'd   5
For nothing but to dance and vex mankind,
What wiser thing could our great Monarch do
Than root ambition out by showing you?
You can the most aspiring thoughts pull down,
For who would have his wife to have his crown?   10

3–4. This ball was a public one, held, presumably, at Worcester House. See note to line 34.

421

With a white vizard you may cheat our eyes;
You know a black one would be no disguise.
See in her mouth a sparkling diamond shine!
The first good thing that e'er came from that mine.
Heav'n some great curse upon that hand dispense,   15
That for th' increase of mischief sent her hence!
How gracefully she moves and strives to lug
A weight of riches that might sink the pug!
Such fruits ne'er loaded so deform'd a tree:
Her jewels may be match'd, but never she.   20
If bold Actæon in the waves had seen
In fair Diana's room our puppet Queen,
He would have fled and in his full career,
For greater haste, have wish'd himself a deer,
Preferr'd the bellies of his dogs to hers,   25
And thought 'em the more cleanly sepulchres.
What stupid madman would not choose to have
The settl'd rest and silence of a grave
Rather than such a hell, which always burns,
And from whom Nature forbids all returns?   30
Ormonde looks paler now than when he rid;
Your visit frights him more than Tyburn did.
Fear of your coming does not only make
Worcester's wise Marquis but his house to shake.
What will be next unless you mean to go   35
And dance among your fellow-fiends below?
There, as upon the Stygian Lake you float,
You may o'erset and sink the laden boat,
While we the funeral rites devoutly pay,
And dance for joy that you are danc'd away.   40

18. *pug:* Dwarf. Catherine was short.

21–26. Diana transformed Actæon into a stag and he was torn to pieces by his own hounds.

31–32. For Ormonde's "ride" see *The History of Insipids,* 43–48 and n. I cannot trace the particular encounter alluded to here between him and the Queen.

33–34. Henry Somerset, third Marquis of Worcester (1629–1700), let his house in the Strand to Clarendon until Clarendon House was completed. Worcester House was afterwards used occasionally for special functions, of which the ball seems to have been one. I cannot trace any encounter between the Queen and the "wise Marquis," whom Evelyn described as "a person of great honor, prudence, and estate."

Catherine of Braganza. From an engraving by Hollar.

JOHN WILMOT, EARL OF ROCHESTER

The Earl of Rochester's Verses
for Which he was Banished
(*1675*)

Late in the summer of 1675 Rochester was banished from court at the behest of the Duchess of Portsmouth. He seems to have spent the following year at Woodstock, and his letters to Savile are full of lamentations about the Duchess' displeasure and affirmations of his ignorance as to its cause. In August 1675 he writes, "By that God that made me, I have no more offended her in thought, word, or deed, no more imagined or uttered the least thought to her contempt or prejudice, than I have plotted treason, concealed arms, trained regiments for a rebellion" (*Rochester-Savile Letters*, p. 35).

Whether Rochester was being naïve or disingenuous in his protestations to his intimate friend is a question, but there is little doubt that the cause of the Duchess' indignation and the royal displeasure was the following lampoon, which is dated 1675 in B.M. Add. MS. 23722. In several MSS. as well as in *POAS* the title identifies the poem as the cause of Rochester's banishment. Burnet explains how one day Rochester "being drunk, . . . intended to give the King a libel that he had writ on some ladies, but by mistake he gave him one wrote on himself [i.e. the King]" (*History, 1,* 477).

The title of the poem in *POAS, On King Charles, By the Earl of Rochester, For Which he was Banished the Court and Turned Mountebank,* connects it with another celebrated episode in Rochester's career, his playing the rôle of the quack Doctor Alexander Bendo on Tower Hill.

Ascriptions to Rochester in addition to those recorded in the textual notes occur in Bod. MS. Rawl. D. 924 and Princeton MS. AM 14401. The poem is included in the various editions of *The Miscellaneous Works of the Right Honorable the Late Earls of Rochester and Roscommon* (1st ed., 1707). D. M. Vieth provides important biographical and bibliographical information about the poem in

"Rochester's 'Scepter' Lampoon on Charles II," *PQ*, 37 (1958), 424–32.

THE EARL OF ROCHESTER'S VERSES
FOR WHICH HE WAS BANISHED

In the Isle of Britain, long since famous grown
For breeding the best c——ts in Christendom,
There now does live—ah, let him long survive!—
The easiest King and best-bred man alive.
Him no ambition moves to get renown   5
Like the French fool who wanders up and down,
Starving his soldiers, hazarding his crown.
Peace is his aim, his gentleness is such,
And love he loves, for he loves f——ing much.
Nor are his high desires above his strength: 10
His sceptre and his p——k are of a length,
And she may sway the one who plays with t'other,
And make him little wiser than his brother.
　　The p——ks of kings are like buffoons at court:
We let 'em rule because they make us sport.   15
His is the sauciest one that e'er did swive,
The proudest, peremptoriest p——k alive.
Whate'er religion or his laws say on't,
He'll break through all to come at any c——t.
Restless he rolls about from whore to whore,   20
A merry Monarch, scandalous and poor.
　　"Oh dearest Carwell, dearest of all dears,
The best relief of my declining years,
Oh how I mourn thy fortune and my fate,
To love so well and be belov'd so late!"   25
Yet still his graceless ballocks hung an arse.
Nothing could serve his disobedient tarse.
This to evince it were too long to tell ye,
The painful trick of his laborious Nelly—
While she employs hands, fingers, lips, and thighs   30
To raise the limb which she each night enjoys.
　　I hate all monarchs with the thrones they sit on,
From the hector of France to the cully of Britain.

JOHN LACY

Satire
(*1677*)

This invective against Charles II is ascribed to Rochester in *POAS*, 2 (Case 211 2 a) and appears in *The Works of the Earls of Rochester, Roscommon, and Dorset* (London, 1739). It is reprinted in Quilter Johns' edition of Rochester. Ascriptions in *POAS* are not, however, to be relied on, and the poor quality of this piece suggests the work of an inferior hand. Rochester could hardly have been guilty of the false Charles-Albemarle rhyme with which the poem begins, and the note of honest indignation against the King's sexual promiscuity is alien to him.

In three MSS. (V.&A. Dyce 43, Vienna 14090, and B.M. Harl. 7319) the poem is ascribed to "Mr. Lacy," and it is dated 1677 in the B.M. text. The author was probably John Lacy (d. 1681), a famous comic actor, who also wrote a number of farces, among them a coarse adaptation of *The Taming of the Shrew* called *Sawny the Scot* (1666). In 1667 Lacy incurred the King's anger for abusing the court in the part of the Country Gentleman in Edward Howard's *Change of Crowns* and was committed to the Porter's Lodge. This incident and the fact that Lacy had at one time been Nell Gwynne's dramatic coach and lover may have aroused the animus against the actress and her royal keeper so bitterly expressed in this poem.

The variant title, *Upon Nell Gwynne's and the Duchess of Portsmouth's Naked Pictures,* refers to the celebrated nude portraits attributed to Lely.

SATIRE

Preserv'd by wonder in the oak, O Charles,
And then brought in by the Duke of Albemarle:

1. *the oak:* Boscobel Oak, in which Charles was concealed after the Battle of Worcester.

The first was Providence; the next, all Devil,
Shows thee a compound of both good and evil.
The ill we've too long known, the good's to come,   5
But not expected till the Day of Doom.
　　Was ever prince's soul so meanly poor,
To be enslav'd to ev'ry little whore?
The seaman's needle points always to the pole,
But thine still points to ev'ry craving hole,   10
Which wolf-like in your breast raw flesh devours,
And must be fed all seasons and all hours.
C——t is the mansion house where thou dost swell.
There thou art fix'd as tortoise is to shell,
Whose head peeps out a little now and then   15
To take the air and then creeps in again.
Strong are thy lusts, in c——t th' art always diving,
And I dare swear thou pray'st to die a-swiving.
How poorly squander'st thou thy seed away,
Which should get kings for nations to obey!   20
But thou, poor Prince, so uselessly hast sown it,
That the Creation is asham'd to own it.
Witness the royal line sprung from the belly
Of thine anointed Princess, Madam Nelly,
Whose first employment was with open throat   25
To cry fresh herrings e'en at ten a groat,
Then was by Madam Ross expos'd to town,
(I mean to those that would give half a crown),
Next in the playhouse she took her degree,
As men commence in th' university: 30
No doctors till they've masters been before,
Nor any player but she's first a whore.
Look back and see the people mad with rage
To see the bitch in so high equipage,
And ev'ry day they do the monster see,   35
They let ten thousand curses fall on thee.
Aloud in public streets they use thee thus,
And none dare quell 'em, they're so numerous.

27. *Madam Ross:* A "notorious hag, who inveigled young girls of attractive ap-
pearance not only to sell apples and oranges in the theatres, but to act as decoys for
houses of ill-fame in Lewkenor's Lane" (Dasent, *Nell Gwynne*, p. 36).

Stopping the Bank in thee was only great,
But in a subject it had been a cheat.   40
To pay thy debts what sums canst thou advance,
Now thy exchequer is gone into France
T'enrich a harlot all made up of French,
Not worthy to be call'd a whore but wench?
Cleveland indeed deserv'd that noble name,   45
Whose monstrous lechery exceeds all fame.
The Empress Messalina tir'd in lust at least,
But you could never satisfy this beast.
Cleveland, I say, was much to be admir'd,
For she was never satisfi'd or tir'd.   50
Full forty men a day have swiv'd the whore,
Yet like a bitch she wags her tail for more.
    Where are the bishops? Where's their bawdy court?
Instead of penance they indulge the sport.
The standing in white sheets and penitent stoles,   55
That's only fit for schoolmen and for fools.
Thy base example ruins the whole town,
For all keep whores, from gentleman to clown;
The issue of a wife's unlawful seed,
And none's legitimate but bastard breed.   60
Thou and thy brachs have quite cross'd the strain;
We ne'er shall see a true-bred whelp again.
An honest, lawful wife's turn'd out of doors,
And he most honor has that keeps most whores.
    Heav'ns, to what end is thy lewd life preserv'd?   65
Is there no God or laws to be observ'd?
Nineveh repented after forty days:
Be yet a king and wear the royal bays!
But Jonah's threats can never waken thee:
Repentance is too mean for majesty.   70
    Go practice Heliogabalus's sin:

39. *Stopping the Bank:* The stop of the Exchequer, 1672. See *Nostradamus' Proph-ecy,* 14 and n.

45. *Cleveland:* Barbara Palmer, Duchess of Cleveland. Cf. *Last Instructions,* 79ff.

71. *Heliogabalus* (218–222), a depraved Antonine emperor, played the role of Venus in theatrical performances in his palace. He often dressed as a woman and made a practice of bathing in the women's baths (see Aelius Lampridius, "Antoninus Elaga-balus," *The Scriptores Historiae Augustae,* London & New York, 1924, 2, 104–77).

Forget to be a man and learn to spin,
Go dally with the women and their wheels
Till Nero-like they drag thee out by the heels.
Go read what Mahomet did, that was a thing   75
Did well become the grandeur of a king,
Who, whilst transported with his mistress' charms,
And never pleas'd but in her lovely arms,
Yet when his janizaries wish'd her dead,
With his own hand cut off Irene's head.   80
Make such a practice of thyself as this,
Then shalt thou once more taste of happiness:
Each one will love thee, and the Parliament
Will their unkind and cruel votes repent,
And at thy feet lay open all their purses,   85
And give thee all their pray'rs not mix'd with curses.
All this I wish, who am not yet your friend,
Till like a child you promise to amend.
If not, you'll find your subjects rugged stuff,
But now I think on't, I have said enough.   90

A Proper New Ballad
(*1677*)

After Buckingham's visit with Rochester at Woodstock from about October 20th to the 5th of November, during which *A Familiar Epistle* and *Advice to Apollo* were written, he was invited as Lord High Steward of Oxford to a banquet tendered by the Mayor and Aldermen. On November 5th Thomas Dixon, a Fellow of Queen's, wrote Daniel Fleming as follows: "The Duke of Buckingham, who is Steward for the City of Oxford and has been at Woodstock with the Earl of Rochester and other nobles this fortnight, is expected at Oxford this week, where he is to be entertained by the city with banquets and speeches, which will afford matter both for the Duke and also our university wits, to descant upon" (*HMCR, Le Fleming,* p. 141). The banquet took place the next day, and, as Dixon had prophesied, some university wit "descanted" upon it in *A Proper New Ballad.* Buckingham seems to have assumed for the occasion that peculiar combination of canting godliness and *bonhomie* with which he endeared himself to staunch Nonconformist citizens, as Anthony Wood's account of the occasion suggests:

> The Duke of Bucks, Steward of the City of Oxon, was entertained with a dinner by the citizens of Oxford at Soladell Harding's in All Saints parish. There were with him several country gentlemen who ate up their victuals and in requital spoke liberally at dinner against the university. William Morrell, vintner, was Mayor, but being sick of the gout, Sir Sampson White did the office for him for that time. There is a ballad of his entertainment, which came to £200.
>
> (*Life and Times,* 2, 391, 6 Nov. 1677)

Whether Rochester was among the "country gentlemen" on this mirthful occasion is not known, but he would have been amused by Buckingham's technique as a politician. On this occasion the Duke was probably electioneering on behalf of Brome Whorwood, whom he recommends to the Corporation of Oxford for re-election to Parliament in a letter dated 25 Jan. 1678. The letter thanks the Mayor and Alderman for "the extraordinary marks I have lately received of your kindness" (quoted in Burghclere, *Buckingham,* p. 365). Whorwood, a violent Whig, continued to represent Oxford until 1681.

The citizens of Oxford mentioned in the poem are identified in the notes from *A Chronological Account of all that have Borne Office in the City of Oxford from . . . 1660 to the year 1720 . . . , by B. Cole,* a manuscript at Yale.

A Proper New Ballad appears only in the commonplace book of J. M. Osborn entitled *Wit and Learning.* Its tune is *Cuckolds all A-row,* which the Cavaliers had adopted in the Civil Wars to abuse the citizens of London in various loyal ballads (W. Chappell, *Popular Music of the Olden Time, 1,* 340–42).

A Proper New Ballad Concerning the Reception of His Grace the Duke of Buckingham by the Right Worshipful the Mayor and Aldermen of the City of Oxon. 1677.

To the Tune of "Cuckolds all A-row" or "Tom Tyler"

1.

Now listen, good friends, and I'll tell you how 'twas
That the townsmen of Oxford went to Woodstock race,
To wait on the Duke of Buckingham's Grace
   And invite him to come to the town-a,
   And invite him to come to the town-a.   5

2.

There went Mr. Mayor and Alderman Wright,
Mr. Paynton, the Town Clerk, and Sir Sampson White,
And a great many more fine sparks to invite

---

2. *Woodstock:* A small town eight miles north of Oxford. Rochester's birthplace and country seat, an ancient timber house in the Park of Ditchley was there. Rochester had been Ranger of Woodstock Forest since 1675 (Pinto, *Enthusiast in Wit,* p. 147).

7. *Sir Sampson White:* One of Oxford's five Aldermen in 1677. John *Paynton* was Town Clerk, 1663–84.

His kind Grace to come to the town-a,
His kind Grace to come to the town-a.   10

3.

Away they rode on through village and hamlet,
At as a good rate as their horses could amble at,
Some clad in good frieze, and others in camlet,
   To invite him to come to the town-a,
   To invite him to come to the town-a.   15

4.

And the spokesman of this fair company
It was Mr. Paynton of high degree,
Who made his oration most eloquently
   And invited his Grace to the town-a,
   And invited his Grace to the town-a.   20

5.

For he promised him junkets and all good cheer,
Good wine and good cider, good ale and good beer,
And for anything else he should need not to fear,
   If he would but come to the town-a,
   If he would but come to the town-a.   25

6.

Then out stood the Mayor himself in open view,
And shook him by the hand, as I may shake you,
And swore before George Mr. Paynton said true,
   If he would but come to the town-a,
   If he would but come to the town-a.   30

7.

The Duke never stay'd to consider humdrum,
But presently promis'd them that he would come,
Then he made 'em all drunk, and so sent them home,
   To carry the good news to the town-a,
   To carry the good news to the town-a.   35

The Second Part. To the Same Tune.

13. *camlet:* A kind of deep-piled cloth.
31. *humdrum:* Dull, monotonous talk.

8.

Now when as the Duke he appeared in sight
They all march'd out in their scarlet so bright,
And Carfax bells they did ring out right,
    For the Duke was come to the town-a,
    For the Duke was come to the town-a.   40

9.

Then the Town Clerk stood out in the midst of the street
And prepar'd his oration his Grace for to greet,
Which thus he began in words most sweet,
    For the Duke he was come to the town-a,
    For the Duke he was come to the town-a.   45

10.

Most illustrious Prince, may't please your Worship's Grace,
We are monstrously glad to see your fair face,
And because you were pleas'd to accept of the place
    Of Lord High Steward of the town-a,
    Of Lord High Steward of the town-a.   50

11.

Your Grace in his troubles serv'd his Majesty
With courage, faith, honor, and loyalty,
For which we'll drink your health most heartily,
    Before you go out of the town-a,
    Before you go out of the town-a.   55

12.

And further your Grace did desire lovingly
To set up a Gospel-preaching ministry,
The thing—ah—desir'd by all the godly,
    For your Grace is come to the town-a,
    For your Grace is come to the town-a.   60

38. *Carfax:* A thirteenth-century tower in Oxford.

56–57. An allusion, possibly, to Buckingham's occasional pretences of piety and to his associations with the Nonconformists.

13.

And now I should speak in the city's behalf,
But, faith, I think 'twill not at present be safe,
For I see that already the scholars do laugh,
    At my welcoming you to the town-a,
    At my welcoming you to the town-a.   65

14.

But when we are got together so close,
With each man his bottle of sack at his nose,
O then we may speak it under the rose
    That your Grace is welcome to the town-a,
    That your Grace is welcome to the town-a.   70

15.

And now we'll bring you to the house of Sol Hardin',
Where we have sent meat and drink, pies, puddings, and tarts
        in,
And as for the reck'ning, you shan't pay a farthin',
    Now your Grace is come to the town-a,
    Now your Grace is come to the town-a.   75

16.

For all princes, kings, dukes, and earls that come hither
(Which seldom they do indeed in such bad weather)
His worship the Mayor straight brings in thither,
    As soon as they come to the town-a,
    As soon as they come to the town-a.   80

17.

For Sol is as good a cook as e'er spit joint of meat,
And can make as good hash as your Grace ever eat,
If you please to accept of the poor townsmen's treat,
    Now that you are come to the town-a,
    Now that you are come to the town-a.   85

18.

And further we'll speak in the praise of poor Sol,
Though he never cut commons for college or hall,
Yet he verses shall cap with the best of them all,
    Now that you are come to the town-a,
    Now that you are come to the town-a.   90

19.

O how we rejoice, my Lord, to see this day,
We are ready to leap out of our skins for joy,
Yet when we'd express't we have nothing to say,
    But you are welcome to the town-a,
    But you are welcome to the town-a.   95

20.

We'll ram, damn, and ban, raunt, taunt, and tear,
We'll curse, swear, and stare, and still domineer
To be as like your Grace as any are here,
    If you will but stay in the town-a,
    If you will but stay in the town-a.   100

21.

We'll tope for our lives, and drink and be drunk,
We'll pimp for our wives, and drab with a punk,
We'll cog to the skies, and cheat by the lump,
    To pay for this charge of the town-a,
    To pay for this charge of the town-a.   105

22.

Assist us above the scholars to tease,
We'll worship your Grace the Devil to please,
We'll bawl at the clergy and rough it with ease,
    As sure and as long as you'll side with the town-a,
    As sure and as long as you'll side with the town-a.   110

87. *cut commons:* Carve meat.
96. *ban:* Curse.

23.

All night long we'll caper and revel and sing,
And the waits they shall play, and the bells they shall ring,
And so my Lord Steward, God save the King,
  And you are welcome unto the town-a,
  And you are welcome unto the town-a.   115

24.

The Town Clerk thus ended his loving speech,
And the Duke he thank'd him and scratch'd his breech,
For you would not think how it made it itch
  To be welcom'd thus to the town-a,
  To be welcom'd thus to the town-a.   120

25.

He entered the town then courteously,
And ate and drank with 'em till the clock struck three,
Then he thanked them all most heartily,
  And so he march'd out of the town-a,
  And so he march'd out of the town-a.   125

112. *waits:* A small body of wind instrumentalists maintained by a city or town at the public charge, *obs.*

On his Excellent Friend Mr. Andrew Marvell
(1678)

Marvell died suddenly of a tertian fever on 18 August 1678. According to a contemporary physician, "an ounce of Peruvian bark would have saved him, but instead of that he was given an opiate." The suddenness of his death gave rise to rumors of poisoning.

This tribute to Marvell as a patriot after the high Roman fashion is above all remarkable for being in blank verse. The *DNB* notes, without citing any evidence, that it has been attributed to Sheffield, Duke of Buckinghamshire. On the face of it this ascription is most implausible.

ON HIS EXCELLENT FRIEND MR. ANDREW MARVELL

While lazy prelates lean'd their miter'd heads
On downy pillows, lull'd with wealth and pride,
(Pretending prophecy, yet nought foresee),
Marvell, this island's watchful sentinel,
Stood in the gap and bravely kept his post.   5
When courtiers too in wine and riot slept,
'Twas he th' approach of Rome did first explore,
And the grim monster, arbitrary pow'r,
The ugliest giant ever trod the earth,
Who like Goliath march'd before the host.   10
Truth, wit, and eloquence, his constant friends,
With swift dispatch he to the main-guard sends.
Th' alarum straight their courage did excite,
Which check'd the haughty foes' bold enterprise
And left them halting between hope and fear.   15

7–8. These lines probably refer to Marvell's famous pamphlet, *An Account of the Growth of Popery and Arbitrary Government in England* (1678).
12. *main-guard:* The keeper of a castle.

436

Andrew Marvell. From a painting by an unknown artist.

He like the sacred Hebrew leader stood,
The people's surest guide and prophet too.
Athens may boast of virtuous Socrates,
The chief among the Greeks for moral good;
Rome of her orator, whose fam'd harangues   20
Foil'd the debauched Antony's designs;
We him, and with deep sorrows wail his loss.
But whether Fate or Art untwin'd his thread,
Remains in doubt; Fame's lasting register
Shall leave his name enroll'd as great as theirs   25
Who in Philippi for their country fell.

20–21. Cicero attacked Mark Antony in the senate for his gross excesses and after the establishment of the Triumvirate in 43 B.C. was proscribed and put to death on Antony's instigation.

26. At the Battle of Philippi (42 B.C.) Mark Antony and Octavius Caesar defeated Cassius and Brutus, the chief conspirators who murdered Julius Caesar.

Textual Notes

A NOTE ON THE TEXT

EDITORIAL PROCEDURE in this volume, and to some extent in those which follow, is influenced mainly by two considerations: the indeterminate authority of the texts and the extraordinarily large number of texts extant.

The first consideration derives chiefly from the anonymity and secrecy which surrounded every stage in the production and circulation of most of the poems in this volume. As the Introduction indicates, authors, scribes, and printers took pains to conceal their part in the production and distribution of satires and lampoons, which the government was trying to suppress by vigilance and severe measures. Most of these poems were issued anonymously or pseudonymously; the innumerable scribes who made copies of them are unknown; the proprietors of the unlicensed presses which printed some of them are in all but a few cases untraceable.

Ten or twenty years after their composition, when such poems could be legally published, they were thrown hastily into the press and ascribed, on little or no evidence, to authors whose names might lend prestige to the various volumes of *State Poems* and similar editions thus produced.

There are a few exceptions to this pattern among the poems in this volume, chiefly those pieces acceptable to the government, by Wild, Waller, and Dryden, whose publication was presumably superintended by the authors. One recently-discovered manuscript of Marvell (Bod. MS. Eng. poet. d. 49) was probably compiled from the author's papers and carries some authority, although its inclusion of works by another writer casts some doubt on its textual and canonical authenticity.

With such minor exceptions, however, the poems here published are represented in many manuscripts (on an average, seven or eight), very rarely in broadsheet, and, more frequently, in a late printed volume. None of the texts has any determinable authority, although there does seem to be an order of priority among the following groups:

(1) manuscripts of single poems or broadsheets and other early
editions of single poems.
(2) manuscript collections of poems.
(3) printed collections of poems.

There are exceptions to this order: broadsides published many years
after the known date of composition, and manuscript collections
based on printed collections. As a rule, nevertheless, the collation
of texts shows that manuscripts have far fewer demonstrable errors
than the post-1688 printed texts.

Faced with many versions of a poem, none of them having biblio-
graphical authority, the editor has adopted the following procedures:
(1) The separate manuscript copy, where it exists, has been pre-
ferred to the copy in a manuscript collection, unless the separate
manuscript copy has shown a preponderance of demonstrable errors
or markedly inferior readings. The broadsheet version has been
similarly preferred, unless it is demonstrably much later than the
date of composition. In general, manuscripts have been preferred
to printed collections. (2) The version having the fewest errors of
historical fact, the fewest inconsistencies in meaning, and the fewest
faults of style (especially in matters of meter and rhyme) has been
adopted as the copy text. (3) Demonstrably false and inconsistent
readings in the copy text have been emended, where possible, from
other texts and the emendations recorded. (4) The textual notes
record only verbal variants with meanings distinctly different from
the copy text, although the editor has tried to err on the side of in-
clusiveness in doubtful cases. Where no textual notes are given, no
such variants have been found, with the exception of *Mac Flecknoe*,
where they are readily available in several scholarly editions. (5) The
texts and material in footnotes have been modernized in capitaliza-
tion, spelling (except where rhyme, meter, or sense require retention
of the old orthography), italicization, and punctuation. There is no
virtue in trying to preserve the orthographic and punctuative vagaries
of various unknown scribes, printers, and editors. (6) Proper names,
conventionally indicated in seventeenth-century printed texts of the
poems by letters and dashes, have been supplied from the manu-
scripts. (7) Obscene words have been indicated by initial letters and
dashes, following the practice of the printed texts and manuscripts.

(8) Unless otherwise noted, definitions in the notes are taken from the *Oxford English Dictionary*.

The second consideration which has governed editorial procedure stems from the difficulty of making a complete collection of manuscripts. It has been necessary to proceed with the editing of the poems while manuscripts continued to pour in, because there was no way to determine how many versions of any poem might exist in the vast number of American and foreign collections. A great effort has been made to uncover all collections of such material, large and small, here and abroad, and, in the poems here edited, all known books and manuscripts have been consulted. It is in the nature of things, however, that in some cases superior texts remain undiscovered, and it is hoped that the publication of this volume will bring them to light.

SIGLA

Manuscripts

A. Taylor 1: Manuscript volume (no title) containing satires written between 1666 and 1689, in the collection of Robert Taylor.

B. Folger Shakespeare Library m. b. 12.

C. B.M. Harleian 7315.

D. Bodleian Don. b. 8.

E. Bodleian Eng. Poet. e. 4.

F. Phillips 7440 (Osborn collection, Yale University).

G. Phillips 8301   "   "   "   "

H. Phillips 8302   "   "   "   "

I. B.M. Harleian 6913.

J. Douce 357.

K. Harvard Eng. 585.

M. Harvard Eng. 624.

N. Harvard Eng. 636F.

O. Victoria and Albert Dyce 43.

P. National Library of Vienna 14090.

T. Bodleian Firth c. 15.

U. Bodleian Rawlinson Poet. 173.

W. B.M. Harleian 7316.

X. B.M. Harleian 7317.

Z. B.M. Harleian 7319.

A'. B.M. Additional 21094.

B'. B.M. Additional 34362.

D'. B.M. Additional 29497.

F'. B.M. Additional 23722.

G'. B.M. Egerton 2623.

I'. Ohio State University, Wentworth MS.: "A Choyce Collection of Poems, etc.," bookplate of Thomas Wentworth, Earl of Strafford.

J'. B.M. Sloane 655.

K'. B.M. Burney 390.

L'. All Souls College Codrington 116.

M'. All Souls College Codrington 174.

U'. National Library of Scotland Advocate 19.1.12.

V'. National Library of Scotland Advocate 19.3.4.

W'. Edinburgh University D.

A". Taylor 2: "A Collection of Choyce Poems, Lampoons, and Satyrs from 1673 to 1689, never extant in print," collection of Robert Taylor.

B". Chest II no. 13 (Osborn collection, Yale University).

C". B.M. Additional 18220.

D". Chest II no. 14 (Osborn collection, Yale University).

F''. Chest II no. 3 (Osborn collection, Yale University).

G''. Commonplace book containing poems by the Earl of Rochester *et al.*, Yale University.

I''. B.M. Harleian 7649.

L''. Taylor 3: "Political Poems 1660–1688," collection of Robert Taylor.

R''. Bodleian Eng. Poet. d. 49.

CC. Portland Miscellany: Manuscript miscellany of poems in the collection of the Duke of Portland at Nottingham University.

EE'. Harvard 623F.

Printed Texts

e. A/COLLECTION/OF/POEMS/ON/Affairs of State;/*Viz.*/[10 titles in 2 columns]/——/BY/*A*—— *M*——*L* Esq; and other Eminent Wits./——/ *Most whereof never before Printed.*/——/*LONDON,*/Printed in the Year, M DC LXXXIX.

Case 188(I)(a) 1689

f. A/COLLECTION/OF/POEMS/ON/Affairs of State;/ . . . In the list of titles Dryden's name is spelled normally. Otherwise the title follows that of the first edition.

Case 188(I)(b) 1689

g. THE SECOND PART/OF THE/COLLECTION/OF/POEMS/ON/Affairs of State,/*Viz.*/[21 titles in two columns divided by a single line of rule]/——/By *A*—— *M*——*L* and other eminent Wits./None whereof ever before Printed./——/LONDON, Printed in the Year, 1689.

Case 188(2) 1689

h. THE/THIRD PART/OF THE/COLLECTION/OF/POEMS/ON/Affairs of State./Containing,/Esquire *Marvel*'s further Instructions to/a Painter./ AND/The late Lord *Rochester*'s Farewel./——/LONDON:/Printed in the Year M DC LXXXIX.

Case 188(3) 1689

j. A SECOND/COLLECTION/OF/The Newest and Most Ingenious/POEMS, SATYRS, SONGS, &c./AGAINST/Popery and Tyranny,/Relating to the TIMES./——/Most of which never before Printed./——/[ornament]/——/ LONDON, Printed in the Year M DC LXXXIX.

Case 189(2) 1689

k. A THIRD/COLLECTION/OF/The Newest and Most Ingenious/POEMS, SATYRS, SONGS, &c./AGAINST/Popery and Tyranny,/Relating to the TIMES./——/Most of which never before Printed./——/[group of ornaments]/——/LONDON, Printed in the Year M DC LXXXIX.

Case 189(3) 1689

l. The/Fourth (and Last)/COLLECTION/OF/POEMS, SATYRS, SONGS, &c./CONTAINING,/[11 titles in a single column]/——/Most of which never before Printed./——/LONDON, Printed *Anno Dom.* 1689.

Case 189(4) 1689

m. POEMS/ON/AFFAIRS OF STATE:/FROM/The Time of *Oliver Crom-well, to the/Abdication of K. James* the Second./*Written by the greatest Wits of the Age.*/VIZ./Duke of *Buckingham,*/Earl of *Rochester,*/Lord *Bu*——*st,*/Sir *John Denham,*/*Andrew Marvell,* Esq;/Mr. *Milton,*/Mr. *Dryden,*/Mr. *Sprat,*/Mr. *Waller.*/Mr. *Ayloffe,* &c./——/With some Miscellany Poems by the same:/Most whereof never before Printed./——/*Now carefully examined with the Originals, and/Published without any Castratration.*/——/Printed in the Year 1697.

Case 211(I)(a) 1697

o. POEMS/ON/AFFAIRS OF STATE:/ . . . The title follows that of the first edition.

Case 211(I)(c) 1697

p. POEMS/ON/AFFAIRS OF STATE:/FROM/The Time of *Oliver Crom-well, to the/Abdication of K. James* the Second./*Written by the greatest Wits of the Age.*/VIZ./Duke of *Buckingham,*/Earl of *Rochester,*/Lord *Bu*——*st,*/Sir *John Denham,*/*Andrew Marvell,* Esq;/Mr. *Milton*/Mr. *Dryden,*/Mr. *Sprat,*/Mr. *Waller,*/Mr. *Ayloffe,* &c./——/With some Miscellany Poems by the same:/Most whereof never before Printed./——/*Now carefully examined with the Originals, and/Published without any Castratration.*/——/THE THIRD EDITION, CORRECTED AND MUCH ENLARGED./——/Printed in the Year 1699.

Case 211(I)(d) 1699

q. POEMS/ON/AFFAIRS OF STATE:/ . . . /Lord *Bu*——*st,*/ . . . /THE FOURTH EDITION, CORRECTED AND MUCH ENLARGED./——/ Printed in the Year, 1702.

Case 211(I)(e) 1702

r. POEMS/ON/AFFAIRS OF STATE:/ . . . /Lord *Bu*——*st,*/ . . . /THE FIFTH EDITION, CORRECTED AND MUCH ENLARGED./——/ Printed in the Year 1703.

Case 211 (I)(f) 1703

u. POEMS/ON/AFFAIRS OF STATE,/FROM/The Reign of K. *James* the First,/To this Present Year 1703./Written by the Greatest Wits of the Age,/*VIZ.*/The Duke of *Bucking-/ham.*/The Earl of *Rochester.*/The Earl of *D*——*t.*/Lord *J*——*s.*/Mr. *Milton.*/Mr. *Marvel.*/Mr. *St. J*——*n.*/Mr. *John Dryden.*/Dr. *G*——*th.*/Mr. *Toland.*/Mr. *Hughes.*/Mr. *F*——*e.*/Mr. *Finch.*/M. *Harcourt.*/Mr. *T*——*n,* &c./——/*Many of which never before Publish'd.*/——/VOL. II./——/Printed in the Year 1703.

Case 211(2)(a) 1703

x. POEMS/ON/AFFAIRS OF STATE,/From 1640. to this present/Year 1704./*Written by the greatest Wits of the Age,*/VIZ./The late Duke of/*Buckingham,*/Duke of *D*——*re,*/Late E. of *Rochester,*/Earl of *D*——*t,*/Lord *J*——*rys,*/Ld *Hal*——*x,*/*Andrew Marvel,* Esq;/Col. *M*——*d*——*t,*/Mr. *St. J*——*ns,*/Mr. *Hambden,*/Sir *Fleet Shepherd,*/Mr. *Dryden,*/Mr. *St*——*y,*/Mr.

Pr——r,/Dr. *G——th, &c.*/——/*Most of which were never before publish'd.*/ ——/VOL. III./——/Printed in the Year 1704.

Case 211(3)(a) 1704

b'. POEMS/ON/Affairs of STATE:/FROM/OLIVER CROMWELL,/To this present time. Written by the/greatest Wits of the Age, *Viz.*/Lord *Rochester,*/ Lord *D——t,*/Lord *C——ts,*/Duke of *Buckingham,*/Dr. *K.*/Dr. *Wild,*/Sir *Charles S——dly,*/Sir *Fleetwood S——d,*/Mr. *Dryden,*/Mr. *Prior,*/Charles Blount, Esq;*/Mr. *Wicherly,*/Mr. *Shadwell,*/Mr. *Tho Brown,*/Capt Ayloffe.*/ Mr. *H——bt,*/——/PART III./——/With other Miscellany POEMS;/And a new Session of the present/POETS. The whole never before/Printed./ ——/Printed in the Year, 1698.

Case 215 1698

c'. A New/COLLECTION/OF/POEMS/Relating to/STATE AFFAIRS,/ FROM/OLIVER CROMWELL/To this present Time:/By the Greatest/ Wits of the Age:/Wherein, not only those that are Contain'd in/the Three Volumes already Published are/incerted, but also large Additions of chiefest/Note, never before Published./The whole from their respective Originals,/without Castration./= =/LONDON,/Printed in the Year, M DCC V.

Case 237 1705

d'. THE/*Miscellaneous WORKS*/Of His Grace/*GEORGE,* Late Duke of *Buckingham.*/——/In Two Volumes./ . . . /*LONDON*/ . . . 1707.

Case 232(I)(b) 1707

e'. THE/WORKS/of His Grace,/George Villiers,/Late Duke of Buckingham./ In Two Volumes./ . . . /The Third Edition . . . /LONDON . . . 1715.

r'. Rochester's *Poems on Several Occasions,* ed. James Thorpe. Princeton, New Jersey: Princeton University Press, 1950.

u'. Robert Wild, *Iter Boreale,* 1671.

Wing 2138

a''. THE/Second Advice/*TO A*/PAINTER,/For Drawing the/HISTORY/Of our/*NAVALL* Business;/*In Imitation of Mr.* WALLER./——/Being the last Work of Sir John DENHAM./——/Printed in the Year, 1667.

B.M. 11623.r.57

1

b''. THE/Second, and Third Advice/*TO A*/PAINTER,/For Drawing the HISTORY/Of our/*NAVALL* Actions,/The two last years, 1665. And 1666./*In Answer to Mr.* WALLER./——/——*Pictoribus atque Poetis,*/ Quidlibet Audendi semper fuit potestas./Humano Capiti cervicem pictor equinam,/Jungere si velit——/Horat. de Arte Poet./——/A. Breda, 1667.

Wing 2258

B.M. 11623.r.57

2

c''. DIRECTIONS/TO A/PAINTER,/FOR/Describing our Naval Business:/
In Imitation of Mr. *WALLER./BEING/*The Last Works/OF/Sir IOHN
DENHAM./——/Whereunto is annexed,/*CLARINDONS* *H*ouse-Warm-
ing./By an Unknown AUTHOR./——/Printed in the Year 1667.

Huntington Library #122032

d''. The same with manuscript annotations.

Bodleian Gough. London. 14.

p''. THE/WORKS/OF/*JOHN SHEFFIELD,*/EARL OF MULGRAVE,/MAR-
QUIS OF NORMANBY,/AND/DUKE OF BUCKINGHAM./ . . . /LON-
DON/ . . . 1723.

Iter Boreale 4–19

Copy text: Iter Boreale . . . London . . . 1660.

Collation: Iter Boreale. With other Select Poems: being an Exact Collection of all hitherto Extant . . . London . . . 1671.

54. *so heal*] to heal *1671.* 75. *followers*] fellowers *1671.* 156. *shriek'd*] shriek *1671.* 165. *these*] those *1671.* 182. *this rest*] his rest *1671.* 188. *exorcise*] exercise *1671.*

The Second Advice to a Painter 36–53

Copy text: R″.

Collation: A, C, D, E, M, F′, M′, F″, R″, a″, b″, c″.

Title: The Second Advice to a Painter/ 1665 *F′. Directions to a Painter.* By Sir John Denham *c″.* The Second Advice to a Painter for Drawing the History of our Naval Business in Imitation of Mr. Waller. [Supposed to be Written by Sir J. Denham. *C, A.*] Being the Last Work of Sir John Denham *D* [Printed in the Year 1667 *a″*]. The Second Advice to a Painter for Drawing the History of our Naval Business [In the two last years 1665 and 1666. *F″*] in Answer to Mr. Waller *b″.* The Second Advice to a Painter for drawing the History of our Naval Fight in Imitation of Mr. Waller. 1665 June *M′.*

2. *Waller only*] only Waller *E.* 4. What made the actors tremble when they saw *F′.* 7–8. First in fit distance of the prospect feign/ Brave Allin tilting at the coast of Spain *E. main*] vain *R″.* 8. *tilting at the coast*] tilling all the coasts *D. coast*] Court *C.* 11–12. *Omitted F′.* 21. So] See *a″*; For *b″.* 22. *prove*] are *R″.* 23. *feign'd*] gain'd *F′, E.* 27–28. *Omitted all except A, C, F′.* 30. Use nothing but ultramarinish blue *R″.* 31–32. To pay his fees the silver trumpet spends,/And boatswain's whistle for his place depends *all except E, a″.* 32. And without swains whistles for his place depends *a″.* 37–38. Muscovy sells us hemp and Denmark tar,/Pitch, cordage; Sweden, copper; Münster, war *E, F′.* 39–40. Ashley, prize; {Gawden victuals / Warwick customs} Carteret/Sells pay, but Coventry does sell the fleet *R″.* 45. Then win respect to foggy Opdam's gout *E.* 49. *they*] he *F′.* 55. *tail*] trail *c″.* 60. *caracole*] carry coal *all except E, F′, R″.* 61–62. *Omitted E, F′.* 65. *properties*] proper toys *E*; fopperies *errata c″.* 71. Ne'er did Mark Antony in Pharos Isle *E, F′.* 75. Now, Painter, let thy cunning all appear *E, F′.* 76. *parting*] panting *a″.* 77. For alas she hath but a short delight *a″, b″.* 81. To Penn much, Brouncker more, most Coventry *c″.* 82. For they she knew were more afraid than she [he *A, C*] *D, M, F′, M′, a″, b″*; For they she knew were all more 'fraid than he *F″, c″.* 83–88. *Omitted F′.* 88. *men*] him *M, a″, b″, c″*; omitted *M′.* 91–100. *Omitted F′.* 97. *twinging*] homingen *C.* 99. *trait'ress*] cursed *M, a″, b″.* 104. *pirates*] puppets *M, a″, b″.*

107–08. *Omitted D, F', M', a", c".*   115. *very*] ev'ry *R".*   118. *rupture*]
tympany *E, F'.*   119. *bears*] devours *M, F", a", b".*   120. *tuns*] tons *D.*
121–26. *Omitted F'.*   125. Both which presaging, yet keep still in sight *M,*
a", b". gorge] George *M'.*   125–26. *Omitted D.*   129. *At*] Of *E.*   130.
squeasy] easy *M', R", c";* queasy *A, C, D.*   133. *While*] Which *E.*   139.
wall] jail *E;* hall *A, C, M, a", b".*   141. *be*] *Omitted R".*   143. *cannon*]
powder *E.*   144. *brimstone*] sulphur *E, F'.*   155. *wrath dispute*] reach dis-
pute *c";* reach debute *R".*   157–72. *Omitted F'.*   175–76. *Omitted F'.*
178. And still fights Opdam in the shades below *all except c", R".*   182. *con-*
tact] contract *all except D, M, F', M".*   183. *An untaught*] When a rude *E,*
F'.   187. *fearless*] peerless *all except A, E, M, F", c". distains*] disdains *A,*
M', F", a"; bestains *M, b".*   189. *Berkeley*] Bartlet *c".*   190. *royal Har-*
ding's] royal Hasting's *M.*   191–94. *Omitted E, F'.*   197. The Dutch
Auranea careless at us sail'd *R". Urania*] Auranea *all except F', M'.*   201–02.
Omitted E, F'.   205. *be on*] but one *D.*   209–10. *Omitted E, F'.*   217–
24. *Omitted F'.*   228. Mins, Tiddenham, and Sansom bravely fell *F'. Sam-*
sun] Lawson *A, C, D, a".*   233–34. *Omitted F'.*   241–42. *Omitted E, F'.*
242. *wheel*] reel *all except D, M, a", b", c".*   247–50. *Omitted F'.*   248. *its*]
and *A, a", b";* it *all others.*   253–54. To Bergen we with confidence made
haste/ And th' secret spoils by hope already taste *c".*   255. *Though*] Tom *E, F'.*
265. *Omitted M';* With far more state and sureness curtains drew *A, C. Cuttance*
true] cutting true *F';* curtains drew *D, M, F", a", b".*   275. *His*] Our *E.*
278. *nought*] ought *F'.*   279–82. *Omitted E.*   286. Aboard the Admiral was
reach'd and di'd *M, b". reach'd*] shot *A, C.*   287–310. *Omitted F'.*   288.
our] his *c".*   295–310. *Follow 368 F'.*   306. *officers*] officer *E.*   314. *Slips*
to the] Ships into *M, M', F', c";* Shifts to *a";* Slips into *A, C, F", b";* Slips to
D; Steps into *E.*   317–40. *Omitted F'. Follow 368 A, C, D, a".*   320. *bains*]
banns *D, E, c";* banes *A, C, M, a";* bands *M'.*   330. *regenerate*] degenerate
M'.   348. *in*] by *E, M', F", R".*   355. *art*] a *D, E, M, F", R", a", b".*
357. *Or if our sun*] O may our sun *c";* Art thou our sun *M'.*   368. *cards*]
cares *M, a", b".*

Divination   55–66

Copy text: E.

Collation: E, I".

Title: Divination/ with Lilly the Astrologer/ who/ should be Author of a Sec-
ond Advice to a Painter *I".* Divination. In answer to the Advice *E.*

23. *Or earth*] On earth *I".*   26. *He*] It *I".*   29. *guilt (I")*] grief *E.*   32.
put] breed *I".*   33. *crown*] stuff'd *I".*   38. *a popular*] the popular *I".*
39. *whip*] nip *E.*   45. *of*] if *I".*   47. Produce me the subscriber, sign'd by
us *I".*   48. *or*] but *I".*   61. *brains*] brain *I".*   62. *but's loyalty*] but loy-
alty *I".*   66. *runs*] flows *I". true*] truce *E. Hill*] Rill *E.*   80. That in a true;
this a more glittering ray *I".*   84. *Bristol*] Bristow *I".*   94. *or*] nor *I".*
95–104. *Omitted in I" and two lines inserted after l.* 94: Bays down unhappy

Sandwich: sets a snarl/ Upon Prince Rupert and Duke Albemarle.   100. *ease*]
cease *E*.   111. *revile*] to revile *I″*.   116. *fetch*] steal *I″*.   135. *your title*]
the title *I″*.   141. *like*] as *I″*.   146. *though still*] though shell *E*.   151.
don't] now *I″*.   152. *which*] that *I″*.   157. *Him*] He *I″*.   169. *Though't's*
fit] Though fit *I″*.   170. *her late*] this late *I″*.   187. *break thy*] and thy *E*.
191. Whatever faithful subjects seek to hide *I″*.   204. *rebuilt*] be built *E*.
217. *realms*] lands *I″*.   224. *a native Hollander*] the native Hollanders *I″*.
230. *unplant*] displant *I″*.   232. *till he*] till they *I″*.   243. *force*] war *I″*.
245. *near*] ne'er *I″*.   249. *discovering*] discerning *I″*.   250. Imperial Sov-
ereign of the seas and isles *I″*.   259. *pasteboard*] painted *I″*.   263–68. *Omit-*
ted I″.   269. *thou seem'st*] she seems *I″*.   270. *thy*] her *I″*.   271. *he . . .*
himself]   they . . . themselves *E*.   272. *Himself . . . himself*] Themselves
. . . themselves *E*.   284. *block up*] hedge up *I″*.

The Third Advice to a Painter   68–87

Copy text: R″.

Collation: C, E, M, F′, M′, F″, R″, k, b″, c″.

Title: The Third Advice to a Painter on our Last Summer's Success with
[against *F′*] French and Dutch. 1666 *F″*. The Third Advice to a Painter *C*. The
Third Advice to a Painter on our Last Summer's Success with French and Dutch.
1666. Written by the same hand as the former was *b″*. Directions to a Painter.
By Sir John Denham *c″, k*.

6. *marshall'd shells*] muscle-shells *c″, k, M′*.   10. *how we do yet less*] what we
do in less *all others*.   25. *airy*] earthy *F″, F′, b″*.   28. *Toulon*] Taloon *c″,*
k.   56. *whirling*] flaming *E, F″, F′, b″*.   64. *consort*] courage *F′*.   68.
deaf] dead *all except R″, F″, F′, b″, M*. *Fate*] state *c″, k, M*.   72. *skill is*]
conduct's *F″, F′*.   76. *Bricol'd*] Brusled *F″, F′, b″*; Bricolles *M′*; Recoil'd *all*
others.   80. *foible*] feeble *all others*. *Achilles' heel*] Chittereale *b″*.   93.
soon] since *all except C, F′, b″, M′*.   101. *losing rooks*] cheated rooks *E*;
parents mock'd *c″, k*.   105. *our scorn*] th' story *c″, k*.   110. *Berkeley*]
Bartlet *c″, k*.   111. Though others that surviv'd the corps and neer *b″, M*.
112. *petrifi'd*] putrifi'd *F″, C, b″, M*.   132. *137–38 follow E, c″, k*.   138. *jaw*]
maw *all except c″, k, M′*.   141. *late*] safe *F″, F′*.   150. *second*] other
F″, F′.   177. *much*] most *R″*.   178. *porter*] coachman *E, c″, k, M*.   180.
With *Honi soit qui mal* she bravely wrought *b″, M*.   181. *the Gen'ral's*] she-
Gen'ral's *R″*.   192. *snuffling*] snuffing *R″*.   196. *spirit*] fiendly *E, c″*;
friendly *k*.   199. *she-Albemarle*] the Albemarle *c″, k*.   212. *snap*] fall *all*
except M′, R″.   232. *the same measures*] the small manners *c″, k*.   240.
to content] for contents *F″, C, F′, M′*; for consents *R″*.   245. *ere*] and *all ex-*
cept F″, C, M′, R″.   253–54. *Omitted b″*.   266. *spill*] fill *all except b″,*
M, M′, F′.   267. Yet after four days' fight they clearly saw *all except b″,*
M, M′.   278. *magnifies*] multiplies *M′*.   284. *his own*] the Court *M*.
300. *chink*] thinks *F″, b″, M*. *start*] impart *E, F′, c″, k*.   319–20. *Omitted b″,*
M.   330. *from.*] omitted *R″*.   369–70. *Order reversed E, c″, k*.   370. *cut*]

cuff *F″*; hem *E*, *c″*, *k*.   386. *Gold*] hot *F″*, *F′*; cold *C*; omitted *b″*, *M*.   392. *we*] he *E*, *F′*, *F″*, *C*.   403. *Virginian*] New England *E*, *F′*, *k*.   407. *light*] tight *R″*.   408. *huff*] stuff *M′*.   417. *against*] among *E*, *F″*.   421–22. Omitted *c″*, *k*.   426. *lies*] dies *R″*.   439. *couns'llors*] councels *c″*, *k*.   450. *gales*] calms *all others*.   452. *needle's*] vocal *F″*, *F′*.   456. *she painted*] the painter *c″*, *k*. *After 456 M′ notes:* 8bre: ye 1st 1666.

Clarendon's Housewarming   88–96

Copy text: R″

Collation: A, C, J, O, P, F′, R″, d″.

Title: The Housewarming to the Chancellor *A, C*. A Housewarming to Chancellor Hyde *O, P*.

4. *season*] reason *J*.   7. *brume*] spume *J*.   9. *buy*] build *J*.   21. *fitter*] after *all except F′*.   23. *That she begg'd*] That she had *J, P*. *She*] he *d″*.   24. *an Hyde*] a Hyde *A*.   33. *cattle*] chattel *all except J, F′*.   37. And henceforth like Pharaoh he Israel oppress'd *all except F′*.   38. *make*] omitted *al except J, F′, d″*.   38. *infest*] distress'd *d″*.   43. *mold*] mole *all texts*. 45. *easier*] easiest *all except F′*.   47. *friends*] friend *R″*.   48. To grudge him for timber who fram'd him the war *R″*.   49. *m.n.* Allen Broderick, Allen Apsley *A, C, O*.   50. The two Allens when join'd ply him with gallons *F′*. 51. The two Allens that save his injustice with balance *A, C, O, P*.   58. *cheap*] cheaper *R″*.   61. *then*] they *A, C, P*. *advice*] device *F′*. *assay'd*] essay'd *A*.   66. *Summ'ners*] Sinners *J, d″, R″*.   68. *dairies club*] clubs dairy *R″*.   69. *Bellings*] Beakns *d″*; Beekings *J*.   70. *Were*] Where *R″*. *Clutterbuck's, Agar's, and Kipps'*] Clutterbuck, Eagers & Kipps *d″*; Clutterbuggs Eyes and Lipps *A, C*; Clutterbucks Eyes and Lipps *O, P*. *Agar's*] Ayers *J*. *Kipps'*] Pepys *F′*.   76. Not tho' the whole Parliament would kiss him behind *all except J*; No, not though the Parliament should kiss him behind *J*. *No*] Not *R″*. 79. *the leads*] his head *J*.   83. *sat*] was late *A, C, O, P*.   84. *Chancellor's*] Chancellor *R″*.   88. *excellent*] famous *J*.   91. And shows 'em the top by a regal [royal *J*] gold ball *all except F′*.   95. *metropolis*] metropolitan *J*. 96. And till there you remove it shall never want burning *all except F′*.   98. *this*] our *A*.   101. *buildings*] builders *R″*.   103. *its*] his *R″*.   104. *expatiation*] expectation *A, C, O, P*.   108. At Tybourn arrive and save the Tower barge *A, C, O, P*.   111. When like the whole ox with public good cheer *A, C, O, P*.

The Last Instructions to a Painter   99–139

Copy text: R″

Collation: R″, Osborn MS., h, m.

Title: September 1667 *MS*. The Last Instructions to a Painter, about the Dutch Wars 1667. By A. Marvell, Esq. *m*.

4. *It*] If't *MS., m.*   11. *Sketching*] Stretching *MS.*   15. *out*] up *MS.*   19.
guiltless] guilty *MS.*   29. *soup*] sauce *MS.*   32. *pleasure*] pleasure's *m.*
34. *chine*] chin *m.*   38. *treat*] cheat *m.*   42. *were*] wear *R".*   53. *assay'd*]
essay'd *m.*   60. To make her classen D——s once malleable *h;* To make her
glassen Duke but malleable *MS.*; To make her glassen Duke once malleable *m.*
75. *revolves*] resolves *MS.*   88. *looks*] locks *m.*   104. *Campaspe*] blank *MS.*
105. *tables*] tablets *m.*   109. *trick-track*] tick-tack *MS., m.*   123. *So*] Sad
MS.   136. And on all trades, like as a war, she feeds *MS.*   146. *Bugger'd*]
Proceeds *MS.*   181. *coif*] wife *MS., m.*   182. *Mitre*] mitred *m.*   187, *rab-*
ble] rubble *h.*   192. *still to*] to do *m.*   203. *Cart'ret*] Cartwright *MS.*
209. *drinkers*] drunkards *m.*   221. *were*] was *MS., m.*   222. *sea-cod*] sea-
god *MS.*   249. *strid*] stood *MS., m.*   261. *Williams*] William *MS.*   265.
How'rd on's birth, wit, strength, courage much presumes *R".*   271. *theirs*]
there's *MS., h.*   286. *th' unknown*] the known *MS.*   290. *think*] thing *MS.,*
m.   292. *counsel*] council *m.*   309. *Where force had*] Wheresoe'er that *MS.*
321. *ropes untwine*] rope untwines *h.*   338. *bitter*] magic *all others.*   357.
'gainst] to *h, R".*   364. *else*] then *MS., m.*   383. *just*] first *MS.*   388.
crimes] broils *MS.;* brawls *m.*   417. *well*] men *MS., m.*   422. *But*] That *R".*
424. *so*] to *h, m.*   434. *'twere*] were *MS.*   451. *instructs*] intrusts *MS., m.*
461. *order'd*] order *h, R".*   463–64. *Omitted R".*   467. *laughter's*] laugh-
terous *MS.*   475. But still this hope him solac'd ere they come *MS.*   485.
lov'd] thought *MS.*   494. *banquiers*] banquers *MS.;* bankers *m.*   497. *cir-*
cling] sucking *m.*   500. *that's*] cheats *m.*   513. *If*] Do *m.*   522. *would*]
of *MS., m.*   536. *complacence*] complaisance *h.*   556. *calm*] cold *MS.*
559. *Such*] So *MS., m.*   566. *bullets*] bullet *R".*   603. *on*] or *MS.*   607.
ill-defended] ill-deserted *h, m.*   624. After the robber of her whelps does yell
MS.   649–96. *Omitted m.*   655. *as*] has *all others.*   717. *Furs*] Fir *m;*
Firres *MS.*   753. *moan*] mourn *m.*   764. *her*] here *h.*   771. Who'd not
pursue when the Dutch fleet was beat? *MS.*   780. *unrepaired*] unprepared *m.*
802. He's ablest speaker who of law has least *MS.*   803. *less*] least *MS.*
804. And he for counsellor who hath least wit *MS.* *couns'llor*] chanc'lor *m.*
809. *council*] counsel *h.*   817. *De Ruyter*] Ruyter *h, R".*   823. *job*] go *MS.*
833. With sun and choler all come up adust *MS.*   876. *in in*] in to *MS., m.*
888. *dark*] dart *m.*   897. *anguish*] anger *MS.*   903. *her touch*] her hand
MS.; a touch *m.*   904. *airy*] angry *MS.*   907. *startling*] startled *MS.*   909.
door] ear *MS.*   911. *fled*] led *h.*   912. *he lies*] he's laid *MS.*   921.
ghastly] ghostly *MS., m.*   930. *enclose*] disclose *MS.* *depths*] depth *MS.*
938. *will*] would *MS.*   943. *well*] will *h.*   950. *to*] in *m.*   951. *prease*]
please *R", h;* press *m.*   977. *earthquakes*] earthquake *R".*   980. *hoard*]
hide *MS.*   982. *ras'd*] rac'd *m.*   984. *Nor guilt to flattery bind*] Whom
neither flatt'ry binds *h.*   985. *gen'rous*] omitted *h.*   986. With counsels
their large souls supply *h.*   988. *stare*] share *MS.*

At end of text: By A.M. *m.*

Fourth Advice to a Painter   141–146

Copy text: E.

Collation: F″, E, C, M, A, D, F′, U′, c″, G, k.

Title: The Fourth Advice to a Painter for carrying on his piece from London's conflagration to the burning of our Ships at Chatham by the Dutch Anno Domini 1667 *F″.* The Fourth Advice or New Instructions to a Painter *C.* Another Advice to the Painter *D.* The Fourth Advice 1668 *F′.* Directions to a Painter. By Sir John Denham *c″.*

1. *giv'n*] done *C.*   3. *wiser*] wise *M, F′. treasure*] treasury *C, A.*   9. *once destin'd*] design'd once *E.*   18. *rulers*] masters *all except c″, k.*   21. *the same*] such a *F″.*   22. *not*] omitted *F″.*   43. Or though the anger, hate, or folly rather *C.*   53. *confess'd*] thought best *C, A;* profess'd *F′.*   64. *base*] late *C. submission*] commission *C.*   65. *These*] Thus *E. state*] coast *F″.*   68. *politicians here*] politicians' lives *F′.*   73. I leave, then Painter let thy art describe a story *F″.*   74. *Shaming*] Staining *G.*   90. *from the*] boist'rous *G.* 93. *break*] force *G.*   94. *unmann'd*] remain'd *F″.*   108. *honor*] tenor *F″.* 114. *Useless*] Unless *C, F′.*   117. *reigns*] designs *F′.*   119. Surprising Chatham makes Whitehall appear *F″, F′.*   121–22. Make that defense if that thou canst seem more/ Than pride and sloth and ignorance there before *F″.*   125–28. *Follow 136 F′.*   127. *Henry's*] Harry's *c″.*   127–28. *Follow 136 F″, D.* 129–36. *Omitted C, M, A.*   129–32. *Follow 142 c″, k.*   130. Rome as it burnt, and as it burnt he play'd *F″.*   133–36. *Omitted c″, k.*   136. His fucking [swiving *F′*] then prov'd [proves *D*] useless as his chain *F″.*   140. *fear*] heat *F″, C.*   141. *here*] not *E, c″.*   142. That sure's as ill to them as the disease *F″.*

At end of text: Marvel 1667 *U′.*

Fifth Advice to a Painter   146–152

Copy text: E.

Collation: M, F′, c″, U′, k, E.

Title: Directions to a Painter. By Sir John Denham *c″.*

3. *you*] all *k.*   15. *now*] new *F′.*   29. *their*] her *F′.*   33–156. *Omitted F′.* 56. *m.n.* Sprage *M.*   60. *Romewards*] homewards *M, c″, k.*   61. *parlier*] parley *E.*   76. *foe*] toe *k. Lines after 142 missing from E.   143–56 added from M.*   155. *imbellis*] imbelli *M;* imbelliae *c″.*

The Downfall of the Chancellor   158

Copy text: C.

Collation: C, D, B', F", A, F', K', O, B", o.

F', K' begin with:

> Pacto uno, binis thalamis, belloque triformi,
> lege empta, Gallis repetundis, fraude telonio,
> Principis edicto, populi prece, voce senatus,
> regnum prodidit, aedes condidit, exuit ostrum.

2. *broker . . . ruin*] ruin . . . breaker *F"*.   3. *divider*] deluder *B'*.   6. *His*] By's *D*; And's *B"*. *to the heir*] now himself *F"*. *is tumbl'd*] himself pull'd *C, A, O*.   7. *affronter*] despiser *B', F', K', B"*; imposter *o*.   9. *and*] omitted *C, D, B', F", A, O, B"*. *abus'd*] omitted *F', K'*.   10. *expect*] believe *D, B', F", F', K'*.   11–12. *Omitted F"*.   13–26. *Omitted O*.   15. *to*] do *D, B', F", F', B"*.   18. *Rump*] Trump *C*.   19. *wither'd*] injur'd *F"*.   24. Three millions will be found to make him chief *F", F', K'*. *for their relief*] to make him chief *B', B"*.   25–26. *B', F', K', o omit and substitute the following:*

> Of sacrilege, ambition, lust and pride,
> All comprehended in the name of Hyde
> For which his due reward I'd almost said
> The nation may most justly claim his head.

The King's Vows   159–162

Copy text: B'.

Collation: B', P, B, D", F", B", R", A', D', C", O, r.

Title: Royal Resolutions *P, B, A', O*, By A. Marvell, Esq. *r*. A Lampoon writ by the Lord Buckhurst: 1667 *D"*. A Prophetic Lampoon made Anno 1659 by the Duke of Buckingham relating to what would happen under King Charles the Second *D'*. A Libelous Poem *C"*. The Vows *R"*.

1. *low*] an *P, B, F", A', D', C", O, R", r*.   2. *our stomach*] bowels *P, B, F", A', O, r*.   3. *Our pockets*] And stomach *P, B, F", A', D', O, r;* Our stomach *R"*.   5. *Made these vows*] Did swear *P, B, A', O, r*.   6. *I see*] he saw *R"*.   10. *fine*] long *P, B, A', O, r*.   15. *displease me*] refuse *F"*.   25. *making*] marrying *P, B, A', O, r*.   27. And shall be successor to me or Gerrard *P, B, A', O, r*.   34–35. I'll have a council that sit always still/And give me a licence to do what I will *P, B, A', O*.   35. *what I will*] what they will *D'*.   37. *fine*] French *P, B, A', O*.   *After 37 B, A', O, r insert:*

> My insolent brother shall bear all the sway.
> If Parliaments murmur I'll send him away,
> And call him again as soon as I may.

40–42. *Omitted R″, C″.*   44. My bawds shall ambassadors be far and near
P, B, A′, O; My bawds call ambassadors far and near *r.*   53. Where many
strange fowl shall feed and enjoy *P, B, A′, O, r;* Where the drake shall the duck
with freedom enjoy *D″.*   54. *O adds the following:*

17.

The ancient nobility I will lay by,
And new ones create their rooms to supply,
And they shall raise fortunes for my own fry.

18.

Someone I'll advance from a common descent
So high he shall hector the Parliament
And all wholesome laws for the public prevent.

19.

And I will assert him to such a degree
That all his foul treasons, though daring and high,
Under my hand and seal shall have indemnity.

20.

I'll wholly abandon all public affairs
And pass all my time with buffoons and play'rs,
And saunter to Nelly when I should be at pray'rs.

Substantially the same additions occur in B, P, B′.

At end of text: Anonnymous. Communicat fr. T. W. May 20: 1670 *C″.*

Further Advice to a Painter   164–167

Copy text: J.

Collation: D, J, F′, L′, U′, B″, F″, m.

Title: A New Advice to the Painter 1674 *F′.* On the Council that Sat at Arling-
ton's House for the Cutting off of Coventry's nose *L′.* A New Advice to the
Painter 1670 *D, F′.* Further Instructions to a Painter. By A. Marvell, Esq. 1670
m. 5th Advice to a Painter *F″.* On the Parliament *B″.*

3. *holy]* pious *F′.*   4. *weeping]* mourning *F′.*   7. *work of state]* works of
fate *L′.*   10. *pathic]* punk *F″.*   13–16. Omitted *U′, F″, D, F′, m.*   17.
bar] door *D, F″.*   21. *great]* grave *F″, D;* brave *F′. that]* then *L′. can]* did
U′, F″.   25–26. Omitted *L′, D, F′, F″, B″, m.*   29. *next]* scene *F′.*   29–
30. Omitted *F″. After line 28 F″ inserts:* Next draw the figure of a council
board.   33. *Capacious]* Captious *J. with]* and *J. replete]* repeat *J, L′, m.*
35. *Thus]* That *J, m.*   36. *Gives [That give U′]* all his fearful neighbors
strange alarms *m. Frightens]* Threatens *L′, F″.*   37. *glorious bacchanals]*
bacchanalias *B″.*   38. *a]* the *J.*   41–42. Omitted *F″.*   43. Omitted *m.*

47–50. *Omitted here and inserted after l. 54 F'*.   48. *tool of state*] fool of state *F', F"*; fool of fate *U'*. *m.n.* Ld. Hollis *F'*.   49. *Two*] Four *D, F"*. *five*] first *U', m.*   50. *aim at*] dream of *F"*.   51–54. *Omitted F"*.   55. Whilst positive walks like Woodcock in the park *m. walks*] leads *B", L', F'*. *m.n.* Dr. Robt. Howard, Ld. St. Johns *F'*.   56. *m.n.* Bucknall *F'*.   58. *to debate the City*] to be beat in the city *all except L'*.   59–64. *Omitted U', D, F", F', m.*   60. *turncoat*] coward *L'*.

At end of text: Marvell *U'*; A. Marvell *m*.

The Haymarket Hectors   169–171

Copy text: C.

Collation: A, C, D, J, F', R", x.

2. *will*] did *D*.   11. And for sweet variety thought it expedien *R"*.   22. *lend*] send *A, C, D, J*.   24. His Monmouth, [his *R"*] Life-guard, O'Brien, and Sandys *A, C*.   25. *all the fears*] the romance *J, F', R"*.   29. Nay, farewell the subsidies so she may cloven try *R"*. *she*] he *A, C, D, x*.   30. *nostrils*] nose *C*.   38. In Monmouth and in Carlo *R"*.   40. The sons of Mary and Barlo *R"*.   42. Might they not well have spar'd the noses of others *R"*.   44. *voice*] vote *D, F'*; tongue *J, R"*.   47. *mention*] motion *D, J*.

On the Three Dukes Killing the Beadle   172–174

Copy text: G.

Collation: G, D, D", J, F', m.

Title: As given m. No title G. A true and perfect Relation of a bold and Saucy Beadle, being upon the watch on Saturday night 25th of Febr. who was fairly killed by two Dukes *D*. A true and perfect relation how a bold and saucy Beadle being upon the watch Sunday morning 26 Feb: 1670/71 was killed very fairly by 3 Dukes [*J*], Monmouth, Albemarle, Somerset *D"*. A watchman killed by the D. Somerset, D. Albemarle, D. Monmouth *F'*.

3. *m.n.* Whetstone's Park *J*.   4. *gentle*] genteel *m*.   5. *m.n.* St. James's *J*.   7. *gleek*] brace *D*. *m.n.* Monmouth, Albemarle and Somerset *J*.   8. *bloody*] cloudy *D*.   13. *sad*] bad *F'*.   14. When she was sick to lose even all she had *F'*.   15. *from*] with *D", J, m*.   19. *a*] *omitted G*.   26. *stand*] stay *m*.   28. *puts*] put *G*.   31. The fiddlers end, and so doth all the sport *D"*; The fiddlers wit increaseth all the sport *F'*.   35. Yet shall Whitehall make innocent the good *D"*.   36. *men*] youths *F'*.   37. *m.n.* Hyde Park *J*.   41–42. *Follow 36 D*.

Upon the Beadle   174–176

Copy text: D.

Collation: D, F".

Title: Another on the Same Subject D [Follows "Near Holborn lies a park of great renown"].

12. *bare*] their bare D.   13. *especially*] especiall D.   27. That from their hopeful youth such fruits may come F".   44. *gallant*] brave D.   45. *their politic heads*] that statesman's head F".   58. *late*] *omitted* D.   61–70. *Omitted* F".

Upon Blood's Attempt to Steal the Crown   178

Copy text: R".

Collation: A, C, J, O, P, B", C", D", F", R", m.

Attribution: Marvell C, J, R", m.

1. *rents*] land J; rent m.   2. *English*] imperial D".   4. *No mask so fit*] The fittest mask *all other texts.*   8. *bishop's*] prelate's m.

On the Prorogation   179–184

Copy Text: B".

Collation: A, B, O, C, P, B', F', F", B", D, g.

Note: The texts of *On the Prorogation* may be arranged in three groups: A, B, C, O, and P agree substantively with each other; so do B', F', F", and g; and so do B" and D. To simplify the textual notes A will represent the first group, B' the second, and B" the third. Where one version varies substantively from its group this variant is noted.

Title: On the Prorogation of the Eighteen-Years Parliament, or Club of Unanimous Voters g. Upon the Prorogation of the Parliament Twice F". A Complaint of a Prorogued Parliament Man F'. On the Prorogation by Proclamation D. Upon the Prorogation of a Parliament before the Last Prorogation was Expired B'.

1. Prorogue upon prorogue, damn'd rogues and whores A.   7–8. *Omitted* B'.   9. *fobb'd*] fool'd A, F'; serv'd B', g.   10. *ten*] twelve *all except* B", D.   19. Unjust elections cull'd and took much pains F'.   20. *the Parliament*] a Parliament man A, B, C, O; a member of P.   21. Heal'd Coventry's slit [split F'] nose and through our fears B', F", g; Cut Coventry's nose and cropp'd his ears A, B, C, O; Cut Coventry's nose and cropp'd off both his ears P.   23. *Omitted* g.   32. *patriots*] patriarchs A. *After 35* B', F', g *insert:* They need not hector more 'gainst Hogen-Mogen/And feel like us the plague of a proroguing.   76. *But of some medley cut*] But some middle cut B".

99–100. *Omitted B', F', g.*   102. *when*] whom *A, F", D.*   111. *For*] well
B'.   112. Unless Fanatics [Fans *B', F', F"*] lend, or money from France be
sent *A;* If Saints lend not or cash from France be sent *g.*   113–14. *Omitted
A.*   115. *foregame*] fair game *A.*   117–34. *Omitted B'.*   121–22. *Omitted
A.*   124. *Thames*] hands *D.*   126. Moon shines at noonday and at night
the sun *A.*   137. *to be prorogued*] rogued *B".*

At end of text: Dec. 29th 1671 *B".*

Nostradamus' Prophecy   186–188

Copy text: L'.

Collation: D, B', L', B", f, m.

Title: An Ancient Prophecy Written Originally in French by Nosterdam and
Now Done into English. 6 Jan. 1671. *B'.* An Ancient Prophecy of Nostradamus
Rendered into English *L'.* The Prophecy of Nostre Dame Written in French,
Now Done into English. January 1671/2. *D.* An Old Prophecy of Nostradamus
Written Originally in French, Now Turned into English by *B".* Nostradamus's
Prophecy. By A. M. *f;* by A. Marvell Esq. *m.*

1. Her faults and follies London's doom shall fix *f, m;* The blood of the just
London's firm doom shall fix *D, B", B'.*   2. *she must sink*] cover it *B', D,
B".*   3. *Fire-balls*] Firebrands *B".*   6. With high aspiring head towards
those skies *B', D, B".*   7. *thing*] trick *D, B', B".*   10. Saving their own,
shall give the rest away *f, m.*   11. *by th' easy people*] the sov'reign people *D,
B', B".*   12. *the King and Parliament*] their King in Parliament *D;* both to
King and Parliament *B";* the King by Parliament *f, m.*   13. *Villainy*] villains
f, m.   15. *come*] shall use *D, B', B".*   16. Yet play the courtesans behind
the scenes *D.*   17. When sodomy prime ministers make sport *B". Sodomy*]
so doing *L'.*   22. *th' Exchequer*] one's father *D.*   23. When declarations,
lies, and ev'ry oath *f, m. lie*] vows *B'.*   25. *shall be at Brentford town*] at
Brentford shall be known *B';* shall be at Brentford known *B". After line 26 D,
B', B" insert:*

> When public faith and vows and payments stop,
> Then London, lately burn'd, shall be blown up,
> And wooden shoes shall come to be the wear,
> When Cerberus shall be the Treasurer,
> London shall see, for it will come to pass,
> A greater thief than Alexander was.

*49–50 follow this passage D, B', B". In B" "Poet Bayes" is written at the end of
the text.*   27–48. *Omitted B"; appear as a separate poem entitled "A Libel"
D.*   29. *seal's*] seat's *f, m.*   28. *and whom*] omitted *L'.*   30. *starch'd*]
harsh *f, m.*   35. The Lord Treasurer shall in one year *B'.*   36. *rich*] fat
f, m.   41. *th' English*] London *B'.*   42. *Gallic*] Latin *f, m.*   44. To fill
his empty treasury they must toil *D.*   45. *toil*] sigh *f, m.*

The Dream of the Cabal: A Prophetic Satire.   192–203
Anno 1672.

Copy text: j.

Collation: A, B, C, H, O, F', K', j, m.

Title: The Gambol, or A Dream of the Grand Cabal F', K'; A Dream H.
The following Prologue occurs in m:

> Whoever looks about and minds things well,
>   And on affairs abroad doth take a view,
> May think the story which I here do tell
>   Was never dreamt, it falleth out so true.
> I do confess it's something hard to find
>   A crooked path directly in the dark;
> And while a man's asleep you know he's blind,
>   And can't easily hit on a mark.
> Well, be it so, yet this you know is right:
> What's seen i'th' day is dreamt again at night.
> A dream I hope will no wise man offend,
> Nor will it treason be (I trow) to lend
> A copy of my dream unto my friend.
>   Cabal, beware your shins,
>   For thus my tale begins.

22. *m.n.* Buckingham F', m.   30. Spawn [Spoil F'] of the people, always mak-
ing rents *all MSS. except* H.   35. *m.n.* Ormond F', m.   40. *'Tis*] 'Twas
all MSS.   46. Above my valor to let tongue break my neck H; I no ways like
my tongue should break my neck j, m.   48. *m.n.* Lauderdale F', m.   56.
hoop] lop H, F', K'; faw A, B, C, O.   59. *Na siller*] No money j, m.   61.
gin] gang H, j, m.   69. *m.n.* Arlington F', K', m.   75–76. *Omitted all MSS.
except* H.   85. *travail*] travel O, F', j, m.   87. How first to court, cajole, and
bribe for fear B; Now force, cajole, and court and bribe for fear j, m.   105.
m.n. Chancell. Shafts. m.   108. *m.n.* Ashley Cooper F'.   155. *abas'd*] abus'd
all MSS.   165. *then*] therefore H, j, m.   169–70. *Order reversed* F', K'.
179. *m.n.* Clifford F', K', m.   184. *rumbling*] rambling *all MSS.*   194. Must
first appear this kingdom to beguile j, m.   206. *Omitted* C.   215. *m.n.*
Lauderdale F', K', m.   218. *Omitted* F'.   221. *work*] works j, m.   225.
m.n. Clifford F', m.   243. *pay'th*] say'th A, B, C, O, F'.   244. *solemn*] pub-
lic F', K'.

After 252 H inserts:

> In th'army too I doubt 'twill sacred Sir
> Bring ill luck for to be singular
> For to Scotch or English I can't consent
> Th'one their King betray'd th'other their Parliament
> But honest Irish that so worthily

Hath bore the name of rebel for's loyalty
And rather chose upon himself to bring
That hateful name than burthen would his King
In unsuspected numbers they may come
From every port like French and till your drum
You beat may private and on half-pay live
Like them till you your orders out shall give
The safety of yourself great Sir and throne
Condemn your trusting to the French alone
Tis fit that some that do you sovereign call
Should mixed be with them and not French all
And no subject have you so true so just
As Irish are for them you safe may trust
They punctually comport with royal will
Save whom you please and whom you please shall kill
If there be reason as perhaps there may
The City once again in ashes lay
They readily will do't and strew each street
With ghastly flames and blood of all they meet
Where fore you must the Catholics restore
To the ancient glory they had heretofore
These are the tools alone will fit our plot
When what I've named Nature herself hath not
What others say or think I take no care
To serve your Crown alone my studies are

253. *m.n.* Ormond *F'*, *O*; added in contemporary hand *m. check'd*] snubb'd
A, C, O.   255–56. *Omitted all MSS. except H.*   262. *yourself*] your land
j, m.   265. *lie*] fall *A, B, C, O, j, m.* That it as well as I exploded shall *A, B, C,
O, j, m.*   299. *not*] no *j.*   313–14. *Omitted all MSS. except H.*   318.
same] some *j. whoops*] hoops *j, m.*   320. *you*] them *C, j, m.*   321. *a Monck*]
as Monck *j, m.*   326. *e'en*] omitted *j, m.*   329. The law doth fence you,
you're secure from fear *F', K'.*   335. *that*] will *all MSS.*   342. *and prince
may*] as prince doth *A, C, H*; . . . does *B, O.*   352. *we to*] unto *C, j, m.*
360. *m.n.* Clifford *F'*; added in contemporary hand *m.*   379. *six of seven*] five
or six *j, m.*

The Banished Priests' Farewell to   204–210
The House of Commons

Copy text: D.

Collation: D, L'.

Title: The Roman Catholicks Farewell to the Parliament March 29th 1673 *L'.*
18. *run*] move *L'.*   19. *If*] And if *D.*   22. *great and proudest*] bold and
crafty *L'.*   25. Made but your folly appear the more *D.*   54. *sacred*] secret
L'.   57. You can substantiate a wench, what you *L'. After 60 L' inserts:* What,

shall such silly fools as you decree/What creed, what doctrine must believed be?
67. *lastly*] beastly *L'*.   74. *huff*] snuff *L'*.   82. *Omitted L'*.   88. *to*] do *D*.
After 104 L' inserts:

> For if not we then theirs the right,
> And not your monstrous church hermaphrodite,
> That like a mule between a horse and ass
> 'Twixt Puritan and we begotten was
> And false to both your grisly mothers cry
> In fear and fool of dame and sire fly.

After 106 L' inserts:

> The country Jug and Robin may admire
> The part of their sirreverence esquire.

After 112 L' inserts:

> Or majesty shall slap you in the chops
> With an old proclamation fit for fops,
> And banish us as he did in sixty-six.
> Please will an easy people easy tricks;
> Our work you have done much against the grain.
> May not yours be so before you come again.
> Great fart, farewell! Your noise and crack is broke,
> And all dissolv'd into a stinking smoke.

113–14. *Omitted L'*.

His Highness' Conversion by Father Patrick   211–212

Copy text: D.

Collation: D, L', U', G, F", k, o.

Title: The Dispute between his Highness and Dr. Patrick upon the Change of
his Religion *L'*. The Dispute (1673) *U'*. The Dispute. By the E. of R———r. 1673
k, o.

1. *Between*] Betwixt *U', L', F", G, k, o*.   2. *weighty*] mighty *F", U'*.   3.
And religion the theme] Religion was the theme *L', U', k, o*; Religion the theme
F".   5–8. *Omitted F"*.   5. When I dare boldly say, if the truth were but
known *U', k, o. had his Highness*] if the D. had *G*.   6. *Patrick's*] Patrick *D,
L', k, o*.   7. *He'd have call'd it*] It had been *D*.   8. To have chang'd from
a good one to one that [that which *L', k, o*] is worse *U'*.   9–18. *Omitted L',
U', k, o*.   13–16. *Omitted F"*.   17–18. *follow line 26 F"*.   20. *the Father*]
Father Patrick *F", L', U' G*; S. Patrick *k, o*.   21. *Were* [Was *F"*], first, Sir,
they cheat you and leave you in the lurch *L', U', k, o*.   22. *any*] omitted *D*.
23. And next unto that he averr'd for a certain *L', U', k, o*.   24. *ours*] our
Church *G*.   25. At which two reasons, so deep and profound *L', U', k, o*.
27. For now I both see and plainly do find *F". And straight*] But at last *L'*; But

at length *U', k, o.* 29. That it is not your reason nor will can afford *L';* It is not your reason nor wit can afford *U', k, o;* wit nor learning *D. wit*] will *U'.* 31. *that somewhere 'tis*] he somewhere has [hath *L'*] *F", G, k, o.* 33–34. *Omitted U', L', k, o.* 35. *matter*] dispute *U', L', k, o.* 37. *this matter*] the cause *U', L', k, o;* this business *F";* it just *G. At end of text:* Rochester *U'.*

Advice to a Painter to Draw the Duke by   214–219

Copy text: D.

Collation: A, C, D, G, J, X, F', L', B", F", R", 1679, f, m.

Title: Advice to the Painter *J.* An Advice to the Painter how he may Draw the D. of York *F'.* Advice to a Painter to Draw a Duke by. By H. Savile. Printed 1679 *C.* Advice to a Painter. By A. M., Esq. *f;* by A. Marvell, Esq. *m.*

3. *in triumph*] in council *R", 1679.* 4. *abhorring*] abjuring *1679.* 6. *Omitted f, X.* 7. *him falling*] his Highness *f, m.* 9–10. *m.n.* the Pope, Father Patrick, Earl of Danby, the Irish *X.* 15. Arm'd with blood, zeal, and blessing from thy hand *A, C;* Arm'd with gold, zeal, and blessings from your hands *F';* Thus arm'd with zeal and blessings from your hands *f, m.* 18. *wise*] Powis *J. m.n.* Fitzgerard and Scott in Ireland *X. Fitzgerald*] Fitchgarrett *G.* 21. *in a more glorious cause*] in such a noble cause *J;* in such a glorious cause *D, F', B".* 22. As to destroy religion and their laws *F';* As to destroy their liberties and laws *J, D, B".* 24. *their parchment precedents*] Parliaments, presidents *F', f;* their pertinent presidents *J;* their parchments, presidents *A, C;* Parliaments and presidents *X.* 25. *men*] ever *D;* even *B";* e'er *m.* 29. *guide*] bride *A, C.* 31. *Occurs in L' and m only.* 33–34. *Omitted J.* 34. *soil*] spoil *f.* 35. We'll have those villains in our nation press'd *J.* 36. *And I do*] You and I *D, R", 1679.* 37. *m.n.* Lord Mordaunt, now Earl of Monmouth. He went Admiral of the Fleet to fetch the Duchess of York from Modena in Italy to be married to the Duke of York who then had the pox *X.* 38. *Conveying*] Convoying *D.* 40. Does now in baseness and in Pop'ry

chestnut

join *A, C.* 41. *golden*] golden *R".* 45. *the tained Churchill*] now painted Churchill *A, C. m.n.* Madame Churchill his Mrs. *X.* 49. *jealous*] zealous *L'.* 67–74. *Omitted 1679.* 67. *m.n.* Earl of Tyrconnel *X.* 71. His sword is all, his argument's in his look *G, L'. and his*] not his *f, m.* 76. *m.n.* Cardinal Howard at Rome, brother to the Duke of Norfolk *X.* 78. His sense, his soul, his squinting of his eye *D.* 79. *m.n.* Ld. Bellasis *X.* 85–86. *Omitted J.* 87. Now, Painter, show the Cabal of the plot *J.* 88. *Fitzgerald*] Fitchgarrett *G.* 89. Are these fit heads to overthrow a state? *A, C, G, L'.* 94. *all their hands*] bloody hands *A, C.* 101–18. *Omitted f.* 103. *pleasure*] plenty *J, R".* 106. *Betray'd*] Destroyed *D, F'.* 112. *But to a zealous*] But such a jealous *J.* 118. *retrieve*] survive *D.*

A Charge to the Grand Inquest of England, 1674   221–227

Copy text: o.

Collation: A, C, B', o.

Title: Upon the Parliament *A, C.* On the Pensionary House of Commons *B'.*

9. Then Howard, Birch, Lee, Coventry, and Meers *B'. Powle*] Seymour *C, A.*
10. *Temple*] Powle *B'. Marvell*] S—— *o.*   29. *explore*] implore *o.*   40.
Omitted B'.   42. *Milton*] Selden *o;* Maton *A.*   43. *fail to*] fail *o, C.*   45.
privilege is] privileges or *C, A.*   54. *in*] on *o.*   56. *sitting*] sit in *o.*   58.
you] they *o.*   59. *Omitted C, A, B'.*   70. *full throats*] foul mouth *C, A, B'.*
72. *regal*] royal *o.*   76. *corrupt*] *Omitted C, A, B'.*   78. *of*] full of *o.*
79. *noise*] those *C, A.*   87–90. *Follow l. 102 o.*   92. *one*] once *o.*   104.
address] redress *o.*   108. *though least*] for last *C, A;* for least *B'.*   110. Tho'
one [none *A, B'*] of you have bravely taken in hand *C.*   117. In pride of
grace at once your [the *A*] easier and your [the *A*] nobler prey *C.*   119. *so*
lash'd] to lash *o.*   120. *friendly*] friend by *o.*   137. *your*] their *o.*   138.
your] their *o.*   142. *Omitted A, C.*   144. *Where*] And to *o.*   146. *low*
spheres] lower sphere *o.*

Britannia and Raleigh   228–236

Copy text: J.

Collation: A, C, D, J, X, F', J', L', R", e, m.

Attribution: Marvell *C, X, e, m;* Mr. Ayloff *R".*

2. *yielded*] quitted *X.*   6. *in*] to *A, C, F'.*   9. What pow'r does free me
from my happy rest *F'.*   10. *unseemly*] untimely *all except J.*   16. *suffer-*
ings] sufferers *A, C, D, X, R".*   17. *Howard*] Leigh *A, C, F', X;* Lee *D, R".*
Garr'way] Galloway *X.*   18. Till Osborne's golden cheats I shall detect *C;*
And Osborne's golden cheats shall be detect *D;* Thus Osborne's golden cheat I
shall detect *X, E, m;* Til golden Osborn's cheats shall be detect *R". m.n.* Mar-
quess of Camarshen *X.*   19. *leave*] love *F'.*   20. *cut-nose guards* the life-
guards *F'.*   24. *master's*] martyr's *all except D;* martyr'd *D.*   39. *turn'd*]
read *A, C, D, X.*   41. *by learning tyrants' lore*] by cruel tyrant lore *X;* by
handling tyrant's lore *A, C;* for weaving tyrant's lore *D.*   43. *reign*] race *X,*
e, m.   47. *endless*] and great *X, e, m;* nor less *F'.*   51. *his canker'd*] the in-
fected *F'.*   52–53. *Omitted F'.*   54. *confirm*] perform *X, e, m.*   57. So
mounted on a bright celestial car *X, e, m. triumphal*] celestial *R".*   62. *arm*]
hand *A, C, D, X, e, m.*   63. *her right*] the ancient *F'.*   66. *bred*] burst *J'.*
67. *Jove's loud rav'nous curs*] all the people do *D.* loud] lewd *C, X, e, m.*   68.
Horror] Tortures *all texts.*   76. *of the*] to brave *R".*   77. chills all their
hearts, their active heat controls *all texts.*   82–83. If not o'er-aw'd: this new-
found holy cheat,/ Those pious frauds too slight t'insnare the Brave *X, e, m.*
83–84. *Omitted F'.*   84. Are proper acts of long-ear'd rout t'inslave *X, e, m.*

89. *scorn*] own *J.*   92. *impostors*] impostures *all texts.*   94. So boundless
law in its full power shines *X.*   96. *baby-bonds*] childish bands *F'.*   102–
04. *Omitted D, R''.*   107. *disguis'd*] omitted *D.*   113. *head*] age *X, e, m.*
114. *boys*] prigs *X, e.*   125. *pagod*] biggots *A, R'', C, D, X, e, m.*   128.
Fiend] Feign'd *A, C, F'.*   129. Thus the state's right marr'd by this hellish
court *X.*   134. *again*] blank *J. scandal*] shame *F'.*   141–42. *Omitted X, e.*
143. *learn'd*] Fop's *F'.*   147. *oil*] juice *A, C, X;* ill *F', J', L'.*   153–54. *Omit-
ted X, e, m.*   153. *stinking Scottish*] base tyrannic *m.*   154. *for*] and *C.*
155. *No!*] omitted *X, e, m.*   161. Shall eternize a glorious lasting name *X, e,
m.*   166–67. *Omitted L'.*   167. *stews*] shews *R''.*   170. *Carwells*] Corn-
wells *X;* Corwells *e. Pembrokes*] Portsms *m. Nells*] Neils *e.*   172. *Messaline*]
Teg *A, C;* Tigiline *F';* Tegoline *X, e, m;* Tegelina *L;* Tegeline *J', R''. Acte's*]
Arteria's *X, e, m;* Artesia *A, C;* Acteas *L';* Artesia's *R''.*   173. Who yield to
these in lewdness, lust, and fame [shame *C, A*], *X, e, m.*   183. Balm in their
wounds and shall their life restore *X, e, m.*   189. *lead chain'd*] bear slain *X,
e.*   195. *tyrant*] serpent *X, e.*

At end of text: Sic vaticinatur, etc. *D.*

Upon his Majesty's being made Free of the City   237–242

Copy text: C.

Collation: A, B, C, D, O, P, U', R'', g, m.

Title: **On the Lord Mayor and Court of Aldermen Presenting the Late King
and Duke of York each with a Copy of their Freedoms, Anno. Dom.** 1674 *g;* By
A. Marvell, Esq. *m.* The City Maggot *D.*

1. *Londoners*] Londoner *C, O, P.*   9. *'em*] on *C, O, P.*   10–12. Themselves
they've bereft/ Of the little wealth [wit *g*] they had left/ To make an offering
of their freedom *U', m.*   15. *heeding*] trading *A, B, C, P, O;* breeding *g;* head-
ing *m.*   23. *much*] ten times *g, m.*   24. When none but such fools would
receive him *g, m.*   33. When he should on his books be poring *R''.*   35.
constant] wanton *D.*   37–42. *Omitted g, m.*   51. *But molested the*] To vex
his poor *g, m.*   54. To his Cleveland, his Nelly and Carwell *C, O, P.*
55–60. *Omitted U'.*   57. That had not fear taught him sobriety *g, m.*
58–60. *D.* And the House was so barr'd/With guard upon guard,/He had
burglar'd all their propriety *A, B, C, O, P.*   61–62. Such a plot was laid/Had
not Ashley betray'd *U', g, m.*   64–66. *m.n.* The Duke of York's trumpet and
a footman of the King's took away a citizen's wife from him in the street *U'.*
64. *your wives*] Cheapside *R''.*   66. *the soldiers*] foot-boys *g, m. your*] their
C, O.   77. *Two*] Three *A, B, C, O, P.*   79–84. *Omitted D.*   82–83. And
do not mistrust/He may once grow more just *g, m.*   84. When he's worn of
his follies and vices *g, m.*   86. *that which*] that *C, B, O.*   90. *carriage*]
gristle *D, R'', g, m.*   94. *Grace trow*] fair show *C, D;* grave show *R''.*   95.
A-proroguing go *B, O;* A-proroguing I trow *P.*   96. *pyx*] pex *C.*   97–114.

Omitted g.   97–108. *Omitted m.*   100. *if ever*] before *all but R".*   103–
08. *Omitted U'.*   103. *your*] our *C.*   108. *we've had*] we have *C.*   114.
To charters, our king, and sovereign *A, C;* To his country or to his sovereign
g, m.   117. *color*] cull out *g, m.*   120. With the wife of religion Italian
C.   121–26. *Omitted U', g, m.*   121. *ye*] the *C.*   131. *I see*] See *C.*
132. *Untill*] unless *C.*

The History of Insipids   243–251

Copy text: B".

Collation: A, C, D, J, O, P, U, F', J', L', U', B", F", CC, j, m.

Title: The Chronicle from Ra: Gregge jun'. 8 March 77/8 *B".* The History of
the Times *A, C;* By the E. of Rochester *J* [added in another hand]. The History
of Insipids. A Lampoon by Ld. Rochester *U.* The History of Insipids, A Lam-
poon. 1676 *j;* By the Lord Roch——r *m.*

2. *miracle*] glory *CC.*   13. *Our*] Old *U.*   14. *Espoused*] Has paid off *F'.*
15. *resolves*] ventures *D.*   24. *Pope*] omitted *U, j, m.*   25–30. *Follow 36
O, P.*   30. *wise*] wish't *L'.*   31–36. *Follow 24 O, P.*   32. *some*] done *F'.*
34. *Charles*] *J*—— *j, m;* *J*——mes *U.*   35. *m.n.* Atkins, North, Wood *O, P.*
36. *m.n.* Crew and Compton *O, P.*   38. *Preferring*] Preserving *U, L', j, m.*
42. *grace*] love *O, P.*   49. *sots*] Scots *A, C.*   51. *votes*] voices *B".*   54.
prorogue, prorogue] adjourn and prorogue *B".*   56. *betray'd*] the trade *O, P,
L'.*   60. *them all*] the knaves *U, F", j, m.*   61–66. *Follow 90 O, P.*   61.
Yet, Charles, do not thy mind oppress *O, P.*   62. *victories were*] victory is ours
B".   66. *beat*] base *F".* brave] bravest *B".*   68. *master*] sov'reign *A, C, D,
U, F', F", j, m.*   75. *three days parling*] three days prating *L', F";* seven days
prating *O, P.*   77. *Dane*] Don *F".*   79–84. *Omitted F", O, P.*   79.
sweetly] neatly *F'.*   80. *baffle*] business *F', B".*   83. *call'd*] haul'd *A, C;*
hal'd *CC.*   85–90. *Follow 96 O, P.*   93. And must have Charles reign ab-
solute *F".*   95–96. Has not the French King made us fools/Taking in
Maastricht with our tools? *j, m.*   96. *taking*] his taking of *B".* *m.n.* Mon-
mouth *CC.*   100. *of*] and *O, P.*   104. *his*] this *B".*   106. *only*] worse
than *B".*   109–14. *Omitted O, P.*   115. *wise*] grave *A, C, D, U, J, F", j,
m.*   126. *subjects*] English *J.*   127. Panders, pimps, bastards, royal whores
O, P. *upstarts*] upstart treasurers *B", D, J, F', F", CC.* *pimps*] omitted *CC.*   132.
But a small blessing to the nation *U, j, m.*   135. *work*] sport *U, j, m.*   138.
Grown wise by wrongs we shall abhor you *U, j, m.*   141. *Charles and*] treach-
erous *U, j, m.*   145–50. *U, j, m, read:*

<blockquote>

That false rapacious wolf of France,
   The scourge of Europe and its curse,
Who at his subjects' cry does dance,
   And study how to make them worse,
To say such kings, Lord, rule by thee
Were most prodigious blasphemy.

</blockquote>

154. *public*] subjects *U, j, m.*   162. *most*] best *F", CC.*   164. *brutish*] British
A, C, O, P, F', L', CC.   167–68. And be no more like wretched frogs/Mis'rably
king'd with storks and logs *O, P, L'.*   168. *wretched*] ruin'd *D.*

At end of text: 1675 *D.*

<h2 style="text-align:center">The Chequer Inn   253–261</h2>

Copy Text: R".

Collation: A, B, C, D, O, P, T, Z, I', W', A", B", D", R", x.

Title: The Chequer Inn, or A Pleasant New Ballad to the Tune of I tell thee,
Dick. By Mr. H. Savile. 1674. *A", T.* The Chequer Inn. By Mr. H. Savile 1673 *B.*
1675 *Z.* 1674 *I'.* The Exchequer Inn, or the Supper made by Thomas Earl of
Danby upon the Parliament's Clearing of Him A.D. 1675. *D".*

Note: A and *C* agree with *x* unless otherwise noted.

9. *m.n.* Wallingford House over against Whitehall let by the D. of Buckingham
to the E— of Danby then Ld. Treasurer, who treated the Commons there *A",*
T, I', B.   13. *host*] oast *D.*   19. *wex*] vex *D, x;* wex *A, C.*   21. *hoards*]
heaps *x.*   27. *'Twill fail him*] A will fall *P.*   28. *claw*] pay *all except A, C,*
D", x.   39. *him*] been *x.*   42. And have been well requited *P;* Had they
been so requited *B.*   46. Therefore I needs must speak my mind *x. fin'd*]
kind *x.*   54. *m.n.* A doorkeeper of the House of Commons *B.*   63. *did*] her
B, O, P, T, Z, I', A".   65. *fain*] forc'd *x.*   71. *sky*] sun *x.*   77. To plant
us with his government *A, P.* After *l.* 84 *D, B", x* insert *ll. 103–32.*   86. *out-*
roar'd] on's sword *D.*   91. Yet worse than he was none of those *B, O, P, Z,*
I', A".   92. *as meat*] have meat *A".*   106. *pellets*] sallets *A".*   110. *chear*]
cheat *B, O, T, Z, I', A".*   111. With butt'ry ware and larder *A".*   112.
provant] trovant *O;* prov'nder *x.*   113. He had sew'd on too, to's hose *A".*
132. *chop-cheer*] chop-share *A";* crop-cheer *B", D", x.*   133. *Hanmers*] Ham-
mers *A";* Hammonds *P.* Harbords] Herberts *x.*   141. *rick'd*] till'd *P;* tick't
T, I', A"; reach'd *D;* built *B".*   142. *feast*] treat *A".*   147. *Papists*]
Papishes *x.*   151. *host*] oast *D.*   154. *physic*] visick *x.*   158. Till King
kiss'd both oastess and oast *D.*

At end of text: Andrew Marvell *Z.* 1675 *D.* 20 Dec. 1675 *B".*

<h2 style="text-align:center">The Answer   261–262</h2>

Copy Text: x.

Collation: A, C, D, W, B', x.

Title: Upon the Rump or the Last Long Parliament *B'.* On K. Charles the
Second's Pension Parliament *W.* Supplement to the Chequer Inn *D.*

1. *such*] our *D; representatives*] representation *A, C, W.*   2. That ruin us,
our bearns and wives *W.*   6. *to undo*] but to cheat *W.*   10. So Rowley
when he gold does lack *W.*

The Royal Buss   263–265

Copy text: J.

Collation: J, D, B', L', F'', o.

Title: The Royal Buss. 1679 *B'*.

3. *rife a*] full as *P*; rais'd a *L'*; fallen a *F''*.   6. Are only great in guilt, not pow'rs *D, F''*.   7–8. *Omitted J.*   10. *puss*] blank *B'*; buss *L', F'', o.*   11. *tippet*] tyrant *D, F''*.   13. *them*] him *J, F'', o.*   14. *Carwell's*] Portsm——h's *o*.   22. And then the Queen cri'd foh! unto him *D*; And when the quean laid arse unto him *F''*.   29. *flippant*] frequent *B'*.   33. Whilst they suppli'd his pimps with pay *F''*.   42. *fence*] force *o*.   43–44. *Omitted D.*   49–50. *Omitted J.*   53–54. *Omitted L'*.   60. *or*] and *J*.   65. *Carwell*] Portsmouth *o*.   69. *red hot*] forced *B'*.   70. *Parliament*] Commons *o*.

On the Statue Erected by Sir Robert Viner   267–269

Copy text: F''.

Collation: A, C, D, O, P, F', J', U', B'', F'', L'', R'', CC, f, o.

Title: Upon Sir Robert Viner's setting up the King's Statue in Woolchurch Market *F', R''*. A Copy of Verses made upon Sir Robert Viner Erecting the King's Statue in White Marble on Horseback at Woolchurch and his Keeping it Covered and not Exposing it to Public View till on the King's Birthday *Margoliouth MS.* [not seen]. On Sir Robert Viner's setting up the King's Statue in Stocks Market 1673 *L''*.

1. *cities*] citizens *CC, f, o*.   3. *statue*] statute *F''*.   4. *bankers*] a broker *o*.   5. *knightly and generous*] mighty and gracious *o*.   6. *King and a steed*] King on a steed *CC, f, o*.   9. *But now*] By all *CC, f, o*.   10. To be as revenge and as malice forecast *f, o*.   12. *monster*] monkey *CC, f, o*.   14. *affirm*] assure *CC, f, o*.   15–18. *Omitted U'*.   17. *disguis'd*] disfigur'd *A, C, D, F', O, J', L''*; design'd *B''*.   19. *is*] in *F''*.   20. *much firmer*] much finer *A, C, O, P*; better *J'*; more faster *f*; much faster *CC, o*; firmer *F''*.   21–24. *Omitted U'*.   25. Surely this statue is more dangerous far *CC, f, o*.   31. And alleges the thing is none of his own *CC, f, o*.   33. *Sir Knight*] Sir Robert *o*.   36. *and*] or *F''*.   39. *Omitted U'*. Or is he in his Cabal in his —— set? *f*; Or is he now in his Cabal closely set? *o*. *this*] his *F''*.   42. *Jack-pudding*] black pudding *F', F''*.   45. *beams*] errors *f, o*.   49. The King will not think of restoring his bankers *P*.   49–50. *Omitted f, o*.   51. If the judges and Parliament do not him enrich *f, o*.   54. For the graver at work does reform him thus long *F''*; to mend him thus long *U'*; 'Tis the graver at work to reform him so long *o*.   57. *restore us our King*] pray give us our King *CC, f, o*.   58. As ever you hope for December in spring *F''*.   60. We had better have him than his P——'d [P——fy'd *CC*] brother *f*; We had better have him than his bigotted brother *o*.

The Statue at Charing Cross 270-273

Copy text: J.

Collation: A, B, C, D, O, P, B', U', W', R'', b', x.

Title: Upon the Statue of Brass of King Charles the first on Horseback to be set up at Charing Cross *J*. On the Statue at Charing Cross *B*. Verses on the Statue at Charing Cross of King Charles the first. 1675 *D*.

2. *blinded*] buffl'd *B', R''*.   4. *is*] be *J, D*.   8. *legally*] lately *B, P, W'*. 10. Since a guard and a garden could not one defend *A, B, C, D, x*.   12. *Any monument*] Any more to know *C, b', x*.   13. *sheathing*] shelt'ring *C, b', x*. 21. *loyally*] legally *A, C, b', x*.   22. When their pensions are lost to be fed with a sight *B, P*.   24. *ere long*] shortly *J*. *forty and eight*] eighty and eight *A, C, b'*.   30. That the Treasurer the trick thought to try o'er again *B, P*. 36. *far*] long *A, B, C, D*.   40. *guineas*] guinny *J*.   41. *The housewifely*] The hussy my *P*. *nice*] wise *A, B'*.   44. *And we've lost*] Though we lose *A, C;* So we lose *D*.   45. *Berties*] parties *A, C, b', x;* Bartus *B';* Bartues *D;* Bertues *B, P*.   52. As would the next sessions reimburse him with use *C, D, b', x*.

A Dialogue between the Two Horses 275-283

Copy text: B'

Collation: A, B, C, D, J, B', F', L', U', W', MS. belonging to Cleanth Brooks, g, m.

Title: A Dialogue between Two Horses. By A. M.——l, Esq. *g;* By A. Marvell, Esq. 1674 *m*.

7. *fellow'd*] follow'd *C*.   14. *oracular*] articulate *F', m*.   16. When images speak to devotes of their shrine *A, C*.   17. *ne'er*] well *D*.   24. In a dialogue between two inanimate horses *m*.   33. *that*] then *m*.   37-38. *Omitted L'*. 39. *silence*] forth *g, m*. *After 42 m inserts:*

> The money of widows and orphans employ'd,
> And the bankers quite broke to maintain the whore's pride.

51-52. *Omitted g*.   55. *seiz'd*] broke *U', W'*.   59-60. *Follow 61-62 F'*. 59. *consume*] devour *D*.   68. *Omitted g*.   71. *that placed*] placed *B'*. *After 74 m inserts:*

> To see them that suffer both for father and son,
> And help'd to bring the latter to his throne;
> That with their lives and estates did loyally serve,
> And yet for all this can nothing deserve:
> The King looks not on 'em, preferment's deni'd 'em,
> The Roundheads insult, and the courtiers deride 'em;
> And none gets preferments but who will betray
> Their country to ruin—'tis that ope's the way.

75. *To*] Of *B'*.   76. *rascally*] spurious *L'*.   83. *publicans*] burgesses *Brooks
MS.*, *m*.   85. *Then baser*] How base are *m*.   86. *Court*] Country *m*.   87–
88. *Omitted B'*.   93–94. *Omitted L'*.   95. *send for*] admit of *L'*. *After 96
m inserts*:

  C. The misses take place and advanc'd to be duchess,
    With pomp great as queens in their coach and six horses;
    Their bastards made dukes, earls, viscounts and lords,
    And all the high titles that honor affords—
  W. While these brats and their mothers do live in such plenty,
    The nation's impov'rish'd, and the Chequer quite empty;
    And though war was pretended when the money was lent,
    More on whores than in ships or in war hath been spent.

101. *rebuked*] reproved *D*.   107–08. *Omitted W'*.   111. *steals*] strays *g, m*.
113. In very dark nights sometimes you may find him *g, m*.   115. *Peace*] Pause
Brooks MS., g, m.   126. And I alike do value my life and the state *Brooks
MS*.   127. *Though*] *Omitted B'*.   135–36. *Omitted g*.   139. *a*] of a *B'*.
149. *A Tudor! A Tudor!*] Oh Tudor, Tudor *B'*.   152. *write newsbooks*]
writes newsbook *B'*.   159–62. *Omitted g, m*.   168. *horribly*] humbly *g, m*.
169. *monarchy's*] tyranny's *g, m*.   176. *crimes*] faults *g, m*. *their*] their own
g, m.   181–88. *Omitted A, C*.   188. *brandy and ale*] wine, brandy, and
ale *U'*.

Marvell's Ghost   285–286

Copy text: D.

Collation: A, D, L', C, F', D", k, m.

Title: Marvell's Ghost. 1679 *L'*. Andrew Marvell's Ghost: Aug. 1678 *D"*. Mar-
vell's Ghost. By Mr. Jo. Ayloffe *k, m*.

1. *banks*] lake *all except D*.   3. *as*] by *all except D. sate*] late *k, m*.   5.
sense] scene *D"*.   10. *stain*] shame *k, m*.   11. *spurious*] omitted *k*.   23.
persecuting] presenting *F'*.   24. *laid waste*] destroy'd *all except D*.   25. *in-
cest, murder*] incests, murders *D*.   27. *And villainies*] Such villains shall *D"*.
32. *reclaim*] restrain *L'*.   35. *first*] e'er *all except D*.   42. *ills*] isle *k*.

A Poem upon the Imprisonment of Mr. Calamy in Newgate 289–293

Copy text: u'.

Collation: u', brs. (1663).

Title: Brs. *adds:* By Robert Wild D. D. author of the late *Iter Boreale*.

14. *sat*] set *brs*.   62. *Nonconformists*] Nonconformist *brs*.   64. *can*] can't
brs.   70. *swap*] swaft *brs*.

The Geneva Ballad   313–317

Copy text: 1674 brs.

Collation: 1674 brs., 1678 brs.

25. *like*] with *1678*.   98. *Presbyter*] blank *1674, 1678*.

The Session of the Poets   327–337

Copy text: D.

Collation: D, J, O, P, G', K', V', F", m.

Title: The Session of the Poets, to the tune of Cook Laurel *m;* Sessions of Poets *D;* A New Ballad to the Old Tune of Cook Laurel *K'.*

Note: The order of stanzas varies widely. In some MSS. some of the stanzas are given as "the Second Part," but the arrangement is not as satisfactory as that given in our copy text (*D*) and in the first printed version (*m*).

4. *abuses*] abusers *m.*   9. *that*] had *m.*   10. *A*] And a *m.*   16. *a peer*] as partners *O.*   21. *Oyez being call'd*] The court being set *J, V', F";* The court being call'd *K'.*   22. *suit*] court *O, P, G', F", m.*   27. *his*] him his. *After 32 m insert:*

> Humorous Weeden came in a pet,
>   And for the laurel began to splutter,
> But Apollo chid him, and bid him first get
>   A muse not so common as Mrs. Rutter.

35. *Gifford*] Clifford *G', K', F", m.*   45. *Savoy-missing Cowley came*] Cowley came modestly *J, O, P, G', K', V', F";* Savage-missing Cowley *m;* Cowley came mildly *D.*   46. *bad*] good *F".*   46–48. *O, P read:*

> To whom Apollo straight reach'd forth the bays,
> But the chief of the senate did strongly urge for't
> That ere he was crown'd he might explain his plays.

47. *good*] bad *F", m. After 48 O, P insert:*

> For they were in the dark as to language and plot,
>   Which made Apollo to laugh out loud,
> And bid 'em admire what they understood not,
>   For he should have the laurel in spite of the crowd.
>
> But with rev'rence to Apollo he still put it by,
>   And urg'd to bestow it on one was more fit,
> And as he departed with smiles did reply
>   'Twas pity his fancy outlevell'd his wit.

53. *Cotton*] Charles Cotton *K'.*   55. *but*] not *V', F". Virgil*] verses *O.*   66. *swear*] swagger *K'.*   78. *Shirley*] shortly *J.*   85. Newcastle and's horse for

entrance next strives *O, P, G', K', V', F''*, *m*. *for entrance next*] next for entrance *D*.   87. *m.n*. [*on Nature's posset-maker*] so his lady calls it in her poems *D;* A word used by my lady in her poems *G'*.   96. *bow*] go *J, O, P, G', K', V', F''*, *m*.   97. *labor deserv'd*] age deserv'd *D, G;* endeavor deserv'd *J;* age desir'd *m*.   99. *bald*] bold *O, P, K', V', F''*, *m*.   100. *perr'wig*] peruke *O, P*.   109. *An asterisk refers to these verses on a subsequent page in V':*

> Buckhurst alleg'd his descent from a wit,
>   But that title was quickly found to be frail;
> By his grandfather's copy he claimed it,
>   But his father, it seems, had cut off the entail.
>
> Sidley had something to show of his own
>   And offer'd to lay it upon the table,
> But when his evidence came to be shown,
>   It appear'd to be nothing but a fool's bable.

110. *put*] dispute *m*.   121. *Denham*] Jack Denham *J, F''*.   131. *his*] on's *D*. 134. *God damn*] damn *m*.   139. *The Secret*] The Secrets *m*.   144. *wott*] wot *O;* sot *J, P, G', K', V', F''*, *m*.   149. Sir Thomas Clarges laid claim to the bays *K'*.   150. *arrogant*] insolent *O*.   151. *Swearing*] Protesting *K'*. 153. *V' adds the following lines in margin:*

> So Apollo pinn'd his ears to make 'em fit
> To the circumversion of his nose and wit.

154. *help'd*] helps *G';* had a hand in *V'*. Help'd by Will D'Avenant as some do suppose *J*.   155. *crop off*] crop *D*.   158. But Apollo to recompense such a bold sot *O, P*. *After 158 J, V' add:*

> To Berkenhead Phoebus himself had a quarrel,
>   And before all the court, he plainly did show it,
> For he ask'd him how he could stand [pretend *V'*] to the quarrel,
>   Unless as a liar he were kin to a poet.

161. *appeal'd*] appear'd *D*.   161. *and the*] from the *O, P;* in the *F''*. *After 164 O, P add:*

> Apollo at last in pity decreed
>   This Cambridge poet the bays should wear
> For dancing a jig, but chiefly, indeed,
>   Because of all poets he had the best hair.

169–72. *Omitted m*.

On Mr. Edward Howard   338–339

Copy text: G''.

Collation: D, E, J, C'', G'', r'.

Title and ascription: By ye Ld. B: *G''.* Charles Ld. Buckhurst, now E. Dorsett *E*.

Made by Ld. Buckhurst *C"*. On Mr. Edward Howard's poeme, the Ld. Buck-
hurst ye supposed Author *D. Ascribed to "B" J.*

3. *throw*] fling *D, J, C"*.   4. *On*] At *D, E, J, C"*.   5. Ned Howard's like
tierce claret, which begins to pall *E*.   11. *Ned*] heart *D, E, J, C"*.   12.
breed in carrin] feed on carrion *E*.   19–20. *Omitted and inserted after l. 27*
D, E, J, C".   28. *nimbler*] quicker *E*.   32. *arrant*] errant *E, C", G"*.

At end of text: Communicat a Dr Sim: Patrick Sept. 6, 1669 *C"*.

On the Same Author upon   339–340
his *"British Princes"*

Copy text: G".

Collation: E, G", r'.

Ascription: E. A. *E*. By Major Aston *G"*.

8. *witty*] quiet *E*.   15. *runs*] flings *E*.   22. *cast*] throw *E*.

On the Same Author upon his   340–341
"New Utopia"

Copy text: G".

Collation: E, N, U, G", r'.

Ascriptions: Charles L. Buckhurst *E*. By the E. of Dorset *U*. By Mr. Hen: Savill
G". Whitherley *N*.

2. *Flecknoe*] fluence *E, r'*.   3. *stock*] mass *U*; rock *all others*.   6. *assistance*]
assurance *E, r'*.   7. No, they fly higher; yet thy muse is such *U*.   10. *own*]
read *r'*.   14. With bullock liver and some stinking fish *N*.   21. *Laugh'd*]
Hiss'd *U*.   22. *And*] Are *U*.   26. *reams*] rhymes *E, r'*.   34. Thy plays
like blind born puppies should be drown'd *N*.   35. *not*] that *U*.   36. Unto
the son of an heroic lord *N*.   38. *Drench'd*] Drest *N; herself*] thyself *U*.

Ephelia to Bajazet

Copy text: r'.

Collation: D", G", C' ", G', U, r'.

Title: Ephelia (a Deserted Lover) to Bajazet, Which May Serve as a Caveat to
Women. By Ld. Ro. *U*.

15. *great*] fierce *C' ", G'*.   20. *or fondness*] weaker or *D", C' ", G'*.   23.
What lost I not] I know not what *C' "*.   30. *his*] such *C' "*.   31. *charms*]
shame *C' "*.   32. *melted*] melting *C' "*.   38. *need*] durst *C' "*.   39. *No*]
Now *D", G'; act*] look *C' "*.   47. *shatter'd*] crumbl'd *D"*.   49. *show*] vow
C' ".   51. *love*] frame *D", C' ", G'*.   55. *meet*] make *G'*.

A Very Heroical Epistle in Answer to Ephelia   346–347

Copy text: r'.

Collation: D", G", CC, G', r'.
12. *constrain*] contain *CC, G'*.   39. *Thy crowding*] *The crouching D", CC,*
G'.   50. *dares*] does *r'*.

An Epistolary Essay from M. G. to O. B.   349–351
upon their Mutual Poems

Copy text: r'.

Collation: G'', N, CC, r'.

Title: An Epistolary Essay very delightful and solid from ye L^d: R: to ye L^d: M:
upon their Mutual Poems *G''*; To my Lord Mulgrave from Rochester. An
Epistolary Essay from M. G. to O. B. upon their Mutual Poems *N*; From E. R.
to L. M. *CC.*

3. *With*] Which *r'*.   7. *thanks*] praise *N*.   11. *t'have writ*] to fight *CC*.
41. Runns in a costive and insipid strain *N*.   58–59. Is fain to starve the
numerous traine below/That those above may make the greater show *N*.   65.
Omitted N.   78. *that's*] there's *r'*.   87. But men will censure you, 'tis two
to one *r'*.

At end of text: Rochester *N*.

A Session of the Poets   352–356

Copy text: G''.

Collation: D, N, U, D'', G'', e', r'.

Title: A Session of the Poets. Supposed to be written by Elk. Settle *G''*. A trial
of the Poets for the Bays. In Imitation of a Satyr in Boileau. By the D. of Buck-
ingham *U*; By the Duke of Buckingham and the Earl of Rochester *e'*; The Ses-
sions of Poets: 1676/7 *D''.*

1. *grow*] grew *r'*.   2. *clam'rous a crowd*] num'rous a brood *D*.   4. *a*] new
D''.   5. The poets and wits at this general call *N, D''*.   6. *Had drawn 'em
together*] Assembl'd together *D''*.   7. *thronging*] gaping *N, D''*. *gap'd*] strove
D''; ask'd *N*.   10. *ancient grave wit*] great ancient poet *N, D''*.   13. *so gave
him leave*] therefore thought fit *N, D''*.   14. *when*] now his *D''*; now *r'*.
15. No sooner was this grave [great *N*] author set by *D''*.   16. *got*] straight
D''.   17. He needs must confess of all men that e'er writ *N, D''*.   18. *fancy*]
humor *N, D''*.   21. *Brawny*] Mr. *N, D''*.   26. The next Tom Shadwell began
for to wallow *D''*.   37. Nat Lee was the next stepp'd in for a price *D''*; Nat
Lee was the next stepp'd in for a prize *N*.   41–42. *Omitted N, D''*.   43. *Yet
owning he had sense*] But knowing he had reason *N, D''*.   48. *Damn him*]
Gadzwounds *D''*; God Domma *G''*; God damme *D, N, r'*.   49. *Ballocks*] Bo *D''*.
51. *modest*] harmless *D, N*.   58. *prudently*] therefore *N*.   66. *gravely*]
gently *N*.   68. *man's life*] mankind *N*.   71–72. *Omitted N, D''*.   71.
Aphra] Astrua *N*.   74. *ace*] arse *D''*.   77. *acknowledg'd 'twas hard to*] con-
sider'd he could not *N, D''*.   79. He said if she made conquests and charms her
pretence *D''*.   81. *At last Mamamouchi came*] The next Mamamouchi comes
D''; Anababalutha put *r'*; Annabalatha put *D*; Marababalashu put *G''*.   83–100.
Omitted D''.   84. *Protesting*] Pretending *N*.   86. *With other pretenders*]
And many more poets *N*.   91. By the Nine sisters he solemnly swore *D*. *sacred*]
omitted *N, G'', r'*.   96. *E'en told 'em*] Tom told him *U*.

An Allusion to Horace 358–363

Copy text: D".

Collation: N, B', J', C", D", G", r'.

Title: An Imitation of the Tenth Satire, Horace I Lib. *N.* A Satyr against the present poets. Being an allusion to Horace Satyr X, Book I: Nempe incomposito dixi pedi &c. Written by the Earl of Rochester. 1677 *D".* 1–4. *Omitted G".* 3. *found*] fond *N.* 5–7. *sir added at end of each line D".* 14. *assembling a vast crowd*] and idle senseless crowd *C".* 16. Though e'en] Though I own *B'.* 17. *and the*] of the *J'.* 27. With epithets, 'twill soften their discourse *B'.* 28–29. *partly illegible J'.* 29. *morosest*] moros *r'*; remotest *B'*; longest *C".* 33. *sheer*] clear *C".* 34. *swift*] sweet *D".* 36. *jaded*] jade *J'.* *loose*] light *B'.* 38. *slave*] knave *N.* 40. *lash'd*] whipt *N.* 45. Great proofs of nature's force but none of art *B'*; *line illegible J'.* 57. *enforce*] in force *J'*; in farce *B'.* 58. *or*] and *D".* 59. *would*] could *N, J', D".* 61. *mannerly*] Mannerly *D".* 62. *by springs*] with things *N.* 65. *a resistless charm*] irresistless charms *N. line illegible J'.* 67. *kindle*] tinder [?] *J'.* 69. *vanquish'd*] languishing *N*; conquer'd *C".* 70. *all night*] at night *B'.* 74. *his*] and *N, D".* 78. *excellencies*] excellences *N.* 79. *temples*] temple *D".* 80. *best*] least *B'*; well *C".* 85. *justness*] justice *C".* 89. *choice*] gross *B'.* 90. *or*] not *C".* 92. *loose slattern*] loose slattern'd *N*; lewd slattern *J'.* 94. *Prove you*] Proves you *J'*; Prove him *N.* 98. *securely*] firmly *B'.* 99. *well read o'er thrice at least*] thrice read over at the least *N.* 102. *rout*] court *D".* 103. *line illegible J'.* 109. *in*] of *N, r'.* 118. *poor-fed*] poor-led *B', C".* 119. *scraps*] suppers *B'. cry*] carry *J', D".* 120. *loathe*] hate *N.* 121–22. If S——, S——, S——, W——,/ G——, B——, B——, B—— *r'.* 123. *Omitted D".* 124. *censure*] sense for *C".*

At end of poem: Rochester *N;* Ld. Rochester *C".*

In Defense of Satire 364–370

Copy text: D.

Collation: D, N, B', G', D", G", EE', d', r'.

Title: A Satyr upon the Follies of the Men of the Age by the Duke of Buckingham, ascribed falsely to the Earl of R. *d'.* In Defense of Satyr, writ by Sir Carr Scroope 1677 *D".*

24. *Here*] How *D. gain*] game *G".* 28. *m.n.* Capt. Aston *D"*; Sir John Fenwick *EE'.* 29. *m.n.* Sir Edw. Bash *D".* 32. *m.n.* Captain Aston *EE'.* 35. *noise*] vice *N. m.n.* Phil. E. Pemb. *D".* 36. *m.n.* Sir George Huet *EE'.* 38. *m.n.* Sir George Hewet and Mrs. Marshall *D".* 52. *frolics*] quarrels *G", d', r'. m.n.* Ld. Rochester Epsom *D"*; Earle of Rochester *EE'.* 54. *m.n.* Capt. Downs killd *D"*; Captain Downes *EE'.* 59. *seek*] set *D".* 61. *Sotus*] Scotus *D"*; Solus *D, B'. m.n.* Mr. Griffin *N, D", EE'.* 62. *Porus*] Ponis *D. m.n.* E. St. Albans *D"*; Sir R. Bovy *EE'.* 63. *new*] ne'er *D.* 77. *Simius*] Simms *D"*;

Simons *N;* Sinnus *B'. m.n.* Frank Newport *D'';* Mr. Newport Sir E. Bash *EE'.*
78. *Alidore's*] Abdy's *D'';* Alidon's *D. m.n.* Ld. Culpeper *N. m.n.* Sr. John
Abdy. Mrs. Michell Michell *D''.*   79. *m.n.* Ld. Cornw. Ld. Culpeper. Sue
Willis. Churchill Brouncker *D''.*   81. *Frightens*] Frights *D.*   89. *heights*]
lights *all texts except D.*   91. *m.n.* D. Monmouth *D'';* Prince Rupert *EE'.*
93. *m.n.* Sr. Tho. Armstrong *D'';* Mr. Loftus *EE'.*   96. *m.n.* Ld. Gerard
crossed out and Mulgrave *written in by another hand N. m.n.* Mulgrave *D''.*
104. *m.n.* Coll. Russell *D'';* Earl of St. Albans *EE'.*   105. *m.n.* Ld. Chancellor
N. m.n. Ld. Chancellor Finch *D'' florid*] fond *D''. flam*] flame *B', D''.*   106.
tries to sham] cries out shame *B';* tries to shame *D''.*

On the Supposed Author of a Late Poem   371–372
"In Defense of Satire"

Copy text: r'.

Collation: W', D'', G'', r', N.

Title: On the Supposed Author of the Defense of Satire, 1677 *D''.*

5. *on man*] unman *D''.*   10. *ass*] ape *D'', N.*   25. *maid*] nymph *D''.*   33.
canst] must *D''.*   34. *entirely but*] entire but for *N.*

At end of text: Writ by the Lord Rochester *D'';* Roch. *N;* Rochester *W'.*

The Author's Reply   373

Copy text: D''.

Collation: N, W', D'', G'', r'.

Title: The Answer *r'.* Answered by Sir Charles Scroope *W'.*

2. *ill*] bad *r', N, G''.*   4. *all thy*] full of *r', N, W', G''.*   5. Thou canst hurt
no man's fame with thy ill word *G'', r'. name*] fame *N, W'.*

On Poet Ninny   374–375

Copy text: r'.

Collation: D'', G'', CC, G', r'.

19. *modish*] modest *r'.*

A Familiar Epistle to Mr. Julian,   388–391
Secretary to the Muses

Copy text: I.

Collation: F, I, J, O, P, T, Z, G', I', J', U', W', A'', D'', L'', R'', x.

Title: A Familiar Epistle to Mr. Julian, Secretary to the Muses. 1677 *Z.*
4. *empti'd*] employ'd, *J, G', D'';* display'd *O.*   5. *wight*] knight *L''.*   16.

m.n. Sir George Etherege *A"*.   17. *he*] she *F*.   20. *main*] one *F*.   21.
winter] summer *T, Z, I', U', D", R"*.   24. *m.n.* Sir Carr Scroope *U'*.   36.
cheeks] face *F, I, T, Z, I', U', A", D"*.   40. *dare*] dares *I*.   42. *least*]
best *J, O, P, G', J', D", x*.   46. *parts*] man *G', D"*.   50. *chants*] courts *T,
Z, I', U', A", R"*.   51. *bubbling*] boiling *T, Z, I', U', A", R"*; dabbling *F*.
52. The froth at last breaks out into a song *F*.   57. *squinting*] squeezing *F, O,
P, W', x*; squeamish *J, J'*.   60. *pen*] wit *F, W', L"*.   62. *have*] has *I*.
65. *What*] Such *F*.   67. *detest*] detests *F*.   72. *He*] But *F, I, P, Z, I', U',
W', A", L", R"*.   83. *morning*] morning's *F*.   99. *mother*] mistress *I*.

At end of text: The knight which is the subject of this satyr is Sir Carr Scroope,
who died 1680. John Dryden *Z, I', U'*; John Dryden. The knight in this satyr is
Sir Carr Scroope, who died 1680 *T*.

Advice to Apollo   393–395

Copy text: O.

Collation: O, U', m.

Title: Advice to Apollo, 1678 *m*.

14. *thought*] thoughts *m*.   21. *and*] or *m*.   26. *our*] the *m*.   38. *darts*]
dart *m*.   41. *Would*] And *m*.   44. *so*] still *m*.   46. Omitted *U', m*.   48.
charity] charity then *m*.

An Essay upon Satire   401–413

Copy text: D.

Collation: D, F, I, B', F', K', U', l, m, c', p".

Date: 1679 *F'*., 1680 *B'*, 1675 *p"*.

Ascription: J. Dr——en, Esquire *l, m*; Earl of Mulgrave *c'*; and Mr. Dryden
added by Pope in his copy of c'.

15. *took*] look *D*.   20. *aim*] hit *I, F, c'*.   25. *grossest*] hardest *F'*; greatest
F, I. declaim] disclaim *l, m, c'*.   34. *wisest*] nicest *F'*.   39. *each*] this *B'*.
40. *greater*] greatest *F', K'*; other *I*.   42. *correction*] connection *I*; convic-
tion *F*.   44. *fool*] fop *F, I*.   45. *too*] omitted *D*.   50. *dancing*] gaudy
I, F.   52. *Of such a*] Or of the *F', K'*.   55. *not*] omitted *D*.   57. *courtier*]
courtiers *D*.   59. *so too*] too too *B', l, m, c'*.   61. *shall*] omitted *D*. mis-
tresses] ministers *K'*.   62. *and*] or *l, m, c'*.   68. *loyal*] royal *D, U'*.   70.
and] how *l, m*.   71. *rail*] rule *B'*.   76. *At council set*] Th'at councils sit *D*.
83. *sharper*] larger *F'*.   84. *m.n.* Buckingham *F'*; Bucks *B'*.   95. Though
he had left mankind to be destroy'd *D*.   99. *friends*] friend *l, m, c'*.   101.
own] old *B', U', l, m, c'*.   102. *m.n.* Shaftesbury *B', F', K'. little*] omitted
D.   118. Omitted *I. wretches*] bodies *F*.   122. *m.n.* Halifax *F', K'*; E of
E——x *c'*.   131. *odd*] old *U'*.   133. I'll pay him justly and admire him too
F, I.   135. *wittily*] wittingly *F, K'*.   137. *Refin'dly*] Willingly *K'*; Un-

friendly *U'*.   143. *theirs*] those *F, m, c'*; these *l*.   145. *Polytropos'*] Folly
Tropus *F, I*; folly Tropet *B*; folly Tropos *F', l, m*; folly Tropet's *K'*; Polu
Tropos *U'*. *m.n.* Lord Chancellor *F'*; Chanc. *F, B'*.   157. By those who scarce
had wit enough to show it *I*.   158. For some sit silent and condemn the
weaker *I, F*.   162. *Omitted K'*.   172. *still they feign*] they design *D*.
188. *he*] she *l*.   192. *his brisker*] his better *K'*; he in former *F, I*.   194.
Mulgrave] blank *K'*.   202. *Petworth*] Belworth *K'*. *sorrow*] horror *F'*.   221.
common] woman's *U'*.   226. *is*] in *D*.   226–29. *Omitted F, I*.   229.
Howe] Hall *all except F'*.   235. *so much*] just the *D*.   236. *as*] is *F, I, l,
m, c'*.   240. *motion*] action *l, m, c'*.   248. *their*] her *l, m, c'*.   250. *his*]
that's *F, I*.   255. *injuring*] injury *U', l, m, c'*.   256. *left out*] forgot *U'*.
264. *works*] words *F, I*.   265. *here*] there *D*.   271. *who*] Omitted *D*.
273. *can*] can't *l, m, c'*.

My Lord All-Pride   414–415

Copy text: r'.

Collation: D", G", CC, G', r'.

1. *loath'd*] loath *G'*.   3. *scribbler*] scribble *D", G'*.   5. *in*] with *D"*.   7.
his brain's] and brains *CC*.   8. *rake*] take *G", r'*.   17. With breath and
ev'ry other loathesome mark *G'*.   22. *like Harlequin to jest*] like Harlequins
to jest *D", CC, G'*; like Harlequin in jest *r'*.   26. *off*] of *G'*.

Nell Gwynne   420

Copy text: X.

Collation: X, g.

3. She has got a trick to *(rest of line blank) g*.

The Queen's Ball   421–422

Copy text: A.

Collation: A, C, D, L', U', W', F", x.

Title: To Her Majesty upon her Dancing. Anno 1670. *D*. The Queen's Ballat *A*.
1. *great*] dear *D, F"*.   4. *to*] and *F"*.   6. *to dance*] dance, pray *L'*; to dance
and pray *U', W'*.   9. *most*] more *L'*.   11. *vizard*] vizor *x*.   12. *would*]
will *D, F"*.   14. *came*] sprung *F"*.   15. Heavens some great care upon that
head dispense *F"*.   16. That for th' increase of nonsense takes it thence *A,
C, D, L', F", x*.   17. *strives*] strains *F"*.   18. *the pug*] poor pug *D*.   19.
loaded] grew on *F"*.   21. *bold*] old *A*.   22. *puppet*] gypsy *D, F"*; puggy *L'*;
pupsy *U', W'*.   24. *deer*] bear *F"*.   26. *cleanly*] heavenly *F"*.   28. *settl'd*]
quiet *U', W'*.   30. And from whence Nature expects no returns *D*.   34. *to*]
too *x*.   35. *mean*] please *x*; intend *C*.   36. *fellow-fiends*] fellow-friends *x*.
38. You may curvet and overturn the boat *D, F"*; You may o'erset and overturn
the boat *L'*; You may o'erset or overturn the boat *W'*.

The Earl of Rochester's Verses   424
For Which he was Banished

Copy text: P.

Collation: A, C, D, G, N, P, U, X, F', m.

Title and ascription: A base copy. Rochester *D.* Verses by the Lord Rochester *N.* On King Charles, by the Earl of Rochester, for which he was banish'd the Court and turned Mountebank *m.* Lord Rochester's Lampoon on King Charles for which he was banished the Court and turn'd Mountebank *U.* By the Lord Rochester. 1675 *F'.*

1–2. There is a monarch in an isle, say some/that has the bravest of cunts in Christendom *N.*   1. *grown*] known *U, m.*   3. There not long since liv'd (oh! may he live and thrive) *D;* Not long since reign'd, Oh! may he long survive *A, X;* There reigns, and long may he reign and thrive *m.*   6. *fool*] King *U, m.*   7. *soldiers*] subjects *U, m;* people *A, C, D, X, F'.*   8–9. *Omitted U, m.*   11. *a*] an equal *P.*   12. And she that plays with one may play with t'other *G, P.*   *After 13 D, U, X, F', m insert 32–3. D adds:*

> The hector wins towns by money, not trenches.
> The cully he conquers all the pretty wenches.
> He victory and honor refuses,
> And rather than a crown, a cunt he chooses.

13–14. Poor Prince, thy p——, like the buffoons at court,/It governs thee, because it makes thee sport *m.*   16–17. *Omitted U, m.*   16. *His*] He *P.*   18–19. Though safety, law, religion, life lay on't,/'Twould break through all to make its way to c——t *A, C, U, m.*   *After 19 F' inserts:*

> As soon as up down the back stairs he jogs,
> Follow'd by's pimps and bastards, his best friends, and dogs.

After 20 A, C, X insert: With dog and bastard always going before.   21. Grown impotent and scandalously poor *F'. After 21 D inserts:* With a damn'd crew to whores he jogs/ Of bastards, pimps, buffoons, and dogs.   22–25. *U, m read:*

> To Carwell, the most dear of all thy dears,
> The sure relief of thy declining years,
> Oft he bewails his fortune and her fate,
> To love so well and to be lov'd so late.

24. *my fate*] thy fate *G, P.*   24–25. *Omitted F'.*   25. *ballocks*] buttocks *U, m. After 25 D, U, X, F', m insert:* For when in her he settles well his t——.   27. *Omitted D, U, X, F', m.* But ill agreeing with his limber tarse *A, C.*   29. *trick*] chops *P.*   30. Hands, fingers, arms, mouths, c——t, and thighs *G, P. After 33 D adds:* Ah, generous Sir! long may you survive,/ For we shall never have such liberty to swive. *After 33 X adds:*

The hector wins towns by money, not trenches.
The cully conquers all the pretty wenches.
He business and honor both refuses,
And rather a cunt than a crown he chooses,
A generous sir. Oh! may he long survive,
For we ne'er shall have such liberty to swive.

Satire   425–428

Copy text: P.

Collation: J, O, P, U, Z, F', L', u.

Title: Satyr. Mr. Lacy *O, P.* Satyr. Mr. Lacy. 1677 *Z.* Nell Gwynne's and the Duchess of Portsmouth's Naked Pictures *J, F', L'.* A Satyr by the Ld. Rochester which K. Charles took out of his Pocket *U, u.*

Note: U seems merely a copy of the printed text (*u*).

9. *always*] nobly, *J, O, Z, F', L';* nimbly *U, u.*   11. *in thy breast*] in the flesh *F', L';* in that breast *u.*   20. *Which*] Who *U, u.*   23. *line*] lives *U, u.*   27. *Ross*] Rose *P.*   31–32. *Omitted J, F', L'.*   35. *monster*] monsters *P.*   36. *They let*] That lets *P.*   37. *Aloud*] Allow'd *U, u.*   39–40. *Omitted J.*   42. *gone into*] remov'd to *J, U, F', L', u.*   46. *monstrous*] minutes *all except U, u.*   48. Thou ne'er couldst have to satisfy the beast *P. this*] the *P.*   50. Who though she has been satisfi'd and tir'd *J, L';* Although she has been satisfi'd and tir'd *O, Z.*   51. *has swiv'd*] provided for *U, u;* provide *O, Z, F', L'.*   53. Where are the bishops, where's their bawdy court? *J, O, F', L';* Where are the bishops now, where are their bawdy court? *U, u. their*] the *P.*   55. For standing in white sheets their penance cools *J, U, F', L', u. penitent stoles*] penitential stools *O, Z.*   56. *schoolmen*] Frenchmen *J, U, F', L', u;* Scotchmen *O, Z.*   57–64. *Omitted J, U, F', L', u.*   60. *bastard*] mongrel *O, Z.*   80. *Irene's*] Arenia's *O, P, Z;* Ariana's *J, L'.*   84. *cruel*] stubborn *J, U, F', L', u.*   87. *Who am not yet*] Although I'm not *U, F', u.*

On His Excellent Friend Mr. Andrew Marvell   436–437

Copy text: q.

Collation: U', m, o, p, q.

Title: Andrew] Anth. *m, o;* And. *p.* On his Excellent Friend Mr. Andrew Marvell deceased. 1677 *U'. All texts date poem 1677.*

INDEX OF FIRST LINES

GENERAL INDEX

COMPILED BY ELIANE SCHENKER

The cue words "cited," "biographical note," "explained," "identified," and "mentioned" indicate that the person or subject appears in a footnote to the page listed.